SACRIFICE, CULT, AND ATONEMENT IN EARLY JUDAISM AND CHRISTIANITY

RESOURCES FOR BIBLICAL STUDY

Editor
Marvin A. Sweeney, Old Testament/Hebrew Bible

Number 85

SACRIFICE, CULT, AND ATONEMENT IN EARLY JUDAISM AND CHRISTIANITY

Constituents and Critique

Edited by
Henrietta L. Wiley and Christian A. Eberhart

SBL PRESS

Atlanta

Copyright © 2017 by SBL Press

All rights reserved. No part of this work may be reproduced or transmitted in any form or by any means, electronic or mechanical, including photocopying and recording, or by means of any information storage or retrieval system, except as may be expressly permitted by the 1976 Copyright Act or in writing from the publisher. Requests for permission should be addressed in writing to the Rights and Permissions Office, SBL Press, 825 Houston Mill Road, Atlanta, GA 30329 USA.

Library of Congress Cataloging-in-Publication Data

Names: Eberhart, Christian, editor. | Wiley, Henrietta L., editor.
Title: Sacrifice, cult, and atonement in early Judaism and Christianity : constituents and critique / edited by Henrietta L. Wiley and Christian A. Eberhart.
Description: Atlanta : SBL Press, [2017] | Series: Resources for biblical study ; Number 85 | "This volume features a selection of presentations delivered at annual conferences of the Society of Biblical Literature for the Sacrifice, Cult, and Atonement section between the years 2011 and 2014"—Introduction. | Includes bibliographical references and index.
Identifiers: LCCN 2017009199 (print) | LCCN 2017010558 (ebook) | ISBN 9781628371550 (pbk. : alk. paper) | ISBN 9780884141914 (hardcover : alk. paper) | ISBN 9780884141907 (ebook)
Subjects: LCSH: Sacrifice—Judaism—Congresses. | Temple of Jerusalem (Jerusalem)—Congresses. | Purity, Ritual—Congresses. | Atonement—Congresses. | Atonement (Judaism)—Congresses.
Classification: LCC BM715 .S23 2017 (print) | LCC BM715 (ebook) | DDC 296.4/92—dc23
LC record available at https://lccn.loc.gov/2017009199

Printed on acid-free paper.

Contents

Acknowledgments vi
Abbreviations ix

Introduction: Constituents and Critique of Sacrifice, Cult, and
Atonement in Early Judaism and Christianity
    Christian A. Eberhart 1

Part 1: Purification: Perspectives from the Torah and the Dead Sea Scrolls

The Purgation of Persons through the Purification Offering
    Joshua M. Vis 33

"She Shall Remain in (Accordance to) Her Blood-of-Purification":
Ritual Dynamics of Defilement and Purification in Leviticus 12
    Dorothea Erbele-Küster 59

Accessing Holiness via Ritual Ablutions in the Dead Sea Scrolls and
Related Literature
    Hannah K. Harrington 71

Part 2: Sacrifice: Ritual Aspects and Prophetic Critique

A Reexamination of the Ancient Israelite Gesture of Hand Placement
    David Calabro 99

"I Will Not Accept Them": Sacrifice and Reciprocity in the
Prophetic Literature
    Aaron Glaim 125

Prophetic Cult-Criticism in Support of Sacrificial Worship?
The Case of Jeremiah
    Göran Eidevall 151

"What to Me Is the Multitude of Your Sacrifices?": Exploring the
  Critique of Sacrificial Cult and the Metaphors for YHWH
  in the Prophetic Lawsuit (Micah 6:1–8 and Isaiah 1:1–20)
  Ma. Maricel S. Ibita 169

Part 3: Atonement: Alternative Concepts

To Atone or Not to Atone: Remarks on the Day of Atonement
  Rituals according to Leviticus 16 and the Meaning
  of Atonement
  Christian A. Eberhart 197

Cultic Action and Cultic Function in Second Temple Jewish
  Martyrologies: The Jewish Martyrs as Israel's Yom Kippur
  Jarvis J. Williams..233

Resistance Is Not Futile: Restraint as Cultic Action in
  2 Thessalonians 2:1–12
  Ross E. Winkle..265

Part 4: Temple and Priesthood: Rethinking Sacred Authority

Pillars, Foundations, and Stones: Individual Believers as
  Constituent Parts of the Early Christian Communal Temple
  Timothy Wardle..289

"Not One Stone Will Be Left on Another": The Destruction of the
  Temple and the Crucifixion of Jesus in Mark's Gospel
  Nicole Wilkinson Duran 311

"You Are What You Wear": The Dress and Identity of Jesus as
  High Priest in John's Apocalypse
  Ross E. Winkle..327

Bibliography...347
List of Contributors..393
Ancient Sources Index...399
Subject Index...425

Acknowledgments

This volume makes the scholarly work of the Sacrifice, Cult, and Atonement section, which until 2016 convened once a year at the Annual Meeting of the Society of Biblical Literature, available to a wider academic audience. As chairs of this program unit, we wish to thank the members of the steering committee Bill Gilders, Steve Finlan, Jason Tatlock, and Nicole Duran for their collaboration. They have pursued the themes of this program section with scholarly rigor and professional engagement for almost a decade. We have experienced their team spirit, felt their enthusiasm, benefitted from their expertise, and appreciated their creative ideas. We would also like to express our deep gratitude to the multitude of biblical scholars who contributed their research first through presentations and then in writing.

Moreover, we are very thankful to Bob Buller and Nicole L. Tilford of SBL Press for their continued interest in the topic of this collection of essays and the pleasant cooperation during the process of its production and to Marvin A. Sweeney, Hebrew Bible Editor of Society of Biblical Literature Resources for Biblical Study, who adopted the present volume into this series. Special thanks are directed to Wipf & Stock/Pickwick for the kindness of granting permissions to reprint a chapter of the book by Jarvis J. Williams, *Christ Died For Our Sins: Representation and Substitution in Romans and Their Jewish Martyrological Background* (Eugene, OR: Pickwick, 2015), under the title "Representation and Substitution in Second Temple Jewish Martyrologies." It provides a fitting contribution to the section on the theme of atonement in the present volume.

We gratefully acknowledge that the following funds were made available to support the finalization of the manuscript and its preparation for publication: first, a Project Completion Grant by the College of Liberal Arts and Social Sciences at the University of Houston; we are grateful to Anadeli Bencomo, Associate Dean for Faculty and Research at this college, for her continued support. A second book completion grant was graciously awarded from the Pangborn Fund by the School of Arts, Sciences, and Business at Notre Dame of Maryland University. Our thanks go particularly to Sabita Persaud, Chair of the Committee for Faculty Research and Development at NDMU, for her enthusiasm and support for this project.

We would also like to express our gratitude to Monika C. Müller, Lektorat TextTradition // Academic Bible Services, Friedrichsdorf (Germany), and Robert Matthew Calhoun, Houston (TX), for providing excellent editorial assistance, helping with the task of proof reading, compiling the indexes, and giving much valuable advice. We gratefully acknowledge the assistance of Robert Gaddie, student at the University of Houston, who aided with the task of proofreading. We thank James W. Watts of Syracuse University, who has been an experienced mentor for this Annual Conference section of the Society of Biblical Literature and a good friend for more than a decade. Finally we are specifically grateful to the Lanier Theological Library (Houston, Texas), its founders Mark and Becky Lanier, and its director Charles Mickey for their support and generosity during the work of finalizing this volume.

Christian A. Eberhart (Houston, Texas)
Henrietta L. Wiley (Baltimore, Maryland)

Abbreviations

AB	Anchor Bible
ABD	*Anchor Bible Dictionary*. Edited by David N. Freedman. 6 vols. New York: Doubleday, 1992.
Avot R. Nat.	Avot de Rabbi Nathan
ABRL	Anchor Bible Reference Library
AcBib	Academia Biblica
adj.	adjective, adjectival
ADPV	Abhandlungen des Deutschen Palästina-Vereins
Ag. Ap.	Josephus, *Against Apion*
AGJU	Arbeiten zur Geschichte des antiken Judentums und des Urchristentums
AJA	*American Journal of Archaeology*
ALD	Aramaic Levi Document
ALGHJ	Arbeiten zur Literatur und Geschichte des hellenistischen Judentums
AmJTh	*American Journal of Theology*
AnBib	Analecta Biblica
Ant.	Josephus, *Jewish Antiquities*
AOAT	Alter Orient und Altes Testament
AOTC	Abingdon Old Testament Commentaries
ARA	*Annual Review of Anthropology*
ASSM	Accordia Specialist Studies on the Mediterranean
AThR	*Anglican Theological Review*
AUSS	*Andrews University Seminary Studies*
BA	*Biblical Archaeologist*
BARIS	British Archaeological Reports, International Series
Barn.	Barnabas
BBB	Bonner biblische Beiträge
BBRSup	Bulletin for Biblical Research Supplements
BCBC	Believers Church Bible Commentary

BDAG	Bauer, W., F. W. Danker, W. F. Arndt, and F. W. Gingrich. *Greek-English Lexicon of the New Testament and Other Early Christian Literature*. 3rd ed. Chicago: University of Chicago Press, 2000.
BDB	Brown, Francis, Samuel R. Driver, and Charles A. Briggs. *A Hebrew and English Lexicon of the Old Testament*. Oxford: Clarendon, 1907.
BETL	Bibliotheca Ephemeridum Theologicarum Lovaniensium
BEvTh	Beiträge zur evangelischen Theologie
Bib	*Biblica*
BiBe	Biblische Beiträge
BibInt	Biblical Interpretation Series
BibOr	Biblica et Orientalia
Bik.	Bikkurim
BJS	Brown Judaic Studies
BJSUCSD	Biblical and Judaic Studies from the University of California, San Diego
BK	*Bibel und Kirche*
BKAT	Biblischer Kommentar. Altes Testament
BN	*Biblische Notizen*
BRLJ	Brill Reference Library of Judaism
BSCS	Brill Septuagint Commentary Series
BTB	*Biblical Theology Bulletin*
BTS	Biblical Tools and Studies
BW	Bible and Women
BZAW	Beihefte zur Zeitschrift für die alttestamentliche Wissenschaft
CA	*Current Anthropology*
CAD	*The Assyrian Dictionary of the Oriental Institute of the University of Chicago*. Chicago: Oriental Institute of the University of Chicago, 1956–2006
CBÅ	*Collegium Biblicum Årsskrift*
CBET	Contributions to Biblical Exegesis and Theology
CC	Continental Commentary
CD	Cairo Genizah copy of the Damascus Document
CEJL	Commentaries on Early Jewish Literature
CeS	Civilisations et sociétés
CJA	Christianity and Judaism in Antiquity

CogSci	*Cognitive Science*
Comp. Nic. Crass.	*Comparatio Niciae et Crassi*
ConBNT	Coniectanea Biblica: New Testament Series
ConcC	Concordia Commentary
const.	construct
CQS	Companion to the Qumran Scrolls
CSSH	*Comparative Studies in Society and History*
CTRJ	*Clothing and Textiles Research Journal*
DCH	*Dictionary of Classical Hebrew*. Edited by David J. A. Clines. 9 vols. Sheffield: Sheffield Phoenix Press, 1993–2014.
DCLS	Deuterocanonical and Cognate Literature Studies
Decal.	Philo, *De decalogo*
def.	definition
DHR	Dynamics in the History of Religions
DJD	Discoveries in the Judaean Desert
DiKi	Dialog der Kirchen
DSD	*Dead Sea Discoveries*
EAC	Entretiens sur l'antiquité classique
EBR	*Encyclopedia of the Bible and Its Reception*. Edited by Hans-Josef Klauck et al. Berlin: de Gruyter, 2009–
ECHC	Early Christianity in Its Hellenistic Context
EdF	Erträge der Forschung
EeC	Études et Commentaires
EFN	Estudios de filología neotestamentaria
EJL	Early Judaism and Its Literature
EncJu1	*Encyclopaedia Judaica*. 17 vols. New York: Macmillan, 1971–1982.
Ep.	*Epistula(e)*
Eph.	Ignatius, *To the Ephesians*
ET	English Translation
ETL	*Ephemerides Theologicae Lovanienses*
ETS	Erfurter theologische Studien
EvT	*Evangelische Theologie*
Exod. Rab.	Rabbah Exodus
ExpTim	*Expository Times*
FAT	Forschungen zum Alten Testament
fem.	feminine
FF	Foundations and Facets

FRLANT	Forschungen zur Religion und Literatur des Alten und Neuen Testaments
Fug.	Philo, *De fuga et inventione*
G&H	*Gender & History*
GDR	Gorgias Dissertations in Religion
Gen. Apoc.	Genesis Apocryphon
GesB17	Wilhelm Gesenius. *Hebräisches und Aramäisches Wörterbuch zum Alten Testament: bearbeitet von F. Buhl.* 17th ed. Berlin: Springer, 1962.
GK	Wilhelm Gesenius. *Hebräische Grammatik, völlig umgearbeitet von Emil Kautzsch.* 28th ed. Leipzig: Vogel, 1909.
GKC	*Gesenius' Hebrew Grammar.* Edited by Emil Kautzsch. Translated by Arthur E. Cowley. 2nd ed. Oxford: Clarendon, 1910.
GNS	Good News Studies
Gos. Pet.	Gospel of Peter
GTBS	Gütersloher Taschenbücher Siebenstern
H	Holiness Code text
Hag.	Hagigah
HALOT	Koehler, L., W. Baumgartner, and J. J. Stamm. *The Hebrew and Aramaic Lexicon of the Old Testament.* Translated and edited under the supervision of M. E. J. Richardson. 4 vols. Leiden, 1994–1999
HB	Hebrew Bible
HBM	Hebrew Bible Monographs
HBT	*Horizons in Biblical Theology*
HCOT	Historical Commentary on the Old Testament
HdO	Handbook of Oriental Studies
HDR	Harvard Dissertations in Religion
Her.	Philo, *Quis rerum divinarum heres sit*
Herm. Sim.	Shepherd of Hermas, Similitude(s)
Herm. Vis.	Shepherd of Hermas, Vision(s)
HNT	Handbuch zum Neuen Testament
HNTC	Harper's New Testament Commentary
Hor.	Horayot
HR	*History of Religions*
HThKAT	Herders Theologischer Kommentar zum Alten Testament

HTR	*Harvard Theological Review*
HTS	Harvard Theological Studies
HUCA	*Hebrew Union College Annual*
HvTSt	*Hervormde teologiese studies*
IBC	Interpretation: A Bible Commentary for Teaching and Preaching
ICC	International Critical Commentary
IEJ	*Israel Exploration Journal*
Il.	Homer, *Iliad*
inf.	infinitive
ITC	International Theological Commentary
ITSRS	Italian Texts and Studies on Religion and Society
IVPNTC	InterVarsity Press New Testament Commentary Series
JANER	*Journal of Ancient Near Eastern Religions*
JANESCU	*Journal of the Ancient Near Eastern Society of the Columbia University*
JAOS	*Journal of the American Oriental Society*
JBL	*Journal of Biblical Literature*
JCC	Jewish Culture and Contexts
JCPS	Jewish and Christian Perspectives Series
JEH	*Journal of Ecclesiastical History*
JSHJ	*Journal for the Study of the Historical Jesus*
JSHRZ	Jüdische Schriften aus hellenistisch-römischer Zeit
JSJ	*Journal for the Study of Judaism in the Persian, Hellenistic, and Roman Periods*
JSJSup	Journal for the Study of Judaism Supplement Series
JSNT	*Journal for the Study of the New Testament*
JSNTSup	Journal for the Study of the New Testament Supplement Series
JSOT	*Journal for the Study of the Old Testament*
JSOTSup	Journal for the Study of the Old Testament Supplement Series.
JTS	*Journal of Theological Studies*
Jub.	Jubilees
J.W.	Josephus, *Jewish War*
KAW	Kulturgeschichte der antiken Welt
KEK	Kritisch-exegetischer Kommentar über das Neue Testament

Ker.	Kerithot
LAB	Liber antiquitatum biblicarum
LAE	The Life of Adam and Eve
LCL	Loeb Classical Library
LDiff	lectio difficilior
Leg.	Philo, *Legum allegoriae*
Legat.	Philo, *Legatio ad Gaium*
Let. Aris.	Letter of Aristeas
Leuc. Clit.	*Leucippe et Clitophon*
LHBOTS	Library of Hebrew Bible/Old Testament Studies
Life	Josephus, *The Life*
lit.	literally
LNTS	Library of New Testament Studies
LSJ	Lidell, Henry George, Robert Scott, Henry Stuart Jones. *A Greek-English Lexicon*. 9th ed. with revised supplements. Oxford: Clarendon, 1996.
LSRS	Lincoln Studies in Religion and Society
LXX	Septuagint
Magn.	Ignatius, *Epistle to the Magnesians*
masc.	masculine
MBT	Münsterische Beiträge zur Theologie
Mek.	Mekilta
Menah.	Menahot
Mid.	Middot
Midr.	Midrash
MNTC	Moffatt New Testament Commentary
Mos.	Philo, *De vita Mosis*
MS(S)	manuscript(s)
MT	Masoretic Text
MThZ	*Münchener Theologische Zeitschrift*
Mut.	Philo, *De mutatione nominum*
NCB	New Century Bible Commentary
NCBC	New Cambridge Bible Commentary
NCCS	New Covenant Commentary Series
Neot	*Neotestamentica*
NICNT	New International Commentary on the New Testament
NICOT	New International Commentary on the Old Testament

NIDB	*New Interpreter's Dictionary of the Bible*. Edited by Katherine Doob Sakenfield. 5 vols. Nashville: Abingdon, 2006–2009.
NIGTC	New International Greek Testament Commentary
NIVAC	New International Version Application Commentary
NovT	*Novum Testamentum*
NovTSup	Supplements to Novum Testamentum
NSBT	New Studies in Biblical Theology
NSKAT	Neuer Stuttgarter Kommentar, Altes Testament
NTC	New Testament in Context
NTD	Das Neue Testament Deutsch
NTG	Neue theologische Grundrisse
NTL	New Testament Library
NTM	New Testament Monographs
NTR	New Testament Readings
NTS	*New Testament Studies*
NTSI	New Testament and the Scriptures of Israel
NTT	New Testament Theology
OBO	Orbis Biblicus et Orientalis
OCM	Oxford Classical Monographs
Od.	Homer, *Odyssey*
ORA	Orientalische Religionen der Antike
orig.	original (meaning)
OTE	*Old Testament Essays*
OTL	Old Testament Library
OTM	Old Testament Monographs
OTMes	Old Testament Message
OTS	Old Testament Studies
P	Priestly text
Parab	*Parabola*
par(r).	parallel(s)
PastPsy	*Pastoral Psychology*
PC	Proclamation Commentaries
per.	person
Pesiq. Rab.	Pesiqta Rabbati
PGM	*Papyri Graecae Magicae: Die greichischen Zauberpapyri*. Edited by Karl Preisendanz. 2nd ed. Stuttgart: Teubner, 1973–1974.

Phld.	Ignatius, *Epistle to the Philadelphians*
PHSC	Perspectives on Hebrew Scriptures and Its Contexts
PIBA	*Proceedings of the Irish Biblical Association*
pl.	plural
Po	Popular interpretation
poss.	possessive
Pr	Priestly author
pron.	pronoun, pronominal
Ps.	Pseudo
Pss. Sol.	Psalms of Solomon
Quaest. conv.	Plutarch, *Quaestionum convivialum libri IX*
QD	Quaestiones Disputatae
QE	Philo, *Questiones et solutiones in Exodum*
QVO	*Quaderni di Vicino Oriente*
RAC	*Reallexikon für Antike und Christentum.* Edited by Theodor Klauser et al. Stuttgart: Hiersemann, 1950–
RB	*Revue Biblique*
RBL	*Review of Biblical Literature*
RBS	Resources for Biblical Study
RechBib	Recherches bibliques
RelSoc	Religion and Society
RevQ	*Revue de Qumran*
RFCC	Religion in the First Christian Centuries
RGG[4]	*Religion in Geschichte und Gegenwart.* Edited by Hans Dieter Betz. 4th ed. Tübingen: Mohr Siebeck, 1998–2007.
RivBibSup	Rivista biblica supplementi
RNT	Regensburger Neues Testament
RŠ	Rabbi Šimʿon bar Yoḥai
RVV	Religionsgeschichtliche Versuche und Vorarbeiten
Shabb.	Shabbat
SAC	Studies in Antiquity and Christianity
SAOC	Studies in Ancient Oriental Civilization
SBFLA	*Studi Biblici Franciscani Liber Annus*
SBLDS	Society of Biblical Literature Dissertation Series
SBLStBL	Society of Biblical Literature Studies in Biblical Literature
SBS	Stuttgarter Bibelstudien

sc.	scilicet ("namely"/"supply")
SCS	Septuagint and Cognate Studies
Sheqal.	Sheqalim
SHBC	Smyth & Helwys Bible Commentary
SHJ	Studying the Historical Jesus
Sib. Or.	Sibylline Oracle
sg.	singular
SJLA	Studies in Judaism in Late Antiquity
SMEA	*Studi Micenei ed Egeo-Anatolici*
SNTSMS	Society for New Testament Studies Monograph Series
SNTSU	*Studien zum Neuen Testament und seiner Umwelt*
Somn.	Philo, *De somniis*
Spec.	Philo, *De specialibus legibus*
SPIB	Scripta Pontificii Instituti Biblici
SSEI	Smithsonian Series in Ethnographic Inquiry
StBibLit	Studies in Biblical Literature (Lang)
STDJ	Studies on the Texts from the Desert of Judah
STW	Suhrkamp Taschenbuch Wissenschaft
SubBi	Subsidia Biblica
suf.	suffix
SUNT	Studien zur Umwelt des Neuen Testaments
T. Levi	Testament of Levi
T. Yom.	Tevul Yom
TBN	Themes in Biblical Narrative
TDNT	*Theological Dictionary of the New Testament.* Edited by Gerhard Kittel and Gerhard Friedrich. Translated by Geoffrey W. Bromiley. 10 vols. Grand Rapids: Eerdmans, 1964–1976.
TDOT	*Theological Dictionary of the Old Testament.* Edited by G. Johannes Botterweck and Helmer Ringgren. Translated by John T. Wills et al. 15 vols. Grand Rapids: Eerdmans, 1974–2006.
Tg. Ps.-J.	Targum Pseudo-Jonathan
Th.	Theodotion
Tim.	Plutarch, *Timoleon*
TJT	*Toronto Journal of Theology*
TLOT	*Theological Lexicon of the Old Testament.* Edited by Ernst Jenni and Claus Westermann. Translated by

	Mark E. Biddle. 3 vols. Peabody, MA: Hendrickson, 1997.
TNTC	Tyndale New Testament Commentaries
TRE	*Theologische Realenzyklopädie.* Edited by G. Krause and G. Müller. Berlin: de Gruyter, 1977–2006.
UCOP	University of Cambridge Oriental Publications
VE	*Vox Evangelica*
VEccl	*Verbum et Ecclesia*
VT	*Vetus Testamentum*
VTSup	Vetus Testamentum Supplement Series.
WA	*D. Martin Luthers Werke: Kritische Gesamtausgabe.* Weimar: Böhlau, 1883–.
WAWSup	Writing from the Ancient World Supplement Series
WBC	Word Biblical Commentary
WesBibComp	Westminster Bible Companion
WiBiLex	*Das wissenschaftliche Bibellexikon im Internet.* www.wibilex.de.
WMANT	Wissenschaftliche Monographien zum Alten und Neuen Testament
WUNT	Wissenschaftliche Untersuchungen zum Neuen Testament
Yad.	Yadayim
Yevam.	Yevamot
YREAL	Yearbook of Research in English and American Literature
ZAW	*Zeitschrift für die alttestamentliche Wissenschaft*
ZBK	Zürcher Bibelkommentare
Zebah.	Zebahim
ZECNT	Zondervan Exegetical Commentary on the New Testament
ZNT	*Zeitschrift für Neues Testament*
ZPE	*Zeitschrift für Papyrologie und Epigraphik*
ZTK	*Zeitschrift für Theologie und Kirche*

Introduction:
Constituents and Critique of Sacrifice, Cult, and Atonement in Early Judaism and Christianity

Christian A. Eberhart

This volume features a selection of presentations delivered at annual conferences of the Society of Biblical Literature for the Sacrifice, Cult, and Atonement section between the years 2011 and 2014. The objective of this program unit was the study of the practices, interpretations, and reception history of sacrifice and cult in early Judaism, Christianity, and their larger cultural contexts (ancient Near East and Greco-Roman antiquity). I am delighted that this book makes the presentations dedicated to these topics, and with them the work of this section, available to a wider academic audience. It is thus a sequel to the volume *Ritual and Metaphor: Sacrifice in the Bible* that I previously edited for the scholarly series Resources for Biblical Study.[1]

All the contributions to this volume deal with the cult at the Jerusalem temple that epitomized the religious, cultural, and sociopolitical identity of Judaism throughout different time periods. They do this in different ways. Some contributors explore the rich spectrum of constitutive practices and concepts, such as purification rituals, sacrifices, atonement, or sacred authorities at the temple. They examine specific aspects of these practices and concepts with the goal of investigating their meanings and interpreting them for modern readers. Other contributions are concerned

---

1. *Ritual and Metaphor: Sacrifice in the Bible*, ed. Christian A. Eberhart, RBS 68 (Atlanta: Society of Biblical Literature, 2011); I am grateful for the positive reception that this volume found; see, e.g., the book reviews by John Dunnill (Review of *Ritual and Metaphor: Sacrifice in the Bible*, ed. Christian A. Eberhart, *RBL* [2012]: http://tinyurl.com/SBL0393b) and by Greg Carey (Review of *Ritual and Metaphor: Sacrifice in the Bible*, ed. Christian A. Eberhart, *RBL* [2012]: http://tinyurl.com/SBL0393b).

with conceptual alternatives to sacrifice. Some of these alternatives seek to critique these established traditions and endeavor to renegotiate them, whereas others utilize metaphorization and spiritualization so as to employ the suggestive potential of these traditions as terminological and ideological resources. However, these critical and creative responses are valuable in their own right, as they help modern scholars recognize how past interpreters understood the constitutive practices and concepts. Such perspectives are manifest in traditions developed in, for example, Jewish prophetic books, the Dead Sea Scrolls, and early Christian literature. They all attest to the continuing relevance of the legacy of the Jewish cult even after the destruction of the Second Temple in 70 CE and specifically explore the multifaceted ways in which Judaism and Christianity are structurally and conceptually related.

1. History of Research: Ritual Sacrifice

The scholarly study of these topics is, of course, by no means new. For centuries anthropologists, biblical scholars, classicists, historians, and others have studied particularly sacrifice and atonement from different perspectives and with different methods, yet a consensus is not in sight.[2] Even the general statement that both concepts might serve to reconcile or mediate between the human and the divine realm has recently been questioned by classicists and proponents of ritual theory, who limit the focus of inquiry to anthropological, social, and cultural perspectives. This is a rather new development in a seasoned struggle for comprehension.

The topic of sacrifice has been studied especially across multiple religions and cultures of the ancient Mediterranean and/or the so-called ancient Near East. Three aspects were of particular importance across the centuries: First, whether or not sacrifice could be considered an inevitable characteristic of "human nature" or their culture; second, whether sacrificial rituals in the Hebrew Bible/Old Testament informed the concept of the sacrifice of Jesus/the Eucharist (or Last Supper, Lord's Supper, etc.). The third aspect, namely, that of atonement or the "inner efficacy" of sacrifice, shall be discussed in its own paragraph below.

---

2. This is the assessment of, e.g., Josef Drexler, *Die Illusion des Opfers: Ein wissenschaftlicher Überblick über die wichtigsten Opfertheorien ausgehend vom deleuzianischen Polyperspektivismusmodell*, Münchener Ethnologische Abhandlungen 12 (Munich: Akademischer Verlag, 1993), 1.

The first of these three topics was addressed by Thomas Aquinas (Tommaso d'Aquino, 1225–1274 CE), the great medieval Dominican friar and scholastic theologian. One of his objectives as a scholar of the Roman Catholic Church was the merger of theological teachings with classical philosophy, specifically the works of Aristotle. He believed that the revelation of God happened through nature, which is why he encouraged its study in all of its aspects to grasp and experience salvation. In his comprehensive *chef-d'œuvre*, the *Summa Theologica*, therefore, Aquinas engaged in a kind of comparative investigation of sacrifice in both Old and New Testament and in Greco-Roman and other cultures. The crucial point of his study was how humans honor God. Borrowing from Aristotle and Augustine, he concluded that all humans, whether Hebrews, Christians, Greeks, Romans, or pagans, do so when performing sacrificial rituals. Thus sacrifice belongs to human nature and can be considered a universal gesture of devotion to God.[3] Aquinas also claimed sacrifice as the conceptual background of the Eucharist. Fred S. Naiden describes the difference between either one as follows: "The altar remained the place of sacrifice, the celebrant placed the offering there, incense burned, and worshippers watched. Yet the animals were gone, and the bread and wine were part of a meal more important than any Greek feast. Bloodshed was gone in one way, but not in another, for its redemptive effect was more important than before."[4] Thus the sacrifices of Greco-Roman antiquity and of the Old Testament, particularly those of the Day of Atonement, foreshadowed various facets and the content of one of the seven sacraments of Roman Catholicism. In the celebration of the Eucharist, Roman Catholic priests were understood to transform bread and wine into the body and blood of Jesus Christ through a process called "transubstantiation" (Latin *transsubstantiatio*). It implied that the external appearances (accidents) of bread and wine remain unchanged. In this way, priests were understood to continuously repeat the sacrifice of Christ at the climax of every mass.

A few centuries later, the Spanish Dominican Bartolomé de las Casas (1484–1566), one of the first advocates for universal human rights, once again compared biblical and pagan sacrifice. During the Valladolid debate in 1550–1551, Las Casas defended the Native Americans of the West

---

3. Thomas Aquinas, *Summa Theologica* 2.2. q. 85 a. 1–4; http://tinyurl.com/SBL0393a. Cf. Fred S. Naiden, *Smoke Signals for the Gods: Ancient Greek Sacrifice from the Archaic through Roman Periods* (Oxford: Oxford University Press, 2013), 289–90.

4. Naiden, *Smoke Signals*, 290.

Indies against the charge that they were uncivilized and lacked social order. Although they practiced animal sacrifice and even human sacrifice, Las Casas argued, much like Aquinas, that sacrifice was in principle universal and a natural human gesture of devotion.[5] According to him, this would be an effective basis for the Spanish to convert the natives since all they needed to do was assist them in replacing their sacrificial practices with the sacrifice of Christ.[6]

The Reformation revisited and modified the Roman Catholic interpretation of the Eucharist. It especially rejected the concept of transubstantiation that formed the basis of the repeated sacrifice of Jesus Christ during the Eucharist. While maintaining that Jesus Christ was really present in bread and wine, the German monk and academic professor Martin Luther (1483–1546) distinguished, in his 1528 work "Vom Abendmahl Christi: Bekenntnis" ("On the Last Supper of Christ: Confession"), between three different modes of Christ's existence: a bodily one, an imperceptible spiritual one, and a heavenly one. Luther saw Christ as the principle of creation; he argued, among other things, that the spiritual Christ was present in all expressions of the created world, which would include bread and wine.[7] Thus the Lutheran Reformation affirmed the real presence of Jesus Christ during the Eucharist "in, with, and under" bread and wine while dismissing the concept of transubstantiation and the idea that Christ was sacrificed repeatedly. Looking at the Bible as its doctrinal norm (*norma normata*), Lutherans instead held the opinion that only "one appeasing sacrifice existed in the world" (*unicum tantum in mundo fuit sacrificium propitiatorium*),[8] namely, the death of Christ on the cross. The Swiss Reformation agreed with the latter, but differed on the interpretation of the sacrament. For the French theologian John (Jean) Calvin (1509–1564), the Eucharist was only a symbol for, and an act of, commemoration of the death of Christ who, since his ascension, was in heaven with God the

---

5. Bartolomé de las Casas, *In Defense of the Indians: The Defense of the Most Reverend Lord, Don Fray Bartolomé de las Casas, of the Order of Preachers, Late Bishop of Chiapa, against the Persecutors and Slanderers of the Peoples of the New World Discovered across the Seas*, trans. Stafford Poole (DeKalb: Northern Illinois University Press, 1974), 222–25, 238.

6. Cf. Naiden, *Smoke Signals*, 292.

7. Martin Luther, "Vom Abendmahl Christi: Bekenntnis (1528)," WA 26:335–37.

8. Philip Melanchthon, *Apologia Confessionis* 24:22.

Father.[9] With Calvin, the Swiss Reformation therefore also rejected the idea of the real presence of Christ.

Georg Wilhelm Friedrich Hegel (1770–1831), a German philosopher of the late Enlightenment, was a Lutheran, but that does not mean that he espoused Luther's views on the matter. As a representative of a transcendental idealism based on Immanuel Kant and borrowing from Baruch Spinoza, Hegel developed a philosophical system that centered on the concept of an absolute and all-encompassing God. Through an emphasis on logic and the philosophy of the spirit/mind, he tried to overcome dualistic structures such as nature and mind, human and divine, or even God Father and Son.[10] What does that mean for his understanding of sacrifice? For Hegel, the sacrificial victim actually symbolizes the divine, and a sacrificial meal is an attempt of humans to unite with the divine. It is upon humans, however, to recognize that these dialectic structures do not exist and to transcend them. Without a real distinction between the human and the divine, therefore, any type of offering to a god is meaningless. Naiden aptly concludes that, for Hegel, "there is no wrong way or wrong god. The act of sacrifice requires a victim in whom the worshipper can see himself, but no single, unique victim such as Christ."[11] In the framework of his idealistic philosophy, Hegel thus "liquidated" sacrifice.[12]

Since the second half of the nineteenth century, endeavors of theorizing about sacrifice were still motivated by comparative interests, yet a new emphasis on understanding "primitive" inclinations in the history of humanity and explaining Christian concepts of sacrifice began to emerge.[13]

---

9. Jean Calvin, *Institution de la religion chrestienne: en laquelle est comprinse une somme de pieté, et quasi tout ce qui est necessaire a congnoistre en la doctrine de salut; Quatrième livre: L'existence de l'Église* (Geneva: Michel Du Bois, 1541).

10. Cf. Walter Jaeschke, "Hegel, Georg Wilhelm Friedrich," *RGG*⁴ 3:1505–6; Peter C. Hodgson, "Hegel, Georg Wilhelm Friedrich," *EBR* 11:705–8.

11. Naiden, *Smoke Signals*, 308.

12. Ibid., 310.

13. See Albert Stöckl, *Das Opfer nach seinem Wesen und seiner Geschichte* (Mainz: Kirchheim, 1861); Ernst von Lasaulx, *Die Sühnopfer der Griechen und Römer und ihr Verhältnis zum Einen auf Golgatha: Ein Beitrag zur Religionsphilosophie* (Würzburg: Voigt & Mocker, 1841); Hermann Th. Wangemann, *Das Opfer nach Lehre der heiligen Schrift Alten und Neuen Testaments: Eine apologetische Darstellung des biblisch-kirchlichen Opferbegriffs* (Berlin: Schultze, 1866); Friedrich Max Müller, *Lectures on the Origin of Religion as Illustrated by the Religions of India: Delivered in the Chapter House, Westminster Abbey, in April, May, and June, 1878*, Hibbert Lectures (London:

Specifically the discovery of evolutionary descent by Charles Robert Darwin (1809–1882) spurred the application of a similar line of reasoning in the realm of religious and biblical studies.[14] Thus the English anthropologist Edward Burnett Tylor, for instance, suggested in 1871 that primitive humans considered sacrifices as gifts for the gods through which they attempted to exercise influence on them and find favor; further developed civilizations no longer needed such archaic ways of interaction with the divine realm.[15] The biblical scholar George Buchanan Gray later adopted this general approach to sacrifice. He claimed that comprehensive terminology for sacrifices found in the Hebrew Bible warrants such an understanding; he maintained this interpretation over against ideas of communion associated with sacrifice.[16] The latter was, for instance, the approach presented by William Robertson Smith, a Scottish orientalist who understood Semitic sacrifices in relation to concepts of taboo and their social setting as communal meals. Robertson Smith described sacrifices as joyful events that affirmed the unity among clan members and with deities, who were seen as ancestors. The life-sustaining power of sacrifices helped to form groups of kin; the essential basis of this process was a form of mystical or sacramental communion.[17]

Longmans, Green & Co., 1878); Henri Hubert and Marcel Mauss, "Essai sur la nature et la fonction du sacrifice," *Année Sociologique* 2 (1899): 29–138; W. Robertson Smith, *Lectures on the Religion of the Semites*, Burnett Lectures 1888–1889 (London: Black, 1894).

14. It is worth mentioning that, during the years of exploration aboard the HMS *Beagle*, Darwin himself kept private notebooks in which he tried to find "equivalence between biblical and evolutionary doctrines" (James Moore, "Darwin, Charles: I. Darwin and the Bible," *EBR* 6:165).

15. Eduard B. Tylor, *Primitive Culture* (London: Murray, 1920), 2:375.

16. George Buchanan Gray, *Sacrifice in the Old Testament: Its Theory and Practice* (New York: Ktav, 1971 [first published 1925]), 32, et al. Gray, while maintaining this general interpretation, acknowledges a certain variety: "But some Jewish sacrifices were doubtless in origin and remained, or if not so in origin became, more than gifts to God; they represent a combination of rites, some of which sprang out of entirely other conceptions, and in some cases continued to symbolize other conceptions—of fellowship with the deity perhaps, of propitiation, of purification" (32–33).

17. Robertson Smith, *Lectures*. See also the description in Alfred Marx, "Le sacrifice israélite de 1750 à nos jours: Histoire de la recherché" (PhD diss., Université de Strasbourg, 1977), 202–6. In developing his theory of sacrifice, Robertson Smith favored the concept of sacramental communion over the idea of reconciliation (cf. Peter W. Coxon, "Smith, William Robertson," *TRE* 31:409).

The Scottish social anthropologist James G. Frazer adopted key concepts of the approach of Robertson Smith, who was his personal friend, throughout his influential work *The Golden Bough*.[18] This comparative study describes more generally how religion evolved from a level of primitive belief in superstition and magic to higher forms of faith that eventually culminated in the rise of science.[19] Frazer also explored sacrificial rituals, positing that rituals as such, not related myths, were the basis of religion. He especially proposed the interpretation of sacrifices as totems, that is, representations of ancestral groups or other spiritual beings. Communal sacrificial meals then sustained the life of a clan through the consumption of these spiritually relevant beings.

However, the proximity of the sacrificial cult in the Hebrew Bible to that of other ancient Near Eastern cultures and religions was not always appreciated. Julius Wellhausen, a German biblical scholar and orientalist who laid the foundations for much of modern source-criticism, specifically of the Pentateuch, openly articulated his disregard for the cult of Israel and its sacrificial rituals. In a monograph published in 1882, he called the cult "the pagan element" that Israel adopted from the Canaanites and that presented a "continuous danger for morality and monotheism," which is why the prophets fought against it but did not succeed in abolishing it.[20] Such negative assessments were shared by others after him, for example by Ludwig Köhler, who wrote in 1935 that the sacrificial cult was no part of divine revelation.[21]

---

18. James G. Frazer, *The Golden Bough: A Study in Magic and Religion*, 3rd ed. (London: Macmillan, 1911–1915). Frazer's work has a peculiar publication history. It was originally published in two volumes in the year 1890; a revised edition extended to three volumes appeared in 1900; its most voluminous edition of no less than twelve volumes occurred between 1911 and 1915. Finally an abridged version in one volume appeared in 1927 (all editions London: Macmillan).

19. Cf. Hans Wißmann, "Frazer, James George," *EBR* 9:633.

20. Julius Wellhausen, *Israelitische und jüdische Geschichte*, 9th ed. (Berlin: de Gruyter, 1958), 174: "Der Kultus war das heidnische Element in der Religion Jahves, größtenteils erst bei der Einwanderung in Palästina von den Kanaaniten entlehnt; und er blieb vor dem Exil immer das Band, welches Israel mit dem Heidentum verknüpfte, eine stete Gefahr für die Moral und den Monotheismus."

21. Ludwig Köhler, *Theologie des Alten Testaments*, 4th ed., NTG (Tübingen: Mohr Siebeck 1966), 186. See also the pertinent remarks by Adrian Schenker, "Einführung," in *Studien zu Opfer und Kult im Alten Testament*, FAT 3 (Tübingen: Mohr Siebeck, 1992), v.

Yet Wellhausen also shared other insights about the sacrificial cult of Israel, which he separated into a preexilic and a postexilic period. He considered the preexilic cult as simple and spontaneous; the postexilic cult, on the other hand, was abstract, artificial, and characterized by strict observance of laws. The oldest type of sacrifice was the burnt offering, sacrificed entirely as an expression of devotion to God. Another frequent form was the meal offering, given out of gratitude to God and accompanied by a joyous feast. Wellhausen points out that a close reading of the sacrificial regulations yields that the actual offering to God is accomplished in the burning rite rather than in blood rites. Such rituals accompanied the daily life of ancient Israel. A significant dissociation and estrangement occurred after the centralization of the cult and after the exile. This period saw especially the development of two new types of expiatory sacrifice, namely, sin offering and guilt offering. With them, blood rites that were performed to propitiate God came to dominate the cult.[22]

Another important comparative study of sacrifice was the lengthy article "Essai sur la nature et la fonction du sacrifice," which soon rose to the status of a classic.[23] Coauthored by the French sociologists and anthropologists Henri Hubert and Marcel Mauss, this work on sacrifice in the Hebrew Bible and in Hinduism claims a different focus, namely, consecration of the victim through which the sacrificial object passes from the profane domain to the religious one: "Il est bien certain, en effet, que le sacrifice implique toujours une consécration ; dans tout sacrifice, un objet passe du domaine commun dans le domaine religieux ; il est consacré."[24] The moment of slaughter of the victim is the specific moment of transition; slaughter and the destruction of the sacrificial object are, therefore, essential and the climax of sacrifice.[25] Through consumption of the sacrificial meat, religious communities partake in turn of the sacredness "accumulated" there.

The focus Hubert and Mauss put on the slaughter of sacrificial animals was readily adopted and further emphasized in subsequent theorizing; however, the focus shifted more to the analysis of Greek epics and ritual practices. In the first half of the twentieth century, the Swiss classicist

---

22. Wellhausen, *Israelitische und jüdische Geschichte*, 173. Cf. Marx, "Sacrifice israélite," 169–75.
23. Hubert and Mauss, "Essai."
24. Ibid., 36–37.
25. Ibid., 67, 71–75.

Karl Meuli suggested that prehistoric hunting practices are the origin of a number of certain phenomena in Greek sacrificial rituals, such as paying homage to the animal's carcass.[26] "Meuli first coined the term *Unschuldskomödie* (comedy of innocence); this is a kind of 'staging' during the sacrificial ritual, by which worshippers try to hide and deny the slaughter of the victim."[27] Later, the French literary historian and social anthropologist René Girard and the German classical philologist Walter Burkert published seminal works almost at the same time that continued this line of inquiry. Drawing likewise on ancient Greek drama and Western literary classics, Girard set out to develop a comprehensive theory of human society according to which all humans envy their neighbors and imitate them; Girard calls such comportment "mimetic desire" and suggests that it leads to periodic conflict. Unaware of the true origins of these conflicts, humans tend to identify outsiders of society—typically members of cultural, racial, or religious minorities—to hold them responsible for these crises. They make them scapegoats and seek to get rid of the problems by chasing them away or even killing them. Girard posits that such "generative violence"[28] is at the heart of sacrifice, which needs to be seen as a ritualized reenactment of such mob violence against "others." Thus sacrifice is in essence an act of collective murder.[29] Girard now goes on to apply these insights to the passion and death of Jesus, which he interprets as an act of expulsion. While the mechanism of generative violence remains concealed in Hebrew Bible sacrifices, the New Testament gospels reveal this very process by stating the innocence of Jesus and describing the mob violence directed against him. Girard thus construes the death on the cross as nonsacrificial; Jesus died against the sacrificial mechanism in order to

---

26. Karl Meuli, "Griechische Opferbräuche," in *Phylobolia: Festschrift für Peter von der Mühll zum 60. Geburtstag am 1. August 1945*, ed. Olof Gigon and Karl Meuli (Basel: Schwabe, 1946), 185–288.

27. Maria-Zoe Petropoulou, *Animal Sacrifice in Ancient Greek Religion, Judaism, and Christianity, 100 BC–AD 200*, OCM (Oxford: Oxford University Press, 2008), 7.

28. René Girard, *Violence and the Sacred*, trans. Patrick Gregory (Baltimore: Johns Hopkins University Press, 1977), 19, 93. Cf. Raymond Schwager, "Christ's Death and the Prophetic Critique of Sacrifice," *Semeia* 33 (1985): 109–23.

29. Girard, *Violence*; Girard, *Des choses cachées depuis la fondation du monde* (Paris: Grasset, 1979); Girard, "Generative Scapegoating," in *Violent Origins: Walter Burkert, René Girard, and Jonathan Z. Smith on Ritual Killing and Cultural Formation*, ed. Robert G. Hamerton-Kelly (Stanford, CA: Stanford University Press, 1987), 73–105.

break the vicious circle of generative violence forever.[30] According to him, any interpretation of the death of Jesus as a sacrifice is a relapse to concepts found in the Hebrew Bible or in pagan cultures.[31] Several Christian scholars have been receptive to Girard's understanding of sacrifice, especially his claim that Jesus exposed mechanisms of generative violence in order to "end sacrifice."

Burkert's approach to sacrifice features a similar focus on violence and murder, which is already manifest in the Latin title *Homo Necans* (which means "The Killing Human") of his foundational 1972 book on the subject.[32] In this study, Burkert discusses ancient Greek myths in search of "biological" origins of sacrifice, which he discovers in Palaeolithic hunting practices. These were not only expedient to provide food for the community, which implies that the sustenance of the group's lives came at the expense of an animal's death. Because of the need to cooperate, the coordination of a hunting party had also a consolidating effect on human clans. As the kill marks the moment of success, ritual animal slaughter was originally instituted in the context of sacrifices to commemorate this decisive moment. In the development of his thesis, Burkert acknowledges the influence of the scholarship of Meuli.[33] Thus a progressive line of theorizing can be drawn from Hubert and Mauss via Meuli to Girard and Burkert that gradually emphasized violence and killing at the center of sacrifice.[34]

However, more recent scholarship has demonstrated that the link between sacrifice in ancient Greece or other cultures and killing or violence does not need to be seen as imperative. Particularly French scholars have recognized sacrifice as belonging to, or rather being part of a communal meal, which became its own conceptual paradigm. The classi-

---

30. Girard, *Choses cachée*, 203–46.

31. Ibid., 246–85.

32. The full title of the German original is *Homo Necans: Interpretationen altgriechischer Opferriten und Mythen*, RVV 34 (Berlin: de Gruyter, 1972). The English version was published as *Homo Necans: The Anthropology of Ancient Greek Sacrificial Ritual and Myth*, trans. Peter Bing (Berkeley: University of California Press, 1983). See also Walter Burkert, *Kulte des Altertums: Biologische Grundlagen der Religion* (Munich: Beck, 1998), 181: "Die zentrale Handlung im antiken Opfer ist das 'heilige' Schlachten eines Tieres" ("The central activity in ancient sacrifice is the 'sacred' slaughter of an animal.").

33. Cf. Burkert, *Kulte des Altertums*, 139.

34. Cf. David Frankfurter, "Ritual as Accusation and Atrocity: Satanic Ritual Abuse, Gnostic Libertinism, and Primal Murders," *HR* 40 (2001): 352–80.

cists and cultural historians Jean-Pierre Vernant and Marcel Detienne (who is from Belgium) were attentive to the struggle of ancient societies for food and to the fact that sacrificial animals were customarily comestible. Informed by the structuralism of Claude Lévi-Strauss, their studies of Greek sacrifice no longer focus on the historical development of rituals over time but on the sociopolitical functions of sacrificial meals.[35] As Naiden aptly defines the contrast to previous theorizing, Burkert posited that sacrifice created solidarity, while Vernant and Detienne "replied that solidarity created sacrifice."[36] French biblical scholarship has also adopted such an emphasis. One representative is Alfred Marx, who summarizes his comprehensive study on Old Testament sacrifice with a statement that it is a festive communal gathering of the faithful with the purpose of honoring God: "Le sacrifice est un repas festif auquel les fidèles convient Yhwh et qu'ils offrent en vue de l'honorer et de lui rendre hommage."[37] It is this approach that has allowed scholars to realize the simple fact that not all sacrifice in ancient Israel or other cultures is animal sacrifice and that not all sacrificial material is meat. Marx therefore published an entire monograph on the importance of cereal offerings in the Old Testament.[38] It is also Marx who reinserts the religious dimension into the study of sacrifice by mentioning the role God plays in all of this. Recently, Naiden published a book advocating for the same in the study of ancient Greek sacrifice.[39]

Yet this is exactly the point that has generally been questioned in the context of a final approach to sacrifice to be briefly surveyed here, namely, in ritual theory. Puzzled by the multitude of scholarly "answers" to the question of what sacrifice is, some have come to doubt the basic tenet that sacrifices must be seen as representing something else within a larger interpretive framework. Why, they ask, can a sacrificial ritual not simply

---

35. Cf. Marcel Detienne, "Pratiques culinaires et esprit de sacrifice," in *La cuisine du sacrifice en pays grec*, eds. Marcel Detienne and Jean-Pierre Vernant, Bibliothèque des histoires (Paris: Gallimard, 1979), 7–35; Jean-Pierre Vernant, "Théorie générale du sacrifice et mise à mort dans la θυσία grecque," in *Le sacrifice dans l'Antiquité: Huit exposés suivis de discussions; Vandœuvres-Genève, 25–30 août 1980*, ed. J. Rudhardt and O. Reverdin, EnAC 27 (Geneva: Fondation Hardt, 1981), 1–21.

36. Naiden, *Smoke Signals*, 12.

37. Alfred Marx, *Les systèmes sacrificiels de l'Ancien Testament: Formes et fonctions du culte sacrificiel à Yhwh*, VTSup 105 (Leiden: Brill, 2005), 221.

38. Alfred Marx, *Les offrandes végétales dans l'Ancien Testament: Du tribut d'hommage au repas eschatologique*, VTSup 57 (Leiden: Brill, 1994).

39. Naiden, *Smoke Signals*.

be what it is, a ritual? A ritual, they argue, consists of actions and gestures that immediately convey meaning. This approach, which resembles ideas first proposed by Frazer, makes use of a sociocultural perspective and particularly explores certain "latent functions" of ritual activities.[40] One of its stated goals is transcending the specificity of rituals in individual cultures and religions in order to understand them "as a universal factor in human behavior," as the Israeli philosopher Ithamar Gruenwald puts it.[41] This approach has been used above all to posit that ritual gestures inscribe the status of cult authorities such as priests, to indicate access to subsequent meal rites, and to define hierarchies at the social, ethical and ritual level.[42]

2. History of Research: Atonement

Another topic related to sacrifice, but not identical with it, is atonement. For a first attempt of defining it, atonement can appear as the function or effect of sacrificial rituals. As such it frequently occurs in Hebrew Bible texts; the Hebrew term employed for this purpose is usually כפר *piel* (typically translated as "to atone"). However, in modern scholarly parlance the term atonement is commonly deployed as a comprehensive soteriological term and theological-conceptual abstraction denoting salvation in a broad sense, especially through the death of Jesus Christ in light of his resurrection. Both usages of the term are thus incompatible; this terminological ambivalence has characterized the history of research.[43]

Another important factor was the theory of atonement as vicarious satisfaction developed by the Benedictine abbot and philosopher/theologian Anselm of Canterbury (1033–1109). Adopting Augustine's doctrine of original sin, Anselm posits that all humans are sinners; they owe God, their creator, full obedience and veneration but fall short of it. This results

---

40. Cf. William K. Gilders, *Blood Ritual in the Hebrew Bible: Meaning and Power* (Baltimore: Johns Hopkins University Press, 2004), 6, 141, 181–91.

41. Ithamar Gruenwald, *Rituals and Ritual Theory in Ancient Israel*, BRLJ 10 (Leiden: Brill, 2003), 184.

42. For a more comprehensive description of ritual theory, see the pertinent sections in my contribution, "To Atone or Not to Atone: Remarks on the Day of Atonement Rituals according to Leviticus 16 and the Meaning of Atonement," in this volume.

43. Cf. Günter Röhser, "Sühne II: Biblisch 2. Neues Testament," *RGG*[4] 7:1844–45; Christian A. Eberhart, "Atonement: II. New Testament," *EBR* 3:32–42, esp. 32–33.

in an obligation of indemnification that cannot be fulfilled. Yet God cannot simply suspend the punishment because of his infinite justice. Due to this dilemma, all of humanity would deserve destruction. God did not, however, create humans for eternal punishment but for salvation. Only a divine being could achieve on behalf of humans what they were incapable of; this answers the question of incarnation, namely, why God became human (see the title of Anselm's book *Cur Deus homo*—"Why God [Became] Human"). So how can the just punishment be prevented and humans be saved? According to Anselm, the divine-human Jesus Christ vicariously takes on the punishment of death for all humans.[44]

Anselm chose this particular conceptual background to convey the doctrine of atonement in categories that were accessible to his contemporaries. Referring to Roman legal and imperial structures that he considered to be universal, Anselm depicted God as an overlord of the world or a Roman magistrate. For centuries to come, his interpretation set a standard that other interpreters either followed or rejected. The Dutch lawyer and theologian Hugo Grotius (Huig de Groot, 1583–1645), for example, advocated for the primacy of reason and developed an international legal corpus based on a notion of common sense.[45] Like many before him, he compared biblical sacrifice to that of pagans. He argued that neither human sacrifice nor the sacrifice of Jesus should be despised as murder; how could it be, since it was God who demanded the latter from Jesus in order to obtain indemnification for humans? Somewhat similar to Anselm, Grotius described the sacrifice of Christ as third-party indemnification. In principle, he reasoned that comparable categories applied to sacrifices of the Greeks or the Aztecs. To Grotius, they were inferior offerings for inferior gods, but they were not worthless as such.[46] Grotius thus attributed a certain status to these other religions.

Karl Christian Wilhelm Felix Bähr, a German pastor, presented a different approach to atonement in his voluminous study *Symbolism of the Mosaic Cult* published early in the nineteenth century.[47] Bähr assumed

---

44. See Ludwig Hödl, "Anselm von Canterbury," *TRE* 2:759–78, esp. 774–75; Gillian R. Evans, "Anselm von Canterbury," *RGG*⁴ 1:515–16.

45. See Christoph Link, "Grotius, Hugo," *RGG*⁴ 3:1303.

46. Hugo Grotius, *Defensio fidei catholicae de satisfactione Christi adversus Faustum Socinum* (Salmurii: Pean, 1675); cf. Naiden, *Smoke Signals*, 292–93.

47. Karl C. W. F. Bähr, *Symbolik des Mosaischen Cultus*, 2 vols. (Heidelberg: Mohr, 1837–1839).

that the information in the books Exodus, Leviticus, and Numbers about the sacrificial cult yields a complete and harmonious system. This cult is the external representation of the theological system of Israelite religion; both correspond to each other in that the latter is the symbolic meaning of the former.[48] Bähr regards atonement as the solution to the separation between the earthly and the heavenly realm, which the process of sacrifice overcomes. In particular, he suggests that atonement, as the specific effect of sacrificial blood rites, accomplishes this through a process of substitution. For Bähr, one Hebrew Bible verse is the key for this interpretation as it locates the "soul" of a sacrificial animal in its blood, which God has destined for atonement on the altar (Lev 17:11). So Bähr assumes that the human soul is being transferred to the sacrificial animal while the offerer leans one hand on its head. When the priest then takes the blood of the animal and applies it within the sanctuary, Bähr suggests that it contains and transports the human soul. Hence the goal of the ritual is to establish contact, or communion, between the soul and the sanctuary, which is the place of God's presence.[49] In the process, the animal substitutes for the human who cannot immediately approach the sanctuary.

According to Bähr's understanding, blood rites are of prime importance in early Judaism to achieve atonement. His theory constituted a decisive revision of the legal categories that dominated Anselm's theory of vicarious satisfactory atonement, although it retained some of the penal aspects. Bähr's alternative remained characteristic and prominent in many future theories of atonement, for example, that of Johann Heinrich Kurtz, a school teacher in religious education, who claimed that all sacrificial blood rites had expiatory functions.[50] Kurtz places, however, more emphasis on animal slaughter, which he considers an essential element of sacrifice. He suggests that it represents, in dramatic fashion, the punishment of the sinner that the animal takes on in vicarious fashion.[51] Burdened with sin, the sinner's soul is transferred to the sacrificial animal when the offerer leans his hand on the head of the sacrificial animal; its subsequent

---

48. Ibid., 1:21–23.
49. Ibid., 2:199–201; see also Marx, "Sacrifice israélite," 84–87.
50. J. H. Kurtz, *Das mosaische Opfer: Ein Beitrag zur Symbolik des mosaischen Cultus; Mit besonderer Berücksichtigung der neuesten Bearbeitung dieses Gegenstandes in der "Symbolik des mosaischen Cultus" von Dr. K. Chr. W. Fr. Bähr* (Mitau: Lucas, 1842), 12–13, 32–33, 45.
51. Ibid., 33–34, 74–80.

death then liberates the sinner from everything that separated him/her from God.⁵²

A number of different aspects were added to such theories. Ernst von Lasaulx, a German philologist and politician, claimed that a similar emphasis on atonement is attested in a variety of religious traditions, for example, those of ancient Greece and Rome.⁵³ The Reformed pastor Christoph Hermann Hasenkamp published a shorter study on sacrifice at approximately the same time Bähr's two volumes appeared.⁵⁴ For Hasenkamp, the Hebrew Bible does not depict God as a merciless judge; rather, God is loving and eager to forgive. Against common misconceptions, Hasenkamp observes that the Hebrew verb כפר *piel* ("to atone") never features God as its object. Therefore the sacrificial cult should not be construed as a human attempt to propitiate God; instead it is an institution of God's grace for the benefit of humans.⁵⁵ Based on this particular observation, Hasenkamp goes on to question the vicarious nature of the suffering and death of Jesus Christ according to the New Testament.⁵⁶ He furthermore assumes that the hand-leaning rite during the sacrificial ritual cannot be strictly connected to a consciousness of sin or signify the transmission of sins since this gesture also occurs in types of sacrifice offered to express gratitude to God. Finally, he notes that even expiatory sacrifices are only prescribed for minor and inadvertent sins according to Lev 4–5, which means that sacrifice does not mitigate in situations that could cost a human life.⁵⁷

Wellhausen's understanding of sacrifice as such has already been summarized above. For him, the postexilic cult was associated with a degree of estrangement; it also witnessed two new types of expiatory sacrifice, namely, sin offering and guilt offering. Only in this period did blood rites become central in the cult; with them the overall interpretation of cultic activities shifted from the idea of bringing offerings to please God to that

---

52. Ibid., 64–74.
53. Von Lasaulx, *Sühnopfer der Griechen und Römer*.
54. Christoph Hermann Hasenkamp, "Ueber die Opfer: Resultate einer biblisch-philosophischen Untersuchung," *Die Wahrheit der Gottseligkeit* 1.1 (1827): 7–33; 1.3 (1829): 245–349.
55. Ibid., 265–66.
56. Ibid., 268–309.
57. Ibid., 312–15; see also Marx, "Sacrifice israélite," 109–10.

of a medium to obtain forgiveness, instituted by God and to be strictly observed by all.[58]

The detailed description of this period in the history of interpretation shows that it already features most of the relevant parameters of the subsequent discussion on the topic. The major objective was to overcome Anselm of Canterbury's theory of atonement as vicarious satisfaction in legal and penal categories.[59] The gradual understanding of the sacrificial cult in its own terms, the interpretation of sacrifices as offerings or gifts to God, and the redefinition of certain ritual activities and gestures (hand-leaning rite, animal slaughter) and their relative importance to the ritual were salient features in this quest.

Theories of vicarious satisfaction were, nevertheless, proposed later on. An example is Alexis Medebielle's study, which has been praised for its positive impact on Roman Catholic exegesis and theology.[60] Against Protestant and rationalist exegetes, Medebielle ventures to defend the truth based on the Bible.[61] He recognizes already Noah's burnt offering after the deluge (Gen 8:20–21) as propitiatory. His broad coverage of both sin offering and guilt offering, and his analysis of the verse of Lev 17:11 in particular reveal that, through the blood rite, the life of the animal victim is substituted for that of the human.[62] This substitution, however, applies to all types of blood sacrifice. According to Medebielle, these expiatory sacrifices also provide satisfaction to God. The purpose of the hand-leaning gesture is the transfer of sin to the sacrificial animal, the slaughter of the victim the sinner's punishment.[63] Medebielle concludes with the remark that vicarious satisfaction has been instituted by God to foreshadow the true satisfaction realized in Christ.[64]

Predominantly Christian scholars have tried, for some time, to apply theories of sacrifice that pertain to the Hebrew Bible to christological and soteriological concepts. The specific question is how these theories inform

---

58. Wellhausen, *Israelitische und jüdische Geschichte*, esp. 172–74; see also Marx, "Sacrifice israélite," 169–75.

59. See Marx, "Sacrifice israélite," 293.

60. Alexis Medebielle, *L'expiation dans l'Ancien et le Nouveau Testament*, SPIB, vol. 1 (Rome: Institut Biblique Pontifical, 1924). See Leopold Sabourin, *Rédemption sacrificielle: Une enquête exégétique*, Studia 11 (Brussels: de Brouwer, 1961), 174.

61. Medebielle, *L'expiation dans l'Ancien et le Nouveau Testament*, 1:4.

62. Ibid., 133–36.

63. Ibid., 142–43, 147–58.

64. Ibid., 164–65.

the notion of the "sacrifice of Jesus" and/or the Eucharist. Such theorizing typically falls under the category of atonement as a comprehensive soteriological term and theological-conceptual abstraction. However, the fact that it is not fully compatible with the concept of atonement as the effect of ritual activity in the Hebrew Bible is not always sufficiently realized. For example, the British biblical scholar Vincent Taylor published a study that juxtaposes a discussion of Old Testament sacrifice with chapters on the Eucharist and atonement.[65] As for the former, Taylor suggests that the words of institution require both moral obedience of the individual and the belief that the body and blood of Christ are being consumed.[66] As for the latter, he explains that the atonement of Jesus is, first, the obedient self-offering of Jesus to the Father's will, second, his submission to God's judgment upon sin, and third, the expression of the perfect penitence of Jesus for all of the sins of humanity.[67]

The explicit application of the traditional Jewish sacrificial cult to christological concepts is the topic of the Epistle to the Hebrews. This New Testament text—a sermon or "word of exhortation" (Heb 13:22) rather than a letter—features a unique christological approach. It depicts Jesus as superior to a variety of traditional Jewish spiritual authorities and institutions such as angels, Moses, the high priest Aaron, and the sacrificial cult. It thus promises the inauguration of a better cultic order (8:1–10:18) and a better spiritual experience (10:19–13:25). The anonymous author of Hebrews develops this comprehensive and complex argument through the claim that Jesus is both high priest at a heavenly sanctuary and the ultimate sacrifice "once and for all." Most New Testament occurrences of the terms "blood," "sacrifice," and "to atone" are found in Hebrews. However, scholars have faced the continuous challenge that the author of Hebrews significantly alters these traditional Jewish concepts for their christological application.[68]

---

65. Vincent Taylor, *Jesus and His Sacrifice: A Study of the Passion-Sayings in the Gospels* (London: Macmillan, 1948).

66. Ibid., 214–5: "The words [of institution] indicate that the proving, of which [1 Cor 11:28] speaks, has an intellectual as well as a moral character. The man is not only to examine his motives and his conduct, but also whether he has perceived what is involved in eating the bread and in drinking the cup. The implication is that it is upon this kind of self-examination that the opportunity presented to him in the Eucharist depends; only so are the bread and the wine the body and the blood of Christ for him."

67. Ibid., 299–312.

68. See Wilfrid Stott, "The Conception of 'Offering' in the Epistle to the Hebrews,"

Such conceptualization and theorizing did not go without rebuttal. On the one hand, some have complained that notions of vicarious satisfaction are no longer comprehensible in modernity. The German New Testament scholar Rudolf Bultmann, for instance, famously called the idea of a divine being who atones for the sins of humanity through his blood "primitive mythology" that requires demythologization and existential interpretation.[69] On the other hand, New Testament concepts of biblical atonement or Christ's expiatory sacrifice were often criticized as conveying the image of a vengeful, violent, or blood-thirsty God.[70] Stephen Finlan writes about the "widespread dismay regarding the received doctrines of atonement" and thinks that incarnation and *theosis* (the idea of deification of humanity widely popular in Eastern Orthodox Christianity) are more important concepts for Christianity.[71]

In light of various challenges against atonement, several scholars reviewed its cultic basics in the Hebrew Bible. The German biblical scholar

---

NTS 9 (1962): 62–67; Walter E. Brooks, "The Perpetuity of Christ's Sacrifice in the Epistle to the Hebrews," *JBL* 89 (1970): 205–14; Mathias Rissi, *Die Theologie des Hebräerbriefs: Ihre Verankerung in der Situation des Verfassers und seiner Leser*, WUNT 41 (Tübingen: Mohr Siebeck, 1987), 72–78; A. N. Chester, "Hebrews: the Final Sacrifice," in *Sacrifice and Redemption: Durham Essays in Theology*, ed. S. W. Sykes (Cambridge: Cambridge University Press, 1991), 57–72; Richard W. Johnson, *Going outside the Camp: The Sociological Function of the Levitical Critique in the Epistle to the Hebrews*, JSNTSup 209 (London: Sheffield Academic, 2001); Susan Haber, "From Priestly Torah to Christ Cultus: The Re-Vision of Covenant and Cult in Hebrews," *JSNT* 28 (2005): 105–24; Craig R. Koester, "God's Purposes and Christ's Saving Work According to Hebrews," in *Salvation in the New Testament: Perspectives on Soteriology*, ed. Jan G. van der Watt, NovTSup 121 (Leiden: Brill, 2005), 361–87; Christian A. Eberhart, "Characteristics of Sacrificial Metaphors in Hebrews," in *Hebrews: Contemporary Methods, New Insights*, ed. Gabriella Gelardini, BibInt 75 (Leiden: Brill, 2005), 37–64; Eberhart, *Kultmetaphorik und Christologie: Opfer- und Sühneterminologie im Neuen Testament*, WUNT 306 (Tübingen: Mohr Siebeck, 2013), 131–56; Stephen Finlan, "Spiritualization of Sacrifice in Paul and Hebrews," in Eberhart, *Ritual and Metaphor*, 83–97.

69. Rudolf Bultmann, *Neues Testament und Mythologie: Das Problem der Entmythologisierung der neutestamentlichen Verkündigung*, ed. Eberhard Jüngel, BEvTh 96 (Munich: Kaiser, 1988), 19.

70. Cf. S. Mark Heim, *Saved from Sacrifice: A Theology of the Cross* (Grand Rapids: Eerdmans, 2006), 21–29.

71. Stephen Finlan, *Problems with Atonement: The Origins of, and Controversy about, the Atonement Doctrine* (Collegeville, MN: Liturgical Press, 2005), 1, 3–5, 117–24. See also Finlan, *Background and Contents of Paul's Cultic Atonement Metaphors*, AcBib 19 (Atlanta: Society of Biblical Literature, 2004).

Klaus Koch still defines it as vicarious, but no longer mentions satisfaction. For him, the sin offering is no sacrifice offered by humans but a ritual for the extermination of sin instituted by God.[72] It "works" vicariously: the hand-leaning rite transfers sin to the sacrificial animal that is killed instead of the human. The paradigm of this ritual and thus of atonement is the scapegoat ritual in Lev 16:20–22, which features a hand-leaning gesture and the death of the animal in its own right.[73] Rolf Rendtorff, another German biblical scholar, dedicated much of his research to the study of sacrifice.[74] He assumed that the order of sacrifices corresponds to their importance in the Israelite cult; hence the privileged place of the burnt offering. Nevertheless, he offered a detailed analysis of all types of sacrifice, including the cereal offering. Regarding the sin offering, Rendtorff recognized a historical development from a purification ritual of the altar to one that had expiatory functions for humans.[75] Only the ritual on the Day of Atonement features sin offerings that purify both the altar and humans. In general, this type of sacrifice came to dominate the entire cult system of Israel and orient it toward the Day of Atonement.[76] Like Koch, he speculates that the hand-leaning gesture could derive from the scapegoat ritual.

A theory of atonement that has become very influential in the theology of Germany is that of the biblical scholar Hartmut Gese; it was in turn further developed by his student Bernd Janowski.[77] It features, however, mostly elements and insights that others have proposed previously.

---

72. Klaus Koch, "Sühne und Sündenvergebung um die Wende von der exilischen zur nach-exilischen Zeit," *EvT* 26 (1966): 217–39, esp. 230–31.

73. Ibid., 225–31; Koch, "Die Eigenart der priesterschriftlichen Sinaigesetzgebung," *ZTK* 55 (1958): 47; see also Christian Eberhart, *Studien zur Bedeutung der Opfer im Alten Testament: Die Signifikanz von Blut- und Verbrennungsriten im kultischen Rahmen*, WMANT 94 (Neukirchen-Vluyn: Neukirchener Verlag, 2002), 230–31.

74. Rendtorff wrote his doctoral dissertation on literary genres in the Priestly Code (Rolf Rendtorff, *Die Gesetze in der Priesterschrift: Eine gattungsgeschichtliche Untersuchung*, FRLANT 62 [Göttingen: Vandenhoeck & Ruprecht, 1954]); it focuses specifically on sacrificial rituals. He then presented a study of the history of sacrifice (*Studien zur Geschichte des Opfers im Alten Israel*, WMANT 24 [Neukirchen-Vluyn: Neukirchener Verlag, 1967]), again proposing a close literary analysis of Hebrew Bible texts. Later he started a commentary on Leviticus (*Leviticus 1,1–10,20*, BKAT 3.1 [Neukirchen-Vluyn: Neukirchener, 2004]), which was to remain unfinished.

75. Rendtorff, *Gesetze in der Priesterschrift*, 199–241; Rendtorff, *Leviticus*, 210–14.

76. Rendtorff, *Gesetze in der Priesterschrift*, 217–22.

77. Hartmut Gese, "Die Sühne," in *Zur biblischen Theologie: Alttestamentliche Vorträge*, 2nd ed. (Tübingen: Mohr Siebeck, 1983), 85–106; Bernd Janowski, *Sühne als*

According to Gese, the postexilic cult is significantly different from the preexilic one and characterized by a gradual development toward atonement; this idea was proposed earlier by both Wellhausen and Rendtorff. Then a number of elements known from the work of Bähr (and some also from that of Kurtz) recur as well: Gese interprets Lev 17:11 to mean that the offerer seeking atonement transfers his soul, which contains his sin, to the sacrificial animal and identifies with it. The subsequent blood application rite at the sanctuary establishes contact between the soul of the human and the place of divine presence.[78] The human is thus existentially incorporated into the holy and encounters God.[79] Janowski adds that the expiatory cult is no means to propitiate God; instead it has been instituted by God for the salvation of humans (see similar ideas by Koch).[80] God provides life through death.[81] Gese finally claims that the salvific meaning of the death of Jesus can only be articulated with the concept of cultic atonement ("Die Heilsbedeutung des Todes Jesu ist nur mit dem Sühnegedanken zu fassen").[82]

Partially spurred by a renewed interest in biblical theology, these ideas have frequently been adopted in New Testament scholarship and beyond, for instance by Gerhard Barth, Ulrich Wilckens, Helmut Merklein, Otfried Hofius, and James D. G. Dunn, who all posit that New Testament passages about the "blood" of Jesus (e.g., Rom 3:25; 5:9; 1 Cor 10:16; 11:25, 27; Eph 2:13; Col 1:20; 1 Pet 1:19; Heb 9:12, 14; 10:19, 29; Rev 7:1) refer directly to cultic atonement categories of the Hebrew Bible.[83] The main differences

---

Heilsgeschehen: Traditions- und religionsgeschichtliche Studien zur Sühnetheologie der Priesterschrift, 2nd ed., WMANT 55 (Neukirchen-Vluyn: Neukirchener, 2000).

78. Gese, "Sühne," 98–99, 101–3.
79. Ibid., 97, 99, 104.
80. Janowski, *Sühne als Heilsgeschehen*, 358–59.
81. Ibid., 362.
82. Gese, "Die Sühne," 105.
83. See Gerhard Barth, *Der Tod Jesu Christi im Verständnis des Neuen Testaments* (Neukirchen-Vluyn: Neukirchener Verlag, 1992), 47; Ulrich Wilckens, *Der Brief an die Römer: Röm 1–5*, EKK 6.1 (Neukirchen-Vluyn: Neukirchener Verlag, 1978), 240; Helmut Merklein, "Der Sühnetod Jesu nach dem Zeugnis des Neuen Testaments," in *Versöhnung in der jüdischen und christlichen Liturgie*, ed. David H. Ellenson et al., QD 124 (Freiburg: Herder, 1990), 155–83; Merklein, "Der Tod Jesu als stellvertretender Sühnetod: Entwicklung und Gehalt einer zentralen neutestamentlichen Aussage," in *Studien zu Jesus und Paulus*, WUNT 43 (Tübingen: Mohr Siebeck, 1987), 181–91; Otfried Hofius, "Sühne und Versöhnung: Zum paulinischen Verständnis des

are, according to Hofius, that God alone is active in the new expiatory sacrifice of the crucifixion and that this sacrifice needs no further repetitions.[84] More recently, Thomas Knöppler presented a comprehensive overview of New Testament atonement concepts based on the ideas of Gese and Janowski.[85] The last decades saw a number of conferences and other research endeavors dedicated to these broad christological and soteriological topics, yielding a variety of publications.[86]

Occasionally, scholars took note of the fact that a sacrificial or expiatory interpretation of the death of Jesus on the cross is at odds with the passion narrative. Ferdinand Hahn, for instance, observes that the death on a cross was by no means a cultic event and that the theme of sacrifice is mostly absent from christological passages in the New Testament (with the exception of Hebrews).[87] Nevertheless, Hahn claims that the vicarious expiatory suffering and death of Jesus are widely attested.[88] Cilliers Breytenbach disputed this opinion based on the observation that the Greek lexeme ἱλάσκομαι, "to atone," is rare in New Testament soteriological concepts and distinct from καταλλάσσω, "to reconcile," which references

---

Kreuzestodes Jesu," in *Paulusstudien*, WUNT 51 (Tübingen: Mohr Siebeck, 1989), 33; Hofius, "Sühne IV: Neues Testament," *TRE* 32:342–47, esp. 342–43; James D. G. Dunn, *Romans 1–8*, WBC 38A (Dallas: Word, 1988), 181.

84. Hofius, "Sühne und Versöhnung," 48–49.

85. Thomas Knöppler, *Sühne im Neuen Testament: Studien zum urchristlichen Verständnis der Heilsbedeutung des Todes Jesu*, WMANT 88 (Neukirchen-Vluyn: Neukirchener Verlag, 2001).

86. See, e.g., M. F. C. Bourdillon and M. Fortes, eds., *Sacrifice* (London: Academic Press, 1980); Karl Lehmann and Edmund Schlink, eds., *Das Opfer Jesu Christi und seine Gegenwart in der Kirche: Klärungen zum Opfercharakter des Herrenmahls*, DiKi 3 (Freiburg im Breisgau: Herder; Göttingen: Vandenhoeck & Ruprecht, 1983); S. W. Sykes, ed., *Sacrifice and Redemption: Durham Essays in Theology* (Cambridge: Cambridge University Press, 1991); Roger T. Beckwith and Martin J. Selman, eds., *Sacrifice in the Bible* (Carlisle: Paternoster, 1995); Bernd Janowski and Michael Welker, eds., *Opfer: Theologische und kulturelle Kontexte*, STW 1454 (Frankfurt am Main: Suhrkamp, 2000); Ann W. Astell and Sandor Goodhart, eds., *Sacrifice, Scripture, and Substitution: Readings in Ancient Judaism and Christianity*, CJA 18 (Notre Dame: University of Notre Dame, 2011); Eberhart, *Ritual and Metaphor*.

87. Ferdinand Hahn, "Das Verständnis des Opfers im Neuen Testament," in Lehmann, *Opfer Jesu Christi*, 51–91, esp. 72–73.

88. Ibid., 73: "Nun fällt aber auf, daß im Unterschied zu irgendwelchen der Opfertradition entnommenen Vorstellungen die Auffassung von Jesu Tod als einem stellvertretenden Sühneleiden einen überaus breiten Raum einnimmt."

secular categories.[89] This discussion had analogies in English scholarship, which uses the term "atonement" even more widely than German scholarship to refer to the entirety of New Testament soteriology concepts. Here the argument was put forth that the lexeme ἱλάσκομαι cannot account for the various facets of New Testament soteriology.[90] Since then individual studies on several of the New Testament soteriological motifs have demonstrated their independent character.

In recent decades, alternative approaches to cultic atonement in the Hebrew Bible were developed by, for example, Adrian Schenker, who holds that atonement consists of tokens of reconciliation in case of human conflict. According to him, sacrificial atonement is modeled on the paradigm of secular processes of reconciliation, which requires that the guilty party acknowledges wrongdoing and offers an object of value in exchange. Thus all sacrifices are essentially gifts for God who then no longer insists on punishment. Sacrificial blood that is applied in Israel's sanctuary is a special sign of such human desire to be reconciled.[91] Calling the sin offering "purification offering," the Jewish rabbi and biblical scholar Jacob Milgrom suggests that sacrificial blood effects ritual cleansing of sancta, which are subject to defilement themselves in Jewish thought. Like Rendtorff, he thus acknowledges the effect of this type of sacrifice on the sanctuary; he questions, on the other hand, any further effect on the offerer.[92] Furthermore, recent scholarship has challenged two of the main points of much of scholarly theorizing on Hebrew Bible sacrifice and atonement of the twentieth century. For instance, Christian Eberhart and Kathryn

---

89. Cilliers Breytenbach, *Versöhnung: Eine Studie zur paulinischen Soteriologie*, WMANT 60 (Neukirchen-Vluyn: Neukirchener Verlag, 1989); Berytenbach, "Versöhnung, Stellvertretung und Sühne: Semantische und traditionsgeschichtliche Bemerkungen am Beispiel der paulinischen Briefe," *NTS* 39 (1993): 59–79.

90. Megory Anderson and Philip Culbertson, "The Inadequacy of the Christian Doctrine of Atonement in Light of Levitical Sin Offering," *AThR* 68 (1986): 303–28; Bradley H. McLean, "The Absence of an Atoning Sacrifice in Paul's Soteriology," *NTS* 38 (1992): 531–53.

91. Adrian Schenker, *Versöhnung und Sühne: Wege gewaltfreier Konfliktlösung im Alten Testament; mit einem Ausblick auf das Neue Testament*, BiBe 15 (Fribourg: Schweizer Katholisches Bibelwerk, 1981), 55–79, 102–4; Schenker, "Das Zeichen des Blutes und die Gewißheit der Vergebung im Alten Testament: Die sühnende Funktion des Blutes auf dem Altar nach Lev 17.10–12," *MThZ* 43 (1983): 195–213.

92. Jacob Milgrom, *Leviticus 1–16: A New Translation with Introduction and Commentary*, AB 3 (New York: Doubleday, 1991), 1033.

McClymond proposed that the slaughter of animals, which has attracted much attention since Hubert and Mauss, has been overrated in the interpretation of sacrifice and that blood application rites, which have been the focus of scholarship since the works of Bähr and Wellhausen, should not be construed as the main components of sacrificial rituals. Rather, sacrificial rituals consist of a variety of elements; their investigation requires a polythetic approach to incorporate previously neglected aspects and to yield a more holistic view of sacrificial rituals.[93]

Some biblical scholars have applied Milgrom's approach to New Testament sacrificial terminology in christological contexts.[94] Against general claims that "atonement" is the dominant image or concept of early Christian soteriology, some scholars now favor the view that diverse New Testament soteriological images articulate each in their own creative ways the gospel of Jesus Christ.[95] Others specifically question to what degree and how the notion of substitution is a constitutive category of New Testament christology.[96]

---

93. Eberhart, *Studien zur Bedeutung der Opfer*; Eberhart, "A Neglected Feature of Sacrifice in the Hebrew Bible: Remarks on the Burning Rite on the Altar," *HTR* 97 (2004): 485–93; Kathryn McClymond, *Beyond Sacred Violence: A Comparative Study of Sacrifice* (Baltimore: Johns Hopkins University Press, 2008), 61: "A comprehensive approach to sacrifice has to incorporate *all* the offering substances employed in a sacrificial system" (emphasis original).

94. See, e.g., Wolfgang Kraus, *Der Tod Jesu als Heiligtumsweihe: Eine Untersuchung zum Umfeld der Sühnevorstellung im Römer 3,25-26a*, WMANT 66 (Neukirchen-Vluyn: Neukirchener Verlag, 1991); Kraus, "Der Tod Jesu als Sühnetod bei Paulus: Überlegungen zur neueren Diskussion," *ZNT* 3 (1999): 20–30; Kraus, "Der Erweis der Gerechtigkeit Gottes im Tode Jesu nach Röm 3,24-26," in *Judaistik und Neutestamentliche Wissenschaft: Standorte—Grenzen—Beziehungen*, ed. Lutz Doering, Hans-Günther Waubke, and Florian Wilk, FRLANT 226 (Göttingen: Vandenhoeck & Ruprecht, 2008), 211–13; Eberhart, *Kultmetaphorik und Christologie*, 78–130.

95. See, e.g., Olivette Genest, "L'interprétation de la mort de Jésus en situation discursive: Un cas-type; l'articulation des figures de cette mort en 1-2 Corinthiens," *NTS* 34 (1988): 506–35; Cilliers Breytenbach, "'Christus starb für uns': Zur Tradition und paulinischen Rezeption der sogenannten 'Sterbeformeln,'" *NTS* 49 (2003): 447–75; Breytenbach, "Gnädigstimmen und opferkultische Sühne im Urchristentum und seiner Umwelt," in Janowski, *Opfer*, 217–43.

96. See Günter Röhser, *Stellvertretung im Neuen Testament*, SBS 195 (Stuttgart: Katholisches Bibelwerk, 2002); Jens Schröter, "Sühne, Stellvertretung und Opfer: Zur Verwendung analytischer Kategorien zur Deutung des Todes Jesu," in *Deutungen des Todes Jesu im Neuen Testament*, ed. Jörg Frey and Jens Schröter, WUNT 181 (Tübingen: Mohr Siebeck, 2005), 51–71.

An exploration of the constituents and critique of sacrifice and atonement in early Judaism and Christianity covers both a lot of territory (which includes the cultures and religions of the ancient Near East) and a vast period of time (approximately a millennium). It touches upon what is foundational and still essential to Jews and Christians in their religions and worship experiences. Persistent problems along the way are that the modern usage of the term "sacrifice" is as ambivalent as that of the term "atonement"; it is linked to the further problem that the temple and its cult, which are the "home" of these terms, ceased to exist almost two millennia ago. Hence an ongoing challenge will be to remember past institutions and to honor them. A lot of biblical research has been dedicated to these themes. This is also what the contributions to the present volume are all about.

3. Outline of the Present Volume

This collection of essays deals with the constitutive aspects of and critical voices regarding sacrifice, cult, and atonement in early Judaism and Christianity. Its contributions are all set in the matrix of terminological and conceptual investigation of the cult of Second Temple Judaism; this cult shaped, among other things, early Christian endeavors of comprehending the ignominious death of Jesus as an act of divine salvation. The voices assembled in this volume thus explore history, probe old structural and conceptual connections, and trace the development of new insights.

In the first section, this volume features perspectives from the Torah and the Dead Sea Scrolls on the theme of purification; two of its three contributions deal with the effect that the blood of sin offerings has according to different text traditions. Joshua M. Vis is specifically interested in the terminological nuances in sin offering rituals as they can be observed in the regulations for the Day of Atonement (Lev 16:1–28) and the law of the sin offering (4:1–5:13). He notes that the authors of the latter have used key grammatical and syntactical features as well as theological and relational ideas drawn from the description of the sin offerings in Lev 16. According to Vis, the passage Lev 16:1–28 is the earliest text on the sin offering; it employs the Hebrew verb and prepositions כפר + על and כפר + את as functional equivalents. This assumption is corroborated through the identification of the privative, not causative, מן following the כפר-phrase throughout Lev 16. The same features appear throughout Lev 4:1–

5:13, further attesting to the validity of such an analysis. Vis concludes that the offerer of the sin offering, referred to by כפר + על, is the object being purged of (privative מן) sin/guilt in the law of Lev 4:1–5:13.

Dorothea Erbele-Küster focuses on the torah regulation about purification of women after parturition in Lev 12, which contains the peculiar directive that, in such a situation, the woman "shall remain in the blood of purification" according to the Hebrew text of verse 4. These words convey the complex function that blood has in the purification ritual; further contributing aspects are time, blood flow, offerings, and the cultic engagement of the woman as a priest. Erbele-Küster notes that the Hebrew expression "blood of purification" puzzled already the early Greek translators, as the LXX renders it as "impure blood." The reception history of this passage shows that the Greek conception of "im-purity" and of the purification ritual are major reasons for this textual change.

Concluding this section, Hannah K. Harrington examines dynamics of purification in the Dead Sea Scrolls and related literature, specifically how ablution rituals allow access to holiness. The function of ritual ablutions, both in biblical and postbiblical literature, was not just to remove specific bodily impurities; in some cases, such impurities were not even a factor. Therefore, Harrington explores the function of ritual ablutions to facilitate access to levels of holiness in Second Temple texts, especially in the Dead Sea Scrolls. She observes that this stance toward ritual ablutions is supported by scriptural antecedents, a variety of Second Temple and rabbinic texts, as well as by the archaeological record.

The second section of this volume centers on a variety of ritual aspects and the so-called prophetic critique of the institution of sacrifice. David Calabro reexamines the ancient Israelite hand placement gesture, which played an important role in the sacrificial cult as well as in other ritual contexts. Contrary to most scholars, he suggests that this gesture was carried out with both hands. Calabro examines the phrase סמך ידים על ("lay the hands upon") and observes that the noun is consistently featured in the dual. After the disappearance of the temple cult, the consistent nature of this gesture was obscured by a number of factors, including linguistic change and a method of vocalization that followed the consonantal text in an ad hoc manner. These factors ultimately led to modern reconstructions of the gesture as sometimes one-handed, sometimes two-handed. Calabro refutes this understanding and goes on to reexamine also the function of this ritual gesture, which effects the assignment of the recipient to a particular "position in an organizational order."

Aaron Glaim investigates biblical texts commonly considered to present a prophetic critique of sacrifice. He observes that they typically depict God's pitiless punishment of the Israelites and Judeans with brutal military defeat and other calamities, which would be incommensurate with any divine acceptance of sacrifices. Hence Glaim suggests that prophetic discourse of this kind actually functions as an apology for the cult of YHWH. Prophetic rhetoric provides an explanation as to how Israel and Judah could suffer devastating military defeats when sacrifices were being offered without challenging the overall efficacy of sacrificial practice. The argument is not that sacrifices as such are ineffective, rather that they are ineffective when YHWH is angry. According to Glaim, this premise helps to explain why prophetic texts were embraced by later authorities who might well have had strong connections to the Jerusalem temple cult.

Göran Eidevall arrives at somewhat related conclusions in his study of two issues which are rarely brought together in exegetical discussions, namely, the interpretation of prophetic denunciations of sacrifice, on the one hand, and the question of theological coherence in the book of Jeremiah, on the other. He argues that the cult-critical passages in the book of Jeremiah need not be seen as incompatible with those passages promoting sacrifices. On the basis of rhetorical analysis of the relevant passages, Eidevall suggests that the final editors of this prophetic book had a basically positive attitude to the sacrificial cult and created a certain degree of coherence regarding cultic issues by means of a chronological principle. Whereas passages that reject sacrifices always refer to the past (that is, to the cult before 586 BCE in Solomon's temple), passages accepting or even promoting sacrifices consistently refer to the future (that is, to the postexilic cult in the Second Temple).

Ma. Maricel S. Ibita explores the critique of the sacrificial cult and the metaphors for YHWH in prophetic lawsuit passages such as Mic 6:1–8 and Isa 1:1–20. She proposes that the issue stems from Israel's mistaken and forgotten identity, which is related to who YHWH is and who the people are for YHWH. Employing blending theory, Ibita notes that the metaphors depict YHWH as suzerain king and father. The most important characteristics of YHWH that emerge from this study are elucidated by insights from social values palpable in the biblical text, showing that authentic worship goes beyond the multitude of sacrifice one can offer.

The three contributions in the third section of this volume explore the multifaceted nature of atonement in the Hebrew Bible and alternative concepts. Christian A. Eberhart examines the connection of various rituals at the "Day of Atonement" in Lev 16 with the effect of atonement. Using information from sacrificial rituals in Lev 1–7, he investigates blood application rites and burning rites in sacrificial rituals of that festival. Proceeding to a discussion of the scapegoat ritual, Eberhart develops a broad conceptualization of atonement so as to include aspects such as elimination rituals and the sacrificial burning rite. He also reviews recent proposals from a sociocultural perspective that make "latent" functions of these rituals visible and compares these functions to their explicit or manifest purposes. Finally, he explores how early Christian texts deploy atonement terminology and concepts from the Day of Atonement.

Jarvis J. Williams argues that the Jewish martyrs in martyrologies of Second Temple Judaism functioned as Israel's Yom Kippur. He corroborates his thesis by presenting support that the martyrs' torah-observant lives provided the appropriate cultic action; thus their representative and substitutionary deaths for Israel functioned to achieve national purification. By cultic action, Williams means the appropriate performance of the Levitical cultic rituals as prescribed by YHWH in Leviticus and reiterated elsewhere in the Hebrew Bible. By cultic function, he means the positive results achieved for the community as a result of the appropriate cultic action (e.g., forgiveness, reconciliation, expiation, propitiation, atonement).

According to Ross E. Winkle's reading of 2 Thessalonians, resistance is not futile. Chapter 2 of this New Testament text contains an enigmatic reference to a figure described as the "restrainer," which Winkle understands as an oblique allusion to the figure of Michael in Dan 10:13, 21, and 12:1. The dynamic description of Michael in the book of Daniel, along with the later understanding in various Jewish traditions of Michael as a high priestly, intercessory figure, would make sense as the potential background for the restrainer in 2 Thess 2, particularly when one is cognizant of the various descriptions of priestly restraint against disaster and evil. The priesthood was sometimes characterized by martial overtones, military action, and warfare. The language of both Dan 12 and 2 Thess 2 allow for Michael's and the restrainer's activity to cease, and the cessation of Michael's activity of restraint would thus refer to the cessation of his high priestly ministry of spiritual warfare and resistance to and restraint of evil. Winkle proposes that Daniel's "time of trouble" (12:1) would then ensue, mirroring the reference to the climactic rise and activity of the Thessalonian man of lawlessness.

A fourth and final section deals with aspects and concepts derived from the temple building and its priesthood in order to reframe sacred authority. Tim Wardle analyzes how the sectarians at Qumran and the early Christians appropriated temple terminology and applied it to their respective communities. In so doing, both groups declared that God's presence now infused them, and purity and holiness were now expected. Wardle observes, however, that the early Christians went one step further in assigning specific structural terminology—that of pillars, stones, and foundations—to individual members of the community. The decision to apply temple architecture to individual members of the Christian community was rooted in Jewish Scriptures, developed along christological lines, and served both to create and reinforce communal identity.

Nicole Wilkinson Duran explores the prediction of Jesus in Mark's Gospel that "not one stone will be left on another" in the framework of the destruction of the temple and the crucifixion. She notes that scholars attuned to themes of sacrifice in this gospel have tended to see Jesus as inherently opposed to the rituals and laws of the purity system, including temple sacrifice and indeed the temple itself. While there is clearly a tension between Jesus and what the gospel perceives as his ritual and religious environment, Duran questions whether Jesus, according to Mark, expresses genuine opposition to the temple, to sacrifice, or to the purity system. Taking note of the readings of both Bruce Chilton and Girardian scholars, she argues that this gospel affirms the logic of sacrifice in much the same way that Hebrew narrative did and does not celebrate the temple's destruction as a kind of liberation, but grieves the event as it grieves the crucifixion.

In his second contribution to this volume, Ross E. Winkle assesses the identity of Jesus as high priest in John's Apocalypse by looking specifically at Rev 1:13. This verse has been the focus of contentious arguments both for and against understanding the identity of Jesus Christ as high priest on account of the clothing imagery described there. Clothing or dress communicates many data to observers, and a key piece is role-related identity. According to Winkle, an analysis of both the foot-length robe and the belt/sash that Jesus, the one "like a Son of Man," wears indicates that he has a high priestly role-related identity. He concludes that the Epistle to the Hebrews is not the only document within the New Testament describing or portraying Jesus as high priest.

This volume features contributions by scholars from multiple academic disciplines and different geographical areas. These scholars explore terminology, aspects, and concepts of the ancient Israelite and early Jewish religion and their creative application in early Christianity. They likewise scrutinize how sacrifice and atonement as key concepts of the temple cult were both transcended and transformed after the destruction of the Second Temple in 70 CE. Hence the concepts of sacrifice and atonement have permeated religious ideas and secular rhetoric throughout the ages, causing fascination and perplexity alike. While the contributions to the present volume offer no systematic exposition of sacrifice and atonement in biblical literature, it is the hope of the editors that they will help to appreciate and better comprehend the sanctuary and its worship, which epitomized the religion of ancient Israel and Judah and which became the foundation of ongoing learned reflections in rabbinic Judaism and a central conceptual resource in Christianity.

Part 1
Purification: Perspectives from the Torah and the Dead Sea Scrolls

The Purgation of Persons through the Purification Offering*

Joshua M. Vis

Introduction

In Lev 16:1–28, a text widely regarded as one of the earliest from the Priestly Source, בעד + כפר refers exclusively to חטאת offerings made to purge (כפר) the sancta "on behalf of" Aaron, his house, and the people (Lev 16:6, 11, 17). The clear objective of the חטאת offerings of Yom Kippur, according to Lev 16:1–28, is to purge the sancta "on behalf of" (בעד) the Israelites. The passage never uses the preposition על in this manner in Lev 16:1–28. Instead, in two places (Lev 16:16, 18), על + כפר identifies the purged sancta. In these cases, על functions just as the definite direct object marker does in Lev 16:20, where again sancta are the objects of purgation. Leviticus 16:16 also employs privative מן after the על + כפר clause to mark exactly what items (מטמאת בני ישראל ומפשעיהם) are purged from the sanctuary. This construction with מן, after על + כפר, not only occurs here in Lev 16:16, which further strengthens the case that על + כפר can and does mark the object purged, but also in Lev 16:30 and 34 and a variety of places throughout Lev 1–16. All told, the proper reading of these prepositions (בעד, על, מן) in Lev 16:1–28, and then throughout Lev 1–16, reveals that while חטאת offerings originally functioned to purge the sancta on Yom Kippur, they subsequently had the purpose of purging persons from sins and uncleanness, as evidenced especially in Lev 4:1–5:13.

---

* Portions of this article were previously published in my dissertation: Joshua M. Vis, "The Purification Offering of Leviticus and the Sacrificial Offering of Jesus" (PhD diss., Duke University, 2012).

The Use of Prepositions in Leviticus 16

The prepositions used in relation to the חטאת offering and verb כפר give us a clear picture of the function of the חטאת offering throughout the ritual. Aaron consistently effects purgation (כפר) "on behalf of" (בעד) himself/his house and the congregation with the חטאת offerings on Yom Kippur (Lev 16:6, 11, 17). Furthermore, Aaron purges (כפר) parts of the sanctuary, marked either with the definite direct object marker את (Lev 16:20, 33 [H]) or with על (Lev 16:16, 18), which clearly is functionally equivalent to את, marking the object of כפר. Throughout Lev 16:1–28, the prepositions בעד and על never appear interchangeably; that is, a person is never the object of על, and the sancta is never the object of בעד. However, in the addition from the writer of the Holiness Code, the Israelites are the object of the preposition על with the verb כפר (Lev 16:30, 33, 34). The shift from various sancta as the objects of כפר (marked either by את or על) to the Israelites as the objects (marked by על) of כפר comes as a surprise and requires explanation. Nevertheless, just as in 16:1–28, Lev 16:30, 33, and 34 also clearly show that the objects of purgation can be marked with כפר + על or כפר + את.

Jacob Milgrom muddies the waters on the use of prepositions in Lev 16 in his primary discussion of his hypothesis regarding the function of the חטאת offering.

> When the object is nonhuman, כפר takes the preposition על or ב or a direct object. For example, all three usages are attested in the purging of the adytum on the Day of Purgation (16:16, 20), and they must be understood literally, for the כפר rite takes place on (על) the כפרת and on the floor before it, in (ב) the adytum, or it can be said that the entire room (את) is purged (כפר; cf. also 6:23; 16:10, 33; Exod 30:10).... When the object of כפר is a person, however, it is never expressed as a direct object but requires the prepositions על or בעד. Both signify "on behalf of" (16:6, 24, 30, 33; Num 8:12, 21), but they are not entirely synonymous. The difference is that על can only refer to persons other than the subject, but when the subject wishes to refer to himself he must use בעד (e.g., 9:7; 16:6, 11, 24; Ezek 45:22).[1]

---

1. Jacob Milgrom, *Leviticus 1–16: A New Translation with Introduction and Commentary*, AB 3 (New York: Doubleday, 1991), 255.

With one exception (Exod 30:10, with "its [the altar's] horns" as the object of על along with the verb כפר), the preposition על after the verb כפר marks the object for which כפר is accomplished. Milgrom's example above, where he states that "the כפר rite takes place on (על) the כפרת," is misleading. Although על appears with כפרת in 16:14 (a verse Milgrom neglects to list), כפר stands nowhere in this verse, thus על + כפר does not occur with כפרת as Milgrom appears to indicate above. Furthermore, I do not accept Milgrom's last point concerning על and בעד. In Lev 16:1–28, every חטאת offering for a person, be it the priest, his family, or the people, happens "on behalf of," בעד, the person. The preposition בעד + person is not simply reserved for sacrifices Aaron makes on his behalf, as Lev 16:17 shows. The crucial difference in usage between בעד and על is that על, along with the definite direct object marker (את), can mark the purged object. The preposition בעד appears with כפר not only in Lev 16:6, 11, 17, but also in Lev 9:7 where it takes the second-person singular pronoun (referring to Aaron) as its object alongside the entire people of Israel. If the Priestly writer wishes to communicate that כפר happens "on behalf of" a person, meaning another object is purged on a person's behalf, בעד is used, not על. Milgrom fails to mention that על also marks sancta as the object of כפר, as in Lev 16:16 (וכפר על־הקדש) and Lev 16:18 (וכפר עליו), with the third-person masculine pronoun on על referring back to המזבח. Milgrom concludes that in Lev 16:16, על functions like the definite direct object marker (את) when he translates the phrase in this way: "Thus he shall purge the adytum."[2] Milgrom curiously does not translate על in Lev 16:18 in this same way. Instead he concludes: "Whereas the preposition על after כפר always means 'for, on behalf of' if the object is human, it can literally mean 'on, upon' if the object is nonhuman (see vv. 10, 16 and ch. 4 Comment B)."[3] I quoted Milgrom's translation of this same construction in 16:16 above, where he translates על + כפר, marking הקדש, as if על functions like the definite direct object marker את. While it is true that על + כפר can sometimes mean literally "on, upon," this cannot be the case in Lev 16:18. Leviticus 16:20 settles it when it marks הקדש and המזבח with the definite direct object marker (את) after the verb כפר. Therefore, in both 16:16 with כפר על־הקדש and in 16:18 with (המזבח) כפר עליו, על must have a meaning similar to the definite direct object marker (את),

---

2. Ibid., 1010.
3. Ibid., 1036.

lest we conclude that Lev 16:16 and 16:18 are communicating something different than 16:20.

One can adduce further proofs for reading על + כפר as functionally equivalent to את + כפר in Lev 16:1–28 (as well as 16:29–34a). Milgrom notes that the placing of blood on the horns of the altar in Lev 16:19 purifies it (וטהרו), while the seven-fold sprinkling of blood on the altar consecrates it (וקדשו, Lev 16:19).[4] The command in Lev 16:18 to עליו + כפר (המזבח), the phrase about which Milgrom and I disagree, precedes all of this. Milgrom notes this same sequence in Exod 29:36–37, where the altar is first purged (Milgrom cites both the verb חטא and כפר to support the notion of purging) and then consecrated.[5] In both cases, Milgrom argues that the altar is purged, but he denies that על + כפר is the key phrase alerting the reader to purgation and to the object of said purgation. We need only look to the rest of 16:18 and the following verse to see:

1. One of the two goals of these חטאת offerings (a combination of the blood of the bull for Aaron and his house and the blood of the goat for the people) is to declare it (the altar) clean (וטהרו);
2. The only action done "upon" the altar is a seven-fold sprinkling of blood (16:19), which must be the action of (re)consecration, the second goal of these חטאת offerings.

"The daubing of the altar horns purifies the altar and the sevenfold sprinkling of the altar consecrates it." Milgrom continues: "Support for this sequence is found in the prescription for the altar's consecration (Exod 29:36–37): first it is purged (חטא, כפר) and then it is consecrated (קדש, משח)."[6] Milgrom's distinction is certainly correct, but such a distinction requires that עליו + וכפר in Lev 16:18 be rendered as "and purge it [the altar]." Exodus 29:36–37 confirms this reading by demonstrating that the order of operations is to purge and then to consecrate. Furthermore, both of these verses have the combination of על + כפר functioning equivalently to את + כפר with the altar as the object of purgation.

Also relevant in this context are the phrases וחטאת על־המזבח בכפרך עליו in Exod 29:36 and שבעת ימים תכפר על־המזבח וקדשת אתו in verse

---

4. Ibid., 1037.
5. Ibid.
6. Ibid.

37. In both phrases, the altar (המזבח) is the object of עַל, not אֵת, and yet the understanding clearly is "you shall purge the altar."[7] In verse 37, the כפר-phrase precedes, but is paired with, the קדש-phrase: the altar is purged and then consecrated. Verse 36 has כפר+עַל with the altar as the object, and again עַל functions like אֵת, with the proper rendering of the phrase as follows: "You shall offer a sin offering upon the altar when you purge it."

While the following phrase in Exod 29:36, וחטאת עַל־המזבח, might communicate that the altar is purged, this is unlikely because it would be the only case in which חטא + עַל, instead of חטא + אֵת (Lev 8:15; 14:49, 52; Ezek 43:20, 22; 45:18), means "to purge or purify," rather than "to offer a sin offering upon." As discussed above, the same issue arises in Lev 16:18–19, this time with כפר and טהר. In Lev 16:18, Aaron "shall go out to the altar that is before YHWH and purge it [כפר עליו]. He shall take some of the blood of the bull and some of the blood of the ram and put it on the horns of the altar all around." Leviticus 16:19 reads: "He shall sprinkle some of the blood with his finger seven times. Thus he shall declare it clean [וטהרו] and consecrate it from the uncleanness of the Israelites." Milgrom renders וטהרו as "Thus he shall purify it," which is indeed a possible translation. However, throughout Lev 1–16, this same verb, in the *piel* (in places, with the exact same pointing and 3rd masc. sg. objective suffix, as marked below with an asterisk), appears a number of times and is rendered by Milgrom as "he shall declare it/him clean" (13:6*, 13, 17, 23*, 28*, 34, 37*, 58; 14:7*, 48). Ezekiel 43:26 has the same construction with כפר followed by טהר: יכפרו את־המזבח וטהרו אתו טהר. The altar (המזבח) has the definite direct object marker, leaving no confusion about the proper translation of כפר and the entire phrase: "They shall purge the altar." It is thus highly unlikely that the טהר-phrase after the כפר-phrase—both here in Ezek 43:26 and in Lev 16:18–19—means "and cleanse it," as Milgrom renders it, but rather "and they/he shall declare it clean." The altar is not cleansed twice, but purged and then declared clean.

One final textual component provides support for my reading of Lev 16:18: the summary in verse 19b of what Aaron has accomplished. First, he purges the altar through the placing of blood upon the horns of the altar, and declares it clean from the uncleanness of the Israelites. Then, he (re)consecrates the altar by sprinkling blood on it seven times, which

---

7. Unless otherwise noted, all translations are mine.

matches the sevenfold sprinkling of oil done by Moses in Lev 8:11 at the original consecration of the altar. As mentioned above, Milgrom asserts that the procedure is purgation and then consecration. However, Milgrom has neglected to see that the only action done on (על) the altar is the sprinkling of the blood (והזה עליו), the action of (re)consecration. The other actions were done on the horns of the altar (על־קרנות המזבח), not the altar itself. As Milgrom himself states: "The notion that the same application of the blood of the purification offering can simultaneously decontaminate and consecrate is intrinsically wrong. The realms of impurity and holiness are incompatible with each other and their admixture is lethal (e.g., 15:31; ch. 4, Comment C)."[8] Yet Milgrom's translation of Lev 16:18–19 requires such an equation. If purgation is effected "upon the altar," as Milgrom would have us believe, then the sevenfold sprinkling would have to be the action effecting this purgation, as it is the only action done "upon the altar." But this cannot be so. Clearly the placement of blood upon the horns of the altar "effects purgation," thus purgation is not effected "upon the altar," but "upon its horns." The only possible explanation, then, is that על + כפר in Lev 16:18 and כפר על־המזבח in Exod 29:36–37 communicates "purge it/the altar" just as it does in Lev 16:16. In Lev 16:1–28, then, את + כפר or על + כפר conveys the direct purgation of an object.

Baruch Levine similarly analyzes the phrases את + כפר and על + כפר in Lev 16. Levine concludes:

> In fact, in the cultic texts even the older construction, i.e., כפר + direct object seems to have the same functional force as כפר + indirect object,[9] when it conveys the spatial process. Thus, מכפר את־הקדש "from purifying the sanctuary," in Leviticus 16:20 (compare verse 33) refers to the same ritual acts to which וכפר על־הקדש in verse 16 refers. The graphics of the direct object construction are admittedly more binding physically, but as the relationship between action and consequence is concerned, there is no difference.[10]

It is not clear to me why Levine views the את + כפר equation as older than על + כפר, for, as he notes, they both appear in Lev 16, and I see no

---

8. Ibid., 524.

9. Levine considers כפר + preposition as equivalent to כפר + indirect object.

10. Baruch Levine, *In the Presence of the Lord: A Study of Cult and Some Cultic Terms in Ancient Israel*, SJLA 5 (Brill: Leiden, 1974), 66.

reason to suppose that Lev 16:20 reflects an older tradition (and thus an older construction) than Lev 16:16. Levine seems to make this determination based on the fact that "in Akkadian, *kapāru/kuppuru* tends to take the direct object, whereas in biblical Hebrew more often than not, כפר is constructed with an indirect object, introduced by the independent prepositions על and בעד, and with the prefixed preposition ל."[11] As Levine notes, כפר + ל occurs only once in P or H, in Num 35:33 (an H text), which is not a cultic context.[12] The construction כפר + ל occurs here because this text focuses on blood as the defiling material that must be purged from the land, and not on the land as the object that needs purgation.

Num 35:33
ולא־תחניפו את־הארץ אשר אתם בה כי הדם הוא יחניף את־הארץ ולארץ
לא־יכפר לדם אשר שפך־בה כי־אם בדם שפכו:

For it is the blood that pollutes the land, and for the land, it will not be purged of the blood that was shed on it except by the blood of the one who shed it.

Thus כפר + ל is not parallel in meaning to either כפר + בעד or כפר + על, nor does it appear frequently in the Priestly material. כפר + בעד itself occurs only in Lev 9:7 and four times in Lev 16 (vv. 6, 11, 17, and 24). Although כפר + בעד in Lev 9:7 appears to refer to both the purification offering and the burnt offering, as in 16:24, it is a reference only to the burnt offering. Again, this combination of כפר+ בעד is very infrequent and should not be viewed as equivalent to the use of כפר + על, which is the preferred combination throughout the Priestly material and which is used differently than בעד. Furthermore, neither כפר + בעד nor כפר + ל occur in a situation where either construction could equate with כפר + את (also very rarely used in P, it should be noted, only 16:20, 33). Levine thus fails to recognize that, in P, it is only כפר + על that is functionally equivalent to כפר + את.

Although Roy Gane concludes that the offerer is purged in Lev 4:1–5:13, he surprisingly misses the equation of כפר + על and כפר + את. Instead, Gane agrees with Milgrom concerning the equation of על and בעד:

---

11. Ibid., 63.
12. Ibid., 58 n. 10.

Whereas כפר is always followed by על in cases of physical impurities, formulas concerned with moral faults also employ the preposition בעד in contexts that include officiating by the high priest on behalf of himself (9:7; 16:6, 11, 17, 24). So it appears that lack of בעד in formulas of חטאת sacrifices that are solely for physical impurities is due to the lack of a case in which a priest reflexively removes his own physical impurity by simultaneously functioning as offerer and officiant.[13]

Gane's adoption of Milgrom's hypothesis about על and בעד is not only surprising given that Gane argues for the purgation of offerers in all cases but Yom Kippur (the same argument I will make), but also because recognition of the equation of כפר + על and כפר + את allows for a simple refutation of what Gane says here. First, not all of the verses where כפר + בעד occurs (Lev 9:7; 16:6, 11, 17, 24) use this phrase to refer to an offering of the high priest on his own behalf.

Lev 9:7: וכפר בעדך ובעד העם

Lev 16:6: וכפר בעדו ובעד ביתו

Lev 16:11: וכפר בעדו ובעד ביתו

Lev 16:17: וכפר בעדו ובעד ביתו ובעד כל־קהל ישראל

Lev 16:24: וכפר בעדו ובעד העם

In each verse, בעד indeed indicates the offering by the high priest on his own behalf; but it also indicates the offering by the high priest on behalf of his house (16:6, 11, 17) or on behalf of the Israelites (9:7; 16:17, 24). One could argue that the offering for the house of the high priest benefits the high priest, and indeed the sacrifice of the same animal in Lev 16 accomplishes כפר for both, and thus בעד is rightly used with בית. But the same explanation does not apply in the case of the offerings for the Israelites in 9:7; 16:17, 24. If בעד is reserved for offerings that benefit the high priest, then על should have been used to mark העם in 9:7 and 16:24 and כל־קהל ישראל in 16:17, unless, as I argue, בעד + כפר refers to an offering on a

---

13. Roy Gane, *Cult and Character: Purification Offerings, Day of Atonement, and Theodicy* (Winona Lake, IN: Eisenbrauns, 2005), 123.

person's or persons' behalf for the benefit (the purgation) of the sanctuary. This is certainly the case in Lev 16 (something upon which Milgrom, Gane, and I agree). Furthermore, while Lev 16 is concerned with moral faults, it is also concerned with impurity (16:16 contains מטמאת בני ישראל along with ומפשעיהם לכל-חטאתם). This fact calls into question this statement from Gane: "Whereas כפר is always followed by על in cases of physical impurities, formulas concerned with moral faults also employ the preposition בעד." Gane, like Milgrom, has simply misunderstood the distinction between the usage of כפר + בעד and כפר + על. The text does not restrict the combination of כפר+בעד to the high priest offering a sacrifice on his own behalf, nor does it apply only to offerings concerning moral faults. This verb-and-preposition combination happens when a חטאת offering is brought on behalf of an Israelite or a group of Israelites for the purpose of purging some part of the sanctuary.

A few other texts outside of the Priestly texts merit mention. Ezekiel 43:25–26, mentioned briefly above, is similar to Exod 29:36–37. Both texts command a seven-day cleansing of the altar through חטאת offerings, as well as its consecration (Ezek 43:26 uses מלא יד, while Exod 29:37 uses the *piel* of קדש). Ezekiel 43:26 uses את to mark the altar as the object of כפר (יכפרו את-המזבח), while Exod 29:37 uses על (תכפר על-המזבח), again attesting to the fact that כפר + על and כפר + את are functionally equivalent. Jeremiah 18:23 (אל-תכפר על-עונם) and Ps 79:9 (וכפר על-חטאתינו) also both clearly use כפר+על as "purge" and with על marking the object. In Jer 18:23, אל-תכפר על-עונם ("do not purge their iniquity") is followed by and in partial parallelism with וחטאתם מלפניך אל-תמחי ("and do not blot out their sin from before you"). The pairing of a כפר phrase with a phrase containing חטאת certainly seems like an intentional allusion to sacrifice, and it also attests to a relationship between כפר and מחה, which has such meanings as "wipe, blot out." This verse adds further proof to the legitimacy of the meaning "purge" for כפר. Thus, כפר + על can unquestionably equate with כפר + את, and כפר + על is not similar to כפר + בעד. When one perceives the relationships between the prepositions and את in this way, then the understanding of the function of the חטאת offering here in Lev 16, as well as in Lev 4:1–5:13 and Lev 17, becomes much clearer, as the following section will begin to explain.

Leviticus 16:29–34a: Understanding the Addition from the Author of the Holiness Code

The final section of Lev 16 quite clearly comes from the Holiness Code. The shift in addressees in 16:29 provides the first clue: the text speaks directly to the people for the first time. Remarks Milgrom:

> Heretofore, they were referred to in the third person. Moreover, they played no part whatever in the sanctuary ritual. Even their offerings were brought not by them but by Aaron. ... Thus this switch to second-person, direct address to Israel is the first of several signs that this and the following verses comprise an appendix to the text.[14]

Furthermore, Christophe Nihan points to a number of terminological changes in Lev 16:29–34a:

> In particular, the inner-sanctum is referred to as מקדש הקדש (v. 33) instead of הקדש in v. 2–28 (see v. 2, 3, 16, 17, 20, 23, 27); the community is referred to by the phrase עם הקהל (v. 33) instead of עם (v. 15, 24) or קהל (v. 17); the verb כפר Piel, when it has persons as subjects, is systematically constructed with על (see v. 30, 33, 34), whereas Lev 16:1–28 always uses בעד.[15]

Specific mention of the native (אזרח) and the resident alien (גר) in 16:29 offers further proof of H's authorship. These two nouns appear together in H five times (Lev 17:15; 18:26; 19:34; 23:42; 24:16) and neither noun appears in Lev 1:1–16:28. Finally, Lev 16:29–34a is unmistakably similar to Lev 23:26–32. Nihan notes: "The parallel is particularly striking in 16:31, which is the literal equivalent to Lev 23:32a, but there are numerous additional similarities between the two laws, especially in 16:29–31."[16] Aside from the terminological differences, some important and surprising thematic and theological differences emerge. Leviticus 16:30 asserts that the aim of Yom Kippur is "to purify you (the Israelites) [לטהר אתכם] of all your sins [מכל חטאתיכם]." The full verse (16:30) reads: "For on this day, he shall purge you [יכפר עליכם] to purify you [לטהר אתכם] of all of

---

14. Milgrom, *Leviticus 1–16*, 1054.
15. Christophe Nihan, *From Priestly Torah to Pentateuch: A Study in the Composition of the Book of Leviticus*, FAT 2/25 (Tübingen: Mohr Siebeck, 2007), 347.
16. Ibid., 348.

your sins [מכל חטאתיכם];¹⁷ you shall be declared pure before YHWH." For the first time in Lev 16, the people (here, referred to with the 2nd pl. pronominal suffix) are the objects of כפר. The construction is כפר + על, but as in Lev 16:16 and 16:18, I argue that the sense is clearly the same as כפר + את. Leviticus 16:34a also supports my reading of 16:30. While Lev 16:30 has the verb לטהר ("to purify") between יכפר עליכם ("he shall purge you") and מכל חטאתיכם ("of all your sins"), Lev:16:34a has לכפר על־בני ישראל מכל־חטאתם, in which the preposition מן follows directly after the על + כפר phrase. In both cases, along with translating על + כפר as functioning parallel to כפר + את, I perceive מן as privative, creating a clear cause and effect between the action of כפר and the result of cleanliness for the people. If one were to translate this as Milgrom does, "shall purgation be effected on your behalf to purify you of all your sins (Lev 16:30)" and "to effect purgation on behalf of the Israelites for all their sins (Lev 16:34a)," one still must account for the odd fact that this verse asserts that the people are purified. Moreover, not only does Milgrom's translation of the מן differ in each verse, but his translation leads to a disconnected cause and effect; purgation is effected for the people (which means that the sancta is purged), which somehow leads to the purification of the people.

Gane's discussion of the use of the preposition מן in conjunction with כפר phrases throughout the Priestly material is instructive in a number of places where כפר occurs in Lev 1–16, but here I want to shed light on Lev 16:30 and 16:34a. Gane begins with two passages on physical ritual impurities (Lev 12:7; 14:19) and shows that in each case the proper reading of the מן is privative. Leviticus 12:7 addresses the case of the new mother, and Gane points out that the result clause for the כפר process is וטהרה ממקר דמיה: the מן must be translated as "from"—the woman "shall be pure from the source of her blood." Gane explains,

> Following וטהרה, "and then she shall be pure," מן does not refer to impure blood coming "from" its genital source. Rather, the real force of מן here can only be *privative*, a usage derived from the overall concept of separation that is basic to this preposition…: as a result of the priest's performing

---

17. Although the atnach appears on אתכם, I am translating it as though the proper break comes after חטאתיכם. I simply disagree with the Masoretes on this. Milgrom also renders the break as I do (*Leviticus 1–16*, 1011).

כפר on her behalf (עליה),[18] the parturient becomes pure in the sense that she is freed/separated *"from"* (מן) her physical ritual impurity, which is identified in terms of its physical cause as her "source of blood." This does not refer to physical healing, of course, because her flow of blood had already stopped before she brought her sacrifices (vv. 4–6). Rather, the sacrificial process removes residual ritual impurity from her.[19]

Milgrom also translates as Gane suggests here, rendering ממקר דמיה as "from her source of blood."[20] In this case, then, we have a very clear example of a חטאת offering, along with an עולה offering, benefiting the offerer, and not the altar.[21] Gane goes on to show that the same construction occurs in Lev 14:19, which has the following: ועשה הכהן את־החטאת וכפר על־המטהר מטמאתו. Again, we have the preposition מן in a very similar construction as Lev 12:7, although here מן marks the result of the verb כפר, whereas in Lev 12:7 it marks the result of טהר. Milgrom renders מן in Lev 4:19 as "for" (a causative sense of מן): "The priest shall then offer the purification offering and effect purgation for the one being purified for his impurity."[22] I disagree with Milgrom's translation of וכפר על־המטהר, which should instead be rendered "and purge the one being purified." Moreover, with Gane, I also think Milgrom's rendering of מן as causative is highly unlikely. As Gane points out, the dynamics of Lev 12:7 and Lev 14:19 are the same, and so too are the results. Not only does Lev 14:19 identify the offerer as המטהר ("the one being purified"), but the following verse ends with the pronouncement וטהר, "And he shall be pure." Gane rightly concludes: "The bottom line for Lev 14:19 is that a privative meaning of מן in מטמאתו makes perfect sense in this context, where the idea of removing evil[23] from the offerer is implied anyway. Therefore, there is no reason to complicate the plain sense by understanding this preposition differently than in 12:7, where the privative meaning is positively required."[24]

---

18. Here again, I think that על is marking the direct object of כפר, and thus the priest is not performing כפר on her behalf, but rather the priest "purges her."

19. Gane, *Cult and Character*, 112–13 (emphasis original).

20. Milgrom, *Leviticus 1–16*, 761.

21. Gane, *Cult and Character*, 114.

22. Milgrom, *Leviticus 1–16*, 828.

23. This is too strong a term. There is no evidence that impurity is evil. Gane labels it as such because he is accepting Milgrom's translation of כפר in Lev 14:20 as "make expiation for him."

24. Gane, *Cult and Character*, 115.

All of this brings me to Lev 16:34a, where the same construction occurs: לכפר על־בני ישראל מכל־חטאתם. Remarking on Lev 16:30, Gane writes:

> But Lev 16:30 provides direct evidence that is overpowering: מן follows the verb טהר in the "result" column, where it can only be privative, as in 12:7.... Leviticus 16:30 is stronger than 12:7 because it has טהר in *pi'el*, followed by the direct object that refers to the collective offerer (here the entire Israelite community) as in Num 8:21 (the Levites). The conclusion is inescapable: the כפר process removes moral faults from the offerer(s).[25]

In the same way that the privative מן in Lev 12:7, coming after the verb טהר, sheds light on Lev 14:9 (מן + כפר), Lev 16:30, also with privative מן and טהר, sheds light on Lev 16:34a, which has כפר + מן. Leviticus 16:30 has already stated that one of the goals, in fact the main goal according to H, of Yom Kippur is to purify (לטהר) the Israelites so that they (here literally 2nd pl., "you") will be declared pure (תטהרו). In Lev 16:34a, as in Lev 12:7, and 14:9, using the causative sense of מן clearly "complicate[s] the plain sense."

My reading, in which the people are purged and thus clean, is internally coherent, but it still faces the difficulty of explaining why and how H reports that the people are cleansed. Why does the writer of H conclude that the main goal of Yom Kippur is to purge the Israelites, making them clean? My analysis of Lev 16:1–28 concludes that only the goat for Azazel effected purgation for the Israelites by purging Aaron of the sins he carries on behalf of the people. Leviticus 16:33 indeed confirms that the sanctuary, tent of meeting, and the altar are purged, just as Lev 16:20 states. In this way, the addition from H and the original Priestly text are in accord. Leviticus 16:29–34a lends further evidence to my theory that על + כפר and את + כפר are functionally equivalent. I have already discussed how על + כפר in Lev 16:30 and 16:34a clearly indicates that the proper translation is "to purge you (pl.)/the people" due to the privative מן following the כפר phrases in these verses. Leviticus 16:33 also confirms that על + כפר and את + כפר are functionally equivalent, as את marks the sancta that are purged, and על the persons that are purged. Milgrom, of course, sees this difference between sancta marked with את + כפר and persons marked with על + כפר as an indication that what is accomplished for sancta and what is accomplished for persons are distinct. Milgrom translates 16:33:

---

25. Ibid., 125–26.

"He shall purge the holiest part of the sanctuary, and he shall purge the Tent of Meeting and the altar; he shall effect purgation for the priests and for all the people of the congregation."[26] Not only has the use of כפר + על in Lev 16:1–28 shown Milgrom to be in error, but Lev 16:30 and 34a have also decisively shown that one of the purposes of Yom Kippur, for the author of H, is "to purge the Israelites of [privative מן] all their sins" (לכפר על־בני ישראל מכל־חטאתם). Only once a year can all of the Israelites "be declared pure before YHWH" (לפני יהוה תטהרו).

The final piece of the puzzle relates to how H believes the people become pure through the rituals of Yom Kippur. A few issues are in play and chapter 3 of my dissertation covers these issues in greater detail.[27] For this article, it will suffice to present some of my conclusions in order to explain H's addition in Lev 16. One issue concerns the sanctuary, which I have argued is purged only once a year, on Yom Kippur. Milgrom believes it is cleansed through every חטאת offering, those of Yom Kippur as well as those offered throughout the year, whose procedure is explicated in Lev 4:1–5:13. I contend that the חטאת offerings of Lev 4:1–5:13, however, purge the offerer(s) and not the sancta. Just as כפר + על functions as an equivalent alternative to כפר + את throughout Lev 16, so too does it function in this way in Lev 4:1–5:13. This fact, combined with the use of the privative מן on חטאת (meaning "sin" and following כפר + על) in Lev 4:26, 5:6 and 5:10, as well as the use of the preposition על to mark the sins purged in Lev 4:35 and 5:13, further supports the conclusion that the offerer is purged by the חטאת offerings of Lev 4:1–5:13. This occasional purgation for persons results not in the offerer being declared pure (טהר), as in Lev 16:34a, but in the offerer being forgiven (נסלח, see Lev 4:20, 26, 31, 35; 5:10, 13). Thus the rituals of Yom Kippur, in the eyes of H, have the ability to move the offerer from a state of forgiveness to a state of ritual purity. Gane, too, sees a two-phase movement for the Israelites, as sinners move from sinful to forgiven, due to the recurring purification offerings described in Lev 4:1–5:13, and then forgiven to "(morally) pure (טהר; v. 30 [Lev 16])" on Yom Kippur.[28] However, while Gane recognizes the possibility that כפר + על may be functionally equivalent to כפר + את, he does not argue for this.[29] Even though Gane notes that כפר + על followed by הקדש

---

26. Milgrom, *Leviticus 1–16*, 1011.
27. Vis, "Purification Offering," 93–134.
28. Gane, *Cult and Character*, 275.
29. Ibid., 139.

in Lev 16:16 must mean simply "purge the adytum," he is unwilling to part with Milgrom on the equivalency of כפר + על and כפר + בעד.³⁰

My contention is that the purgation of the sanctuary, sullied from the sins of people, and the purgation of Aaron, the representative of the people, allows for the purification of all of the Israelites.³¹ The relationship between the Israelites and the sanctuary means that one cannot be clean while the other remains sullied. It is clear that the sins and uncleanness of the Israelites sully the sanctuary. Leviticus 16 communicates this truth without equivocation. Leviticus 4:1–5:13 shows that the reverse is also true. The actions done to the sanctuary can affect the people. The manipulation of sacrifices within and upon the sancta can purge the people of the stain of sin. The addition from H in Lev 16 communicates that the people can only be clean when the sanctuary is clean. Moreover the purgation of Aaron, Israel's representative (and thus of all the Israelites), on Yom Kippur encompasses all of Israel's sins, covering any heretofore not dealt with by means of the sacrificial system, either through neglect or because of the system's inability to purge such sins. Together, through the purgation of the sanctuary and the purgation of Aaron via the goat for Azazel, H communicates that the rituals of Yom Kippur make the Israelites pure before YHWH.

This understanding of Lev 16:29–34a also informs the important H text Lev 17:11, the only place in P or H which explains the rationale for sacrifice. I have shown that this verse agrees with the rest of Leviticus in its affirmation that כפר means "purge."³² I translate the key Hebrew phrase as follows: "And I have placed it [the blood] upon the altar to purge your spirits" (ואני נתתיו לכם על־המזבח לכפר על־נפשתיכם).³³ As was shown above, Lev 16:30 and 34a make it clear that כפר is done so as to cleanse

---

30. Ibid.

31. Vis, "Purification Offering," 109–24, argues that the goat for Azazel purges Aaron of the sins he carries as the representative of the Israelites, including פשעים, transgressions (Lev 16:16, 21), understood as wanton, brazen sins that cannot be purged by any other method.

32. Ibid., 204–30.

33. Ibid., 204–9, 221–27, explains my translation of נפש as spirit, not in the sense of something separate from the body, but as in the sense of "the animating force that sustains the creature"; see Yitzhaq Feder, *Blood Expiation in Hittite and Biblical Ritual: Origins, Context, and Meaning*, WAWSup 2 (Atlanta: Society of Biblical Literature, 2011), 197. This is why I believe that H concludes that it is specifically the נפש of the offerer that is purged.

the people. Thus in Lev 16:30 and 34a, an H text, the meaning of כפר must be understood as "purge." The concept of ransom, which some scholars believe is the proper understanding of כפר in 17:11 ("to ransom for your lives"),[34] cannot be the meaning of כפר in Lev 16:30. The commandment in Lev 16:29 to "deny your spirits" (תענו את־נפשתיכם) is given because it is exactly this part, the נפש of the people, that is cleansed on Yom Kippur.[35]

The Use of Prepositions in Lev 4:1–5:13

Throughout these verses, which give instructions for the חטאת offerings throughout the year, the prepositions על and מן continue to be of utmost importance. Unlike in Lev 16:1–28, the preposition בעד never occurs. As was shown above, בעד is used with כפר to mark the person(s) for whom the purgation is carried out. It never marks the object of purgation. The exclusion of בעד throughout Lev 4:1–5:13 is thus extremely telling, as is the use of על and מן throughout. The Priestly authors of 4:1–5:13 have used the logic of the חטאת offering as a purgative offering in Lev 16, but they have shifted the object of purgation from the sancta to the offerer(s). They have not, however, shifted the use of the phrase על + כפר (marking the object purged) or בעד + כפר (marking the person[s] for whom purgation is accomplished, not the object purged) or the preposition מן after the כפר-phrase. If the offerers of Lev 4:1–5:13 were not the objects of purgation, as Milgrom suggests,[36] the authors would have used כפר + בעד to mark the offerer, not כפר + על. Because of this grammatical consistency with Lev 16, the goal of the חטאת offering of 4:1–5:13 becomes clear. The reality of a relationship between the sancta and the Israelites as explicated in Lev 16 is assumed, but the cause and effect is reversed. Whereas Yom Kippur attested to the people's ability to soil the sancta, the recurring חטאת offering attests to the ability of the sancta to purge the people. Similar ritual procedures as those carried out on Yom Kippur are utilized to purge the offerer.

Throughout Lev 4:1–5:13, the person for whom the priest effects כפר is always marked with כפר + על. In fact, for every חטאת-offering prescrip-

---

34. Jacob Milgrom (*Leviticus 17–22: A New Translation with Introduction and Commentary*, AB 3A [New York: Doubleday, 2000], 1474) and Baruch Levine (*Presence of the Lord*, 67–68) take this view.

35. Vis, "Purification Offering," 132–33.

36. Milgrom, *Leviticus 1–16*, 253–58.

tion in this section (4:20, 26, 31, 35; 5:6, 10, 13), the כפר formula is exactly the same: וכפר עליו הכהן. The one exception is Lev 4:20, which has the entire congregation represented by the elders and thus has the masculine plural third-person suffix on על. I have already discussed my reasoning for reading these phrases as expressing the purgation of the offerer, which means translating the phrase: "Thus the priest shall purge him." While the use of את would make such a reading definitive, the Priestly writers used את and על interchangeably, as has been shown above (see Lev 16:16, 18, 30, 33, 34), and thus either can mark the object for which purgation is effected. For the Priestly writers of Lev 16, there does not appear to be any conceptual difference between marking the adytum (הקדש), for example, with כפר + על (as in Lev 16:16) or כפר + את (as in Lev 16:20). Thus the authors of Lev 4:1–5:13 would have known that כפר + על and כפר + את could be used interchangeably because they would have seen a text very similar to Lev 16. Perhaps because of the indirect way in which offerers were purged, through rituals that only came into physical contact with sancta and not the offerer, these Priestly authors chose to use כפר + על exclusively when the object of purgation was a person. With both כפר + על and כפר + את at their disposal, these Priestly authors selected the collocation that still expressed the novelty of this new use of the חטאת offering (purging persons instead of sancta), while also acknowledging, ever so subtly, that the ritual process of this חטאת offering achieves its desired effect obliquely on account of the relationship between the people and the sancta. Baruch Levine also notes that כפר + על and כפר + את "have the same functional force," although he does not carefully articulate how these two phrases are distinct from כפר + בעד.[37] However, Levine does speculate similarly as I have concerning כפר + על when he suggests "that [כפר] + direct object was not employed by the cultic writers in connection with humans or the substance of the sacrifices precisely because it was desired to avoid the associations of the older usage, wherein [כפר] meant simply 'to wipe off, cleanse,' implying automatic effects."[38] Certainly "wipe off" as a translation of כפר in Lev 4:1–5:13 would create confusion. "Cleanse" is not quite as problematic, although it too will not work in Lev 4:1–5:13, but not for the same reason that Levine thinks. While "purge" (my preferred translation of כפר) and "cleanse" are rather similar, the חטאת of

---

37. Levine, *Presence of the Lord*, 66. See also Levine's larger discussion in ibid., 63–67.

38. Ibid., 66.

Lev 4:1–5:13 leads to forgiveness for the offerer. It does not result in the purity of the offerer, thus my preference for "purge." Nonetheless, regardless of the correct understanding of כפר, presented with the choice of two functionally equivalent collocations, על + כפר and את + כפר, the authors of Lev 4:1–5:13 chose to use על + כפר exclusively in order to acknowledge the indirect nature of the purgation effected by this חטאת offering.

In Lev 4:26 and 5:6, 10, the use of the privative מן provides further evidence for the understanding of על + כפר as functionally equivalent to את + כפר. The crucial phrases in these three verses are as follows:

Lev 4:26: וכפר עליו הכהן מחטאתו ונסלח לו

Lev 5:6: וכפר עליו הכהן מחטאתו

Lev 5:10: וכפר עליו הכהן מחטאתו אשר־חטא ונסלח לו

In each of these cases, the preposition מן follows immediately after the כפר-phrase and is attached to the noun חטאתו ("his sin"). I contend that the מן should be understood as privative and thus translated as "from/of his sin." In all three of these cases, then, I render the Hebrew as: "Thus the priest shall purge him of his sin." Gane also notes the importance of מן, which he too thinks is privative in these cases, as it is throughout Lev 1–16, whether the offering addresses a moral or a physical problem. Gane produces a very extensive table in which he tabulates "components of language governed by כפר in pentateuchal prescription/descriptions of purification offerings, plus the results of כפר if they are given."[39] To be clear, in all of the cases below in which מן occurs in either the evil⇐prep. column (4:26; 5:6, 10; 14:19; 15:15, 30; 16:16, 34) or the result column (12:7; 16:30), Gane argues, as do I, that the מן should be understood privatively.[40]

Table Key: kind of case: C = consecration, P = physical ritual impurity, M = moral fault), (kind of obj.: S = sanctuary/sancta, O = offerer; spaces are left blank when the object is unspecified or unclear.

---

39. Gane, *Cult and Character*, 109.
40. See Gane's argument, ibid., 106–35.

Table 1: Components of Language Governed by כפר

ref.	kind of case	result	evil⇐prep.	locus	kind of obj.	obj.⇐prep. or direct obj.	כפר + subj.
Exod 29:36	C				S	עליו	בכפרך
Exod 29:37	C				S	על־המזבח	הכפר
Exod 30:10	M + P			על־קרנתיו			וכפר אהרן
Exod 30:10	M + P				S	עליו	יכפר
Lev 4:20	M	וכפר להם			O	מהם	וכפר
Lev 4:26	M	וכפר לו	מחטאתו		O	עליו	וכפר ... הכהן
Lev 4:31	M	וכפר לו	מחטאתו		O	עליו	וכפר ... הכהן
Lev 4:35	M	וכפר לו	על־חטאתו		O	עליו	וכפר ... הכהן
Lev 5:6	M	וכפר לו	מחטאתו		O	עליו	וכפר ... הכהן
Lev 5:10	M	וכפר לו	מחטאתו אשר־חטא		O	עליו	וכפר ... הכהן
Lev 5:13	M	וכפר לו	על־חטאתו אשר־חטא מחטאתו		O	עליו	וכפר ... הכהן
Lev 6:23	M			מקדש			לכפר
Lev 7:7	M/P				S	בו יכפר	יכפר
Lev 8:15	C				O	עליו	לכפר
Lev 9:7	M				O	בעדך ובעד העם	וכפר
Lev 9:7	M				O	בעדם	וכפר
Lev 10:17	M			לפני יהוה	O	עליהם	לכפר
Lev 12:7	P	וכפרה ממקר דמיה			O	עליה	וכפר

ref.	kind of case	result	evil⇐prep.	locus	kind of obj.	obj.⇐prep. or direct obj.	כפר + subj.
Lev 12:8	P	וטהרה			O	עליה	וכפר ... הכהן
Lev 14:19	P		מטמאתו		O	על המטהר	וכפר
Lev 14:31	P			לפני יהוה	O	על המטהר	וכפר
Lev 15:15	P		מזובו	לפני יהוה	O	עליו	וכפר ... הכהן
Lev 15:30	P		מטמאת זובה		O	עליה	וכפר ... הכהן
Lev 16:6	M + P				O	בעדו ובעד ביתו	וכפר
Lev 16:10	M			עליו	[O]*		לכפר
Lev 16:11	M + P				O	בעדו ובעד ביתו	וכפר
Lev 16:16	M + P		מטמאת בני ישראל ומפשעיהם לכל חטאתם		S	על הקדש	וכפר
Lev 16:17	M + P			בקדש	S		לכפר
Lev 16:17	M + P				O	בעדו ובעד ביתו ובעד כל קהל ישראל	וכפר
Lev 16:18	M + P				S	עליו	וכפר
Lev 16:20	M + P				S		וכלה
Lev 16:27	M + P			בהם	O	בהם	לכפר
Lev 16:30	M	לטהר אתכם מכל חטאתיכם	אתכם מכל חטאתיכם		O	עליכם	יכפר

THE PURGATION OF PERSONS

ref.	kind of case	result	evil⇐prep.	locus	kind of obj.	obj.⇐prep. or direct obj.	כפר + subj.
Lev 16:32	M + P					את־מקדש הקדש ואת־אהל מועד	כהן [הכהן]
Lev 16:33	M + P				S	ואת־המזבח	יכפר
Lev 16:33	M + P				S		יכפר
Lev 16:33	M + P		על־בני ישראל		O	על כל־עם הקהל	יכפר
Lev 16:34	M		מכל־חטאתם		O	על־בני ישראל	יכפר
Lev 23:28	M + P			לפני יהוה אלהיכם	O	עליכם	יכפר
Num 6:11	M		מאשר חטא על־הנפש		O	עליו	וכפר
Num 8:12	P	לכפר			O	על־הלוים	יכפר
Num 8:21	P	ויכפר עלהם			O	עליהם	לכפר
Num 15:25	M				O	על־כל־עדת בני ישראל	ונכפר
Num 15:28	M				O	על־הנפש השגגת בחטאה בשגגה לפני יהוה	וכפר [הכהן]
Num 15:28	M	וכפר לו			O	עליו	יכפר
Num 28:22	M/P?				O	עליכם	לכפר
Num 28:30	M/P?				O	עליכם	לכפר
Num 29:5	M/P?				O	עליכם	לכפר

* Gane leaves this space blank, but I have marked it as affecting the offerer. I contend that Aaron is the object of purgation in this case.

As the table makes clear, מן is the favored preposition for marking the problem for which כפר is needed. Of the twelve places[41] where the problem is marked, in only two instances is another preposition used; I will discuss those below. Furthermore, Lev 12:7 and 16:30 should be included in this conversation. Despite the fact that these verses have מן governed by the verb טהר and thus appear in their own column, they are clearly indications of the privative מן being used in connection with כפר. These verses have כפר in tandem with טהר, and following טהר is the preposition מן marking what is purged/cleansed from the offerer(s). As for Lev 4:26 and 5:10, which use the privative מן, we also learn that this purgation leads to the forgiveness of the offerer, the end result of all cases in Lev 4:1–5:13, as will be discussed below.

In the four other verses in Lev 4:1–5:13 that report that the priest effects כפר and the offerer is forgiven (4:20, 31, 35; 5:13), the preposition מן does not occur. In Lev 4:20 and 4:31, the text has no reference to the sin committed but simply reports purgation and forgiveness (i.e., Lev 4:20, וכפר עלהם הכהן ונסלח להם). However, in Lev 4:35 and 5:13 the preposition לו is used to specify the sin for which purgation is needed.

Lev 4:35: וכפר עליו הכהן על־חטאתו אשר־חטא ונסלח לו

Lev 5:13: וכפר עליו הכהן על־חטאתו אשר־חטא מאחת מאלה ונסלח לו

These two verses, and specifically the clauses beginning with על־חטאתו, represent a challenge to my theory of the function of the recurring חטאת offering. The challenge concerns the proper understanding of מן as privative (my reading) or causative (Milgrom's reading). As Gane points out, "there is no privative על."[42] For this reason, and to maintain the integrity of his thesis (i.e., sancta are purged by the חטאת offerings of Lev 4:1–5:13, not the offerers), Milgrom asserts that על in the cases above (Lev 4:35; 5:13) and מן (understood causatively) in 4:26; 5:6, 10 are equivalent.[43]

---

41. I include Lev 12:7 and 16:30 even though, as you can see, Gane places them in the "result" column of his table and not the "evil⇐prep." column. However, Gane does discuss these two passages at length and believes that they do belong in the conversation about the privative מן.

42. Gane, *Cult and Character*, 125.

43. Milgrom, *Leviticus 1–16*, 251.

Thus, in all of these cases, Milgrom can translate the prepositions as "for." However, Milgrom does not do so in all the cases involving מן. As we have seen, Milgrom translates the מן as privative in Lev 12:7 (here מן follows טהר directly, which follows כפר), 16:16, 16:30 (again, טהר interrupts מן and כפר) and 16:34a. Gane sees the problem Milgrom faces quite clearly:

> Leviticus 16:16 and 30 are in the context of the Day of Atonement ceremonies, regarding which vv. 16, 18, 20, and 33 explicitly state that the sanctuary and its sancta are purged by means of the special purification offerings....[44] So there is no need for Milgrom to avoid the privative sense of מן here. In fact, this reading reinforces his contention that purification offerings remove evil from the sanctuary and its sancta. But taking מן the same way in other contexts would be devastating to his thesis that purification offerings always purge the sanctuary and its sancta rather than the offerer.[45]

For this reason, Milgrom cannot be consistent in his rendering of מן after כפר-phrases.

My thesis faces the challenge of explaining the presence of על after כפר-phrases in Lev 4:35 and 5:13. Ultimately, I concur with Gane when he states that "מן and על in the evil⇐prep. formulaic position are not synonymous. While the former is best rendered 'from,' the latter means 'concerning' ['because of,' in my opinion], a more indirect idea found only with moral faults, but not with the less abstract physical ritual impurities."[46] Gane finds support in Lev 16:30 where this phrase occurs: יכפר עליכם לטהר אתכם מכל חטאתיכם. Gane, Milgrom, and I agree on the usage of מן as privative in this phrase, which Milgrom renders as "to purify you of all your sins."[47] If מן is privative here, then it must also be so in the many other places where it marks the evil purged from offerers throughout Lev 1–16. Therefore מן and על cannot be synonymous in Lev 4:1–5:13. While I agree with Gane on this last point, it must be noted that Lev 16:30 comes from

---

44. Leviticus 16:33 also states that the people are purged if one understands that את and על are functional equivalents following כפר.

45. Gane, *Cult and Character*, 119.

46. Gane, *Cult and Character*, 126. I do not believe one can confidently say that in the minds of the Priestly writers physical ritual impurities were less abstract than moral impurities. In terms of sacrificial procedure, they were treated almost identically (see Lev 12:8; 14:19, 31; 15:15, 30).

47. Milgrom, *Leviticus 1–16*, 1011.

H, while Lev 4:1–5:13 comes from P. Gane acknowledges this somewhat, and responds: "While 16:30, which Milgrom also assigns to H, involves factors that are unique to the Day of Atonement, my point here is that its use of מן in language closely following כפר is consistent with what we find elsewhere in pentateuchal cultic laws."[48] Gane's point is solid, but not unassailable. As he also points out, aside from the source critical issue, טהר comes between כפר and the מן in question. On this last point, Lev 16:34a is helpful. The phrasing is very similar to 16:30, but טהר is not included here: והיתה־זאת לכם לחקת עולם לכפר על־בני ישראל מכל־חטאתם אחת בשנה. Considering Lev 16:30, I submit that the half-verse be rendered: "This shall be for you an everlasting statute: to purge the Israelites of all their sins once a year." Combine this with the syntax of verses like Lev 12:7, 15:15, 30, 16:16, and the case for the privative מן is very strong. As mentioned above, of the twelve cases in Leviticus which state the source or problem for which כפר is needed, ten of these cases use מן, while only two cases use על (4:35; 5:13). In three of the cases with מן (Lev 12:7; 16:16, and 16:30), Milgrom translates the מן as privative.[49] Thus even Milgrom does not think the מן and על are equivalent in all of these cases. I would also add that my work shows that על + כפר and את + כפר function equivalently, which only strengthens the case for the privative מן in Lev 4:26, 5:6, and 5:10. Ironically, my articulation of the equivalency of על + כפר and כפר + את also makes less crucial the issue of the privative or causative מן in comparison to the similar clauses with the preposition על in Lev 4:1–5:13. Once it is understood that the offerer is the object of purgation, which כפר + על makes clear throughout Lev 4:1–5:13, whether the offerer is purged "of/from" his sin or "because of" his sin (or both) is not crucial. Either way, the offerer is purged because the offerer committed wrongdoing.

Conclusion

The authors of the חטאת offerings detailed in Lev 4:1–5:13 have used key grammatical and syntactical features, as well as theological and relational ideas drawn from the description of the חטאת offerings in Lev 16. Leviticus 16:1–28, the earliest text on the purification offering, uses על + כפר and כפר + את as functional equivalents. Furthermore, the identification

---

48. Gane, *Cult and Character*, 118.
49. Milgrom, *Leviticus 1–16*, 761, 1033, 1056.

of the privative, not causative, מן following the כפר-phrase throughout Lev 16, strengthens my conclusion of the functional equivalency of כפר + על and כפר + את. These same features appear throughout Lev 4:1–5:13, further attesting to the validity of my analysis of them in chapter 16. In 4:1–5:13, it becomes clear that the offerer of the חטאת offering, marked by כפר + על, is the object being purged of (privative מן) the sin/guilt the offerer is carrying.

"She Shall Remain in (Accordance to) Her Blood-of-Purification": Ritual Dynamics of Defilement and Purification in Leviticus 12

Dorothea Erbele-Küster

According to Lev 12, the regulations for the postpartum woman include a seven-day period of cultic impurity of a woman who delivered a male child, followed by a second, unrelated period of thirty-three days (v. 4a) or, for female offspring, sixty-six days (v. 5b), in which the woman must remain in her "blood of purification" or "of purity." The translation depends on whether one should understand the Hebrew word טהרה as a process or a state. These regulations touch upon the fundamental question of how cultic purity and impurity are conceptualized in the literary unit to which Lev 12 belongs, namely, Lev 11–15. The common topic of these chapters is that the body must be compliant with the cult in order to be brought near to God. Scholars have proposed a number of competing interpretations,[1] a circumstance that the texts themselves may have encouraged precisely through their silence on their underlying rationale. The passage does not imply a material understanding of im/purity, as it addresses neither the length of the bleedings, nor the physical characteristics of the blood. As we shall see, טהרה functions as an essentially cultic term, referring to

---

1. For an overview, see Dorothea Erbele-Küster, "Die Körperbestimmungen in Lev 11–15," in *Menschenbilder und Körperkonzepte im Alten Israel, Ägypten und im Alten Orient*, ed. Angelika Berlejung, Jan Dietrich, and Joachim F. Quack, ORA 9 (Tübingen: Mohr Siebeck, 2012), 209–24; Christophe Nihan, "Forms and Function of Purity in Leviticus," in *Purity and the Forming of Religious Traditions in the Ancient Mediterranean World and Ancient Judaism*, ed. Christian Frevel and Christophe Nihan, DHR 3 (Leiden: Brill, 2013), 311–68.

anything that complies with the regulations of the cult—that is, in other words, ritually pure.[2]

Reading Rituals and Their Dynamics

In recent years biblical scholars have argued for a distinction between text and ritual, noting the difficulties created through the intertwined nature of the written text and its performance.[3] In other words, *texts are not rituals and rituals are not texts*.[4] Focusing on the textuality of the ritual held after a woman has given birth to a child, I seek to unfold the roles of the different agents involved in the ritual. This methodological approach shifts the focus from the symbolic meaning of the ritual and its underlying concept of purity to descriptions of the ritual actions and roles of the agents.[5]

The phrasing of the Hebrew text of Lev 12 quoted in the title expresses the complex role that the blood of the parturient plays in the purification ritual. It obviously puzzled the first translators into Greek, as the LXX declares that the woman shall remain "in her impure blood" (12:4, 5). I shall therefore analyze the LXX version after examination of the MT.

The text raises questions such as: How does the text conceive of impurity and the purification process? In what sense does the woman "remain in" the blood of purification/purity? How should one understand the preposition ב "in," "in accordance to/with?" Finally, how does the text envision the purification ritual in connection with the blood of purification/purity? We shall see that the instructions for the rite include several agents, factors such as time, blood flow, and the cultic engagement of the woman and the

---

2. See Dorothea Erbele-Küster, "Gender and Cult: 'Pure' and 'Impure' as Gender-Relevant Categories," in *Torah*, ed. Irmtraud Fischer and Mercedes Navarro Puerto, BW 1 (Atlanta: Society of Biblical Literature, 2011), 375–406.

3. William K. Gilders, *Blood Ritual in the Hebrew Bible: Meaning and Power* (Baltimore: Johns Hopkins University Press, 2004); James W. Watts, *Ritual and Rhetoric in Leviticus: From Sacrifice to Scripture* (Cambridge: Cambridge University Press, 2007); Hanna Liss, "Ritual Purity and the Construction of Identity," in *The Books of Leviticus and Numbers*, ed. Thomas Römer, BETL 215 (Leuven: Peeters, 2008), 329–54; Brian D. Bibb, *Ritual Words and Narrative Worlds in Leviticus*, LHBOTS 480 (London: T&T Clark, 2009); Wesley J. Bergen, *Reading Ritual: Leviticus in Postmodern Culture*, JSOTSup 417 (New York: T&T Clark, 2010).

4. Watts, *Ritual and Rhetoric in Leviticus*, 29.

5. Cf. Christian Frevel and Christophe Nihan, "Introduction," in *Purity and the Forming*, 9–10.

priest (i.e., offerings).[6] Careful analysis of the role of the individual agents will show how they interact in the dynamics of the purification ritual.

I shall therefore sift through Lev 12, which is a clearly defined unit. The introductory divine speech formula in verse 1 opens the regulations. Verse 7 closes the chapter and yields an interpretive clue. An appendix governing the case of a woman of lower social and economic standing follows in verse 8. Together with Lev 15, the material on the postpartum woman in Lev 12 forms a bracket around the regulations about surface eruptions (Lev 13 and 14).[7] It envisions the birth of a male descendant (v. 2) and of a female (v. 5). The text revolves around the childbearing woman, with only one interruption: the command to circumcise the male newborn (v. 3).

Remaining in Accordance with the Blood of Purification

In Lev 12:2 the woman's condition after giving birth is compared to that during her menstrual period (כימי נדת) and thus implicitly connected to Lev 15:19–26, which concerns the woman's monthly bleeding. Leviticus 12:2b reads: "she is cult-disabled (impure) for seven days—according to the days of her unstable condition of menstruation she is cult-disabled."[8] This seven-day period of impurity is followed by a second, unrelated period of thirty-three days (v. 4a) or sixty-six days (v. 5b), depending on the sex of the child, in which the woman is supposed to remain "according to" the blood of purification/purity (טהרה). In Lev 12:4b, 6 the masculine noun is used (טָהֳרָהּ).[9] The suffixed personal pronoun establishes a firm link between this process and the woman. The preceding specifications of the number of the "days of her purity/purification" underline the idea of a process. The text suggests that the woman's postpartum bleedings last shorter or longer depending on the newborn's sex, seven plus thirty-three

---

6. The role of God in the ritual within the symbolic system shall not be highlighted as this article is focusing on the ritual acts.

7. Cf. Erbele-Küster, *Körperbestimmungen*. Christophe Nihan, *From Priestly Torah to Pentateuch: A Study in the Composition of the Book of Leviticus*, FAT 2/25 (Tübingen: Mohr Siebeck, 2007), 301 holds that "Lev 12 probably belonged initially together with Lev 15."

8. Unless otherwise noted, all translations are the author's.

9. The form is analyzed by some as an inf. const. (e.g., Jacob Milgrom, *Leviticus 1–16: A New Translation with Introduction and Commentary* [AB 3; New York: Doubleday, 1991], 755); cf. GesB[17], 435.

days for a boy and twice that long for a girl. This in turn indicates that the blood serves as the carrier of either purity or impurity.

The word for blood in this construct chain is in the plural, which elsewhere in the MT connotes spilled blood and, by extension, blood guilt.[10] The phrasing "to remain in" the blood of purification does not mean that she is confined to the domestic sphere.[11] The text itself defines the expression as a separation from cultic objects and from the sanctuary (v. 4). The verb ישב occurs with two different prepositions: ב in verse 4 and על in verse 5b. The preposition ב usually designates a physical location, "in."[12] Applied to Lev 12:4, this would mean literally that the woman sits in the blood. A different interpretation, however, suggests itself as regards the use of על in verse 5b. This preposition denotes not only spatial proximity but also an underlying reason that could be rendered in its abstract meaning: "As prep. upon, and hence on the ground of, according to, on account of, on behalf of."[13] Furthermore, the use of two different prepositions makes it clear that one should not understand the construction in terms of space alone, but rather causally or instrumentally. Thus she shall remain "according to" the blood of purification.

Hence, in line with the *Dictionary of Classical Hebrew*, which suggests the translation "*blood of*, perh. requiring, *purification*,"[14] I understand the term as denoting a process. This goes along with the expression in the second part of the verse, "until the days of her purification are completed,"[15] stressing the time span.

---

10. See Dorothea Erbele-Küster, "Blutschuld," in *WiBiLex* (Stuttgart: Deutsche Bibelgesellschaft, 2015), http://tinyurl.com/SBL0393f; Christian Eberhart, "Blood I. Ancient Near East and Hebrew Bible/Old Testament," *EBR* 4:201–12.

11. GesB[17], 323.

12. Carl Brockelmann, *Hebräische Syntax* (Neukirchen-Vluyn: Neukirchener Verlag, 1956), §106a, and Paul Joüon and Takamitsu Muraoka, *A Grammar of Biblical Hebrew*, SubBi 27 (Rome: Biblical Institute Press, 2006), 3:§113c.

13. BDB, 752. See also Joüon, *Grammar*, 3:§113f.

14. *DCH* 3:348–49.

15. The Masoretic vocalization adds the suffix of the 3rd fem. sg. to the masc. noun טֹהַר, the suffix being recognizable in the *mappiq* in the final ה (as in v. 6a). A different form (without the *mappiq*) is found in vv. 4a, 5b, where the fem. noun טָהֳרָה is used.

Purification Offering

After her period of cultic ineligiblity has passed, the text directs the parturient to perform a cultic activity at the entrance of the tent of meeting.[16] The woman is to bring a sheep and a dove (v. 6) or, as equivalent, two doves or turtledoves (v. 8), to the priest for a burnt offering (עלה) and a purification offering (חטאת). The animals are either a quadruped or a winged creature; among the former the sex is specified.[17] Leviticus 1:2 characterizes the עלה as קרבן (from the root קרב, *qal* "approach," *hiphil* "offer"), that is, as an offering presented before God or at the altar. Distinct from the voluntary עלה, Lev 4 introduces the חטאת as an obligatory method of expiating for unintentional violations of the commandments. The term חטאת is equivocal, capable of designating either the trespass incurred or the ritual means of removing it.[18] It derives from the privative *piel* stem ("absolve, purify, de-sin") of a root whose *qal* stem means "to sin" or "to trespass." In order to express this idea, as opposed to the common translation of חטאת with "sin offering," interpreters have proposed more adequate renderings, such as "purification offering" or "reintegration rite."[19]

---

16. Judith Romney Wegner, "'Coming before the Lord': The Exclusion of Women from the Public Domain of the Israelite Priestly Cult," in *The Book of Leviticus: Composition and Reception*, ed. Rolf Rendtorff and Robert A. Kugler, VTSup 93 (Leiden: Brill, 2003), 453 argues that although women are required to perform cultic activity at the entrance of the tent of meeting, their access to the divine is restricted: they are never said to come "before YHWH," as in Lev 15:14.

17. See Naphtali S. Meshel, *The "Grammar"of Sacrifice: A Generativist Study of the Israelite Sacrificial System in the Priestly Writings with a "Grammar" of Σ* (Oxford: Oxford University Press 2014), 33–35. Nicole J. Ruane, *Sacrifice and Gender in Biblical Law* (Cambridge: Cambridge University Press 2013), 40–76 discusses the question of the gender of sacrificial animals and the preponderance of male animals among them.

18. Ina Willi-Plein, *Opfer und Kult im alttestamentlichen Israel: Textbefragungen und Zwischenergebnisse*, SBS 153 (Stuttgart: Katholisches Bibelwerk, 1993), 97; and Rolf Rendtorff, *Leviticus1,1–10,20*, BKAT 3.1 (Neukirchen-Vluyn: Neukirchener Verlag, 2004), 148.

19. The translation of חטאת as "sin offering" emphasizes the *qal* meaning of the root חטא, "to sin." Rendtorff, *Leviticus*, 220 argues for retaining this translation, although he emphasizes that the double meaning of the word (i.e., both the trespass and its removal) must always be kept in mind. For the translation of חטאת as "purification offerring," see Jacob Milgrom, "Sin-Offering or Purification-Offering?," *VT* 21 (1971): 237–39; and Milgrom, *Leviticus 1–16*, 253–54. Thomas Hieke, *Levitikus: Erster Teilband: 1–15*, HThKAT (Freiburg im Breisgau: Herder, 2014), 88–92 proposes

Except for the plant-based חטאת, all forms of this rite exceed the specifications for the עלה with the addition of ritual manipulations of the victim's blood, which is applied to the horns of the altar and, in the case of a purification offering on the part of the entire community, to the curtain that conceals the inner sanctum of the tent (Lev 5:5–7, 18, 25, 30, 34). The remaining blood is then poured out at the base of the altar. As the sacrificial regulations in Lev 1–7 show, the blood manipulation lies in the hands of the priest mediating the offerer's access to the altar.[20] The recurring formula underlines the significance of the entire ritual: "And he [the priest] performs the purification ritual for her [him] and it is forgiven her [him]" (vv. 26, 31, 35). Thus, while Lev 5 characterizes the purpose of the offering as cleansing and forgiveness, the purification offering (חטאת) in Lev 12 is part of a rite of cleansing and reintegration into the cultic community,[21] without any connection to sin (similarly the Nazirite vow in Num 6 or the inauguration of the altar in Lev 8:15).

Deciphering the Ritual Agents

By analyzing the different actions within the ritual, we have already started identifying the distinct agents.[22] Ritual agency has a decisive position in the proper function of a ritual. As mentioned above, the text presupposes various agents, both personal and impersonal. Their roles shall now be deciphered more specifically in order to sketch the dynamics of the ritual as envisioned by the text.

Interpreters have commonly viewed the blood (ritual) as the decisive factor of the procedure,[23] although they have had difficulties explaining

---

"Entsündigungsopfer." For the translation of חטאת as "reintegration rite," see Alfred Marx, "Sacrifice pour les péchés ou rite de passage? Quelques réflexions sur la fonction du ḥaṭṭā't," *RB* 96 (1989): 27–48.

20. Gilders, *Blood Ritual in the Hebrew Bible*, 78–81.

21. For this reason Marx, "Sacrifice," interprets חטאת not as sacrificial offering but as "rite de passage." Willi-Plein, *Opfer und Kult*, 96–98 also classifies חטאת not as a sacrifice but as a ritual.

22. For a general discussion on objects, actions, participants, and language involved in biblical ritual, see Gerald A. Klingbeil, *Bridging the Gap: Ritual and Ritual Texts in the Bible*, BBRSup 1 (Winona Lake, IN: Eisenbrauns 2007), 174–204.

23. See Milgrom, *Leviticus 1–16*, 254–58, 1031–34, and Erhard Gerstenberger, *Leviticus: A Commentary*, OTL (Louisville: Westminster John Knox, 1996), 59–60, regarding sin offerings in general.

the effect of the ritual "detergent." If one opts for this, then, in the special case of Lev 12, the woman's blood must be taken into consideration and related to the blood of the offering.²⁴ On the other hand, the poverty exception, which permits a plant-based offering for the חטאת (Lev 5:11–13), challenges the idea of the centrality of blood for the sacrificial rite, for in cases of hardship both the purification and reintegration do not depend on blood. Moreover, one must consider the dual structure of the ritual in Lev 12: in addition to a חטאת an עלה is required, contradicting the characterization of the latter in Lev 1 as a purely voluntary offering.²⁵

We can therefore conclude that the declaratory formula, "and she is in compliance with the cult," suggests the interpretation of the חטאת in Lev 12 as a purification offering. Its effect is anticipated by the woman's loss of reproductive blood (of purification) during and after delivery, and by the passage of the required amount of time.

The purification offering of Lev 12 marks the transition from the prior condition of cultic impurity, which is a time of separation from the sanctuary, to the condition of cultic purity and hence of reintegration into the ritual community. These instructions for women presuppose that ordinarily they are cultically active, despite their lack of the sign of circumcision. Verse 7a then describes the priest's activity thus: "He brings it into YHWH's presence and completes the purification ritual for her." The first verb (קרב *hiphil*) can denote the entire offering procedure, or it can simply mean the physical presentation prior to slaughter (cf. Lev 1:3).²⁶ The appendix governing the case of a woman of lower social and economic standing (Lev 12:8) uses another verb (כפר *piel*) to describe the priestly agency. It has the technical meaning "to remove cultic impurity" or "to restore to cultic eligibility." In its brevity, the formula, "the priest completes the purification procedure for her, and she is pure," in Lev 12:7, 8 alludes to other passages within Leviticus, especially the offering laws. Nevertheless,

---

24. Ruane, *Sacrifice and Gender*, 142–44, 166–69 speaks of "reproductive blood."

25. On Lev 1 and its informational gaps, which indicate that certain acts are performed by the offerer, see Dorothea Erbele-Küster, "Reading as an Act of Offering: Reconsidering the Genre of Leviticus 1," in *The Actuality of Sacrifice: Past and Present*, ed. Alberdina Houtman et al., JCPS 28 (Leiden: Brill, 2014), 34–46.

26. In a similar vein, Christian A. Eberhart, "Sacrifice? Holy Smoke!," in *Ritual and Metaphor: Sacrifice in the Bible*, ed. Christian A. Eberhart, RBS 68 (Atlanta: Society of Biblical Literature, 2011), 23 understands the verb as a comprehensive term for the approach to the sanctuary.

Lev 12 uses כפר *piel* differently than Lev 4–5 do. In the latter passages, the verb denotes the removal or forgiveness of individual guilt, frequently in connection with the expression "and her/his sin is forgiven."[27]

The verb כפר *piel* occurs in Lev 12:7, 8 with the preposition על and the third-person feminine singular suffix. The preposition על frequently denotes the person or group on whose behalf the ritual is performed.[28] Leviticus 12, like Lev 1–7, gives no further indication of the means of purification or of the condition from which the person is purified. The idea may also be implicit of a physical cleansing or contact. Nevertheless, the key idea involves neither a concrete location nor a specific physical act. In Leviticus כפר *piel* denotes a priestly activity without specifying details.[29] The כפר formula serves both to mark the conclusion of the ritual and to interpret it.

Picking up the question of agency within the dynamics of defilement and purification, we can see another shift toward the end. In contrast to the ritual procedure, whose agent is named (the priest), the closing comment "and she is pure" (vv. 7, 8) qualifies its subject but describes no action

---

27. Rendtorff, *Leviticus*, 176–78 speaks of a ritual and technical use of *kipper* and translates it as "to complete the act of atonement." In Lev 4:46 it forms an interpretive formula of the ritual together with "to forgive"; cf. Christian Eberhart, *Studien zur Bedeutung der Opfer im Alten Testament: Die Signifikanz von Blut- und Verbrennungsriten im kultischen Rahmen*, WMANT 94 (Neukirchen-Vluyn: Neukirchener Verlag, 2002), 128, 168; Bernd Janowski, *Sühne als Heilsgeschehen: Traditions- und religionsgeschichtliche Studien zur Sühnetheologie der Priesterschrift*, 2nd ed., WMANT 55 (Neukirchen-Vluyn: Neukirchener Verlag, 2000), 250–52.

28. Cf. Exod 30:15, 16; Lev 1:4; 4:20, 26, 31, 35; 5:6, 10, 13, 16, 18, 26; 8:34; 10:7; 14:18, 19, 20, 21, 29, 31; 15:25, 30; 16:30, 33b, 34; 17:11a; 19:22; 23:28; Num 5:8; 6:11; 8:12, 19, 21; 15:25, 28; 17:11, 12; 25:13; 28:22, 30; 29:5; 31:50; Ezek 45:15; Neh 10:34; 1 Chr 6:34; and 2 Chr 29:24. The preposition בעד can perform the same function. In very few passages does על combine with an impersonal object such as the altar or the sanctuary (for the differences between the prepositions cf. Nobuyoshi Kiuchi, *The Purification Offering in the Priestly Literature: Its Meaning and Function*, JSOTSup 56 [Sheffield: Sheffield Academic, 1987], 88–89).

29. Rendtorff, *Leviticus*, 176–78 speaks of a ritual and technical use of *kipper* and translates it as "to complete the act of atonement." In Lev 4:46, it forms an interpretive formula of the ritual together with "to forgive" (cf. Eberhart, *Studien zur Bedeutung der Opfer*, 128, 168. According to James W. Watts, *Leviticus 1–10*, HCOT [Leuven: Peeters, 2013], 326 the deployment of the verb in Leviticus stresses the "the book's concern to persuade worshippers of the necessity and benefits of priests' monopoly over cultic service").

on her part. The direction of communication changes over the course of the passage; the priest does not figure in the final declaration.

The summary formula "and she is ritually pure as a result of the source of her blood" (v. 7, וטהרה ממקר דמיה), following the sacrificial ritual, cannot be taken to mean that what the woman has been purified of is her (impure) issue of blood, since earlier there was mention of "blood of purification."

How, then, are we to understand the preposition מן in the phrase "the woman is pure *from* (מן) the flow of her blood"? The preposition מן indicates a separating movement: "(away) from," "(out) from within."[30] The frequent causative use of the preposition ("because, as a result of") rests on this meaning of "going out, emerging from."[31] The text says not only that the woman was cult-disabled because of her flow of blood, but also, and more importantly, that she is ritually pure "from out of" the flow, that is, as a result of it.

The LXX Rendering of Leviticus 12

The comparison of the Greek translations to the Hebrew MT, being aware that the text the first translators referred to was different, provides an illuminating example of how language serves and reflects the specific cultural construction of ritual dynamics. Most strikingly, in contrast to the MT, the LXX speaks in verses 4 and 5 of the woman's remaining in "her impure blood" and not "the blood of purification." Nevertheless, some among the uncial manuscripts (stemming from the fourth or fifth century) as well as numerous miniscules speak of pure blood. Possibly the majuscule manuscripts that John Wevers follows in his edition of the LXX understood the blood in terms of an impure secretion whose expulsion was necessary for purification and healing.[32] This annihilates the ambiguity enclosed in the Hebrew text.

---

30. GesB[17], 435; and Brockelmann, *Hebräische Syntax*, §111–12.

31. GK, §119z.

32. I differ here from John W. Wevers, *Notes on the Greek Text of Leviticus*, SCS 44 (Atlanta: Scholars Press, 1997), 166–67, who essentially denies this shift. Regarding the few Greek MSS that deviate from the LXX by using a form of καθαρός (in the pure blood), Wevers posits a misunderstanding (167), because for him, impurity is a key characteristic of menstruation (for further criticism of Wevers's position see also Kristin De Troyer, "Blood: A Threat to Holiness or towards (another) Holiness?," in

For "the days of her purification" the Greek chooses a term that alludes to the previously drawn analogy with menstruation, κάθαρσις being a *terminus technicus* for the latter.[33] Soranus speaks of menstruation as a "catharsis": "since, as some people say excreting blood from bodily excessive matter, it effects a purgation of the body. In most women the menstrual flux is pure blood"[34]—which means it is not mixed with other substances. This shows that classical antiquity did not associate menstruation with impurity as opposed to purification, either.

The Greek-speaking recipients, however, struggled with the conception of ritual impurity as reflected in the Hebrew text. With its translation of the Hebrew roots טמא and טהר as a pair of opposites based on the same lexical stem, the LXX created its own concept of (im)purity, which subsequently wielded a powerful influence even over the understanding of the Hebrew text.

The LXX's reference to "impure blood" in Lev 12 became significant within the reception history in two ways: first, in contrast to the MT, the LXX divests the woman's blood of any cleansing role; and second, through its language it reduces impurity to a nonentity, to something privative, a negative condition. Likewise it minimizes the dynamics of the purification ritual wherein the woman has her share.

In addition to its differing interpretation of the concept of "im-purity," the Greek text also introduces peculiarities into the purification ritual itself. In connection with the ritual procedure in verse 7 we read: "And the priest completes the atonement ritual for her and purifies her." In other words, the LXX explicitly identifies the subject of the ritual action: the priest. Besides this, in contrast to the MT's "result-oriented" final statement ("and she is pure"), the LXX treats the declaration of purity as a discrete act on the priest's part. In verse 8, the future passive καθαρισθήσεται ("she shall be purified") has, in contrast to the MT, not such a strong declarative and confirmatory character.

Wholly Woman, Holy Blood. A Feminist Critique of Purity and Impurity, ed. Kristin De Troyer et al., SAC [Harrisburg, PA: Trinity Press International, 2003], 45–64, esp. 58).

33. Cf. Wilhelm Pape, *Griechisch-Deutsches Handwörterbuch*, 3rd ed. (Braunschweig: Vieweg, 1880), 310: "monatliche Reinigung."

34. Soranus Ephesius, *Soranus' Gynecology*, trans. from the Greek with an introduction by Owsei Temkin (Baltimore: Johns Hopkins Press, 1991), 16 f IV.

Concluding Remarks on the Ritual Dynamics

The regulation in Lev 12 inscribes two differently qualified postpartum periods into the female body. While the first (seven or fourteen day) period can be seen as a static condition of impurity (vv. 2, 5a), the second (of thirty-three or sixty-six days) may be understood as a process of purification. The text characterizes the latter period by the phrases "blood of purification" (vv. 4, 5) and "the time of her purification" (vv. 5, 6). Both expressions suggest that the postpartum loss of blood is itself a purifying process. Hellenistic Greek texts regard the menstrual period, like pregnancy, as essential to women's health.[35] The period depends on the sex of the child, not on the length of her postpartum bleeding. Nor is blood as such located on the side of the impure. Already during the period of cultic noncompliance, the passage mentions the blood of purification (Lev 12:4, 5).

The differentiation into two periods of seven plus thirty-three days (or fourteen plus sixty-six days) is thus based less on the bodily secretions of the woman who has given birth than on the intention to distinguish two phases of a ritual. Following van Gennep's division into *rites de séparation* and *rites de marge*, the seven or fourteen days represent a separation ritual, while the thirty-three or sixty-six days of the blood of purification constitute a transformation ritual.[36] The purification offering of Lev 12 marks the transition from the old condition of cultic impurity, which is a time of separation from the sanctuary, to the condition of purity and hence of reintegration into the ritual community.[37] In contrast to the beginning of the text, where biological terms refer to the newborn's gender, the sacrifical instruction speaks of a "son" or a "daughter," words that express social and family relationships. This shows that, as part of the mother's ritual reintegration, the infants too are received into the social group.

---

35. Cf. Ann Ellis Hanson, "The Medical Writer's Woman," in *Before Sexuality: The Construction of Erotic Experience in the Ancient Greek World*, ed. David M. Halperin, John J. Winkler, and Froma I. Zeitlin (Princeton: Princeton University Press, 1990), 309–337 esp. 317.

36. Arnold van Gennep, *Les rites de passage* (Paris: Picard, 1909).

37. Cf. Angelika Dierichs, *Von der Götter Geburt und der Frauen Niederkunft* (Mainz: von Zabern, 2002), 213–14, who describes ancient Greek ritual practices, namely purification rituals and dedicatory gifts for goddesses who have given birth.

The purification ritual in Lev 12 is a dynamic, multilayered and ambivalent process: the period of cultic impurity is accompanied by the blood of purification. The formulation is decisive: the woman is not purified "of" (or "from")[38] her blood flow, but rather by means of or as a result of it. After the specified time has passed, the woman returns to a state of ritual purity thanks to her "spring," or in medical terms, as a result of the residual bleeding of her womb.[39]

The (ritual) declaration of cultic compliance is a performative act in itself, in which purification and declaration of being pure, the pure and the impure converge. Thus the declaration marks just the final point of a long dynamic. We can observe that a ritual-technical use of טהרה can stand for the ritual itself in other instances, as in Lev 13:7; 14:2, 23; 15:13.

Our analysis has shed light on both the priestly purity system and the sacrificial system, as well as their interrelatedness, by deciphering the multilayered ritual agency.[40] The dynamic of the purification (ritual) lies in the interrelatedness of corporeal, physical, and cultic processes in time and place. One could speak of a "triangular relationship established between the offerer, the altar (Yahweh), and the priests."[41] A plurality of elements influences the dynamics of purification: the body of the woman, the timespan, her offering, and the sanctification of the offering through the priest. Decisive is therefore not just the declarative act of the priest; the "woman is focalized as an agent responsible for protecting a system."[42] The human agency lies in the hands of both the priest and the woman.

---

38. Roy E. Gane, *Cult and Character: Purification Offerings, Day of Atonement, and Theodicy* (Winona Lake, IN: Eisenbrauns, 2005), 112–20 translates מן here in a privative sense.

39. Ursula Rapp, "The Heritage of Old Testament Impurity Laws: Gender as a Question of How to Focus on Women," in *Gender and Religion: European Studies*, ed. Kari E. Børresen, Sara Cabibbo, and Edith Specht, Quaderni 2 (Rome: Catocci, 2001), 29–40, esp. 32, proposes an overarching meaning of מקור as postpartum bleeding.

40. Jonathan Klawans, *Purity, Sacrifice and the Temple: Symbolism and Supersessionism in the Study of Ancient Judaism* (Oxford: Oxford University Press, 2006) urges the analysis of ritual structures of sacrifice and purity in tandem.

41. Gilders, *Blood Ritual in the Hebrew Bible*, 82.

42. Deborah L. Ellens, *Women in the Sex Texts of Leviticus and Deuteronomy: A Comparitive Conceptual Analysis*, LHBOTS 458 (New York: T&T Clark, 2008), 8, concluding on the so-called "Sex Texts" in Leviticus in general.

Accessing Holiness via Ritual Ablutions in the Dead Sea Scrolls and Related Literature

Hannah K. Harrington

Introduction

The function of ritual ablutions in Second Temple times cannot be reduced to simply the removal of ritual impurity, as discussions of holiness and purity in ancient Judaism usually claim.[1] To be sure, in the priestly texts of the Bible, washing functioned primarily to remove ritual impurity, for example, corpse contagion, sexual discharges, and scale disease (e.g., Lev 11–15; Num 19). Scholars have even noted a correlation between ritual

---

1. See, e.g., the systems of ritual purification in several recent commentaries and monographs which delineate the removal of impurity by ablutions but do not discuss the power of ablutions to move a person further into holier space or activities, cf. Jonathan Klawans, *Impurity and Sin in Ancient Judaism* (Oxford: Oxford University, 2000); Hyam Maccoby, *Ritual and Morality: The Ritual Purity System and its Place in Judaism* (Cambridge: Cambridge University, 1999); Jay Sklar, *Sin, Impurity, Sacrifice, Atonement: The Priestly Conceptions*, HBM 2 (Sheffield: Sheffield Phoenix, 2005); Ian C. Werrett, *Ritual Purity and the Dead Sea Scrolls*, STDJ 72 (Leiden: Brill, 2007); David P. Wright, *The Disposal of Impurity: Elimination Rites in the Bible and in Hittite and Mesopotamian Literature*, SBLDS 10 (Atlanta: Scholars Press, 1987); see also Tikva Frymer-Kensky, "Pollution, Purification and Purgation in Biblical Israel," in *The Word of the Lord Shall Go Forth: Essays in Honor of David Noel Freeman in Celebration of His Sixtieth Birthday*, ed. Carol L. Meyers and Michael Patrick O'Connor (Winona Lake, IN: Eisenbrauns, 1983), 399–414; Cana Werman, "The Concept of Holiness and the Requirements of Purity in Second Temple and Tannaitic Literature," in *Purity and Holiness: The Heritage of Leviticus*, ed. Marcel J. H. M. Poorthuis and Joshua Schwartz, JCPS 2 (Leiden: Brill, 2000), 163–79. Jacob Milgrom, *Leviticus 1–16: A New Translation with Introduction and Commentary*, AB 3 (New York: Doubleday, 1991), recognizes this power, but focuses primarily on the role of ablutions in removing ritual impurity.

ablutions and the removal of specific stages of impurity.[2] However, many Jews in antiquity were also making efforts to access greater holiness beyond just a status of purity. Ritual ablutions functioned as a means of access to facilitate participation in a more intense realm of holiness.[3] This essay explores three categories of data which reveal that ablutions often aided the acquisition of holiness in Second Temple times: (1) Dead Sea Scrolls and scriptural antecedents; (2) related Second Temple traditions; (3) archaeological data from the Temple Mount.

Definitions

At the outset of this discussion, it is important to define "holiness" and distinguish between it and "purity" in the Pentateuch.[4] Accordingly, holi-

---

2. Milgrom, *Leviticus 1-16*, 842-43, 859, 969-76, 991-1000, discusses the removal of scale-disease in stages. The first bath removes the ability of the scale-diseased person to contaminate others by sharing the same roof. Thus, he can return to the community without fear of contaminating others by entering a building or sharing any kind of overhang with them. The second bath eliminates contamination power by direct contact to all persons and vessels, but the impurity is still potent to sacred items. At the end of the scale-diseased person's purification, sacrifices remove all residual impurity. Milgrom also discusses the stages of ablutions particularly among the Qumran sect, Jacob Milgrom, "First Day Ablutions in Qumran," in *The Madrid Qumran Congress: Proceedings of the International Congress on the Dead Sea Scrolls, Madrid 18-21 March, 1991*, ed. Julio Trebolle Barrera and Luis V. Montaner, STDJ 11 (Leiden: Brill, 1992), 2:561-70.

3. Philip Jenson, *Graded Holiness: A Key to the Priestly Conception of the World*, JSOTSup 106 (Sheffield: JSOT Press, 1992) provides a helpful schema of "zones of holiness" in the priestly narrative, 89-93. Areas of greater holiness are outlined in m. Kelim 1:1-4 and ritual immersions are performed to gain access to holier items and space by ritual immersions. E.g., before eating ordinary food, tithes, and priestly contributions (*terumah*), people are expected to wash hands; before eating sacred food, they are expected to ritually immerse and wait for sunset (m. Hag. 2:5; cf. 3:1-2) (See discussion below). However, since the Mishnah was not produced until the third century CE, it is often sidelined for earlier periods of study. F. Schmidt, *La pensée du temple, de Jérusalem à Qoumrân: Identité et lien social dans le judaïsme ancien* (Paris: Édition du Seuil, 1994), 143-57, tries to correlate levels of holiness according to the Qumran sect with the views of the rabbis.

4. The Holiness traditions of Leviticus teach the notion that Israel must achieve holiness through obedience to the commandments of Yahweh; cf. Jacob Milgrom's comments on Lev 20:8 in *Leviticus 17-22: A New Translation with Introduction and Commentary*, AB 3A (New York: Doubleday, 2000), 1740. Deuteronomy, on the other

ness is viewed as the essence of God himself (Lev 20:3; 22:32; cf. 1 Sam 2:2).[5] *Qadosh*, "separated one," describes his uniqueness as the deity vis-à-vis humanity. This separation is most obvious in the fact that Yahweh, unlike his creation, is not subject to death and decay.[6] This distinction between divinity and mortality represents a chasm that human beings cannot bridge. But holiness is not just a state of divine perfection and withdrawal; rather it is an all-consuming power with an unshakeable will. The Bible generally treats divine holiness as a dynamic force before which all creation trembles (Exod 15:11; 1 Sam 6:20; Pss 96:9; 111:9; Isa 6:3).[7] The Holy One exercises himself on behalf of his people but always retains the prerogative to do as he sees fit (cf. Hos 11:9). Thus, approaching holiness is a dangerous proposition (Exod 33:20; Num 4:20; 18:3; Judg 13:22; 1 Kgs 19:13), and as set forth in the priestly literature, it is unapproachable except through proper channels and restrictions.[8]

---

hand, emphasizes Israel's holiness by election (Deut 7:1–6). Milgrom explains that in the traditions of the Priests (P) as well as Deuteronomy (D), holiness is an inherent state, but in the Holiness Code, the concept is dynamic: "Lay persons can attain it, and priests must sustain it, for holiness is diminished or enhanced by either violating or obeying the divine commandments" (*Leviticus 17–22*, 1740–41). Naomi Koltun-Fromm, *Hermeneutics of Holiness: Ancient Jewish and Christian Notions of Sexuality and Religious Community* (Oxford: Oxford University Press, 2010), 6–9, 32, distinguishes these definitions by the terms "achieved holiness" versus "ascribed holiness."

5. Cf. Milgrom, *Leviticus 17–22*, 1712, explains that throughout the Hebrew Bible, "Holiness is his [Yahweh's] quintessential nature..., distinguishing him from all beings.... It acts as the agency of his will. If certain things are termed holy ... they are so by virtue of divine dispensation. Moreover, this designation is always subject to recall." See also ibid., 1735.

6. Ibid., 1720–23, emphasizes the polarities of holiness and impurity representing the forces of life and death, respectively; David P. Wright stresses the process of decay and death as part of human mortality, the antonym of divinity: "Unclean and Clean (OT)," *ABD* 6:729–41. See also, Roy Gane, *Cult and Character: Purification Offerings, Day of Atonement, and Theodicy* (Winona Lake, IN: Eisenbrauns, 2005), 201; Maccoby, *Ritual and Morality*, 31–32.

7. John Armstrong, *The Idea of Holiness and the Humane Response: A Study of the Concept of Holiness and Its Social Consequences* (London: Allen & Unwin, 1981), 6–7. This strong connection between power and sanctity continues throughout the New Testament and rabbinic literature and is apparent as well in Greco-Roman literature, see the discussion in Hannah K. Harrington, *Holiness: Rabbinic Judaism and the Graeco-Roman World*, RFCC (London: Routledge, 2001), 20–26.

8. Milgrom, *Leviticus 1–16*, 730. For further discussion of the elements of holi-

Yet with all of these challenges, Leviticus clearly states that Israel must emulate the divine holiness (Lev 11:45; 19:2). This *imitatio dei* command translates into a quest for purity of person, in both ritual and ethical senses. Leviticus 11 treats purity as a ritual matter that Israel must observe after contact with various dead creatures, emphasizing the effort to separate themselves from the realm of death when they come into contact with the holy giver of life. Leviticus 18–19, in which the command to be holy recurs, focuses on ethical purity in human relationships, especially in the area of sexuality.

Purity is understood as the absence of impurity (both ritual and moral), a state that Israel must maintain in order to stand in the presence of Yahweh. The holiness of Yahweh, which provides Israel both blessing and danger, must not be compromised by bringing impurity into its zone. From a ritual perspective this includes such actions as entering sacred space or handling sacred food while in a bodily impure condition (see Lev 11–15; Num 19). From a moral perspective, ethics are an essential part of holiness, and Israel is sanctified only as she commits to them (Lev 19:1–4; 20:2–8). Repeated disobedience to the commandments of God, whether cultic or ethical, will bring disaster on the nation (Lev 18:28–29; 26:14–39).[9]

During Second Temple times, as discussed below, many Jews pursued a greater holiness beyond the simple biblical requirements of purity. It will become apparent that this effort was an attempt to engage Yahweh's power for a variety of purposes.

Scrolls and Scriptural Antecedents

The Dead Sea Scrolls reveal a Jewish community with a heightened concern for impurity. From harvesting and eating ordinary food in a state of ritual purity (4Q284a 1, 4) to ascribing impurity upward to the source of a stream of liquid because it had flowed onto an impure substance (4QMMT B 55–58), this sect held inordinately stringent views on purity.[10] Moreover,

---

ness and the dichotomy between Yahweh's perfection and power on the one hand, and his ethical goodness toward his people on the other; see Harrington, *Holiness*, 11–44.

9. For more on the nature of holiness vis-à-vis purity, see Milgrom, *Leviticus 17–22*, 1721.

10. For additional examples of these and other sectarian purity regulations, see Hannah K. Harrington, *The Purity Texts*, CQS 5 (London: T&T Clark, 2004).

these Jews utilized ritual ablutions not only for removal of ritual impurity but also as part of an effort to access greater holiness.[11] There are several contexts in which ritual washing functions in this quest for holiness: (1) before initiation and advancement into higher levels of holiness, (2) before entering the sanctuary, (3) before atonement; (4) before revelation; and (5) before the eschaton.

Ritual Ablutions as a Marker for Initiation and Advancement

In order to become a member of the community, the Qumran sect required an initiation ritual that began a series of tests of the novitiate's character, each level of which was demarcated by restrictions regarding food and drink. According to the Community Rule:

> He [the novitiate] must not touch the pure food of the many while they examine him regarding his spirit and his deeds until he has completed a full year.... He must not touch the drink of the Many until he has completed a second year among the men of the Community.... They shall enter him in the Rule according to his rank ... for purity and for intermingling his possessions. (1QS VI, 16–22; cf. also CD XV, 15; 4Q265 1 II, 3–9)[12]

Most scholars identify the Qumran sectarians as a group of Essenes. In Josephus's description of Essene initiation (*J.W.* 2.139), it is the "waters of purification" that mark stages in the novitiate process and admit him to the "purity," that is, the pure food and drink of the sect. Lawrence H. Schiffman puts it this way: "The new member gradually became less and less impure through the initiation process."[13] Each ritual ablution thus allows

---

11. Koltun-Fromm, *Hermeneutics of Holiness*, 64 n. 3 refers to the Qumran sect's version of holiness as "achieved holiness" rather than "assumed holiness." In other words, the sect did not consider a Jew automatically holy on the basis of race alone, but the Jew achieved holiness only by adhering to the laws of the sect and its special interpretation of Scripture.
12. Unless otherwise specified, all translations are the author's.
13. Lawrence H. Schiffman, *Sectarian Law in the Dead Sea Scrolls: Courts, Testimony and the Penal Code*, BJS 33 (Chico, CA: Scholars Press, 1983), 216. To be sure, there is a density of meanings in ritual ablutions, see the survey of ritual theory in John J. Collins, "Prayer and the Meaning of Ritual," in *Prayer and Poetry in the Dead Sea Scrolls and Related Literature: Essays in Honor of Eileen Schuller on the Occasion of Her 65th Birthday*, ed. Jeremy Penner, Ken M. Penner, and Cecilia Wassen, STDJ 98

the candidate greater access to the holy community. The water ritual initates the new member into a series of tests that give him new levels of access to the holy community. These ablutions are not for the removal of specific biblical impurities that require accompanying rituals, including a wait for sunset and, in some cases, the use of ash of the red heifer. Rather these ablutions mark off entry into a holier status.

Moreover, this usage of ablutions to mark stages of advancement into the sect does not stop, according to Josephus, with the initiation process. Rather, impurity labels continue to distinguish junior members from senior members. Those at the top of the ladder of moral integrity that touch those of lower rank become ritually impure (*J.W.* 2.150). Apparently, as one matures in moral character, sensitivity to impurity increases. Surely, all of these members maintained ritual purity according to biblical norms, and all had entered the sect through the novitiate procedure of purifications and moral tests; still there were further levels of holiness to be accessed.

The rabbis are well aware of the power of ablutions to move a person into another level of access to holy things. The Mishnah states: "They wash the hands for eating unconsecrated food, tithe, and *terumah*; and for eating food in the status of Holy Things they immerse" (m. Hag. 2:5). The writer goes on to spell out levels of access marked by immersions:

> He who immerses for the eating of unconsecrated food and is thereby confirmed as suitable for eating unconsecrated food is prohibited from eating tithe. [If] he immersed for eating tithe and is thereby confirmed as suitable for eating tithe, he is prohibited from eating *terumah*. [If] he immersed for eating *terumah* and is thereby confirmed as suitable for eating *terumah*, he is prohibited from eating food in the status of holy things. [If] he immersed for eating food in the status of holy things and is thereby confirmed as suitable for eating food in the status of holy things, he is prohibited from engaging in the preparation of purification water. (m. Hag. 2:6).

Where do the sectarians and the rabbis get this notion of initial and progressive levels of holiness demarcated by ablutions and labels of impurity? Eyal Regev recognizes the sectarians' commitment to the biblical regula-

---

(Leiden: Brill, 2012), 84. Collins explains that repeated rituals of washing "dramatized the separation of the members from the outside world, which was viewed as defiled."

tions of bodily purifications but claims that they, unlike the early Pharisees and rabbis, infused these rituals with a devotional quality in order to gain atonement from God.[14] Regev further claims that the sectarians "dramatized their role and obligations in these rituals in a manner that created a distinctive concept of ritual purity that emphasized their superior purity and morality."[15] Regev is surely correct that the sectarians were concerned with morality as well as ritual in the pursuit of holiness, as indeed is Scripture (Lev 19:2–20:26; cf. Ps 24:4). But why do both the sectarians and the later rabbis link the ritual of washing to levels of holiness? In my view, this is not just a sociological phenomenon, but an adaptation of a usage of ritual ablutions already found in Scripture. In fact, as Vered Noam notes, much of what seems to be superogatory purity practices in the Scrolls derives simply from the authors' conservative reading of Scripture.[16]

The concept of the initiation of Israel to a holier status by means of water purification is already in the Hebrew Bible. Leviticus 8 describes an induction ceremony for the priests that included ablutions: Moses washes Aaron and his son in water (Lev 8:6) as a part of the ritual that moves them from the ordinary sphere into a holy one. Also, the induction ceremony for the Levites, even though they are laity, requires water purification, which seems to move them into some level of holiness even though not into the status of priests. Indeed the Levites are called *tenufah*, "an elevation offering before the LORD." This action involves ritual immersion and laundering of clothes as well as a hand-laying ceremony (Num 8:21). These rituals sanctify, that is, set apart, the Levites from other Israelites and authorize them to handle sancta in service to the priests (Num 8:6–7). Similarly, at Qumran, the initiation ritual served as the gateway through which an individual, whose "spirit and deeds" passed muster, entered into a new life of service to God.

---

14. Eyal Regev, *Sectarianism in Qumran: A Cross-Cultural Perspective*, RelSoc 45 (Berlin: de Gruyter, 2007), 130–31. I am not convinced by Regev's stark dichotomy between the rabbis' technical and the sectarians' vibrant views of ritual purification, 149, 154–61; see Hannah K. Harrington, "Examining Rabbinic Halakha through the Lens of Qumran," in *The Qumran Legal Texts between the Hebrew Bible and Its Interpretation*, ed. Kristin De Troyer and Armin Lange, CBET 61 (Leuven: Peeters, 2011), 137–56.

15. Regev, *Sectarianism in Qumran*, 131. According to Regev, the sect felt the need to introduce a "moral ritual."

16. Vered Noam, "Stringency in Qumran: A Reassessment," *JSJ* 40 (2009): 342–55.

Ritual Ablutions before Entry into the Sanctuary

The assembly of the holy community is viewed by the sect as a surrogate temple and officiating priesthood, and so on some level initiation is entry into the sanctuary (cf. 4Q174 1-2, 21 1, 1-10; 1QS V, 20; IX, 2).[17] But some texts also refer to the temple building as a place of maximum sanctity. In the Temple Scroll, for example, the entire temple city is considered on a par with the sanctity of the temple itself (11Q19 XLV, 11-18), and double purifications are required for entry into it. The semen-impure, for example, must bathe a second time on the third day of his purification (11Q19 XLV, 7-12). This three-day process probably derives from other three-day purifications in Scripture, such as the three days of purification before the Sinaitic revelation (Exod 19:14-16), and three days of purification before the Jordan River crossing (Josh 3:2).[18] But why does the Temple Scroll require two immersions? Possibly, following Yigael Yadin, semen impurity was absolved with one ablution, as required by Lev 15:16, but the second ablution was in preparation to engage with holiness, which, according to the Temple Scroll, permeated the entire space of the temple city.[19]

The notion that entry to the temple and its levels of holiness can be unlocked by immersions comes from the rituals of the biblical priests. In the tabernacle system, washing of hands and feet was required before any priest officiated or entered the tent (Exod 30:20). To be sure, no impure person could enter the tabernacle court, so, according to the system, the

---

17. For more on the community as temple, see Devorah Dimant, "4QFlorilegium and the Idea of the Community as Temple," in *Hellenica et Judaica: Hommage à Valentin Nikiprowetzky*, ed. André Caquot, Mireille Hadas-Lebel, and J. Riaud (Leuven: Peeters, 1986), 165-89; George J. Brooke, "Miqdash Adam, Eden and the Qumran Community," in *Gemeinde ohne Tempel: Zur Substituierung und Transformation des Jerusalemer Tempels und seines Kults im Alten Testament, antiken Judentum und frühen Christentum*, ed. Beate Ego, Armin Lange, and Peter Pilhofer, WUNT 118 (Tübingen: Mohr Siebeck, 1999), 285-302; Harrington, *Purity Texts*, 15-16.

18. Three-day periods were often anticipations of other special engagements with holiness, e.g., Esther's fasting for divine favor preceded her approach to the king (Esth 4:16). Also, Ezra and Nehemiah both wait three days in Jerusalem before beginning their work at the temple or its surroundings in the City of David (Ezra 8:32-33; Neh 2:11-12).

19. Yigael Yadin, *The Temple Scroll* (Jerusalem: Israel Exploration Society, 1977-1983) 2:192.

priests would already have washed themselves before entering the complex. Apparently, the ablutions before entering the tent authorized the priest to access a higher level of holiness. The Talmud records differing views as to the function of the priestly immersions (y. Yoma 3:3–4, 40b–c and b. Yoma 30a–b). Ben Zoma views these immersions as rituals that distinguish between profane and sacred realms (cf. Maimonides, *Hilkhot beit haMiqdash* 5:4–5), but R. Yehuda considers them to be a safeguard against possible ritual impurity. In light of the fact that no impure person would have been allowed entry into the tabernacle court, the priest, who is already in the court, probably performed ablutions not to cleanse ritual impurity but to access more intense holiness.[20]

Most prominent are the multiple washings of the high priest on the Day of Atonement. According to the Mishnah, on the Day of Atonement the high priest immerses himself five times (once before each of the holy rituals) and washes his hands and feet ten times (m. Yoma 3:3). Milgrom calculates only two immersions and six washings of hands and feet in Lev 16, but he states that the Mishnah is probably accurate for the actual practice of the Herodian temple.[21] Surely these immersions within the sacred precincts were not all for the removal of possible ritual impurity.

The matter is not limited to the priests. Another strong model for the effect of multiple immersions comes from rules pertaining to the laity. As noted above, the scale-diseased person performs multiple immersions, first to remove his contagion within the ordinary sphere and, second, to allow him back into his house on the seventh day to prepare for offering his sacrifice on the next day. The rabbis express perplexity (b. Yoma 31a) as to why R. Yehuda asserted that a scale-diseased person must also immerse immediately before his entrance into the temple courts since he has just performed a purifying bath the night before. Their solution is that everyone must immerse in order to set their minds on the fact that they are entering the temple. The Mishnah states explicitly: "No one can enter into the priestly court to officiate even if he is pure until he immerses" (m. Yoma 3:3). This attitude is confirmed centuries earlier by the writer of Aramaic Levi: "When you rise to enter the house of God, bathe in water and

---

20. Milgrom, *Leviticus 1–16*, 753 discusses the ban on impurity within the tabernacle court; see also his discussion of degrees of holy space within the tabernacle complex, ibid., 614.

21. Milgrom, *Leviticus 1–16*, 1018.

then put on the priestly vestments" (ALD 18).[22] This too is the mindset emphasized among the Scrolls; ritual immersion prepares for the reception of holiness.

Ritual Ablutions before Atonement

Among the Scrolls, ritual bathing is also necessary for the holiness that brings atonement even without the temple. The sectarians' self-identification was one of constant impurity due to their inherent sinful state. According to the Hodayot, the Thanksgiving Hymns, human beings are ontologically flawed, each individual being "guilty of sin from his mother's womb to old age" (1QH[a] IV, 27–30, 35). Impurity is a fact of life since each person is "a structure of dust fashioned with water; his counsel is the [iniquity] of sin, shame of dishonor and so[urce] of impurity, and a depraved spirit rules over him" (1QH[a] V, 20–22). Since impurity is the default status of humanity, ritual purification is an ongoing requirement. The same author prays that as he is purifying his hands, the holy spirit, which God has graciously placed within him, will purge his inner being:

> And because I know that You have recorded the spirit of the righteous, I myself have chosen to purify my hands in accordance with your wil[l]. The soul of your servant a[bho]rs every work of injustice. I know that no one can be righteous apart from you. And I entreat your favor by that spirit which you have placed within [me], to fulfill your [mer]cy with [your] servant for[ever], to purify me by your holy spirit, and to bring me near by your will according to the greatness of your mercy. (1QH[a] VIII, 18–21)

The supplicant identifies himself with the righteous and those who abhor injustice, thus he seeks a higher level of holiness when he asks, as he washes his hands, to be drawn in line with God's will by the spirit's purifying power (cf. also 11Q5 XIX, 13–14).

The Community Rule explicitly connects ritual purification and atonement. The writer emphasizes that no ablutions can remove the impurity of one who rejects the Community's laws, but for the humble that accept the

---

22. Joseph M. Baumgarten, "Some 'Qumranic' Observations on the Aramaic Levi Document," in *Sefer Moshe: The Moshe Weinfeld Jubilee Volume; Studies in the Bible and the Ancient Near East, Qumran, and Post-biblical Judaism*, ed. Chaim Cohen, Avi Hurvitz, and Shalom Paul (Winona Lake, IN: Eisenbrauns, 2004), 397.

authority of the community, ritual washing will be effective (1QS III, 6-8; 4Q255 II, 1-4). The author goes on to state that the holy spirit will purify him from sin, and ritual ablutions will purify his body:

> But by the holy spirit of the community, in its truth, he can be purified [יטהר] from all of his sins and through an upright and humble attitude his sin may be atoned, and by humbling himself before all God's laws his flesh can be purified [יטהר] by sprinkling with waters of purgation and sanctified [יתקדש] by purifying waters. (1QS III, 10-13)

The synonymous interchanging of the verbs "purify" (יטהר) and "sanctify" (יתקדש) reveals the interconnectedness of ritual and moral purification here. The author does not accept one without the other; the two are inextricably linked in the process of repentance.[23] The same attitude holds true for the Damascus Document, which expresses the matter negatively: the word of a transgressor is not believed unless he has been ritually purified (CD X, 2; cf. 1QS V, 14-20, even possessions of a sinner are impure).

Given the sect's self-identification as a sanctuary and eternal priesthood, members would no doubt have been cleansed from ritual impurities as soon as they occurred with the necessary waits for sunset and, if required, other ritual actions. The only ritual impurity mentioned here is that caused by sin for which there is no wait until sunset. Indeed, in 4Q texts the blessing comes directly after washing while the cleansed person was standing in the water: "And then he shall enter the water.... And he shall say in response, Blessed are y[ou]" (4Q414 2 II, 5-6; 4Q512 42-44 II). The ablution thus does not remove specific ritual impurities, but invites the holy spirit to purify an individual's inner being. Or, as Joseph M. Baumgarten puts it: "Far from being merely external acts ... these purifications were viewed as the means by which the holy spirit restores the corporate purity of Israel."[24]

---

23. Joseph M. Baumgarten, "Tohorot," in *Qumran Cave 4. XXV: Halakhic Texts*, ed. J. Baumgarten et al. (Oxford: Clarendon, 1999), 83-92, argues, on the basis of 4Q274-279 and 4Q512, that the sectarians mandated the special waters of purgation biblically required only for corpse impurity, for other ritual impurities as well.

24. Joseph M. Baumgarten, "The Purification Liturgies," in *The Dead Sea Scrolls after Fifty Years: A Comprehensive Assessment*, ed. Peter Flint and James C. Vanderkam (Leiden: Brill), 2:211; see also Baumgarten, "The Law and Spirit of Purity at Qumran," in *The Bible and the Dead Sea Scrolls: The Second Princeton Symposium on Judaism*

Once again, the need for ablutions takes its cue from Scripture. Moral impurity causes a deficiency and distance that both human attitude and ritual methods ameliorate.[25] Some patriarchs, according to Scripture, immersed and offered sacrifices after transgression in order to appease the deity. Both Job and Jacob order their families to wash themselves before attending expiatory sacrifices. Job explains: "It may be that my sons have sinned" (Job 1:6); in Jacob's case the idolatry is evident, as he orders his household: "Put away the strange gods that are among you, and be pure, and change your garments" (Gen 35:1–3). Humility and repentance played a large role in Naaman's healing, which likewise was preceded by bathing in the Jordan River (2 Kgs 5:14). As in these examples where no temple was available, so also among the sectarians ritual washing still accompanies prayer and blessings.

Since the Qumran sect regarded itself as a replacement for the temple cult, at least temporarily, prayer substituted for sacrifice (1QS IX, 4–5). Baumgarten notes that in several scrolls ritual washing precedes the recitation of prayers. Indeed in Cave Four texts the blessing comes only after washing and is offered while the purifying person is standing in the water. Baumgarten argues: "Ritual purity is required for their recital."[26] However, if the concern was ritual impurity, a wait for sunset would be involved. Here the purifying person washes and immediately blesses God. My claim is that the purifying person has already performed the required ablutions and waited for sunset. This new washing is like the washing preceding the offering of a sacrifice in the temple. Just as washings preceded the offering of sacrifices at the altar, so the sect performed ablutions before offering the "sacrifice of praise."[27]

---

and Christian Origins, ed. James H. Charlesworth (Waco, TX: Baylor University Press, 2006), 2:93–105.

25. In fact, the atonement process in Leviticus and Numbers is largely a ritual purification accompanied by repentance and restitution (cf. Lev 5:5; 18:27–29; Num 15:28–30).

26. Baumgarten, "Some 'Qumranic' Observations," 394.

27. Daniel K. Falk, "Qumran Prayer Texts and the Temple," in *Sapiential, Liturgical and Poetical Texts from Qumran: Proceedings of the Third Meeting of the International Organization for Qumran Studies, Oslo 1998: Published in Memory of Maurice Baillet*, ed. Daniel K. Falk et al., STDJ 35 (Leiden: Brill, 2000), 106–26.

Ritual Ablutions before Revelation

Water purification for the authors of the Scrolls anticipates engagement with holiness not only for initiation, atonement, and temple access, but also for the experience of divine revelation. According to Josephus, the Essenes, who are most likely linked to the Scroll authors, required ritual purification as a prerequisite for the reception of prophecy: they utilized the books of the prophets and also "various forms of purification" (*J.W.* 2.159). One fragmentary text from Qumran, in particular, supports the practice of ritual washing as a preparation for divine revelation. 4Q213a (4QAramaic Levi^a) corroborates the existence of the Testament of Levi at Qumran which, when combined, gives an account of purification before divine revelation:

> [Then] I [washed my clothing and purified them with pure water,] [and] I bath[ed all over in living water, so making] all [my ways correct. Then] I raised my eyes [and face] to heaven, [I opened my mouth and spoke,] and my fingers and hands [I spread out properly in front of the holy angels. So I prayed and] said. (4Q213a 1 I, 6–10 with the Testament of Levi, Mount Athos MS in brackets)

In this passage, bathing precedes Levi's entreaty before the holy angels. In the next column, his purification and supplication are rewarded with a supernatural vision in which he is ushered into heaven: "Then I saw visions […] in the appearance of this vision, I saw [the] heav[en opened, and I saw a mountain] underneath me, high, reaching up to heaven […] to me the gates of heaven, and an angel [said to me: Enter Levi…]."[28]

The revelation at Sinai provides the model for expectation of divine revelation after purification. Here all Israel is told to "sanctify" themselves in the sense of ritual purification, even laundering and abstaining from sexual intercourse, as the necessary preparation to stand in the presence of God and receive the law (Exod 19:14). Although Scripture does not explicitly command immersions, all of the ancient Jewish interpreters understand

---

28. Scholars differ regarding the purpose of the ablution. James Davila ("Heavenly Ascents in the Dead Sea Scrolls," in Flint, *The Dead Sea Scrolls after Fifty Years*, 2:466–69) says that the immersion may have been preparatory for the vision; Baumgarten ("Some 'Qumranic' Observations," 397) argues that the ablution is preparatory to the prayer since there is a piece of text between the prayer and the vision.

the biblical requirement of laundering to include bodily immersion (Mek. Yitro; Mek. RŠ 96–97; Philo, *Decal.* 11; b. Ker. 9a; b. Yevam. 46a; y. Shabb. 9.12a). According to rabbinic legend, even Moses immersed before the revelation and finally had to separate permanently from his wife so he could be pure and ready constantly for additional revelation (b. Shabb. 87a, 88b; Avot R. Nat. 2).

These immersions are probably not for the removal of the impurities discussed in Lev 11–15, for example, seminal discharge and corpse impurity, because it seems likely that these impurities would have been taken care of separately and beforehand. As Schiffman has argued, the Qumranites lived in expectation of this messianic era in the present, and so required the constant purification of all impurity in their ranks. Indeed, the impurities of Lev 11–15 require a wait for sunset for complete purification (e.g., 11:15), a matter about which the sect is emphatic even where it is not explicit in Scripture (cf., e.g., MMT B 71–72 and Lev 14:19–20). Divine revelation immediately follows the ablutions of Levi in the text above. Thus his purification seems to be anticipatory of holiness rather than for the removal of impurity.

There is strong biblical precedent for ritual washings before reception of supernatural revelation and power. The miracles of the quail (Num 11:18), crossing the Jordan (Josh 3:5) and the divine revelation of the results of the lot-casting (Josh 7:13–14) are all preceded by sanctification, which in nonpriestly texts, indicates ritual ablutions.[29] Indeed, troops achieve victory in battle only if they maintain purity (Deut 23:9–14). Most of these examples occur over a three-day period in order to allow time for the sun to set and for the residual impurity to wear off completely.[30] The issue of waiting for sunset apparently became a bone of contention in ancient times, because several scrolls insist upon it (4QMMT B 71–72; 11Q19 L, 12–16; 4Q266 9 II, 1–4). We know from rabbinic literature that many Jews allowed the purifying person access to all but sacred things immediately after washing (m. T Yom 2:2–3).[31]

---

29. The report that Bathsheba רוחצת "bathes" (2 Sam 11:2), later explained as מתקדשת "sanctifies herself" after her menstrual impurity (2 Sam 11:4), supports this deduction; see Milgrom, *Leviticus 1–16*, 965.

30. Ibid., 966–67.

31. For the prerabbinic date of this concept, see Thomas Kazen, *Issues of Impurity in Early Judaism*, ConBNT 45 (Winona Lake, IN: Eisenbrauns, 2010), 88–89, 99, who argues that first day ablutions were not a sectarian development but a "systemic

The mystics of the *hekhalot* texts (dated as early as the first century CE) form a close parallel to the Qumran sectarians, since both were trying to influence/contact the angels. In these text immersions play an important role in facilitating various adjurations. The ritual for drawing down the Sar ha-Torah, for example, demands twenty-four immersions daily. Another Sar ha-Torah ritual requires immersions in a river every morning and evening for nine days.[32]

Purification before the Eschaton

The Dead Sea Scrolls clearly portray ritual purification as preparation for the eschaton. According to the War Scroll, a great war in the messianic era will be fought in heaven and on earth engaging both natural and supernatural forces. Because angels will be present in this battle, those impure from a sexual discharge are not allowed to participate (1QM VII, 3–6). Also, the Rule of the Congregation prohibits any ritually impure person from serving on the eschatological council (1Q28a II, 2– 4; cf. Lev 5:3; 7:21). Schiffman argues that the Qumranites lived in expectation of this messianic era at all times, and so required the constant purification of impurity in their ranks.[33]

Purification for at least some Jews carried eschatological significance and played a role in the resurrection of the dead. According to the writer of Hodayot:

> For our glory's sake you have purified [טהרת] man from transgression, so that he can purify himself [להתקדש] for you from all impure abominations [תואבות נדה] and the guilt of unfaithfulness, so as to be joined wi[th] the children of your truth; in the lot with your holy ones, that bodies, covered with worms of the dead, might rise up from the dust to an et[ernal] council; from a perverse spirit to your understanding. (1QH XIX, 10–13)

---

necessity" for dealing with long periods of impurity; cf. also Hannah K. Harrington, "Leniency in the Temple Scroll's Purity Law? Another Look," *Henoch* 36 (2014): 35–49.

32. For further discussion and references of these texts, see Rebecca M. Lesses, *Ritual Practices to Gain Power: Angels, Incantations, and Revelation in Early Jewish Mysticism*, HTS 44 (Harrisburg, PA: Trinity Press International, 1998) 132–60.

33. Lawrence H. Schiffman, "Purity and Perfection: Exclusion from the Council of the Community in the *Serekh ha-'Edah*," in *Biblical Archaeology Today*, ed. J. Amitai (Jerusalem: Israel Exploration Society, 1985), 373–89.

Although this text does not refer explictly to washing, like the Community Rule it interweaves the terms and concepts of ritual purity and sanctification. Purification is holistic, referring not simply to the removal of ritual impurity, but to a complete eradication of guilt and perversion so that a person can join the company of the holy angels and enjoy the blessings of the eschaton. The ultimate goal of purification here is nothing short of resurrection from the dead. Seen in this light, this text foreshadows later rabbinic levels of piety in the saying that ritual purity leads to separation and then to holiness and eventually to the holy spirit and the resurrection of the dead (m. Sotah 9:15).

The connection between water purification and the outpouring of the spirit of God at the eschaton is a biblical principle. Just as the spirit worked in conjunction with water to effect the first creation (Gen 1:2), so also at the eschatological rejuvenation. In fact, the eschaton opens with the divine purification of Israel: the prophet Zechariah promises the outpouring of the spirit culminating in the divine fountain that will purify Israel (Zech 12:10; 13:1). Ezekiel especially links the eschatological purification with a new creation: God will sprinkle pure water on wayward Israel to purify her of sin, giving her a new heart and a new spirit (Ezek 36:25).[34] Furthermore, the notion that purification precedes the eschaton is not a complete abstraction. Rather, with the emphasis on ritual purification in water prevalent in so many forms of Second Temple Judaism, for example, before atonement, before temple entry, and other holy activities, Jews would have associated these purity terms with both physical and moral cleansing.[35]

In summary, the Qumran sect performed ritual ablutions not only to maintain purity but also to facilitate access to more intense levels of holiness. This conclusion is based upon: (1) the diverse contexts in which ritual ablutions were performed not to remove a specific ritual impurity with its requisite wait for sunset but to engage in a holy activity or access a level of holiness; and (2) the biblical precedent, both priestly and lay, of immersions performed by ritually pure persons in pursuit of greater holiness or authorization for access to more sacred areas.

---

34. John R. Levison, *Filled with the Spirit* (Grand Rapids: Eerdmans, 2009), 206.

35. See Baumgarten, "The Purification Liturgies," 208–11 for further discussion with examples from Cave 4 Qumran texts (e.g., 4Q414 10 VII; 4Q504 1–2 V, 15; 4Q512) on the intermingling of purification terms for ritual and moral cleansing.

Related Second Temple Traditions

One might argue that this emphasis on ritual immersion in a quest for holiness was limited to the biblical interpretations and traditions of a few sectarians who wrote the Dead Sea Scrolls and, in some cases, later rabbis. However, the Scripture was the property of all Jewish religious groups in Second Temple times, and the power of ritual ablutions to help move a person into a level of holiness appears elsewhere as well.[36]

In some Second Temple texts, purification rituals accompany atonement even without the sanctuary. According to LAE 6–7, the penitent pleads for forgiveness as he immerses in water although nowhere near the temple. Adam says to Eve, "Stand clothed in the water up to [your] neck, and let no speech come out of your mouth, because we are unworthy to entreat the Lord since our lips are unclean." Similarly, the Sib. Or. 4:165–68 calls for immersion of the whole body in rivers followed by prayer for forgiveness, and the penitent spreads forth his hands to God. No waiting for full removal of impurity is recorded in either of these cases. Moreover, the Testament of Levi explains that it is in the water that divine cleansing takes place: "And the spirit of understanding and sanctification shall rest upon him in the water (T. Levi 18:7 [Brownlee]). Before Levi prays that the Lord make known to him the "spirit of holiness," he is obligated to bathe (T. Levi 2:3; cf. Jud 12:7–8).[37]

The Mishnah reports a group of Jews called "Morning Bathers" because they immersed before morning prayers, but states that the Phari-

---

36. Jonathan D. Lawrence, *Washing in Water: Trajectories of Ritual Bathing in the Hebrew Bible and Second Temple Literature*, AcBib 23 (Atlanta: Society of Biblical Literature, 2006), 196, sees ritual purity as originally a preparation for a single encounter with God, which was later institutionalized into cultic systems that preserved purity for the community's encounters with God. He points to various uses of immersion in Second Temple Judaism: initiation, before prayer, before eating, before Sabbath and festivals. This diversity of usages of washing leads him to assert that washing was not just a ritual but carried a spiritual quality, 201; for an opposing view see Hartmut Stegemann, "The Qumran Essenes: Local Members of the Main Jewish Union in Late Second Temple Times," in Trebolle Barrera, *Madrid Qumran Congress*, 1:110: "Nor did the bath have any sacramental meaning such as forgiveness of sins, but provided only ritual purity."

37. Lawrence, *Washing in Water*, 110, suggests that this passage describes a preparation for theophany.

sees considered this practice unnecessary (m. Yad. 2:20).[38] That is not to say that the Pharisees did not care if one was pure or not before prayer, but that they assumed that the individual already performed ablutions after impurity, and thus a second ablution would have been superogatory.

One of the most interesting examples of water purification preceding holy activity comes from the New Testament and is roughly contemporary with the Qumran sectarians: the Baptist traditions, recorded in all four gospels and by Josephus. In these accounts of Jesus's baptism, ablutions anticipate holiness in most of the ways discussed above.

Ritual Ablutions as a Marker for Initiation and Advancement

Significantly, Jesus's baptism inducts him into a life of ministry, as it did the biblical priests and Levites. According to Matthew, it is while he is standing in the purifying water of the Jordan River that the Spirit of God rests upon him and consecrates him for ministry (Matt 3:16–17). Baptism moves him from the ordinary sphere to a consecrated one. In the Fourth Gospel, water also works in anticipation of the Spirit to bring about the "new birth" that Jesus requires of his followers (John 3:5: "You must be born of water and spirit"). So too the humbling ablutions of foot washing inaugurate a new life of service for the disciples (John 13:1–17).

Raymond Brown recognizes the association of ritual ablutions and initiation into the people of God and claims that it is the unique contribution of the Fourth Gospel: "It is John who tells us that through baptismal water God begets children unto himself and pours forth upon them his Spirit (John 3:5; 7:37–39)."[39] Water and Spirit are used in conjunction with each other to effect this initiation; both elements fulfill a single objective.[40] Indeed, the gospels' notion that new life follows baptism is not unusual in light of biblical and Qumran precedents.[41]

---

38. Baumgarten, "Some 'Qumranic' Observations," 395–96.

39. Raymond Brown, *An Introduction to the Gospel of John*, ed. Francis J. Moloney, ABRL (New York: Doubleday, 2003), 234.

40. Larry Paul Jones, *The Symbol of Water in the Gospel of John*, JSNTSup 145 (Sheffield: Sheffield Academic, 1997), 70, translates this phrase epexegetically in which water and Spirit function together; Wai Yee Ng, *Water Symbolism in John: An Eschatological Interpretation*, StBibLit 15 (New York: Lang, 2001), 66, sees both a ritualistic and figurative usage of the water symbol.

41. Cf. also Hermann Lichtenberger, "The Dead Sea Scrolls and John the Baptist: Reflections on Josephus' Account of John the Baptist," in *The Dead Sea Scrolls: Forty*

Ritual Ablutions before Atonement

Scholars debate the role of atonement, or lack of it, in John's baptism. Walter Wink denies that John's baptism effected atonement because that was the role of the divine Christ. Rather, he claims that John's baptism was "solely for the purpose of manifesting to the world its need for the purification which Christ alone brings (John 1:31)."[42] Nevertheless, John's baptism is specifically termed *baptisma metanoias* by both Mark and Luke (Mark 1:4; Luke 3:3). James Charlesworth is probably correct that, as at Qumran, water did not by itself effect atonement, but it contributed to a person's experience of repentance by expressing a desire for cleaning and dependence on God's grace. This "baptism of repentance for the forgiveness of sins," was part of the repentance process.[43] John does not specify any ritual impurities nor does he send any of these penitents to the temple to offer atoning sacrifices. The examples from the Dead Sea Scrolls discussed above suggest that baptism was considered by many Jews in Second Temple times as an invitation to God's spirit to enter and perform his work of inner purification.

Josephus sees it from a slightly different perspective as "a consecration of the body implying that the soul was already thoroughly cleansed by righteous behavior" (*Ant.* 19.116–119). However, at least in Luke's account, there is no opportunity yet for the penitent to have demonstrated righteous living, rather they have just been rebuked by John for unrighteous acts, and are seeking baptism as part of the repentance process (Luke 3:7–14). Still, Josephus's point is well taken that ritual ablutions cannot purify the inner person; the sectarians of Qumran would agree (cf. 1QS III, 4–12).

Years of Research, ed. Devorah Dimant and Uriel Rappaport, STDJ 10 (Leiden: Brill, 1992), 340–46.

42. See Walter Wink, *John the Baptist in the Gospel Tradition*, SNTSMS 7 (Cambridge: Cambridge University Press, 1968), 90, "If Jesus is the Lamb of God who takes away the sins of the world ([John] 1:29, 36), then clearly John's baptism can no longer be for the forgiveness of sins. We see him baptize no one, nor is he once called 'the Baptist' in this Gospel."

43. See James H. Charlesworth, "John the Baptizer and Qumran Barriers in Light of the Rule of the Community," in *The Provo International Conference on the Dead Sea Scrolls: Technological Innovations, New Texts, and Reformulated Issues*, ed. Donald W. Parry and Eugene Ulrich, STDJ 30 (Leiden: Brill, 1999), 353–78, esp. 357–58.

With respect to Jesus, however, baptism did not mean that he was being purified from sin or impurity. Indeed, Jesus is never depicted as impure by the Gospel writers, and in the Fourth Gospel he is presented as the "Lamb who takes away sin and impurity" (John 1:29). Rather, his baptism prepares him for a special engagement with holiness. As John A. T. Robinson points out, in the case of Jesus, water baptism pointed to the Spirit "which was to consecrate the coming one for his mission (John 1:31), the ultimate divine mission of taking away the sin of the world (John 1:29) and of pouring out upon believers the holy spirit of God (John 1:33)."[44]

Ritual Ablutions before Revelation

The Fourth Gospel presents John the Baptist performing ritual ablutions in preparation for the revelation of the Word incarnate: "So that he should be made known to Israel, that is why I am baptizing with water" (John 1:31). According to Matthew and Luke, the revelation of the Spirit and the divine voice confirming Jesus as God's Son occur immediately after he emerges from the water (Matt 3:16; Luke 3:21–22).

This act of divine revelation reminds one of the quintessential revelation in the Hebrew Bible, the giving of the law at Mount Sinai.[45] Just as that foundational experience of ancient Israel was preceded by ritual purification in preparation for a holy encounter with God (Exod 19:14–15), similarly, the revelation of Jesus as the Son of God does not happen without proper preparation. According to John 1, ritual ablutions are still the gateway that invites an engagement with holiness.[46]

---

44. John A. T. Robinson, "The Baptism of John and the Qumran Community: Testing a Hypothesis," in *Twelve New Testament Studies*, SBT 34 (London: SCM, 1962), 24.

45. Lawrence, *Washing in Water*, 186–87 n. 2, agrees that John's baptism could be seen as a preparation for theophany since he was preaching of the coming Kingdom of God; see also Joan Taylor, *The Immerser: John the Baptist within Second Temple Judaism*, SHJ (Grand Rapids: Eerdmans, 1997), 3.

46. Paul reflects the same trend of thought when he says that all Israel was purified in the Red Sea and then they all ate spiritual food (manna) and drank miraculous water (1 Cor 10:1–3). Israel's "baptism" in the Red Sea initiated a new and holier phase of life when she began to experience divine provision of manna and quail.

Purification before the Eschaton

The baptism of Jesus can also be seen as an eschatological event.[47] According to Luke, John prophesies Jesus's mission of eschatological judgment collecting the "wheat" and burning the "chaff" (Luke 3:17). John's message warned of divine judgment about to occur, as well as expressed hope that a messianic figure would emerge soon to bring rescue to the Jews (Luke 3:4-9). But do ritual ablutions form a part, if only in preparation, of this end time phenomenon? Indeed, if one examines the priestly traditions of the Torah, there does not seem to be a place for eschatological concepts in the purity system.[48] Nevertheless, with the data presented above from the Dead Sea Scrolls and other contemporary Jewish literature, it becomes apparent that ablutions did form a part of messianic expectation.

According to Luke, crowds, including even tax collectors, responded to John's preaching by seeking ritual purification in water in an effort to "flee from the wrath to come" (Luke 3:7, 12). As Robert Webb puts it: "John's baptism is the final opportunity to prepare for the eschatological judgment and restoration to be brought by the expected figure."[49] Baptism expresses that hope for eschatological deliverance.

Furthermore, John's ministry of baptism was necessary, among other reasons, in order to provide a context in which the messiah could emerge. According to the Fourth Gospel, John was able to identify the messiah

---

47. Bruce Chilton, "Yohanan the Purifier and His Immersion," in *TJT* 14.2 (1998): 211 n. 45, sees John's baptism as a purification ritual with eschatological overtones; see also Otto Böcher, "Johannes der Täufer," *TRE* 17:175.

48. Cf. Catherine Murphy, *John the Baptist: Prophet of Purity for a New Age*, Interfaces (Collegeville, MN: Liturgical Press, 2003), 60: "Nowhere in Jewish tradition was baptism associated with the messiah or the end times, notwithstanding the interrogation of John by priests and Levites in the Fourth Gospel (John 1:19-28). This is discontinuous with Jewish tradition and therefore more likely to be a historical innovation, at least of the evangelists' and perhaps of John's"; see also Taylor, *Immerser*, 9. Against this position, Chilton claims that, while John's baptism was definitely ritual bathing and did not bring atonement, it "was driven by an eschatological expectation; not necessarily of a messiah but of divine judgment. Of all the statements attributed to Yohanan, the claim that after him a baptism of spirit was to come stands out as possibly authentic," "Yohanan the Purifier," 207-11.

49. Robert Webb, "John the Baptist and His Relationship to Jesus," in *Studying the Historical Jesus: Evaluations of the State of Current Research*, ed. Bruce Chilton and Craig A. Evans, NTTS 19 (Leiden: Brill, 1998), 196.

during the course of baptism: "I myself did not know him, but he who sent me to baptize with water said to me, 'He on whom you see the Spirit descend and remain, this is he who baptizes with the Holy Spirit'" (John 1:33; also 1:41). According to this text, the process of baptism was prerequisite for identifying the messiah and receiving his blessings, in particular, the baptism of the Spirit.[50] Robinson goes so far as to suggest that John was baptizing "precisely to force the eschatological issue … to set the last things in motion by his baptism of water" (see John 1:26, 31, 33).[51] If so, the Qumran sectarians would have understood John's reasoning; purification prepared for eschatological blessing. They too regarded themselves as living in eschatological times and anticipated not only the appearance of the messiah(s) but also a holy war against the forces of darkness. Ritual purity was an important prerequisite for their success (see above).

In summary, the Baptist traditions reflect the vibrant understanding of ritual ablutions reflected in late Second Temple Judaism. As in the purity texts found at Qumran, ritual washing in the gospels precedes and facilitates a variety of outcomes including initiation into a new life of ministry, atonement from sin, divine revelation, and eschatological blessing.

Archaeology of the Temple Mount

Recent archaeology weighs into the discussion of ritual immersion as an act that anticipates an encounter with holiness. According to archaeologists, dozens of ritual baths have been excavated to the south and west of the Temple Mount that date from Herodian or Hasmonean times.[52] At

---

50. According to Ng, John's identification of Jesus during baptism is the fountainhead to the "subsequent and successive use of water symbolism" throughout the Fourth Gospel, where water often symbolizes eschatological blessing, see, in particular, Ng's discussion of John 3:30, *Water Symbolism in John*, 60.

51. Robinson, "Baptism of John," 24. Ng, *Water Symbolism in John*, 68, puts it well: "Just as John the Baptist prepared the way for the eschatological Christ ([John] 2:23), his baptism anticipates salvific cleansing of the eschatological kingdom. So water anticipates the eschatological means of purification which the gospel eventually comes to reveal as the Holy Spirit ([John] 7:37–39)." For more on the Fourth Gospel's understanding of ritual ablutions and holiness, see Hannah K. Harrington, "Purification in the Fourth Gospel in Light of Qumran," *John, Qumran, and the Dead Sea Scrolls: Sixty Years of Discovery and Debate*, ed. Tom Thatcher and Mary Coloe, EJL 32 (Atlanta: Society of Bible Literature, 2011), 117–38.

52. Eyal Regev, "The Ritual Baths Near the Temple Mount and Extra-Purification

least ten of these ritual baths have been identified in close proximity to the Temple Mount.[53] It is clear from the archaeological context of these ritual baths that they were built for public use and were intended to serve those who wished to immerse before entering the temple.[54]

According to Ronny Reich, there are likely at least two more ritual baths on the Temple Mount itself. Reich claims that two subterranean chambers of the Temple Mount north of the southern wall but south of the Women's Court and *ḥēl* (rampart) are probably ritual baths.[55] This information correlates with the report of the Mishnah which mentions ritual immersion of the priests on the Temple Mount itself (m. Sheqal. 8:4; m. Yoma 3:2–6; 7:3–4; Tamid 1:1; m. Mid. 1:6; see also m. Hag. 2:6; 3:1). This means that even those who had purified already upon entering the temple complex probably immersed again before officiating or participating in the inner court or within the Court of the Women.

Regev makes a compelling argument that the ritual baths at the Temple Mount cannot be for use by ritually impure persons by the conventional definitions of Lev 11–15, for example, seminal discharge, menstruation, corpse impurity, because these persons would still have to wait for sunset in order to enter the sacred areas. Halakhic evidence indicates that most of the pilgrims, even those labeled as *ʿam-haʾaretz*, "people of the land," because they did not usually observe ritual purity throughout the year and were not trustworthy in matters of tithes, took care of their ritual purity before reaching Jerusalem. Thus, he concludes that visitors to the temple came already ritually pure but then performed extra purifications in order

---

before Entering the Temple Courts," *IEJ* 55 (2005): 194–204, utilizes the work of several archaeologists, including the unpublished excavation report of Benjamin Mazar, and the dissertation of Ronny Reich, "Miqwa'ot (Jewish ritual immersion baths) in Eretz-Israel in the Second Temple and the Mishna and Talmud Periods" (Hebrew) (PhD diss., Hebrew University of Jerusalem, 1990), 87–93, 218–30.

53. Two small baths were located near the southern wall of the Temple Mount, between the stairways of the Huldah gates (dimensions: 3 x 4.8 m.; 1.4 x 4 m) with others nearby, see Ronny Reich, "Two Possible *Miqwāʾōt* on the Temple Mount," *IEJ* 39 (1989): 63–65; Benjamin Mazar, *The Mountain of the Lord* (Garden City, NY: Doubleday, 1975), 146; Reich, "*Miqwaʾot* in Eretz-Israel," 220, nos. 17y and 18y. Near the southwestern corner of the Temple Mount, in the vicinity of Robinson's Arch, five ritual baths were excavated in the spaces beneath the monumental staircase.

54. Reich, "*Miqwaʾot* in Eretz-Israel," 89.

55. Reich, "Two Possible *Miqwāʾōt* on the Temple Mount," 63–65.

to enter holy area.⁵⁶ Regev also refers to Paul's ritual immersion immediately before entering temple precincts without waiting for sunset.⁵⁷

On the other hand, Yonatan Adler does not see these purifications at the Temple Mount to be extra but as necessary to remove rabbinic, not biblical impurities, for which no wait for sunset is required.⁵⁸ Adler argues that the rabbis required immersion if one was preparing to offer food or other contributions to the temple. But this is just the point: before engaging the holiness of the temple, immersion additional to the simple removal of impurity was required. Adler objects to calling this an extra purification, but it is surely additional to the simple removal of the impurities of Lev 11–15. In any case, both Regev and Adler agree that biblical impurities that required sunset had to be purified before one ever approached the Temple Mount, or else the individual could not use the ritual baths there in order to proceed into the sacred courts.

Conclusion

In light of the foregoing data it becomes apparent that ritual ablutions in Second Temple times were not just for the removal of impurity, but were also utilized as a tool to help an individual prepare for special holy experiences. The ritual bath was a mechanism that gave the participant proper status to engage a level of holiness. In this regard, the Dead Sea Scroll authors are supported by many biblical traditions, some priestly and some lay, which emphasize the effectuality of ritual purification not only to remove ritual impurity but to anticipate acts and levels of holiness. Those

---

56. For purification on the way to Jerusalem or before the beginning of the journey, see m. Bik. 3:2; t. Bik. 2.8. According to the Mishnah, in order to facilitate purification on the way to Jerusalem, ritual baths were fixed and the burials were marked in the beginning of Adar, before the Passover pilgrimage (m. Sheqal. 1:1; cf. m. Hag. 3:6). See Aharon Oppenheimer, *The ʿAm ha-ʾAretz: A Study in the Social History of the Jewish People in the Hellenistic-Roman Period*, trans. I. H. Levine, ALGHJ 8 (Leiden: Brill, 1977), 92–94, 159–60.

57. Regev, "Ritual Baths Near the Temple Mount," 198–99: "According to Acts 21:24–26, Paul followed the order of James and the Elders of the Jerusalem Church and immersed immediately before entering the Temple. Luke, or perhaps his source, may have regarded this as the prevalent practice.... His immersion seems to serve as a preparation rite before entering the Women's Court."

58. Yonatan Adler, "The Ritual Baths near the Temple Mount and Extra-Purification before Entering the Temple Courts: A Reply to Eyal Regev," *IEJ* 56 (2006): 209–15.

immersing in water anticipated such divine blessings as: initiation into a holy people, entry into sacred space, atonement, divine revelation, miracles, and the coming of the messiah. Ritual purification of this nature is evidenced not only in the Bible and the Dead Sea Scrolls but is supported by data from other Second Temple literature, the New Testament, rabbinic sources, and the archaeological record.

Part 2
Sacrifice: Ritual Aspects and Prophetic Critique

A Reexamination of the Ancient Israelite Gesture of Hand Placement

David Calabro

Introduction

Hand placement (also known as imposition of hands, laying on of hands, and hand-leaning),[1] a prescribed ritual gesture in which a priest lays his hands on the head of a person or animal, is attested twenty-three times in the Hebrew Bible.[2] It is also attested sporadically in other early Jewish

---

1. The more commonly used terms are "imposition of hands" and "laying on of hands," which represent the traditional usage in English-speaking religious communities. Jacob Milgrom introduced the term "hand-leaning" in *Leviticus 1–16: A New Translation with Introduction and Commentary*, AB 3 (New York: Doubleday, 1991), 133, 150, and others have subsequently adopted it, notably William H. C. Propp, *Exodus 19–40: A New Translation with Introduction and Commentary*, AB 2A (New York: Doubleday, 2006), 457 (on Exodus 29:10: "shall press their hands," with explicit reference to Milgrom); Roy E. Gane, *Cult and Character: Purification Offerings, Day of Atonement, and Theodicy* (Winona Lake, IN: Eisenbrauns, 2005), 244–46. Milgrom argues that the verb סמך, usually rendered "lay" or "place," actually "implies pressure" and is thus different from שית and שים, the verbs used for Jacob's gesture of blessing in Gen 48:14, 17, 18. Although Milgrom's interpretation is certainly in line with late antique Jewish sources, it seems to me to lean too heavily on these sources and to press the biblical evidence too far; his review of other biblical examples of סמך does not preclude the idea that the "pressure" could be only the weight of the hands, so that "placement," "imposition," and "laying" would be acceptable translations. The term I use here, "hand placement," is used by David P. Wright in his article "The Gesture of Hand Placement in the Hebrew Bible and in Hittite Literature," *JAOS* 106 (1986): 433–46, and I find it to be felicitous both in its conciseness and in its resonance with the notion of "placing" the object of the gesture in a particular status or role (for which I argue below).

2. Exod 29:10, 15, 19; Lev 1:4; 3:2, 8, 13; 4:4, 15, 24, 29, 33; 8:14, 18, 22; 16:21;

texts.³ A chain of interpreters, including René Péter in 1977, Bernd Janowski in 1982, David P. Wright in 1986, and Jacob Milgrom in 1991, have argued that there are actually two different gestures of hand placement, with one involving only a single hand and the other both hands. The two gestures, according to these interpreters, have different functions.⁴ This theory has been very influential, as shown in more recent studies, almost all of which accept the basic division into two formally distinct gestures, even if they differ as to the significance of the division.⁵ However, a fresh consideration of the evidence in light of the textual witnesses and in light of Biblical Hebrew grammar suggests that, on the contrary, there was only one gesture, which involved the placement of both hands. I will present arguments for this new (or, actually, old) analysis of the gesture's form. Then I will explore its meaning based on a new examination of context.

24:14; Num 8:10, 12; 27:18, 23; Deut 34:9; 2 Chr 29:23. In some cases, the head is not explicitly mentioned as the body part on which the hands are laid. However, in each of these cases, textual parallels with more explicit instances make it clear that the gesture uniformly involves laying the hands on the other's head.

3. LXX Lev 1:10 (hand placement gesture not in the Hebrew); Sus 1:34; Jub 25:14; Gen. Apoc. (1QapGen ar) 20:21–22, 28–29.

4. René Péter, "L'imposition des mains dans l'ancien testament," *VT* 27 (1977): 48–55; Bernd Janowski, *Sühne als Heilsgeschehen: Traditions- und religionsgeschichtliche Studien zur Sühnetheologie der Priesterschrift*, 2nd ed., WMANT 55 (Neukirchen-Vluyn: Neukirchener Verlag, 2000), 199–221; Wright, "Gesture of Hand Placement," 433–46; Wright, "Hands, Laying On of: Old Testament," *ABD* 3:47–48; Milgrom, *Leviticus 1–16*, 151.

5. See Stephen Finlan, *The Background and Contents of Paul's Cultic Atonement Metaphors*, AcBib 19 (Atlanta: Society of Biblical Literature, 2004), 86–93; Gane, *Cult and Character*, 244–46; JoAnn Scurlock, "The Techniques of the Sacrifice of Animals in Ancient Israel and Ancient Mesopotamia: New Insights through Comparison, Part 1," *AUSS* 44 (2006): 25; Clayton David Robinson, "The Laying On of Hands, with Special Reference to the Reception of the Holy Spirit in the New Testament" (PhD diss., Fuller Theological Seminary, 2008). Among the rare dissenting voices, see M. Kiuchi, *The Purification Offering in the Priestly Literature: Its Meaning and Function*, JSOTSup 56 (Sheffield: Sheffield Academic, 1987), 112–19 (Kiuchi accepts the formal distinction proposed by Péter as "possible," but he asserts that there is no difference in meaning); Propp, *Exodus 19–40*, 457.

Textual Analysis

Before confronting the previous proposals concerning hand placement, it is useful to review the textual evidence for this gesture in the Hebrew Bible. The passages mentioning the gesture (translated according to the vocalization of the received MT) are the following:

Exod 29:10

והקרבת את־הפר לפני אהל מועד וסמך אהרן ובניו את־ידיהם על־ראש הפר

You shall bring the bull before the tent of meeting. Then Aaron and his sons shall lay their hands on the bull's head.[6]

Exod 29:15

ואת־האיל האחד תקח וסמכו אהרן ובניו את־ידיהם על־ראש האיל

You shall take the first ram, and Aaron and his sons shall lay their hands on the ram's head.

Exod 29:19

ולקחת את האיל השני וסמך אהרן ובניו את־ידיהם על־ראש האיל

You shall take the second ram, and Aaron and his sons shall lay their hands on the ram's head.

Lev 1:4

וסמך ידו על ראש העלה ונרצה לו לכפר עליו

He shall lay his hand on the head of the burnt offering, and it will be accepted on his behalf to make atonement for him.

Lev 3:2

וסמך ידו על־ראש קרבנו ושחטו פתח אהל מועד וזרקו בני אהרן הכהנים את־הדם על־המזבח סביב

He shall lay his hand on the head of his offering and shall slaughter it at the door of the tent of meeting. Then the sons of Aaron, the priests, shall sprinkle[7] the blood on the altar on all sides.

---

6. Translations from Hebrew and Greek are my own unless otherwise noted.
7. Possible meanings of the verb זרק include "toss," "throw," "scatter abundantly," "dash," and "pour." The meaning "sprinkle" for the cultic disposal of blood is found in *HALOT*, 283, def. 2, and it agrees with the Akkadian cognate *zarāqu* "sprinkle, strew." See further BDB, 284.

Lev 3:8

וסמך את־ידו על־ראש קרבנו ושחט אתו לפני אהל מועד וזרקו בני אהרן את־דמו על־המזבח סביב

He shall lay his hand on the head of his offering and shall slaughter it before the tent of meeting. Then the sons of Aaron shall sprinkle its blood on the altar on all sides.

Lev 3:13

וסמך את־ידו על־ראשו ושחט אתו לפני אהל מועד וזרקו בני אהרן את־דמו על־המזבח סביב

He shall lay his hand on its head and shall slaughter it before the tent of meeting. Then the sons of Aaron shall sprinkle its blood on the altar on all sides.

Lev 4:4

והביא את־הפר אל־פתח אהל מועד לפני ה׳ וסמך את־ידו על־ראש הפר ושחט את־הפר לפני ה׳

He shall bring the bull to the door of the tent of meeting before Yahweh. Then he shall lay his hand on the bull's head and shall slaughter the bull before Yahweh.

Lev 4:15

וסמכו זקני העדה את־ידיהם על־ראש הפר לפני ה׳ ושחט את־הפר לפני ה׳

The elders of the congregation shall lay their hands on the bull's head before Yahweh, and one shall slaughter the bull before Yahweh.

Lev 4:24

וסמך ידו על־ראש השעיר ושחט אתו במקום אשר־ישחט את העלה לפני ה׳ חטאת הוא

He shall lay his hand on the goat's head and shall slaughter it in the place where one slaughters the burnt offering before Yahweh. It is a sin offering.

Lev 4:29

וסמך את־ידו על ראש החטאת ושחט את־החטאת במקום העלה

He shall lay his hand on the head of the sin offering and shall slaughter the sin offering in the (same) place (as) the burnt offering.

Lev 4:33

וסמך את־ידו על ראש החטאת ושחט אתה לחטאת במקום אשר ישחט את־העלה

He shall lay his hand on the head of the sin offering and shall slaughter it as a sin offering in the place where one slaughters the burnt offering.

Lev 8:14

ויגש את פר החטאת ויסמך אהרן ובניו את־ידיהם על־ראש פר החטאת

He brought near the bull of the sin offering. Then Aaron and his sons laid their hands on the head of the bull of the sin offering.

Lev 8:18

ויקרב את איל העלה ויסמכו אהרן ובניו את־ידיהם על־ראש האיל

He brought the ram of the burnt offering. Then Aaron and his sons laid their hands on the ram's head.

Lev 8:22

ויקרב את־האיל השני איל המלאים ויסמכו אהרן ובניו את־ידיהם על־ראש האיל

He brought the second ram, the ram of the ordination rite. Then Aaron and his sons laid their hands on the ram's head.

Lev 16:21

וסמך אהרן את־שתי ידו על ראש השעיר החי והתודה עליו את־כל־עונת בני ישראל ואת־כל־פשעיהם לכל־חטאתם ונתן אתם על־ראש השעיר ושלח ביד־איש עתי המדברה

Aaron shall lay his two hands on the head of the living goat and shall confess over it all the iniquities and wickedness of the children of Israel—that is, all their sins—putting them on the head of the goat. Then he shall send it away into the wilderness by means of an appointed man.

Lev 24:14

הוצא את־המקלל אל־מחוץ למחנה וסמכו כל־השמעים את־ידיהם על־ראשו ורגמו אתו כל־העדה

Take the blasphemer outside the camp. Then all who heard (the blasphemy) shall lay their hands on his head, and the whole congregation shall stone him.

Num 8:10

והקרבת את־הלוים לפני ה' וסמכו בני־ישראל את־ידיהם על־הלוים

You shall bring the Levites before Yahweh. Then the children of Israel shall lay their hands on the Levites.

Num 8:12

והלוים יסמכו את־ידיהם על ראש הפרים ועשה את־האחד חטאת ואת־האחד עלה לה' לכפר על־הלוים

The Levites shall lay their hands on the heads of the bulls. Offer one as a sin offering and the other as a burnt offering to Yahweh to make atonement for the Levites.

Num 27:18

ויאמר ה׳ אל־משה קח־לך את־יהושע בן־נון איש אשר־רוח בו וסמכת את־ידך עליו

Yahweh said to Moses, "Take Joshua the son of Nun, a man in whom is the spirit, and lay your hand on him."

Num 27:23

וסמך את־ידיו עליו ויצוהו כאשר דבר ה׳ ביד־משה

He laid his hands on him and commanded him, according to what Yahweh had spoken by means of Moses.

Deut 34:9

ויהושע בן־נון מלא רוח חכמה כי־סמך משה את־ידיו עליו וישמעו אליו בני־ישראל ויעשו כאשר צוה ה׳ את־משה

Joshua the son of Nun was filled with the spirit of wisdom, for Moses had laid his hands on him. The children of Israel listened to him and did as Yahweh had commanded Moses.

2 Chr 29:23

ויגישו את־שעירי החטאת לפני המלך והקהל ויסמכו ידיהם עליהם

They brought the goats of the sin offering near before the king. Then the congregation laid their hands on them.

In these passages, the basic Hebrew idiom for the gesture of hand placement is (ים)סמך יד "lay the hand(s)." In all but the last four passages (Num 27:18, 23; Deut 34:9; 2 Chr 29:23), the head is explicitly mentioned as the object of the placement of hands; the full phrase used is על (ים)סמך יד ראש (מקבל) "lay the hand(s) on the head of RECIPIENT," where RECIPIENT is a person or animal.

Two further examples of ritual hand placement occur in the LXX. In Lev 1:10, a plus not found in the Hebrew text mentions that an offerer of small cattle should lay his hand on the animal's head (making this verse more closely parallel to v. 4). In Sus 1:34, two elders lay their hands on Susanna's head before bearing (false) testimony against her.[8] These verses read in the Greek as follows:

---

8. The rationale for the use of this gesture here may derive from analogy with the procedure for the blasphemer in Lev 24:14.

Lev 1:10 (LXX)
ἄρσεν ἄμωμον προσάξει αὐτὸ [καὶ ἐπιθήσει τὴν χεῖρα ἐπὶ τὴν κεφαλὴν αὐτοῦ]⁹
He shall bring it as a male without blemish, [and he shall put (his) hand on its head].

Sus 1:34
ἀναστάντες δὲ οἱ δύο πρεσβῦται ἐν μέσῳ τῷ λαῷ ἔθηκαν τὰς χεῖρας ἐπὶ τὴν κεφαλὴν αὐτῆς¹⁰
Then the two elders stood up in the midst of the people and put their hands on her head.

The contexts in which the gesture of hand placement occurs in these passages can be divided into six clearly-defined categories based on who performs the gesture to whom and on what occasion:

1. Offerer to animal in the sacrificial cult: Exod 29:10, 15, 19; Lev 1:4, 10 (LXX); 3:2, 8, 13; 4:4, 15, 24, 29, 33; 8:14, 18, 22; Num 8:12; 2 Chr 29:23
2. Aaron to the scapegoat on the Day of Atonement: Lev 16:21
3. Congregation to blasphemer at the latter's execution: Lev 24:14
4. Israelites to Levites at the consecration of the latter: Num 8:10
5. Moses to Joshua at the latter's installation: Num 27:18, 23; Deut 34:9
6. Elders to Susanna to testify against the latter: Sus 1:34

In the discussion below, examples of the gesture will be referred to by these categories, except where the discussion concentrates on a specific verse.

In the analysis of Péter, Janowski, Wright, and Milgrom, the texts in category 1 describe a one-handed gesture. Péter's formulation of the purpose of this one-handed gesture combines the functions of attribution and substitution under the French term *identification*, which corresponds to

---

9. The brackets enclose the portion not found in the MT.
10. The version quoted is that of Theodotion. Codex Chisianus 88 contains considerable variation: (1) the agent of the gesture is not only the elders but also an unspecified number of judges; (2) the personal pronoun is used in the phrase mentioning the hands, thus τὰς χεῖρας αὐτῶν; and (3) the genitive τῆς κεφαλῆς is used after the preposition ἐπί instead of the accusative τὴν κεφαλήν. These variants are not germane to the present discussion. Both texts agree in the plural number of hands: τὰς χεῖρας.

Janowski's term *Identifizierung*.[11] The analysis by Wright and Milgrom, following Roland de Vaux[12] and further grounded in comparison with Hittite ritual texts, is that it expresses attribution: it is like saying "this is mine," making it clear to God that the animal being offered belongs to the offerer and not to the ritual specialist who performs the sacrifice.[13] Wright also goes beyond Péter in decisively placing category 4 with this gesture; he sees the gesture here as serving "to demonstrate that the Levites are the Israelites' offering to God and that the benefit of the dedication of the Levites and their ensuing service is to accrue to the Israelites."[14]

Meanwhile, according to both Péter and Wright, categories 2, 3, and 5 belong with the two-handed gesture. Here again, Péter and Wright differ as to the meaning of the gesture. Péter believes that it "expresses the transfer of some thing from the agent to the recipient."[15] Wright, however, considers this to be a legal gesture of designation; it is like saying "this is the one," officially pointing out the intended recipient of sin, guilt, or authority.[16]

This brief foray into the interpretations of hand placement by Péter, Janowski, Wright, and Milgrom shows that the understanding of hand placement in ancient Israelite ritual follows the analysis of the gesture's form in the various contexts in which the gesture occurs. Although difference in the form of a gesture does not necessarily imply difference in function, it does increase the likelihood of a difference in function, especially if the two forms of the gesture line up with clearly divergent contexts.[17] It is

---

11. In Péter's words, the gesture expresses "une idée d'identification entre l'offrant et l'animal offert: l'offrant affirme par ce geste que c'est bien lui qui offre l'animal, et, en quelque sorte, qu'il s'offre lui-même au travers de la victime" (Péter, "Imposition des mains," 52); see also Janowski, *Sühne als Heilsgeschehen*, 215–21; Wright, "Gesture of Hand Placement," 437.

12. Roland de Vaux, *Studies in Old Testament Sacrifice* (Cardiff: University of Wales Press, 1964), 28: "In placing his hand on the animal's head, the offerer attests that this victim is *his* indeed, that the sacrifice which is about to be presented by the priest is offered in *his* name, and that the benefits accruing from it will return to *him*" (emphasis original).

13. Wright, "Gesture of Hand Placement," 438–44; Milgrom, *Leviticus 1–16*, 152–53.

14. Wright, "Gesture of Hand Placement," 439.

15. In Péter's words, "exprimant le transfert de quelque chose du sujet sur le destinataire." Péter, "Imposition des mains," 54–55.

16. Wright, "Gesture of Hand Placement," 435–36.

17. Several interpreters have suggested that the distinction between one and two hands in hand placement either does not affect the meaning or corresponds to a sym-

therefore a priority to sort carefully through the textual sources to determine whether the cumulative evidence points to two gestures or one.

Table 1 shows the textual evidence for the biblical attestations of סמך יד, arranged by category. The third column shows the spelling of the MT, the fourth column the evidence from the Dead Sea Scrolls, and the fifth column the reading of the LXX.

Table 1. Textual Evidence for Number of Hands in Hand Placement

Reference	Subject	Masoretic	DSS	LXX
Category 1				
Exod 29:10	plural	יְדֵיהֶם	—	τὰς χεῖρας αὐτῶν
Exod 29:15	plural	יְדֵיהֶם	—	τὰς χεῖρας αὐτῶν
Exod 29:19	plural	יְדֵיהֶם	—	τὰς χεῖρας αὐτῶν
Lev 1:4	singular	יָדוֹ	י[ד]ו̊ (4Q25)	τὴν χεῖρα
Lev 1:10	singular	---	—	τὴν χεῖρα
Lev 3:2	singular	יָדוֹ	יד̊[ו] (4Q25)	τὰς χεῖρας
Lev 3:8	singular	יָדוֹ	—	τὰς χεῖρας
Lev 3:13	singular	יָדוֹ	—	τὰς χεῖρας
Lev 4:4	singular	יָדוֹ	ידו (4Q25)	τὴν χεῖρα αὐτοῦ
Lev 4:15	plural	יְדֵיהֶם	—	τὰς χεῖρας αὐτῶν
Lev 4:24	singular	יָדוֹ	—	τὴν χεῖρα
Lev 4:29	singular	יָדוֹ	—	τὴν χεῖρα
Lev 4:33	singular	יָדוֹ	—	τὴν χεῖρα
Lev 8:14	plural	יְדֵיהֶם	—	τὰς χεῖρας
Lev 8:18	plural	יְדֵיהֶם	—	τὰς χεῖρας αὐτῶν
Lev 8:22	plural	יְדֵיהֶם	—	τὰς χεῖρας αὐτῶν
Num 8:12	plural	יְדֵיהֶם	—	τὰς χεῖρας
2 Chr 29:23	plural	יְדֵיהֶם	—	τὰς χεῖρας αὐτῶν

bolic distinction of quantity (signifying greater solemnity, greater "emphasis," or the sins of more people). See Kiuchi, *Purification Offering*, 113, 180 n. 7; Gane, *Cult and Character*, 244–45; Scurlock, "Techniques of the Sacrifice of Animals," 25.

Reference	Subject	Masoretic	DSS	LXX
Category 2				
Lev 16:21	singular	שְׁתֵּי יָדָו	שתי יד[..] (4Q23)	τὰς χεῖρας αὐτοῦ
Category 3				
Lev 24:14	plural	יְדֵיהֶם	—	τὰς χεῖρας αὐτῶν
Category 4				
Num 8:10	plural	יְדֵיהֶם	ידי[ה]ם̊ (4Q23)	τὰς χεῖρας αὐτῶν
Category 5				
Num 27:18	singular	יָדְךָ	[יד]כֿה (4Q27)	τὰς χεῖράς σου
Num 27:23	singular	יָדָיו	ידיו (4Q27)	τὰς χεῖρας αὐτοῦ
Deut 34:9	singular	יָדָיו	—	τὰς χεῖρας αὐτοῦ
Category 6				
Sus 1:34	plural	—	—	τὰς χεῖρας (αὐτῶν)

In the analysis of Péter and Wright, the crucial category is the first one, which is also the largest, that of laying hands on an animal in the sacrificial cult. In the third column of table 1, we can see that there are basically two options for this category in the consonantal text: ידיהם "their hands," with a plural pronoun suffix; and ידי, with a singular pronoun suffix. The vocalized text consistently interprets the second form as יָדוֹ "his hand." This is the point of departure for Péter's and Wright's theory that the gesture in this category involved only one hand. They accordingly analyze the longer form as a distributive plural, meaning "one hand of each of them." In Wright's words, "Other instances of hand placement in sacrifice have 'hands' (plural) in the text, but this is only because the subject is plural, each person laying one hand on the animal."[18]

However, some considerations raise doubt about this theory. Going back to the first category in table 1, the three verses in Lev 3 are rendered with plural "hands" in the LXX: τὰς χεῖρας, "his hands." This disagrees with the vocalized MT. This textual variant in the LXX is not consistently carried through, and it could be explained as a sporadic attempt to harmonize the text with such passages as Lev 16:21; Num 27:23; and Deut 34:9, where

---

18. Wright, "Gesture of Hand Placement," 436.

the gesture is definitely two-handed. But it is also possible that the LXX variant reflects an earlier plural reading.[19]

In addition, postbiblical textual sources make it clear that, in the Second Temple period, the סמיכה or hand-placement ritual on the sacrificial animal was to be performed with two hands. Philo Judaeus, who lived in Alexandria in the late first century BCE and the early first century CE, included a description of this rite in his treatise *De specialis legibus*, and there the individual offerer is clearly described as using both hands:

ἔπειτα δ' ἀπονιψάμενος ὁ προσάγων τὰς χεῖρας ἐπιφερέτω τῇ τοῦ ἱερείου κεφαλῇ. καὶ μετὰ ταῦτα λαβών τις τῶν ἱερέων καταθυέτω καὶ φιάλην ἕτερος ὑποσχὼν καὶ δεξάμενος τοῦ αἵματος ἐν κύκλῳ περιϊὼν τὸν βωμὸν ἐπιρραινέτω.... τὰς δὲ ἐπιτιθεμένας τῇ τοῦ ζῴου κεφαλῇ χεῖρας δεῖγμα σαφέστατον εἶναι συμβέβηκε πράξεων ἀνυπαιτίων καὶ βίου μηδὲν ἐπιφερομένου τῶν εἰς κατηγορίαν ἀλλὰ τοῖς τῆς φύσεως νόμοις καὶ θεσμοῖς συνᾴδοντος ... ὡς ἅμα τῇ τῶν χειρῶν ἐπιθέσει δύνασθαί τινα παρρησιασάμενον ἐκ καθαροῦ τοῦ συνειδότος τοιαῦτα εἰπεῖν. αἱ χεῖρες αὗται οὔτε δῶρον ἐπ' ἀδίκοις ἔλαβον οὔτε τὰς ἐξ ἁρπαγῆς καὶ πλεονεξίας διανομὰς οὔτε αἵματος ἀθῴου προσήψαντο

Then the person bringing the offering must wash his hands and lay (them) on the victim's head. After this, one of the priests must take (it) and slaughter (it), while another holds a vessel underneath, and after catching some of the blood, he must go in a circle around the altar and

---

19. Linguistic evidence and the dates of extant papyri support the assumption that the Pentateuch was the first portion of the Hebrew Bible to be rendered into Greek; it seems to have been translated sometime between the middle of the third century and the middle of the second century BCE. Thus the Greek text of the Pentateuch far predates the Masoretic vocalization of the Hebrew Bible (which seems to have taken place around 700 CE, the oldest extant pointed manuscripts dating to the ninth century CE). This strengthens the possibility that the plural reading "hands" in Lev 3 represents a faithful transmission of the original reading. The fact that other portions of the Pentateuch have the singular "hand" does not represent a challenge to this theory, since our current LXX text is most likely a composite of the efforts of many translators, even within individual books. Some translators may have been more erudite than others. On the date of the Greek translation of the Pentateuch and of other biblical books, see J. A. L. Lee, *A Lexical Study of the Septuagint Version of the Pentateuch*, SCS 14 (Chico, CA: Scholars Press, 1983), 129–44; Timothy Michael Law, *When God Spoke Greek: The Septuagint and the Making of the Christian Bible* (Oxford: Oxford University Press, 2013), 35–36, 42, 45–49; Siegfried Kreuzer, *The Bible in Greek: Translation, Transmission, and Theology of the Septuagint*, SCS 63 (Atlanta: SBL Press, 2015), 20–22.

sprinkle (it) thereon.... In the hands laid on the animal's head there happens to be the clearest pattern of blameless actions, and of a life not burdened by things that incur accusation, but rather (a life) in harmony with the laws and ordinances of nature ... so that as soon as he does the laying on of hands, he can speak boldly out of a pure conscience and say thus: "These hands have neither taken a gift to do injustice, nor (taken) the proceeds of robbery and greediness, nor have they meddled with innocent blood." (*Spec.* 1.198–204)

Philo's witness regarding the use of both hands agrees with the Mishnah:

הכול סומכין חוץ מחירש שוטה וקטן וסומא ונוכרי והעבד והשליח והאישה וסמיכה שיירי מצוה על הראש בשתי ידיים ובמקום שסומכין שוחטין ותכף לסמיכה שחיטה

All may perform hand placement, except for deaf-mute people, insane people, minors, blind people, foreigners, slaves, agents, and women. Hand placement is a secondary commandment, (performed) on the head and with both hands. (The animal) is slaughtered on the spot where hand placement is performed, and the slaughtering follows the hand placement in immediate succession. (m. Menaḥ. 9:8)

The Tosefta, followed by the Talmud Bavli, also clearly describes hand placement in the offering ritual as employing both hands:

כיצד סומך זבח עומד בצפון ופניו במערב סומך ופניו במערב מניח שתי ידיו על גבי קרניו של זבח ולא היה מניח ידיו על גבי זבח ולא היה מניח ידיו זו על גבי זו ולא היה דבר חוצץ בין ידים לקרנות

How does one lay (his hands on the sacrificial animal)? The sacrificial animal stands to the north, its face to the west, and he lays (his hands on the animal) to the west, his face to the west. He rests his two hands on the ridge of the horns of the sacrificial animal. He does not rest his hands on the sacrificial animal's back, nor does he rest his hands one on top of the other, nor does anything intervene between the (two) hands and the horns. (t. Menaḥ. 10:12 ≈ b. Yoma 36a)[20]

---

20. The parallel passage in the Talmud reads like the Tosefta, except that the one doing hand placement is said to stand "on the east, his face to the west" (והסומך עומד במזרח ופניו למערב). The description in both texts means that the animal and the one doing hand placement both face toward the temple building, the location of God's throne, with the one doing hand placement standing behind the animal's head. The animal is positioned with its face turned sideways, so that the one doing the hand placement can stand directly behind its head without having to mount the animal.

Of course, neither of these observations constitutes proof that hand placement in the biblical period always involved two hands and not one. It is possible to imagine that there were originally two distinct gestures, one involving both hands and the other involving only one, and that these two gestures merged in the Second Temple period, so that the two-handed variety was eventually used in the contexts in which the one-handed variety had previously been used. A careful reexamination of the biblical data, however, suggests a simpler scenario in which the gesture uniformly employed both hands in the period before the Babylonian exile as well as in the Second Temple period. There are three main reasons for this.

First, the only passage in which the addition of the word שתי "two" makes the use of two hands indisputable, Lev 16:21, has a defective writing of the plural "hands": ידי. If it were not for the explicit mention of "two hands," one would easily read the consonantal text's ידי as a reference to one hand. This raises the possibility that ידי in the other passages is also a defective writing (such defective writings are actually quite common in this part of the Pentateuch)[21] and that the vocalization as a singular in these passages is simply based on an ad hoc reading of the consonantal text.

Other passages support this idea. In Num 27:18, Yahweh's command to perform the gesture includes the form ידך, which is vocalized in the MT as יָדְךָ, "your hand." But in verse 23, where the command is fulfilled, the consonantal text has ידיו (with the letter *yod* as a *mater lectionis*), which can only mean "his hands," so it is vocalized accordingly. The LXX in verses 18 and 23 and the reference to the same event in Deut 34:9 likewise describe a two-handed gesture.[22] A similar example appears in Lev 9:22, where Aaron performs the priestly blessing gesture. The consonantal text has ידו, but this is vocalized as יָדָיו "his hands." Evidently, Aaron's gesture was recognized as נשיאת הידיים "the lifting of hands" (for the priestly blessing), a gesture that would have been familiar from the synagogue service at the time when the vowel points were added to the Hebrew text (around 700 CE).[23] This shows that the usual method in pointing defectively written

---

21. Cf. Francis I. Andersen and A. Dean Forbes, *Spelling in the Hebrew Bible* (Rome: Biblical Institute Press, 1986), 62; James Barr, *The Variable Spellings of the Hebrew Bible* (Oxford: Oxford University Press, 1989), 131–37.

22. Both Péter and Wright agree that ידך in v. 18 is a defectively spelled dual; Péter, "Imposition des mains," 49–51; Wright, "Gesture of Hand Placement," 435.

23. By contrast, the ritual of hand placement in the sacrificial cult of the Second

examples of the word יד "hand" in ritual hand gestures was to go with the singular in every case, except in specific instances where the dual was obvious. In the case of hand placement, this method was facilitated by the fact that instances of ידו cluster in certain chapters (Lev 1; 3; 4), while instances of ידיהם (which, as I argue below, indicate the dual) cluster in other chapters (Exod 29; Lev 8).24

The argument that ידו in these instances is to be read as יָדָיו on the basis of the defective writing in Lev 16:21 emerges already in the Babylonian Talmud, where it is attributed to Resh Lakish (b. Menah. 93b, commenting on the Mishnah passage quoted above). While this supports my approach to the consonantal text in descriptions of hand placement, it is also significant for what it implies about the knowledge of this gesture after the destruction of the Second Temple. As early as the third century CE, the reading of the phrase describing hand placement had become a matter of speculative discussion. The Talmudic passage bases the argument on comparison between scriptural passages, not tradition. The very fact that the issue was open to discussion implies that both the gesture itself and the correct pronunciation of the phrase used to describe it had been forgotten.

Even later, in the medieval period, Ibn Ezra in his commentary on Lev 1:4 argued the opposite, that ידו in cultic hand placement indicates only one hand: the manner of sacrifice differs from the manner of the scapegoat ritual, and therefore, since only the prescription for the scapegoat includes the word שתי "two," the ritual for the sacrificial animal must involve only one hand (a curious argument, to be sure). Ibn Ezra's work (twelfth century CE) follows the vocalization of the MT chronologically. Another source from the same general time period, Targum Pseudo-Jonathan, likewise reads the descriptions of hand placement as referring only to the right hand.25 These medieval sources anticipate the arguments of scholars like

---

Temple was no longer a living practice and was thus subject to ambiguity, although hand placement was still used in other contexts; see Arnold Ehrhardt, "Jewish and Christian Ordination," *JEH* 5 (1954): 125–38.

24. The one exception is ידיהם in Lev 4:15, nine verses removed from the nearest occurrence of ידו.

25. In Lev 1:4; 3:2, 8, 13; 4:4, 24, 29, 33, Targum Pseudo-Jonathan reads יד ימיניה "his right hand" (with slight orthographic variants in some instances) in place of the MT's ידו. In most cases in which the MT reads ידיהם "their hands," Targum Pseudo-Jonathan simply translates literally; however, in two places, the targum specifies "their right hands": Lev 8:14 (ידיהון ימיני), Lev 8:18 (יד ימינהון). Note that the earlier Targum Onqelos, unlike Pseudo-Jonathan, strictly agrees with the MT.

Péter. Again, however, they are based on speculation and not on tradition; their value is therefore secondary to the earlier sources like Philo, the Mishnah, and the Tosefta, which most likely reflect the actual practice of the Second Temple period.

Second, the idea that יְדֵיהֶם means "one hand of each of them" presupposes the existence of a plural form *יָדִים "hands." Yet there is no independent evidence for the existence of such a form in Hebrew. There is a plural form יָדוֹת, though it is only used in figurative senses.[26] Comparative evidence from Ugaritic and Akkadian supports the argument that יְדֵיהֶם is the expected dual, not plural, form. Plurals of the cognates of יָד are rare, and when they occur, they generally have the feminine ending *-āt (Hebrew -ôt).[27] Interestingly, in a later period, Syriac and Arabic diverge from the older Semitic languages in this respect, attesting plural forms similar to the putative Hebrew *יָדִים.[28] In this light, it may be significant that Ibn Ezra's commentary and Targum Pseudo-Jonathan were both created in an environment in which Arabic and Late Aramaic (including Syriac) were the predominant Semitic languages (we will return to this below).

Third, the analysis of יְדֵיהֶם as a plural form conflicts with the typical grammatical treatment of body parts in Biblical Hebrew. It is a lesser-known, but nevertheless firmly established, aspect of Hebrew grammar that the words for body parts and other "inalienably possessed" things, when bound to a plural genitive, tend to remain grammatically singular or dual, depending on whether the possessor is using one or two of them.[29]

---

26. BDB, 388. The figurative senses include "portion, share"; "tenon" (of the portable tabernacle wall boards); and "axletree" (of a chariot). This problem is noted by Péter, "Imposition des mains," 52 n. 10.

27. In Akkadian, the forms are *idum* "hand, arm," dual *idān* (oblique *idīn*), plural *idātum*, as in *kakkašu la padâ ana idāt bēlūtiya ušatmiḫ* "he entrusted his merciless weapon to my lordly arms" (CAD 7:10–16). For Ugaritic, singular *yd*, dual *ydm*, plural *ydt*, the latter only in the sense of "rations," as in *šbʿ ydty b ṣʿ* "seven are the rations of my plate" (Gregorio Del Olmo Lete and Joaquín Sanmartín, *Dictionary of the Ugaritic Language in the Alphabetic Tradition*, HdO 67 [Leiden: Brill, 2015], 2:952–54). See also Hebrew כַּף "palm, hand," dual כַּפַּיִם, plural כַּפּוֹת; זְרוֹעַ "arm," plural זְרֹעוֹת.

28. Arabic has a dual form *yadāni* and plural forms *yudiyyun, yadiyyun, yidiyyun, ʾaydin*. Syriac has plural forms ܐܝܕܝܢ (absolute; emphatic = ܐܝܕܝܐ) and ܐܝܕܘܬܐ, the latter being for metaphorical extensions.

29. An example of this phenomenon in the construct state may be seen in Num 8:12, cited above: רֹאשׁ הַפָּרִים, literally "the head of the bulls," meaning the head of each bull. For singular יָד "hand" with a plural possessor, see 2 Sam 18:28; Ezra 10:18–19.

This explains the above-noted fact that plural forms of the word יד are very rare, except in figurative (and therefore alienable) uses. The pattern for inalienable nouns is distinct compared to alienable nouns, like houses, spears, and books, which are always plural when the possessor is plural.

Thus, when one wants to say "one hand of each of them," the pattern is to use a singular noun followed by a plural suffix: יָדָם, literally "their hand"; also יֶדְכֶם "your (pl.) hand" and יָדֵנוּ "our hand."[30] Table 2 lays out the various attested forms, with the number of biblical attestations shown in the right column. There are no instances where the corresponding non-singular forms יְדֵיהֶם, יְדֵיכֶם, and יָדֵינוּ have to be taken as distributive plurals, and a dual interpretation is usually preferable. For example, we can contrast Exod 29:20 and 30:19:

> You shall take some of its blood and put it on the right earlobes of Aaron and his sons, on the thumbs of their right hands [בֹּהֶן יָדָם הַיְמָנִית], and on the big toes of their right feet. (Exod 29:20 ≈ Lev 8:24)

> Aaron and his sons shall wash (both of) their hands and feet with it [אֶת־יְדֵיהֶם וְאֶת־רַגְלֵיהֶם]. (Exod 30:19 ≈ Exod 30:21; 40:31; Deut 21:6)

In Exod 29:20, only one thumb (the right one) of each priest is anointed with the blood, so the body part noun is in the singular. In Exod 30:19, both hands and both feet of each priest are washed, so the body part nouns are in the dual. These examples also include the nouns רגל "foot" and בהן "thumb, big toe," which show the same pattern. Table 2 shows examples of singular body part nouns with plural pronoun suffixes, with the total number of attestations in the Hebrew Bible for each form.

Examples with poss. pron. suf. are treated below. As far as I am aware, Hebrew grammars do not note this phenomenon. However, it is noted for a kindred Afroasiatic language, ancient Egyptian, in Alan H. Gardiner, *Egyptian Grammar: Being an Introduction to the Study of Hieroglyphs*, 3rd ed. (Oxford: Griffith Institute, 2005), § 510. The term "genitive of inalienable possession" is used in Bruce K. Waltke and Michael Patrick O'Connor, *Introduction to Biblical Hebrew Syntax* (Winona Lake, IN: Eisenbrauns, 1990), § 9.5.1h, but without discussion of the grammatical aspects of this category. In a forthcoming article, I discuss this phenomenon in early Semitic languages and in Egyptian, together with its cultural implications: David Calabro, "Inalienable Possession in Early Egypto-Semitic Genitive Constructions," *QVO* 12 (2017): 91–106.

30. See Propp, *Exodus*, 457.

Table 2. Singular Body Part Nouns with Plural Suffixes

Form	Translation	Number
יָדָם	"their hand" → one hand of each of them	30
יֶדְכֶם	"your (pl.) hand" → one hand of each of you	7
יָדֵנוּ	"our hand" → one hand of each of us	1
רַגְלָם	"their foot" → one foot of each of them	4
רַגְלְכֶם	"your (pl.) foot" → one foot of each of you	2
רַגְלֵנוּ	"our foot" → one foot of each of us	1
רֹאשָׁם	"their (masc.) head" → the head of each of them	14
רֹאשָׁן	"their (fem.) head" → the head of each of them	1
רֹאשְׁכֶם	"your head" → the head of each of you	1
רֹאשֵׁנוּ	"our head" → the head of each of us	1

As shown in table 2, the pattern also applies to nonpaired body parts, like ראש "head," which takes forms such as רֹאשָׁם, literally "their head." The forms רָאשִׁים "heads," רָאשֵׁיהֶם "their heads," and רָאשֵׁיכֶם "your heads" typically refer to alienable things that are similar to heads, like "tops," "gates," "chiefs," or the like. One interesting case is 2 Kgs 10:7, in which רָאשֵׁיהֶם refers to people's heads that have been cut off, thus becoming "alienable" heads!

There are some exceptions to this pattern, especially in the book of Ezekiel.[31] Nevertheless, the pattern is regular enough, especially in the Pentateuch, to be considered a general rule. Thus the expected meaning of ידיהם is "both hands of each of them." A striking example of the general rule is found in Exod 29:9–10, where we have יד־בניו, literally "the hand of his sons," immediately preceding a description of hand placement with ידיהם.

The grammatical treatment of inalienable nouns becomes more relaxed in later stages of Hebrew, as in Arabic and Late Aramaic. This coincides with the attestation of plural forms of the word "hand" analogous to the putative Hebrew *יָדִים in Arabic and Syriac. The form ידיהם in descriptions of hand placement could thus be understood as a plural form,

---

31. For the noun ראש, see Lev 10:6; Job 2:12; Ezek 1:22; 7:18; 24:23; 27:30; 32:27; 44:20.

meaning "one hand of each of them," if read according to the usage of Semitic languages in the medieval period (rather than according to Biblical Hebrew usage). This provides the necessary background to understand the interpretations of Ibn Ezra and Targum Pseudo-Jonathan, which innovatively understood the gesture to involve only one hand.

To summarize, the prescribed ritual gesture of hand placement most likely employed both hands in every case, including categories 1 and 4 (the offering of a sacrificial animal and the consecration of Levites). The writing ידו in the consonantal text of Lev 1, 3, and 4 should be understood as a defective writing of the dual, as is certainly the case with ידי in Lev 9:22 and 16:21 and with ידך in Num 27:18. The vocalization of ידו as a singular in other cases is most likely due to an erroneous ad hoc reading of the consonantal text. Moreover, the word ידיהם should be understood to mean "both hands of each of them," not "one hand of each of them." If the latter meaning were intended, according to regular Biblical Hebrew grammatical usage, the form ידם would have been used. All of this applies to the meaning of the text as understood in the biblical period. Following this early period, we see a diachronic shift from preservation of the original understanding of the gesture (in Philo, the Mishnah, the Tosefta, and secondarily in the Talmud) to misunderstanding (in the vocalized MT, Ibn Ezra, and Targum Pseudo-Jonathan), the latter being occasioned by loss of the actual rite and by linguistic changes that obscured the meaning of the biblical phrases.

Function of the Gesture

The renewed understanding of the gesture's form invites us to revisit the embattled issue of the gesture's function. Overviews of prior interpretations of hand placement can be found in the works of Wright, Milgrom, Rendtorff, and Gane.[32] Basically, the interpretations that have been proposed can be grouped into five major categories:

1. *Manumissio* or devoting to deity: equivalent to saying, "This is God's."
2. Transfer (of sin, authority, etc.)

---

32. Wright, "Gesture of Hand Placement," 437; Milgrom, *Leviticus*, 151; Rolf Rendtorff, *Leviticus 1,1–10,20*, BKAT 3.1 (Neukirchen-Vluyn: Neukirchener Verlag, 2004), 40–44; Gane, *Cult and Character*, 244–45.

3. Identification or substitution: equivalent to saying, "This represents me."
4. Designation: equivalent to saying, "This is the one."
5. Attribution: equivalent to saying, "This is mine."

The second interpretation, that of transfer, is perhaps the most common, appearing both in older studies and in more recent ones. This interpretation is influenced by the texts describing the installation of Joshua and, in some cases, by comparison with the laying on of hands by Jesus and the apostles in the New Testament. Part of the force of this interpretation comes from the fact that it can apply to all contexts, as long as the thing that is transferred is understood to be variable. The other four interpretations tend to work in some contexts but not as well in others. While some interpreters apply a single meaning to all examples of hand placement (with varying degrees of success), others divide the instances of hand placement into groups based on the form of the gesture or on contextual criteria, applying a different meaning to each group. A summary of some prior interpretations is given in table 3.[33]

---

33. Friedrich Nitzsch, *Die Idee und die Stufen des Opferkultus* (Kiel: Universitäts-Buchhandlung, 1889), 16; W. Robertson Smith, *Lectures on the Religion of the Semites*, Burnett Lectures 1888–1889 (London: Black, 1894), 239, 422–23; Paul Volz, "Die Handauflegung beim Opfer," *ZAW* 21 (1901): 93–100; Henry Preserved Smith, "The Laying-On of Hands," *AmJT* 17 (1913): 47–62; Heinrich Vorwahl, *Die Gebärdensprache im Alten Testament* (Berlin: Ebering, 1932), 38–39; de Vaux, *Studies in Old Testament Sacrifice*, 28; Péter, "Imposition des mains," 48–55; Janowski, *Sühne als Heilsgeschehen*, 199–221; Wright, "Gesture of Hand Placement," 433–46; Kiuchi, *Purification Offering*, 112–19, 180–82; Baruch Levine, *Leviticus* ויקרא: *The Traditional Hebrew Text with the New JPS Translation*, JPS Torah Commentary (Philadelphia: Jewish Publication Society, 1989), 5–6, 201; Levine, *Numbers 1–20: A New Translation with Introduction and Commentary*, AB 4A (New York: Doubleday, 1993), 269–70, 275–76; Milgrom, *Leviticus*, 150–53; Finlan, *Background and Contents*, 86–93; Gane, *Cult and Character*, 244–46; Robinson, "Laying On of Hands."

Table 3. Selected Modern Interpretations of Hand Placement

Interpreter	Date	Context	Number of hands	Function
Friedrich Nitzsch	1889	sacrifice	not specified	*manumissio*, ceding offerer's property to God
W. Robertson Smith	1889	sacrifice	both*	devoting animal to deity; Po: laying community's sin on animal's head; Pr: simple identification between parties
		"blessing or consecration" (precise context uncertain)	both*	simple identification between parties
		scapegoat	both*	laying community's sin on animal's head
Paul Volz	1901	installation of Joshua, sacrifice, scapegoat	both/single*	transfer (*Übertragung*) of holy power, sin-stuff, curse, or impurity
		sacrifice (Exod 29; Lev 3; 8); consecration of Levites	both/single*	copy of offering rite without transfer function
Henry Preserved Smith	1913	sacrifice	both/single*	Orig.: partaking of sanctity of animal; Pr: "simply the essential part of the act of slaying"
		scapegoat, blasphemer	both/single*	transfer of guilt
Heinrich Vorwahl	1932	all	not specified	forms connection for flow of mana between offerer, offering, and God
Roland de Vaux	1964	scapegoat	single*	laying people's sins on animal
		sacrifice	single*	attesting that animal belongs to offerer
		sacrifice	single	identification
René Péter	1977	scapegoat, blasphemer, installation of Joshua	both	transfer

A REEXAMINATION OF THE ANCIENT ISRAELITE GESTURE

Interpreter	Date	Context	Number of hands	Function
Bernd Janowski	1982	sacrifice	single	identification between offerer and animal (*Subjekt-Übertragung*), allowing sinful offerer to die vicariously through animal
		installation of Joshua	both	transfer of authority or charisma (*Subjekt-Übertragung*)
		blasphemer	single/both	indicating "it was this one"
		scapegoat	both	magical transfer of *materia peccans*
David Wright	1986	sacrifice, consecration of Levites	single	attribution
		scapegoat, blasphemer, installation of Joshua	both	designation
N. Kiuchi	1987	scapegoat, sacrifice	single/both	substitution
Baruch Levine	1989, 1993	all	single/both*	assigning for use in specific rite; terms *assign*, *designate*, and *consign* used interchangeably
Jacob Milgrom	1991	sacrifice	single	ownership
		scapegoat	both	transference
Stephen Finlan	2004	sacrifice	single	identifying the giver
		scapegoat	both	transfer of sin-stuff
Roy Gane	2005	sacrifice	single	identification of ownership
		scapegoat	both	identification of route of transfer
Clayton Robinson	2008	all	both/single	transfer or transmission

Note: The asterisk (*) indicates that the number of hands is assumed without argument. Abbreviations: Orig. = original meaning; Po = popular interpretation; Pr = priestly author (in Exodus, Leviticus, and Numbers).

Three main problems recur in previous analyses of hand placement. First, there is the assumption of a neat one-to-one correlation between form and function. This assumption lies behind interpretations that propose two different gesture forms, a one-handed form and a two-handed form, each with one and only one distinct meaning. In reality, a gesture may have at least as many functions as there are contexts, while gestures of different form may have functions that are interrelated or even basically the same. Although I have endeavored to show that biblical hand placement had only one form (using two hands), this does not mean that there is only one function, especially since there are different contexts. By the same token, the assertion of a single form does not automatically negate the interpretations put forward by those who have assumed that there are two different forms.

Second, there is the assumption that interpretations are mutually exclusive when, in fact, they are not. Scholars writing on hand placement have tended to elevate a single interpretation as if there can be only one correct meaning. However, the real-life situation in the biblical world was likely more complex. Different people in the society likely held different interpretations of the same gesture. Some of those interpretations may have aligned with different social strata, religious viewpoints, and locations in space and time. Both Robertson Smith and Propp draw a distinction between the priestly author's viewpoint of hand placement and the popular understanding of the gesture.[34] Responding to Milgrom's idea that the placement of a single hand on the sacrificial animal signifies ownership, which idea Milgrom adopts "by the process of elimination," Propp writes the following: "While this may be P's rationale ... I would remain open-minded as to popular understandings of the ceremony. None of the interpretations proffered above excludes the others."[35] Even beyond the differences of interpretation between people, a single person could have applied different interpretations to different aspects of the same gesture. For example, a gesture can accomplish one thing (like designating a suc-

---

34. Robertson Smith, *Lectures*, 422; Propp, *Exodus*, 458.

35. Milgrom, *Leviticus*, 151–52; Propp, *Exodus*, 458. A potentially problematic aspect of Propp's statement is the category of "popular understanding," which could become a catch-all for interpretations that seem to make sense but are unsupported by the texts themselves (which belong exclusively to the priestly corpus). One can, however, view "popular understanding" as a term for the different interpretations transmitted in the priestly texts, some of which may have been held in common with other segments of society.

cessor) while resembling another (like placing a crown). These interpretations are not contradictory, although combining them certainly makes the gesture more nuanced and less flat.

Third, many try to fit ancient practice within a framework of logical relationships that is characteristic of modern Western philosophy. These relationships are embodied in the terms used, such as *identification*, *designation*, and *attribution*. To be sure, some of these functions follow so naturally from the available evidence that they are virtually truisms. The function of designation, for example, arises naturally from the direct contact involved in hand placement (which unambiguously points out the recipient) and from the fact that the gesture immediately precedes further ritual performance on the recipient. Likewise, since the protocol of sacrifice assumes that the animal receiving hand placement belongs to the one making the offering and is to be accepted on his behalf (Lev 1:2–4), the gesture would tend to carry an attributive function. One may question, however, whether these functions were salient for ancient Israelites. Equivalents of these words are not attested in Biblical Hebrew, let alone in the texts describing hand placement. Ultimately, one must reconcile the outsider view by which we determine what the ancient rituals *mean* with the insider textual formulations that disclose what these rituals *meant*.

A close reading of the Hebrew texts, with careful attention to words and phrases that are structurally aligned with descriptions of the gesture, offers the most accurate method for disclosing ancient understandings of hand placement. This method has been employed to a limited extent by past interpreters, mostly to champion a single interpretation above others, the others being then excluded or subordinated in a logical or diachronic schema. However, the method acquires a more satisfactory conclusion by equal application in multiple texts, thereby disclosing various mutually complementary interpretations.

Much has been written about the clause ונרצה לו לכפר עליו "and it will be accepted on his behalf to make atonement for him." The discussions center on the way in which the animal mediates atonement for the one performing the gesture, some appealing (desperately, in my opinion) to the meaning of the word לו "on his behalf."[36] Attention to the other word choices, however, reveals that the text focuses not on what the gesture does to the animal, but rather on the gesture's form as a similitude of atone-

---

36. Smith, "Laying-On of Hands," 56; Kiuchi, *Purification Offering*, 117.

ment. In the phrase לכפר עליו "to make atonement for him," the verb כפר is semantically linked to the concept of covering.[37] The laying of hands on the animal's head is seen as an iconic symbol of "covering over" the sins of the one making the offering, the head being the locus where sins are accumulated (cf. the expression בראש "in/on the head" in Josh 2:19; Judg 9:57; 1 Sam 25:39). Just as the offerer covers the animal's head with his hands, Yahweh, having accepted the offering, will cover the person's sins.

It has been recognized for some time that the phrase וסמכת את־ידך עליו "you shall lay your hands[38] on him" in Num 27:18–20 is grammatically and semantically parallel to ונתת מהודך עליו "you shall put some of your power on him." This lends support to the transfer interpretation, since the notion of "putting X upon Y" is a close equivalent to the notion of transfer, or "carrying X across to Y." The phrase נתן על "to put upon" is also used in reference to putting the community's sins on the head of the scapegoat in Lev 16:21. Similarly, in Deut 34:9, the image of Joshua being "filled with the spirit of wisdom" is connected, through the conjunction כי "for," with Moses's gesture of hand placement. The phrase נתן על contributes a distinctive nuance to the concept of transfer, indicating that what is transferred becomes like a material possession that one can wear (like a crown), rather than something that permeates the soul or the blood (the verb מלא "fill" in Deut 34:9, of course, carries a different nuance).

However, further application of this method of close reading yields an interpretation that nobody, to my knowledge, has suggested previously. In Num 27:16, Moses asks Yahweh to "appoint" (יפקד) a man over the congregation. In verse 18, Yahweh responds by telling Moses to "take Joshua the son of Nun … and lay your hands on him, then have him stand before Eleazar the priest and before the whole congregation." This sequence suggests that at least one function of hand placement was to "appoint" a person or thing. The Levites, on whom the gesture of hand placement was performed (Num 8:10), are also described as being "appointed" to their offices with verbs from the same root פקד (Num 1:50; Neh 7:1; see also Num 3:10, referring to the sons of Aaron). Other passages also associate various forms of touching with פקד, especially with God as the agent.[39]

---

37. BDB, 497–98; *HALOT*, 493–94. Contrast the comments of Scurlock, "Techniques of the Sacrifice of Animals," 25–26 n. 61.

38. For the plural "hands" instead of the MT's singular, see the discussion above.

39. See Ps 80:15–16, 18 (Eng. vv. 14–15, 17), where the Psalmist's request that God "visit [פקד] this vine, the stock that your right hand planted, the son whom

Stuart Creason has recently treated the rich semantics of the verb פקד in detail. According to him, the verb's basic meaning is "to assign a person or a thing to what the subject believes is its proper or appropriate status or position in an organizational order," or more succinctly, "to put something where it is supposed to be in the overall scheme of things."[40] On the basis of the passages from Numbers mentioned above, one could posit that hand placement is the "gesture of פקד," a way of appointing a person or animal to a particular status or role. This function could apply to all of the biblical attestations of hand placement. One assigns the sacrificial animal to its proper status as an offering to the deity, one assigns the scapegoat to its proper status as such, and so on.[41] This does not exclude other interpretations, although it may be that the function of פקד was more closely linked to the gesture of hand placement itself than to any one context.

The difference between this and the notion of "designation" is subtle but nonetheless significant. While the designation function is basically deictic (it is like saying "this is the one"), the function of פקד is performative, effecting a new status for the recipient in and through the rite itself. The function of "assigning" the recipient for use in a specified rite, as argued by Levine, is also similar. However, Levine's argumentation depends on other factors, such as a somewhat idiosyncratic translation

---

you strengthened" is semantically parallel to his request, "let your hand be on the man at your right hand, on the son of man whom you strengthened." See also Jer 1:9–10: "Yahweh stretched out his hand and touched my mouth, and Yahweh said to me, 'Behold, I hereby put my words in your mouth; see, this day I hereby appoint you [הפקדתיך] over the nations and over the kingdoms, to uproot and to tear down, to destroy and to overthrow, to build and to plant.'" Whereas the prescribed ritual gesture performed by humans invariably uses two hands (according to my argument above), God often uses just one hand when he touches humans. (Here in Jer 1:9–10, it does not seem likely that the gesture was originally two-handed, even though a defective spelling of "hands" in the consonantal text is theoretically possible.)

40. Stuart Creason, "PQD Revisited," in *Studies in Semitic and Afroasiatic Linguistics Presented to Gene B. Gragg*, ed. Cynthia L. Miller, SAOC 60 (Chicago: Oriental Institute of the University of Chicago, 2007), 30.

41. Wright has noticed that the gesture seems to be performed only on large entities; meal offerings, e.g., do not require hand placement (Wright, "Gesture of Hand Placement," 439). From the perspective of the present interpretation, the difference in distribution of the gesture could result from the fact that smaller entities are easily manipulated, so they can be put in their proper places through elevation (as in the תנופה or "elevation offering") or through handing over from one person to the next across graded boundaries.

of the verb עשה "to make" and spoken formulas that accompanied hand placement as described in the Mishnah. Overall, the evidence adduced by Levine lends support to the function of the gesture that I have proposed. By using a Biblical Hebrew term (פקד) to explain the function of the ancient Israelite gesture, this interpretation avoids the potential pitfalls of using modern Western philosophical terms, like *identification*, *designation*, and *attribution*, to describe ancient Israelite ritual practices.

Conclusion

I have argued that the Israelite gesture of hand placement, which played an important role in the temple sacrificial cult as well as in other ritual contexts, was a single gesture employing both hands. The gesture was denoted by the phrase סמך ידים על "lay the hands upon," with the noun consistently in the dual. After the disappearance of the temple cult, a number of factors obscured the consistent nature of this gesture, including linguistic change and a method of vocalization that followed the consonantal text in an ad hoc manner. These factors ultimately led to modern reconstructions of the gesture as sometimes one-handed, sometimes two-handed.

The simpler reconstruction of the gesture's form enables a more accurate explanation of its function. Some interpretations of the meaning, such as the interpretation as a similitude of atonement, as well as the idea of "putting (sin, authority, etc.) upon" another (similar to "transfer"), find support in some but not all contexts. Interpretations such as these may have been abundant in ancient times, inasmuch as people may view their own ritual actions within a present context and not in terms of other contexts in which the same actions are repeated. However, an interpretation as a gesture effecting the assignment of the recipient to a particular "position in an organizational order," according to the semantics of the verb פקד, works well in all attested instances of the gesture, at least as far as cultic use is concerned.[42] These interpretations, I have argued, take us closer to an emic understanding of this gesture in ancient Israelite practice.

---

42. Noncultic uses of hand placement are mentioned in some biblical and extra-biblical narratives, specifically Gen 48:14, 17, 18 (with the Hebrew idioms שית ידים and שים ידים instead of סמך ידים); Jub. 25:14; and 1QapGen ar 20:21–22, 28–29. The contexts in these instances include blessing (Jacob to Ephraim and Manasseh in Gen 48; Rebekah to Jacob in Jub. 25) and healing (Abram to the Pharaoh in 1QapGen ar).

"I Will Not Accept Them":
Sacrifice and Reciprocity in the Prophetic Literature

Aaron Glaim

In this article, I argue that the biblical texts from which modern scholars have adduced a "prophetic critique of sacrifice" actually do not contain some generalized or categorical critique of sacrifice as a mode of religious practice.[1] Rather, I interpret the biblical prophetic texts that portray Yahweh rejecting, hating, or abhorring Israelite or Judean sacrifices in a straightforward and technical manner: What Yahweh is rejecting in these texts are the sacrificial gifts of the Judeans and Israelites in the periods immediately before he visits harsh punishments upon them. Yahweh's rejection of sacrifices is a consequence of broken relations with his people, and is particular to specific historical moments. No prophetic text depicts Yahweh making durable theological pronouncements against the practice of sacrifice. To turn the matter on its head, I would suggest that the depiction of Yahweh favorably accepting Israelite and Judean

---

1. After presenting an early version of this article at the 2012 International Meeting of the Society of Biblical Literature in Amsterdam, I was introduced to Prof. Göran Eidevall of Uppsala University, who had arrived at conclusions similar to my own on the topic of sacrifice in prophetic rhetoric, but whose excellent book had not yet appeared in print. See now Göran Eidevall, *Sacrificial Rhetoric in the Prophetic Literature of the Hebrew Bible* (Lewiston, NY: Mellen, 2012). Eidevall's approach is largely in accord with my own: "If sacrifices are offered within the framework of a reciprocal human-divine relationship, the sacrificial system will always allow for the possibility that some sacrifices are rejected by the deity. Some of the so-called cult-critical passages are best explained as total but situational rejection of the cult.... Their main rhetorical function can be construed either as threat (because YHWH has cut off all cultic commun[icat]ion) or as retrospective explanation (YHWH is in control, the destruction of his temple[s] was a punishment for the people's iniquities and this was announced in advance by his prophets)" (215–16).

sacrifices immediately before their respective defeats at the hands of the Assyrians or Babylonians—"foretold" in all of the prophetic texts that I treat—would have entailed that Yahweh is either capricious or weak, unwilling or unable to help Israel and Judah despite his acceptance of their gifts. In fact, the dominant historiographical strategy in prophetic texts explains Israelite and Judean military defeats as angry punishments from Yahweh.[2] In support of this point, I show that several biblical texts state or presume that the acceptance of both sacrifices and noncultic gifts is incommensurate with angry punishments or an enduring state of hostility, for this acceptance signals relatively favorable relations and a lack of ill will on the part of the receiving party. I submit that this interpretation yields a more rhetorically coherent, historically plausible, and intellectually satisfying reading of the prophetic literature.

My approach differs from contemporary scholarship on this topic in three ways. First, many interpreters treat the practice of sacrifice as a largely static "ritual [to be] performed"[3] or as "worship"[4] akin to a modern church liturgy or synagogue service. Hence, they regard the depiction of Yahweh's rejection of sacrifices as an indictment of ritual in general. Biblical texts, however, consistently state or presume that the practice of sacrifice is an active and transactional process wherein humans offer sacrifices to God, who might accept or reject them depending on the circumstances. The portrait of Yahweh rejecting sacrifices thus adheres to sacrificial logic and does not, as a matter of course, constitute some critique of ritual in general or sacrifice as a particular mode of worship.

My approach secondly differs from several scholars who have suggested that prophetic texts oppose the institution of animal sacrifice at state sanctuaries because it was an unfair economic burden imposed upon the poor by the "ruling classes."[5] Scholars must read between the lines of the texts to arrive at this conclusion. Joseph Blenkinsopp takes up this position in his discussion of Amos in *A History of Prophecy in Israel*:

---

2. See Nathaniel B. Levtow, *Images of Others: Iconic Politics in Ancient Israel*, BJSUCSD 11 (Winona Lake, IN: Eisenbrauns, 2008). This is also a Deuteronomistic strategy (e.g., 2 Kgs 17:20).

3. Jonathan Klawans, Purity, *Sacrifice and the Temple: Symbolism and Supersessionism in the Study of Ancient Judaism* (Oxford: Oxford University Press, 2006), 98.

4. Joseph Blenkinsopp, *A History of Prophecy in Israel*, 2nd ed. (Louisville: Westminster John Knox, 1996), 80.

5. Ibid., 93.

[Amos's] point seems to be that worship was (as it still is) a very powerful way of legitimating the current political and social status quo. Quite simply, Amos was not taken in by the religiosity of his contemporaries. A further and more specific point is that state cults were wealthy and complex operations, owning land, employing slaves, and supported by contributions, not all voluntary, from the population at large. Cultic personnel were, in addition, tax exempt, and the sacrificial system must have represented a significant drain on commodities and livestock; all of which will help to explain the frequent denunciations of priests and the sacrificial cult in the prophetic literature.[6]

Blenkinsopp's observations about the privileged position of state cults in ancient political economies are correct, but firm evidence does not exist for the proposition that Yahweh's rejection of animal sacrifices in prophetic texts is a function of an underlying critique of exploitative socioeconomic arrangements. The texts simply do not advance this point in any observable manner. Jonathan Klawans proposes a similar argument in *Purity, Sacrifice and the Temple*. Klawans interprets Mal 1:13, wherein Yahweh asserts that he will not accept a stolen offering, as encoding a general indictment of exploitative economic conditions that extends across the prophetic corpus:

> The prophets' "rejection" of sacrifice was deeply connected to their belief that Israel was economically rotten to the core.... One who has taken unjustly from the poor cannot properly *give* anything, and therefore the "sacrifice" offered by such a person is anathema.[7]

---

6. Ibid., 80. He echoes this argument in Blenkinsopp, *Isaiah 1–39: A New Translation with Introduction and Commentary*, AB 19 (New York: Doubleday, 2000), 184, "Critique of worship continues another protest theme common to the first generation of classical prophecy.... Primary targets of these attacks in the eighth century prophets are state cults in both kingdoms (Bethel, Dan, Samaria, Jerusalem) that not only provided religious legitimation for an expansive and oppressive state apparatus but also imposed heavy economic burdens of their own. Temple personnel in the service of the state were tax exempt, economic support of the cult was not optional, and the sacrificial system represented a significant drain on livestock.... Animal sacrifice seems to have aroused the strongest negative reaction ... no doubt because it could be so easily exploited to the advantage of temple personnel."

7. Klawans, *Purity, Sacrifice and the Temple*, 87. Klawans focuses on theft, but Mal 1 puts forth several reasons in explaining why Israelite sacrifices are unacceptable: "[You] offer polluted food on my altar.... When you offer a blind [victim] for sacrifice is it not evil? Or a lame or a sick one, is it not evil?" (1:7–8).

128   GLAIM

> The prophets—or, at least, some of them—found sacrifice offensive because they believed that those who were offering gifts had themselves stolen them. The concern with property renders it impossible altogether to distinguish between a ritual violation and an ethical wrong. Sacrificing a stolen animal is, at one and the same time, both ethically and ritually wrong.[8]

These arguments are coherent and perhaps appealing to some modern readers who are concerned with social justice and uncomfortable with animal sacrifice; nevertheless, they lack direct textual support. No biblical prophetic text ever articulates the argument that Yahweh opposes the practice of sacrifice because it places an exploitative and onerous burden on the poor. The book of Amos indeed criticizes wealthy Israelites for their abuses against the poor, and it also depicts them reposing at sanctuaries.[9] As I detail below, however, Amos has Yahweh rejecting Israelite sacrifices not because of their expensive cost, but as a punishment for specific ethical and cultic violations.

Indeed, all of the prophetic texts that assert Yahweh's rejection of sacrifices clearly and explicitly portray him as angry and preparing violent retributions for Israel or Judah, often in immediately adjacent passages. From a schematic perspective, I would suggest that participation in positive reciprocity is incompatible with negative reciprocity; one does not accept gifts from a person whom one is actively and angrily punishing, at least not in good faith. Although sacrifices are occasionally said to exacerbate Yahweh's wrath—namely because he is vexed at receiving presents but not obedience—they are never identified as the root cause of Yahweh's anger. Most prophetic texts trace Yahweh's anger to ethical abuses, idolatry, violations of the covenant, or some combination of these factors.

The final way in which my approach differs from some contemporary accounts is that I do not regard the prophetic literature as speaking to some longstanding dispute between priests and prophets on the one hand, and ethics and ritual on the other. Although Klawans treats this issue with more caution and nuance than much previous scholarship, he,

---

8. Ibid., 98.

9. Amos 2:8: "They recline on garments held in pledge beside every altar; they drink the wine of those who have been fined in the house of their God." There is no criticism of sacrifice here. (Here and subsequently, all translations of the biblical text are my own.)

too, ultimately concludes: "In short, I believe that the disputes between priests and prophets were indeed real."[10] Klawans continues: "The prophets hold the people to an ideal moral standard, while the priests seek to operate and maintain social institutions that serve these people's needs."[11] Ronald Hendel has recently offered a forceful defense of this position that warrants extended consideration.[12] Hendel argues that prior to the "prophetic critique" of the eighth and seventh centuries, sacrifices and related rituals enjoyed the unquestioned status of *doxa*:

> Prior to these prophetic critiques it was uncommon—or perhaps even unthinkable—to question the validity of customary Israelite rituals, including festivals, sacrifices, prayers, and hymns. These practices belonged to the domain of what the sociologist Pierre Bourdieu calls *doxa* (Greek for "opinion, notion, expectation"). The *doxa* of a culture are [sic] the unquestioned assumptions and practices of everyday life, which since they are unspoken are not subject to argument or dispute.[13]

Before the appearance of Amos and other likeminded prophets, Hendel argues, it was customary for Israelites to assume that Yahweh "delights in" ritual activities, especially sacrifices.[14] As evidence for this position, Hendel cites Gen 4:3–5, in which Cain and Abel offer sacrifices, "but no reason or justifications are given for this practice.... As *doxa*, sacrificial offerings in

---

10. Klawans, *Purity, Sacrifice and the Temple*, 98.
11. Ibid., 100.
12. Ronald S. Hendel, "Away from Ritual: The Prophetic Critique," in *Social Theory and the Study of Israelite Religion: Essays in Retrospect and Prospect*, ed. Saul M. Olyan, RBS 71 (Atlanta: Society of Biblical Literature, 2012), 59–80. See also Ronald S. Hendel, "Prophets, Priests, and the Efficacy of Ritual," in *Pomegranates and Golden Bells: Studies in Biblical, Jewish, and Near Eastern Ritual, Law, and Literature in Honor of Jacob Milgrom*, ed. David P. Wright, David Noel Freedman, and Avi Hurvitz (Winona Lake, IN: Eisenbrauns, 1995), 185–98; "Whereas the priests see a correspondence and mutuality between ritual and ethics, the classical prophets *contrast* the ethical with the ritual.... What is most remarkable in these is not the prophets' denunciations of ritual per se, but their emphatic contrast between ritual and ethics. This contrast reflects a perspective utterly alien to that of the priests.... We might say that the religious views of the prophets are not merely opposed, but are in a sense incommensurate. These priests and prophets are not talking *to* each other on the relationship between ritual and ethics, but are talking *past* each other" (190–91, emphasis original).
13. Hendel, "Away from Ritual," 63.
14. Ibid., 60.

Genesis are simply part of ordinary practice, an unquestioned norm of the commonsense world, a self-evident proposition."[15] The prophets, by contrast, were "religious radicals and eccentrics" whose "social forms were … at variance with the social forms of the majority."[16] By virtue of their eccentric and radical status, the prophets had the capability to "step outside the *doxa* of their contemporaries and cast these conventional habits into radical doubt."[17] From this outsider position, prophets such as Amos, Isaiah, and Jeremiah drew a binary distinction between ritual and ethics that was absolute and irreversible:

> They seem to agree that the ritual practices of their contemporaries are worthless. Each makes a strong contrast between ritual and ethics, such that the *doxa* of ritual is not only brought into question, but is rejected in contrast to the ethical virtues that Yhwh requires. This strong binary contrast between ritual and ethical practices is a striking feature of these prophetic texts.[18]

While Hendel notes that sacrifice is thought of as a reciprocal process,[19] he does not consider that both acceptance and rejection are readily intelligible outcomes of this process. To my mind, the rejection of sacrifices does not imply a violation of unquestioned assumptions about the practice of sacrifice, as Hendel argues. Many biblical cultic texts explicitly consider the possibility that Yahweh might not accept a sacrifice (e.g., Lev 22:20, 23). In the text that Hendel cites as evidence for the unquestionable status of sacrifice, Yahweh actually rejects Cain's sacrifice. Furthermore, this instance of rejection employs terminology similar to that which occurs in Amos 5:22, the centerpiece of Hendel's argument: "Yahweh looked [favorably] upon [וישע] Abel and his tribute [מנחה], but as for Cain and his tribute, Yahweh did not look upon it" (לא שעה; Gen 4:4–5). Compare Amos 5:22: "As for the sacrifice [שלם] of your fatted cattle, I will not look upon [it] [לא אביט]." Just as Yahweh might accept Abel's sacrifice while rejecting Cain's in Gen 4:3–5, it is conceivable that prophetic depictions

---

15. Ibid., 64.
16. Ibid., 78, 79.
17. Ibid., 71.
18. Ibid., 69.
19. Ibid., 62: "By withholding his positive reception of these rites, he [Yahweh] nullifies their effectiveness. They become empty gestures, gifts with no recipient and no reciprocity."

of Yahweh's rejection of sacrifices at particular historical crises do not preclude his acceptance of sacrifices at others. As I discuss below, texts within the books of Isaiah and Jeremiah—both of which Hendel cites as participating in the condemnation of ritual—outline future scenarios in which Yahweh will favorably accept sacrifices again.[20]

In contrast to the stark differentiation that Hendel and Klawans draw between priests and prophets, the so-called "prophetic critique of sacrifice" functions rather as an apology for the cultus, despite occasional scenes in prophetic literature of priests and prophets in conflict (e.g., Amos 7:10–17). In my reading, prophetic texts provide an explanation as to why Yahweh would allow his people to be defeated and his temples destroyed during periods in which sacrifices regularly continued at his earthly sanctuaries. This explanation does not challenge or undermine the basic reciprocal logic of sacrificial practice; rather, prophetic rhetoric iterates this logic. This observation helps to make sense of the facts that several prophets were also priests and that prophetic texts were ultimately collected, redacted, and canonized by enfranchised Jerusalem priests or by those very close to them.[21]

In fact, the books of Hosea (3:4–5), Micah (4:1–13), Isaiah (27:13; 19:19–20; 56:6–7; 60:7), Jeremiah (17:24–26; 33:17–18), and Ezekiel (20:40–44; 43:27) contain prophecies about the restoration of Jerusalem and Yahweh's house on Mount Zion. Several of these texts even prophesy the restoration of sacrifice. Ezekiel's temple vision states that after the purification of the altar "the priests will make your ascending offerings and your sacrifices, and I will accept you [ורצאתי אתכם]" (43:27). Ezekiel 20:40–44 states that after the Israelites have been sufficiently punished for their misdeeds (v. 44) and show remorse (v. 43), Yahweh will accept their sacrifices yet again:

> (v. 40) On my holy mountain, on the mountain heights of Israel, says my lord Yahweh, all the house of Israel, all of it, shall serve me in the land. There I will accept them [ארצם], and there I will seek your contributions

---

20. The irrevocability that Hendel picks up on in Amos 5:21–24 may reflect the historical fact that the kingdom of Israel was eradicated by Assyria in 721 BCE. Note that no such condemnation appears in Amos's oracle against the kingdom of Judah (Amos 2:4–5), which also suffered at the hands of the Assyrians and which also operated a state sacrificial cult.

21. Klawans, *Purity, Sacrifice and the Temple*, 97.

and your tithes along with all your holy things [i.e., sacrifices]. (v. 41) With a pleasing aroma [בריח ניחח] I will accept you [ארצה אתכם].

Adumbrating the argument below, this text draws a distinction between a period of punishment in which Yahweh will not accept sacrifices and a subsequent period in which hostility has subsided and Yahweh accepts sacrifices yet again. A text from Trito-Isaiah similarly underscores the significance of acceptance: "I will bring [foreigners] to my holy mountain and make them joyful in my house of prayer, their ascending offerings and sacrifices will be acceptable [לרצון] on my altar, for my house shall be called a house of prayer for all people" (Isa 56:7). In this vision of a restored Jerusalem temple, Yahweh will accept not only Israelite sacrifices, but also the sacrifices of non-Israelites (Isa 56:6).[22] Another passage from Trito-Isaiah makes a similar claim about the renewed temple: "Every flock of Kedar will be gathered for you; the rams of Nebioth will minister to you [ישרתונך]. They will ascend on my altar with acceptance [על רצון] and I shall glorify the house of my glory" (Isa 60:7). A later verse explains this development: "For in my anger I attacked you, but in my favor [ברצוני] I have compassion for you" (v. 10). Malachi, too, refers to a time when sacrifices will please Yahweh yet again: "The tribute of Judah and Jerusalem shall be pleasing [ערבה] to Yahweh, as in the days of yore, years long past" (3:4). In spite of the alleged prophetic departure from priestly conceptions and priorities, the passages above employ cultic terms and adhere to the reciprocal logic of sacrifice as they narrate ruptures and reconciliations in Yahweh's relationship with Israel.[23]

---

22. On this passage see Joseph Blenkinsopp, *Isaiah 56–66: A New Translation with Introduction and Commentary*, AB 19B (New York: Doubleday, 2003), 129–43; Saul Olyan, *Rites and Rank: Hierarchy in Biblical Representations of Cult* (Princeton: Princeton University Press, 2000), 91, 119. Isaiah 66:21 suggests that Yahweh will take "priests and Levites" from the nations.

23. See also Isa 43:23–24, which treats the interruption of sacrifices brought about by the destruction of the Jerusalem temple as part and parcel of a wider interruption in the relationship between Yahweh and Israel: "You have not brought me the small cattle of your ascending offerings, nor have you honored me with your sacrifices. I have not burdened you with [the offering of] tribute, nor wearied you with frankincense. You have not purchased calamus [for incense] with money, nor have you satiated me with the fat of sacrifices. Rather, you have burdened me with your offenses and wearied me with your iniquities."

Several biblical texts comment upon the capabilities and limitations of both sacrifices and noncultic gifts to effect reconciliation between aggrieved parties. It is well known that expiatory sacrifices might "wipe away" (כפר) unintentional offenses committed by their offerer, resulting in forgiveness (Lev 4–5; Num 15:22–29). Several narrative texts state that noncultic gifts, too, have the potential to "wipe away" (כפר) certain offenses in some situations. This potential is presumed, but not realized, in the following exchange between David and the Gibeonites:

> David said to the Gibeonites, "What shall I do for you? With what shall I wipe away [במה אכפר] [Saul's offense]?" The Gibeonites said to him, "It is not a matter of silver or gold with Saul and his household." (2 Sam 21:3–4)

Gifts of silver and gold, like sacrifices, cannot remedy every offense; in this case the Gibeonites find satisfaction only when seven of Saul's descendants are impaled on poles. The potential for gifts to effect reconciliation meets successful realization in the narrative of Jacob's flight from Esau (Gen 32–33). The relevant portion of the narrative has Esau in pursuit of Jacob, who is in fear of his life (32:8) and the lives of his family (32:12) because of his appropriation of their father Isaac's blessing (Gen 27). Esau, who has pledged to kill Jacob (27:41), is approaching with four hundred men (32:7). Jacob instructs his servants to meet Esau and offer him "tribute" (מנחה; 32:14, 19), a common term also for sacrifices. Jacob's stated goal in providing the tribute—to "wipe away" his brother's anger—forges a connection to sacrificial terminology. When the brothers meet, Jacob bows to Esau seven times, they embrace, and Esau asks about the gifts. Jacob answers that they are intended "to find favor in the eyes of my lord" (33:8). At first Esau refuses the tribute, but Jacob presses the issue (33:10–11):

> Jacob said, "No, if I have found favor in your eyes, then take my tribute from me for thus have I seen your face as though seeing the face of God, and you accept me.[24] Please take my gift that has been brought for you, for Yahweh has been gracious to me and I have everything." [Jacob] urged him and [Esau] took it.

---

24. Interestingly, as in Judg 13 (discussed immediately below), the danger of having looked upon a divine being is negated by that figure's acceptance of the beholder.

Jacob's strategy for placating his aggrieved and dangerous brother consists of expressing subordination through words and gestures and persuading Esau to accept his gift. Esau accepts the gift and the two part on favorable terms, which illustrates the causal or signaling relationship between the acceptance of gifts and a lack of hostile intent.

The idea that Yahweh's acceptance of sacrifices similarly indicates a lack of hostile intent appears in Judg 13:23. Judges 13 narrates the divine announcement of Samson's birth to his parents, Manoah and his wife. The announcement comes by way of two surreptitious angelic visits. After the second of these visits, Manoah invites the angelic messenger to stay while he and his wife prepare a kid goat. The messenger refuses the invitation to dine, but tells Manoah: "If you make an ascending offering, make it for Yahweh" (v. 16). Manoah does just this (vv. 19–23):

> Manoah took the kid and the tribute and he offered it up on the rock for Yahweh, creating a wonder as Manoah and his wife were looking on. When the flame ascended from the altar to the sky, Yahweh's messenger ascended on the flame of the altar. Yahweh's messenger was no longer visible to Manoah and his wife. Then he knew that it had been a messenger of Yahweh. Manoah said to his wife, "Surely we shall die for we have seen a god." But his wife said to him, "If Yahweh had wanted to kill us, he would not have taken an ascending offering and tribute from our hands, nor would he have shown us all of these things, nor would he have announced this at this time."

Manoah realizes that he and his wife have looked upon a divine being, putting their lives in danger. His wife points out that Yahweh's acceptance of the sacrifice, confirmed here as in Judg 6:21–23 by the altar flame ascending into the sky, indicates that he does not wish to kill the one offering the sacrifice: "If Yahweh had wanted to kill us, he would not have taken an ascending offering and tribute from our hands." Her inference is correct: "The woman bore a son, and she named him Samson. The boy grew and Yahweh blessed him" (v. 24). Yahweh's acceptance of the sacrificial gift signals favorable relations and a lack of hostile intent on his part.

Also relevant in explicating the logic and efficacy of sacrificial practice are the numerous statements that sacrifices produce a pleasing aroma (ריח נחוח) for Yahweh. Elements of the flood narrative in Gen 6–8 shed light on the meaning of this phrase. In Gen 6:7 Yahweh sees that people have become wicked and makes the following resolution: "I shall wipe the humans that I created from the face of the earth … for I am sorry that I made them." According to the J account, Yahweh rescinds his deadly resolution, but only after he has smelled the pleasing aroma of Noah's sacrifices:

> Noah built an altar to Yahweh, and he took of every kind of clean cattle, and of every kind of clean bird, and he offered up ascending offerings to Yahweh on the altar. Yahweh smelled [וירח] the pleasing aroma [ריח הניחח] and Yahweh said to himself, "Never again will I curse the earth on account of humankind ... never again will I strike down every living thing as I have done" (Gen 8:20–21).

This text suggests a causal relationship between the pleasing aroma of the sacrifices and Yahweh's resolution no longer to wreak destruction on the earth; in other words, the aroma of the sacrifices effects Yahweh's placation. In 1 Sam 26:19, David suggests that Yahweh should "smell tribute" (ירח מנחה) if Yahweh has stirred Saul against him, which implies that the smell of the sacrificial tribute might have a soothing effect on him.

With these wider observations about the preconditions and effects of sacrifice in mind, I turn now to the prophetic evidence. I treat each of the texts that are commonly associated with the "prophetic critique of sacrifice": Amos 5:21–27; Hos 6:4–7 and 8:13; Isa 1:10–17; Jer 6:20 and 7:21; and Mic 6:6–8. I point out three features of each of these texts. First, none criticizes the offering of sacrifices as a mode of religious practice; rather, the texts assert variously and often scathingly that Yahweh rejects Israelite and Judean sacrifices because he is angry. Second, the texts are embedded in larger rhetorical units that spell out the reasons for his anger with Israel or Judah: ethical abuses, "idolatry," and covenant violations. Third, the texts assert that Yahweh is beyond placation and resolute in his judgment to execute harsh punishments against Israel and Judah. This invariably entails military defeat, subjugation to foreign peoples, and exile.

The text most frequently associated with the prophetic critique of sacrifice is Amos 5:21–27. The verses immediately preceding the passage set forth a scenario of imminent doom in which Yahweh has resolved to punish the Northern Kingdom of Israel:

> My lord Yahweh, god of hosts, has spoken thus: there will be mourning in all the streets, and they will say, "Oh, no!" in public places. They will call the farmer to mourning and the wailers to wail. There will be mourning in all the vineyards, for I will pass through your midst, said Yahweh. Pity the ones who desire the day of Yahweh, for the day of Yahweh is darkness, not light. It is as if a man fled from a lion and ran into a bear

and he got home and leaned his arm on the wall and a snake bit him. Is not the day of Yahweh darkness and not light, gloom without brightness? (Amos 5:16–20)

Much of the earlier content in the chapter—indeed, much of the content from Amos 2:6 onward—serves to explain Yahweh's rationale for punishing the kingdom of Israel on this coming "day of Yahweh." The indictment centers on the Israelites' ethical abuses:

> They hate the one who adjudicates in the gate, and they abhor the one who speaks with integrity ... you trample the poor, and impose a levy of grain from him.... I know your transgressions are many and your offenses are great. Afflicting the innocent and taking bribes, they cast aside the poor in the gate. (Amos 5:9–12)

Yahweh's rejection of Israelite sacrifices in the following passage is commensurate with his anger and resolution to punish the kingdom of Israel (Amos 5:21–27):

> (v. 21) I hate, I reject [מאסתי] your pilgrimage festivals [חגיכם]; I will not smell [לא אריח] your assembly feasts. (v. 22) If you offer me ascending offerings and your tribute, I will not accept [them] [לא ארצה]. I will not look upon the sacrifice [שלם] of your fatted cattle. (v. 23) Remove the noise of your songs from my presence; I will not listen to the music of your instruments. (v. 24) But let justice [משפט] roll down like water; righteousness [צדקה] like an ever-flowing torrent.[25] (v. 25) Did you offer me sacrifices [זבחים] and tribute in the wilderness for forty years, O House of Israel? (v. 26) You will carry your images of Sakkut your king and Kewan,[26] your gods whom you made for yourselves, (v. 27) and I shall drive you into exile beyond Damascus, he says, Yahweh God of Armies is his name.

In verse 21, Yahweh asserts that he hates and rejects Israelite pilgrimage festivals and will not "smell" Israelite feasts, likely referring to the sacrifices offered on these occasions. The verb "smell" is the same as that employed in Gen 8:21 and 1 Sam 26:19, texts which imply that the aroma of sacrifices might pacify Yahweh's anger. Next, he avers that he will not accept Israelite

---

25. Another possible rendering is: "But let judgment [משפט] roll down like water; vindication [צדקה] like an ever-flowing torrent."
26. Omitting כוכב, "star."

ascending offerings, nor will he "look upon"—another idiom for acceptance—their sacrifice of fatted cattle. The verb "accept" (רצה) is the same as that employed in cultic expositions of sacrificial regulations, where it implies the possibility of rejection if certain preconditions are not met.[27] Yahweh also expresses his displeasure with Israelite songs and music, components of festival practices that accompanied the offering of sacrifices in efforts to attract Yahweh's presence or to invoke his remembrance of Israel.[28] In my reading, the assertions that Yahweh will not accept or even consider Israelite sacrifices and music express his implacability and resolution to punish Israel rather than generic criticism of ritual activities.

A common reading of verse 24 has it express the need for social justice and moral uprightness, both of which are sorely lacking in the kingdom of Israel according to earlier passages in Amos.[29] It is also possible that the verse refers to the coming punishment of the Israelites. The nouns justice/judgment (משפט) and righteousness/vindication (צדקה) are common in forensic contexts and may refer to punishments that will roll down like a torrential flashflood. Verse 25, which is often considered a Deuteronomistic insertion,[30] implies that sacrifices were not offered in the desert wanderings of the Israelites, contradicting the Pentateuch's account. Wolff argues that the upshot of this verse is not that sacrifices are problematic, but rather that "the time in the wilderness was the time of absolute faithfulness," when gifts were unnecessary to mediate the relationship between Yahweh and Israel.[31] Another possibility is that an earlier version of the pentateuchal

---

27. E.g., Lev 1:4, 7:18, 19:5–7, 22:19–23.

28. E.g., Num 10:9–10: "When you go to war against your enemy in your land, you shall blow the trumpets and be remembered in the presence of Yahweh your god and you shall be rescued from your enemies. On the day of your rejoicing and during your festivals and new moons you shall blow the trumpets over your ascending offerings and your slain sacrifices and they shall be a reminder in the presence of your god; I am Yahweh your god." See also 2 Chr 5:12.

29. For the traditional reading, see, e.g., J. Philip Hyatt, "The Translation and Meaning of Amos 5:23–24," *ZAW* 68 (1956): 17–24.

30. Hans W. Wolff, *Joel and Amos: A Commentary on the Books of the Prophets Joel and Amos*, Hermeneia (Philadelphia: Fortress, 1977), 264–65, argues that the pairing, "sacrifices and tribute" (זבחים ומנחה) is a late formulation and that "tribute" (מנחה) in the eighth century referred to sacrifices in general rather than to grain-based accompaniments. He also argues that the only other assertion that the Israelites did not sacrifice in the desert occurs in a Deuteronomistic addition to Jeremiah (7:21–23).

31. Ibid., 265.

narrative did not include the Priestly material that appears from Exod 24 onward. Verse 26 ironically ties the offense of worshiping foreign gods to the punishment for this and other offenses: the Israelites will carry the standards of Kewan and Sakkut into captivity beyond Damascus.[32]

Whereas many scholars have cited Amos 5 in claiming that there is a durable and generic renunciation of animal sacrifice or cultic ritual in the prophetic literature, two scholarly commentaries of Amos arrive at a different conclusion, namely that the condemnation is historically specific and targets the offerers rather than the offerings. Hans W. Wolff suggests that the passage was "probably proclaimed at the state sanctuary at Bethel.... Speaking as the messenger of Yahweh, Amos proclaims to his audience the sweeping rejection of all their cult offerings."[33] Quoting Gerhard von Rad, Wolff summarizes Amos 5:21–27 as an "announcement of punishment upon those who despise God's commands and at the same time deceive themselves by presuming to maintain through the cultus a stable relationship with God."[34] David Noel Freedman and Francis Andersen arrive at a similar conclusion in their commentary on Amos:

> The prophets have too often been portrayed as modern freethinking rationalist monotheists who rejected the cult entirely on the grounds that it was a vestige of primitive conceptions of deity and worship. There is little doubt that they believed that obedience was better than sacrifice and that doing justice and righteousness was more important than practicing the liturgy. Still, it is difficult to imagine, especially in that setting, that they wished to do away with public worship at the temple or the great festivals, with their multiform sacrifices and other rites.[35]

---

32. Ibid.
33. Ibid., 262–63.
34. Ibid., 266. "Amos has not merely issued a cultic decision of limited applicability [i.e., Yahweh will always reject the sacrifices of the wicked]. On the other hand, neither has he presented fundamental deliberations on the cultus as such" (267).
35. Francis I. Andersen and David N. Freedman, *Amos: A New Introduction with Notes and Commentary*, AB 24A (New York: Doubleday, 1989), 559. "They [the prophets] did not advocate the abolition of the cult but rather regarded the impending destruction of the nation and its temple as God's final judgment and his punishment for persistent apostasy. The end of the cult was proclaimed as a judgment visited by a justly angry God on his people, not as a goal to be devoutly wished and sought" (540). In their comment to Amos 4:4, Andersen and Freedman write: "Some commentators have read this and similar critiques throughout the prophets as an indictment of the cultus as such, but that judgment is too categorical. The attitude of the prophets to the

Neither Wolff nor Anderson and Freedman explicate the reciprocal dimension of prophetic portrayals of rejected sacrifices, nor do they extend their readings across the prophetic corpus; nevertheless, they argue that Amos 5:21–27 is historically specific and directed at offensive people rather than cultic practices.

Unlike other prophetic corpora, the book of Amos does not include any prophecy about the restoration of Yahweh's house or the resumption of cultic practices. This might reflect Amos's preoccupation with the Northern Kingdom of Israel, whose capital and cult sites became anathema to the priesthood in Jerusalem. Amos 3:14 prophesies the violent desecration of the altar at Bethel: "On the day that I punish the transgressions of Israel I will also punish the altar of Bethel, and the horns of the altar will be cut off and fall to the ground." Other passages prophesy against the Israelite sanctuary at Gilgal (4:4; 5:5) and the Judean sanctuary at Beersheba (5:5). Jerusalem, however, is described as Yahweh's dwelling place (1:2), and the restoration of the "booth of David" is foretold (9:11–15).

I turn now to two passages from the book of Hosea, which, like the book of Amos, is set in the eighth century during the period of Assyrian ascendancy. The first passage enunciates the treachery of the Israelites and Judeans (6:4–7):

> (v. 4) What shall I do with you, Ephraim? What shall I do with you, Judah? Your covenant loyalty is like morning mist, like dew that disappears in the early morning. (v. 5) I have cut them down with the prophets; I have killed them with the words of my mouth. Your judgments go forth like light. (v. 6) I desire loyalty, not a slain sacrifice; knowledge of God more than ascending offerings. (v. 7) But they, like humankind [כאדם], have violated the covenant; they have betrayed me.

Verses 4 and 7 allege that the Israelites have violated Yahweh's covenant. Verse 5 mentions violent punishments and divine judgments that Yahweh has already visited upon them on this account. These verses make it plain that the social framework of the passage is one of exasperation and retribution. James Mays has argued that verse 6 expresses Hosea's radical rejection of sacrifice and ritual:

---

political and religious institutions and officials of Israel was ambivalent. They could commend or condemn as occasion required. This passage is not a general rejection of all the festivals; it is a specific pronouncement against a particular festivity, a national celebration" (434).

> In his election of Israel Yahweh had not meant to found one more religion of ritual by which men might manage the divine; he had intended to become absolute Lord of all life. In the eighth century, sacrifice was the essential religious act; Hosea's hearers probably could not conceive of religion apart from sacrifice. The declaration rejecting sacrifice must have sounded radical and nihilistic.... The formulation is probably rooted in the long struggle between the Mosaic Yahwism of the amphictyonic league and the characteristic cult of Canaan.[36]

In my reading, however, verse 6 subordinates sacrifice to obedience and does not criticize the practice: Yahweh wants covenant loyalty but receives betrayal along with sacrificial gifts.[37] Andersen and Freedman arrive at a similar conclusion in their commentary to Hosea:

> This verse [v. 6] has often been quoted as proof that the prophets, or Hosea at least, made a radical break with the cult, maintaining that it was never part of Yahweh's purpose for his people. [According to this interpretation, they] were to serve him solely by loyalty and knowledge, by obedience to the ethical provisions of the covenant. It is a plea to inwardness and morality as the sum of religion. The point at issue is whether the prophets in the eighth century came to the think of the cult as extraneous or even deleterious to Israel's relationship with Yahweh. It seems rather that sacrifice is not denigrated; it is simply put in second place.[38]

Indeed, the following verses contain a series of further indictments that explain Yahweh's anger: the priests are murderers (6:9); Israel has been defiled by fornication (6:10); they have committed acts of wickedness and falsehood (7:1–3); they are adulterers (7:4). The looming punishments that Yahweh has in store for Israel are described in detail: "I will spread my net upon them; I will take them down like a [predatory] bird; I will admonish them in accordance with the proclamation to their assembly. Pity them, for they have strayed from me; theirs is destruction for they have rebelled against me" (7:12–13). Two verses in the following chapter add idolatry to the indictment: "With their silver and their gold they have made images

---

36. James L. Mays, *Hosea*, OTL (Philadelphia: Westminster, 1969), 98.

37. This is similar to 1 Sam 15:22–23. See Francis I. Andersen and David N. Freedman, *Hosea: A New Translation with Introduction and Commentary*, AB 24 (Garden City, NY: Doubleday, 1980), 431: "It seems certain that Hosea has in mind the oracle of 1 Sam 15:22–23."

38. Ibid., 430.

for themselves, in order that they might be cut down. [Yahweh] rejects your calf, Samaria; my anger is kindled against them" (8:4b–5a).

This framework of transgression, rage, and impending punishments sets the scene for the second passage: "As for the sacrifices that are my gifts [זבחי הבהבי],[39] let them sacrifice the flesh and eat it [themselves]. Yahweh does not accept them [לא רצם]. Now he will remember their misdeed and punish their offenses; they shall return to Egypt" (8:13). The argument here is apparently that those offering sacrifices might as well eat the meat of the sacrificial animals themselves rather than offering it to Yahweh, for he would reject it and it would go to waste. This implies that on other, more favorable occasions sacrificial meat might indeed be put to good use as a gift for Yahweh.

Hosea also prophesies against the Israelite shrines at Bethel and Gilgal.[40] Hosea 13:2 criticizes the Israelites for making cast images of silver and kissing calves, referring to the calves at Bethel and Dan. The rejection of these sanctuaries precludes the favorable resumption of sacrifices at these sites. On the other hand, Hos 3:4–5 appears to prophesy a time when the Israelites might resume cultic activities in Jerusalem:

> The Israelites will live for a long time without a king, without a prince, without sacrifice [זבח], without a pillar, without ephod, without teraphim. Afterward, the Israelites will repent and seek Yahweh their god and David their king and they will revere Yahweh and his goodness in future days. (Hos 3:4–5)

Despite some ambiguity, the passage seems to imply that after a period without king or cultus, the Israelites from the Northern Kingdom will return to the Davidic kingdom in Judah and "seek Yahweh," perhaps by offering sacrifices at the Jerusalem temple.

Like the passages from Amos and Hosea above, Isa 1:10–17 is also set in the period of Assyrian domination, though its particular target is

---

39. Reading the hapax legomenon הבהבי as "my gifts," derived from the root יהב "give." Andersen and Freedman, *Hosea*, 510, prefer to derive the word from the root אהב "love," thus yielding "beloved children," a reference to child sacrifice.

40. For Bethel, see Hos 10:14–15: "As Shalman[eser] destroyed Beth Arbel on a day of war, with mothers struck down upon their children, so shall it happen for you, Bethel, because of your wickedness." 10:5 and 4:15 refer to Bethel not as "the house of God" but as "a house of iniquity." For Gilgal, see Hos 12:11: "They sacrificed bulls in Gilgal; their altars shall be heaps in the furrows of the fields."

the kingdom of Judah. The wider poetic oracle in which this passage is embedded portrays a scenario in which the kingdom of Judah has been found guilty of serious offenses and has already begun to receive violent punishments. Yahweh summons celestial witnesses against Judah, invoking a forensic context of judgment: "Listen, Heavens; take note, Earth, for Yahweh has spoken: 'I have raised children; I have brought them up, but they have rebelled against me'" (v. 2). Unlike oxen who recognize their masters, the Israelites do not recognize their master, Yahweh (v. 3). Their condemnation continues: "O offending nation, a people burdened with iniquity, seed of evildoers, children of corruptors, they have abandoned Yahweh. They despise the holy one of Israel; they have turned their backs [on him]" (v. 4). The following verses employ a bodily metaphor to express the deservedness and physical violence of their punishments: "Where shall you be struck next?—you continue to stray. Your head is injured and your heart is faint. From the sole of the foot to the head, nothing is sound: welts and gashes, wounds and injuries" (1:5-6). The following verse moves from the metaphor to its referent, Judah's military defeat: "Your country is desolate; your cities have been burned by fire. As for your land, strangers devour it in front of you; it is desolate, as though overturned by strangers" (v. 7). A later verse reasserts the principle of rebellion and punishment through military defeat: "If you refuse and rebel you shall be destroyed by the sword" (v. 20).

Referring to the Assyrian campaign against Judah, verses 8 and 9 describe Jerusalem as a booth in a vineyard (v. 8), "a small remnant" of a once great kingdom, preserved by Yahweh though it should have perished like Sodom and Gomorrah (v. 9). Isaiah 1:10-17 speaks to the leaders of Sodom and Gomorrah, that is, the leaders of the Judean territories that have already been ravaged by the invading Assyrian army:

> (v. 10) Listen to the word of Yahweh, leaders of Sodom; pay heed to the instruction of our god, people of Gomorrah. (v. 11) For what purpose is this multitude of your slain offerings? says Yahweh. Am I satisfied with ascending offerings of rams and fat of fatted cattle? I have no desire for the blood of bulls, or lambs, or goats. (v. 12) When you come to appear before me, who requested this from you, trampling my courts? (v. 13) Bring no more false tribute [מנחת־שוא]; it is abominable incense to me. (v. 14) New moon and Sabbath and the proclaiming of assemblies—I cannot bear iniquity and assembly feast. My very person hates your new moons and your appointed feasts; they are a burden upon me that I am weary of carrying. (v. 15) When you spread out your hands [in supplica-

tion] I will hide my eyes from you; when you multiply prayers I will not listen; your hands are full of blood. (v. 16) Wash up, make yourselves clean, get your wicked deeds away from me, cease from doing evil, (v. 17) learn to do good, seek justice, relieve the oppressed, vindicate the orphan, and plead for the widow.

As Blenkinsopp has suggested, efforts to seek Yahweh's favor through the offering of sacrifices would have intensified during military crises such as the Assyrian invasion.[41] Nevertheless, the sacrifices offered by the "leaders of Sodom" and "people of Gomorrah" are to no avail; they do not satisfy Yahweh and will not avert his punishments. Yahweh loathes even the presence of such people in his sanctuary's courts.

Brevard Childs has argued that this passage constitutes "a sharp polemic against Jerusalem's thriving cultic practice."[42] This polemic "represents a powerful minority voice within Israel's religion without any clear parallels in ancient Near Eastern sources."[43] After noting that "the hypothesis from the nineteenth century that the prophets were opposed to sacrifice in principle has been rejected," Childs extends the hypothesis, claiming that the passage represents an attack on all ritual practices: "[Yahweh] is disgusted before this tedious ordeal, and is even filled with 'revulsion' toward Israel's carefully orchestrated rituals.... The prophetic attack is highly specific ... and is directed to this moment of deep religious distortion within Jerusalem."[44] Several features of the passage, however, suggest that Yahweh's qualms with the various cultic practices mentioned therein stem from the culpability of those performing them rather than his appraisal of their inherent religious merit. Yahweh does not reject tribute *tout court*; rather, he has no desire for "false tribute," which does not express submission and obedience to its receiver. New moons, Sabbaths, and festivals are a "burden" to Yahweh because he is weary of keeping up his side of relationship with a rebellious and iniquitous partner. Yahweh refuses to consider Israelite prayers because those praying with outstretched arms are culpable––their "hands are full of blood"––not because he takes issue with prayer as a mode of religious practice. Verses 16 and 17 then spell out the ethical and forensic preconditions that are necessary

---

41. Blenkinsopp, *Isaiah 1–39*, 184. See also 1 Sam 7:8–10.
42. Brevard S. Childs, *Isaiah*, OTL (Louisville: Westminster John Knox, 2001), 19.
43. Ibid.
44. Ibid.

in order to reestablish a productive relationship between the Israelites and Yahweh their national god.⁴⁵

The book of Micah is also situated in the period of Assyrian ascendancy and likewise pronounces doom against Israel and Judah. Micah 6:6–8, which scholars often associate with the prophetic critique of sacrifice, poses a rhetorical question and offers a response:

> (v. 6) With what shall I come before Yahweh and prostrate myself to the God of heights; shall I come before him with ascending offerings, with calves a year old? (v. 7) Will Yahweh accept [הירצה] thousands of rams, myriad rivers of oil? Shall I give him my firstborn for my rebellion, the fruit of my body for my offense? (v. 8) He has told you, O human, what is good, and what Yahweh seeks from you: to act justly, and to love loyalty, and to walk humbly with your god.

While this passage has been interpreted as criticizing the practice of sacrifice, its upshot seems rather that sacrifices, no matter their quality or quantity, cannot take the place of justice and loyalty to Yahweh.⁴⁶ As with the passages from the other prophetic corpora treated above, the verses preceding this passage invoke a context of litigation:

---

45. Two passages in Isa 1–39 suggest that Yahweh might resume cultic relations with the Israelites once again after a period of punishment and reconciliation. Isaiah 27:13 states that after the iniquity of Jacob has been "expiated" (יכפר) through the punishment of exile (27:8–9), "a great trumpet will be blown, and those lost in the land of Assyria and those banished to the land of Egypt will come and prostrate themselves [השתחוו] to Yahweh on the holy mountain at Jerusalem." While this verse does not mention sacrifices specifically, prostrations often accompanied the offering of sacrifices in cultic contexts (e.g., 1 Sam 1; Mic 6:6). The second passage describes the future reconciliation of Yahweh and the Egyptians, who will offer him sacrifices: "Yahweh will make himself known to Egypt, and the Egyptians will know Yahweh at that time. They will serve [him] with sacrifices and tribute [ועבדו זבח ומנחה]; they will make a vow to Yahweh and redeem it [ונדרו נדר ליהוה ושלמו]" (Isa 19:19–21).

46. Francis I. Andersen and David Noel Freedman, *Micah: A New Translation with Introduction and Commentary*, AB 24E (New York: Doubleday, 2000), 528: "To say that the prescription in Mic 6:8 is 'good' could imply that the other proposal in v. 7 [i.e., the offering of sacrifices] is 'bad.' This is the common reading, [according to which this passage represents] another place where reconciliation with God through sacrifice is rejected.... But, the comparative meaning of [good] implies that the suggestion in v. 7 is good, but the one in v. 8 is 'better.'"

> Hear now what Yahweh says: Arise, plead your case [ריב] to the mountains, let the hills hear what you have to say. Listen, O mountains, to Yahweh's case [ריב], and [you], O foundations of the earth. For Yahweh has a dispute [ריב] with his people, and he will plead with Israel. O my people, what have I done to you? How have I wearied you? Testify against me! (6:1–3).

Yahweh then reminds the Israelites that he redeemed them from the house of bondage in Egypt and rescued them from King Balak of Moab (6:4), implying that Israel owes him an enormous debt of gratitude. Later verses pronounce the guilt of the Israelites and their coming punishments: "The wealthy ones [of the city] are full of malice and its inhabitants have spoken lies. Their tongue is treacherous in their mouth. I, for my part, have begun to attack you, to ruin [you] on account of your offenses" (vv. 12–13). More specific pronouncements of accusation and punishment appear in verse 16: "Omri's statutes are observed, and all the practices of the house Ahab, and you walk in their counsel. Therefore, I will ruin you and make you an object of derision, and you will bear the disgrace of my people."

The book of Jeremiah contains two passages that scholars have adduced as evidence for the prophetic critique. Jeremiah 6:20 portrays Yahweh turning his nose up at the incense and sacrifices offered by the Judeans. The immediate context of this verse contains all of the rhetorical elements present in the passages above:

> (v. 16) Thus says Yahweh: stand in the streets and look around, ask for the old paths—Which one is the good way?—and walk in it so that you might find rest. But they said, "We will not walk." (v. 17) I set watchmen over you—Listen for the sound of the horn!—But they said, "We will not listen." (v. 18) Therefore let the nations hear and let the council know what is in store for them. (v. 19) Hear, O earth: I am about to bring evil upon this people, the fruit of their contrivances, for they have not heeded my words and they have rejected my instruction. (v. 20) For what purpose does this frankincense come to me, calamus [incense] from a distant land? Your ascending offerings are not acceptable [לא לרצון], your slain offerings are not pleasing [לא ערבו] to me. (v. 21) Therefore Yahweh has spoken thus: I am furnishing stumbling blocks for this people, fathers and sons together will stumble against them, a resident and his neighbor, and they shall perish.

Verse 20 is embedded in a rhetorical unit that articulates Judah's disobedience (vv. 16–17), judgment (vv. 18–19), and punishment (v. 21). The upshot of verse 20, then, is that the incense and sacrifices of the Judeans can neither avert nor suspend Yahweh's judgments. In my reading, this verse asserts Yahweh's implacability and resolution to punish the Judeans in spite of their gifts, rather than a generic appraisal of cultic practices.[47] Earlier verses in the chapter support this reading. The punishment of military defeat for Judah and Jerusalem is anticipated in verse 6: "Cut down [Jerusalem's] trees and build siege ramps against Jerusalem. This is the city to be punished, it is oppression from inside out." Verse 11 vividly describes Yahweh's anger: "I [Yahweh] am full of the fury of Yahweh; I am weary of containing it." Verse 15 meanwhile reiterates the culpability of the Judeans: "They shall be put to shame because they have committed abomination. They neither feel shame nor know how to be humiliated. Therefore they shall fall among the fallen; they will be brought low at the time I punish them."

The following chapter of Jeremiah contains another verse strongly associated with the prophetic critique of sacrifice. Jeremiah 7:21 states that the Judeans ought to eat the meat of their ascending offerings themselves rather than incinerating it for Yahweh, implying that it would be wasted on him.[48] Jack Lundbom has argued that this verse constitutes "a strident attack on Temple sacrifice"[49] and evidence that "Jeremiah thinks sacrifices really ought to cease."[50] Like Jer 6:20, however, the surrounding verses

---

47. Jack R. Lundbom, *Jeremiah 1–20: A New Introduction with Translation and Commentary*, AB 21A (New York: Doubleday, 1999), 438: "Yahweh is not averse to Temple worship per se. The reason it no longer delights him is that people have rejected his word." Lundbom is nevertheless somewhat uncertain about the rhetorical contours of the passage: "Do temple sacrifices not require [frankincense and good cane]? Does not Yahweh savor their swell smells? Yahweh says these no longer please him. Why? We are not told. But when this oracle is taken together with the previous oracle the answer becomes clear. People have not heeded his words and have rejected his teaching" (440). I submit that consideration of the role of offerings in the social context of human-divine reciprocity explains why the sacrifices no longer please Yahweh.

48. This echoes Hos 8:13.

49. Lundbom, *Jeremiah 1–20*, 485. He continues: "[The] point is that obedience is more important than sacrifice.... He is being ironic. Were he given to straight talk he would tell the people simply to cease making sacrifices, for Yahweh no longer accepts them" (ibid.).

50. Ibid., 481, adding: "Both whole burnt offerings and sacrifices are mentioned in 6:20, where Temple worship comes in again for censure and for the same reason as here: simultaneous disregard for Yahweh's word (v. 19).... [Sacrifices are] not pleasing to Yahweh.... [P]eople may just as well go ahead and eat the meat of both."

depict both the culpability of the Judeans and Yahweh's unshakable resolution to punish them:

> (v. 16) As for you [Jeremiah], do not pray on behalf of this people, do not raise a cry or prayer on their behalf, and do not intercede with me, for I will not listen to you. (v. 17) Do you not see what they are doing in the cities of Judah and in the streets of Jerusalem? (v. 18) The children gather wood, the fathers light the fire, and the women knead dough to make cakes for the Queen of Heaven. They offer libations to other gods so that they might vex me. (v. 19) But is it I that they vex--says Yahweh--not themselves, to their own humiliation? (v. 20) Therefore thus says my lord Yahweh: My furious anger will be poured out on this place, on human beings and animals, on the trees of the field and the fruit of the earth; it will burn unquenched. (v. 21) Thus says Yahweh of Armies, God of Israel: As for your ascending offerings, snatch them away [ספו] with your slain sacrifices and eat meat. (v. 22) For I did not speak to your ancestors or command them, when I brought them out of the land of Egypt, concerning ascending offerings and slain sacrifices.[51] (v. 23) Rather, this is what I commanded them: "Heed my voice, and I will become your god, and you will become my people; walk in the all the ways that I command you, so that things go well for you." (v. 24) Yet they did not obey.

In verse 16, Yahweh instructs Jeremiah not to attempt to intercede on behalf of the Judeans because he is absolutely resolute in his decision to punish the Judeans for their idolatry (v. 18) and disobedience (v. 24). Yahweh's refusal to accept Judean sacrifices amounts to a similar pronouncement: just as Yahweh will not consider Jeremiah's intercessory prayers, so he will not consider the sacrificial gifts of the Judeans which they intend to avert the coming calamity. Just as Yahweh's refusal to consider prayers in this particular context of disobedience, judgment, and punishment does not amount to an attack on prayer, so too his refusal to accept Judean sacrifices does not amount to an attack on sacrifice; both are expressions of utter implacability. Jeremiah 14:11–12 reiterates this dual assertion almost identically, except that it also mentions fasting, and is to be interpreted in like manner.[52]

---

51. See my discussion of Amos 5:25 above.
52. Jeremiah 14:11–12: "Yahweh said to me: Do not pray on behalf of this people for their benefit. When they fast, I do not listen to their cry. When they offer ascending offerings and tribute, I do not accept them. Rather, by sword, by famine, and by plague I am eradicating them." See Lundbom, *Jeremiah 1–20*, 706-7: "A fast is carried out at

Two later passages in the book of Jeremiah associate the offering of sacrifices with amicable relations between Yahweh and Judah in both pre-exilic and postexilic contexts. This feature of the text undermines the argument that the book of Jeremiah encodes a durable pronouncement against the practice of sacrifice. Jeremiah 17:24–26, which speaks to a preexilic context,[53] states that if the Judeans are obedient to Yahweh, then Jerusalem will be inhabited forever and people will offer sacrifices there:

> (v. 24) Now if you obey me, says Yahweh, not carrying a load through the gates of this city on the Sabbath, sanctifying the Sabbath without doing any work on it, (v. 25) then there will enter the gates of this city kings to sit on the throne of David, riding on chariots and horses, they and their officials, the men of Judah and the inhabitants of Jerusalem, and this city shall be inhabited forever (v. 26). They will come from the cities of Judah, from around Jerusalem, from Benjamin, from the Shephelah, from the hill country, from the Negev, bringing ascending offerings and slain offerings, tribute and incense, and thank offerings to the temple of Yahweh.

In Jer 33:17–18, which speaks to a postexilic context,[54] Yahweh asserts that in a future period of reconciliation "for David there will never cease to be a man to sit on the throne of the house of Israel; for the Levite priests there will never cease to be a man in my presence to offer ascending offerings, incense, and tribute, and to offer slain sacrifices continually." Lundbom

---

a time of personal or national emergency, i.e., a drought, famine, plague, sickness, death, or if the land is threatened by enemy invasion.... Fasting is done to supplicate divine favor, which here is being denied." Lundbom continues: "In ordinary human affairs [tribute; Heb. מנחה] is a 'present' one gives to secure the favor of another, not unlike today's box of candy or bouquet of flowers.... In Jeremiah, Yahweh rejects offerings and sacrifices because people disregard his word and the covenant demands (6:19–20; 7:21–23; 11:15)" (707).

53. Ibid., 808: "These words are then spoken before sacrificial worship comes under censure (6:20; 7:21–26), reflecting early preaching by the prophet that looked for a joyful return of northern exiles to Zion for the yearly festivals (31:2–14), at which time Yahweh 'will feast the priest's appetite with abundance' (v. 14)."

54. Jack R. Lundbom, *Jeremiah 21–36: A New Translation with Introduction and Commentary*, AB 21B (New York: Doubleday, 2004), 541: "This oracle promises a continuation of Judah's royal and priestly lines, for which reason many commentators deny it to Jeremiah and date it to the post-exilic period. But a post-exilic date is not required; the oracle need only postdate the fall of Jerusalem."

deems this passage "a stark reversal of Jeremiah's earlier words in 6:20, 7:21, and 14:12."[55] Following my reading of these passages, however, there is no need to posit any such stark reversal. Yahweh only rejects the sacrifices of the Judeans in periods when he is planning or executing violent punishments against them; at other times the offering and acceptance of licit (nonidolatrous) sacrifices is an integral part of a well-functioning relationship between Yahweh and his people.

To conclude: I have argued above that the texts that are thought to express a "prophetic critique of sacrifice" do no such thing, nor do they speak to a longstanding dispute between priests and prophets. These texts depict Yahweh furiously and pitilessly punishing the Israelites and Judeans with brutal military defeat and other calamities, which is incommensurate with his simultaneous acceptance of their sacrifices. I have suggested that prophetic discourse of this kind actually functions as an apology for the cult of Yahweh. Prophetic rhetoric provides an explanation as to how Israel and Judah could suffer devastating military defeats when sacrifices were being offered without challenging the overall efficacy of sacrificial practice. The argument is not that sacrifices are ineffective but rather that they are ineffective when Yahweh is angry. This in turn helps to explain why prophetic texts were embraced by later authorities who might well have had strong connections to the Jerusalem temple cult.

---

55. Lundbom, *Jeremiah 21–36*, 541.

Prophetic Cult-Criticism in Support of Sacrificial Worship? The Case of Jeremiah

Göran Eidevall

Introduction

Some prophecies in the book of Jeremiah seem to declare that YHWH denounces the sacrificial cult in its entirety (Jer 6:20; 7:21). By contrast, other passages (17:26; 33:10–11, 18) appear to promote the bringing of sacrifices as a perfectly legitimate means of worshiping YHWH.

Such discrepancies are usually explained in redaction-critical terms. Arguably, though, such an explanation is not entirely satisfactory. It is indeed likely that the book of Jeremiah contains several editorial layers. However, linking cult-critical and procultic oracles to separate editorial strands does not help us understand why the final editors decided to include both cult-critical and procultic utterances. In other theological matters of crucial importance, such as the worship of other gods, the book of Jeremiah can be characterized as relatively coherent. Hence, a different explanation is called for.

In this study I intend to show that the cult-critical prophecies are in fact compatible with the procultic passages. Drawing on recent works on rejected sacrifice, I will show that this phenomenon need not imply a negative attitude toward sacrifices as such. On the basis of a pioneering study by Lena-Sofia Tiemeyer on attitudes toward priests in the book of Jeremiah,[1] it will be argued that the key to understanding the juxtaposition of pro-cultic and cult-critical prophecies lies in recognizing a certain chronological principle followed by the editors. Whereas passages

---

1. Lena-Sofia Tiemeyer, "The Priests and the Temple Cult in the Book of Jeremiah," in *Prophecy in the Book of Jeremiah*, ed. Hans M. Barstad and Reinhard G. Kratz, BZAW 388 (Berlin: de Gruyter, 2009), 233–64.

denouncing sacrifices always refer to the past, passages promoting sacrifices consistently refer to the future.

Prophetic Cult Critique and the Phenomenon of Rejected Sacrifice

Recent studies have demonstrated that the act of bringing sacrifices to a deity is in several respects analogous to gift-giving, which can be seen as an essential ingredient in social interaction between humans in all known cultures.[2] The keyword, in both cases, is *reciprocity*. In a reciprocal relationship, one is never forced to accept a gift, but refusing to do so could signal dissatisfaction with the relationship. According to the biblical authors, human beings did not have the power to control YHWH, or to determine the actions of the deity. Hence, the possibility of rejection would seem to be a corollary of ancient Israelite sacrificial logic.[3] Contrary to a widespread opinion, therefore, declarations to the effect that the deity does not accept what is being offered may in fact be perfectly compatible with a positive attitude to sacrificial cult.

It needs to be pointed out that the phenomenon of rejected sacrifice is not restricted to religious practice in ancient Israel and Judah. Cases of rejection are attested in texts from Ugarit, as well as in a number of sources from ancient Greece, as shown by Fred Naiden.[4] Within the Hebrew Bible, moreover, the occurrence of this phenomenon is not confined to the prophetic literature. It constitutes a literary and/or theological motif in several narratives. To mention just a few examples, rejected sacrifice plays a crucial role in the following episodes: Cain and Abel (Gen 4), the rebellion of Korah (Num 16), and the encounter between Samuel and Saul in 1 Sam 15. The latter episode is instructive. Saul's sacrifice is turned down, but the main point is that Saul *himself* is rejected by YHWH: "he has also rejected you from being king" (1 Sam 15:23b, NRSV). Judging from these and simi-

---

2. See Daniel Ullucci, *The Christian Rejection of Animal Sacrifice* (Oxford: Oxford University Press, 2012), 24–30. The same arguments are presented in Daniel Ullucci, "Contesting the Meaning of Animal Sacrifice," in *Ancient Mediterranean Sacrifice*, ed. Jennifer W. Knust and Zsuzsanna Várhelyi (Oxford: Oxford University Press, 2011), 55–74, esp. 62–67.

3. For a more elaborate discussion along these lines, see Göran Eidevall, *Sacrificial Rhetoric in the Prophetic Literature in the Hebrew Bible* (Lewiston, NY: Mellen, 2012), 38–48.

4. Fred S. Naiden, "Rejected Sacrifice in Greek and Hebrew Religion," *JANER* 6 (2006): 189–223.

lar textual examples, the biblical authors held the view that disobedience could lead to divine unwillingness to accept sacrificial gifts from certain persons, or in certain situations. Conversely, rejected sacrifice was interpreted as evidence of a renunciation of the reciprocal relationship with the deity. Against this background, however, there is no reason to assume that situational declarations of rejection would imply that sacrifices as such are being condemned.

Contrasting Attitudes toward Sacrifice and the Issue of Coherence in the Book of Jeremiah

Anyone studying the topic of sacrificial cult in the book of Jeremiah runs the risk of getting confused. In some passages, all sacrifices seem to be rejected, even if they are offered to YHWH exclusively, in the Jerusalem temple. According to Jer 6:20, this is what YHWH spoke through his mouthpiece: "Your burnt offerings are not acceptable, and your sacrifices do not please me." Other passages, however, seem to regard sacrifices as an integral part of worship. For instance, in Jer 17:26, the reference to people "bringing burnt offering, sacrifice, grain offering and incense, bringing thank offering to the house of YHWH" is part of a prophecy depicting an ideal future. As Terence Fretheim notes in his commentary, the utterance in Jer 17:26 seems to stand in contrast to 6:20, since "the various offerings and sacrifices are here understood to be pleasing to God."[5] Before discussing these textual passages in more detail, it might be helpful to provide a short introduction to the current scholarly discussion on degrees of coherence within the book of Jeremiah.

Within historic-critical scholarship, the standard solution to problems of inconsistency has been to ascribe the conflicting utterances to different redactional layers.[6] It has been customary to regard the final product as lacking theological coherence. John Bright has described the

---

5. Terence E. Fretheim, *Jeremiah*, SHBC 15 (Macon, GA: Smith & Helwys, 2002), 264.

6. For a helpful overview, see Thomas Römer, "The Formation of the Book of Jeremiah as a Supplement to the So-called Deuteronomistic History," in *The Production of Prophecy: Constructing Prophecy and Prophets in Yehud*, ed. Diana Edelman and Ehud Ben Zvi, Bible World (London: Equinox, 2009), 168–71. See also Ronald Troxel, *The Prophetic Literature: From Oracles to Books* (Malden, MA: Wiley-Blackwell, 2012), 208–24.

book of Jeremiah as "a hopeless hodgepodge thrown together without any discernible principle of arrangement at all."[7] Similar statements have been made by other commentators, for instance by Robert Carroll: "Whatever the more sanguine commentators on Jeremiah may think, I am still of the opinion that the book of Jeremiah is a very difficult, confused and confusing text."[8]

I do not find such a perspective on the book of Jeremiah entirely satisfactory. Let me be clear on this matter, though: I am not against redaction criticism, and I am certainly not defending the position that this prophetic book is characterized by authorial unity. There are compelling reasons to assume that the book of Jeremiah is the result of a long and complex process, reaching into the Hellenistic era. Above all, the book shows traces of substantial Deuteronomistic editing during and/or after the exile.[9]

In my opinion, however, the main alternative to authorial unity is not necessarily complete disorder or far-reaching ideological disunity. One may ask: Is it reasonable to assume that the editors accepted the juxtaposition of mutually contradictory statements concerning such a central issue as the temple cult? Or, is it conceivable that they simply overlooked the fact that the collection they had created contained such disturbing disagreement? I do not think so. After all, these editors did not include mutually exclusive statements concerning the issue of worshiping other gods. One might also ask: What were the intended readers of the book supposed to do? Were they encouraged to perform regular sacrificial rites in the rebuilt Jerusalem temple, or were they rather supposed to refrain from such activities altogether?

As pointed out by a growing number of scholars, the book of Jeremiah displays a rather high degree of coherence, despite its long and complex

---

7. John Bright, *Jeremiah: A New Translation with Introduction and Commentary*, AB 21 (New York: Doubleday, 1965), lvi.

8. Robert P. Carroll, "Halfway through a Dark Wood: Reflections on Jeremiah 25," in *Troubling Jeremiah*, ed. A. R. P. Diamond, L. Stulman, and Kathleen M. O'Connor, JSOTSup 260 (Sheffield: Sheffield Academic, 1999), 73–86 (quotation on p. 75). See also William McKane, *Introduction and Commentary on Jeremiah I–XXV*, vol. 1 of *A Critical and Exegetical Commentary on Jeremiah*, ICC (Edinburgh: T&T Clark, 1986), lxxxiii.

9. Thus many Jeremiah scholars; see, e.g., Römer, "Formation," and Winfried Thiel, *Die deuteronomistische Redaktion von Jeremia 1–25*, WMANT 41 (Neukirchen-Vluyn: Neukirchener Verlag, 1973).

editorial history. Thus, Louis Stulman speaks of "theological coherence amidst the chaos."[10] In his introduction to *Reading the Book of Jeremiah: A Search for Coherence*, Martin Kessler states, in a similar vein, that the contributors "have tried to show that, in spite of paradoxes created by multiple voices, the work demonstrates a unity of purpose and coherence that should be taken seriously."[11] Notably, though, the topic of sacrifices is not treated in this anthology. Hence it remains an open question whether the book's statements concerning the cult would fit into such a picture of coherence. However, the thought-provoking study by Tiemeyer indicates that they do.[12]

Tiemeyer's solution to the problem of apparent inconsistency is simple but ingenious. Focusing on shifting attitudes towards priests within this prophetic book, she finds that there is a chronological division between critical and affirmative prophecies: "the book of Jeremiah distinguishes between past and future priests ... texts that betray a critical disposition towards the priests and/or the cult are found in passages that speak about the pre-exilic situation ... texts that view the priests and/or the cult positively are found in passages that speak about the future."[13] In this paper, I wish to follow-up Tiemeyer's study and to develop this line of argumentation, focusing on the seemingly conflicting attitudes toward sacrifice within the book. My main thesis can be summarized as follows: those who were responsible for the final edition(s) of the book of Jeremiah had a basically positive attitude toward the sacrificial cult. Whereas passages that reject sacrifices always refer to the past (that is, to the cult before 586 BCE), passages accepting or even promoting sacrifices consistently refer to the future (that is, to the postexilic cult in the Second Temple era). A third group of passages, which would seem to relativize the role of sacrifices, refer to the present, templeless situation of (some of) the addressees, either during the exile or later (addressing diaspora communities).

---

10. Louis Stulman, *Jeremiah*, AOTC (Nashville: Abingdon, 2005), 13.
11. Martin Kessler, "Editor's Introduction," in *Reading the Book of Jeremiah: A Search for Coherence*, ed. Martin Kessler (Winona Lake, IN: Eisenbrauns, 2004), xii.
12. Tiemeyer, "Priests."
13. Ibid., 234.

Cult-Critical Passages in Jeremiah: Sacrifices of the Past

Jeremiah 6:20

> What (is) this to me—frankincense that comes from Sheba, and sweet cane from a distant land? Your burnt offerings [עלותיכם] are not acceptable, and your sacrifices [זבחיכם] do not please me. (Jer 6:20)[14]

The utterance in Jer 6:20 is connected to the preceding unit, consisting of verses 16–19, and immediately followed by a prediction of disaster (in v. 21).[15] It contains an explicit declaration of rejection, which looks like a negated priestly formula, using two technical terms for divine acceptance of offerings: לרצון ("acceptable," see Lev 1:3; 22:19–21, etc.) and ערב ("to please," see Hos 9:4; Mal 3:4).[16] In addition to the burnt offering (עלה) and the sacrifice of communion (זבח), which were the two main types of animal sacrifice, frankincense and sweet cane are mentioned—two imported luxury products that were used as ingredients in the sacrificial cult.

According to some scholars, Jer 6:20 expresses a general repudiation of *all* sacrificial cult. Fretheim remarks: "given the 'therefore' that follows in v. 21, these offerings are considered a reason for judgment."[17] However, the primary reason for judgment is arguably stated in verse 19: "as for my teaching, they have rejected it." The rhetorical effect created by the editor who combined these two prophecies is unmistakable.[18] One may almost speak of poetic justice: YHWH rejected the sacrifices offered to him by

---

14. Unless otherwise noted, all translations are mine.
15. See Jack R. Lundbom, *Jeremiah 1-20: A New Translation with Introduction and Commentary*, AB 21A (New York: Doubleday, 1999), 433. See also Werner H. Schmidt, *Das Buch Jeremia: Kapitel 1-20*, ATD 20 (Göttingen: Vandenhoeck & Ruprecht, 2008), 165–67. Robert P. Carroll, *Jeremiah: A Commentary*, OTL (London: SCM, 1986), 200, describes 6:16–21 as a "mosaic," consisting of "different fragments ... put together by a Deuteronomistic editor."
16. See, e.g., William L. Holladay, *Jeremiah 1: A Commentary on the Book of the Prophet Jeremiah, Chapters 1-25*, Hermeneia (Minneapolis: Fortress, 1986), 223. See also Schmidt, *Buch Jeremia*, 168, on Jer 6:20 as an instance of prophetic adaption of the vocabulary (as well as the role) of the priests.
17. Fretheim, *Jeremiah*, 125; see also Walter Brueggemann, *To Pluck up, To Tear down: A Commentary on the Book of Jeremiah 1-25*, ITC (Grand Rapids: Eerdmans, 1988), 70: "In place of the torah, Israel has substituted cultic action."
18. One should also note the distinct Deuteronomistic tendency of v. 19; see Schmidt, *Buch Jeremia*, 167.

worshipers who had rejected his torah.[19] In other words, the rejection of the cult is part of the punishment. But this need not entail that the cultic actions were regarded as crimes.

Nothing in the wording of this utterance, or in its immediate context, suggests that sacrifices *as such* are thought to be against YHWH's will. It is imperative to observe the exact formulations in verse 20. The deity rejects "*your* burnt offerings" and "*your*" sacrifices. In other words, the language is relational.[20] Since the ensuing announcement that "neighbor and friend shall perish" (v. 21) pertains to a specific situation, it seems preferable to understand the declaration of rejection as being situational, too.

According to a quite plausible understanding of Jer 6:20, this oracle states that all the efforts made by the addressees in order to appease YHWH have been futile.[21] Even the most precious offerings are said to be of no avail. However, this is not due to a divine dislike for sacrificial gifts. It is because the reciprocal relationship between YHWH and the people of Judah has collapsed. I suggest that the main message of 6:20 can be paraphrased as follows: It does not matter *what* you offer, as long as it comes from *you*.[22] For postexilic readers, it was probably evident that this declaration of rejected sacrifice referred to the conditions prevailing *before* the destruction of the temple in 586 BCE. But they might of course serve as a warning to later generations, as well.

The example of Jer 6:20 shows that prophetic rejection of sacrifice tended to be tied to a specific situation, and therefore did not imply a

---

19. Similarly Carroll, *Jeremiah*, 201, and Lundbom, *Jeremiah 1–20*, 438.

20. The emphatic use of the 1st per. sing. pron. (לִי, twice) is balanced by the use of the pron. suf. for the 2nd per. pl. (כֶם-, also twice). As suggested by Schmidt, *Buch Jeremia*, 168, the expression "your sacrifices" may have a distancing effect. However, the use of such rhetoric seems to presuppose the notion of an intimate relationship.

21. With Jack R. Lundbom, *Jeremiah: A Study in Ancient Hebrew Rhetoric*, 2nd ed. (Winona Lake, IN: Eisenbrauns, 1997), 440. See also McKane, *Introduction*, 151, and Schmidt, *Buch Jeremia*, 168. Georg Fischer, *Jeremia 1–25*, HThKAT (Freiburg im Breisgau: Herder, 2005), 275, has called attention to the contrast between, on the one hand, the people's apparent contempt for YHWH's will (v. 19), and, on the other hand, their ostentatious efforts to impress the deity by means of imported goods (v. 20).

22. Thus also Tiemeyer, "Priests," 260, who has made the following apt comment: "Jer 6:20 does … not reject sacrifices *per se*, but only those of *that generation* owing to their disobedience. God's mind is made up and sacrifices, however exquisite, cannot alter his decision" (emphasis original).

general repudiation of all sacrificial cult. But is it possible, as indicated by the title of this paper, to interpret announcements of rejected sacrifices as actively supporting the notion of sacrifice as a vital means of communication with the deity? I think so. The next passage to be considered, Jer 14:11–12, is a case in point.

Jeremiah 14:11–12

> YHWH said to me: "Do not pray for the welfare of this people. When they fast, I am not going to listen to their cry, and when they offer burnt offering [עלה] and grain offering [מנחה], I am not going to accept them. Instead, I am going to destroy them by the sword, by famine, and by pestilence." (Jer 14:11–12)

The passage Jer 14:11–12 belongs to a unit consisting of Jer 14:10–16, which is sometimes ascribed to a Deuteronomistic redactor.[23] I find it likely that this passage was composed after 586 BCE.[24]

Like Jer 6:19–20, this oracle underlines that all efforts to prevent the disaster will be in vain.[25] Both animal sacrifices (עלה) and vegetal offerings (מנחה) are mentioned in verse 12a. However, the argument put forward in verses 11–12 does not focus solely on sacrifice. Fasting and prayer are mentioned as well. Obviously the point is not that such actions were seen as per definition inappropriate or ineffective. On the contrary, this text presupposes that the prophet/writer and the addressees agreed that, together with prophetic oracles, these three—praying, fasting, and bringing sacrifices—were the main legitimate forms of communication with YHWH. The astonishing message of the prophet is that none of this is going to help. Because of the people's sinfulness and disobedience (v. 10), YHWH is determined to destroy them (v. 12b). The severity of this extreme situation is underlined by the preceding announcement. Implying that such intervention might have been efficacious, because of Jeremiah's

---

23. Thus, e.g., McKane, *Introduction*, 326–28. See also Tiemeyer, "Priests," 259.

24. See Carroll, *Jeremiah*, 313: "the city had already fallen and therefore nothing could have worked. That factor allowed the traditionists great scope for developing their theological explanations."

25. In my opinion Carroll, *Jeremiah*, 313, has summarized the message conveyed by 14:11–12 aptly: "Whatever the people may do, whether fast ... or offer sacrifice, it is not acceptable."

righteousness, verse 11 informs the reader that YHWH had prohibited prophetic intercession (cf. Jer 7:16 and 11:14).[26]

According to my analysis, this text supports the sacrificial system. It explains how the disaster in 586 BCE could happen, and how the temple could be destroyed, without presenting YHWH as powerless—and without undermining the cultic institutions! To readers in the Second Temple era it describes an exceptional situation in the past. They are, I suggest, encouraged to sacrifice and to fast—but also to stay away from iniquity, in order to avoid a repetition. Only against the backdrop of such a basically positive stance toward sacrifice can we appreciate the rhetorical force of the next example, Jer 7:21.

Jeremiah 7:21

> Thus says YHWH of hosts, the god of Israel: "Heap your burnt offerings [עלותיכם] upon your sacrifices [זבחיכם], and eat meat!" (Jer 7:21)

The oracle preserved in Jer 7:21 belongs to a larger unit, consisting of verses 21–28.[27] However, redaction critical studies have shown that while verse 21 probably originated before 586 BCE, verses 22–28 most likely represent a somewhat later stage.[28] I find it likely that the original setting of 7:21 was similar to that of the so-called temple sermon in Jer 7:1–15*.[29]

The provocative recommendation uttered in 7:21, "Heap your burnt offerings upon your sacrifices, and eat meat!," has been characterized as

---

26. See also Jer 15:1; see further the excursus in Schmidt, *Buch Jeremia*, 265–67.

27. Holladay, *Jeremiah 1*, 259, and Lundbom, *Jeremiah 1–20*, 479–80.

28. Schmidt, *Buch Jeremia*, 183–86, and Thiel, *Deuteronomistische Redaktion*, 121–28.

29. With Armin Lange, "Gebotsobservanz statt Opferkult: Zur Kultpolemik in Jer 7,1–8,3," in *Gemeinde ohne Tempel: Zur Substituierung und Transformation des Jerusalemer Tempels und seines Kults im Alten Testament, antiken Judentum und frühen Christentum*, ed. Beate Ego, Armin Lange, and Peter Pilhofer, WUNT 118 (Tübingen: Mohr Siebeck, 1999), 24–27. See also Schmidt, *Buch Jeremia*, 185. Interpretation is, of course, always contingent on contextualization. Reading Jer 7:21 in the light of 7:16–20 (a passage which I do not regard as relevant, since it appears to be later than vv. 1–15* and v. 21, and addresses quite different issues), Hans Barstad, *The Religious Polemics of Amos: Studies in the Preaching of Am 2, 7B-8 ; 4,1-13 ; 5,1-27 ; 6, 4-7 ; 8, 14*, VTSup 34 (Leiden: Brill, 1984), 116, maintains that "Jeremiah's dissatisfaction with the cult is caused by its 'pagan' or syncretistic usages."

a "parody of priestly torah."[30] The reader is arguably prompted to take it as an instance of irony, since heeding such a command would amount to sacrilege.[31] The two main types of animal sacrifice are mentioned in this utterance: עלה ("burnt offering") and זבח ("sacrifice"). As is well known, the most significant difference between them is that in the עלה no part of the meat was eaten by the human participants (instead exactly everything was burnt on the altar, and transmitted to the deity), whereas the זבח sacrifice would always involve a communal meal. Against this background, it is indeed striking that Jer 7:21 appears to say that the addressees need not make any distinction at all between these two types of offering: they can eat the deity's meat as well![32]

I suggest that this remarkable (and, most likely, ironical) piece of advice should be read in the light of the "temple sermon" in Jer 7:1–15.[33] As indicated by 7:1–7, the Jerusalem temple was supposed to serve as the dwelling of YHWH. But because of the people's transgressions, we are told in 7:8–15, this sanctuary is now destined for destruction. YHWH is about to withdraw from his dwelling. In such a situation, the oracle in 7:21 declares that cultic regulations do not matter anymore. This implies that the cult has ceased to be efficacious.[34] However, it would be erroneous to

---

30. Cited from Holladay, *Jeremiah 1*, 259, who adds that Jer 7:21 can also be read as "a parody of Deut 12:6–7, 15, 20, 27." Similarly Schmidt, *Buch Jeremia*, 184.

31. See Carroll, *Jeremiah*, 214, and Fischer, *Jeremia 1–25*, 309. According to Lundbom, *Jeremiah 1–20*, 481, the prophet/author uses the rhetorical figure of *epitrope*, which Lundbom then explains as follows: "Jeremiah thinks sacrifices really ought to cease, yet he urges people to continue making them."

32. Tiemeyer, "Priests," 261, speaks of "fine distinctions," but this is probably to underestimate the provocative aspect of Jer 7:21. Thiel, *Deuteronomistische Redaktion*, 122, suggests that YHWH is being generous, as he gives up his share of the meal and offers it to the human participants ("Jahwe verzichtet auf seinen Anteil am Opfer, stellt ihn den Opferteilnehmern zum Mahl zur Verfügung"). In my opinion, however, such an interpretation of Jer 7:21 misses the mark. It would be more to the point to say that YHWH here deprives the people of all cultic means to attain divine favor; see Peter C. Craigie, Page H. Kelley and Joel F. Drinkard, Jr., *Jeremiah 1–25*, WBC 26 (Waco, TX: Word, 1991), 124: "both meats were to be eaten; the implication is that both were rejected by God, to whom ostensibly they were offered, and thus they might as well be eaten by the foolish humans offering them."

33. For further arguments, see Lange, "Gebotsobservanz," 24 –27.

34. According to Carroll, *Jeremiah*, 216, v. 21 is "not a command to do something illicit, such as eating the holy flesh, but an indication that sacrifice is now no more than a domestic meal."

deduce that the prophet/editor meant to say that the temple cult was a mistake from its very beginning. The point is rather that in the prevailing situation, sacrifices cannot prevent the imminent catastrophe. Therefore the cult has lost its raison d'être. In its absurdity, this oracle addresses an absurd situation. It is too late. So why bother about a strict ritual performance?

For the editors of the book of Jeremiah, however, and for the first readers of the book, this absurd situation belonged to the past. Therefore, they would probably see the oracle in 7:21 as compatible with prophecies endorsing the renewed sacrificial cult in the rebuilt temple (such as Jer 17:26; 33:10–11, 18; see below).

Relativizing Sacrifice: Worship in the Situation of Exile and Diaspora

Jeremiah 7:22–23

> For I did not speak to your fathers, nor did I command them concerning burnt offering and sacrifice, when I brought them out of the land of Egypt, but I gave them this command: Obey my voice, and I will be your God and you will be my people; walk in all the ways I command you, so that it may be well with you. (Jer 7:22–23)

The argumentation which is developed in 7:22–23 (as part of 7:21–28) can be understood as a theological reflection inspired by verse 21, which reinterprets this ironic utterance (see above) in a Deuteronomistic vein.[35]

In verse 22 we find the rather startling statement that YHWH did not give any commands concerning עלה (burnt offerings) or זבח (sacrifices of the communion type) to the exodus generation. It has sometimes been asserted that this passage depicts the ancestors' time in the wilderness as a period without sacrificial worship.[36] But that is hardly correct. On a closer examination, the point made is that this was a period without

---

35. Thiel, *Deuteronomistische Redaktion*, 121–28. See also Carroll, *Jeremiah*, 215, and Schmidt, *Buch Jeremia*, 183–86. Besides the general theological tendency of vv. 22–28, the main argument for this position consists in the observation that this passage is replete with motifs, formulations, and phrases that smack of Deuteronomy and Deuteronomistic literature.

36. So, e.g., Hans W. Wolff, *Joel and Amos: A Commentary on the Books of the Prophets Joel and Amos*, trans. W. Janzen, S. D. McBride Jr., and C. A. Muenchow, Hermeneia (Philadelphia: Fortress, 1977), 264. Thus also, more recently, John Barton,

any *regulations* concerning animal sacrifice.[37] In other words, the exodus generation had no *obligation* to bring offerings to YHWH. As pointed out by Moshe Weinfeld and other scholars, Jer 7:22 can in fact be reconciled with some Pentateuch traditions, although it seems to be at odds with the Priestly account.[38] According to Deuteronomy, the divine decrees given on Mount Horeb (= Sinai) consisted only of the Decalogue. Therefore, it was possible to maintain that cultic observance was of *secondary* importance and subordinated to the demand in verse 23: "Obey my voice, and I will be your God, and you will be my people; and walk in all the ways I command you, so that it may be well with you." However, this does not mean that cultic observance is seen as *unimportant*. In my opinion, therefore, Walter Brueggemann goes too far in his interpretation of Jer 7:22-23, as he contends that "it is asserted that the God of Israel has never been interested in sacrificial liturgy."[39] I also disagree with Fretheim, who claims that these two verses "set up a contrast between the offering of sacrifices and walking in God's commandments."[40]

"The Prophets and the Cult," in *Temple and Worship in Biblical Israel*, ed. John Day, LHBOTS 422 (London: T&T Clark, 2005), 120.

37. This has, of course, been pointed out by other scholars. See, e.g., Fischer, *Jeremia 1-25*, 309-10, and Schmidt, *Buch Jeremia*, 185. In my opinion, though, Helen Schüngel-Straumann, *Gottesbild und Kultkritik vorexilischer Propheten*, SBS 60 (Stuttgart: Katholisches Bibelwerk, 1972), 42-43, overstates this point when she concludes that, according to Jer 7:22, all regulations concerning sacrifice are purely human inventions. In that case, this prophetic utterance would be in conflict not only with P, but also with the traditions recounted in Deuteronomy and the Deuteronomistic literature.

38. Moshe Weinfeld, "Jeremiah and the Spiritual Metamorphosis of Israel," *ZAW* 88 (1976): 53-54. See also Carroll, *Jeremiah*, 215-16, Lange, "Gottesobservanz," 28, Lundbom, *Jeremiah 1-20*, 481-82, and Ina Willi-Plein, *Opfer und Kult im alttestamentlichen Israel: Textbefragungen und Zwischenergebnisse*, SBS 153 (Stuttgart: Katholisches Bibelwerk, 1993), 146. An attempt to reconcile Jer 7:22 also with the Priestly account has been made by Jacob Milgrom, "Concerning Jeremiah's Repudiation of Sacrifice," *ZAW* 89 (1977): 273-75. See also Jacob Milgrom, *Leviticus 1-16: A New Translation with Introduction and Commentary*, AB 3 (New York: Doubleday, 1991), 482-85. For a pointed critique of Milgrom's harmonizing attempt, which assumes that Jer 7:22 (as well as 7:21) is merely concerned with a certain combination of sacrifices, see Eidevall, *Sacrificial Rhetoric*, 151-53. See also Jonathan Klawans, *Purity, Sacrifice, and the Temple: Symbolism and Supersessionism in the Study of Ancient Judaism* (Oxford: Oxford University Press, 2006), 81-82.

39. Brueggemann, *To Pluck up*, 79.

40. Fretheim, *Jeremiah*, 139.

As pointed out by several other scholars, the message in Jer 7:22–23 is primarily about priorities. Obedience, it is asserted, is *more* important than sacrifices, but the latter are not rejected.[41] However, the depiction of the nation's past as a time without cultic regulations and obligations (at least concerning the main types of sacrifice) certainly implies that it would be possible to worship YHWH also without sacrifices. We may thus speak of a tendency to relativize the role of sacrifices. How can such a tendency be explained?

If this text was composed during the period of the Babylonian exile or later, it can be regarded as an attempt to solve a problem that must have been of vital importance for worshipers of YHWH wishing to continue to interact with this deity in a situation where they had no access to a functioning and legitimate cult. During the exile, the problem could have been formulated as follows: How can we maintain contact with YHWH when the temple in Jerusalem has been destroyed?[42] After the exile, the question would rather have been: Is it possible to perform legitimate worship of YHWH in the diaspora? The answer given by Jer 7:22–23 is informed by Deuteronomistic theology. I suggest that the following paraphrase captures the main thrust: "You can remain the people of YHWH, also without access to sacrificial cult, as long as you obey the primary commandments." In practice, as suggested by Thiel, this passage would seem to advocate a torah-centered worship, perfectly adapted to the reality of diaspora communities.[43]

---

41. Tiemeyer, "Priests," 261, expresses this well: "Rather, the central message of Jer 7:21–23 concerns having one's *priorities* right: obedience to God first and sacrifices second" (emphasis original); similarly Weinfeld, "Jeremiah and the Spiritual," 52–55. In his commentary on Jer 7:22–23, Lundbom, *Jeremiah 1–20*, 482, refers to the stylistic feature called *distributio*, "where a first statement is negated, *only* to emphasize a second statement that matters more" (emphasis original).

42. It is likely that sacrificial worship continued in Judah during the exile (see Jer 41:5), and one cannot exclude the possibility that one or more cultic sites dedicated to YHWH existed in Babylonia; see Eidevall, *Sacrificial Rhetoric*, 145–46. However, the problem would still remain for those (probably including the writer responsible for Jer 7:22–28) who adhered to the principle of cultic centralization laid down in Deut 12 (which was allegedly enforced and implemented by King Josiah)

43. See Thiel, *Deuteronomistische Redaktion*, 127, who thinks that this passage advocates some kind of "Wortgottesdienst." However, such an interpretation does not necessarily entail that that the author was opposed to sacrificial cult in a rebuilt temple in Jerusalem. The following comment by Barstad, *Religious Polemics*, 116, would

If the passage Jer 7:22–28 can be called diaspora-oriented, the passages from the book of Jeremiah that I am going to discuss in the concluding section of this paper display a decidedly Jerusalem-centered perspective. Rather than relativizing the sacrificial cult, they affirm its centrality. Since the message of these prophecies is straightforward—there are no great scholarly controversies regarding their interpretation—I will treat them quite briefly.

Prophecies Promoting the Sacrificial Cult

Jeremiah 17:26

> They will come from the towns of Judah and from the surroundings of Jerusalem, from the land of Benjamin and the lowland, from the hill country and the Negev, bringing burnt offering [עולה], sacrifice [זבח], grain offering [מנחה], and incense [לבונה], bringing thank offering [תודה] to the house of YHWH. (Jer 17:26)

The sermon comprising Jer 17:19–27 was probably written in the post-monarchic period, perhaps during the time of Nehemiah.[44] It purports to provide a key to the history of Judah. Above all, it explains what happened in 586 BCE. In addition, it opens up a hopeful perspective for future generations (that is, for the addressees).

According to the author, the secret lies in keeping the Sabbath: no burdens should be carried through the city gates on that day. Previous generations had failed to realize this (vv. 22–23). However, a strict Sabbath observance would seem to guarantee a state of never-ending prosperity (vv. 24–26). Three aspects of this glorious future are mentioned: Davidic rulership, perennial inhabitation, and a flourishing cult (v. 26).

In Jer 17:19–27, the sacrificial cult is not seen as a burden. On the contrary, it looks like a reward. In verse 26 it seems to be taken for granted

---

therefore seem to be an overstatement: "The conclusion we have to draw from this passage in Jeremiah is that the cultic sacrifices seem to be without any religious value."

44. Thus e.g., Bright, *Jeremiah*, 120, Holladay, *Jeremiah 1*, 509, and Schmidt, *Buch Jeremia*, 308. Cf. also McKane, *Introduction*, 416–19. As observed by Carroll, *Jeremiah*, 367, the style of this passage is "typically Deuteronomistic." Tiemeyer, "Priests," 263, notes that "the focus on sacrifices would fit the concerns of the Jerusalem community of the rebuilt temple." According to Fischer, *Jeremia 1–25*, the whole book of Jeremiah should be regarded as a postexilic product.

that, in the ideal future, all the sacrifices brought from various corners of Judah will be accepted by YHWH.[45] Jerusalem's fate is here contingent on Sabbath observance, rather than on sacrifices.[46] Nevertheless, this text clearly promotes the cult performed in the rebuilt Jerusalem temple.

Jeremiah 33:10–11

> Thus says YHWH: In this place, of which you are saying "It is desolate without humans and animals," in the towns of Judah and the streets of Jerusalem that are deserted without inhabitants, neither humans nor animals, (there) will be heard once more: the voice of joy and the voice of gladness, the voice of the bridegroom and the voice of the bride, the voice of those who say "Give thanks to YHWH, for YHWH is good, for his kindness (lasts) forever," while they are bringing thank offering(s) [תודה] to the house of YHWH. Yes, I will restore the fortunes of the lands as it was before, says YHWH. (Jer 33:10–11)

The passage Jer 33:1–13 can be categorized as a prophecy of salvation. It is probably of postexilic origin.[47] In verse 10 the land is described as desolate and uninhabited, presumably due to extensive deportations (this is one of the texts that have given rise to the myth of the empty land).[48] But all this, the reader is told, is about to change. According to verse 11, the streets of the deserted cities will once again be filled by people. In a reversal of the previous reversal, happiness will return to the land (cf. Jer 7:34; 16:9; 25:10).[49] In the near future there are going to be wedding parties again, as well as cultic feasts. On the latter occasions, the songs of praise will be accompanied by thank offerings (תודה).[50] In this passage

---

45. See Fischer, *Jeremia 1–25*, 568, and Tiemeyer, "Priests," 263.

46. Apparently, this text is based upon the idea that Sabbath observance provides a more constant and reliable basis for the relationship between YHWH and the people than the sacrificial cult. Whereas temples may be demolished, the Sabbath recurs regularly every week.

47. With, e.g., Carroll, *Jeremiah*, 634.

48. See further Hans Barstad, *The Myth of the Empty Land: A Study in the History and Archaeology of Judah during the "Exilic" Period* (Oslo: Scandinavian University Press, 1996).

49. See William Holladay, *Jeremiah: 2: A Commentary on the Book of the Prophet Jeremiah, Chapters 26–52*, Hermeneia (Minneapolis: Fortress, 1989), 224.

50. According to all dictionaries, the lexeme תודה (*tôdâ*) can denote both "thanksgiving" and "thank offering." In accordance with this, William McKane, *Jer-*

the primary function of sacrifice is to express gratitude. At the same time, the restoration of the cult (in the Second Temple era) is seen as a joyous event in itself.[51]

Jeremiah 33:18

> The Levitical priests will never lack someone (standing) before me, offering burnt offerings [עולה], burning grain offerings [מנחה], and preparing sacrifices [זבח], every day. (Jer 33:18)

Jeremiah 33:14–26 is evidently of very late postexilic provenience. This is indicated by style and content, as well as by the fact that the entire prophecy is missing in the LXX version.[52] Its topic is the restoration of vital political and cultic institutions. According to this text, there will always be Levitical priests in the temple, taking care of the daily offerings, including burnt offerings, grain offerings, and זבח sacrifices (v. 18). The prospect of uninterrupted cultic service is proclaimed as good news. A functioning sacrificial cult is thus seen as an integral part of the utopia. Notably, there is no hint in this text of the possibility that sacrifices might be rejected.

It would of course be preposterous to maintain that the utterance in Jer 33:18 shares the theological outlook of Jer 6:20 (see above). Still, these utterances do not contradict each other, since they refer to different historical situations. According to the editors of this prophetic book, the sacrificial cult of the First Temple era was doomed (6:20; see also 7:21; 14:11–12). By contrast, great expectations were attached to the cult of the Second Temple era (33:18; see also 17:26; 33:11).

---

emiah XXVI-LII, vol. 2 of *A Critical and Exegetical Commentary on Jeremiah*, ICC (Edinburgh: T&T Clark, 1996), 859, treats תודה in Jer 33:11 as ambiguous: "a reference to hymnic praise in a cultic context and probably to the bringing of thank-offerings to the temple." However, in Jer 33:11 it is almost certain that this word refers to sacrifices. Otherwise this statement would become strangely tautological. Moreover, whereas verbal praise is regularly *uttered* in the temple, one would not expect a formulation to the effect that praise is brought to the temple.

51. Jack R. Lundbom, *Jeremiah 21–36: A New Translation with Introduction and Commentary*, AB 21B (New York: Doubleday, 2004), 535.

52. Thus e.g., Carroll, *Jeremiah*, 638, and Holladay, *Jeremiah 2*, 229–30. Tiemeyer, "Priests," 254, has cited additional arguments in favor of a late postexilic date, pointing out that several visions with similar content are found in Jewish texts from the Hellenistic era.

Conclusion

In this essay I have shown that it is possible to find a certain degree of coherence in the admittedly diverging statements on sacrifices that have been juxtaposed in the book of Jeremiah. The key lies in recognizing the importance of a certain chronological dividing line drawn by the editors. For them, there was a fundamental difference between the preexilic and the postexilic situation. Whereas the cult of the past (that is, in Solomon's temple), with special emphasis on the last decades of the monarchy, is vehemently denounced, the attitude toward the future cult (in the Second Temple era) is consistently positive. However, in some passages, such as Jer 7:22–23, the significance of the sacrificial cult appears to be relativized and downplayed. This can be explained as an adaptation to the realities experienced by some of the book's addressees, namely those who belonged to communities in the diaspora.

"What to Me Is the Multitude of Your Sacrifices?" Exploring the Critique of Sacrificial Cult and the Metaphors for YHWH in the Prophetic Lawsuit (Micah 6:1–8 and Isaiah 1:1–20)

Ma. Maricel S. Ibita

Introduction

The courtroom drama, which the prophets employ to highlight problems in YHWH-Israel relations, contains YHWH's charges of covenant violation evidenced by social injustice, indictment and threats, and critique of sacrifices. This synchronic investigation on the prophetic critique of the cult focuses on metaphors for YHWH in the ריב or "prophetic lawsuit," namely, as suzerain king in Mic 6:1–8 and as father in Isa 1:1–20. From this perspective, I suggest that the core issue relates to YHWH's and Israel's identity. To demonstrate this proposition, I will explore YHWH's apparent negation of Israel's sacrifice in these texts by first providing a brief overview of the metaphors for YHWH as father and as king from the perspective of blending theory. Then I will investigate the different characteristics of YHWH as king and father and the probable biblical ideals behind them. Finally, this preliminary information will be used in discerning the dynamics between the covenant partners and how the critique on sacrifice in these so-called prophetic lawsuit texts is centered on YHWH's and Israel's identities.

Blending Theory and Metaphors for YHWH as King and Father

George Lakoff and Mark Johnson explain that "metaphor is one of our most important tools for trying to comprehend partially what cannot be comprehended totally: our feelings, aesthetic experiences, moral practices, and spiritual awareness."[1] It is, therefore, no wonder that in the Old Testament, the intelligibility and persuasiveness of the prophetic message is couched in the "language of proverbial wisdom, courtroom process, religious expression, popular songs, or any other well-known traditional expressions."[2]

From the viewpoint of cognitive linguistics, the use of metaphor is not only ornamental but conceptual, that is, "metaphor is a matter of thinking," or of understanding one conceptual domain (the target) in terms of another (the source).[3] *Conceptual domain* refers to any coherent organization of experience. *Source domain* is the conceptual domain that provides the structure for the metaphor and whereby we understand another more unknown domain of the metaphor, for example, "king" or "father." *Target domain* is the conceptual domain that is being examined and is understood by the more concrete, known domain, for example, "YHWH." In other words, metaphor in cognitive linguistics is employed not just in speaking rhetorically but also in thinking through and reasoning about something.[4] It is structured as TARGET IS SOURCE, or in this investigation, YHWH IS KING and YHWH is FATHER.[5]

Blending theory, a further development in cognitive linguistics' understanding of metaphor, proposes that there are at least four mental spaces involved in a metaphor. *Mental spaces* or *input spaces* are "small conceptual packets constructed as we think and talk, for purposes of local understanding and action."[6] Figure 1 shows the blend with the initial first and second mental spaces corresponding to the aforementioned source and

---

1. George Lakoff and Mark Johnson, *Metaphors We Live By* (Chicago: University of Chicago Press, 2003), 188.

2. Gene M. Tucker, "Prophetic Speech," *Int* 32 (1978): 35.

3. Lakoff and Johnson, *Metaphors We Live By*, 5. See also George Lakoff, "The Contemporary Theory of Metaphor," in *Metaphor and Thought*, ed. Andrew Ortony, 2nd ed. (New York: Cambridge University Press, 1993), 202–51; Mary Therese DesCamp and Eve E. Sweetser, "Metaphors for God: Why and How Do Our Choices Matter for Humans? The Application of Contemporary Cognitive Linguistics Research to the Debate on God and Metaphor," *PastPsy* 53 (2005): 215.

4. Lakoff, "Contemporary Theory," 208–9.

5. Ibid., 207; DesCamp and Sweetser, "Metaphors for God," 216 n.18. In this investigation, I will follow the usual notation and naming devices for metaphorical mapping across conceptual domains by using small caps to highlight the metaphorical concept.

6. Gilles Fauconnier and Mark Turner, "Conceptual Integration Networks," *CogSci* 22 (1998): 137.

target domains.[7] These input spaces yield a *generic space* that maps onto each of the input spaces and include what are common, yet nonspecific, between them. For example, it generates that "YHWH" and "king" or "father" are "agents with characteristics." The fourth and most innovative part of the theory is the *blended space*, which includes the generic structure captured in the generic space yet incorporates more specific structure. What is thus developed in the blended space is an emergent structure not present in the two input spaces but has much more elaborate and concrete properties than the generic space as I will show below.[8]

In Mary Therese Des-Camp and Eve Sweetser's application of blending theory on the metaphors for God in the Bible, they analyzed "44 metaphors in the Hebrew scriptures and 50 from the Christian scriptures."[9] They present an initial blend of GOD IS POTTER followed by a number of charts showing the *source domain input* and the resulting *blend* since the uniform *target domain* in every metaphor is mostly God as agent and Israel as object.[10] Their other sample blends from the Hebrew Scriptures are GOD IS KING (Ps 5:1), GOD IS ROCK (Deut 32:4), GOD IS BEAR (Hos 13:8; Lam 3), GOD IS WOMAN (Isa 49:15), and GOD IS FATHER (Deut 32:6).

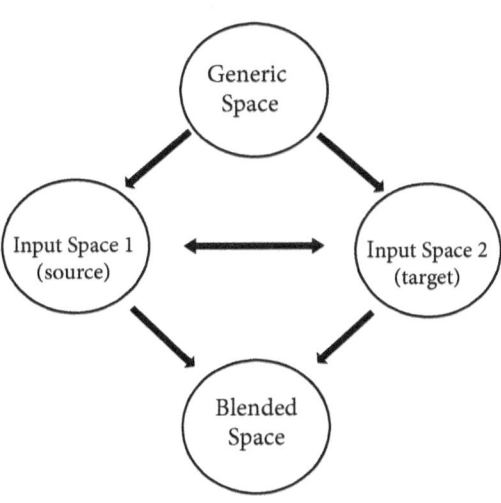

Figure 1: Basic Blend

---

7. See ibid., 137–43; DesCamp and Sweetser, "Metaphors for God," 218–19.

8. For the visual representation, see Fauconnier and Turner, "Conceptual Integration Networks"; and Bonnie Howe, *Because You Bear This Name: Conceptual Metaphor and the Moral Meaning of 1 Peter*, BibInt 81 (Leiden: Brill, 2006), 86.

9. DesCamp and Sweetser, "Metaphors for God," 226. As DesCamp and Sweetser did not specify what "Hebrew scriptures" and "Christian scriptures" comprise exactly, I presume that they mean the Hebrew Bible when they speak of "Hebrew scriptures" and the New Testament canon when they refer to "Christian scriptures." I will also use these distinctions for the rest of the essay.

10. Ibid., 226–29.

DesCamp and Sweetser also compile the characteristics often invoked in these forty-four metaphors and reexamine the metaphors to see which of them incorporate most of the traits. The most frequently used and the "most important characteristics of God in the eyes of the Hebrew scripture writers" include the following: the ability to protect and nurture, the ability to maintain mutual asymmetric relationship, the ability to exert physical control over an entity, the ability to change the state or essence of an entity, the capacity of authority and power, and the capacity to destroy.[11]

Of the metaphors that exhibit these traits, GOD IS KING and GOD IS FATHER dominate all the characteristics. The reason could be because parent-child relationship is one of the strongest and earliest experiences of nurturance by humans.[12] The same holds true for the ancient Israelites' experience of having a king who generally has power of life and death over his subjects.[13] Thus, on the level of the basic unit of society, "father" may be a representative figure for God while on the societal level it is "king."[14] These two popular images are what we encounter in the texts of Mic 6:1–8 and Isa 1:2–20.[15] Given the most common characteristics of God as king and father in these texts, the blends of YHWH IS KING (Mic 6:1–8) and YHWH IS FATHER (Isa 1:2–20) metaphors may be presented as in the figures on the following page.

These metaphors for YHWH as king and father are related to the basic royal metaphor THE COSMOS IS A STATE.[16] In this metaphor, Job Y. Jindo explains, the source domain of human polity is mapped onto the target

---

11. Ibid., 229.
12. Ibid., 234. For a contrasting opinion on the preponderance of this metaphor in the Hebrew Scriptures, see Annette M. Böckler, "Unser Vater," in *Metaphor in the Hebrew Bible*, ed. Pierre Van Hecke, BETL 187 (Leuven: University Press/ Peeters, 2005), 249–61.
13. DesCamp and Sweetser, "Metaphors for God," 234. On the metaphorical understanding of this concept, see Marc Zvi Brettler, *God Is King: Understanding an Israelite Metaphor*, JSOTSup 76 (Sheffield: JSOT Press, 1989); Anne Moore, *Moving beyond Symbol and Myth: Understanding the Kingship of God of the Hebrew Bible through Metaphor*, StBibLit 99 (New York: Lang, 2009).
14. DesCamp and Sweetser, "Metaphors for God," 229.
15. Unless otherwise stated, the English translation used in this contribution comes from the NRSV.
16. Job Y. Jindo, *Biblical Metaphor Reconsidered: A Cognitive Approach to Poetic Prophecy in Jeremiah 1–24*, HSM 64 (Winona Lake, IN: Eisenbrauns, 2010), 77, 81, 95–99.

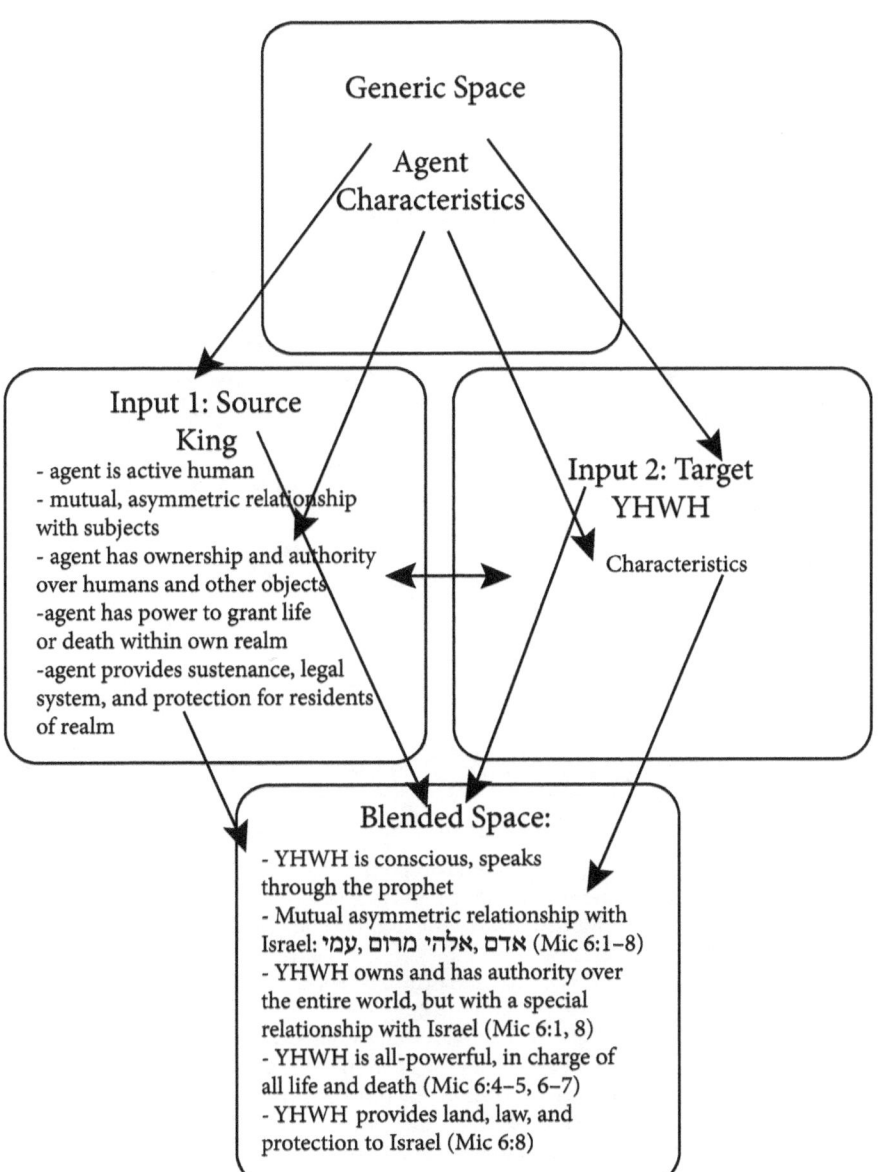

Figure 2: YHWH IS KING Metaphor in Micah 6:1–8

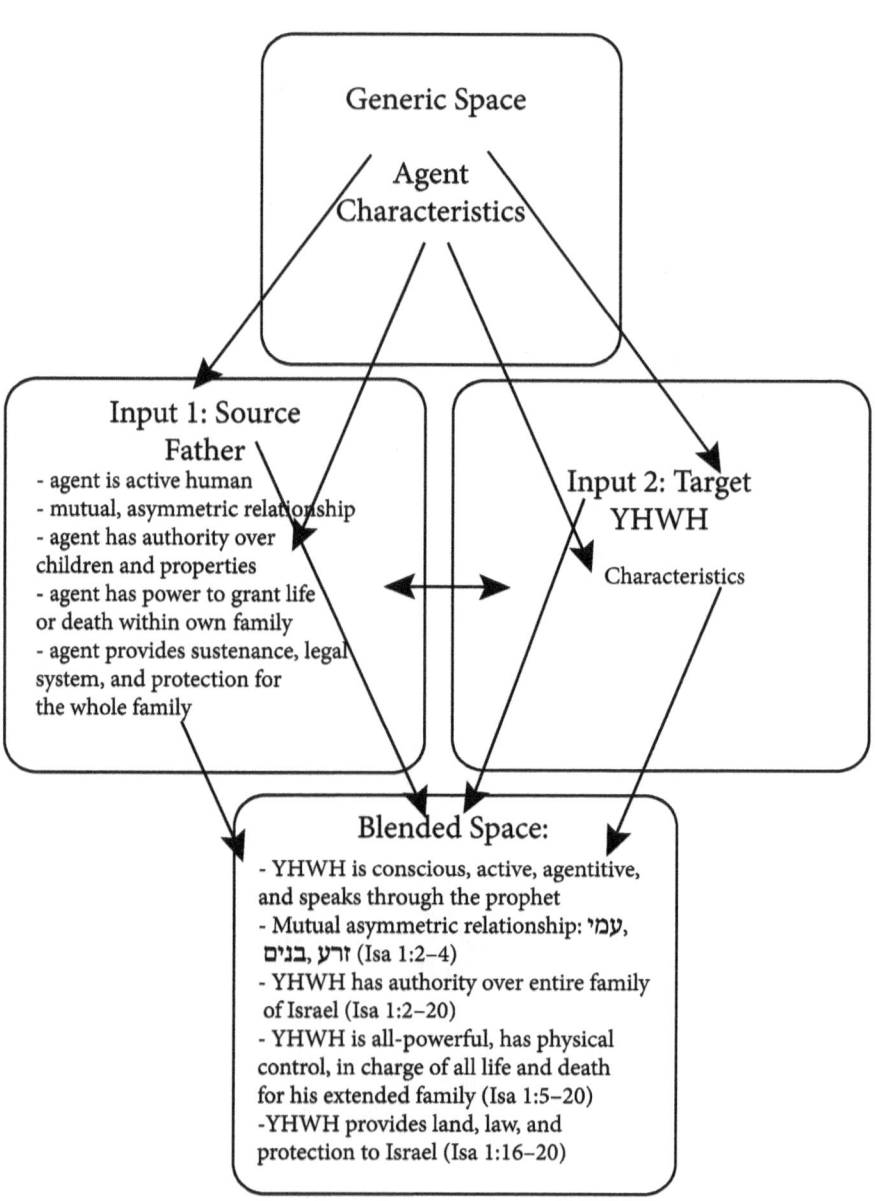

Figure 3: YHWH IS KING Metaphor in Isaiah 1:2–20

domain of the cosmos, which gives rise to the specific metaphors THE PROMISED LAND IS YHWH'S ESTATE and THE HOUSEHOLD IS A FATHER'S DOMAIN.[17] In this organization, the focus is spatial. When one parallels this blending operation with the role or function of the divine, the complementary metaphors YHWH IS KING and YHWH IS FATHER emerge. This royal metaphor concept fits the wide range of God's characteristics according to DesCamp and Sweetser into what Jindo calls a "destruction model." He explains that "in the ancient Near East (including Israel), catastrophic events in the terrestrial world were perceived as emanating from the celestial sphere," especially from the divine assembly which "was the highest authority in the universe."[18] He affirms the long observed concern of the divine assembly in the ancient Near East and in the Hebrew Scriptures for the preservation of cosmic harmony. Repeated and intolerable disruption of this harmony leads the divine assembly "to operate as a judicial organ in order to consider, and counter, such disruption."[19] As a metaphor can also be perceived by considering its *frame* (e.g., "school") or its constituent elements (e.g., teacher, students, classroom, etc.) of which consist its *script* or the diachronic conception of an event (e.g., going to school, having classes, taking examinations, etc.), Jindo identifies four scenes in the script of cosmic order and several actors composing the frame.[20] First, the case is brought before the members of the assembly who carefully consider it and find enough reason to decree that the defendant is culpable (*the judicial decision or lawsuit*). Next, the members send a destructive agent who causes the devastation of the defendant and those who live in his/her land (*destruction*). This is followed by someone tasked to mourn for the destruction of the city or the land (*lamentation/aftermath*). Finally, Jindo argues that other compositions end with a positive scene or a promise of *restoration*. As a whole, the frame is thus made up of the "plaintiff," the "judge," the "defendant," the "intercessor" or "advocate," and the "executioner." In addition, the figure of the "lamenter" is vital because many of

---

17. See ibid., 77–83.
18. Ibid., 75, 76. See also Thorkild Jacobsen, "Mesopotamia," in *The Intellectual Adventure of Ancient Man: An Essay on Speculative Thought in the Ancient Near East*, ed. Henri Frankfort et al. (Chicago: University of Chicago Press, 1946), 136.
19. Jindo, *Biblical Metaphor*, 78.
20. See ibid., 50–51, 78–79. On frame and script, see Friedrich Ungerer and Hans-Jörg Schmid, *An Introduction to Cognitive Linguistics*, 2nd ed., Learning about Language (Harlow: Longman, 2006), 207–56.

these materials depict a lament scene.²¹ Jindo, however, cautions that while all these actors and scenes are important in the development of the drama on the conceptual level, the various perspectives from where the biblical authors want to project it make a difference in presenting the events and actors in the different texts.²² I will demonstrate this point in our comparison and contrast of the texts of Mic 6:1–8 and Isa 1:1–20, which conceptualize YHWH as king and father, respectively. Both texts deal with the violation of cosmic order through the broken covenant as seen in the literary contexts of Mic 6 and Isa 1 where YHWH as king and father demands rectification. In these texts, Jindo's destruction model complements the investigations of DesCamp and Sweetser on the most important characteristics of YHWH. Examination of the social background discernible in the texts further clarifies this interplay.

Social Background for the Most Important Traits of God in the Hebrew Scriptures

As Jindo explains, violation of cosmic order merits action from the gods, which can take the form of judicial action. Within the framework of legal relations between YHWH and Israel (suzerain–vassal, husband–wife, father–children), the ריב or prophetic lawsuit settles the violation of the covenant between them along with its punishment or its repair.²³ The ריב also contains critique of worship and sacrifices (Mic 6:6–8; Isa 1:10–17; Ps 50).²⁴ These prophetic criticisms function as a divine "no" to these practices.²⁵ Since rituals communicate social significance (the worldview of a particular group) and a social function (the group's moral system), probable social values palpable in these texts critical of worship deserve some

---

21. Jindo, *Biblical Metaphor*, 78–79.
22. Ibid., 79.
23. For an overview of the ריב and its *Sitz im Leben*, see Kirsten Nielsen, *Yahweh as Prosecutor and Judge: An Investigation of the Prophetic Lawsuit (Rîb-Pattern)*, JSOTSup 9 (Sheffield: JSOT Press, 1978); Alan S. Bandy, *The Prophetic Lawsuit in the Book of Revelation*, NTM 29 (Sheffield: Sheffield Phoenix, 2010), 24–58.
24. Frank H. Gorman, "Sacrifices and Offerings," *NIDB* 5:29. See 1 Sam 15:22–23; 29:13–14; Jer 6:16–21; 7:21–26; Hos 6:6; Amos 5:21–24; Ps 40:6.
25. See Bryan D. Bibb, "The Prophetic Critique of Ritual in Old Testament Theology," in *The Priests in the Prophets: The Portrayal of Priests, Prophets and Other Religious Specialists in the Latter Prophets*, ed. Lester L. Grabbe and Alice Ogden Bellis, JSOTSup 408 (London: T&T Clark, 2004), 33.

attention.²⁶ The most important traits of God in the Hebrew Scriptures, as seen in the metaphors GOD IS KING and GOD IS FATHER, can be classified in three groups: protection and nurturance as the aim, authority as the source of power, and mutual asymmetric relationship, physical control, change of state or essence, and power to punish or destroy as its manifestations. These traits may also be understood within the context of the social values of dyadism, patronage, and honor and shame.

Dyadism, Patronage, Honor and Shame in Micah 6:1–8 and Isaiah 1:1–20

Characters in the Bible are sometimes presented as persons embedded in their community where they find life's meaning in their family, neighbors, friends, and acquaintances.²⁷ Their self-identity was primarily corporate rather than individualistic as exemplified by "Isaiah son of Amos" or "Micah of Moresheth."²⁸ This identification in relation to someone or something is called *dyadism*.²⁹ This concept determines people's understanding of their identity, roles and status in society, their duties and rights, and what is honorable and shameful societal behavior.³⁰ In a dyadic society, individual actions have consequences for the good or for ill of the group.³¹ Their survival and honor depend on how people conduct and behave according to the approved norms and rules of the society.

---

26. See David Janzen, *The Social Meanings of Sacrifice in the Hebrew Bible: A Study of Four Writings*, BZAW 344 (Berlin: de Gruyter, 2004), 4. Ronald Simkins explains that a "worldview encompasses the mental functioning that directs the human actions. It is the cognitive basis for human interaction with the social and physical environments.... It is a view of the world, a way of looking at reality.... A people's worldview shapes and is shaped by their social and physical environments." See Ronald Simkins, *Creator and Creation: Nature in the Worldview of Ancient Israel* (Peabody, MA: Hendrickson, 1994), 23–24.

27. See Alec Basson, "'Friends Becoming Foes': A Case of Social Rejection in Psalm 31," *VEccl* 27 (2006): 403.

28. See Sarah J. Dille, "Honor Restored: Honor, Shame and God as Redeeming Kinsman in Second Isaiah," in *Relating to the Text: Interdisciplinary and Form-Critical Insights on the Bible*, ed. Timothy J. Sandoval and Carleen Mandolfo, JSOTSup 384 (London: T&T Clark, 2003), 233–34.

29. See Jerome H. Neyrey, "Dyadism," in *Handbook of Biblical Social Values*, ed. John J. Pilch and Bruce J. Malina (Peabody, MA: Hendrickson, 2009), 53–56.

30. See Jerome H. Neyrey, "Group Orientation," in Pilch, *Handbook of Biblical Social Values*, 94–98.

31. Basson, "Friends Becoming Foes," 403.

The leaders are held responsible since they embody the whole people, but the whole community suffers punishment when leaders commit mistakes (Isa 1:2–8, 10; Mic 6:6–7).³² The three most important societal organizations—בית־אב ("house of the father/family"), משפחה ("clan"), and שבט ("tribe")—were all based on kinship structures.³³ Thus, kinship terminology "provided the only language for expressing legal, political, and religious institutions."³⁴ For example, the following kinship vocatives appear in Micah and Isaiah: "My people [עמי], what have I done to you?" (Mic 6:3); "but Israel does not know, my people [עמי] do not understand" (Isa 1:3); "Sons [בנים] I have reared and raised" (Isa 1:2); "evil offspring [זרע], corrupt sons [בנים]" (Isa 1:4).

Related with group orientation is the concept of fictive kinship between patron and client, which parallels that of father-children relation (Isa 1:2–3).³⁵ According to Bruce Malina, *patronage* is "a social, institutional arrangement by means of which economic, political, or religious institutional relationships are outfitted with an overarching quality of kinship or family feeling."³⁶ He explains:

> To survive in some meaningful way in such societies, patronage emerged to the mutual satisfaction of both: clients had their needs met, especially in fortuitous and irregular situations, while patrons receive grants of honor and the accolades of benefaction. Patrons were to treat clients as family members might, with both having special concern for each other's

---

32. K. C. Hanson, "When the King Crosses the Line: Royal Deviance and Restitution in Levantine Ideologies," *BTB* 26 (1996): 20.

33. See Basson, "Friends Becoming Foes," 404; Bruce J. Malina, "Mediterranean Sacrifice: Dimensions of Domestic and Political Religion," *BTB* 26 (1996): 28.

34. Frank Moore Cross, "Kinship and Covenant in Ancient Israel," in *From Epic to Canon: History and Literature in Ancient Israel* (Baltimore: Johns Hopkins University Press, 1998), 3.

35. See T. R. Hobbs, "Reflections on Honor, Shame, and Covenant Relations," *JBL* 116 (1997): 501–3; Bruce J. Malina, "Patronage," in Pilch, *Handbook of Biblical Social Values*, 151–55; John J. Pilch, "'Beat His Ribs While He Is Young' (Sir 30:12): A Window on the Mediterranean World," *BTB* 23 (1993): 101–13; Pilch, "Parenting," in Pilch, *Handbook of Biblical Social Values*, 145–48.

36. Malina, "Patronage," 151. For an overview on this topic, see Samuel N. Eisenstadt and Luis Roniger, *Patrons, Clients and Friends: Interpersonal Relations and the Structure of Trust in Society* (New York: Cambridge University Press, 1984).

welfare, even though separated sometimes by vast differences in status and power.[37]

Patron-client relationship becomes even more important in the context of limited goods—honor, protection, and material benefits, to name a few—as it covers the lowliest and loftiest of social relationships.[38] "Limited good," according to Jerome Neyrey, is a peasant concept that views humans as subject to nature and goods as not perpetual.[39] When one gains, someone else loses out.[40] This is shameful and threatening for the community.[41] An honorable patron ascertains that goods are shared among the clients (Isa 1:16). Failure to deliver these indispensable goods of safety, esteem, and basic necessities to one's clients results in shame for both parties.[42] Micah 6:1–8 and Isa 1:2–20 contrast the honorable patron YHWH as suzerain king/father with the shameful Israel as vassal/son.

Honor and shame relate to a person's or group's public claim to worth in the areas of power, sexual status, and religion. *Honor* is public acknowledgment of such status while *shame* is public denial and repudiation of such assertion.[43] John J. Pilch explains that honor may be passively *ascribed* when one is born into the family's honorable status; it may also be *acquired* by means of a social game of "challenge and response."[44] Shame relates with honor in two ways. It safeguards honor by having a "positive sensitivity to one's honor and honor rating" or a "sense of shame."[45] It jeopardizes honor "when an honorable person is dishonored or fails to guard or maintain personal honor" or when one behaves

---

37. Malina, "Patronage," 152–53. See also Bruce J. Malina, "Authoritarianism," in Pilch, *Handbook of Biblical Social Values*, 12–19.

38. Hobbs, "Reflections," 502.

39. Jerome H. Neyrey, "Limited Good," in Pilch, *Handbook of Biblical Social Values*, 123.

40. Ibid., 123–25.

41. For a contemporary implication of this value, see Paul Trawick and Alf Hornborg, "Revisiting the Image of Limited Good: On Sustainability, Thermodynamics, and the Illusion of Creating Wealth," *CA* 56 (2015): 1–27.

42. Hobbs, "Reflections," 502–3.

43. Joseph Plevnik, "Honor/Shame," in Pilch, *Handbook of Biblical Social Values*, 106. For an overview, see Halvor Moxnes, "Honor and Shame," *BTB* 23 (1993): 167–76.

44. John J. Pilch, *Introducing the Cultural Context of the Old Testament*, Hear the Word! 1 (Eugene, OR: Wipf & Stock, 2007), 53.

45. Ibid.

dishonorably by acting "shamelessly" or by "having no shame."[46] In the aforementioned texts, YHWH ascribes honor to Israel by the kinship terminologies already mentioned.[47] However, the exhortation to remember who YHWH is for them (Mic 6:5, Isa 1:2-4) and the critique of who Israel had become (Isa 1:2-10) are shameful accusations. The prophetic denunciations of sacrifices (Isa 1:13-16) relate to what Malina calls a first-degree challenge to honor. It involves the "extreme and total dishonor of another with no revocation possible."[48] This challenge is manifested in the total degradation of a person through the deprivation of what is needed for an honorable status, in other words, the components of the second half of the Decalogue.[49] Serious and fatal consequences accompany loss of honor or being shamed.[50]

Honor is also symbolized by blood (within one's blood family) and by name (by some kind of interdependence, cooperation, and shared enterprise which also depend on one's honor rating). The latter plays a role in covenantal relationship or in reciprocal suzerain-vassal relations.[51] Israel is honored by having YHWH as its "suzerain par excellence."[52] Their defeat, misfortune, and calamities constitute the shame of YHWH's abandonment.[53] The prophets ground these humiliations in the people's disobedience to the covenant (Mic 6:3-5, 8; Isa 1:3-4, 10-20), reliance on wrong allies (Mic 6:13; Isa 2:6-3:26), or disloyalty and rebellion against

---

46. Ibid.

47. See Dille, "Honor Restored," 234.

48. Bruce J. Malina, *The New Testament World: Insights from Cultural Anthropology*, 3rd ed., rev. and expanded (Louisville: Westminster John Knox, 2001), 44. Second degree challenge to honor consists of significant deprivation of honor with revocation possible such as restoring stolen items, or making monetary restitution for seducing one's unbetrothed, unmarried daughter, etc. Third and lowest degree comprises of the regular and ordinary interactions such as repaying a gift with one of equal or better value, interfamily marriages, etc.

49. Ibid. See also T. R. Hobbs, "Reflections on 'The Poor' and the Old Testament," *ExpTim* 100 (1989): 291-94.

50. Pilch, *Cultural Context*, 53. See, e.g., T. M. Lemos, "Shame and Mutilation of Enemies in the Hebrew Bible," *JBL* 125 (2006): 225-41; John T. Strong, "Egypt's Shameful Death and the House of Israel's Exodus from Sheol (Ezekiel 32.17-32 and 37.1-14)," *JSOT* 34 (2010): 475-504.

51. Malina, *New Testament World*, 37.

52. Saul M. Olyan, "Honor, Shame, and Covenant Relations in Ancient Israel and Its Environment," *JBL* 115 (1996): 205.

53. Plevnik, "Honor/Shame," 108.

the patron (Mic 6:1–5; Isa 1:2–8, 20).[54] As a human suzerain is shamed by a vassal, YHWH also responds by diminishing the honor of his worshipers.[55] This aspect of honor and shame is reflected in Hanson's discussion on royal deviance and restitution.[56] He cites Patrick Considine's study that enumerates various references to the causes, manifestations, and remedies of "divine wrath" from ancient eastern Mediterranean societies.[57] Causes of divine wrath include refusal to undertake a god's request or command (Ezek 20:1–38), challenge to a god's power by a human being (Exod 32:1–9; 1 Sam 15:8–9), the suffering of a god's favorite or slighting of a god's representative (Gen 12:3; 1 Sam 15:1–3; 1 Sam 17:41–51), infringement of a moral code (Gen 18:16–19:29), taking the side of a god's enemy, and the breaking of a covenant with a god (Ps 50; Mic 6:14–16). God's wrath is perceived through natural calamities like failure of crops, plagues, or storm or fire (Exod 7:2–11:10; 12:29–32), theophany (Ps 50:1–5; Mic 1:2–16), frustration of ambition (Job 5:12; Pss 33:10; 146:9), a champion is engaged, physical ill-treatment (2 Kgs 19:20–28), and a punishment that fits the crime (Jer 11:1–17). God's anger is abated or remedied through prevention of occasions that lead to this condition (Isa 1:17), disarming address (Gen 18:22–33; Exod 32:9–14, 30–34), removing the cause of wrath (Isa 1:16), prayer and sacrifice (Ps 32; Ps 51), conciliatory response (Joel 2:12–27), and seriously fearing the consequences of divine wrath (Jon 3:5–10).

These causes of divine wrath may also be classified as disruptions of cosmic harmony that undermine the deity's honor. Micah 6:1–8 and Isa 1:1–20 show the infringement of moral code and broken covenant that dishonor those who are afflicted, which shames YHWH, the ultimate suzerain/patron of the king in biblical social hierarchy.[58] The riposte of YHWH against the threats on his honor is active shaming of Israel physically (ill treatment, Isa 1:5–6), politically (military invasion and conquest,

---

54. Ibid., 108, 109. See also Niels Peter Lemche, "Kings and Clients : On Loyalty between the Ruler and the Ruled in Ancient 'Israel,'" *Semeia* 66 (1994): 119–32; John D. W. Watts, *Isaiah 1–33*, WBC 24 (Waco, TX: Word, 1985), 17.

55. P. J. Botha, "Honor and Shame as Keys to the Interpretation of Malachi," *OTE* 14 (2001): 396.

56. Hanson, "When the King," 11–25.

57. See Patrick Considine, "The Theme of Divine Wrath in Ancient East Mediterranean Literature," *SMEA* 8 (1969): 85–159; Hanson, "When the King," 20.

58. See Hanson, "When the King," 22.

Isa 1:20, Mic 1:8; 6:9–16),[59] and religiously (demonstrated by the ריב as a theophany, Mic 6:1–8; Isa 1:2–20).

For Malina, to seek legal justice among equals or to be brought to court by a subordinate is dishonorable.[60] To bring an equal to court should be a last resort, since publicizing the offense aggravates the dishonor it brings. Moreover, "(1) to go to court demonstrates inequality, vulnerability, and puts one's own honor in jeopardy; (2) court procedure allows those who deprive you of honor to gloat over your predicament; and (3) to have the court obtain recompense or ask for an apology from another is dishonoring in itself, implying that one cannot deal with one's equals."[61] This does not happen in Mic 6:1–8 and Isa 1:2–20. As an honorable suzerain king/patron who brings a case against his shameful vassal/client, YHWH exposes Israel to cosmic and social opinion (Isa 1:2–8, 10, 15–16; Mic 6:1–2, 8). Their asymmetric relations are highlighted as YHWH, as king and father, disciplines his subordinates (Mic 6:13–16; Isa 1:5–8). These actions enhance YHWH's reputation as a benevolent suzerain king and patron as he continues to offer Israel forgiveness and the chance to have their honor restored by reinstatement of their covenant partnership (Isa 1:18–20; Mic 6:8).[62] YHWH abides by the culturally accepted resolution that reconciliation and restoration of peace in the community occur through a mediator known to the community.[63] The prophet fulfils this task by facilitating the ריב, which paves the way toward the restoration of the honor of the vulnerable among the people. It also upholds the covenant stipulations by preventing the deterioration of social conditions (Isa 1:15–16), removing the cause of wrath (Isa 1:13, 16–18), providing a conciliatory response (Isa 1:18–20; Mic 6:3, 8), and instilling fear of consequences (Isa 1:19–20; Mic 6:13–16). Nevertheless, one wonders why the disarming address to YHWH, prayer, and sacrifice (Isa 1:11–15; Mic 6:6–7) are met with complete rejection. Further consideration of the most important characteristics of YHWH as king and father from the perspective of dyadism, patronage, and honor and shame might offer more clues on this cultic reproach.

---

59. See Lyn M. Bechtel, "Shame as a Sanction of Social Control in Biblical Israel: Judicial, Political, and Social Shaming," *JSOT* 16 (1991): 63–70.
60. Malina, *New Testament World*, 43.
61. Ibid.
62. See John J. Pilch, "Forgiveness," *The Cultural Dictionary of the Bible* (Collegeville, MN: Liturgical Press, 1999), 61–62.
63. See Pilch, *Cultural Context*, 63–64.

YHWH's Aim of Providing Sustenance and Protection for Israel

Insofar as sacrifice has to do with the interaction of persons in a society,[64] it is justified that YHWH prefers the more demanding and community-sustaining covenantal obedience rather than the hyperbolic amount of animal sacrifice and cultic acts:

Micah 6:6–8
6a With what shall I come before YHWH
6b Bow myself before God on High
6c Shall I come before him with burnt offerings,
6d With calves a year old?
7a Will he be pleased, YHWH, with thousands of rams,
7b With ten thousands rivers of oil?
7c Shall I give my firstborn for my transgression,
7d Fruit of my body for the sin of my life?
6:8a He has told you, o mortal, what is good
6:8b And what YHWH requires of you;
6:8c Only to do justice and to love loyalty
6:8d And to walk attentively with your God.

Isaiah 1:11–15
11a What to me is the abundance of your sacrifices?
11b the Lord says;
11c Sated I am with burnt offerings of rams
11d and fat of fatlings;
11e and the blood of young bulls, and of lambs, and of goats
11f I do not delight in.
12a When you come before my face,
12b Who seek these from your hand?
12c Trample my courts no more;
13a bringing offerings is futile
13b the odor of burning sacrifice is an abomination to me
13c New moon and Sabbath and calling of convocations
13d I cannot endure assemblies with wickedness.
14a Your new moon and appointed times
14b My soul hates;
14c They have become upon me a burden
14d I am weary bearing them.

---

64. Malina, "Mediterranean Sacrifice," 37.

15a When you stretch out your hands
15b I will hide my eyes from you
15c When you also make many prayers
15d I will not listen:
15e Your hands are full of blood!

The list in Mic 6:6–7 ironically parallels the enumeration of YHWH's righteous deeds for Israel's liberation in verses 4–5. It shows to what extent the community would go to bargain with or buy off YHWH.[65] Even if the sacrifice of one's firstborn, the fruit of one's body, is an extreme legal, biological, and relational sacrifice, YHWH prefers covenantal obedience (Mic 6:8).[66] In Isa 1:20, even if Israel's dishonorable deeds merit death, YHWH offers reconciliation through the life-giving obedience to the covenant. These texts say "No!" to inducement of any material offerings (Mic 6:6–7; Isa 1:11–14) and influence, whether nonverbal (stretched-out hands) or verbal (many prayers) (Isa 1:15). The words תפלה "prayer," or פלל, "to pray," denote "to place a case or situation before God for consideration or assessment," and "assume God as a righteous judge who assesses every case 'graciously.'"[67] They signify whom YHWH listens to: the חמוץ ("oppressed"), יתום ("orphan"), and אלמנה ("widow"). YHWH tasks the king/leaders to fulfill their principal functions of intervening in cases of oppression and protecting widows and orphans as substitute אב.[68] "*God's reputation is at stake* in what happens to those servants of the Lord who cry out in affliction and oppression."[69] As YHWH is divine patron/king/father to Israel (Mic 6:4–5, Isa 1:2), so the leaders as vassals/fathers also need to provide for the people/children (Mic 6:8; Isa 1:16–17). A "life of

---

65. See Walter Brueggemann, Sharon D. Parks, and Thomas H. Groome, *To Act Justly, Love Tenderly, Walk Humbly: An Agenda for Ministers* (New York: Paulist, 1986), 14; Bruce K. Waltke, *A Commentary on Micah* (Grand Rapids: Eerdmans, 2007), 387–88.

66. See Francis I. Andersen and David Noel Freedman, *Micah: A New Translation with Introduction and Commentary*, AB 24E (New York: Doubleday, 2000), 524.

67. Augustine Pagolu, *The Religion of the Patriarchs*, JSOTSup 277 (Sheffield: Sheffield Academic, 1998), 99.

68. See Raymond Westbrook, "Social Justice in the Near East," in *The Shared Traditions*, vol. 1 of *Law from Tigris to the Tiber: The Writings of Raymond Westbrook*, ed. Bruce Wells and F. Rachel Magdalene, (Winona Lake, IN: Eisenbrauns, 2009), 145.

69. Patrick D. Miller, *They Cried to the Lord: The Form and Theology of Biblical Prayer* (Minneapolis: Fortress, 1994), 120 (emphasis original).

willing obedience to his covenant requirements" means forgiveness of sins.⁷⁰ Until it is done, sacrifice insults YHWH.⁷¹

YHWH's Authority over Israel

The mutual asymmetric relationship in YHWH-Israel relations means shared identity between the covenant partners. This mutuality is based on Israel's honorable kinship with YHWH as the uses of בנים (Isa 1:2,4), עמי (Isa 1:3; Mic 6:3, 5), זרע (Isa 1:4) attest. Nevertheless, the pathos-filled vocative עמי in Mic 6:3, 5 urges Israel to "remember" (זכר) and to "know" (ידע) YHWH's "saving acts" (צדקות יהוה).⁷² Isaiah 1:3–4 presents how Israel as עמי has actively forsaken YHWH, despised the Holy One of Israel, and became utterly estranged.⁷³ The designation עמי with the verb ידע also recalls Amos 3:2 which associates ידע with suzerain-vassal relations from Hittite, Akkadian, and Ugaritic texts, as well as some letters from Amarna and Mari.⁷⁴ לא ידע violates suzerain-vassal/patron-client relations and shames the superior. YHWH, through the prophet, has to protect his honor as a divine patron/suzerain-king/father.

---

70. Ernest C. Lucas, "Sacrifice in the Prophets," in *Sacrifice in the Bible*, ed. Roger T. Beckwith and Martin J. Selman (Grand Rapids: Baker, 1995), 65.

71. See John Barton, "The Prophets and the Cult," in *Temple and Worship in Biblical Israel*, ed. John Day, LHBOTS 422 (London: T&T Clark, 2005), 120.

72. For this translation of צדקות יהוה, see Leslie C. Allen, *The Books of Joel, Obadiah, Jonah, and Micah*, NICOT (Grand Rapids: Eerdmans, 1976), 362; Bruce Vawter, *Amos, Hosea, Micah with an Introduction to Classical Prophecy*, OTMes 7 (Wilmington, DE: Glazier, 1981), 159. Johnson acknowledges that for some scholars, ṣdq is "virtually synonymous with deliverance and salvation." For him, Yahweh's ṣedāqā "is a positive, beneficent activity directed toward human beings, who are then its recipients (Ps 24:5). The appropriate human response is to confess, extol, and praise Yahweh's righteousness," citing Mic 6:5; 7:9 as sample texts among others; see Bo Johnson, "צָדַק," *TDOT* 12:243, 254.

73. On the use of עמי in Micah and Isaiah, see Gary Stansell, *Micah and Isaiah: A Form and Tradition Historical Comparison*, SBLDS 85 (Atlanta: Scholars Press, 1988), 117–21.

74. Delbert R. Hillers, "Therefore I Will Punish You," in *Covenant: The History of a Biblical Idea*, Seminars in the History of Ideas (Baltimore: Johns Hopkins University Press, 1969), 121–22; Herbert B. Huffmon, "The Treaty Background of Hebrew Yādaʿ," *BASOR* 181 (1966): 31–37; Herbert B. Huffmon and Simon B. Parker, "A Further Note on the Treaty Background of Hebrew Yādaʿ," *BASOR* 184 (1966): 36–38.

As a suzerain who journeyed with Israel in Mic 6:4–5, the reference אלהי מרום ("God on high") in Mic 6:6 becomes problematic when it is read in "an indignant and almost hysterical tone."[75] It nuances the drifting away of the relationship or the arrogance of the wicked to YHWH's distance (Ps 10:5). Nevertheless, the general vocative אדם (Mic 6:8) reminds Israel of their identity as creatures and vassal of Suzerain-YHWH (Mic 6:3–5) who cannot simply dispense of animals, vegetation, and humans at their will (Mic 6:6–7), even if the killing of a living being to celebrate life affirms ingroup/outgroup boundary markers.[76] It also reminds Israel that YHWH to whom they bow down (כפף) and who they think needs the sacrifices (Mic 6:6–7), prefers doing justice, loving kindness, and walking *with* God as what are truly necessary (Mic 6:8). The total well-being of the community is what brings honor to YHWH.

In Isa 1:4, the development of Israel from being גוי to עם to זרע to בנים shows how YHWH ascribes honor to Israel. It also demonstrates their deterioration in identity and estrangement from YHWH:

> Ah, sinful nation,
> people laden with iniquity,
> evil offspring,
> corrupt sons.
> They have forsaken the Lord,
> They have spurned the Holy One of Israel, they are utterly estranged,
> from whom they are utterly estranged.

The appellations קציני סדם (rulers of Sodom) and עם עמרה (people of Gomorrah) likewise shake up Israel's self-identity that they are unlike Sodom and Gomorrah (Isa 1:9–10). They have now received "the most abhorrent name imaginable, the most despicable, deplorable name available (cf. Jer. 23:14; Ezek. 16:46–49; Hos 11:8; Amos 4:11)."[77] The multitude of their animal sacrifices and prayers symbolizes the immensity of their sins (Isa 1:11–15). While their bloodied hands relate to the offerings, the succeeding commands qualify that they also led to subjugation of the

---

75. See Philip Peter Jenson, *Obadiah, Jonah, Micah: A Theological Commentary*, LHBOTS 496 (New York: T&T Clark, 2008), 167.

76. Malina, "Mediterranean Sacrifice," 41, 42; Jacob Milgrom, "A Prolegomenon to Leviticus 17:11," *JBL* 90 (1971): 155.

77. Walter Brueggemann, *Isaiah 1–39*, WesBibComp (Louisville: Westminster John Knox, 1998), 17.

oppressed, orphans, and widows (Isa 1:16–17). The use of plural verbs regards Israel as a "completely abhorred community that is summoned to listen one more time" to the Holy One of Israel.[78] YHWH's quintessential characteristic of holiness that permeates all aspects of his being and presence impels Israel to likewise be holy in their being and doing.[79]

Israel's identity (Isa 1:2–8, 10; Mic 6:5) is the reason behind the rejection of sacrifice. The multitude of sacrifices cannot automatically rectify the shameful deterioration of whom Israel has become (Isa 1:11–15). The problem lies not in the sacrifice but in the one who sacrifices, culminating in the vivid image of bloodied hands, which is closely connected with those who are victimized (Isa 1:15–16). To lay a hand or to press on the head of the sacrifice (Lev 1:4; 3:2, 8, 13; 4:4, 15, 24; 16:21) suggests identification or ownership or that "the worshipper's sins were symbolically transferred to the animal."[80] If the problem is the way of being and doing of the worshiper, so the offerings also become tarnished. YHWH rejects communion rooted in pretense, dishonesty, and disobedience.[81]

Manifestations of YHWH's Authority over Israel

The third group of YHWH's most important characteristics in the Hebrew Scripture is manifested in his authority as king and father. These traits include YHWH's demand for Israel's transformation, physical control, and destructive traits. Below is a consideration of these qualities in Mic 6:1–8 and Isa 1:1–20.

The Change of Essence or Transformation of the Worshiper

For corporate Israel in Mic 6:7, the purpose of the overwhelming quantity and quality of the sacrifice is to be cleansed of Israel's פשע and חטאת. These justifications relate to the propitiatory and expiatory elements of

---

78. Ibid.
79. See Saul M. Olyan, *Rites and Rank: Hierarchy in Biblical Representations of Cult* (Princeton: Princeton University Press, 2000), 17; Reinhard G. Kratz, "Israel in the Book of Isaiah," *JSOT* 31 (2006): 111.
80. David Peterson, *Engaging with God: A Biblical Theology of Worship* (Downers Grove, IL: IVP Academic, 1992), 40; Gordon J. Wenham, "The Theology of Old Testament Sacrifice," in Beckwith, *Sacrifice in the Bible*, 79.
81. Brueggemann, *Isaiah*, 18.

the עלה.⁸² While עלה expresses the worshiper's total consecration, allegiance, commitment, and self-surrender to YHWH,⁸³ its usages in Micah and Isaiah seem "to appease divine wrath, and thus induce forgiveness of the corrupt deeds of the kings."⁸⁴ YHWH, therefore, rejects (Isa 1:15–16) and corrects this notion (Mic 6:8). Instead of עלה, YHWH favors actions as seen in the use of יכח (niphal, cohortative) and ריב as means for Israel to cleanse itself of its scarlet- and crimson-red sin symbolized by bloodied hands (Isa 1:15, 18–19) and as a way for Israel to restore its memory of YHWH's suzerain kingship (Mic 6:5). In Isa 1:10, 16–17, the corrections that come from דבר־יהוה and תורת אלהינו command cessation of the victimization inside and outside the cultic sphere. "Torah, which for Isaiah is synonymous with the word of YHWH (1:10), does not make victims in cult offerings or in any sort of violence."⁸⁵ In Mic 6:6–8, right relationship with YHWH and social order hinge on knowing YHWH and obeying the covenant.⁸⁶

As the question on the needed transformation of the worshiper is addressed, the issue of the identity and essence of YHWH must also be resolved. Instead of having a transforming worship for the community, Israel's sacrifices change the identity of who YHWH is for them by their trampling (רמס) of YHWH's court (Isa 1:12).⁸⁷ The use of רמס is frequent in prophetic accusations and YHWH's judgment such as in Isa 1:12 and in how the "powerful carelessly foul the pasturage and water supply with their feet, leaving no food or drink for the weak members of the flock" (see Ezek 34:18–19).⁸⁸ The hand to feet movement describes the desecration of the holy place (Isa 1:12, 15), justifies why YHWH would not respond to

---

82. See Pagolu, *Religion of the Patriarchs*, 46.

83. Wenham, "Theology of Old Testament Sacrifice," 82–83.

84. Paul Heger, *The Three Biblical Altar Laws: Developments in the Sacrificial Cult in Practice and Theology; Political and Economic Background*, BZAW 279 (Berlin: de Gruyter, 1999), 275–76.

85. James G. Williams, "Kings and Prophets: Sacred Lot and Divine Calling," in *The Bible, Violence, and the Sacred: Liberation from the Myth of Sanctioned Violence* (Valley Forge, PA: Trinity Press International, 1995), 152.

86. Ibid., 154.

87. I have dealt with the question of YHWH's identity in Ps 50:21 in Ma. Maricel S. Ibita, "'O Israel, I Will Testify against You': Intensification and Narrativity in the Lament-Lawsuit of the 'Unsilent' God in Psalm 50," in *The Composition of the Book of Psalms*, ed. Erich Zenger, BETL 238 (Leuven: Peeters, 2010), 537–49.

88. E.-J. Waschke, "רָמַס," *TDOT* 13:510.

them (Isa 1:14–15), and commands the need for change (Isa 1:16; Mic 6:8). Saul Olyan explains:

> The locus of the cult, the sanctuary, whether represented as tent shrine or tabernacle, temple complex or high place, is, in essence, holy space. Set apart from common territory, the sanctuary, however described, is the dwelling place on earth of the deity, who is himself quintessentially holy. The implements of the sanctuary, including its altar for burnt offerings, are likewise sanctified, as are the priests who oversee the sanctuary's operation and many of the offerings that Israelites bring to it.[89]

Therefore,

> worshipers, too, must be sanctified or must sanctify themselves (*hitqaddēš*) before coming into contact with holy space or holy things. The holiness of the sanctuary may be threatened with either profanation or pollution. Profanation, the transformation of what is holy into what is common, means, in the case of the sanctuary, the transformation of Yhwh's holy abode into common territory, and, therefore, space no longer set apart for the deity's dwelling and his worship.[90]

When this situation happens,

> Pollution of the sanctuary, through the introduction of a defiled person or thing into its space, would render the *sanctuary utterly unfit for the deity's dwelling or service* and would require elaborate rites of purification to return the sanctuary to its previous clean and holy status. It is a major duty of cultic servants to prevent the entry of uncleanness into the sanctuary sphere and likewise to prevent the occurrence of any illegitimate profanation. Thus, we see the concern witnessed in biblical texts to maintain the distinctions holy/common and clean/unclean, to keep what is holy from illegitimate profanation and to guard it from contact with polluting persons and things. *These distinctions make Yhwh's presence possible in the cult; they allow him to dwell with Israel and accept his rightful due as Israel's national god and suzerain.*[91]

---

89. Olyan, *Rites and Rank*, 16.
90. Ibid.
91. Ibid., emphasis added.

Trampling YHWH's court, therefore, shames YHWH and casts out the Holy One of Israel from his sanctuary. It results not just in Israel's estrangement from YHWH but also in YHWH's estrangement from Israel (Isa 1:4).

YHWH's Physical Control over the Worshiper

The second manifestation of YHWH's authority as king and father is his physical control over the worshiper. John Barton observes that except for Mic 6:6, sacrifices were accompanied by feasting and celebration among the preexilic prophets.[92] Read against the backdrop of YHWH's call for weeping and mourning (Isa 22:12–13) and the coming disaster (Mic 3:12), the cultic denunciation might be "mainly part of the prophets' condemnation of excessive luxury, display and self-indulgence."[93] YHWH as teacher of right worship and sacrifice demands transformation of the community through his exercise of control over Israel. Primarily, YHWH instructs them how to deal with evil, from general to specific actions:

> Wash yourselves,
> Make yourselves clean,
> Take away the evil of your deeds from before my eyes;
> cease to do evil. (Isa 1:16)

The command to wash refers to the bloodied hand of the sacrificer. It characterizes Israel as a blemished body that has become an abomination (Isa 1:6).[94] Compared to a sacrificial animal, it is still clean but has become unfit for sacrifice.[95] Thus,

> Israel must engage in ritual purification because it has been defiled and made unacceptable to the holy God (v. 16). The "washing" here to be done is the same as that which David offers in Psalm 51:2, only here it is Israel who must wash, that is, the whole people.... Life with Yahweh must be undefiled, and the community must use the available means to become ritually acceptable.[96]

---

92. Barton, "Prophets and the Cult," 119.
93. Ibid., 120; Johanna Stiebert, *The Construction of Shame in the Hebrew Bible*, JSOTSup 346 (New York: Sheffield Academic, 2002), 91 n. 11.
94. See Olyan, *Rites and Rank*, 103.
95. Ibid., 104.
96. Brueggemann, *Isaiah*, 18–19.

Ritual acceptance or rejection is important personally, economically, socially and religiously.[97] As Olyan underlines:

> Exclusion from cultic and quasi-cultic ritual settings means, in effect, separation from what texts represent as the primary locus for slaughter and meat consumption, for praising and petitioning Yhwh, the national god, and for the regular rehearsal of the national story of origins. These are ritual contexts in which the social order is made and remade. In a word, loss of access to the sanctuary and its analogues is nothing less than a serious hardship for those excluded.[98]

For this reason, the second group of instructions lists more proactive measures to include the socially excluded, so that those who are ritually excluded can more authentically participate in worship:

> learn to do good; seek justice,
> rescue the oppressed, reprove the ruthless,
> defend the orphan,
> plead contend for the widow. (Isa 1:17)

> to do justice and to love loyalty
> and to walk attentively with your God. (Mic. 6:8)

Addressed to the leaders, the recipients of these general to specific actions are the marginalized of the society who are subject to "political exclusion and economic exploitation."[99] These measures that touch every facet of Israel's life—right worship (*holiness*) and right neighbor practice (*righteousness*)—make living honorable.[100] It also means living honorably with and thereby bestowing honor to YHWH the patron/suzerain king/father.

YHWH's Destructive Power

The third manifestation of YHWH's authority as king and father is the use of destructive power. The *niphal* cohortative נוכחה (Isa 1:18) exposes

---

97. See Olyan, *Rites and Rank*, 55, 62.
98. Ibid., 115.
99. Brueggemann, *Isaiah*, 19.
100. Ibid.

the shameful inability of Israel to feed and protect the people.[101] However, it also paves the way for an honorable life in the community as YHWH shows benevolence by means of negotiation: "let us argue it out."[102] Here the prophetic lawsuit functions as a ritual-sacrificial moment for Israel to be cleansed of its iniquity and bloodied hands (Isa 1:15). Since white is a color of innocence and honor, it signifies the bestowal of an honorable status again.[103]

Isaiah 1:19-20 functions doubly as proposals and as verdicts. Willingness and obedience lead to honorable, safe and well-provided life with YHWH as evidenced by eating the good of the land. Refusal and rebellion lead to shame and death as signified by being eaten by either the Assyrian or Babylonian sword.[104] The offer of YHWH, the Holy One of Israel, addresses and resolves the various aspects of sin: relational (broken relationship, Mic 6:3; Isa 1:2-4), social (disturbance of shalom, Mic 6:9-12; Isa 1:16-17), covenantal (rebellion against authority, Mic 6:5, 8, 16; Isa 1:4, 18-20), legal (guilt that necessitates punishment, Mic 6:13-16), ritual (uncleanness and pollution, Mic 6:7-8; Isa 1:10-20), emotional (shame and disgrace on oneself and/or God, Mic 6:1-8; Isa 1:2-20), historical (an accumulating burden, e.g., the "exile," Mic 6:16; Isa 1:7-9, 20), and final (death, Mic 6:13-16; Isa 1:20).[105] Rebellion as "active resistance" blocks all of these aspects and results in shameful estrangement.[106]

Conclusion: The Functions of Sacrificial Critiques from the Perspective of the Metaphors YHWH IS KING and YHWH IS FATHER

As seen in the brief examination above, the prophetic denunciation of sacrifice does not advocate for a nonritualistic religion.[107] Bryan Bibb

---

101. See Don C. Benjamin, "An Anthropology of Prophecy," *BTB* 21 (1991): 139-41.

102. Watts, *Isaiah*, 22.

103. Brueggemann, *Isaiah*, 20; Raphael Patai, *The Arab Mind* (New York: Scribner, 1973), 86, 101-2.

104. Ronald Ernest Clements, *Isaiah 1-39*, NCBC (London: Marshall, Morgan & Scott, 1980), 35; Brueggemann, *Isaiah*, 17.

105. See Christopher J. H. Wright, "Atonement in the Old Testament," in *The Atonement Debate: Papers from the London Symposium on the Theology of Atonement*, ed. Derek Tidball, David Hilborn, and Justin Thacker (Grand Rapids: Zondervan, 2008), 69-71.

106. See Brueggemann, *Isaiah*, 13.

107. John N. Oswalt, *The Book of Isaiah: Chapters 1-39*, NICOT (Grand Rapids: Eerdmans, 1986), 95.

places it within the larger context of prophetic rhetorical strategy where the prophet aims "to convict the audience of their sinful activities, to express God's dim view of the situation, and to explain what God plans to do about it."[108] This investigation of the prophets' cultic reproach from the perspective of blending theory opens us to think and reason from the viewpoint of YHWH as king and father. By exploring the most important characteristics of YHWH present in these metaphors within the context of biblical social values, we discover that YHWH's aim is to maintain cosmic order by nurturing and protecting Israel. Conceptualized as king or father, YHWH has authority over Israel, who is considered a vassal (Mic 6:1–8) or as sons/children (Isa 1:2–10). Their mutual asymmetrical relations are manifested in YHWH's physical control over Israel, his capacity to transform Israel, and when necessary, his use of destructive power to maintain cosmic order.

One way of addressing disturbance in the cosmic order is the ריב or prophetic lawsuit that deals with the broken covenant and includes critique of the cult. In both Mic 6:1–8 and Isa 1:2–20 the reason behind the cultic reproach is not about the sacrifice itself but the forgotten and mistaken identities of the covenant partners.

First, Israel as the one who sacrifices, that is, the worshiper who is vassal or child, has forgotten who he/she is. Sacrifice expresses visually that the most important concept in Israel's self-understanding is the covenant and its principles.[109] Every animal chosen for sacrifice reminisces how YHWH chose Israel (Mic 6:4–5; Isa 1:2–4) and every sacrifice reminds Israel of the command to be holy as YHWH is (Mic 6:8; Isa 1:10–20).[110]

Second, Israel's perceived need of YHWH for sacrifice distorts the long-held identity of YHWH for Israel. This important issue is reiterated in the exhortations for Israel to once again know YHWH (Mic 6:5; Isa 1:2–4, 11–12). Mic 6:5 employs זכר ("to remember") and ידע ("to know"), while Isa 1:3 negatively declares that YHWH's people לא ידע ("does not know") and לא התבונן ("does not understand"). The historical recall (Mic 6:4–5; Isa 1:2) reviews Israel's self-identity and YHWH's kinship with them. In Micah, Israel's concept of YHWH as אלהי מרום is corrected in Mic 6:8 through the exhortation that the people walk *with* their God (עם־אלהיך). In Isaiah, the reference to YHWH as the Holy One *of* Israel (קדוש ישראל)

---

108. Bibb, "Prophetic Critique," 34.
109. Wenham, "Theology of Old Testament Sacrifice," 84.
110. Ibid.

is in itself a dyadic and group-oriented expression of YHWH's identity. The historical recall shows how YHWH as king and as a father acted as an honorable patron for Israel. This asymmetric relation legitimizes YHWH's demand from Israel to take care of their oppressed, orphans, and widows.[111] The rhetorical and conceptual impacts are sharpened as the ריב functions like a double-edged sword. Though it causes shame to both YHWH and Israel, YHWH's benevolent patronage provides the chance to bring honor back to Israel. Both texts present YHWH as pathos-filled because of the plight of עמי (Isa 1:2–8) and the silent charge that Israel has against YHWH (Mic 6:3). The texts urge Israel to remember the צדקות יהוה in the past and impel them to negotiate with YHWH in the present (Mic 6:5; Isa 1:18).

Third, while the exploration of the biblical social values of dyadism, patron-client relation, and honor and shame elucidates the range of characteristics found in the metaphors YHWH IS KING and YHWH IS FATHER and the reason behind the cultic criticism, it also exposes the identities of those who were made anonymous in Israel's forgetfulness of their own identity and of who YHWH is for them: the oppressed, the orphans, and the widows. The honorable status of the covenant and the covenant partners are measured and maintained by ceasing the evil done to the marginalized, by starting to do good and to seek justice for the vulnerable. Concretely, it means rescuing the oppressed, defending the orphan, and pleading for the widow.

In summary, this investigation of the critique of the sacrifices from the perspective of the metaphors YHWH IS KING (Mic 6:1–8) and YHWH IS FATHER (Isa 1:2–10) within the context of biblical social values exposes the core issue in YHWH-Israel relation: the mistaken and forgotten identities of YHWH, Israel, and those who become anonymous when the covenant is broken. Authentic worship intensifies Israel's knowledge of who YHWH is for them and who they are for YHWH. To truly worship YHWH is to be like him: an honorable patron, king, and father—especially to those made vulnerable by the broken covenant. To do otherwise is to shame YHWH and suffer its serious consequences.

---

111. Westbrook, "Social Justice," 145.

Part 3
Atonement: Alternative Concepts

To Atone or Not to Atone:
Remarks on the Day of Atonement Rituals According to Leviticus 16 and the Meaning of Atonement

Christian A. Eberhart

Annual festivals partially determined the religious and cultural identity of Second Temple Judaism.[1] One of them was the "Day of Atonement" (יום הכפרים / ἡμέρα ἐξιλασμοῦ), celebrated on the tenth day of the month of Tishri (Lev 16:29).[2] It differed from the other festivals in that it did not require any pilgrimage to the sanctuary; instead, priests performed rituals at the sanctuary on behalf of the community. For many Jews today this festival, known since medieval times as Yom Kippur (יום כפור), is the holiest day of the year.[3] The Torah features regulations for the Day of Atonement in Lev 23:26–32, which outlines the pertinent obligations of the Israelites,

---

1. See Baruch A. Levine, *Leviticus* ויקרא: *The Traditional Hebrew Text with the New JPS Translation*, JPS Torah Commentary (Philadelphia: Jewish Publication Society, 1989), 261: "These occasions [sc. the Sabbath and religious festivals] are the *sancta*, the religious celebrations that lend to any community its distinctive character and that reinforce its sense of unity and common purpose. They keep the memory of the past alive and enhance the awareness of a common destiny."

2. Depending on the translation of the Hebrew root כפר, this festival may also be called "Day of Purgation"; see, e.g., Jacob Milgrom, *Leviticus 1–16: A New Translation with Introduction and Commentary*, AB 3 (New York: Doubleday, 1991), 1009–84. James W. Watts calls it "Day of Mitigations" (*Leviticus 1–10*, HCOT [Leuven: Peeters, 2013], 13). Not all Jewish groups in antiquity celebrated this festival on the same day. Some Dead Sea Scrolls, e.g., 1QpHab 11:4–8, deal with an implicit calendar schism that would have led to different days of observance of this important event; see Shemaryahu Talmon, "Yom Hakkippurim in the Habakkuk Scroll," *Bib* 32 (1951), 549–63; Joseph M. Baumgarten, "Yom Kippur in the Qumran Scrolls and Second Temple Sources," *DSD* 6 (1999): 185.

3. Already the Jewish sages regarded the Day of Atonement "as the supreme festi-

and in Num 29:7–11, which specifies the types and quantities of sacrifices.[4] In addition, the famous text in Lev 16 contains the ritual of this festival in its entirety. Many scholars today consider this chapter to be the heart of the book of Leviticus.[5] All of these aspects underscore the special importance of the "Day of Atonement" for Judaism past and present.

The name of this festival indicates its religious significance, namely, that it has to do with atonement. However, it already left ancient readers and audiences wondering how this could be imagined. In the Babylonian Talmud, therefore, the tract Yoma, which is dedicated to the Day of Atonement, seeks to answer some of these questions. In doing so, it summarizes: "There is no atonement except through blood" (אין כפרה אלא בדם, b. Yoma 5a; see also b. Zebah. 6a). This motto suggests that blood rites in the context of sacrifices are the only means for obtaining atonement. In the present study, I will show that such an understanding is not fully appropriate. Already a cursory reading of the ritual of the Day of Atonement in Lev 16 shows that atonement is also associated with the goat "for Azazel" (v. 10) which, however, remains well alive (vv. 20b–22). Two other examples from the ritual in Lev 16 reveal a conceptually more intricate

---

val and the greatest day of the year" (Moshe David Herr, "Day of Atonement," *EncJud* 5:1382). The day is sometimes also called יום התענית "Day of Affliction" (CD 6:18–19).

4. A convenient overview of the latter is provided by Jacob Milgrom, *Numbers* במדבר: *The Traditional Hebrew Text with the New JPS Translation*, JPS Torah Commentary (Philadelphia: Jewish Publication Society, 1990), 237.

5. Erich Zenger, "Das Buch Levitikus als Teiltext der Tora/des Pentateuch: Eine synchrone Lektüre mit diachroner Perspektive," in *Levitikus als Buch*, ed. Hans-Josef Fabry and Hans-Winfried Jüngling, BBB 119 (Berlin: Philo, 1999), 47–83, esp. 65–70; Christophe Nihan, *From Priestly Torah to Pentateuch: A Study in the Composition of the Book of Leviticus*, FAT 2/25 (Tübingen: Mohr Siebeck, 2007), 95–99; Didier Luciani, *Sainteté et pardon*, 2 vols., BETL 185, (Leuven: Leuven University Press, 2005), 290–316; Bernd Janowski, "Das Geschenk der Versöhnung: Leviticus 16 als Schlussstein der priesterlichen Kulttheologie," in *The Day of Atonement: Its Interpretations in Early Jewish and Christian Traditions*, ed. Thomas Hieke and Tobias Nicklas, TBN 15 (Leiden: Brill, 2012), 6; Thomas Hieke, *Levitikus: Zweiter Teilband: 16–27*, HThKAT (Freiburg im Breisgau: Herder, 2014), 557–58. According to a different approach, the love commandments in Lev 19 are the central element of the book which is composed on the model of a ring structure; cf. Mary Douglas, "Poetic Structure in Leviticus," in *Pomegranates and Golden Bells: Studies in Biblical, Jewish, and Near Eastern Ritual, Law, and Literature in Honor of Jacob Milgrom*, ed. David P. Wright, David Noel Freedman, and Avi Hurvitz (Winona Lake, IN: Eisenbrauns, 1995), 253; Jacob Milgrom, *Leviticus: A Book of Ritual and Ethics*, CC (Minneapolis: Fortress, 2004), 6–8.

situation: atonement *may* be the result of blood rites, but it *does not need to be*. Instead, atonement is a complex and multifarious concept; it resists reduction to a single definition or translation in both the Hebrew Bible / Old Testament and the New Testament.

In this study, I will examine the connection of various rituals on the "Day of Atonement" as described in Lev 16 with the effect of atonement. I will first explore blood application rites in the context of the sin offering in some depth; second, I will discuss burning rites in sacrificial rituals. Other texts that deal with sacrificial rituals, especially those in Lev 1–7, will inform my investigation of both trajectories. I assume that it is warranted to connect information from these different text bodies for two reasons: First, Lev 1–7 presents comprehensive data on sacrificial rituals that are lacking in Lev 16 (see, e.g., the sparse information on the burnt offering in 16:3, 5, 24). Second, the laws in chapters 1–7 repeatedly feature short declarative formulas such as "this [is] a burnt offering" (עלה הוא / κάρπωμά ἐστιν, 1:13; see also vv. 9, 17) or "this [is] a sin offering for the assembly" (חטאת הקהל הוא / ἁμαρτία συναγωγῆς ἐστιν, 4:21).[6] Such formulas appear mostly at the conclusion of the respective sacrificial laws, suggesting that these in fact comprise the rituals and effects or purposes to which other passages with less extensive information refer.[7] They have the force of definitions. Or, to put it differently, if Lev 1 describes a ritual and declares that "*this* [is] a burnt offering," then the ancient redactor expected the reader/audience to accept that these very regulations apply to later texts such as Lev 16:24 on the burnt offering.

As mentioned above, atonement is also being achieved on the Day of Atonement apart from sacrifices, namely, through the scapegoat ritual. In the course of this essay, therefore, I shall argue that scholars need to broaden their conceptualization of atonement so as to include aspects such as elimination rituals and the sacrificial burning rite. Along the way, I shall discuss recent proposals to interpret these rituals, specifically their "latent" functions, from a sociocultural perspective. I shall also compare them to explicit or manifest purposes of various ritual activities based on

---

6. In this contribution, I am juxtaposing the text versions of the Hebrew Bible and the LXX. I will indicate textual differences by square brackets [...] and occasionally comment on them.

7. See Thomas Hieke, *Levitikus: Erster Teilband: 1–15*, HThKAT (Freiburg im Breisgau: Herder, 2014), 177.

public or official explanations of ancient religious communities who witnessed and performed them.

An epilogue surveys selected aspects of how early Christian authors deployed terminology and concepts from the Day of Atonement. After the destruction of the temple in Jerusalem and the cessation of its cult, such terminology was used metaphorically, yet less often. Nevertheless, one can see the adoption of concepts in line with the explicit purposes of atonement rituals in Lev 16 and the Hebrew Bible / Old Testament in some New Testament christological contexts.

Blood Application Rites in the Context of Sin Offering Rituals

Most biblical instances of the term "to atone / atonement" appear in the Hebrew Bible / Old Testament, where the root כפר occurs 149 times.[8] The majority of these occurrences can be found in the so-called Priestly Source (P).[9] Atonement is, therefore, mostly the result of temple rituals. In what follows, I shall survey a variety of rituals associated with the Day of Atonement.

There is no doubt that the connection between atonement and blood in the above-mentioned rabbinic motto "there is no atonement except through blood" can claim a biblical basis. The sin offering ritual (Lev 4:1–5:13), which describes the application of blood, has the purpose of acquiring atonement (כפר *piel* / ἐξιλάσκομαι) and forgiveness (סלח *niphal* / ἀφίημι) for the person or people offering the sacrifice (4:20, 26, 31, 35).

Blood application rites self-evidently require animals—they obviously do not occur in the ritual of the cereal offering (מנחה / θυσία, Lev 2). Laws for animal sacrifices stipulate the careful selection of an animal. While it must be slaughtered (Lev 1:5; 4:4) and its blood be poured out at the altar base (1:5; 4:7; etc.), the sources associate neither of these ritual activities with any specific effect. It is noteworthy that the sacrificial rituals in Lev 1–7 prescribe actual rites of applying sacrificial blood (4:5–7, 16–18,

---

8. There are 101 verbal and 48 nominal forms of כפר; see Bernd Janowski, *Sühne als Heilsgeschehen: Traditions- und religionsgeschichtliche Studien zur Sühnetheologie der Priesterschrift*, 2nd ed., WMANT 55 (Neukirchen-Vluyn: Neukirchener Verlag, 2000), 105–7. By contrast, only six forms of the lexeme ἱλάσκομαι appear in the New Testament (see the Epilogue below), while the compound ἐξιλάσκομαι ("to atone"), which is frequent in the LXX, is lacking entirely.

9. See Fritz Maass, "כפר *kpr* pi. to atone," *TLOT* 2:626; Hieke, *Levitikus 1–15*, 131.

25, 30, 34) for only one type of sacrifice, the sin offering (חטאת / περὶ τῆς ἁμαρτίας). However, similar blood application rites occasionally occur elsewhere in the context of other types of sacrifices.

The attention to details of the ritual manipulation of blood conveys its importance. The book of Leviticus employs similar terminology throughout: "the priest shall dip his finger in the blood" (וטבל הכהן את־אצבעו בדם / καὶ βάψει ὁ ἱερεὺς τὸν δάκτυλον εἰς τὸ αἷμα, Lev 4:6; see also v. 17), or "the priest shall take of the blood" (ולקח הכהן מדם / καὶ [ἐπιθήσει] ὁ ἱερεὺς ἀπὸ τοῦ αἵματος, 4:25; see also vv. 30, 34). Then the exact type of action is described either as "to sprinkle" (נזה hiphil / [προσ]ραίνω) or "to put/place" (נתן / ἐπιτίθημι). The description of the action depends on the designation of this ritual activity: it can be upon and before the "mercy seat" in the inner sanctum (only on the Day of Atonement, 16:14–15) or, in the outer sanctum, against the veil that separates one from the other, or against the altar of incense, or finally upon the altar of burnt offerings.[10] The pinnacle of these blood application rites are the ceremonies on the Day of Atonement, as conveyed in the following passage about the duties of Aaron, the high priest (Lev 16:15–16a):

ושחט את־שעיר החטאת אשר לעם והביא את־דמו אל־מבית לפרכת
ועשה את־דמו כאשר עשה לדם הפר והזה אתו על־הכפרת ולפני הכפרת:
וכפר על־הקדש מטמאת בני ישראל ומפשעיהם לכל־חטאתם

---

10. Already in the period of Second Temple Judaism, this information did not fully match the historical reality of the sanctuary. According to a variety of traditions, the inner sanctum was empty (Jer 3:16; Josephus, *J.W.* 5.219). When the Roman commander Pompey the Great conquered Jerusalem in 63 BCE to usher in the era of Roman occupation of the province of Judaea, he wanted to crown his victory with a visit to the temple, which he expected to be full of treasures. However, the sanctuary was "devoid of riches and virtually empty aside from a Torah" (Norman Gelb, *Herod the Great: Statesman, Visionary, Tyrant* [Lanham, MD: Rowman & Littlefield, 2013], 9). Later again, the Mishnah relates the following: "Once the ark was taken away, there was a stone from the days of the earlier prophets, and it was called *Shetiyyah*. Its height from the ground was three fingerbreadths. And on it did he [sc. Aaron the high priest] put it [sc. the fire pan]" משנטל הארון אבן היתה שם מימות נביאים הראשונים ושתיה היתה נקראת גבוהה מן הארץ שלש אצבעות ועליה היה נותן, m. Yoma 5:2). See Günter Stemberger, "Yom Kippur in Mishnah Yoma," in Hieke, *Day of Atonement*, 127.

καὶ σφάξει τὸν χίμαρον τὸν περὶ τῆς ἁμαρτίας[11] τὸν περὶ τοῦ λαοῦ ἔναντι κυρίου καὶ εἰσοίσει [ἀπὸ τοῦ αἵματος][12] αὐτοῦ ἐσώτερον τοῦ καταπετάσματος καὶ ποιήσει τὸ αἷμα αὐτοῦ ὃν τρόπον ἐποίησεν τὸ αἷμα τοῦ μόσχου, καὶ ῥανεῖ τὸ αἷμα αὐτοῦ ἐπὶ τὸ ἱλαστήριον κατὰ πρόσωπον τοῦ ἱλαστηρίου καὶ [ἐξιλάσεται τὸ ἅγιον][13] ἀπὸ τῶν ἀκαθαρσιῶν τῶν υἱῶν Ισραηλ καὶ ἀπὸ τῶν ἀδικημάτων αὐτῶν περὶ πασῶν τῶν ἁμαρτιῶν αὐτῶν

He [sc. Aaron, the high priest] shall slaughter the goat of the sin offering that is for the people and bring its blood inside the curtain, and do with its blood as he did with the blood of the bull, and sprinkle it upon the mercy seat and before the mercy seat. Thus he shall make atonement for the sanctuary, because of the uncleannesses of the people of Israel, and because of their transgressions, for all their sins.[14]

These passages from Lev 16 feature regulations for the *performance* of a sin offering, followed by remarks on the intended *purpose*. In verse 15, the audience hears about Aaron, who after offering two sacrifices for his own house now performs the first sacrifice for the congregation of the people of Israel. He brings the blood of the sacrificial animal inside the inner sanctum (sometimes also called "holy of holies"). There he sprinkles it in order to "make atonement for the sanctuary" to which the chamber belongs.

After exiting the sanctuary, the high priest applies some of this blood to each of the four horns of the altar (16:18–19). The text explicitly identi-

---

11. The Greek translation περὶ τῆς ἁμαρτίας for Hebrew חטאת with the sense of "sin offering" is the most frequent one. See the comparative table of terminological equivalents between the MT and LXX in Christian A. Eberhart, *Kultmetaphorik und Christologie: Opfer- und Sühneterminologie im Neuen Testament*, WUNT 306 (Tübingen: Mohr Siebeck, 2013), 208–9; see also Suzanne Daniel, *Recherches sur le vocabulaire du culte dans la Septante*, EeC 61 (Paris: Klincksieck, 1966), 301–16.

12. The rendering "shall bring (some) of its blood" (εἰσοίσει ἀπὸ τοῦ αἵματος αὐτοῦ) in the LXX is more precise than "shall bring its blood" (והביא את־דמו) in the MT as most likely not all of the sacrificial blood was used in this activity; see Martin Vahrenhorst, "Levitikon/Leviticus/Das dritte Buch Mose," in *Septuaginta Deutsch: Erklärungen und Kommentare zum griechischen Alten Testament*, ed. Martin Karrer and Wolfgang Kraus (Stuttgart: Deutsche Bibelgesellschaft, 2011), 1:385.

13. The translation of וכפר על־הקדש without any preposition as καὶ ἐξιλάσεται τὸ ἅγιον ("Thus he shall atone the sanctuary") is noteworthy; it occurs as well in Lev 16:20, 33. It clearly indicates that the Greek translator had a process of purification of the object in mind. The Hebrew wording of the MT conveys this, albeit in a more implicit way.

14. All English translations of biblical and other source passages are my own.

fies the purposes or results: through these rites he "shall make atonement [כפר piel / ἐξιλάσκομαι] for the sanctuary" (16:16; see also vv. 20, 33); he "shall cleanse" (טהר piel / καθαρίζω) and "sanctify" (קדש piel / ἁγιάζω) the altar (v. 19). Although sacrificial blood is always applied to objects according to Lev 16, the priestly texts also know of blood rites on humans. During the ordination ceremonies for Aaron and his sons, the blood of the ram of ordination is put "on the lobe of Aaron's right ear and on the lobes of the right ears of his sons, and on the thumbs of their right hands, and on the big toes of their right feet" (Exod 29:20; see also Lev 8:23–24), in order to "sanctify/consecrate" (קדש piel / ἁγιάζω) the future priests (Exod 29:44; see also 29:21; Lev 8:12, 30). The purification ritual of a "leper" (מצרע / λεπρός) in Lev 14:1–32 requires similar activities.[15] The blood of another type of sacrifice, namely, the guilt offering (אשם / περὶ τῆς πλημμελείας), is smeared in an analogous fashion onto the person who is to be purified from the disease (v. 17); in this way the priest "shall make atonement for him" (וכפר עליו / καὶ ἐξιλάσεται περὶ αὐτοῦ, v. 18b).[16]

The synonyms accompanying the verb "to atone" suggest that atonement has to do with the removal of sin and impurity from the sanctuary and/or humans.[17] Therefore Jacob Milgrom assumes that the sanctuary is subject to defilement itself as an inevitable consequence of human sins

---

15. The frequent translation of Hebrew מצרע as "leper/leprous" for a particular type of skin or surface condition affecting a person or house follows the rendition in LXX with λεπρός. It is, however, questionable because the spectrum of symptoms described in Lev 14 and various other Hebrew Bible texts is broader than that of modern Hansen's disease; see Leon Goldman, Richard S. Moraites, and Karl W. Kitzmiller, "White Spots in Biblical Times," *Archives of Dermatology* 93 (1966): 744–53; Milgrom, *Leviticus 1–16*, 824; Gary B. Ferngren, *Medicine and Religion: A Historical Introduction* (Baltimore: Johns Hopkins University Press, 2014), 33–34.

16. The formula on atonement in Lev 14:18b summarizes the effect of the application rite described in v. 17 (cf. the following translations: LXX, NIV, *Traduction Œcuménique de la Bible*, *Die Bibel nach der Übersetzung Martin Luthers* [1984]). NRSV incorrectly connects וכפר to v. 19.

17. It should be noted that the mention of "sin and impurity" in biblical texts does not necessarily imply the factual occurrence of either one or the other. Both terms are theological interpretive categories that could be attributed to a variety of phenomena for a variety of reasons. Ancient communities of the Near East and beyond generally sought to link negative events such as famine, droughts, defeat in battle, or sickness to supernatural causation and might have retrospectively concluded that "sin" or "impurity" must have occurred because of such phenomena (see Ferngren, *Medicine*, 37–39).

and impurities.[18] Purification through sin offerings happens throughout the year; the rituals on the Day of Atonement, however, also purge for brazen sins.[19]

The "ritual detergent" in cultic contexts is the blood of sacrificial animals. What is the reason for this "special power?" Only one sentence in the Hebrew Bible / Old Testament provides an explicit rationale for how such blood application rites achieve atonement (Lev 17:11):

כי נפש הבשר בדם הוא ואני נתתיו לכם על־המזבח לכפר על־נפשתיכם
כי־הדם הוא בנפש יכפר׃

ἡ γὰρ ψυχὴ [πάσης] σαρκὸς [αἷμα αὐτοῦ] ἐστιν,[20] καὶ ἐγὼ δέδωκα αὐτὸ ὑμῖν ἐπὶ τοῦ θυσιαστηρίου ἐξιλάσκεσθαι περὶ τῶν ψυχῶν ὑμῶν, τὸ γὰρ αἷμα αὐτοῦ [ἀντὶ] τῆς ψυχῆς ἐξιλάσεται.

"For the life of the flesh[21] is in the blood; and I [sc. YHWH] have given it to you on/for the altar in order to make atonement for your lives; because it is the blood that makes atonement through[22] life."

---

18. Milgrom, *Leviticus 1–16*, 1033: "the result of Israel's wrongdoing is the creation of impurity, which then attaches itself to the sanctuary and pollutes it ... then the function of all of the blood manipulations becomes clear: to purge the sanctuary of its accumulated pollution." See also Milgrom, *Ritual and Ethics*, 30.

19. Milgrom, *Ritual and Ethics*, 31: "If, however, individuals have brazenly violated prohibitions, then, once a year, on Yom Kippur, the high priest purges the entire sanctuary, beginning with the inner and holiest area, containing the Ark." The text of Lev 16 does not specify exactly which "type" of sins are being atoned for. Thus already ancient interpreters have held different opinions on this matter. For instance, Josephus hypothesized that sin offerings only addressed inadvertent sins and that guilt offerings would be stipulated for known wrongs (Josephus, *Ant.* 3.230-232; see Watts, *Leviticus 1–10*, 304–12).

20. Through its specific rendering, the LXX identifies "life" and "blood" whereas for the MT, "life" is "in the blood" (cf. Vahrenhorst, "Levitikon," 387).

21. In translations of Lev 17:11, the Hebrew word בשר is often rendered as "creature" (NIV, *Traduction Œcuménique de la Bible*: "créature"), or "body" ("Leib," cf. *Die Bibel nach der Übersetzung Martin Luthers* [1984]). While בשר can certainly have these meanings, the context of Lev 17:11 deals with the prohibition of consuming blood in the process of eating meat. In Lev 17:11, therefore, the proper rendering of בשר is "flesh." This rendering is corroborated by the LXX (σάρξ); see Vahrenhorst, "Levitikon," 387.

22. On the interpretation of the preposition ב as *bet instrumentii* "by means of, through" see Luigi Moraldi, *Espiazione sacrificale e riti espiatori nell'ambiente biblico*

Conveying a genuine aspect of ancient physical anthropology, this passage states that blood is the medium of, or actually contains, the animal's life. Therefore atonement through blood application is, in the end, achieved through life. Other ancient Near Eastern cultures similarly recognize blood as a principal life-force because of various common phenomena: its injury-related loss is fatal, it is shed at childbirth, and menstruation further suggests an obvious link to fertility and reproduction. Blood is then seen in analogy to body fluids such as sperm or mother's milk that appear to contain secret life power. This understanding of blood is evident in various ancient Near East creation myths.[23] In the Hebrew language, this connection is manifest in the similarity of the term דם (blood) and אדם (human being, humanity, man). As the life of a creature, blood belongs to God, the giver of life; hence it is sacred.[24] Finally, in blood application rites, the effect called "atonement" occurs when sacrificial blood is brought into contact with persons or objects; sacrificial blood purges or consecrates upon physical touch.[25]

This understanding of sacrificial blood rites, while certainly not the only one, has received some approval among scholars.[26] However, Christophe

---

e nell'Antico Testamento, AnBib 5 (Rome: Pontifical Biblical Institute, 1956), 237–43; Milgrom, *Leviticus 1–16*, 706–7; Vahrenhorst, "Levitikon," 387.

23. See Jan Bergman and Benjamin Kedar-Kopfstein, "דם," *TDOT* 3:237.

24. In later texts the word "blood," often in conjunction with "flesh," could be used as a synecdoche to refer to a human being as such and, moreover, point to the human predicament of mortality (Sir 14:18; 17:31; Matt 16:17; 1 Cor 15:50; attested also in the Talmud). In other biblical texts, however, it refers specifically to the shedding of blood, i.e., killing, and bloodguilt, i.e., the guilt incurred by bloodshed, often implying the death of innocent people (Gen 9:6; Num 35:33; Hos 12:15 [12:14 ET]).

25. See Christian Eberhart, *Studien zur Bedeutung der Opfer im Alten Testament: Die Signifikanz von Blut- und Verbrennungsriten im kultischen Rahmen*, WMANT 94 (Neukirchen-Vluyn: Neukirchener Verlag, 2002), 165–73, 257–73; Eberhart, "Blood: I. Ancient Near East and Hebrew Bible/Old Testament," *EBR* 4:205–6. If the effect of the ritual occurs at the moment of blood application, then it is *not* the result of the act of animal slaughter *per se*; see Christian Eberhart, "Schlachtung/Schächtung," *WiBiLex* (Stuttgart: Deutsche Bibelgesellschaft, 2006), http://tinyurl.com/SBL0393e.

26. See Friedhelm Hartenstein, "Zur symbolischen Bedeutung des Blutes im Alten Testament," in *Deutungen des Todes Jesu im Neuen Testament*, ed. Jörg Frey and Jens Schröter, WUNT 181 (Tübingen: Mohr Siebeck, 2005), 119–37; Hieke, *Leviticus 1–15*, 255–57; Hieke, *Leviticus 16–27*, 632–34; see also the former view of Christophe Nihan, *From Priestly Torah to Pentateuch*, 186–95. See, moreover, Wolfgang Kraus, "Der Erweis der Gerechtigkeit Gottes im Tode Jesu nach Röm 3,24–26," in *Judaistik*

Nihan has challenged it in a recent essay.[27] Thus I will study his arguments here, although the limited scope of this contribution does not permit a comprehensive analysis. Nihan provides a case for an alternative reading of the meaning of blood rites with specific attention to Lev 4. He first questions Milgrom's view about the *modus operandi* of the sin offering. While he agrees with Milgrom that sins and impurities defile Israel's sanctuary, he questions whether "the disposal of blood must have the same meaning and function in both texts [sc., Lev 4 and 16]."[28] He goes on to assert: "On the contrary, similar rituals may actually take different meanings in different contexts."[29] Nihan then investigates the meaning of prepositions following the verb כפר *piel* with special attention to the regulation about purification of women after parturition in Lev 12:6–7a. The translation of this passage, however, has prompted some debate, so it requires brief consideration:

ובמלאת ימי טהרה לבן או לבת תביא כבש בן־שנתו לעלה ובן־יונה או־
תר לחטאת אל־פתח אהל־מועד אל־הכהן: והקריבו לפני יהוה וכפר עליה
וטהרה ממקר דמיה

καὶ ὅταν ἀναπληρωθῶσιν αἱ ἡμέραι καθάρσεως αὐτῆς ἐφ' υἱῷ ἢ ἐπὶ θυγατρί, προσοίσει ἀμνὸν ἐνιαύσιον [ἄμωμον][30] εἰς ὁλοκαύτωμα[31] καὶ νεοσσὸν

---

und Neutestamentliche Wissenschaft: Standorte—Grenzen—Beziehungen, ed. Lutz Doering, Hans-Günther Waubke, and Florian Wilk, FRLANT 226 (Göttingen: Vandenhoeck & Ruprecht, 2008), 211–13. For summaries of recent studies on sacrificial blood rites, see Eberhart, *Studien zur Bedeutung der Opfer*, 230–51 (with table 9); William K. Gilders, *Blood Ritual in the Hebrew Bible: Meaning and Power* (Baltimore: Johns Hopkins University Press, 2004), 12–25, 49–60, etc.; Christophe Nihan, "The Templization of Israel in Leviticus: Some Remarks on Blood Disposal and *Kipper* in Leviticus 4," in *Text, Time, and Temple: Literary, Historical and Ritual Studies in Leviticus*, ed. Francis Landy, Leigh M. Trevaskis, and Bryan D. Bibb, HBM 64 (Sheffield: Sheffield Phoenix, 2015), 96–120.

27. Nihan, "Templization," 96–120.

28. Ibid., 106.

29. Ibid., 106; see also 113. Nihan refers to Adrian Schenker, "Interprétations récentes et dimensions spécifiques du sacrifice ḥaṭṭāt," *Bib* 75 (1994): 59–70, and Roy E. Gane, *Cult and Character: Purification Offering, Day of Atonement, and Theodicy* (Winona Lake, IN: Eisenbrauns, 2005), 21–24.

30. The LXX adds this word, which is self-evident in ritual contexts (see Vahrenhorst, "Levitikon," 375).

31. The LXX employs a total of six different Greek terms to render Hebrew עלה "burnt offering"; among these ὁλοκαύτωμα is the most frequent one (see the table in Eberhart, *Kultmetaphorik und Christologie*, 208–9).

περιστερᾶς ἢ τρυγόνα περὶ ἁμαρτίας ἐπὶ τὴν θύραν τῆς σκηνῆς τοῦ μαρτυρίου πρὸς τὸν ἱερέα, καὶ [προσοίσει] ἔναντι κυρίου καὶ ἐξιλάσεται περὶ αὐτῆς ὁ ἱερεὺς καὶ [καθαριεῖ αὐτὴν] ἀπὸ τῆς πηγῆς τοῦ αἵματος αὐτῆς.

> When the days of her purification are completed, whether for a son or for a daughter, she shall bring to the priest at the entrance of the tent of meeting a lamb, a year old, for a burnt offering, and a pigeon or a turtledove for a sin offering. He shall offer it before YHWH, and make atonement on her behalf; and she shall be clean due to[32] her flow of blood.

Following Gane, Nihan assumes that Lev 12:7 cannot mean that the altar has been purged from any pollution resulting from the woman's impurity, as Milgrom suggested; on philological grounds, it can only mean "that the woman has been 'purified' from the source of blood."[33] This becomes a precedent of sorts to the claim that atonement in a sin offering can indeed be directed toward a human being. Now Nihan also reads the law of the sin offering in Lev 4 from this vantage point and rejects the notion that it might purge the space of the sanctuary from any pollution.[34] Eventually, he goes one step further and embraces the sociocultural approach of blood rituals proposed by William Gilders, who maintains that the process of ascribing meaning to rituals is always speculative and necessarily employs "gap filling." Therefore Gilders explores Nancy Jay's understanding that an index is a sign connected with its referents not through cultural or religious conventions, but as a matter of fact, and espouses it for the interpretation of blood rituals in the Bible.[35] While Gilders acknowledges that, in the ritual of the sin offering (Lev 4:1–5:13), purification and

---

32. This translation of the Hebrew preposition מן follows the rendering of Lev 12:7a proposed by Dorothea Erbele-Küster, *Körper und Geschlecht: Studien zur Anthropologie von Leviticus 12 und 15*, WMANT 121 (Neukirchen-Vluyn: Neukirchener Verlag, 2008), 20: "und sie ist rein *infolge der* Quelle ihres Blutes" (emphasis added); see also ibid., 40–42. The reasons for this and other translations will be discussed below.

33. Nihan, "Templization," 107.

34. Ibid., 107–8, with reference to Gane, *Cult and Character*, 112–16.

35. Gilders, *Blood Ritual in the Hebrew Bible*, 5–11, 78–84, etc. Hence in the narrative of the covenant at Mount Zion (Exod 24:3–8), Moses's agency in manipulating sacrificial blood indicates his unique status. Likewise during the Passover celebration (Exod 12), the Israelites who apply blood to their doors are "indexed" as those engaged for the Israelites' survival and as people of priestly status. At the same time, such blood rites mark a cultic sphere and "index" access to meal rites (ibid., 43–49).

consecration are explicit or "manifest functions" of blood manipulations based on "public and official explanations," he states that his own attention is devoted to "latent functions" of rituals because "the outside interpreter is also in a position to move beyond the explicit interpretations offered by ritual participants."[36] Such "latent" dimensions of meaning are implied in rituals but never explicitly mentioned; they are usually not recognized by participants in ritual activities. Nihan employs this approach when asserting that sacrificial blood "indexes" the sanctuary's key role for Israel. Moreover, "The application of blood to various areas inside the sanctuary complex connects the guilty party with the deity, while establishing at the same time several basic distinctions and hierarchies at the social, ethical and ritual level."[37]

The approach proposed by Gilders and adopted by Nihan and the specific interpretation of blood application outlined above have enriched biblical studies through special attention to sociocultural dimensions of sacrificial rituals. However, I would like to raise the following critical questions:

1. To begin with, Nihan's argument seems to have a logical problem. He develops his recent position on blood application rites following the interpretation of the statement about the purification of a parturient (Lev 12:7). According to him, the only possible understanding of this passage is that the ritual purifies the parturient from her blood flow.[38] The problem with his view is that, in this short chapter of Leviticus, the blood is twice explicitly called דמי טהרה (lit. "bloods of purity"[39]) (12:4a, 5b). How, therefore, can such pure blood possibly cause impurity *from* which the woman would later need to be purified? This logical problem is already manifest in the LXX, which resorts to rendering בדמי טהרה ("in bloods of purity") as ἐν αἵματι [ἀκαθάρτῳ] [αὐτῆς] ("in her impure blood"),[40] thus *de facto* turning the meaning into its opposite. Admittedly, this passage has puzzled many interpreters. If the literal Hebrew text in Lev 12:4a, 5b

---

36. Ibid., 6, 141; see also ibid., 6, 180, 181–91. For a description of Gilders's position, see Watts, *Leviticus 1–10*, 321–22.

37. Nihan, "Templization," 126.

38. Ibid., 107.

39. Dorothea Erbele-Küster translates "Reinigungsblut" (*Körper*, 20, 40–42). Milgrom proposes "blood purity" (*Leviticus 1–16*, 742, 749); Levine renders "blood purification" and also suggests "pure blood" (*Leviticus*, 73); Hieke has "(vergossenen) Blutes (im Status) der Purifikation" (*Levitikus 1–15*, 441).

40. See Erbele-Küster, *Körper*, 42; Vahrenhorst, "Levitikon," 375.

is to be taken seriously, however, then Dorothea Erbele-Küster's explanation of verse 7 is plausible that the woman after childbirth is indeed purified "through the source of her blood."[41] For the interpretation of blood application rites in the context of the sin offering of the parturient, this understanding means that sacrificial blood might as well have purged the altar from pollution.

2. Adopting a sociocultural approach, Nihan argues that the application of blood at various areas inside the sanctuary complex connects the guilty party, who offers the prescribed sacrifice, with God.[42] This conception, while interesting, creates problems when applied to other blood application rites. How, for instance, is the ritual in Lev 14:14 to be understood where blood of a guilt offering is applied to a "leper" who is being cleansed? If the same ritual logic were to be applied here, would not the person be "connected" to himself?

3. We must ask, furthermore, whether it is warranted to reduce the interpretation of atonement exclusively to the blood application rite at the sanctuary, thus neglecting that the effect articulated by the verb כפר *piel* is not the result of only one ritual component. Nihan actually states that the effect of a sin offering is not just accomplished through its blood rite. However, he does little to employ this insight for his theory of atonement; in his essay, he leaves any ideas on what other ritual activities might contribute to the effect of atonement largely undeveloped.[43]

4. Finally, there appears to be a considerable methodological problem: Nihan questions the expediency of interpretive reflections originating in ancient communities. He considers such explicit statements of the purposes of ritual activities as uncertain because modern scholars have debated them for some time without reaching a consensus; hence he concludes they "are ultimately difficult, if not impossible, to verify."[44] Therefore he ultimately opts for the alternative sociocultural approach based

---

41. Erbele-Küster, *Körper*, 20, 40–42: "infolge der Quelle ihres Blutes." To support this view, Erbele-Küster adopts a *causative* meaning of the Hebrew preposition מן. She explains: "Der Text sagt nicht nur, dass die Frau [sc. the parturient] kultunfähig war aufgrund ihres Blutflusses, sondern vielmehr, dass sie rein ist aus der Quelle ihres Blutes heraus, d.h. infolge des Hervorfließens des Bluts" (ibid., 42).
42. Nihan, "Templization," 126.
43. See Nihan's pertinent comments in ibid., 111–12, 121.
44. Ibid., 95.

on ritual theory.⁴⁵ Yet these two approaches are not methodologically incompatible; they rather belong to different interpretive levels. To state it clearly, I think that the sociocultural analysis of latent dimensions of meanings of blood rites is appealing and plausible in and of itself.⁴⁶ However, it is no direct alternative to the one that is articulated in the Hebrew Bible / Old Testament, which is theological in nature. It is thus methodologically inappropriate to posit that the *explicit interpretation* in biblical texts of blood application rites (which utilizes theological concepts such as "atonement," "purification" from sin and impurity, or "consecration") must be abandoned because one sets out to devise a *sociocultural interpretation* that focuses on *latent* or *implicit* aspects (such as the creation of order, the indication of the status of ritual participants, or the connection of humans to the sanctuary). These interpretive approaches—not to mention historical or psychological ones—do not exclude each other. It is thus not appropriate to claim that one interpretive approach would be incorrect and another one correct.⁴⁷ To the contrary, both are correct, albeit on different interpretive levels.⁴⁸ This will be visualized by the following comparative table.

---

45. See ibid., 120–21.

46. Further questions will nevertheless be raised below.

47. Different interpretive perspectives are listed in, e.g., Thomas Staubli, *Die Bücher Levitikus, Numeri*, NSKAT 3 (Stuttgart: Katholisches Bibelwerk, 1996), 45–46; also Gilders acknowledges the legitimacy of a separate study of both explicit "manifest" and "latent" social-cultural functions of ritual (*Blood Ritual in the Hebrew Bible*, 181–82). Nihan, however, seems to question the usefulness of traditional interpretive approaches due to a lack of corroboration ("Templization," 95). It is not clear to me how the implicit sociocultural interpretation which he employs could actually be "verified"; I would argue that it remains an interpretive possibility like most traditional approaches.

48. A comparison with different biblical text genres will bear this point out. In the well-known narrative of an impending military conflict between Israel and the Philistines near the Valley of Elah (1 Sam 17:1–58), events take an unexpected turn when David approaches the gigantic Goliath, a true epitome of a "figure of fear" (David Jobling, *1 Samuel*, Berit Olam [Collegeville, MN: Liturgical Press, 1998], 219), to tell him: "You come to me with sword and with spear and with javelin; but I am coming to you in the name of YHWH of hosts, God of the ranks of Israel, whom you have defied [ואנכי בא־אליך בשם יהוה צבאות אלהי מערכות ישראל אשר חרפת]. This very day YHWH will deliver you into my hand [היום הזה יסגרך יהוה בידי], and I will strike you down and cut off your head; … so that all the earth may know that there is a god for Israel [וידעו כל־הארץ כי יש אלהים לישראל], and that all this assembly may know

Explicit and implicit (latent) functions of the sin offering ritual

Ritual activities	Explicit (theological) functions	Implicit / latent (sociocultural) functions
Hand-leaning rite (Exod 29:10; Lev 4:4, 15, 24, 29, 33; 8:14)	(None)	Connection (by indexing) to sacrificial animal: probably indicates ownership[49]

---

that YHWH does not save by sword and spear; for this battle belongs to YHWH [וידעו כל־הקהל הזה כי־לא בחרב ובחנית יהושיע יהוה כי ליהוה המלחמה], and he will give you into our hand" (vv. 45–47). After David kills Goliath with his sling and indeed decapitates him, the other Philistines flee in terror and Israel wins the conflict. This popular story can be interpreted in a variety of ways. In the narrative itself, however, David's lengthy speech depicts his motivation to engage in conflict and confront Goliath as uniquely theological, as P. Kyle McCarter Jr., *I Samuel: A New Translation with Introduction, Notes and Commentary*, AB 8 (Garden City, NY: Doubleday, 1980), 295, observes: "Only to Yahweh does he [sc. David] appeal for assistance, and here again his conduct is impeccable: his confidence in the power of his god is absolute." Besides, according to v. 36, David even understands Goliath's insult against Israel's army (v. 10) as being directed toward Israel's God (see A. Graeme Auld, *I and II Samuel: A Commentary*, OTL [Louisville: Westminster John Knox, 2011], 196). The interpreter of this text may nevertheless legitimately inquire whether David has implicit motivations of his own, i.e., to gain status as a successful warrior. Such a sociocultural or psychological interpretation would address latent dimensions of the text, taking into consideration that David's victory over Goliath constituted the start of an impressive military and political career, and a decisive gain in social status. Similar considerations apply to stories such as the conquest of Jericho (Josh 6) or Saul's disobedience after his defeat of the Amalekites (1 Sam 15). With regard to methodology, one interpretation obviously works within the "official" framework of ancient Israelite theology; the other assesses implicit reasons. Yet both lines of inquiry are perfectly valid within their respective argumentative frameworks and of interest in their own right. The legitimacy of different interpretive levels applies, of course, also to other realms, e.g., current-day sports. When German soccer pro Mario Götze was substituted for another player late in the 2014 FIFA World Cup final in Brazil against Argentina, he might have officially cited pride for his country to explain his outstanding efforts that allowed him to score the winning goal for the German team; yet underlying or implicit reasons might just as well have been considerations of his subsequent gain in fame, status, marketability, etc.

49. The hand-leaning rite (Watts translates "hand-pressing" [*Leviticus 1–10*, 189–92]) is understood as an indication of ownership by, e.g., Milgrom, *Leviticus 1–16*, 152; Staubli, *Levitikus, Numeri*, 50; Eberhart, *Studien zur Bedeutung der Opfer*, 265–67. Others interpret it as establishing a connection/relation; see, e.g., Gilders, *Blood Ritual in the Hebrew Bible*, 81; Thomas Hieke, "Der Kult ist für den Menschen da: Auf

Blood application rite (Exod 29:12; Lev 4:5–7, 16–18, 25, 30, 34; 5:9; 8:15; 16:14–15, 18–19)	Atones, purges, consecrates the sanctuary	Connection of the guilty party with the deity; establishes several basic social distinctions
Burning rite on altar of burnt offerings (Exod 29:13; Lev 4:10, 19, 26, 31, 35; 8:16; 16:25)	Pleasing odor for YHWH: appeasement of God through bringing of an "offering"; connection of the guilty party with God	Connection of the offerer / guilty party with the deity through an "offering"; establishes several basic social distinctions[50]

This table juxtaposes explicit theological and implicit/latent sociocultural functions of sacrificial rituals. The comparison shows that the specific function of the blood disposal rite now favored by Nihan is hardly original. The burning rite of portions of sacrificial animals also has a specific effect; it ultimately establishes the quality of the sin offering as an "offering for YHWH" (קרבן ליהוה / δῶρον τῷ κυρίῳ), thus invoking a social or relational dimension. This shall be explored in the next chapter.

Sacrificial Burning Rites on the "Altar of Burnt Offering"

On the Day of Atonement, the high priest "shall come out and offer his burnt offering and the burnt offering of the people, making atonement for himself and for the people" (ויצא ועשה את־עלתו ואת־עלת העם וכפר בעדו ובעד העם / ἐξελθὼν ποιήσει τὸ ὁλοκάρπωμα[51] αὐτοῦ καὶ τὸ ὁλοκάρπωμα τοῦ λαοῦ καὶ ἐξιλάσεται αὐτοῦ [καὶ περὶ τοῦ αὐτοῦ] καὶ καὶ περὶ τοῦ λαοῦ [ὡς περὶ τῶν ἱερέων], Lev 16:24). As this type of sacrifice features no blood application rite, the effect of atonement most likely results from its salient ritual component, namely the burning of the entire animal on the altar of burnt offering.

Spurensuche in den Opfervorschriften von Levitikus 1–10," *BK* 64 (2009), 143–44. I think both views are related: the indication of ownership is the direct basis of the connection between offerer and sacrificial animal.

50. This specific sociocultural interpretation of the burning rite will be explained below.

51. The Greek translation ὁλοκάρπωμα for Hebrew עלה with the sense of "burnt offering" is rare; it occurs only four times in the LXX. See the comparative table of terminological equivalents between the MT and the LXX in Eberhart, *Kultmetaphorik und Christologie*, 208–9.

However, the connection between these two specific sacrificial aspects has not received much scholarly attention in the recent past. Likewise, other types of sacrifice have rather been neglected, even if they occur more frequently in the Hebrew Bible / Old Testament than the sin offering.[52] In what follows, I will show that the investigation of atonement in sacrificial rituals beyond blood application rites helps to understand these other types of sacrifice as well.

The book of Leviticus, featuring the most detailed information on sacrificial rituals, distinguishes the following five types of sacrifice:

1. burnt offering (עלה / ὁλοκαύτωμα, Lev 1);
2. cereal offering / grain offering[53] (מנחה / θυσία, Lev 2);
3. peace offering / fellowship offering / communion offering / well-being offering (זבח שלמים / θυσία σωτηρίου, Lev 3);
4. sin offering / purification offering (חטאת / περὶ τῆς ἁμαρτίας, Lev 4:1–5:13);
5. guilt offering / reparation offering (אשם / περὶ τῆς πλημμελείας, Lev 5:14–6:7 ET; 7:1–7).

All of these five types of sacrifice differ in the description of their material and exact ritual actions.[54] Other terms which appear throughout these rituals interpret these various actions or the rituals in their entirety, or state what their effect on either humans or God is, for example, "being

---

52. On this interesting development in biblical scholarship, see Christian A. Eberhart, "A Neglected Feature of Sacrifice in the Hebrew Bible: Remarks on the Burning Rite on the Altar," *HTR* 97 (2004), 485–93. Exceptions to this scholarly trend are rare. See, e.g., the book by Royden K. Yerkes, *Sacrifice in Greek and Roman Religions and Early Judaism* Hale Lectures (New York: Scribner, 1952), and the publications of Alfred Marx, e.g., "The Theology of the Sacrifice According to Leviticus 1–7," in *The Book of Leviticus: Composition and Reception*, ed. Robert A. Kugler and Rolf Rendtorff, VTSup 93 (Leiden: Brill, 2003, 103–20); Marx, "Familiarité et transcendence: La fonction du sacrifice d'après l'Ancien Testament," in *Studien zu Opfer und Kult im Alten Testament*, ed. Adrian Schenker, FAT 3 (Tübingen: Mohr Siebeck, 1992), 1–13; Marx, *Les systèmes sacrificiels de l'Ancien Testament: Formes et fonctions du culte sacrificiel à Yhwh*, VTSup 105 (Leiden: Brill, 2005).

53. This list features common variations found in English Bible translations and scholarly studies.

54. These differences cannot be explored here. On the individual profiles of the five types of sacrifice in Lev 1–7 see Eberhart, *Studien zur Bedeutung der Opfer*, 16–186; Hieke, *Levitikus 1–15*, 146–330.

acceptable" (רצה, רצון / δέχομαι, δεκτός; Lev 1:3–4; 19:5, 7; 22:19, 20), "pleasing odor" (ריח ניחוח / ὀσμὴ εὐωδίας; Lev 1:9, 13, 17; 4:31; 8:21; etc.), or "to forgive" (סלח niphal / ἀφίημι; Lev 4:20, 26, 31; 5:10, 13). The verb "to atone" (כפר piel / ἐξιλάσκομαι) is one of these interpretive terms. It occurs, for example, in the context of the burnt offering (Lev 1:4; see also 9:7; 16:24). Interestingly, in the sin offering ritual, the formula about atonement and forgiveness (4:20b, 26b, 31b, 35b) always follows the description of the burning rite (4:19–20a, 26a, 31a, 35a), suggesting that blood application and burning rite work together to effect atonement and forgiveness.[55]

Why, then, were sacrificial materials burned on the central "altar of burnt offering"? What is the meaning or purpose of this ritual activity? Also, what is the relation between the effect stated in the biblical texts and the topic of atonement? To answer these questions, I will first make some remarks on the ritual procedure of a sacrificial ritual and, second, scrutinize the explicit statements featured in the texts of the Hebrew Bible / Old Testament.

A considerable amount of scholarly studies has been dedicated to the connection of blood application rites and atonement in sacrificial rituals. Blood application is, however, not the only ritual element to effect atonement in the Hebrew Bible / Old Testament cult. Featuring no such rite, the burnt offering, for example, also effects atonement. I have pointed out elsewhere that animal slaughter, which I think has been overrated in recent studies of the Hebrew Bible / Old Testament cult, does not occur in all of the sacrificial rituals described in Lev 1–7. Therefore it can neither be considered the crucial action nor the key to unlocking the meaning of sacrifices; it rather has preparatory functions. Similar observations pertain to blood application rites. By contrast, the burning rite is common to all types of sacrifice in Lev 1–7: either the entire sacrifice (Lev 1:9, 13, 17) or certain parts of it (2:2, 9; 3:5, 11; 4:8–10, 19–20) are eventually burned on the "altar of burnt offering." I have suggested that this element is the constitutive element of ritual sacrifices.[56] Consisting of wheat, oil, and frankincense, the cereal offering (מנחה, Lev 2 and 6:7–16 [6:14–18 ET]) is a fully valid sacrificial offering (קרבן) that can, according to Lev 5:11–13,

---

55. See Eberhart, *Studien zur Bedeutung der Opfer*, 132–38; Marx, "Theology," 117; Marx, *Systèmes sacrificiels*, 140; Watts, *Leviticus 1–10*, 346.

56. See Eberhart, *Studien zur Bedeutung der Opfer*, 183–184, 318–321; Eberhart, "Neglected Feature," 491, 493.

substitute for a sin offering, which usually requires an animal.[57] This demonstrates not only that a cultic sacrifice can function without killing, but also that atonement is (at least sometimes or partially) achieved through the burning rite, the main ritual activity of the cereal offering (2:2).[58] The Judean sacrificial cult celebrated by Jewish mercenaries at the temple of Elephantine (Yebu) during the sixth century BCE provides a potent example of the importance of this ritual element. According to ancient Aramaic papyri, this cult featured only cereal offerings and frankincense, but no animals. Thus sacrifice can function without victims.

Do Hebrew Bible / Old Testament texts contain information about the meaning or purpose of the burning rite on the main altar? As previously mentioned, this ritual component effects the "pleasing odor for YHWH" (ריח ניחוח ליהוה / ὀσμὴ εὐωδίας τῷ κυρίῳ). The sacrifices given by humans are thus transformed and transported to God in the rising smoke. These dynamics toward God are captured by the comprehensive Hebrew term for offering, קרבן, which means literally "brought near (to God)." It is rendered as δῶρον "gift / offering" in the LXX.[59] In Lev 1–7 this term applies to all five types of sacrifice (Lev 1:2, 3, 10; 2:1, 4; 3:1; 4:23, 28, 32; 5:11; 7:38). By contrast, rituals lacking the burning rite on the main altar do not count as sacrifices. Therefore the Passover (Exod 12:1–28), which is an apotropaic ritual, or the scapegoat (16:10, 20–22), which is an elimination ritual (see below), are absent from the list of sacrifices in Lev 1–7. All five types of sacrifice listed there, however, do effect atonement according to Leviticus and other passages of the Hebrew Bible / Old Testament.[60] This happens partially through the burning rite, which represents the moment when God accepts the sacrifices brought by humans.

---

57. See Eberhart, *Studien zur Bedeutung der Opfer*, 77–88, 207–8.

58. By similar logic Moses appeases God's wrath in order to halt a plague; he advises Aaron to burn incense in a censer (ותן־עליה אש מעל המזבח ושים קטרת / καὶ ἐπίθες ἐπ' αὐτὸ πῦρ ἀπὸ τοῦ θυσιαστηρίου καὶ ἐπίβαλε [ἐπ' αὐτὸ] θυμίαμα), who thus makes atonement for Israel (וכפר עליהם / καὶ ἐξίλασαι περὶ αὐτῶν, Num 17:11–12 [16:46–47 ET]).

59. See Vahrenhorst, "Levitikon," 335–36; Christian Eberhart, "Qorban," *WiBiLex* (Stuttgart: Deutsche Bibelgesellschaft, 2010), http://tinyurl.com/SBL0393d.

60. Burnt offering: Lev 1:4; 9:7; 16:24; grain offering: Lev 9:7; 14:20; 1 Sam 3:14; communion offering: Lev 9:7; 1 Sam 3:14; Ezek 45:15; sin offering: Lev 4:26, 31, 35; 5:13; guilt offering: Lev 5:16, 18. See also Janowski, *Sühne als Heilsgeschehen*, 190–91; Eberhart, *Studien zur Bedeutung der Opfer*, 185–86.

Thomas Hieke aptly describes that the approach conveyed by the term קרבן is intended to establish or renew a relationship with God.[61] It comes as no surprise that people who visit the temple, known to them as the "house of God/YHWH" (1 Sam 3:15; 2 Sam 12:20; 1 Kgs 8:10–11; 2 Chron 24:18, etc.; see also Ps 84), expect to encounter God.[62] If they offer sacrifices there that are burned on the altar, and the effect is articulated by the formula "for a pleasing odor for YHWH," then God is explicitly denoted as a party involved in atonement.[63]

It is clear that this concept initially presupposes an existential separation between humans and God, which the sources articulate in terms of human sins or impurities vis-à-vis a holy God. Another general term for sacrifice is מנחה, which also means "tribute" or "present." Thus even in its cultic usage it highlights the aspect of a status difference between humans and God, who is perceived as a divine king. Sin and impurity necessitate forgiveness, purification, and appeasement; the acknowledgment of the status difference requires a token of homage. The result is "atonement," which denotes a critical positive development in the relationship. William Tyndale coined this term in 1526 to literally mean "at-one-ment."[64] The concept of atonement is thus functionally equivalent and linked to that

---

61. "Der ganze Aufwand hat nicht seinen Sinn und seinen Zweck in sich, sondern ist äußere Ausdrucksform eines personalen, spirituellen Geschehens: die Wiederherstellung der Kommunikation mit JHWH, die Manifestation oder der Zuspruch des göttlichen Wohlgefallens als Grundlage für das Wohlergehen der Menschen.... Hinter der auf Wiederholbarkeit ausgelegten Ritualsprache steht vielmehr die göttliche Offenbarung, dass von Seiten JHWHs ein Weg eröffnet und geschenkt wird, wie eine dauerhafte und erfolgreiche Beziehung zu JHWH zu realisieren ist" (Hieke, *Levitikus 1–15*, 178; see also Alfred Marx, "Opferlogik im alten Israel," in *Opfer: Theologische und kulturelle Kontexte*, ed. Bernd Janowski and Michael Welker, STW 1454 [Frankfurt am Main: Suhrkamp, 2000], 146).

62. See Bernd Janowski, "Der Ort des Lebens: Zur Kultsymbolik des Jerusalemer Tempels," in *Temple Building and Temple Cult: Architecture and Cultic Paraphernalia of Temples in the Levant (2.–1. Mill. B.C.E.)*, ed. Jens Kamlah with Henrike Michelau, ADPV 41 (Wiesbaden: Harrassowitz, 2012), 371–74.

63. The personal dimension of atonement is also manifest in noncultic Hebrew Bible / Old Testament texts where it can specifically designate mediation between human parties in case of controversy; e.g., Jacob provides a "present" (מנחה; Gen 32:21 [32:20 ET]) to prophylactically appease (כפר piel) the "face" of Esau. His goal is reconciliation with Esau and acceptance (see Hieke, *Levitikus 1–15*, 132).

64. See Watts, *Leviticus 1–10*, 345.

of "covenant."⁶⁵ Thomas Staubli mentions that the smoke of the sacrificial cult even creates a visible connection between the earthly and heavenly realms.⁶⁶ This aspect is especially characteristic of the burnt offering, listed first among the five types of sacrifice in Lev 1–7; its Hebrew designation עלה literally means "rising/ascending."⁶⁷

Hence, these observations suggest that the concept of atonement, which aims at reuniting humans and God with the goal of establishing a lasting relationship, is at least in part conveyed in the sacrificial burning rite. To repeat, in the sin offering ritual the recurring formula about atonement and forgiveness (Lev 4:20b, 26b, 31b, 35b) occurs exclusively *after* the description of the burning rite, prompting the assumption that the burning rite contributes to the effect of atonement in the sin offering as well, even if the more distinctive ritual element of this type of sacrifice is the blood application rite discussed above.⁶⁸

---

65. Due to the limited scope of this contribution, only a few aspects can be addressed here; for a more comprehensive discussion, see, e.g., Rolf Rendtorff, *The Covenant Formula: An Exegetical and Theological Investigation*, trans. Margaret Kohl, OTS (Edinburgh: T&T Clark, 1998); Walter Groß, *Zukunft für Israel: Alttestamentliche Bundeskonzepte und die aktuelle Debatte um den Neuen Bund*, SBS 176 (Stuttgart: Katholisches Bibelwerk, 1998); Robert D. Miller II, *Covenant and Grace in the Old Testament: Assyrian Propaganda and Israelite Faith*, PHSC 16 (Piscataway, NJ: Gorgias, 2012). Suffice it to say that, in the Hebrew Bible / Old Testament, covenants are characteristically being instituted in situations of existential threats to humans (fear of destruction of the earth, of childlessness, of sin and impurity, etc.). A covenant then appears as a one-sided promise or a self-imposed obligation of God to assure continuous life for individuals (Gen 15) or care of the earth (Gen 9:12–13). Such covenants can also be founded upon bilateral commitments and may involve ritual sacrifices, as manifest in the covenant ceremony at Mount Sinai (Exod 24:1–11).

66. Staubli, *Levitikus, Numeri*, 51.

67. Milgrom, *Leviticus 1–16*, 172–74; Watts, *Leviticus 1–10*, 184–86.

68. However, the formula "for a pleasing odor for YHWH" that usually accompanies the burning rite occurs just once (Lev 4:31) in all of the sin offering rituals of 4:1–5:13. What might be the reason? The pertinent instruction states: "He [sc. the priest] shall remove all the fat, just as the fat is removed from the lamb of the well-being sacrifice, and the priest shall burn it on the altar upon the offerings by fire of YHWH [והקטיר הכהן אתם המזבחה על אשי יהוה]" (4:35; see also 5:12). As such, it suggests a connection with other types of sacrifice. In fact, on the Day of Atonement the high priest offers sin offerings first (16:11, 15) with their related blood application rites (16:15–16, 18–19). Afterward he offers burnt offerings "to make atonement for himself and for the people" (16:24). Now the instruction continues: "He shall also burn the fat of the sin offering on the altar" (16:25). Hence the ritual of the sin offering

In the early Jewish temple cult, atonement thus denotes a set of diverse human ritual practices in response to divine regulations aimed at overcoming a rift in the vertical relationship. Sacrifices offered outside the context of the Day of Atonement rituals often occur at the conclusion of pilgrimages characterized in and of themselves by large-scale dynamics toward the sanctuary. In the wake of Hezekiah's and Josiah's centralization of the temple cult, the Jewish people had the obligation to participate in three annual pilgrimages at Passover / Unleavened Bread, the Festival of Weeks, and the Festival of Booths (Exod 23:14–17; 34:23; Deut 16:16; 2 Chr 8:13). Centuries later, Philo of Alexandria describes countless groups of pilgrims traveling from remote rural areas to the city of Jerusalem and its temple (*Spec.* 1:68–70; *Leg.* 3:11). Other important occasions such as childbirth also required sacrifices at the sanctuary (Lev 12:6–8). Generally, pilgrimages were cheerful celebrations; the chanting of psalms (e.g., Pss 120–134) accompanied the sometimes lengthy march to the Holy City. Pilgrims brought their sacrifices to the temple in order to offer them through the burning rite to the God of Israel.[69] By their quantity and quality, the sacrifices themselves displayed outwardly the economic and social status, and in their own way also the personal piety, of each person, family, or clan participating in the pilgrimage. Through the act of offering, these sacrifices would finally become manifestations of the connection between humans and God.

Therefore pilgrimages and sacrificial rituals as their conclusion are both characterized by dynamics toward the sanctuary and the God who resides there. The dynamics of the latter are captured in the formula "offering for YHWH" (קרבן ליהוה); the effect of its rising smoke on God is articulated as a "pleasing odor for YHWH" (ריח ניחוח ליהוה). Both aspects imply the connection of the offerer, who might or might not be a guilty party, with God. What, then, are potential sociocultural interpretations of this ritual process? If understood at the interpretive level of immediate contact as "indexes," then the activity of bringing a material

---

was interrupted after the blood application rite. Its fat was not burned right away but after the burnt offering has been burned. If the fat of the sin offering is subsequently placed on the altar, then the description in Leviticus 4:35 is indeed correct: it is burned on the altar with, or upon portions of other types of sacrifice called "offerings by fire."

69. Hence the dynamics conveyed in the Hebrew root קרב ("approach") governs the entire process of the pilgrimage, of which the actual ritual sacrifice called קרבן ("offering") is but the conclusion at the sanctuary.

offering to the sanctuary would forge a "connection" of the offerer with the deity. The burning rite is the moment of culmination through its visible connection between the earthly and the heavenly realm. At the same time, the provisions for different types of sacrifice depending on economic and social status establish and/or reinforce basic social distinctions.

Interestingly, this attempted sociocultural interpretation of what might be latent functions of burning rites has surprising similarities to the one contained in biblical texts. The latter, however, feature explicit linguistic clues regarding this connection through terms like "offering for YHWH," "pleasing odor for YHWH," and so on, making it less speculative. It therefore poses a challenge to the sociocultural analysis of latent dimensions of rituals discussed in the previous chapter, in so far as that one appears to be in part a quasi-duplication of the explicit, theological interpretation of the burning rite.[70] Furthermore, it is clear that the sociocultural interpretation compromises any conceptional idiosyncrasies of blood application rites which are, after all, rather distinct from burning rites. And finally, it may be stressed that the sociocultural analysis of the application rites fails to answer the question of why particularly blood is used for this rite.[71] Other substances deployed in temple rituals are ointment and water. Why then would blood be interpreted as the substance that "indexes" the human-divine connection and/or social status in a special way?

So far in this study, we have seen that atonement is associated with blood application rites on the one hand and with burning rites on the other. Biblical texts feature explicit interpretive reflections of either one, encoding the "native" understandings of their original communities and tradents. These interpretive reflections were naturally set within the cosmological framework of these communities and tradents; they were therefore theological. As we have seen, terminology conceptually related to purification and consecration has been deployed to explain the effect of

---

70. Nihan, however, posits "that it is in the manipulation of the blood of the *ḥaṭṭā't*, more than in any other aspect of the sacrificial rites prescribed in Leviticus, that the ritual, social, political and legal-ethical dimensions that constitute 'Israel' as a community in that book are brought together in connection with the sanctuary" ("Templization," 126).

71. See the pertinent question by Hieke: "Auch wenn der Text selbst keine unmittelbare Auskunft gibt, warum es ausgerechnet das Blut ist, das bei seiner Applikation durch den Priester 'Versöhnung erwirkt', so muss dennoch eine Annäherung an diese Frage versucht werden" (*Levitikus 1–15*, 255).

atonement emerging from blood application rites; in addition, terminology referencing approach and existential connections as well as appeasement has been utilized for burning rites. Both variations articulate the goal of establishing or renewing a relationship between humans and God.

The Scapegoat Ritual

There is, however, yet another element of the Day of Atonement rituals that effects atonement, namely the scapegoat. We encounter it in only a few sentences in Lev 16, situated in the midst of sacrificial rituals. First, Aaron the high priest is to take two goats and bring them to the entrance of the sanctuary. There he casts lots to determine which goat is "for Azazel" (לעזאזל) and which one is to be sacrificed as a sin offering (Lev 16:7–8). One goat "shall be presented alive before YHWH to make atonement over it" (יעמד־חי לפני יהוה לכפר עליו [στήσει αὐτὸν] ζῶντα ἔναντι κυρίου τοῦ ἐξιλάσασθαι [ἐπ'] αὐτοῦ, v. 10).[72] Supplementary information follows later in this chapter (Lev 16:20–22):

וכלה מכפר את־הקדש ואת־אהל מועד ואת־המזבח והקריב את־השעיר החי: וסמך אהרן את־שתי ידו על ראש השעיר החי והתודה עליו את־כל־עונת בני ישראל ואת־כל־פשעיהם לכל־חטאתם ונתן אתם על־ראש השעיר ושלח ביד־איש עתי המדברה: ונשא השעיר עליו את־כל־עונתם אל־ארץ גזרה ושלח את־השעיר במדבר:

---

72. The words לכפר עליו in this specific context have long puzzled interpreters. The problem is that the verb כפר *piel* with the preposition על usually references objects such as the altar (Exod 30:10; Lev 8:15; 16:18) or the inner sanctum (Lev 16:16). This is different in Lev 16:10 where it refers to the animal that will become the scapegoat. The preposition is, therefore, employed in a unique fashion. The lack of consensus illustrates the puzzlement of the interpreters: Levine now translates "to make expiation with it" (*Leviticus*, 103); he formerly chose "in proximity to" for the preposition על (Levine, *In the Presence of the Lord: A Study of Cult and Some Cultic Terms in Ancient Israel*, SJLA 5 [Leiden: Brill, 1974], 80); Milgrom renders "to perform expiation upon it" (*Leviticus 1–16*, 1023); Hieke translates: "auf dass für ihn Versöhnung erwirkt werde" (*Levitikus 16–27*, 561). The perplexity is also manifest in ancient translations; for instance, Targum Pseudo-Jonathan renders "to atone for the sinfulness of the people, the House of Israel" so that the preposition does not refer to the goat at all. The Greek rendition in the LXX exceptionally deploys the preposition ἐπί "at/upon it." Vahrenhorst comments that the translator regards the scapegoat as the means, but not the beneficiary, of atonement ("Levitikon," 384).

καὶ συντελέσει ἐξιλασκόμενος τὸ ἅγιον καὶ τὴν σκηνὴν τοῦ μαρτυρίου καὶ τὸ θυσιαστήριον, [καὶ περὶ τῶν ἱερέων καθαριεῖ,]⁷³ καὶ προσάξει τὸν χίμαρον τὸν ζῶντα. καὶ ἐπιθήσει Ααρων τὰς χεῖρας αὐτοῦ ἐπὶ τὴν κεφαλὴν τοῦ χιμάρου τοῦ ζῶντος καὶ ἐξαγορεύσει ἐπ' αὐτοῦ πάσας τὰς ἀνομίας τῶν υἱῶν Ισραηλ καὶ πάσας τὰς ἀδικίας αὐτῶν καὶ πάσας τὰς ἁμαρτίας αὐτῶν καὶ ἐπιθήσει αὐτὰς ἐπὶ τὴν κεφαλὴν τοῦ χιμάρου τοῦ ζῶντος καὶ ἐξαποστελεῖ ἐν χειρὶ ἀνθρώπου ἑτοίμου εἰς τὴν ἔρημον, καὶ λήμψεται ὁ χίμαρος ἐφ' ἑαυτῷ τὰς ἀδικίας αὐτῶν εἰς γῆν ἄβατον, καὶ ἐξαποστελεῖ τὸν χίμαρον εἰς τὴν ἔρημον.

After he [sc. Aaron, the high priest] has completed making atonement for the sanctuary and the tent of meeting and the altar, he shall present the live goat. Then Aaron shall lay both of his hands on the head of the live goat and confess over it all the iniquities of the people of Israel, and all their transgressions, all their sins, putting them on the head of the goat, and sending it away into the wilderness through a man designated for the task. The goat shall bear on itself all their iniquities to a barren region; and the goat shall be set free in the wilderness.

The sparse information on this ritual allows a few remarks that will help to expand our understanding of the procedures and the achievement of atonement on the Day of Atonement. First, one simply needs to acknowledge that the famous scapegoat ritual is associated with the effect of atonement, although a certain degree of mystification is already evident in ancient translations of the Hebrew text as to how exactly one should imagine the rite to accomplish this.

Second, the scapegoat is not a sacrifice. This has little to do with the obvious fact that the goat is not killed but remains alive; indeed, it is repeatedly called "live goat." As noted above, the constitutive ritual element of a cultic sacrifice is not the activity of slaughter, but the burning rite on the main altar. However, neither of these two activities occurs in the context of the scapegoat ritual; the absence of the latter means that the scapegoat is no cultic sacrifice.⁷⁴ With regard to the absence of the former,⁷⁵ the scape-

---

73. This short phrase is an interpretive addition; see Vahrenhorst, "Levitikon," 385.
74. Hieke, *Levitikus 16–27*, 579 (specifically regarding the aspect that the scapegoat is not being slaughtered).
75. Mary Douglas, "The Go-Away Goat," in Kugler, *Book of Leviticus*, 122: "no violence whatever is committed against the Leviticus scapegoat." This changes toward the end of Second Temple Judaism. The Mishnah tract Yoma relates how the goat is brought into the wilderness to be pushed backwards off a cliff, so that "it did not reach

goat ritual furnishes an example of achieving atonement without any form of killing, and is the first example of this cultic effect outside of sacrificial rituals in Lev 16.

Third, then, we need to ask how this ritual "functions." It starts with a reference to the completion (כלה *piel* / συντελέω, Lev 16:20a) of the atonement process by blood application rites; these words are more than just an incidental note. They explicitly tie the previous ritual procedure to the next for which the "live goat" is being utilized (v. 20b). Now Aaron, the high priest, transfers the sanctuary's pollution and the sins of the people to this animal (v. 21). It happens through a hand-leaning gesture with two hands. The fact that the contents of Aaron's confession are explicitly mentioned leaves no doubt about the intended meaning of this act, contrary to the one-handed gesture in the context of animal sacrifices which lacks any such explanation. The Mishnah, which also knows the two-handed hand-leaning gesture (וסומך שתי ידיו עליו, m. Yoma 6:2), even relates the words of Aaron's confession, which is noteworthy as it allows the only pronouncement of the divine name throughout the year.[76] In addition, it mentions a "scarlet thread (לשון של זהורית) on the head of the goat that was to be sent forth" (4:2),[77] which helps to distinguish this goat from the one for the sin offering and probably symbolizes the transmitted sins and impurities by its color. As for the hand-leaning gesture and the confession of sins, they both reveal that defilement and sins are understood as quasi-material or physical.[78] As such they can be transferred onto a "medium."

---

halfway down the mountain before it broke into pieces" (ולא היה מגיע לחצי ההר עד שנעשה אברים אברים, m. Yoma 6:6). According to Douglas, "this rule is post-biblical, a rabbinical touch. It does not appear anywhere in the text of chapter 16" ("Go-Away Goat," 123).

76. "O Lord, your people, the house of Israel, has committed iniquity, transgressed, and sinned before you. Forgive, O Lord, I pray, the iniquities, transgressions, and sins, which your people, the house of Israel, have committed, transgressed, and sinned before you, as it is written in the torah of Moses, your servant, For on this day shall atonement be made for you to clean you. From all your sins shall you be clean before the Lord" (אנא השם עוו פשעו חטאו לפניך עמך בית ישראל אנא בשם כפר נא לעונות ולפשעים ולחטאים שעוו ושפשעו ושחטאו לפניך עמך בית ישראל ככתוב בתורת משה עבדך לאמר כי ביום הזה יכפר עליכם לטהר אתכם מכל חטאתיכם לפני ה' תטהרו). See Stemberger, "Yom Kippur," 131, 136.

77. Douglas, "Go-Away Goat," 123; Janowski, "Geschenk," 5.

78. Annette Schellenberg, "More than Spirit: On the Physical Dimension in the Priestly Understanding of Holiness," *ZAW* 126 (2014): 170–71.

The scapegoat ritual in Lev 16 concludes with the note that the goat is subsequently sent into the wilderness and "shall be set free" there. It literally "e-scapes" with the burden of Israel's sins and impurities, hence its name.[79] Scholars also classify this type of ritual as elimination ritual, a category that similarly conveys the spatial aspect of the goat carrying something beyond the "border" or "boundary marker," called *limes* in Latin, of human civilization.[80]

If this ritual is not a sacrifice, then one important aspect mentioned above may be revisited here. While sacrificial rituals feature dynamics toward the sanctuary, the scapegoat ritual moves in the opposite direction: it leads away from the sanctuary into the wilderness.[81] In this regard, it is similar to another elimination ritual in Lev 14,[82] which stands in close proximity to chapter 16 in the book of Leviticus. Leviticus 14:1–32 features the above-mentioned purification ritual from some kind of skin or surface condition affecting a person or a house. In either case, the ritual requires two birds, one of which is to be slaughtered. The priest then dips the other bird, together with cedar wood, a scarlet string, and hyssop, into the blood of the first and uses all of these to sprinkle the blood seven times upon the person (v. 7) or house (v. 51). He then releases the living

---

79. This is also implied in the Greek rendering ἀποπομπαῖος ("carrying away") in Lev 16:8 LXX and in the French term *bouc émissaire*. With regard to the scholarly discussion of the past four decades on the topic of the scapegoat, it is important to state that various connotations of humiliation, physical mistreatment, punishment, and potential killing (cf. René Girard, *La violence et le sacré* [Paris: Grasset, 1972]; Girard, "Generative Scapegoating," in *Violent Origins: Walter Burkert, René Girard, and Jonathan Z. Smith on Ritual Killing and Cultural Formation*, ed. Robert G. Hamerton-Kelly [Stanford, CA: Stanford University Press, 1987], 73–105) are absent from both the literal meaning of the term "scapegoat" and from the ritual in Lev 16; see Douglas, "Go-Away Goat," 122–25.

80. Henrike Frey-Anthes, "Sündenbock/Asasel," *WiBiLex* (Stuttgart: Deutsche Bibelgesellschaft), http://tinyurl.com/SBL0393g, §2.1.

81. Stephen Finlan, *The Background and Content of Paul's Cultic Atonement Metaphors*, AcBib 19 (Atlanta: Society of Biblical Literature, 2004), 81–84.

82. Other parallels, mainly from the ancient Near Eastern cultural and religious context, are provided in Bernd Janowski and Gernot Wilhelm, "Der Bock, der die Sünden hinausträgt: Zur Religionsgeschichte des Azazel-Ritus Lev 16,10.21f," in *Religionsgeschichtliche Beziehungen zwischen Kleinasien, Nordsyrien und dem Alten Testament: Internationales Symposion Hamburg 17.–21. März 1990*, ed. Bernd Janowski, Klaus Koch, and Gernot Wilhelm, OBO 129 (Friborg: Presses Universitaires; Göttingen: Vandenhoeck & Ruprecht, 1993), 109–69; Milgrom, *Leviticus 1–16*, 1071–79.

bird. It is interesting that the effect of the blood application rite is stated as "purification" (v. 7), "sin removal," and "atonement" (v. 52); however, the text mentions no effect accompanying the release of the second bird. What is notable here and in the scapegoat ritual is the close connection between the first ritual sequence culminating with blood application and the second one consisting of dispatching the bird, since it seems to suggest that the purification process of the person or object is not sufficient in and of itself. Instead, it apparently requires that the quasi-material defilement, after its separation from the contaminated object, requires transferal to a "medium" in order to be transported into uncultivated territory.[83] Both rituals in Lev 14 and 16, consisting of blood application and dispatch components, could therefore be viewed as complementary halves.

How then does the scapegoat effect atonement on the Day of Atonement? The response to this question is less obvious than in the case of sacrifices, since the one occurrence of the verb "to atone" in Lev 16:10 is not associated with any specific ritual element. It rather seems to reference the scapegoat ritual in its entirety. What, then, does this ritual accomplish? It neither immediately purges sacred objects from defilement, nor is it said to "please" God. However, it appears to conclude whatever is accomplished by the blood application rites in the context of sin offerings. As their "complementary half," the scapegoat carries away the defilement that was released from the sancta, thus finalizing the process of atonement.

Venturing for a moment into the realm of sociocultural interpretation, what would be "latent" meanings of the scapegoat ritual? How might one understand it at the interpretive level of immediate contact as an "index," and what would be its purpose? The first and main point of contact is the gesture of leaning two hands onto the head of the goat. As it is the duty of the high priest, it may once more serve to establish a connection, if only initially. However, the animal—which was incidentally chosen by lot not to be sacrificed so as to "index" the sanctuary's key role and/or connect the guilty party with the deity—is now sent away from the sanctuary into uninhabited territory, thus conveying dissociation. This interpretation receives further corroboration from the observation that another person of lower status is in charge of the latter, not the key representative of the sanctuary. With reflections like these, a sociocultural reading of the scape-

---

83. The close connection between both ritual components has been proposed previously; see Baruch J. Schwartz, "The Bearing of Sin in the Priestly Literature," in Wright, *Pomegranates and Golden Bells*, 18.

goat ritual yields, once again, some notable similarities with the explicit, theological interpretation; it is thus barely innovative.

Conclusion: Atonement on the Day of Atonement in Leviticus 16

I have surveyed three major ritual sequences that effect atonement according to Lev 16: blood application rites that purge Israel's sanctuary from sin and impurities, sacrificial burning rites that transport human offerings to God, and the scapegoat ritual that eliminates sin and impurities and releases them into uninhabited terrain. The text of Lev 16 explicitly connects all three of these respective ritual procedures with atonement: the sin offering as such (vv. 6, 11) and its blood application rite (vv. 16, 17 [2x], 18), the burnt offering (v. 24), and the goat "for Azazel" (v. 10). A redactional note that concludes the Day of Atonement ritual summarizes the effect of all of these distinct rituals with the following words, associating atonement with the various components of the sanctuary and two groups of human beneficiaries (Lev 16:33; see also vv. 32, 34):

וכפר את־מקדש הקדש ואת־אהל מועד ואת־המזבח יכפר ועל הכהנים
ועל־כל־עם הקהל יכפר:

καὶ ἐξιλάσεται τὸ ἅγιον τοῦ ἁγίου καὶ τὴν σκηνὴν τοῦ μαρτυρίου καὶ τὸ θυσιαστήριον ἐξιλάσεται καὶ περὶ τῶν ἱερέων καὶ περὶ πάσης συναγωγῆς ἐξιλάσεται.

And he [sc. Aaron, the high priest] shall make atonement for the holy of holies, and he shall make atonement for the tent of meeting and for the altar, and he shall make atonement for the priests and for all the people of the assembly.

How can one summarize these different methods of achieving atonement conceptually? While the initial disturbance of the divine-human relation can be described in a variety of ways, it always impacts that which is considered holy. It is sometimes described as defilement of the sacred location and its appurtenances, while it has a personal or relational dimension at other times, based on the difference in status between humans and God or the fact that humans belong to the profane world while God is holy. Atonement then happens through rituals that have the effect of purging what has been defiled and the purpose of appeasing God to establish or renew a relationship. The scapegoat ritual, if it complements these previous atonement rituals, finally releases or eliminates the "material" of defilement. Atonement thus emerges as a complex and multifaceted process, necessitating the broadening of later, narrower definitions of atonement. It is accomplished through cult rituals that bridge an existential separation; its agents are priests who function as mediators between humans and God at the sanctuary, God's dwelling place.

The conceptual ambivalence of ritual atonement is manifest in different languages and at various stages of the reception process of biblical texts. For example, the Akkadian *kapāru/kuppuru*, an equivalent of Hebrew כפר, means "to clean" as well as "to smear," conveying the idea of covering sancta defilement.[84] A similar interpretation of the term appears in the Hebrew Bible / Old Testament itself. In a quote from Jer 18:23, the text of Neh 3:37 (4:5 ET) faithfully reproduces its source with the exception of replacing כפר *piel* "to atone" by כסה *piel* "to cover," supplying evidence for the fact that the ancient author of Nehemiah imagined atonement as the covering (not purging/removing) of sin. The LXX deploys a range of different Greek terms to render Hebrew כפר *piel*, each of which links to a specific repertoire of images. Among these terms, the compound verb ἐξιλάσκομαι (Exod 30:15; Lev 16:6, 10, 16; Deut 21:8; etc.) is the most frequent translation with eighty-three occurrences; the simplex ἱλάσκομαι occurs only in Ps 65:4; 78:38; and 79:9. In addition, the LXX uses verbs drawing on other backgrounds, such as ἁγιάζω (Exod 29:33, 36) and καθαρίζω (Exod 29:37; 30:10) connoting "sanctification" and "purification." Thus the concept of "atonement" resists reduction to a single definition or translation; it has therefore been called a "hypernym."[85]

Epilogue: Aspects of Atonement in the New Testament

At this point, I shall juxtapose this study of the Day of Atonement and the explicitly or officially stated functions of its rituals with an examination of how early Christians adopted the concept of atonement. Due to the limited scope of this contribution, however, a brief epilogue must suffice that will survey five selected aspects emerging from the New Testament.

First, the terminology and concepts from temple rituals that effect atonement were obviously being deployed by early Christian authors. This

---

84. Janowski, *Sühne als Heilsgeschehen*, 15–102; Schellenberg, "Spirit," 173.
85. Gilders, *Blood Ritual in the Hebrew Bible*, 137.

is all the more interesting as many of them wrote after the destruction of the temples in Jerusalem and Leontopolis, Egypt, in the later first century CE, tragic events that put an end to any form of Jewish temple cult.[86] However, neither sacrificial rituals and atonement as salient features of Second Temple Judaism nor the substances associated with them became conceptually obsolete. As Watts comments: "this cessation of literal fulfillment did nothing to limit the importance of blood in subsequent religious imagination."[87] From now on, creative ways were being devised for the metaphorical use of such terminology.

Second, it is nonetheless undeniable that atonement terms and concepts occur rather infrequently in New Testament texts. While the Hebrew Bible / Old Testament contains approximately 149 occurrences of the root כפר, only 6 forms of the lexeme ἱλάσκομαι are attested in the New Testament: ἱλάσκομαι ("to atone") (Luke 18:13; Heb 2:17), ἱλαστήριον ("[place of] atonement") (Rom 3:25; Heb 9:5), and ἱλασμός ("atonement") (1 John 2:2; 4:10).[88] In particular, with the exception of Luke 18:13 that does not

---

86. Besides the Jerusalem temple, other Jewish temples existed in the period now commonly called Second Temple Judaism. One of them was built on Elephantine (Aramaic: *Yeb*), an island in the river Nile in Upper Egypt. Dedicated to the God *Yaho*, it served a colony of Judean or Israelite mercenaries. It existed in the fifth century BCE and was probably destroyed in ca. 410 BCE. Another sanctuary existed on Mount Gerizim, built in Persian times as a result of the increasing alienation between the Jewish and Samaritan communities. See Jörg Frey, "Temple and Rival Temples: The Cases of Elephantine, Mt. Gerizim, and Leontopolis," in *Gemeinde ohne Tempel: Zur Substituierung und Transformation des Jerusalemer Tempels und seines Kults im Alten Testament, antiken Judentum und Frühen Christentum*, ed. Beate Ego, Armin Lange, and Peter Pilhofer, WUNT 118 (Tübingen: Mohr Siebeck, 1999), 173–86.

87. Watts, *Leviticus 1–10*, 319.

88. For more comprehensive information, see Eberhart, *Kultmetaphorik und Christologie*, 157–77. Due to this scant attestation of the lexeme ἱλάσκομαι in the New Testament, some scholars challenged claims that atonement could be called a dominant image of Pauline soteriology; see Megory Anderson and Philip Culbertson, "The Inadequacy of the Christian Doctrine of Atonement in Light of Levitical Sin Offering," *AThR* 68 (1986): 303–28; Cilliers Breytenbach, *Versöhnung: Eine Studie zur paulinischen Soteriologie*, WMANT 60 (Neukirchen-Vluyn: Neukirchener Verlag, 1989), 100; Bradley H. McLean, "The Absence of an Atoning Sacrifice in Paul's Soteriology," *NTS* 38 (1992): 531–53. However, most New Testament and scholars employ the term "atonement" (or its German equivalent 'Sühne') differently than Hebrew Bible / Old Testament scholars. While the latter tend to restrict the term to occurrences of the Hebrew root כפר in the Hebrew Bible / Old Testament, New Testament scholars typically use it as an interpretive category and a theological-conceptual abstraction that

occur in a christological context, ἱλάσκομαι is absent from the New Testament gospels.

Third, the terminology and concepts from the Jewish temple cult, when they occur, are consistently employed in line with the explicit or "officially stated" effects found in the priestly texts of the Hebrew Bible / Old Testament. In Rom 3:25, Paul depicts Jesus as the ἱλαστήριον, the "(place of) atonement" associated with the Jewish sanctuary.[89] He attributes one of the key functions of the temple institution to Christ and imagines him as the place of God's presence, thus presupposing the incarnation. This becomes a core image for God's free gift of redemption and justification, illustrating how the gospel can be God's power for the salvation of the faithful.[90] Paul also connects the term ἱλαστήριον with the term "blood" (αἷμα), one of the sacrificial substances that was central to the Day of Atonement. While Paul is not explicit about the question of how the blood of Jesus conveys redemption, 1 John 1:7 states that "the blood of Jesus … cleanses us from all sin." Fully analogous to Second Temple atonement concepts, this image conveys that blood purifies.[91] Some of these aspects converge in the well-known words of institution that Jesus spoke over the eucharistic cup: "For this is my blood of the covenant, which is poured out for many for the forgiveness of sins" (τοῦτο γάρ ἐστιν τὸ αἷμά μου τῆς διαθήκης τὸ περὶ πολλῶν ἐκχυννόμενον εἰς ἄφεσιν ἁμαρτιῶν, Matt

---

conveys an understanding of salvation in its broadest sense expressing the meaning of the death of Jesus, the Christ, in the light of his resurrection, and positing that this event allows humans to be liberated from the state of bondage to sin in order to enter into a renewed relationship with God. See Jörg Frey, "Probleme der Deutung des Todes Jesu in der neutestamentlichen Wissenschaft: Streiflichter zur exegetischen Diskussion," in Frey, *Deutungen des Todes Jesu*, 8. Rabbinic Judaism, where religious acts like repentance (תשבה), prayer, fasting, innocent suffering, the study of the torah, etc. are likewise considered to be ways of obtaining atonement, offers parallels to this development in Christian soteriology; see Anderson and Culbertson, "Inadequacy," 305–15.

89. In Rom 3:25 the rendering of ἱλαστήριον as "place/means of atonement" (NAB; see also "expiation," *Traduction Œcuménique*; "Sühne," *Die Bibel nach der Übersetzung Martin Luthers* 1984) is preferable to "sacrifice of atonement" (NRSV, NIV). In the LXX, ἱλαστήριον is never a "sacrifice of atonement"; the term usually refers to the golden cover of the ark ("mercy seat," Exod 25:17–22; 37:6–9).

90. R. Matthew Calhoun, *Paul's Definitions of the Gospel in Romans 1*, WUNT 2/316 (Tübingen: Mohr Siebeck, 2011), 202.

91. For more comprehensive information, see Eberhart, *Kultmetaphorik und Christologie*, 78–130.

26:28).⁹² According to comments made above on the Hebrew Bible / Old Testament cult, "atonement" occurs upon physical contact. Such physical contact is established in the drinking of the wine during the Eucharist, the liturgical meal celebrated by almost all Christians.

Fourth, overt references to the Day of Atonement are also rare in the New Testament. All those who consider the atoning death of Jesus on the cross as the core of the Christian gospel should note the fact that it actually happened on or near the festival of Passover (on the fifteenth day of the month of Nisan), not on the Day of Atonement. Perhaps this is the reason why early Christian authors barely mention the Day of Atonement.⁹³ Only the (anonymous) author of Hebrews includes an explicit reference to this central Jewish festival, providing first a description of the tabernacle (Heb 9:1–5) and then an abstract of the ritual (vv. 6–7). Here, too, the author refers to concepts of the explicit functions of atonement rituals when saying that "both the tent and all the vessels used in worship" were "sprinkled ... with blood (τῷ αἵματι ... ἐρράντισεν)," which effects purification (vv. 21–22). The conceptual proximity to other blood application rites like that of the Mosaic covenant at Mount Sinai is the reason for the reference to "the blood of the covenant" in verse 20.

Fifth, the New Testament may nevertheless contain a few more subtle allusions to the Day of Atonement, specifically to the scapegoat. Daniel R. Schwartz, for example, points to Paul's statement that "Christ redeemed us from the curse of the law by becoming a curse for us" (Χριστὸς ἡμᾶς ἐξηγόρασεν ἐκ τῆς κατάρας τοῦ νόμου γενόμενος ὑπὲρ ἡμῶν κατάρα, Gal 3:13).⁹⁴ This passage conveys the idea of existential exchange

---

92. Other New Testament passages on the eucharistic cup: Mark 14:24; Luke 22:20; 1 Cor 11:25, 27.

93. Moreover, in light of frequent theological statements that Jesus was, or died as, a "sacrifice" to atone for human sin, it must be mentioned that the historical Jesus was executed by Roman authorities through crucifixion. The *titulus* on the cross (Mark 15:26, par.; different versions in John 19:19; Gos. Pet. 11) indicates that Jesus had been sentenced as a political insurrectionist. A straightforward description of this type of punishment would not yield the conclusion that a sacrifice with any atoning effect had occurred; crucifixion is not a cultic event. See Ruben Zimmermann, "'Deuten' heißt erzählen und übertragen: Narrativität und Metaphorik als zentrale Sprachformen historischer Sinnbildung zum Tod Jesu," in Frey, *Deutungen des Todes Jesu*, 361.

94. Daniel R. Schwartz, "Two Pauline Allusions to the Redemptive Mechanism of the Crucifixion," *JBL* 102 (1983): 260–63 (recently adopted by Daniel Stökl Ben Ezra, "Fasting with Jews, Thinking with Scapegoats: Some Remarks on Yom Kippur in Early

between humans and Christ. It draws on the scapegoat that carries away those human sins and impurities that had been transferred upon it (Lev 16:20–22). In an analogous fashion Jesus Christ, who is considered to be without sin,[95] is understood to assume the sins of humanity, causing a change of status that results in the disposal of sin and human righteousness. Schwartz finds another reference to the scapegoat ritual in Gal 4:4 where Paul uses the Greek verb ἐξαποστέλλω, "to send away." This verb, Schwartz emphasizes, occurs in only two chapters of the LXX, namely in the elimination ritual of Lev 14 and in the scapegoat ritual of Lev 16. He summarizes that, for Paul, "Christ's action was that of a scapegoat."[96] Finally, Stökl Ben Ezra recognizes an allusion to the same ritual in the way Matthew modifies his Markan *Vorlage* in the "Barabbas or Jesus" pericope (Matt 27:15–23). Surprising features are, for instance, the addition of the name "Jesus" to "Barabbas" so that "Jesus Barabbas" is now pitched against "Jesus the Messiah" (v. 17). In the first century CE, the Day of Atonement rituals had evolved in such a fashion that the two goats, one of which was to be sacrificed as a sin offering while the other one was to become the scapegoat, had to be virtually identical (Barn. 7:10a). Matthew might have tried to import this aspect into his passion story by adding the name of Jesus to Barabbas.[97] Furthermore, the red cloak that soldiers later put around the shoulders of Jesus is, according to Matthew, κοκκίνη ("scarlet") (Matt 27:28), no longer πορφύρα ("purple") as in the *Vorlage* (Mark 15:17). Once again, the term "scarlet thread" (לשון של זהורית) was found in the regulations of m. Yoma 4:2 for the cords that were to be tied onto the head of the scapegoat on the Day of Atonement to distinguish it from the one for the sin offering and symbolize the transmitted sins and impurities (see above). Stökl Ben Ezra notes that, in Barn.

Judaism and Christianity, in Particular 4Q541, *Barnabas* 7, Matthew 27 and Acts 27," in Hieke, *Day of Atonement*, 176–78).

95. The statement that Jesus Christ was entirely free of sin is, however, difficult to corroborate given the depiction of his ministry in the Gospels. It may suffice to mention that, according to Mark 2:23–28 and 3:1–6, Jesus effectively violated the fourth commandment to keep the Sabbath day holy, and would have become unclean through physical contact with an impure person according to 5:27–30. Furthermore, Jesus is reported to have disrespected the temple and its worship repeatedly (11:15–19; 13:1–2), thus neglecting core statutes of the torah (Exod 25–40; Lev 1–7).

96. Schwartz, "Pauline Allusions," 261.

97. Stökl Ben Ezra, "Fasting," 182.

7, this Hebrew term is rendered as κοκκίνη.⁹⁸ These and other text signals perhaps allude subtly to an understanding of Jesus as a scapegoat who, as such, carries away human sin. Thus atonement mechanisms that are less central to the Day of Atonement rituals have occasionally been adopted in the New Testament.

---

98. Ibid., 183.

Cultic Action and Cultic Function in Second Temple Jewish Martyrologies: The Jewish Martyrs as Israel's Yom Kippur*

Jarvis J. Williams

Introduction

In this essay, I argue that the Jewish martyrs in Second Temple Jewish martyrologies functioned as Israel's Yom Kippur. I support this thesis by arguing that the martyrs' torah observant lives provided the appropriate cultic action and their representative and substitutionary deaths for Israel functioned to achieve national purification. By cultic action, I mean the appropriate performance of the Levitical cultic rituals as prescribed by YHWH in Leviticus and reiterated elsewhere in the Hebrew Bible. By cultic function, I mean the positive results achieved for the community as a result of the appropriate cultic action (e.g., forgiveness, reconciliation, expiation, propitiation, atonement).

Representation and Substitution in LXX Daniel 3:24–90[1]

One Jewish martyrology is a story about a torah-observant Jew who dies as a martyr at the hands of an antagonist gentile tyrant instead of yielding to

---

* This essay was originally published as ch. 3 in Jarvis J. Williams, *Christ Died For Our Sins: Representation and Substitution in Romans and Their Jewish Martyrological Background* (Eugene, OR: Pickwick, 2015) under the title "Representation and Substitution in Second Temple Jewish Martyrologies." I have reproduced the material here with the permission of Wipf & Stock/Pickwick (www.wipfandstock.com).

1. With slight modifications and fresher insights, the material in this essay comes from Jarvis J. Williams, "Martyr Theology in Hellenistic Judaism," in *Christian Origins and Hellenistic Judaism: Social and Literary Contexts for the New Testament;*

the threat of the authorities, when the tyrant presents the torah-observant Jew with the choice of renouncing his faith or suffering death as a result of his faith.[2] The Jewish martyr dies to accomplish soteriological benefits for the non-torah-observant sinner. The Second Temple texts discussed in this chapter fit within this definition. The first text of investigation is LXX Dan 3.

LXX Dan 3 contains approximately sixty-four more verses than MT Dan 3.[3] The Greek version contains stories and prayers that are absent from the tradition preserved in the MT. The additional verses in the Greek version of Dan 3 consist of LXX Dan 3:24–97. The additions resemble the traditional stories about Daniel in MT Dan 1–6. The author of the LXX versions set the additional stories in the context of the Jewish diaspora; Daniel interacts with foreign monarchs, and Daniel's enemies throw him into the lion's den similar to what MT Dan 6 records.[4]

LXX Dan 3:24–90 inserts the prayer of Azariah and the Song of the Three Jews. LXX Dan 3:24–40 highlights Daniel's three friends, who are identified in the LXX version as Ananias (Shadrach), Azarias (Meshach), and Misael (Abednego), while they prayed as they suffered in Nebuchadnezzar's fiery furnace. They refused to worship a golden statue erected by Nebuchadnezzar in Babylon and instead remained faithful to their God. LXX Dan 3:23 states that Nebuchadnezzar seized the three young men

---

Early Christianity in Its Hellenistic Context, ed. Stanley E. Porter and Andrew W. Pitts, ECHC 2 (Leiden: Brill, 2012), 493–521, esp. 497–500. I have borrowed the overlapping material from Brill with permission.

2. For a definition of Jewish martyrology, see Tessa Rajak, *The Jewish Dialogue with Greece and Rome*, AGJU 48 (Leiden: Brill, 2001), 99–103; Jan W. van Henten, *The Maccabean Martyrs as Saviours of the Jewish People: A Study of 2 and 4 Maccabees*, JSJSup 57 (Leiden: Brill, 1997). In agreement with van Henten (7–13, esp. 8), I define Jewish martyrdom in LXX Dan 3 and in 2 and 4 Maccabees as "a person who in an extremely hostile situation prefers violent death to compliance with a demand of the (usually) pagan authorities. This definition implies that the death of such a person is a structural element in the writing about this martyr. The execution should at least be mentioned." See also Jarvis J. Williams, *Maccabean Martyr Traditions in Paul's Theology of Atonement: Did Martyr Theology Shape Paul's Conception of Jesus's Death* (Eugene, OR: Wipf & Stock, 2010), 3–4 n. 10.

3. Unless otherwise indicated, I use Rahlf's most recent critical edition of the LXX.

4. This information comes from Matthias Henze, "Additions to Daniel," in *Outside the Bible: Ancient Jewish Writings Related to Scripture*, ed. Louis H. Feldman, James L. Kugel, and Lawrence H. Schiffman (New York: Jewish Publication Society, 2013), 1:122.

with fetters and had them thrown into the fiery furnace.⁵ LXX Dan 3:24–25 asserts that the Babylonian king expresses shock when he sees four men (Daniel's three friends and an angel) freely walking unharmed in the fiery furnace. The Greek insertions connect the swift transition from the king's anger and his shock with what happens in the fiery furnace to underscore the miraculous nature of the story.⁶

While Daniel's three friends were in the fiery furnace, they prayed to God while in exile because of the sins of the people. Their prayer acknowledges that Israel suffered the Lord's judgment in exile "because of their sins" (LXX Dan 3:28–37). Azariah blessed the Lord's name and confessed that he was righteous "in all the things" that the Lord had done to them and that the Lord's ways and works were right (LXX Dan 3:27). In LXX Dan 3:28, Azariah continues confessing to the Lord that all of his judgments that he brought upon the holy city were right "because in truth and in judgment you have brought all of these things [upon us] because of our sins" (ὅτι ἐν ἀληθείᾳ καὶ κρίσει ἐπήγαγες πάντα ταῦτα διὰ τὰς ἁμαρτίας ἡμῶν).⁷

To emphasize that the Lord's judgment of exile came upon his people because of their sins, his prayer continues in LXX Dan 3:29 with the words "we have sinned and we have acted lawlessly so that we turned from you and we missed the mark in all things and we did not hear your commandments" (ὅτι ἡμάρτομεν καὶ ἠνομήσαμεν ἀποστῆναι ἀπὸ σοῦ καὶ ἐξημάρτομεν ἐν πᾶσιν καὶ τῶν ἐντολῶν σου οὐκ ἠκούσαμεν). In LXX Dan 3:30–31, Azariah further prays that "we neither treasured up nor did as you commanded to us so that it would be well with us, and all things that you have brought upon us and all things that you have done to us you have done by means of true judgment" (οὐδὲ συνετηρήσαμεν οὐδὲ ἐποιήσαμεν καθὼς ἐνετείλω ἡμῖν ἵνα εὖ ἡμῖν γένηται πάντα ὅσα ἡμῖν ἐπήγαγες καὶ πάντα ὅσα ἐποίησας ἡμῖν ἐν ἀληθινῇ κρίσει ἐποίησας). In LXX Dan 3:32, Azariah confesses, "you have given us over into the hands of lawless enemies, who are the greatest of our enemies and to an unrighteous and most evil king in all of the earth" (καὶ παρέδωκας ἡμᾶς εἰς χεῖρας ἐχθρῶν ἀνόμων ἐχθίστων ἀποστατῶν καὶ βασιλεῖ ἀδίκῳ καὶ πονηροτάτῳ παρὰ πᾶσαν τὴν γῆν).

---

5. καὶ οἱ τρεῖς οὗτοι Σεδραχ Μισαχ καὶ Αβδεναγω ἔπεσον εἰς μέσον τῆς καμίνου τοῦ πυρὸς τῆς καιομένης πεπεδημένοι.

6. Henze, "Additions," 122.

7. Unless otherwise noted, all translations are mine.

In LXX Dan 3:34–35, Azariah begins to pray that God would not break his covenant with his people or withdraw his mercy from them on account of his promise to Abraham, Isaac, and Jacob (μὴ δὴ παραδῷς ἡμᾶς εἰς τέλος διὰ τὸ ὄνομά σου καὶ μὴ διασκεδάσῃς τὴν διαθήκην σου καὶ μὴ ἀποστήσῃς τὸ ἔλεός σου ἀφ' ἡμῶν δι' Αβρααμ τὸν ἠγαπημένον ὑπὸ σοῦ καὶ διὰ Ισαακ τὸν δοῦλόν σου καὶ Ισραηλ τὸν ἅγιόν σου; see also LXX Dan 3:36). In LXX Dan 3:37, Azariah offers a reason for his people in LXX Dan 3:36: "because, O master, we were reduced in the presence of all the gentiles, and we are humble today in all the earth because of our sins" (ὅτι δέσποτα ἐσμικρύνθημεν παρὰ πάντα τὰ ἔθνη καί ἐσμεν ταπεινοὶ ἐν πάσῃ τῇ γῇ σήμερον διὰ τὰς ἁμαρτίας ἡμῶν). Azariah's reference to the humility of "today" refers to the Lord's judgment in exile because of sin, the former of which LXX Dan 1:1–2:49 makes abundantly clear and the latter of which Azariah's prayer crystalizes (LXX Dan 3:28; 3:36–37).

In LXX Dan 3, Azariah and his friends represent the people because he associates them with the sinful nation in exile when he declares that they suffer "because of our sins," even though the text states nowhere that either he or his friends violated torah. He confesses throughout this prayer that "we" have sinned (ἡμάρτομεν) "because of our sins" (διὰ τὰς ἁμαρτίας ἡμῶν; LXX Dan 3:27–28, 37), that "we" have broken the law (ἠνομήσαμεν ἀποστῆναι ἀπὸ σοῦ; LXX Dan 3:28), that "we" have missed the mark (ἐξημάρτομεν; LXX Dan 3:28), that "we" have not listened to the Lord's commands (τῶν ἐντολῶν σου οὐκ ἠκούσαμεν; LXX Dan 3:28), that the Lord has handed "us" over into the hands of wicked people (παρέδωκας ἡμᾶς εἰς χεῖρας ἐχθρῶν ἀνόμων ἐχθίστων ἀποστατῶν καὶ βασιλεῖ ἀδίκῳ καὶ πονηροτάτῳ παρὰ πᾶσαν τὴν γῆν; LXX Dan 3:32), and he prays that the Lord would not destroy him and his people by breaking his covenant with them (καὶ νῦν οὐκ ἔστιν ἡμῖν ἀνοῖξαι τὸ στόμα αἰσχύνη καὶ ὄνειδος ἐγενήθη τοῖς δούλοις σου καὶ τοῖς σεβομένοις σε μὴ δὴ παραδῷς ἡμᾶς εἰς τέλος διὰ τὸ ὄνομά σου καὶ μὴ διασκεδάσῃς τὴν διαθήκην σου; LXX Dan 3:33–36). Yet, Daniel and his three friends were "young ones without blemish" (νεανίσκους οἷς οὐκ ἔστιν ἐν αὐτοῖς μῶμος) since they were compliant with torah both prior to and in exile (LXX Dan 1:4). Therefore, they were not individually to blame for exile since they were "without blemish" (LXX Dan 1:4).

LXX Dan 1:8–19 confirms the faithfulness of Daniel and his three friends to torah in exile when it states that Daniel refused to eat the king's unclean food and to drink his unclean wine. Instead, they complied with torah and refused to defile themselves. Consequently, God gave favor to Daniel (LXX Dan 1:8–9). LXX Dan 1:12–19 suggests that Daniel's three friends complied with Daniel's torah-observance, because Daniel includes them in his plot to deceive the king regarding their refusal to eat the unclean food and to drink the unclean wine (cf. MT Lev 11:1–47; Jub. 22:16–18).[8] Azariah associates himself and his friends with the sinful nation due to the Deuteronomic principle expressed by Moses in Lev 18:5 and repeated in Deuteronomy: obedience to torah brings corporate life to Israel in the land (Deut 5:32–33; 8:1; 11:8–9, 18–25, 28; 28:1–14; 30:15–16), but disobedience to torah results in the Lord's corporate judgment of the people by means of expulsion from the land (Deut 4:25–28; 11:28; 28:15–68; 30:17–20). Both the MT and LXX traditions suggest that Daniel and his three friends were faithful to torah, but their association with the covenant community meant that they suffered exile along with the people, so that they (torah-observers) could identify themselves with the sins of the nation. Thus, Azariah's prayer for the nation in exile represents the corporate cry of the Lord's covenant people in exile.

As Azariah continues his prayer, he urges God to deliver Israel from their national suffering in exile (LXX Dan 3:38–40). He laments that the Davidic monarchy has been abolished and that the temple-cult had been eradicated (καὶ οὐκ ἔστιν ἐν τῷ καιρῷ τούτῳ ἄρχων καὶ προφήτης καὶ ἡγούμενος οὐδὲ ὁλοκαύτωσις οὐδὲ θυσία οὐδὲ προσφορὰ οὐδὲ θυμίαμα οὐ τόπος τοῦ καρπῶσαι ἐναντίον σου καὶ εὑρεῖν ἔλεος; LXX Dan 3:38; see also 2 Kgs 17:22–23; 23:26–25:11; 2 Chr 36:19–20). The eradication of the temple-cult meant the abolishment of a sacrificial means by which to attain God's mercy for the nation since YHWH provided cultic sacrifices of atonement in the Levitical cult to be performed at the temple in order to provide atonement for sin, and since Azariah's prayer connects God's mercy with Levitical cultic language (e.g., ὁλοκαύτωσις ["burnt-offering"], θυσία ["sacrifice"], προσφορά ["offering"], θυμίαμα ["incense"], and καρπῶσαι ["to bear fruit"]).[9] Furthermore, without access to the temple-cult, Israel could neither celebrate daily cultic sacrifices of atonement or the traditional Yom Kippur ritual (Lev 1–6, 16). As a result, the absence of the temple-cult in exile in LXX Dan 3 meant that there was not a means by which or a place at which the Lord's people could perform cultic action to receive his mercy.

---

8. See also 1 Macc 1:11–15, 41–45; 3:58–59; 4:54–60; 2 Macc 5:15–20; Let. Aris. 152–153; Pss. Sol. 2:2; Josephus, *Ant.* 15.417; Acts 21:27.

9. Every word in the above parenthesis occurs in cultic contexts in the LXX (ὁλοκαύτωσις [LXX Lev 6:2]; θυσία [LXX Lev 1:9, 13, 17; 2:1–2, 5–7, 15; 3:1; 5:13; 6:16; Sir 34:18; 35:5; 46:16; 50:13], θυμίαμα [LXX 16:13], and καρπῶσαι [LXX Lev 2:11]).

The prayer of the three friends confirms this when they acknowledge that they did not have a place to offer a sacrificial burnt-offering in order to find God's mercy (προσφορὰ οὐδὲ θυμίαμα οὐ τόπος τοῦ καρπῶσαι ἐναντίον σου καὶ εὑρεῖν ἔλεος; LXX Dan 3:28). This statement alludes to the Levitical cult (LXX Lev 6:2). Thus, the prayer suggests that there is no means by which to receive the Lord's forgiveness through cultic action since the temple-cult's absence is parallel with the friends' statement that there is no place to offer a sacrifice to find God's mercy. In this context, Azariah asks God to use his death and the deaths of his friends to perform the necessary cultic action to provide national cleansing for the covenant community in the place of the temple cult, which LXX Dan 3:39 communicates with the optative προσδεχθείημεν in the statement ἐν ψυχῇ συντετριμμένῃ καὶ πνεύματι τεταπεινωμένῳ προσδεχθείημεν ὡς ἐν ὁλοκαυτώμασι κριῶν καὶ ταύρων καὶ ὡς ἐν μυριάσιν ἀρνῶν πιόνων (LXX Dan 3:39).

Furthermore, Azariah prays that God would use their deaths to cleanse the nation while in exile as long as the temple-cult was ineffective with the prayer "let our sacrifice be in your presence today also to propitiate behind you because there is no shame in those who trust in you so that we would also consecrate behind you" (οὕτω γενέσθω ἡμῶν ἡ θυσία ἐνώπιόν σου σήμερον καὶ ἐξιλάσαι ὄπισθέν σου ὅτι οὐκ ἔστιν αἰσχύνη τοῖς πεποιθόσιν ἐπὶ σοί καὶ τελειῶσαι ὄπισθέν σου; LXX Th. Dan 3:40).[10] Azariah wanted God to receive (προσδεχθείημεν) their deaths "just as" (ὡς) he received the function of the burnt-offerings in the Levitical cult (ὡς ἐν ὁλοκαυτώμασι κριῶν καὶ ταύρων καὶ ὡς ἐν μυριάσιν ἀρνῶν πιόνων). The numerous Levitical cultic words (ὁλοκαύτωσις, θυσία, προσφορά, θυμίαμα, καρπῶσαι, ὁλοκαυτώμασι, and ἐξιλάσαι) applied to Daniel's three friends and their identification with the torah-disobedient nation suggest that they function in the narrative of LXX Th. Dan 3 as proper representatives and substitutionary cultic sacrifices to bring to Israel the mercy (ἔλεος) and cleansing (ἐξιλάσαι) traditionally provided by the temple-cult and Yom Kippur (LXX Th. Dan 3:38–40).

Maccabean Martyrdom in Historical Context[11]

Scholars of Second Temple Judaism are well aware that 1, 2, and 4 Maccabees record that Antiochus Epiphanes IV (henceforth Antiochus) in the

---

10. For a discussion of the text-variant in the different Greek versions, see Williams, "Martyr Theology," 499 n. 12.

11. I am very grateful to Robert Doran for reading and offering critical feedback

second century BCE persecuted and killed many Jews during the Second Temple period because they refused to yield to his Hellenistic reforms and assimilate within Hellenism to the degree he demanded (see 1 Macc 1).[12] Although certain Jews forsook the religion of their fathers by adopting both the cultural and religious practices of the gentiles even before Antiochus's crusade for Hellenism (1 Macc 1:11–15), his reforms were nevertheless radical since he required that all people (Jews and gentiles) everywhere should conform to the Greek way of life (1 Macc 1:20–24, 29–50).[13] He wrote letters and dispatched them throughout his entire kingdom (1 Macc 1:41), which consisted of both Jewish and gentile territories (1 Macc 1:16–19, 41–42). In these letters, he commanded all nations to adopt Greek customs (1 Macc 1:41).

Antiochus's letters declared that Jews and gentiles should become one people and that they should surrender their laws and customs (1 Macc 1:41–42). He required the Jews to adopt "other laws in the land" (νομίμων ἀλλοτρίων τῆς γῆς) besides the torah (1 Macc 1:44). He prohibited the Jews from offering sacrifices and from keeping the Sabbath in compliance with torah (1 Macc 1:44). He commanded the Jews to defile both the temple's holy place and its priests by building altars for other gods besides YHWH (1 Macc 1:45–47). He gave orders that the Jews could no longer circumcise their children, and he demanded them to forget torah's prescriptions for their lives (1 Macc 1:48–49). He offered an unlawful sacrifice on the altar in the temple; he burned the books of the Torah; he executed Jews who

---

to much of the material in this section. I am also grateful to him for his gracious comments about my paper on 2 Maccabees in a personal conversation at the 2011 Annual Meeting of the Society of Biblical Literature in San Francisco, CA after we both gave presentations in the Function of the Apocrypha and Pseudepigrapha on Early Christianity.

12. For a succinct description of Antiochus's policies, see Otto Mørkholm, "Antiochus IV," in *The Cambridge History of Judaism: The Hellenistic Age*, ed. W.D. Davies and Louis Finkelstein (Cambridge: Cambridge University Press, 1989), 2:278–91. I recognize that the reasons behind Antiochus's persecutions are complex. But a basic point that the authors make in 1, 2, and 4 Maccabees is that the persecution was in part the result of the refusal of many Jews to assimilate within Greek culture to the degree that Antiochus desired.

13. 1 Macc 1:11 asserts that renegade Jews approached Antiochus first in pursuit of an alliance with him (ἐν ταῖς ἡμέραις ἐκείναις ἐξῆλθον ἐξ Ισραηλ υἱοὶ παράνομοι καὶ ἀνέπεισαν πολλοὺς λέγοντες πορευθῶμεν καὶ διαθώμεθα διαθήκην μετὰ τῶν ἐθνῶν τῶν κύκλῳ ἡμῶν ὅτι ἀφ᾽ ἧς ἐχωρίσθημεν ἀπ᾽ αὐτῶν εὗρεν ἡμᾶς κακὰ πολλά).

possessed copies of the Torah, and he hung the infants of those Jews who did not obey his reforms (1 Macc 1:54–61).

To ensure full devotion to his demands, Antiochus concluded his letters by asserting that he would kill anyone who refused to act in accordance with his word (1 Macc 1:50). On the one hand, many Jews yielded to Antiochus's edicts and forsook their religion and their God (1 Macc 1:52). On the other hand, other Jews disobeyed Antiochus and remained faithful to their ancestral traditions (1 Macc 1:62–2:28). Torah-observant Jews were resilient in their commitment to their religion even in the face of persecution and death. Neither Antiochus's tortures nor his threats of death persuaded them to abandon their religion (4 Macc 5:1–6:30).[14]

When devout Jews in Jerusalem refused to obey his reforms and the reforms of his compatriots, the gentiles seized the holy city, desecrated the temple, pilfered the holy vessels, and left Jerusalem desolate (1 Macc 1:1–63; cf. 2 Macc 6:1–5). Their plundering devastated Jews throughout the city (1 Macc 1:25–28; cf. 2 Macc 5:11–16). To add insult to injury, two years later, Antiochus deceived many Jews by persuading them that he would extend peace to Israel. He sent a messenger to Judea to execute this deception. Many Jews, unfortunately, believed that Antiochus's gesture of peace was sincere. His deception enabled him to take over Jerusalem a second time (1 Macc 1:29–32).

After his second attack on the city, Antiochus eventually sacked the temple and desecrated it. He also destroyed the books of the Torah and demanded Judea to offer sacrifices to him and to engage in pagan worship (1 Macc 1:33–50). He promised to kill any Jew who obeyed God's law and who refused to yield full allegiance to his new policies (1 Macc 1:33–50; cf. 4 Macc 4:20, 23),[15] and he forbade the Jews from practicing their festivals and from doing anything that uniquely identified them as Jews (2 Macc 6:6).

Antiochus's abolishment of the law and his desecration of the temple meant that Jews could no longer offer acceptable sacrifices of atonement to God as prescribed by him in the torah. Such a prohibition meant that they could not celebrate Yom Kippur. The preceding point is especially true if the latter festival occurred during either the time of Antiochus's desecration or his reforms (1 Macc 1:41–64; 2 Macc 1:5; 5:4, 35; see also Philo,

---

14. Jewish resiliency in the face of persecution and death also appears in the stories of Susanna and Bel and the Dragon.

15. See 1 Macc 1:36–2:13; 4 Macc 1:11; 17:22.

Spec. 1.11.67–69). If Otto Mørkholm is correct that Antiochus suspended temple sacrifices on 15 Chislev (= ca. December 167 BCE)[16] and if this suspension lasted for two full years, then it would have overlapped with the tenth day of Tishri (= September–October), when Yom Kippur would have likely been celebrated.[17] In support of this assertion, in a recent essay, while speaking of Yom Kippur during pre-Antiochus Second Temple Judaism, Albert I. Baumgarten comments that the Jews viewed it as unacceptable to celebrate Yom Kippur on a different date from the one determined by the central temple authorities.[18] The date of celebration enforced by the temple authorities would have likely been the day prescribed by YHWH in the torah since pious Jews zealously devoted to the torah during Antiochus's reign would have honored Moses's prescriptions in the torah regarding this most important Jewish festival until their very death (e.g., 1 Macc 1–2), for, as Philo states, Yom Kippur was the "highest of the festivals" (*Spec.* 2:193–94).[19]

The words of Mattathias during the Maccabean revolt support the assertion that Jews during the revolt would have likely observed Yom Kippur on the exact day prescribed by YHWH in torah, which would have been the tenth day of Tishri (Lev 16:29). After Antiochus threatened the Jews and desecrated the temple (1 Macc 1:10–64), Mattathias responds by saying: "And I and my sons and my brothers will walk in the covenant of our fathers. Far be it from us to forsake the law and the ordinances. We will not obey the king's words so that we would abandon our worship with respect to the right or the left" (1 Macc 2:20–22). By refusing to abandon

---

16. Mørkholm, "Antiochus IV," 286.

17. E. P. Sanders, *Judaism, Practice and Belief: 63 BCE–66 CE* (London: SCM Press, 1992), 140.

18. Albert I. Baumgarten, "Setting the Outer Limits: Temple Policy in the Centuries Prior to Destruction," in *Redefining First-Century Jewish and Christian Identities: Essays in Honor of E. P. Sanders*, ed. Fabian E. Udoh et al. (Notre Dame: University of Notre Dame Press, 2008), 90–92, esp. 91.

19. Daniel Ben Ezra (*The Impact of Yom Kippur on Early Christianity: The Day of Atonement from Second Temple Judaism to the Fifth Century*, WUNT 163 [Tübingen: Mohr Siebeck, 2003], 16) pointed me to the above citation from Philo. For Philo, however, Yom Kippur is "the fast" and not the day of propitiation. For this latter thought, see Markus Tiwald, "Christ as Hilasterion (Rom 3:25): Pauline Theology on the Day of Atonement in the Mirror of Early Jewish Thought," in *The Day of Atonement: Its Interpretation in Early Jewish and Christian Traditions*, ed. Thomas Hieke and Tobias Nicklas, TBN 15 (Leiden: Brill, 2012), 198.

"our worship/service," Mattathias means sacrificial worship as prescribed by YHWH in torah and this sacrificial worship would have included the precise time to celebrate Yom Kippur. Both points seem right because Mattathias utters these words immediately after the king's threat against the Jews who participate in cultic worship in compliance with torah (1 Macc 1:41–47, 51) and immediately after he (Mattathias) vociferates that he and his family would continue to worship YHWH in compliance with torah, even if all of the king's nations should turn away from the "worship/service" of its fathers (1 Macc 2:19–22).

In support of the above, with the exception of two occurrences (LXX Exod 13:5; 3 Macc 4:14), the term λατρείαν ("worship/service") in 1 Macc 2:22 occurs in the LXX in reference to cultic worship. For example, in LXX Exod 12 when giving Moses instructions regarding the feast of Passover, YHWH asserts that Israel will keep this "worship/service" and that when their children ask them about this "worship/service," Israel shall explain to them that it is a Passover (LXX Exod 12:25–26). In LXX Josh 22:27, λατρείαν refers to approaching YHWH with "burnt-offerings," "sacrifices," and "sacrifices of salvation." In LXX 1 Chr 28:13, the Chronicler(s) uses λατρείας in connection with the divisions of the priests and Levites and with the cultic "service" in YHWH's temple.[20]

Appropriate cultic worship at the temple was extremely important for all torah-observant Jews during the Second Temple period because the temple was central to their religious life, which included their social and political status as God's people.[21] The temple was especially essential for Israel's cultic worship during the Second Temple period.[22] The temple symbolized that YHWH dwelt with his people (11QT 25:12–31:10).[23] Thus, the desecration of the temple in Second Temple Judaism suggested both that YHWH no longer dwelt with his people due to the nation's sin (see LXX Dan 3:28–90) and that he put an end to the temple sacrifices and

---

20. In 1 Macc 1:43; 2 Macc 2:19; and 2 Macc 2:22, λατρείας refers to cultic "worship/service."

21. Shaye J. D. Cohen, *From The Maccabees to the Mishnah*, 2nd ed. (Louisville: Westminster John Knox, 2006), 101–2; Jonathan Klawans, *Purity, Sacrifice, and the Temple: Symbolism and Supersessionism in the Study of Ancient Judaism* (Oxford: Oxford University Press, 2006), 103–74.

22. Josephus, *Ag. Ap.* 2.193; Philo, *Spec.* 1.11.67–69.

23. The above citations come from Klawans, *Purity, Sacrifice, and the Temple*, 145–74, esp. 147–48, 153–55.

religious festivals that involved the temple due to the nation's sin (2 Macc 7:33). Consequently, Antiochus's desecration of the temple ended Jewish particularity and identity as they knew it (i.e., their religious life as they practiced it in compliance with the torah in distinction from the nations), and the sacrificial system, especially Yom Kippur, was central to Jewish identity and particularity.[24] Yom Kippur focused on fasting, prayer, and confession and on both individual and corporate atonement for sins (LXX Lev 16:2–34).[25]

Since, therefore, Antiochus desecrated the temple and ended the cult, torah-zealous Jews would have considered the temple unfit for temple worship.[26] They would have considered it to be defiled because of its contamination by the gentiles and apostate Jews (1 Macc 4:36–58; 2 Macc 6:4–6; cf. Acts 21:27),[27] whose contamination would have overlapped with the daily sacrifices and the yearly celebration of Yom Kippur. Torah-observant Jews believed that all sin defiles the temple, especially the sin of mingling with gentiles (Jub. 22:16–22; Let. Aris. 139, 142).[28]

As YHWH prescribed in Lev 1–6 and 16, appropriate cultic action leads to appropriate cultic function. In addition, as YHWH prescribed in Lev 16, during Yom Kippur, the priests would atone for all of their personal transgressions, the transgressions of the people, and the impurities of the holy place because of the impurities of the people (Lev 16:3–28).[29] In Lev 16, YHWH commands Aaron to offer specific animals as atonement for sin, so that the nation and the holy place would be purified

---

24. Sir 50:14–21. See also Sanders, *Judaism*, 143.

25. Jub. 5:17–18; 34:18–19; 11Q5 XXVII, 2–11; Pss. Sol. 3:8; Philo, *Spec.* 193–203; *Mos.* 2.23–24; *Legat.* 306; LAB (Pseudo-Philo) 13:6. See also Daniel K. Falk, "Festivals and Holy Days," in *The Eerdmans Dictionary of Early Judaism*, ed. John J. Collins and Daniel C. Harlow (Grand Rapids: Eerdmans, 2010), 642.

26. For sins that some Second Temple Jews thought would defile the temple and for the relevant primary texts, see Klawans, *Purity, Sacrifice, and the Temple*, 147–74.

27. The above citation of 1 Macc 4:41–59 comes from Lawrence H. Schiffman, *Texts and Traditions: A Source Reader for the Study of Second Temple and Rabbinic Judaism* (Hoboken, NJ: Ktav, 1998), 160–61.

28. The above statement does not imply that Second Temple Jews believed that the sin of mingling with the gentiles was the only sin that defiled the temple; e.g., see texts cited in Klawans, *Purity, Sacrifice, and the Temple*, 147–74.

29. Exod 30:10; Lev 23:27–32; 25:9–10; Num 29:7–11. For a discussion of the rituals of Yom Kippur during both Second Temple and post Second Temple Judaism, see Ben Ezra, *Yom Kippur*, 28–67.

and cleansed (Lev 16:3–34).[30] After YHWH instructs Moses how Aaron should perform the Yom Kippur ritual, he states that the day of the ritual should be celebrated every year for the cleansing of sin (Lev 16:29–30). This cleansing through the offering of blood accompanied by contrition and repentance achieved and symbolized God's forgiveness for the entire nation (Lev 16:29–30; cf. 1QS III, 4).[31]

Later Jewish traditions suggest that during Yom Kippur, Jews devoted themselves to communal confession, penitential prayer, and praise to God for lengthy periods of time.[32] Jubilees 34:18–19 states that Israel should atone for their sins once a year and that Yom Kippur was decreed "so that they might mourn on it on account of their sin and on account of all of their transgression and on account of all their errors in order to purify themselves on this day once a year." Philo expresses that many Jews took up the entire day celebrating Yom Kippur (*Spec.* 2.196). Sirach 50:17–19 states that people fell on their faces to worship the Lord and that the people of the Lord prayed "until the adornment of the Lord was completed and until they completed his service." Such lengthy practices, along with Yom Kippur's cultic sacrifices, were seen by some Jews to effect atonement for sin during the Second Temple period (e.g., 1Q34 2 + 1 6–7).[33] Philo attests to the efficacy of Yom Kippur during this period when he expresses that much prayer was offered on the Day of Atonement to propitiate the Father of the universe to pardon former sins and to ensure new blessings (*Mos.* 2.24).[34]

As to the importance of temple-purity in the Second Temple period, further support emerges from 1 and 2 Maccabees and Josephus. Hanuk-

---

30. See John E. Hartley, *Leviticus*, WBC 4 (Dallas: Word, 1992), 241.

31. These sacrifices were not *ipso facto* efficacious to provide forgiveness, but repentance was the fundamental prerequisite for the efficacy of the sacrifices (see Ps 51; Amos 5:21–22; Hos 6:6; Isa 1:10–17; Mic 6:6–8; Jer 7:21–23). For this point, see Jacob Milgrom, *Cult and Conscience: The Asham and the Priestly Doctrine of Repentance*, SJLA 18 (Leiden: Brill, 1976).

32. For a recent collection of essays devoted to Yom Kippur in early Judaism and in early Christianity, see Hieke, *Day of Atonement*.

33. For additional texts, see Falk, "Festivals and Holy Days," 642.

34. For the importance of long prayers of confession at Yom Kippur in Second Temple Judaism, see also Philo, *Spec.* 1:186; 2:196–199, 203; 7:431. Additionally, as Ben Ezra (*Yom Kippur*, 114) points out, Philo emphasizes the symbolic meanings of Yom Kippur due to his allegorical exegesis, but he likewise maintains the literal meanings and institutions of Yom Kippur.

kah, the Festival of Dedication, memorializes the restoration of the Second Temple and the dedication of the altar by Judas Maccabaeus in 164 BCE during the reign of Antiochus.[35] The feast was celebrated with much feasting, sacrifices, rejoicing, praise, and music due to the restoration and deliverance of the temple from the hands of the gentiles (1 Macc 4:36–59; 2 Macc 1:10–2:18; Josephus, *Ant.* 12.316–326). Regarding the importance of the temple and its purity, Philo describes the purgative rituals of the priest before he entered into the holy of holies (*Somn.* 1.216–217; *Legat.* 306),[36] and he states that "*as God is one*, his temple should also be *one*. In the next place, he does not permit those who desire to perform sacrifices in their own houses to do so, but orders all men to rise up, even from the furthest boundaries of the earth, and to come to this temple" (*Spec.* 2.11.67–69, emphasis added). Philo states elsewhere that Jews would be willing to sacrifice their entire family to preserve the purity of the temple (*Legat.* 308). Josephus says that "there ought to be but one temple for *one God*" (cf. Josephus, *Ag. Ap.* 2.193, emphasis added).

The above comments from 1 and 2 Maccabees, Philo, and Josephus suggest that torah-observant Jews would have therefore withdrawn from the temple when Antiochus desecrated it, for they would offer sacrifices only in a sanctified and purified temple that symbolized the presence of the one and only God of Israel (see Tob 1:4; 1 Macc 4:36–58; Acts 21:27–30).[37] However, since Antiochus forbade the Jews from offering sacrifices and from celebrating their festivals in compliance with torah when he gained control of the temple (1 Macc 1:41–59; 2 Macc 6:4–6), 2 and 4 Maccabees suggest that it was unavailable and unfit for the Jews to practice cultic worship in compliance with the torah (1 Macc 1:41–59). Thus, if there was no temple cult due to its impurity, YHWH's prescribed forms of cultic action would not happen. Without cultic action, then there could be no Yom Kippur ritual.[38] Without the Yom Kippur ritual, there would be no cultic function that offered national purification for the nation's sin. This becomes conspicuous in a Second Temple text like LXX Dan 3:24–90,

---

35. Falk, "Festivals and Holy Days," 644–45, esp. 644.
36. Ibid., 641.
37. See Baumgarten, "Setting the Outer Limits," 92–93.
38. For a list of rabbinic texts that likewise find other means of offering atonement due to the temple's destruction in post–70 CE Judaism, see David Janzen, *The Social Meanings of Sacrifice in the Hebrew Bible: A Study of Four Writings*, BZAW 344 (Berlin: de Gruyter, 2004), 1.

where Daniel's three friends offer themselves as atoning sacrifices for the sins of the nation while in exile without access to the temple. This is likewise true in Tobit, where Tobit expresses, while in exile, that almsgiving accomplishes atonement for sin for those in exile without access to the temple (Tob 4:10–11; 12:9). The preceding traditions offer alternatives to the traditional Yom Kippur cult at the temple because there was no sanctified temple in the land of exile at which Jews could celebrate Yom Kippur.[39]

Jewish Martyrdom and Reconciliation

Second and Fourth Maccabees present the Jewish martyrs as Israel's representatives, substitutes, and as the nation's Yom Kippur. After killing Eleazar in 2 Macc 6, Antiochus compelled a mother and her seven sons to eat unlawful foods (2 Macc 7:1). They were faced with death if they disobeyed. Yet, they rebelled against Antiochus; as a result, each suffered torture and death (2 Macc 7:2–41). While encouraged by his mother to trust God as he faced Antiochus's wrath (2 Macc 7:28–29), the seventh son stated that "we suffer because of our own sins" (ἡμεῖς γὰρ διὰ τὰς ἑαυτῶν ἁμαρτίας πάσχομεν) (2 Macc 7:32; cf. 2 Macc 5:17). His words echo the cry of Daniel's three friends in LXX Dan 3:28–29 and 3:37 (2 Macc 7:32; see also 2 Macc 5:17).[40] The seventh son's confession is almost exactly the same as his old brother (the sixth son), who was martyred earlier in the narrative, in 2 Macc 7:18 (ἡμεῖς γὰρ δι' ἑαυτοὺς ταῦτα πάσχομεν ἁμαρτόντες εἰς τὸν ἑαυτῶν θεόν ἄξια θαυμασμοῦ γέγονεν). Just as the confession of Daniel's three friends, the confession of both the sixth and the seventh sons acknowledges that sin is the foundational reason that the martyrs suffer in the narrative of 2 Maccabees at the hands of Antiochus and that the martyrs' deaths are the foundational reason why God "will be reconciled again to his servants" (εἰ δὲ χάριν ἐπιπλήξεως καὶ παιδείας ὁ ζῶν κύριος ἡμῶν βραχέως ἐπώργισται καὶ πάλιν καταλλαγήσεται τοῖς ἑαυτοῦ δούλοις) (2 Macc 7:33; see also 2 Macc 1:5; 7:37–38; 8:29).

References to the Lord's servants, who were torah-observant Jews, as dying for the soteriological benefit of non-torah-observant sinners

---

39. Ben Ezra (*Yom Kippur*, 115–18) argues that Lev 16 and the Yom Kippur ritual were instructive for the vicarious deaths of the martyrs in 4 Maccabees.

40. Similarly Wolfgang Kraus, *Der Tod Jesu als Heiligtumsweihe: Eine Untersuchung zum Umfeld der Sühnevorstellung in Römer 3,25–26a*, WMANT 66 (Neukirchen-Vluyn: Neukirchener Verlag, 1991), 35.

in 2 Macc 7:33 conceptually connects with Isa 53. Isaiah 53 asserts that YHWH's servant will serve as the means by which the nation's sin is forgiven and the means by which YHWH will declare many righteous to be in the right (LXX 53:4–6, 8, 10–12). Although the verb καταλλαγήσεται in 2 Macc 7:33 is absent in LXX Isa 53, the infinitive δικαιῶσαι and the adjective δίκαιον in LXX Isa 53:11 communicate the concept of reconciliation between God and sinners because the soteriological reality communicated with the words δικαιῶσαι and δίκαιον is the result of the servant's death for the sins of others. In other words, the act of YHWH declaring to be in the right those for whom the servant dies in order to take away their sins results in reconciliation between YHWH and the transgressors for whom the servant dies. In addition to the Isaianic language, 2 Maccabees appropriates Levitical cultic language.

The seventh son's statements that "we suffer because of our sins" and that "he will again be reconciled to his servants" refer to Israel as a nation, which includes the martyrs.[41] This seems right because of the first-person plural ἡμεῖς, the phrase διὰ τὰς ἑαυτῶν ἁμαρτίας, and the first-person plural verb πάσχομεν. The need for God to be reconciled again to his servants reveals that enmity exists between God and his people in the narrative due to the apostasizing of many Jews away from their God to follow Antiochus's Hellenistic policies (1 Macc 1; 2 Macc 5:18; 6:12–16). However, the martyrs were individually innocent of religious apostasy (see 1 Macc 1–2; 2 Macc 7; 4 Macc 6), which is evident by their torah-observance in the face of death. Their suffering was a corollary of their refusal to embrace Greek culture as many of their kinsmen had begun to embrace it (2 Macc 5:1–8:5; 4 Macc 6)[42] The reconciliation needed by their martyrdom is the cessation of God's wrath against the people because of the sin of some within the community and a return of friendship between YHWH and the nation. In this respect, the seventh son interprets the situation of the nation and his brothers in light of Deut 32, and he interprets the vindication of YHWH's

---

41. Against Daniel R. Schwartz, *2 Maccabees*, CEJL (Berlin: de Gruyter, 2008), 314, who without substantiation asserts that 2 Macc 7:32 only refers to the Jews' sins in contrast to 7:33. But, as van Henten (*Maccabean Martyrs*, 137 n. 51) astutely points out, "the verb ἁμαρτόντες occurs only in 2 Macc 7:18 and 10:4, where it also refers to the sinning of the people as a body."

42. A. O'Hagan, "The Martyr in the Fourth Book of the Maccabees," *SBFLA* 24 (1974): 94–120, esp. 108. Against Theofried Baumeister, *Die Anfänge der Theologie des Martyriums*, MBT 45 (Münster: Aschendorff, 1980), 41–42.

servants in Deut 32:36 to be accomplished by means of his faithful death and the faithful deaths of his brothers, who are both *representatives of* and *substitutes for* the nation.

In LXX Deut 32:36a, in his final words to Israel, Moses states that the Lord will vindicate his people, and "he will feel compassion for his servants" (καὶ ἐπὶ τοῖς δούλοις αὐτοῦ παρακληθήσεται), whereas 2 Macc 7:33 stresses that the Lord "will be reconciled again by means of his servants" (καὶ πάλιν καταλλαγήσεται τοῖς ἑαυτοῦ δούλοις). The former accentuates *what* God will do for his people (namely, show them mercy) (see 2 Macc 7:6), but the seventh son's prayer stresses *the means* by which God will show mercy (namely, through his servants, the faithful martyrs). The veracity of the statement that the martyrs would be the means by which God would be reconciled to his nation is strengthened by the noun καταλλαγή and the verb καταλλαγήσεται in 2 Maccabees, both of which always concern reconciliation between the Lord and his people in 2 Maccabees (2 Macc 1:5; 7:33; 8:29).[43]

Before the seventh son utters these words in 2 Macc 7:32-38, the author places a panegyric speech in the mouth of both Eleazar in 2 Macc 6 and in the mouths of the mother and her seven sons in 2 Macc 7. Prior to these speeches, the author lucidly asserts that the sin for which the martyrs suffered torturous death was the nation's rebellion against the torah (2 Macc 5:20–7:32; see also 1 Macc 1:11-15). The respective texts in 2 and 4 Maccabees do not state anywhere that the martyrs themselves actually violated torah along with the rest of the nation. Nevertheless, the "we" in "we suffer because of our sins" (2 Macc 7:32) includes the martyrs along with rebellious Israel for the following reasons: First, the martyrs were members of YHWH's covenant-community for which they suffered (2 Macc 7:16, 30-32, 38). Second, Antiochus is called the adversary of the Hebrews and not simply the adversary of the martyrs (2 Macc 7:31). Third, the martyrological narratives begin with the author's statements about the positive role of suffering in the lives of the Lord's covenant-people (2 Macc 6:12-17).[44] Thus, 2 and 4 Maccabees' presentations of the

---

43. For alternative understandings of reconciliation in 2 Maccabees, see Cilliers Breytenbach, *Versöhnung: Eine Studie zur paulinischen Soteriologie*, WMANT 60 (Neukirchen-Vluyn: Neukirchener Verlag, 1989); Stanley E. Porter, καταλλασσω *in Ancient Greek Literature, with Reference to the Pauline Writings*, EFN 5 (Cordoba: Ediciones El Almendro, 1994).

44. So van Henten, *Maccabean Martyrs*, 139.

martyrs' suffering echo Israel's antecedent Deuteronomic history, thereby fulfilling the Deuteronomic curses set forth in Deut 27–28 and 32 against Israel via the nations due to the disobedience of some within the nation (see Deut 28:1–14 with 28:15–68). The seventh son's words demonstrate that the principle set forth in Leviticus and reiterated in Deuteronomy (namely, when a few in the covenant-community sinned against God and suffered the consequences of their sin, the entire covenant-community including the martyrs suffered the consequences of this sin) was still alive and well in 2 Maccabees. The martyrs' suffering was a result of their refusal to embrace Greek culture as many of their kinsmen had begun to embrace it (2 Macc 5:1–8:5; 4 Macc 6),[45] and their kinsmen's acceptance of Antiochus's Hellenistic regime resulted in God's judgment of the entire nation through Antiochus (see 1 Macc 1), as promised in Deut 28:1–68. Therefore, the martyrological narratives present the seventh son and the other martyrs as representatives of the nation and as substitutes for the nation to pay for Israel's sin, which also became a payment for their sins by virtue of their membership within the covenant-community (cf. 2 Macc 7:32).[46] Second Maccabees 5:1–7:38 supports this interpretation.

As a result of the nation's rebellion against God's law, the temple and the land were dishonored (2 Macc 5:27–6:6). When Antiochus and Menelaus (a Jewish high priest) entered the temple in Jerusalem, they profaned it (2 Macc 5:15–16). To eradicate God's judgment against the nation, the seven sons voluntarily offer themselves to die for Israel to achieve God's forgiveness (2 Macc 7:32–38).[47] Second Maccabees 7:32–38 suggests that

---

45. Against Baumeister, *Anfänge*, 41–42.

46. So Marinus de Jonge, *Christology in Context: The Earliest Christian Response to Jesus* (Philadelphia: Westminster, 1988), 181–82; Ulrich Kellermann, "Zum traditionsgeschichtlichen Problem des stellvertretenden Sühnetodes in 2 Makk 7:37," *BN* 13 (1980): 63–83, esp. 69; van Henten, *Maccabean Martyrs*, 137. Against Sam K. Williams, *Jesus' Death: as Saving Event: The Background and Origin of a Concept*, HDR 2 (Missoula, MT: Scholars Press, 1975), 79 n. 29; David Seeley, *The Noble Death Graeco-Roman Martyrology and Paul's Concept of Salvation*, JSOTSup 28 (Sheffield: JSOT Press, 1990), 87.

47. Similarly Eduard Lohse, *Märtyrer und Gottesknecht: Untersuchungen zur urchristlichen Verkündigung vom Sühntod Jesu Christi*, 2nd ed., FRLANT 46 (Göttingen: Vandenhoeck & Ruprecht, 1963), 67–69; Joachim Gnilka, "Martyriumsparänese und Sühnetod in synoptischen und jüdischen Traditionen," in *Die Kirche des Anfangs: Festschrift für Heinz Schürmann*, ed. Rudolf Schnackenburg (Leipzig: St. Benno, 1977), 223–46; J. Downing, "Jesus and Martyrdom," *JTS* 14 (1963): 279–93, esp. 288–89; van

the seventh son was confident that God would be reconciled again to the nation through the martyrs' deaths because he asserts that God "will be reconciled again to his servants" in 2 Macc 7:33 and because 2 Macc 7:37–38 affirms that the seventh son wants God to end his wrath against the nation by means of the deaths of him and his brothers on behalf of the nation (ἐγὼ δὲ καθάπερ οἱ ἀδελφοί καὶ σῶμα καὶ ψυχὴν προδίδωμι περὶ τῶν πατρίων νόμων ἐπικαλούμενος τὸν θεὸν ἵλεως ταχὺ τῷ ἔθνει γενέσθαι καὶ σὲ μετὰ ἐτασμῶν καὶ μαστίγων ἐξομολογήσασθαι διότι μόνος αὐτὸς θεός ἐστιν ἐν ἐμοὶ δὲ καὶ τοῖς ἀδελφοῖς μου στῆσαι τὴν τοῦ παντοκράτορος ὀργὴν τὴν ἐπὶ τὸ σύμπαν ἡμῶν γένος δικαίως ἐπηγμένην).[48]

The most important parts of the above prayer in 2 Macc 7:37–38 for my thesis are the seventh son's statements "be merciful quickly to the nation" in 7:37 and "to end the wrath of the almighty in me and in my brothers" in 7:38. The grammatical construction in 2 Macc 7:37 is similar to the one in 4 Macc 6:28. Eleazar asks God in the latter text to provide mercy for the nation through his death (ἵλεως γενοῦ τῷ ἔθνει σου). In 2 Macc 7:37, the seventh son prays that God would "quickly be merciful to the nation" (ἵλεως ταχὺ τῷ ἔθνει γενέσθαι) through his death. In both 4 Macc 6:28 and 2 Macc 7:37, the martyrs urge God to grant mercy to the nation through their deaths for it. They offered themselves to God to pay for the nation's sin, which also became a payment for their sin by virtue of their membership within the community (see 2 Macc 7:32). Thus, the function of the martyrs' deaths for Israel parallels the function of Yom Kippur for Israel. That is, the martyrs represent and stand in the place of rebellious Israel, and they are the means by which and the place at which atonement is made for the nation to achieve YHWH's reconciliation, just as the animals stand in the place of Israel (the sacrificial ritual), represent the people (the scapegoat ritual), and are the means by which Israel's sins are purified/covered/atoned during Yom Kippur (Lev 16),[49] just as the Servant stands

---

Henten, *Maccabean Martyrs*, 140–44. Against a sacrificial reading of 2 Macc 7:32–38, see Williams, *Jesus' Death*, 82–88; Jonathan Goldstein, *2 Maccabees: A New Translation with Introduction and Commentary*, AB 41A (Garden City, NY: Doubleday, 1983), 316; Seeley, *Noble Death*, 87–91, 145; H. S. Versnel, "Making Sense of Jesus' Death: The Pagan Contribution," in *Deutungen des Todes Jesu im Neuen Testament*, ed. Jörg Frey and Jens Schröter, WUNT 181 (Tübingen: Mohr Siebeck, 2005), 258–59.

48. Schwartz, *2 Maccabees*, 317.

49. Contra Williams, *Jesus' Death*, 79 n. 29; Seeley, *Noble Death*, 87. Rightly de Jonge, *Christology in Context*, 181–82; Kellermann, "Zum traditionsgeschichtlichen Problem," 69; van Henten, *Maccabean Martyrs*, 137.

in the place of Israel as the means by which the nations' sins are purified/covered/atoned in Isa 53. As the ensuing narrative of 2 Macc 8:1–5 suggests, the martyrs' deaths are the means by which YHWH's wrath ceases against Israel and the means by which reconciliation is achieved in the narrative of 2 Maccabees.[50]

Second Maccabees 5:1–8:5 supports that God fulfilled the seventh son's expectation through the martyrs' deaths, for the latter text states that God was reconciled to the nation after the martyrs die (2 Macc 8:1–5).[51] In light of this, the martyrs' deaths are a foundational reason God ended his wrath against the nation.[52] For example, 2 Macc 1:5 begins with a prayer that God "would be reconciled" to his people and not forsake them during an "evil time" in the first letter in the book prior to the epitome in 2:19–15:37. The "evil time" spoken of in 2 Macc 1:5 probably refers to hellenization on account of the distress that consequently came upon torah-zealous Jews when apostate Jews revolted against the holy city and embraced Antiochus's Hellenistic policies (2 Macc 1:7–8; 2:17–18).

Before the epitome, the author reminds his fellow Jews in Egypt (to whom he is writing) that God has saved his people from the Greek tyrant, restored temple-worship, and he expresses hope that God would soon show his mercy to all Jews scattered throughout the world by gathering them at his holy temple in Judea (2 Macc 2:17–18). The epitome begins with a recounting of how God showed his mercy to the Jews through

---

50. Against Williams, *Jesus' Death*, 83–88; H. W. Surkau, *Martyrien in jüdischer und frühchristilicher Zeit*, FRLANT 36 (Göttingen: Vandenhoeck & Ruprecht, 1938), 59.

51. Schwartz (*2 Maccabees*, 317) observes that 2 Macc 8:4–5 applies 7:38.

52. Jan W. van Henten, "The Tradition-Historical Background of Romans 3:25: A Search for Pagan and Jewish Parallels," in *From Jesus to John: Essays on Jesus and New Testament Christology in Honour of Marinus de Jonge*, ed. Martinus C. de Boer, JSNTSup 84 (Sheffield: JSOT Press, 1993), 117–21, esp. 117. Against Williams, *Jesus' Death*, 85–89; Seeley, *Noble Death*, 88. See also Ulrich Kellermann, *Auferstanden in den Himmel: 2 Makkabäer 7 und die Auferstehung der Märtyrer*, SBS 95 (Stuttgart: Katholisches Bibelwerk, 1979), 54–55; Stephen Anthony Cummins, *Paul and the Crucified Christ in Antioch: Maccabean Martyrdom and Galatians 1 and 2*, SNTSMS 114 (Cambridge: Cambridge University Press, 2000), 88. William H. Brown ("From Holy War to Holy Martyrdom," in *The Quest for the Kingdom of God: Studies in Honor of George E. Mendenhall*, ed. Herbert B. Huffmon, Frank A. Spina, and Alberto R. Green [Winona Lake, IN: Eisenbrauns, 1983], 287–88) states that "Judas and his men are asking God to accept the present national suffering as sufficient, not only to atone for the nation's sins, but as sufficient to invoke his wrath upon the Syrian armies."

Judas and his brothers during the Maccabean crisis (2 Macc 2:19–22), and the author suggests that he intends to set forth this story by summarizing Jason of Cyrene's five-volume work (2 Macc 2:23). The epitome ends with the author asserting that the Hebrews possessed the city of Judea after Judas and his army cut off Nicanor's (a gentile king's) head and cut out his tongue (2 Macc 15:32–37). Thus, reconciliation with God in 1:5, God's mercy and salvation in 2:18, and God's mercy and salvation in 15:37 frame the martyrological sections of the epitome in 6:18–7:42. Such an arrangement could suggest that the author wants to communicate that the reason by which God's reconciliation, mercy, and salvation came to the covenant-community through Judas and his brothers was the faithful martyrs, which the ensuing narrative of 5:1–8:5 supports.[53]

While Antiochus was finishing his second invasion of Egypt in the narrative of 2 Maccabees, he heard that Judea was in revolt (2 Macc 5:1–11). He immediately left Egypt to seize Jerusalem (2 Macc 5:11b–14). Antiochus entered the holy temple and profaned it, for he was oblivious to the fact that God was using him to defile the temple on account of his anger with Israel (2 Macc 5:17–18). Just as the temple suffered pollution and judgment because of the nation's sin, it also experienced God's blessings when he pardoned the nation (2 Macc 5:20a; see also Lev 16:16, 30). Second Maccabees 5:20b states that God's wrath ended, and the glory of Israel was restored to the nation "by means of the reconciliation of the Great Lord" (2 Macc 8:5; see also Lev 9:1–10:2).

After the author describes the reversal of the abominations that Antiochus committed against Israel (2 Macc 5:21–6:11), he discusses why the Jews suffered by means of Antiochus. He offers this explanation immediately before he writes about the martyrdoms of Eleazar, the mother, and her seven sons (2 Macc 6:18–8:2). In 2 Macc 6:12–17, the author urges his readers not to be discouraged by the calamities that God brought against the nation by asserting that he provided the calamities against the nation for her benefit. The author also states that God would soon judge the gentile nations when they reach the full measure of their sins, but he would not deal with Israel in this way. Instead, God judged Israel through Antiochus, and the martyrdom of some was representative of his divine judgment against the entire nation. The author explains that God neither

---

53. In 1 Maccabees, the wrath is ascribed to Antiochus (1:64), and Judas's valor ends wrath against the nation and not his death (3:8). I owe this thought to Schwartz, *2 Maccabees*, 317.

withdrew his mercy from his people nor forsook them (2 Macc 6:13–16). The author, then, highlights the deaths of the martyrs in 2 Macc 6:18–8:2 to demonstrate how God's mercy was achieved for the nation (2 Macc 5:20; 8:5–7). Second Maccabees 6:18–8:5 suggests that God reveals his mercy to Israel by his reconciliatory acts toward the nation, because after the seventh son promises God's future judgment of Antiochus (2 Macc 7:33), he states that he (just as his brothers) offers his life to God with the prayer that he would be merciful to the nation through their deaths (2 Macc 7:37). His optimistic prayer in 2 Macc 7:37 follows the seventh son's confident assertion in 2 Macc 7:33 that the "Lord will be reconciled to his own servants." Subsequent to the author's presentations of the martyrdoms of Eleazar, the mother, and her seven sons (2 Macc 6:18–7:42), the author immediately discusses the response of the torah-zealous Jews to the martyrs' deaths.

In 2 Macc 8, Judas Maccabaeus reappears in the narrative. He and other torah-zealous Jews ask God to be merciful to the martyrs, the temple, and the city (2 Macc 8:2–3). They also pray that the Lord would hear the blood of the martyrs, that he would remember the destruction of the innocent babies, that he would remember the blasphemies against his name, and that he would hate all of the evil committed against Israel (2 Macc 8:4). The reconciliation for which the author prays in 2 Macc 1:5, the mercy of which the author speaks in 2 Macc 2:18, 5:20, 6:12–16, and 15:37, the mercy for which the martyrs die in 2 Macc 7:32–38, and the mercy for which Judas prays in 2 Macc 8:1–4 become a reality when God is reconciled again to the nation by reversing his wrath away from the Jews and against Antiochus and his army (2 Macc 5:1–8:5).[54]

To the contrary, other scholars have argued that the effective prayer of Judas was the means by which the Lord granted mercy and reconciliation to the nation.[55] Indeed, the reconciliation for which the seventh son asserts that his death and the deaths of his brothers would achieve for the nation becomes a reality for Israel in the narrative after Judas's prayer, and God's glory was again restored to both the temple and the nation through their deaths after Judas's prayer. However, to make Judas's prayer the primary basis upon which God becomes reconciled to Israel in the narrative is too narrow of a reading of 5:1–8:5, because God's reconciliation does

---

54. Contra Seeley, *Noble Death*, 87–88.
55. Most recently, Schwartz, *2 Maccabees*, 329.

not take place in this section until *after* the martyrs die (2 Macc 5:20–8:5; 4 Macc 17:21–22).

Judas's prayer was effective. But the exegetical question remains: why is his prayer effective? The narrative suggests that the prayer is efficacious in the narrative because the martyrs died for the nation. Thus, the efficacy of Judas's prayer does not disprove that the martyrs' deaths functioned as Israel's Yom Kippur. In fact, Philo notes that prayers were offered at Yom Kippur, along with fasting, to propitiate God (ἱλασκόμενοι τὸν πατέρα τοῦ παντός) as the participants asked him to forgive their old sins and to bring new blessings (*Mos.* 2:24).

Therefore, the text of 2 Macc 7:32–38 teaches that the martyrs function in the martyrological narratives as representatives of and as substitutes for Israel's sin and that they function as the nation's Yom Kippur for at least six reasons. First, the temple-cult was dysfunctional. Second, the seventh son and his brothers suffered and, eventually, died because of the nation's sin (2 Macc 7:32; see Lev 16:3, 5, 6, 9, 21, 25, 34). Third, the martyrs offered their lives to God in death to achieve reconciliation for the nation (2 Macc 7:37; see Lev 16:30). Fourth, the seventh son asserted that God would again be reconciled to the nation through his death (2 Macc 7:37b; see Lev 16:30). Fifth, the seventh son prayed that God would deliver the nation from his wrath through his death and through the deaths of his brothers (2 Macc 7:38; see Lev 16:30).[56] Sixth, God was reconciled to the nation once again by means of the martyrs' deaths (2 Macc 5:1–8:5; see Lev 16:30).

Jewish Martyrdom, God's Mercy, Satisfaction, and Purification

The evidence that the martyrs functioned as representatives of, as substitutes for, and in the place of Israel's Yom Kippur in the martyrological narratives is even stronger in 4 Maccabees than in 2 Maccabees because of the explicit cultic language applied to the martyrs' deaths. In 4 Maccabees, the author describes the martyrdom of Eleazar in 4 Macc 6 and offers his concluding interpretation regarding the function of their deaths for the nation in 4 Macc 17:21–22. The author describes Eleazar as a scribe of high rank (2 Macc 6:18), from a priestly family, and an expert in the law (4 Macc 5:4,

---

56. Similarly van Henten, *Maccabean Martyrs*, 143–44. Against Williams, *Jesus' Death*, 83–88.

35). Antiochus urges him to disobey the torah and eat swine (2 Macc 6:18; 4 Macc 5:6). Instead, Eleazar voluntarily chooses death. As a result, Antiochus severely tortures him (4 Macc 6:1–8). As he bleeds profusely from the scourges that tore his flesh and from being pierced in his side with a spear (4 Macc 6:6), Eleazar prays that God would use his death to achieve three benefits for Israel: (1) mercy (4 Macc 6:28), (2) satisfaction (4 Macc 6:28), and (3) purification (4 Macc 6:29).

Eleazar's Death and God's Mercy

In the face of death, Eleazar urges God in 4 Macc 6:28 to be merciful to Israel through his death (ἵλεως γενοῦ τῷ ἔθνει σου) (2 Macc 4:1–6:31; 4 Macc 5:4–6:40). Numerous texts throughout 4 Maccabees support that Eleazar's request for mercy is a request for deliverance from God's wrath (2 Macc 4:16–17; 6:12–17; 4 Macc 17:21–22), a wrath that he pours out on Israel in the narrative through Antiochus in order to chasten his people (1 Macc 1:1–64; 2 Macc 6:12–17; 7:32). In 4 Macc 4:19–20, Jason, the high priest, changed the nation's way of life from torah-observance to compliance with the Greek way of life so that he both constructed a gymnasium in Judea and abolished the care of the temple (καὶ ἐξεδιήτησεν τὸ ἔθνος καὶ ἐξεπολίτευσεν ἐπὶ πᾶσαν παρανομίαν ὥστε μὴ μόνον ἐπ᾽ αὐτῇ τῇ ἄκρᾳ τῆς πατρίδος ἡμῶν γυμνάσιον κατασκευάσαι ἀλλὰ καὶ καταλῦσαι τὴν τοῦ ἱεροῦ κηδεμονίαν). As a result, the Lord's divine anger caused Antiochus to make war on Israel (ἐφ᾽ οἷς ἀγανακτήσασα ἡ θεία δίκη αὐτὸν αὐτοῖς τὸν Ἀντίοχον ἐπολέμωσεν) (4 Macc 4:21). Hence, Antiochus issued a decree that anyone practicing Judaism would die (δόγμα ἔθετο ὅπως εἴ τινες αὐτῶν φάνοιεν τῷ πατρίῳ πολιτευόμενοι νόμῳ θάνοιεν) (4 Macc 4:23).

Fourth Maccabees 6:28 supports that Eleazar's prayer urges God to use his death to provide salvation for Israel from God's wrath through Antiochus. He asks God to be satisfied with the martyrs' judgment for the nation (ἀρκεσθεὶς τῇ ἡμετέρᾳ ὑπὲρ αὐτῶν δίκῃ).[57] With this request, Eleazar expresses that he offers his life to God as both a representative of and a substitute for Israel to achieve God's mercy, and he hopes that his provision would satisfy God's wrath against the nation. This interpretation

---

57. For other possible substitutionary uses of ὑπέρ in atonement texts, see LXX Exod 21:20; Lev 26:25; Deut 32:41, 43; Mic 7:9; Wis 1:8; 14:31; 18:11; cf. 1 Macc 5:32; 2 Macc 1:26; 3:32; Rom 5:6–11; 8:32; 1 Cor 1:13; 11:24; 15:3; 2 Cor 5:14–15, 21; Gal 1:4; 2:20–21; 3:13; 1 Thess 5:10.

seems correct for at least three reasons: First, Eleazar offers this petition to God while he faces his judgment for the people and as a representative of the people by means of Antiochus's persecution (4 Macc 6:28; 17:22; see also 1 Macc 6:60; Ps 68:32; Jer 18:4; Dan 4:2). Second, judgment (δίκη) consistently refers to divine judgment throughout 4 Maccabees (4 Macc 4:13, 21; 8:14, 22; 9:9, 15, 32; 11:3; 12:12; 18:22).[58] Third, the author applies the cultic language of blood to Eleazar in 4 Macc 6:29 to refer to the cleansing power of Eleazar's death for the nation.[59]

Eleazar's Death and Israel's Purification

Fourth Maccabees 6:29 states that Eleazar asks God to make his blood Israel's purification (καθάρσιον αὐτῶν ποίησον τὸ ἐμὸν αἷμα).[60] Since Eleazar has already prayed that God would bring mercy to Israel and end his wrath against Israel through his death, Eleazar's request in 4 Macc 6:29 suggests that he urges God to make his death a substitute for the nation's violation of torah to accomplish national purification and salvation. Eleazar's request likewise urges God to let his death function as Israel's Yom Kippur. The substitutionary nature of Eleazar's request is apparent when

---

58. See also 2 Macc 8:11, 13.

59. Since Eleazar's first request that God would be merciful to the nation (ἵλεως γενοῦ τῷ ἔθνει σου) is the main clause in the sentence ἵλεως γενοῦ τῷ ἔθνει σου ἀρκεσθεὶς τῇ ἡμετέρᾳ ὑπὲρ αὐτῶν δίκῃ, the adverbial participial clause (ἀρκεσθεὶς τῇ ἡμετέρᾳ ὑπὲρ αὐτῶν δίκῃ) is a continuation of the first request in 4 Macc 6:28a and likewise takes the tone of a prayer of entreaty, as the first part of the prayer. Other uses of the adjective ἵλεως elsewhere in 4 Maccabees support that in 4 Macc 6:28, Eleazar asks God to accept his death as the means through which he would save the nation from his judgment. E.g., (1) prior to Antiochus's torture of the seven sons in 4 Macc 8:14, he urges them to provide mercy for themselves by eating unclean meat. Obedience to Antiochus would have ensured their salvation from his judgment. (2) In 4 Macc 9:24, as Antiochus inflicts torture upon one of the seven sons, the son exhorts his brothers to follow his example of godliness and he stated that through his godliness God's mercy would save the nation. (3) After the seventh son refuses to obey Antiochus in 4 Macc 12:4–16, he hurls himself into Antiochus's fire that Antiochus used to threaten him and the other brothers. As he entered the fire, the seventh son prays that God would be merciful (ἵλεως) to save the nation through his death (4 Macc 12:17). For other connections in the LXX between God's mercy and deliverance from judgment, see Exod 32:12, 33; Num 14; Deut 21:1–8; 2 Chr 6:25–27, 39; 7:14; Amos 7:2; Jer 5:1, 7; 27:20; 38:34; 43:3.

60. See also 4 Macc 1:11; LXX Dan 3:38–40.

he asks God to make his αἷμα Israel's purification (2 Macc 5:17–18; 6:15; 7:32; 12:42; 4 Macc 5:19; 17:21; see also Lev 16:16, 30),[61] and the function of his death as "the" Yom Kippur for the nation is conspicuously set forth with the words purification and blood and in 17:21–22 when the author states that the martyrs died propitiatory deaths to purify the homeland and to save the nation, language and concepts straight from Lev 16. The blood of the animals in Lev 16 served to purify the nation from all of its sins and to provide salvation from the looming judgment of YHWH if Yom Kippur was not performed in compliance with torah (see Lev 9:1–16:34). Eleazar asks God to use his blood to be Israel's Yom Kippur by granting the nation mercy and satisfaction as a result of his blood (4 Macc 6:28–29), and 4 Macc 17:21–22 in fact states that the martyrs propitiated God, saved the nation, and accomplished national purification for the homeland.

As I have argued elsewhere,[62] καθάρσιον occurs nowhere else in the LXX besides 4 Macc 6:29. However, καθάρισμος is a cognate of καθάρσιον. The latter occurs in the LXX and in the New Testament to refer both to the purification of Israel and to Christians. In both testaments, one receives purification through cultic blood (Exod 29:36; 30:10; see 2 Pet 1:9), through ritual cleansing (Lev 14:32; 15:13; see Mark 1:44; Luke 2:22; 5:14; John 2:6; 3:25), through God's forgiveness (Num 14:18), through the cleansing of holy utensils (1 Chr 23:28), through the purification of the temple (2 Macc 1:18; 2:16, 19; 10:5), or through one's piety (4 Macc 7:6). Eleazar's expertise in the law, his priestly status, and his priestly familial heritage in the narratives of 2 and 4 Maccabeees (2 Macc 6:18; 4 Macc 5:4, 35) suggest that his comments about his death in 4 Macc 6:28–29 are overtly cultic.[63] Moreover, since the narrative of 4 Macccabees states that Antiochus abolished the sacrificial system, killed anyone who yielded allegiance to the torah (1 Macc 1:41–64; 2 Macc 5:4, 35), controlled the temple, and prohibited compliance with the torah (2 Macc 1:5; 7:32–38; 4 Macc 6:28–29; 17:20–21), Eleazar's request likely, then, urges God in 4 Macc 6:28–29 to use his death and the deaths of the other martyrs to substitute for the absence of temple sacrifices, which would have included the Yom Kippur ritual since Antiochus forbade all sacrifices, so that the nation would corporately

---

61. Against Seeley, *Noble Death*, 97–98.
62. Williams, *Maccabean Martyr Traditions*.
63. See also 2 Macc 6:18; 4 Macc 5:4, 35.

experience God's cleansing of forgiveness through the martyrs as the Yom Kippur sacrifices.

Eleazar's Death as a Ransom for Israel

In the final part of his prayer in 4 Macc 6:29b, Eleazar asks God to receive his death as a ransom for the nation (καὶ ἀντίψυχον αὐτῶν λαβὲ τὴν ἐμὴν ψυχήν). The term ἀντίψυχον ("ransom") in 4 Macc 6:29b likewise occurs in 4 Macc 17:21. There the term suggests that the martyrs' deaths purified and saved the nation, because the author connects ἀντίψυχον with both the nation's purification from sin and with its salvation (καὶ διὰ τοῦ αἵματος τῶν εὐσεβῶν ἐκείνων καὶ τοῦ ἱλαστηρίου τοῦ θανάτου αὐτῶν ἡ θεία πρόνοια τὸν Ισραηλ προκακωθέντα διέσωσεν). Furthermore, 4 Macc 6:29b reveals an explicit lexical connection with Yom Kippur with the compound ἀντίψυχον, which occurs as two different words (ἀντὶ τῆς ψυχῆς) in LXX Lev 17:11 in a context where the author discusses Yom Kippur (Lev 16) and the atoning function of blood on behalf of one's life (Lev 17:11).[64]

The restriction not to eat blood in LXX Lev 17:11 due to its redemptive effect for the soul (ἀντὶ τῆς ψυχῆς) includes the blood that atones for sin at Yom Kippur, for in Lev 16–17 YHWH's prohibition not to eat blood emerges to highlight the importance of the function of the animal's blood offered as atonement. This point is supported by YHWH's statement in Lev 16–17 that the blood makes atonement (Lev 16:5–20; 17:12). Similarly, the blood of the martyrs in 4 Macc 6:28–29 and 17:21–22 accomplishes atonement and thereby functions as the nation's Yom Kippur, for the martyrs' blood achieves the same effect as the animals' blood during the Yom Kippur ritual: namely, national purification and salvation (Lev 16:5–34; 4 Macc 17:21–22). The narrator states this in a straightforward way in 4 Macc 17:21–22 with his assertion that the martyrs purified the homeland by means of their deaths (τὴν πατρίδα καθαρισθῆναι ὥσπερ ἀντίψυχον γεγονότας τῆς τοῦ ἔθνους ἁμαρτίας καὶ διὰ τοῦ αἵματος τῶν εὐσεβῶν ἐκείνων καὶ τοῦ ἱλαστηρίου τοῦ θανάτου αὐτῶν ἡ θεία πρόνοια τὸν Ισραηλ προκακωθέντα διέσωσεν).

A function of ἀντίψυχον in 4 Macc 6:29 and 17:21, then, is to communicate that the blood of the martyrs was the required price paid to achieve both Israel's purification and salvation (4 Macc 17:21–22), just as

---

64. So Campbell, *Deliverance*, 650–51.

the sacrificial ritual on Yom Kippur required the blood of the animal to cover/atone the sins of the people (Lev 16).[65] In fact, 4 Macc 17:21 asserts that the homeland was purified "just as" (ὥσπερ) the martyrs became a ransom for the sin of the nation.[66] As I have discussed in detail elsewhere, Williams, followed by Seeley, argued that the author of 4 Maccabees metaphorically means that God received the martyrs' deaths "just as" (ὥσπερ) he received sacrifices since he deemed their deaths as an act of expiation (4 Macc 17:21). The adverb should not be interpreted to mean that their deaths literally expiated sin in the narrative. However, 4 Macc 17:22 speaks against this reading since the author states that "through the blood of these godly ones" (i.e., the martyrs) and "through their propitiatory death," God saved the nation from his wrath (καὶ διὰ τοῦ αἵματος τῶν εὐσεβῶν ἐκείνων καὶ τοῦ ἱλαστηρίου τοῦ θανάτου αὐτῶν ἡ θεία πρόνοια τὸν Ισραηλ προκακωθέντα διέσωσεν). Consequently, the author of 4 Maccabees appears to be echoing Lev 16-17, especially the feast of atonement and the Yom Kippur ritual, when he discusses the martyrs' deaths since he repeatedly uses similar cultic language from Lev 16-17 to describe the function of the martyrs' deaths for the nation in a cultic setting without a functional temple.[67]

4 Maccabees 17:21-22:
The Author's Interpretation of the Martyrs' Deaths

The author of 4 Maccabees interprets the martyrs' deaths to be both sacrificial in nature and a saving event for the nation in 4 Macc 17:21-22 (καὶ τὸν τύραννον τιμωρηθῆναι καὶ τὴν πατρίδα καθαρισθῆναι ὥσπερ ἀντίψυχον γεγονότας τῆς τοῦ ἔθνους ἁμαρτίας καὶ διὰ τοῦ αἵματος τῶν εὐσεβῶν ἐκείνων καὶ τοῦ ἱλαστηρίου τοῦ θανάτου αὐτῶν ἡ θεία πρόνοια τὸν Ισραηλ προκακωθέντα διέσωσεν). He describes their deaths by using the phrase τοῦ

---

65. For a different emphasis, see Rajak, *Jewish Dialogue with Rome and Greece*, 109-11. She argues that the primary function of the ἀντίψυχον in 4 Maccabees "was to establish a connection between persecution, in the Diaspora, and victory, in Palestine, and to bridge the awkward geographical disjunction between two locations."
66. Williams, *Jesus' Death*, 177-78; Seeley, *Noble Death*, 97.
67. Against Kraus, *Tod Jesu*, 38-39. Rightly Campbell, *Deliverance*, 650-51. For further evidence, see 4 Macc 6:28-29; 7:8; 17:10; 17:21-22; 18:4; see also Exod 33:12-34:9; Assumption of Moses 9:6-7; 10:2-10; 2 Macc 5:20-7:38.

ἱλαστηρίου τοῦ θανάτου.[68] The term ἱλαστήριον occurs in 4 Macc 17:22 with other cultic vocabulary (e.g., "sin" [ἁμαρτίας], "blood" [διὰ τοῦ αἵματος], and "to purify" [καθαρισθῆναι]), a cultic concept (ἀντίψυχον γεγονότας τῆς τοῦ ἔθνους ἁμαρτίας), and a soteriological term (διέσωσεν). Additionally, the cultic concept of consecration occurs in 4 Macc 17:19–20 (καὶ γάρ φησιν ὁ Μωυσῆς καὶ πάντες οἱ ἡγιασμένοι ὑπὸ τὰς χεῖράς σουκαὶ οὗτοι οὖν ἁγιασθέντες διὰ θεὸν τετίμηνται οὐ μόνον ταύτῃ τῇ τιμῇ ἀλλὰ καὶ τῷ δι' αὐτοὺς τὸ ἔθνος ἡμῶν τοὺς πολεμίους μὴ ἐπικρατῆσαι). The idea of the consecration of the martyrs in 4 Macc 17:19–20 joins with the other cultic concepts mentioned above to make the context of the martyrs' deaths overtly cultic and similar to Yom Kippur.

Fourth Maccabees 17:22 and Rom 3:25 are the only places in available literature where an author applies ἱλαστήριον to the death of torah-observant Jews in a cultic context for the soteriological benefit of non-torah-observant sinners. The term ἱλαστήριον refers to the mercy seat in contexts in the LXX where priests atoned for sin through the sacrifice of blood (Lev 16:14–15). God commands Israel to put the ἱλαστήριον above the ark of the covenant in the holy of holies, the place where only the high priest could enter (Exod 25:17–20; 37:6). God commands the priest to make atonement on the ἱλαστήριον to provide cleansing for sin (Exod 25:18–22; 31:7; 35:12; 37:6–8; Lev 16:14–15), and God appears above the ἱλαστήριον to show his acceptance of atonement (Exod 25:22; Lev 16:2; Num 7:89). The term also occurs in LXX Ezek 43:14–20 in reference to a place at which atonement takes place by the pouring out of blood.[69]

---

68. In 4 Macc 17:22, a major textual variant exists pertaining to the function of ἱλαστήριον. For a discussion, see Hans-Josef Klauck, *Unterweisung in lehrhafter Form: 4 Makkabäerbuch*, JSKRZ NS 3 (Gütersloh: Mohn, 1989), 753, van Henten, "Tradition-Historical Background," 101–28, esp. 123, and David Arthur DeSilva, *4 Maccabees: Introduction and Commentary on the Greek Text in Codex Sinaiticus*, BSCS (Leiden: Brill, 2006), 250.

69. The occurrence of ἱλαστήριον in the context of 4 Macc 17:21–22 is certainly cultic for the above reasons, but also because the term itself is part of a semantic family of ἱλας- words that often occur in cultic contexts in the LXX that speak of atoning for sin, because these words often translate from the Hebrew root, which often means "to atone," and because some form ἱλαστήριον occurs in Leviticus's prescriptions regarding Yom Kippur (LXX Lev 16:2, 13–15). I am not asserting that the ἱλας-words group always translates from the Hebrew that means "to atone" (see LXX Exod 32:14; 2 Kgs 21:3; 1 Chr 6:34; 2 Chr 29:24; Ps 105:30; Ezek 43:14–20; Zech 7:2; 8:22). I am neither affirming that the ἱλας-words group always conveys the idea of atoning sacrifice (see

In his now famous unpublished doctoral thesis, Daniel P. Bailey argues that ἱλαστήριον in 4 Macc 17:22 and in Rom 3:25 have distinct meanings.[70] The author of 4 Macc 17:22 uses the term consistent with its occurrence in the Hellenistic world (i.e., propitiatory), but Paul uses the term consistent with its occurrence in the biblical world (i.e., mercy seat).[71] According to Bailey, to argue that ἱλαστήριον refers to sacrificial atonement in 4 Macc 17:22 is a mistake. After reviewing the evidence in the relevant Hellenistic literature that supports reading the term as propitiatory, Bailey argues that various inscriptions in the Hellenistic world affirm that ἱλαστηρία were offered either to propitiate the wrath of offended deities or to gain their favor.[72] He also argues that -τηρίον words do not regularly refer to actions, but to places.[73] Bailey concludes that the meaning of ἱλαστήριον in 4 Macc 17:22 as it relates to the martyrs' deaths "should be sought against a non-sacrificial background."[74] According to Bailey, 4 Maccabees nowhere states that the martyrs died as atoning sacrifices for Israel's sin.

Bailey's doctoral thesis is a careful and thorough contribution to scholarship. To my knowledge, it provides the most extensive lexical analysis of ἱλαστήριον based on ancient texts and ancient inscriptions in English-speaking scholarship. Bailey's concern, though, is exclusively a

---

LXX Exod 32:14; Prov 16:14). E.g., ἐξιλάσασθαι is often cultic and often refers to the cleansing that takes places when sins are atoned (LXX Exod 30:10; Lev 1:4; 4:20, 26, 31, 35; 5:6, 10, 13, 16, 18, 26; 6:23; 7:7; 16:29; Num 5:8; 6:11; 8:12, 19, 21; 15:25, 28; 17:11, 12; 28:22, 30; 29:5, 11; 31:50; 1 Kgs 3:14; 2 Kgs 2:13; 1 Chr 6:34; 2 Chr 29:24; 30:18; 2 Esd 20:34; Ps 105:30; Ezek 43:20, 22; 45:17; Sir 3:3, 30; 5:6; 20:28; 28:5; 34:19; 45:16, 23). However, the one occurrence of ἱλάσθη in the LXX is not cultic, and it is altogether void of sacrificial ideas (LXX Exod 32:14). In LXX Exod 32:14, ἐξιλάσασθαι translates from a root that means "to repent" and highlights YHWH's mercy to Israel in spite of the nation's idolatry. Rather, my point is simply that the ἱλας- words often occurs in cultic texts and often speak of sacrificial atonement when this word group occurs with explicit cultic vocabulary, as it does in 4 Macc 17:21–22.

70. Many thanks to Dan for e-mailing me a copy of his dissertation.

71. Daniel P. Bailey, "Jesus as the Mercy Seat: The Semantics and Theology of Paul's Use of Hilasterion in Romans 3:25" (PhD diss., University of Cambridge, 1999), 5–12, esp. 11–12.

72. For the above analysis and summary of Bailey's view, see DeSilva, *4 Maccabees*, 250–51, who cites Bailey ("Mercy Seat," 31–75).

73. Stephen Finlan, *The Background and Contents of Paul's Cultic Atonement Metaphors*, AcBib 19 (Atlanta: Society of Biblical Literature, 2004), 200–3, who cites Bailey.

74. The above quotation comes from DeSilva (*4 Maccabees*, 251), who summarizes Bailey's view.

lexical one. His work seeks to offer a better translation of ἱλαστήριον in Rom 3:25 by analyzing every ancient text and inscription that has lexical affinity to it. I agree with his argument that the occurrence of the same term in different texts (i.e., 4 Macc 17:22 and Rom 3:25) does not necessitate that the term should be translated the same way in both texts. Nevertheless, Bailey's thesis and arguments (if I understand them correctly) seem to pit his lexical analysis against the context within which ἱλαστήριον occurs. Therefore, his analysis prevents the term from conveying its contextual theme.[75] In my view, regardless of how one translates ἱλαστήριον in 4 Macc 17:22, since the term occurs in the same context as several atonement vocabulary and concepts found in Lev 16–17 (i.e., judgment, purification of the nation, ransom, vicarious death, sin, and blood), ἱλαστήριον in 4 Macc 17:22 at least alludes to the Yom Kippur ritual; it at least suggests that the martyrs' deaths are functioning as Israel's Yom Kippur, and it at least suggests that the martyrs die in the narratives as representatives of and as substitutes for Israel.[76]

Fourth Maccabees 6:28–29 speaks of the martyrs' deaths in the context of blood, purification, and ransom. Likewise, 4 Macc 17:21–22 speaks of the martyrs' deaths in the context of purification for the nation, ransom, blood, and salvation.[77] The author's reference to the consecration of the martyrs for God in 4 Macc 17:20 (ἁγιασθέντες διὰ θεόν) and the participle προκακωθέντα in reference to the mistreatment of the nation in 4 Macc 17:22 recall the imagery of setting apart the animals for atonement and the terminology of the afflictions at Yom Kippur (see LXX Lev 16:29–32).[78] Therefore, the contextual evidence in 4 Macc 6:28–29 and 17:21–22 challenges the conclusion that ἱλαστήριον in 4 Maccabees should be understood as a pagan reference to a non-cultic/non-sacrificial background. I suggest that 4 Macc 6:28–29 and 17:21–22 together affirm that the martyrs offered themselves to God as representatives of the nation, as substitutes for the nation, and that the martyrs functioned as Israel's Yom Kippur in the narrative of 4 Maccabees.[79]

---

75. For a similar critique, see also Finlan, *Atonement Metaphors*, 200.
76. Similarly Ben Ezra, *Yom Kippur*, 115. DeSilva (*4 Maccabees*, 250–51) argues that the author uses the cultic language from the Yom Kippur ritual to describe the effect of the martyrs' deaths.
77. DeSilva, *4 Maccabees*, 202.
78. Ben Ezra, *Yom Kippur*, 116.
79. DeSilva, *4 Maccabees*, 202–3. Similarly Marinus de Jonge, "Jesus' Death for

Conclusion

The following eight conclusions can be inferred from the analysis in this chapter. First, Antiochus desecrated the temple and forbade the Jews from offering sacrifices in compliance with torah (1 Macc 1:41-59). As a result, many Jews in the narratives of 2 and 4 Maccabees viewed the temple as unclean and unfit for temple worship until its purification in compliance with torah (see Jub. 22:16-18; Let. Aris. 152-153; Pss. Sol. 2:2; Acts 21:27). Second, in 2 and 4 Maccabees, Antiochus forbade the Jewish people from offering any cultic sacrifices in compliance with torah, which included Yom Kippur (1 Macc 1:41-59). Third, the martyrs suffered and died because of the nation's sin (2 Macc 7:18, 32; 12:39-42; 4 Macc 4:21; 17:21-22), just as the high priest offered the animal's blood for sin on Yom Kippur (Lev 1:1-7:6; 8:18-21; 16:3-24). Fourth, the martyrs' blood was the required price for the nation's national purification, forgiveness, and salvation (2 Macc 7:32-38; 4 Macc 6:28-29; 7:8; 17:21-22), just as the animals' blood was the required price for Israel's forgiveness on Yom Kippur (Lev 16:30). Fifth, the martyrs' deaths provided purification and cleansing for the nation (4 Macc 6:28-29; 17:22), just as the animals' blood provided purification and cleansing for Israel on Yom Kippur (Lev 16:16, 30). Sixth, the martyrs' deaths ended God's wrath against the nation (1 Macc 1:1-64; 2 Macc 7:32-38; 8:5; 4 Macc 17:21-22), just as the animals' blood when appropriately offered at Yom Kippur placated God's wrath against the nation (Lev 9:1-16:30). Seventh, the martyrs died as representatives of and vicariously for the nation (2 Macc 7:18, 32; 4 Macc 4:21; 17:21-22), just as the animals were representatives of and were substitutes for the sins of the nation on Yom Kippur (Lev 16:1-30). Eighth, God judged sin and granted forgiveness through the martyrs' deaths in the narratives (2 Macc 6:12-7:38; 4 Macc 17:21-22), just as YHWH judged sin and granted forgiveness through the animals' deaths on Yom Kippur (Lev 16:1-30).

Others and the Death of the Maccabean Martyrs," in *Text and Testimony: Essays on New Testament and Apocryphal Literature in Honour of A. F. J. Klijn*, ed. Tjitze Baarda et al. (Kampen: Kok, 1988), 142-51, esp. 150-51.

Resistance Is Not Futile: Restraint as Cultic Action in 2 Thessalonians 2:1–12*

Ross E. Winkle

Introduction

Perhaps one of the most famous statements about the boundaries of viable resistance to something unwanted comes from the fictional Captain Jean-Luc Picard of the USS *Enterprise* in the television series *Star Trek: The Next Generation*. In the Season Three cliffhanger in 1990, the alien Borg, a transhuman collective of galactic predators that absorbs or assimilates all species it encounters, abduct Captain Picard and assimilate him, thus creating his new identity as "Locutus of Borg." The Borg then attempt to assimilate the crew of the USS Enterprise, with the ultimate goal of turning all of Earth into a colony of Borg automatons. At a critical juncture during this conflict, newly assimilated Locutus utters those memorable yet terror-inducing words to the *Enterprise* crew: "Resistance is futile."[1]

Here I will argue about resistance from a different direction—that of 2 Thess 2. I will suggest that the enigmatic "restrainer" (ὁ κατέχων) in 2 Thess 2:1–12 alludes to the understanding of high priestly figures as engaged in a martial type of cultic, ongoing resistance to or restraint against evil or disaster. First, the concept of restraint is critical to the argument of the notorious passage in 2 Thess 2:1–12, which describes the nefarious actions of the "man of lawlessness." Second, the figure of Michael, the great angelic prince of Israel in Dan 10–12, provides a reasonable background to the

---

* I would like to thank Dr. Robert Matthew Calhoun for his comments on an earlier draft of this essay.

1. Michael Piller, "The Best of Both Worlds, Part 1," DVD, Episode 26 of Season 3 of *Star Trek: The Next Generation*, directed by Clif Bole (Hollywood, CA: Paramount Pictures, 2013).

"restrainer" who successfully resists and thus restrains the emergence of the man of lawlessness. Third, the dynamic of restraint was an integral element of the work of the priestly cult in protecting against evil, disaster, and wrath from the time of ancient Israel to the New Testament era. Fourth, such cultic restraint was understood and described with martial terminology. Finally, I show that understanding the depiction of Michael in Dan 10–12 as a figure whose activity is martial in description but also cultic and high priestly in nature further illuminates the mysterious and yet striking action of the restrainer in 2 Thess 2 at the juncture at which the man of lawlessness is revealed.

The Problem of the Restrainer

First Thessalonians is probably the earliest of Paul's letters.[2] Second Thessalonians picks up and expands in 2:1–12 what Paul wrote in 1 Thessalonians regarding the eschaton. While 2 Thessalonians has often been neglected because of its short length and similarity to some of the content of 1 Thessalonians, it is this striking reference in 2:1–12 to the climactic actions of the eschatological "man of lawlessness," who ultimately proclaims himself divine but whom Jesus destroys at his coming, that is this epistle's "claim to fame."

These verses in chapter 2 focus on the claim that "the day of the Lord" had already arrived. Instead of the Thessalonian congregation being shaken up or alarmed by such a false report (2:1–2), it needs to realize that the day of the Lord cannot have already arrived, since two things must take place first: (1) the apostasy (ἡ ἀποστασία); and (2) the appearance or revelation of the man of lawlessness (ὁ ἄνθρωπος τῆς ἀνομίας), who will take his seat in the temple of God (2:3–4). This latter figure's appearance on the scene (2:6) will occur once the restrainer is "removed" or "goes out of the middle" (ἐκ μέσου γένηται [2:7]). It would only be after the revelation of the man of lawlessness—whom the text associates with widespread deception—that the Lord Jesus would come and destroy him (2:8–11).

---

2. With regard to the dating of 1 Thessalonians, see, e.g., M. Eugene Boring, *An Introduction to the New Testament: History, Literature, Theology* (Louisville: Westminster John Knox, 2012), 209: "Most constructions of the history of early Christian literature consider 1 Thessalonians to be the earliest New Testament document, and thus the earliest extant piece of Christian writing."

While the identity and actions of the man of lawlessness have captured the attention of numerous exegetes, the identity in this passage of ὁ κατέχων appears more enigmatic and problematic. Seemingly intractable questions about this latter apocalyptic figure have contributed to negative evaluations of the entire passage. William Neil, for example, comments that these verses in 2 Thessalonians are "the weirdest piece of writing in all the epistles."[3] Scholars have advanced numerous suggestions as to the identity of this character, but currently no consensus exists as to whom the terminology may refer. Darrell D. Hannah observes that the identity of the restrainer is "one of this chapter's most tantalizing puzzles, an exegetical conundrum that has baffled readers for centuries," and then, in a display of hyperbole, declares that "the proposed solutions as to the identity of this mysterious figure are legion."[4] Consequently, a kind of exegetical melancholy has set in among many interpreters with regard to the resolution of the identity of the restrainer. Ben Witherington, for instance, notes with a hint of cynicism that "there have been almost as many conjectures about 'the Restrainer' as there have been commentaries on 2 Thessalonians."[5] Beverly Roberts Gaventa warns that attempts to identify the restrainer are "futile."[6] Finally, Helmut Koester lamented that "the identity of [the restrainer] will probably never be solved."[7]

This passage in 2 Thess 2:1–12 contains a number of difficulties, including the use of ellipses, clauses missing direct objects, and rare phraseology. But at least two key facts underscore the interpretational difficulty of the reference to the restrainer in particular. First, in the New Testament outside of 2 Thessalonians, the Greek verb κατέχω has several usages: it can mean "hold back, hinder, prevent from going away" (Luke 4:42; Phlm 13), "hold down, suppress, stifle" or "lay claim to" (Rom 1:18),

---

3. William Neil, *The Epistles of Paul to the Thessalonians*, MNTC 12 (London: Hodder & Stoughton, 1950), 132.

4. Darrell D. Hannah, "The Angelic Restrainer of 2 Thessalonians 2.6–7," in *Calling Time: Religion and Change at the Turn of the Millennium*, ed. Martyn Percy, LSRS 2 (Sheffield: Sheffield Academic, 2000), 29, 30.

5. Ben Witherington III, *1 and 2 Thessalonians: A Socio-rhetorical Commentary* (Grand Rapids: Eerdmans, 2006), 208.

6. Beverly Roberts Gaventa, *First and Second Thessalonians*, IBC (Louisville: John Knox, 1998), 113.

7. Helmut Koester, "From Paul's Eschatology to the Apocalyptic Schemata of 2 Thessalonians," in *The Thessalonian Correspondence*, ed. Raymond F. Collins, BETL 87 (Leuven: Leuven University Press, 1990), 457.

"hold to, hold fast, retain faithfully" (Luke 8:15; 1 Cor 11:2; 15:2; 1 Thess 5:21; Heb 3:6, 14; 10:23), "possess" (2 Cor 6:10), "confine" (Rom 7:6), "take into one's possession, occupy" (Luke 14:9), or "hold course"/"steer toward" (Acts 27:40).[8] Consequently, questions have arisen as to whether "restrainer" is an adequate or correct rendering. Second, the verb first appears as a neuter participle in 2:6 (τὸ κατέχον) and then as a masculine participle in 2:7 (ὁ κατέχων). Why are different genders in the participle used so close together?

The Meaning of κατέχω in 2 Thessalonians

As indicated earlier, scholars have advanced numerous theories as to what and/or whom this enigmatic neuter κατέχον and masculine κατέχων might refer.[9] There are basically two perspectives at opposite ends of the spectrum, seeing the words as referring to either good or evil. Those that view the κατέχον/-ων as an evil power often see the neuter as a reference to rebellion or lawlessness, while they view the masculine as referring to Satan or an eschatological agent of Satan, like the man of lawlessness. Supporters of such an interpretation typically view this as one that best reflects the grammar of the passage.

However, the context and structural flow of the passage here indicate several things with regard to the meaning of this intriguing term: (1) three times in this passage the verb ἀποκαλύπτω ("reveal": 2:3, 6, 8) occurs, all of which refer to one or more evil figures; (2) the verb κατέχω is used to describe something that is happening "now"—something that will cease or stop—before the man of lawlessness is "then" revealed (2:7–8); and (3) this strongly suggests that κατέχω has the basic sense of "hold," with the further nuances of "holding down," "restraining," or "preventing" the revelation of the man.

Consequently, Hannah's observations on this approach are well worth quoting: "Thus taking ὁ κατέχων in a negative sense as 'a hostile occupying

---

8. BDAG, s.v. "κατέχω." All New Testament usages of this verb are transitive except for the one found in Acts 27:40.

9. See the extensive discussion in the commentaries. See also Hannah, "Angelic Restrainer," 31–37; and Colin R. Nicholl, *From Hope to Despair in Thessalonica: Situating 1 and 2 Thessalonians*, SNTSMS 126 (Cambridge: Cambridge University Press, 2004), 228–30 (an earlier version of this essay on pp. 225–49 was published as "Michael, the Restrainer Removed [2 Thess.2:6-7]," *JTS* 51 [April 2000]: 27–53).

power' can be said to be the best grammatical solution, but only, I would contend, in violence to the context. Why, if the ὁ κατέχων is a hostile or evil power, must he be removed for the man of lawlessness to appear?"[10] He then observes that "no ancient Greek interpreter known to us [Hippolytus, John Chrysostom, Theodore of Mopsuestia, Basil of Caesarea, and perhaps Justin Martyr][11] ever understood the two κατέχειν participles in this passage in the sense of 'to possess,' 'to occupy,' 'to overpower,' 'to oppress,' and so on, but rather uniformly understood the participles in the sense of 'to restrain,' 'to check,' 'to hinder.'"[12] This line of argumentation thus again supports the meaning of κατέχον/-ων referring to restraint, and as a result the idea that it refers to an evil character—Satan or one of his agents—loses support. Consequently, I accept the interpretation of the masculine term to refer to this figure as the "restrainer."[13]

Those that see the κατέχον/-ων as good offer a number of interpretations, which divide between human and superhuman possibilities. Among those who advocate a human or intramundane reference, the options include: (1) the Roman emperor or empire; (2) a particular human ruler or the principle of law and order; and (3) Paul or the proclamation of the gospel. Those who advance a superhuman interpretation typically suggest: (1) God or God's will/plan; (2) the Holy Spirit; or (3) an angel.

It is clearly beyond the scope of this paper to evaluate fully all of the arguments for or against each of the above possible interpretations.[14] Rather, I shall examine an interpretation that Hannah and Colin Nicholl have recently revived. This interpretation raises the possibility that the restrainer implicitly refers to the work of Michael, the celestial prince who

---

10. Hannah, "Angelic Restrainer," 35.

11. Ibid., 35 n. 23.

12. Ibid., 35.

13. Josephus uses the verb in a number of places to speak of holding back or preventing something dangerous, bad, or evil (e.g., *Ant.* 14.102, 357; *J.W.* 1.662; 2.11, 40, 213, 214, 267; 3.127; 5.454; 6.260, 345; 7.48; *Life* 1.43, 60).

14. For recent discussion of these options, see, e.g., G. K. Beale, *1-2 Thessalonians*, IVPNTC 13 (Downers Grove, IL: InterVarsity Press, 2003), 213-17; Hannah, "Angelic Restrainer," 31-37; Paul Metzger, *Katechon: II Thess 2,1-12 im Horizont apokalyptischen Denkens*, BZNW 135 (Berlin: de Gruyter, 2005), 15-47; Nicholl, *Hope to Despair*, 228-32; Fritz W. Röcker, *Belial und Katechon: Eine Untersuchung zu 2 Thess 2,1-12 und 1 Thess 4,13-5,11*, WUNT 262 (Tübingen: Mohr Siebeck, 2009), 422-73; and Jeffrey A. D. Weima, *1-2 Thessalonians*, BECNT (Grand Rapids: Baker Academic, 2014), 570-77.

first appears in the Hebrew Bible in the book of Daniel and who is later known in the New Testament as the heavenly archangel.[15]

2 Thessalonians, Daniel, and Michael

Paul frequently utilized the LXX for many of his quotations and allusions.[16] Neither of the Thessalonian letters, however, contains explicit quotations from the Old Testament. Nevertheless, most New Testament scholars believe that these letters are indebted to the Jewish Scriptures in reference to various terms and concepts utilized within them. Since it is nearly universally agreed that 2 Thessalonians is either alluding to or using concepts from Daniel, particularly Dan 11,[17] Dan 10–12 offers an obvious place to look for the allusive background to the restrainer.

There are only two characters in these last three chapters of Daniel that could possibly be reasonably correlated with the restrainer of 2 Thess 2: the unnamed being who personally encounters Daniel and speaks with him in 10:10–12:4; or Michael, to whom the text refers by name three times (10:13, 21; 12:1).

In Dan 10:13, the first reference to Michael, English translations describe him as "*one* of the chief princes" who comes to the help of the first, unnamed being in the latter's opposition or resistance to the Prince of Persia. The Hebrew term אחד, however, can refer not only to a cardi-

---

15. Cf. Hannah ("Angelic Restrainer," 28–45) and Nicholl (*Hope to Despair*, 225–49). For a list of earlier supporters of this view, see ibid., 230 n. 25. See also the support given to this interpretation by Gary S. Shogren, *1 and 2 Thessalonians*, ZECNT (Grand Rapids: Zondervan, 2012), 287–88; Sigve K. Tonstad, "The Restrainer Removed: A Truly Alarming Thought (2 Thess 2:1–12)," *HBT* 29 (2007): 145; and Witherington, *1 and 2 Thessalonians*, 211, 221.

16. See, e.g., Christopher D. Stanley, *Paul and the Language of Scripture: Citation Technique in the Pauline Epistles and Contemporary Literature*, SNTSMS 74 (Cambridge: Cambridge University Press, 1992), 67–68, 254; J. Ross Wagner, "Isaiah in Romans and Galatians," in *Isaiah in the New Testament*, ed. Steve Moyise and Maarten J. J. Menken, NTSI (London: T&T Clark, 2005), 118 n. 9.

17. Reference is made, e.g., to the arrogant and self-exalating nature of the man of lawlessness in 2 Thess 2:4a and his desecration of the temple in 2:4b in relation to the arrogant and self-exalting king of the north in Dan 11:36–37, the abomination of desolation as associated with the temple in Dan 9:27 and 12:11 (cf. 8:13; 11:31), and the "lawless ones" in Dan 12:10. See, e.g., the discussion in Beale, *1–2 Thessalonians*, 206–7; Hannah, "Angelic Restrainer," 42–43; Nicholl, *Hope to Despair*, 232–33, 236–39; and Weima, *1–2 Thessalonians*, 513–14, 517.

nal number ("one") but also to an ordinal number ("first").[18] So the basic question is whether 10:13 is referring to a cardinal number ("one") or an ordinal number ("first"). Because of the focus and priority given to the inhabitants of Judah and Israel among all of the nations in the book of Daniel (not to mention in the rest of the Old Testament),[19] it would seem that Michael, who is also called "your [2nd per. pl.] prince" (שׂרכם [MT]; ὁ ἄρχων ὑμῶν [Th.]; cf. ὁ ἄγγελος [LXX]) when Daniel is later spoken to in 10:21, would be designated as the "first" of the chief princes instead of just "one" of them. But if 10:13 were referring to such an ordinal number, one would normally expect the term ראשון ("first, chief") instead.

In the context of Dan 10, however, the use of אחד makes more sense than ראשון for at least three reasons. First, the use of ראשון would make the resulting phrase (ראשון ... הרשנים ["first of ... the firsts"]) linguistically redundant. Second, in the Hebrew Bible the adjective אחד has an ordinal meaning particularly when *not* used *in association with dates*.[20] Third, the book of Daniel uses the Hebrew אחד or the Aramaic חד slightly more often than ראשון to indicate the ordinal term "first."[21] Use of אחד as an ordinal would thus indicate that Michael was the "*first* of the chief princes."

The last reference to Michael in the book of Daniel occurs in 12:1, which describes him as "the great prince" (השׂר הגדול) who "stands" (or, "protects") "the sons of your people." In light of this reference in 12:1 to Michael as the "great prince," it would again make more sense as the "first" of the chief princes than just "one" of them. This great prince stands up

---

18. This is also true for the Greek term εἷς. While it is frequently translated as "one," it can also mean "first" in the LXX (e.g., Num 1:1; Ezr 3:6; 7:9; 10:16, 17; Dan 1:21 [Th.]; 9:2 [Th.]; Hag 1:1).

19. See, e.g., Dan 1:1 (Judah), 1:2 (Judah), 1:3 (Israel), 1:6 (Judah); 9:7 (Judah and Israel), 9:11 (Israel), and 9:20 (Israel). See also the references to the "Beautiful Land" (i.e., Judah/Israel) in 8:9 and 11:16, 41.

20. See, e.g., Exod 26:4, 24; 28:17; 36:11; 36:29; 39:10; 2 Sam 17:9; Ezek 10:14. Note that several of these describe aspects of the high priest's clothing. See Jacques Doukhan, *Secrets of Daniel: Wisdom and Dreams of a Jewish Prince in Exile* (Hagerstown, MD: Review and Herald, 2000), 163.

21. Ibid. The Hebrew word אחד or Aramaic חד has the adjectival meaning of "first" in Dan 1:21, 7:1 (Aramaic), 9:1, 2, and 11:1 (cf. Ezra 5:13, 6:3 [Aramaic]), while ראשון has that meaning only in 8:21, 10:4, 10:12 and 13. Doukhan notes that "this tendency appears in most postexilic literature because of the influence of Aramaic" (*Secrets of Daniel*, 165 n. 8).

or arises, and immediately there is a horrific "time of trouble" of greater magnitude than has ever been seen.

The Hebrew verb referring to Michael "standing up" in 12:1 (עמד) frequently occurs in the book of Daniel.[22] Within Daniel it has several meanings, such as beginning service (e.g., 1:4, 5, 19), physically standing (e.g., 2:2; 8:3, 15; 10:16), taking a stand against or opposing/resisting someone (e.g., 8:4, 7; 10:13), and coming to power (e.g., 11:2, 3, 4).[23] The word itself has a wider semantic range within the Hebrew Bible, however, and it can also refer to "standing still," "stopping," and "cease moving" (e.g., Josh 10:13; 1 Sam 9:27; 2 Sam 2:28; 2 Kgs 4:6; Nah 2:9 (MT; ET 2:8); and Hab 3:11).[24] In Josh 10:13, for example, the term occurs in synonymous parallelism to the verb דמם: to being silent, still, motionless, or rigid. The verb can also refer to the cessation of an action (2 Kgs 13:18; see also Gen 29:35; 30:9; Jon 1:15).

Daniel 12:1a LXX translates this Hebrew verb with two separate words (καὶ κατὰ τὴν ὥραν ἐκείνην παρελεύσεται Μιχαηλ ὁ ἄγγελος ὁ μέγας ὁ ἑστηκὼς ἐπὶ τοὺς υἱοὺς τοῦ λαοῦ σου).[25] In its description of Michael, it uses the term ἵστημι, which simply indicates that Michael is the one who stands for (or, over) his people. But it also uses another verb, παρέρχομαι ("to go, pass by; come near, arrive"), to describe what Michael does at this critical time. Theodotion's Greek text, however, is different (καὶ ἐν τῷ καιρῷ ἐκεινῷ ἀναστήσεται Μιχαηλ ὁ ἄρχων ὁ μέγας ὁ ἑστηκὼς ἐπὶ τοὺς υἱοὺς τοῦ λαοῦ σου): it uses the verb ἀνίστημι, which instead indicates that Michael "stands up" or "arises" at this critical juncture. In any case, παρέρχομαι can also mean "be no longer available for something" (e.g., Matt 14:15; Acts 27:9; 1 Pet 4:3) as well as "disappear" or "pass away" (e.g., Matt 24:34; Mark 13:31; 2 Cor 5:17).[26] Use of this verb with one of these latter meanings would effectively indicate that Michael *ceases* a certain activity at this point in time. It is possible that the LXX translator thought that this particular verb made sense in context, since immediately after Michael does this, a time of trouble or distress breaks out, such as has never been seen up to that

---

22. Dan 1:4, 5, 19; 2:2; 8:3, 4, 6, 7, 15, 17, 18, 22 (2x), 23, 25; 10:11 (2x), 13, 16, 17; 11:1, 2, 3, 4, 6, 7, 8, 11, 13, 14 (2x), 15 (2x), 16 (2x), 17, 20, 21, 25, 31; 12:1 (2x), 5, 13.

23. On the different meanings of the verb, see Helmer Ringgren, "עָמַד," *TDOT* 11:178–87.

24. Ibid., 183–84 §II.1.n.

25. See the discussion in Nicholl, *Hope to Despair*, 239–41.

26. BDAG, s.v. "παρέρχομαι."

time—in essence, "all hell breaks loose." So it appears that the translator was attempting to mirror one of the latter meaning(s) of the Hebrew verb mentioned earlier (e.g., "stand still" or "stop"; "be silent, still motionless, rigid"). Whatever was meant by the use of παρέρχομαι, the LXX created the possibility for later interpreters to understand Michael departing or ceasing his work in order for a time of trouble or distress to take place.

Moreover, one of the later Jewish revisers of the MT (Aquila or Symmachus) translated the Hebrew verb in MS 233 with the Greek verb ἀναχωρέω (meaning "go away," "withdraw," "retire," "take refuge"; "return"), further substantiating this particular translational interpretation.[27] In addition, Nicholl points out that among later Jewish writings, Rab. Ruth proem 1 (ca. 500 CE) agrees with two rabbis from the third century who concluded that in Dan 12:1 Michael is *not* defending God's people but being silent.[28] Furthermore, the Great Magical Papyrus of Paris, dating from the third or fourth century but probably containing concepts as early as the first century BCE,[29] actually uses the term κατέχων in describing Michael's restraining activity against the great serpent or dragon: καὶ Ὠρίων καὶ ὁ ἐπάνω καθήμενος Μιχαήλ·ἑπτὰ ὑδάτων κρατεῖς καὶ γῆς, κατέχων, ὃν καλέουσι δράκοντα μέγαν ("And Orion and Michael who [sg.] sits on high: you [sg.] hold the seven waters and the earth, keeping in check [or, restraining] the one they call the great serpent" (*PGM* 4.2768-2771).[30] Despite its complicated and tangled conceptual background, it appears to witness an understanding of Michael as a restraining angel.

Thus, there are several compelling reasons why the figure of Michael is an attractive candidate for understanding the restrainer in 2 Thessalonians.[31] First, since it is almost universally held by biblical interpreters that some material in Dan 10–12 stands behind the apocalyptic information in 2 Thess 2, it would be reasonable to look for the literary antecedent for the restrainer in those chapters as opposed to elsewhere. Because Michael

---

27. BDAG, s.v. "ἀναχωρέω." Nicholl, *Hope to Despair*, 242.
28. Ibid., 243.
29. Ibid., 235 n. 45.
30. See the discussion in Hannah, "Angelic Restrainer," 44; Thomas J. Kraus, "Angels in the Magical Papyri: The Classic Example of Michael, the Archangel," in *Angels: The Concept of Celestial Beings—Origins, Development and Reception*, ed. Friedrich V. Reiterer, Tobias Nicklas, Karin Schöpflin, DCLS Yearbook 2007 (Berlin: de Gruyter, 2007), 620; and Nicholl, *Hope to Despair*, 235.
31. See the argumentation in ibid., 230–36 and Hannah, "Angelic Restrainer," 43–45.

explicitly appears by name three times as a key figure in those chapters (10:13, 21; 12:1), Hannah notes that seeing Michael as the implicit restrainer would maintain and support the apocalyptic outlook of 2 Thess 2:1–12 as well as locating the meaning of the restrainer in an authoritative text.[32] Second, angels were often understood as restraining evil, and it was rather common in apocalyptic literature.[33] For instance, in Rev 7:1–3, four angels hold back the four winds of the earth so that they cannot damage the earth, the sea, or any trees. In Rev 9:13–15 the sixth trumpet angel is commanded to release the four angels who have been bound at the river Euphrates. And in another text in Revelation, an angel seizes the dragon, Satan, and binds him with a chain, throws him into the abyss for a thousand years, and locks him in there with a key and seals it over him (20:1–3).[34] The motif of angelic restraint was not only known to the author but would also have likely been recognizable and familiar to his audience. Third, in a similar way Michael effectively holds back and restrains the activity of evil powers in Dan 10–12,[35] and this is essentially the same activity engaged in by the restrainer in 2 Thess 2. Fourth, Michael's stepping aside, withdrawing from, or "suspending his normal activities"[36] of restraint, as apparently understood by the LXX translator of Dan 12:1, occurs almost immediately prior to the Danielic time of trouble, and this would effectively correspond to the period of time in 2 Thessalonians in which the man of lawlessness climactically enters this period of history. Fifth, one can arguably make the case that the Thessalonian congregation was aware of the identity and work of Michael, since in 1 Thess 4:16 Paul asserts that Jesus would return to earth with the voice of the archangel (ἀρχαγγέλου). Jude 9 indicates that Michael is ὁ ἀρχάγγελος ("the archangel"), and Michael was clearly known as such within Second Temple Judaism (e.g., 1 En. 20:1–7; 40:9; 1QM

---

32. Hannah, "Angelic Restrainer," 30, 42.
33. Ibid., 40.
34. See also, e.g., 1 Enoch 10:4, 11–12 (where Raphael and Michael are commanded to bind Azaz'el and Semyaza), Tob 8:3 (where Raphael binds the demon Asmodeus hand and foot), and Jubilees 5:6, 10:7–13, 48:15–19 (where the angel of the presence and other good angels bind and restrain Prince Mastema and various evil angels and demons).
35. Note the language of John E. Goldingay: it is "the heavenly correspondents of these earthly powers" who are "restrained" by Michael and the angel who speaks to Daniel (*Daniel*, WBC 30 [Dallas: Word, 1988], 292–93).
36. Nicholl, *Hope to Despair*, 245.

XVII, 7).³⁷ Finally, sixth, understanding Michael to be the restrainer would be not be unusual in terms of nomenclature and, in fact, little different than Paul referring to Satan not as Satan, or any of his other designations, but instead as ὁ πειράζων ("the tempter") in 1 Thess 3:5.³⁸

The Restrainer as a Cultic Figure

With regard to the book of Daniel, cultic and priestly issues are of great significance.³⁹ Descriptions of—and intertextual relationships between— several visionary figures in Daniel suggest high priestly connotations. For example, it is possible that the figure known as the ὡς υἱὸς ἀνθρώπου ("[one] like a son of man") in Dan 7:13 LXX (כבר אנש [MT]) is a high priestly figure.⁴⁰ His heavenly approach to the Ancient of Days resonates

---

37. For a succinct summary of the various and significant roles attributed to Michael in Jewish thought (such as archangel, defender of Israel, intercessor, military angel, and primary opponent of Satan/Belial), see Nicholl, *Hope to Despair*, 230-32. See also the more extensive treatment in Darrell D. Hannah, *Michael and Christ: Michael Traditions and Angel Christology in Early Christianity*, WUNT 2/109 (Tübingen: Mohr Siebeck, 1999), 15-121.

38. In the Thessalonian correspondence, cf. "Satan" (1 Thess 2:18; 2 Thess 2:9) and "evil one" (2 Thess 3:3). See also Matt 4:3 on Satan as ὁ πειράζων.

39. See André Lacocque, *The Book of Daniel*, trans. David Pellauer (Atlanta: John Knox, 1979), 124-25 ("The vision in chapter 7 has the Temple as its framework"); and Crispin H. T. Fletcher-Louis, "The High Priest as Divine Mediator in the Hebrew Bible: Dan 7:13 as a Test Case," in *Society of Biblical Literature 1997 Seminar Papers*, SBLSP 36 (Atlanta: Scholars Press, 1998), 174 (Dan 7 "is ultimately Temple centered"). In line with this, some have suggested that Daniel writes from a priestly orientation or worldview or is a priest himself. See ibid., 171-72; Fletcher-Louis, "Jesus as the High Priestly Messiah: Part 1," *JSHJ* 4 (2006): 164 n. 32; and Marvin A. Sweeney, "The End of Eschatology in Daniel? Theological and Socio-Political Ramifications of the Changing Contexts of Interpretation," in *Form and Intertextuality in Prophetic and Apocalyptic Literature*, FAT 45 (Tübingen: Mohr Siebeck, 2005), 256-60, who concludes that "the visions of Daniel 7-12 are permeated with priestly imagery, symbolism, and concepts" (p. 260).

40. See Fletcher-Louis, "Divine Mediator," 161-93, who confidently stated: "Glancing at the *Curriculum Vitae* of the candidates for the post described in Dan 7:13-4 [sic] the high priest is the front runner" (ibid., 167). See also Fletcher-Louis, "Jewish Apocalyptic and Apocalypticism," in *The Study of Jesus*, vol. 2 of *Handbook for the Study of the Historical Jesus*, ed. Tom Holmén and Stanley E. Porter (Leiden: Brill, 2011), 1598-1600; Fletcher-Louis, "Jesus as the High Priestly Messiah: Part 2," *JSHJ* 5 (2007): 57-60; Fletcher-Louis, "The Revelation of the Sacral Son of Man: The Genre,

with the earthly approach of the high priest into the most holy place on the yearly Yom Kippur. Furthermore, the later controversy between the Pharisees and the Sadducees over the correct ritual of the high priest on Yom Kippur was integrated into their interpretations of Dan 7, suggesting that they saw this chapter as one with high priestly meaning.[41]

It is also possible that the same cultic figure from Dan 7 should be identified with other figures in Daniel's visions that interpreters have understood to be high priestly in nature. For instance, some have identified this figure in Dan 7 with: (1) the "Prince of the Host"/"Prince of Princes" in Dan 8:11, 25;[42] (2) the striking being Daniel sees in vision in 10:5–6;[43] and/or (3) Michael, the prince of Israel in Dan 10:13, 21; 12:1.[44] No consensus carries the day, however.

History of Religions Context and the Meaning of the Transfiguration," in *Auferstehung—Resurrection: The Fourth Durham-Tübingen Research Symposium: Resurrection, Transfiguration and Exaltation in Old Testament, Ancient Judaism and Early Christianity (Tübingen, September, 1999)*, ed. Friedrich Avemarie and Hermann Lichtenberger, WUNT 135 (Tübingen: Mohr Siebeck, 2001), 257–61; and Lacocque, *Book of Daniel*, 124–26. On the relationship of the ὡς υἱὸς ἀνθρώπου in Daniel 7, Adam (the original "man"), and the high priest, see Fletcher-Louis ("Messiah: Part 1," 172 n. 67). While a celestial judgment takes place in Dan 7 (see 7:10, 22, 26), Yom Kippur was also a day of judgment, one in which the high priest approached YHWH; on this see Roy Gane, *Cult and Character: Purification Offerings, Day of Atonement, and Theodicy* (Winona Lake, IN: Eisenbrauns, 2005), particularly 305–9.

41. See t. Yoma 1:8; b. Yoma 19b; 53a; y. Yoma 1:5, 39a; see also the discussion in Fletcher-Louis ("Divine Mediator," 182–85; "Messiah: Part 2," 59); Jacob Zallel Lauterbach, "A Significant Controversy between the Sadducees and the Pharisees," *HUCA* 4 (1927): 173–205; and Jacob Milgrom, *Leviticus 1–16: A New Translation with Introduction and Commentary*, AB 3 (New York: Doubleday, 1991), 1028–31.

42. E.g., Doukhan, *Secrets of Daniel*, 160; Lacocque, *Book of Daniel*, 162.

43. E.g., Lewis O. Anderson, "The Michael Figure in the Book of Daniel" (PhD diss., Andrews University, 1997), 317–61; Doukhan, *Secrets of Daniel*, 160; Iwan Whiteley, "A Search for Cohesion in the Book of Revelation with Specific Reference to Chapter One" (PhD diss., University of Wales [Lampeter], 2005), 175–76.

44. E.g., John Day, *God's Conflict with the Dragon and the Sea: Echoes of a Canaanite Myth in the Old Testament*, UCOP 35 (Cambridge: Cambridge University Press, 1985), 151–78; Doukhan, *Secrets of Daniel*, 160; Lacocque, *Book of Daniel*, 133–34; Benedikt Otzen, "Michael and Gabriel: Angelological Problems in the Book of Daniel," in *The Scriptures and the Scrolls: Studies in Honour of A. S. van der Woude on the Occasion of His 65th Birthday*, ed. Florentino García Martínez, A. Hilhorst, and C. J. Labuschagne, VTSup 49 (Leiden: Brill, 1992), 118; Nathaniel Schmidt, "The Son of Man in

But in what way(s) could the Thessalonian restrainer be considered cultic? While references to "every so-called god or object of worship" (πάντα λεγόμενον θεὸν ἢ σέβασμα) and "the temple" (τὸν ναόν) in 2 Thess 2:4 certainly lead one into the realm of cultic terminology, the description of the restrainer is not only restrained but incredibly thin. Such being the case, it helps to look again at the proposed background of the restrainer in Dan 10–12.

The description of the activity of Michael and his colleague in Dan 10 is overtly martial in nature. This makes sense, since this last section in Daniel begins in 10:1 with the revelation of a great conflict or war (צבא גדול), and chapter 11 tells of king fighting king. In 10:13 and 20 the LXX, basing its translation on the Hebrew term שר, portrays the initialization of the conflict first against the general or commander of the king/ruler/prince of the (kingdom of the) Persians (ὁ στρατηγὸς βασιλέως Περσῶν, and τοῦ στρατηγοῦ τοῦ βασιλέως Περσῶν [10:13]) and then similarly against such a general or commander of the king of the Persians and of the Greeks (τοῦ στρατηγοῦ τοῦ βασιλέως τῶν Περσῶν, and στρατηγὸς Ἑλλήνων [10:20]).[45] Furthermore, the LXX speaks of the conflict in 10:13 by using the martial verb ἀνθίστημι ("stand up against" [particularly in battle]; "withstand, oppose"),[46] and then in 10:20 uses another martial verb, διαμάχομαι ("fight, strive with, struggle against") to describe the martial action that the Hebrew verb לחם ("fight, do battle, make war") indicates.[47]

But the activity of Michael is not simply martial in nature. As the "first of the chief princes," Michael would be the equivalent of the "prince of princes" (שר־שרים / LXX minus) described several chapters earlier in 8:25,[48] and the "prince of the host" in 8:11. Some have also identified this

---

the Book of Daniel," *JBL* 19 (1900): 22–28; and Zdravko Stefanovic, *Daniel: Wisdom to the Wise: Commentary on the Book of Daniel* (Nampa, ID: Pacific Press, 2007), 389.

45. In fact, Papyrus 967 consequently describes Michael in 10:21 as "the powerful [angelic] general who presides over the sons of your people" (John J. Collins, *Daniel: A Commentary on the Book of Daniel*, Hermeneia [Minneapolis: Fortress, 1993], 362 nn. 31, 51). Theodotion's revision has been corrected toward the Hebrew: "the ruler/prince of the kingdom of the Persians" (ὁ ἄρχων βασιλείας Περσῶν and τοῦ ἄρχοντος βασιλείας Περσῶν [10:13]; and the "ruler/prince of the Persians" (ἄρχοντος Περσῶν) and "the ruler/prince of the Greeks" (ὁ ἄρχων τῶν Ἑλλήνων [10:20]).

46. Theodotion uses the more neutral term ἵστημι ("stand").

47. Theodotion also uses a martial term here: πολεμέω ("fight").

48. See, e.g., Klaus Koch, *Das Buch Daniel*, EdF 144 (Darmstadt: Wissenschaftliche Buchgesellschaft, 1980), 207; Lacocque, *Book of Daniel*, 206; William H. Shea,

person in chapter 8 with the glorious figure in 10:5–6 whose appearance terrified the men with Daniel and left him virtually paralyzed and in a "deep sleep."⁴⁹ This "prince of the host" (שַׂר־הַצָּבָא / ἀρχιστράτηγος) in 8:11 would normally be understood, from a terminological standpoint, as a military figure who commands the heavenly host (8:10). Yet the word שַׂר appears in cultic contexts as well. First, part of the Hebrew designation for him in 8:11 (שַׂר) is used not only in a martial way but also for leading priests in the sanctuary.⁵⁰ Second, the prince of the host has a "sanctuary" (מִקְדָּשׁ / τὸ ἅγιον),⁵¹ And third, he engages in rituals that are "continual" or "regular" (תָּמִיד / LXX minus), terminology used numerous times for various aspects of the sanctuary cult.⁵² Consequently, the combination of these textual and thematic characteristics of the superlative "prince of

---

Daniel: A Reader's Guide (Nampa, ID: Pacific Press, 2005), 181. See also Adela Yarbro Collins, "The Son of Man Tradition and the Book of Revelation," in *The Messiah: Developments in Earliest Judaism and Christianity*, ed. James H. Charlesworth (Minneapolis: Fortress, 1992), 551. Most commentators, however, see the visionary being in 10:5–6 as not Michael but Gabriel (Otzen, "Michael and Gabriel," 116 n. 5).

The visionary figure in Dan 10:5–6 is typically disassociated from the later explicit reference to Michael in the same chapter (10:13, 21); Fletcher-Louis, e.g., calls this possible identification "implausible" ("Divine Mediator," 169–70, here 169). Nevertheless, such an identity association appears legitimate. See, e.g., Doukhan, *Secrets of Daniel*, 159–60; and Winfried Vogel, *The Cultic Motif in the Book of Daniel* (New York: Lang, 2010), 165–68.

49. See, e.g., Doukhan, *Secrets of Daniel*, 159; Martin Pröbstle, "Truth and Terror: A Text-Oriented Analysis of Daniel 8:9–14" (PhD diss., Andrews University, 2006), 704–8 and 730–31.

50. E.g., 1 Chr 15:5–10; 24:5; 27:22; 28:1; 29:6; 2 Chr 36:14; Ezra 8:24, 29. First Chronicles 27:22 and 28:1 would appear to include the leaders of the tribe of Levi.

51. Note, however, that the sanctuary in the LXX is not described as "his."

52. This term appears in many texts in the Hebrew Bible that have a priestly meaning, such as: (1) bread set out on table continually, i.e., Sabbath by Sabbath (Exod 25:30; Lev 24:8; Num 4:7; 2 Chr 2:4); (2) lamps in the sanctuary to burn and be tended continually (Exod 27:20; Lev 24:2–4); (3) the carrying of the names of the sons of Israel in the high priest's breastpiece as a continual memorial (Exod 28:29); (4) the high priest bearing the judgment of the Urim and Thummim over his heart continually (Exod 28:30); (5) the high priest wearing the head ornament continually (Exod 28:38); (6) daily (morning and evening) sacrifices (Exod 29:38–42; Num 28:3; 1 Chr 16:40); (7) incense offering burned continually (Exod 30:8); (8) reference to the altar of burnt offering that it is to burn continually (Lev 6:13); (9) daily sacrifices (Num 4:16; 28:3, 6, 10, 15, 23, 24, 31). The LXX utilizes the word for sacrifice (θυσία), but it does not have the Greek adjective for the Hebrew תָּמִיד.

princes" would appear to point to none other than a high priestly identity. This is apparently how a number of Jewish interpreters saw it, since some segments of Second Temple Judaism and beyond identified Michael as an intercessory, high priestly, figure.[53] If the Thessalonian restrainer alludes to the activity of Michael in Dan 10–12, and if Michael can be equated with the superlative "prince of princes" and the "prince of the host" in Dan 8, then the restrainer could also have a cultic background and identity.

The Martial Context of the Priestly Cult

According to the Hebrew Bible, the priestly cult of ancient Israel, centered in the tribe of Levi, had its origins in violence, starting with the murder of the Shechemites by Levi and his older brother Simeon in order to avenge their sister's rape (Gen 34:1–27). The "sons of Levi" were consecrated to their priestly ministry to YHWH after killing about 3,000 of those who had worshiped the golden calf at Mount Sinai (Exod 32:26–29). The grandson of the high priest Aaron, Phinehas, received the covenant of peace for himself and his descendants because of his zeal for the honor of God expressed in an "atoning" execution via spear of both an Israelite man and a Midianite woman with whom the man had been consorting, thereby halting a plague that had killed 24,000 Israelites (Num 25:1–13). The legacy of the Mushites (the priestly descendants of Moses) was as warriors.[54] Clearly the origins of the priestly ministry were truly drenched in violence and blood.

But the martial imagery attached to the priesthood does not stop there. Along with the "men of war," seven priests with trumpets marched in front of the ark of the covenant in the Israelite campaign against Jericho (Josh 6:2–20). Later, the priest Eli's sons Hophni and Phinehas went with the ark into battle against the Philistines, but the sons were killed, the ark was captured, and the Israelites were defeated (1 Sam 4). In these stories the ark has become a war palladium with the priests as cultic warriors.[55] In the later story of King Uzziah's attempted takeover of the

---

53. E.g., 3 Bar. 11:4–9, 14:2; T. Abraham 14:5–6, 12–13; b. Zebah. 62a; b. Menah. 110a; Exod. Rab. 18:5; Midr. Psalms Ps 134, sect. 1; Pesiq. Rab., Piska 44, sec. 10, etc. See the discussion of these views in Hannah, *Michael and Christ*, 42–45; also Doukhan, *Secrets of Daniel*, 164.

54. See Mark Leuchter, "The Fightin' Mushites," *VT* 62 (2012): 479–500.

55. Ibid., 489, 499; C. L. Seow, "Ark of the Covenant," *ABD* 1:386–93.

priestly prerogative of burning incense in the temple, eighty priests who came with high priest to challenge Uzziah were described as "men of valor [בני־חיל]" (2 Chr 26:17), a term used numerous times in military contexts.[56] In the War Scroll (1QM) from Qumran, those who have leading roles in the eschatological battle against the "sons of darkness" are the priests under the direction of the high priest (e.g., 1QM II, 1–3; XV, 4–7; XVI, 13–14). More examples could be enumerated, all of which show that the cultic responsibilities of the priests were clearly and repeatedly associated with war. Thus martial references in regard to priestly characters should not necessarily be stripped of cultic, ritual meaning, since the martial and the cultic do not cleanly divide into clearly demarcated categories in the Hebrew Bible.

The Restrainer and Cultic Restraint

Priestly ministry included what could be described as oppositional activity, in particular, the restraint of divine wrath from breaking out and destroying sinful humanity. The idea that priestly intercession had a restraining force should not come as a surprise. In the wilderness, members of the priestly tribe of Levi were to camp around the tabernacle to prevent wrath from falling on the Israelites (Num 1:53; see also 18:5). The classic example of this restraining activity is the story in Num 16 about the aftermath of the rebellion of Korah, Nadab, and Abihu, after which the wrath of YHWH broke out against the rebelling Israelites in a plague (16:46). Aaron took his censer, offered incense, and "made atonement" (כפר) for the people (16:47). He "stood between the dead and the living; and the plague was stopped" (16:48 NRSV).[57]

Aaron's use of incense in this event was apotropaic in nature, here not preventing but warding off the wrath of God from further devastation among the Israelites.[58] While recognizing that this was an extraordinary situation for the Israelites in which no particular law prescribed

---

56. See, e.g., Deut 3:18; 1 Chr 5:18; 26:7; 2 Chr 28:6. The term חיל refers to armies numerous times (e.g., 1 Sam 17:20; 2 Sam 8:9; 1 Kgs 15:20).

57. "Made atonement" is the language of a number of English translations (e.g., ESV, NASB, NIV, and NRSV).

58. Kjeld Nielsen, *Incense in Ancient Israel*, VTSup 38 (Leiden: Brill, 1986), 79, 87. The cessation of the plague was translated into Aramaic in Targ. Ps.-J. Num 17:13 using the verb כלא ("I restrain, ward off").

what Aaron should do, Kjeld Nielsen suggests that "the story may reflect a traditional use of incense in times of plagues and perhaps other dangers."[59] This would be similar to what took place on Yom Kippur with regard to the incense utilized by the high priest. In fact, in that series of prescriptions, Lev 16:13 clearly indicates that the use of incense was to cover the mercy seat of the ark so that the high priest would not die.[60] Nielsen indicates that it was for "the sole purpose of preventing the high priest from being killed while executing his duties. The incense cloud provides cover."[61]

What is intriguing is that later reflections on Num 16 make several elements of the story more dramatically martial in tone. For example, in Wis 18:21–25 at least seven words describing the atoning activity of Aaron have strong martial overtones. The author compares Aaron's use of incense with the use of a weapon: he "fought in front with the weapon of his own ministry, prayer and atonement by incense" (προεμάχησεν τὸ τῆς ἰδίας λειτουργίας ὅπλον προσευχὴν καὶ θυμιάματος ἐξιλασμόν [18:21]).[62] Thus, he resisted (ἀντέστη, 18:21) and ultimately conquered the wrath (ἐνίκησεν τὸν χόλον), showing that he was YHWH's servant (θεράπων [18:22]).[63] He did this not through the use of the typical weapons of force (ὅπλων ἐνεργείᾳ [18:22]) but through the use of the weapon of his word—prayer (symbol-

---

59. Nielsen, *Incense*, 79, 87.

60. Ibid., 71, 73, 79, 86.

61. Ibid., 71. See Roy Gane, *Ritual Dynamic Structures*, GDR 2 (Piscataway, NJ: Gorgias, 2004), 177: "the incense [used on the Day of Atonement] is definitely apotropaic." See also Paul Heger, *The Development of the Incense Cult in Israel*, BZAW 245 (Berlin: de Gruyter, 1997), 78.

62. προμαχέω is a *hapax legomenon* in the LXX and can be translated as "fighting in front" or "fighting as one's champion"; see LSJ, s.v. "προμαχέω." In the LXX ὅπλον refers to a specific piece of armor or a weapon, translating the Hebrew terms for a shield (1 Kgs 10:17; 14:26–27; Jer 26:9; Ps 5:13; 90:4) or a spear (Nah 3:3; Hab 3:11). In the plural it is more generic, referring to arms, armor, or weapons (1 Sam 17:7; 2 Kgs 10:2; 2 Chr 21:3; 23:9–10; 32:5; Neh 4:11; Jdt 6:12; 14:11; Wis 18:22; 1 Macc 1:35; 5:43; 6:2, etc.; in the New Testament, see John 18:3; Rom 13:12; 2 Cor 6:7; 10:4). In non-biblical Greek it can also refer to a tool or implement, e.g., rope or cable (Homer, *Od.* 14.346, 21.390), ship's tackling (*Od.* 2.430), blacksmith's tools (*Il.* 18.409, 412), etc. See LSJ, s.v. "ὅπλον." Weapons were, of course, tools or implements of warfare.

63. For ἀνθίστημι in a martial context, see, e.g., the following LXX texts: Lev 26:37; Deut 7:24; 9:2; 11:25; 25:18; 28:7; Josh 1:5; 7:13; 23:9; Judg 2:14; 2 Chr 20:6, 12; Esth 9:2; Dan 11:15–16; Jdt 2:25; 6:4; 11:18; 1 Macc 6:4; 8:11; 11:38; Wis 11:3; Sir 46:6; etc. While θεράπων refers to a servant or attendant, it can also refer to a companion-in-arms, such as a charioteer or other warrior (LSJ, s.v. "θεράπων").

ized by the incense)—comprised of appeals to the oaths and covenants given to his ancestors.[64] Thus he beat back (ἀνέκοψε [18:23]) the wrath because "on his long robe the whole world was depicted, and the glories of the ancestors were engraved on the four rows of stones, and your majesty [the Tetragrammaton] was on the diadem upon his head" (Wis 18:24 NRSV).[65] To these the destroyer yielded (εἶξεν [18:25]), that is, surrendered in battle. Clearly the cultic ritual of Aaron is understood as a martial exercise.

Furthermore, in an encomium on the martyr Eliezar in 4 Macc 7:11, the author compares Eliezar's defeat of his enemies in death (7:4) to this same story of Aaron, whom the author describes as being "armed with the censer" (τῷ θυμιατηρίῳ καθωπλισμένος [7:11]). In this text the emphasis is not—as in Wis 18:24—on the incense but on the censer which held the incense. Yet the martial idea is the same.[66] According to this text, the censer-as-weapon was effective enough that Aaron ultimately "conquered the fiery angel" (τὸν ἐμπυριστὴν ἐνίκησεν ἄγγελον).[67] In the arena of this type of conflict, the high priest did not wield the dress tool of a sword but rather that of an incense-bearing censer.

Other aspects of the priestly cult and/or rituals were also oppositional and apotropaic, warding off God's wrath or some other calamity. For example, the golden bells attached to the hem of the high priest's robe sounded out when he wore them so he would not die (Exod 28:33–35).[68] Furthermore, according to Gideon Bohak, "it seems as if the Tetragrammaton became the apotropaic mark par excellence."[69] The most famous

---

64. On the intersection of prayer and incense, cf. Ps 141:2 (140:2 LXX); Jdt 9:1; Rev 5:8; 8:3–5.

65. ἀνακόπτω is used in terms of driving back, beating back, or restraining an assailant (see LSJ, s.v. "ἀνακόπτω").

66. The term καθοπλίζω in 4 Macc 7:11 is a term frequently found in martial contexts, used to describe a person, group, or animate force armed for battle; see Jer 46:9; 2 Macc 4:40; 15:11 (here, symbolically armed, but described in contrast to military armor); 3 Macc 5:38 (here, elephants); 4 Macc 3:12; 4:10; Luke 11:21. See further 4 Macc 11:22 and 13:16, where the martial imagery is primarily symbolic.

67. The implicit story here is presumably the same one connected with the revolt of Korah, Dathan, and Abiram (Num 16:46–47).

68. Joachim Braun, *Music in Ancient Israel/Palestine: Archaeological, Written, and Comparative Sources* (Grand Rapids: Eerdmans, 2002), 195–96.

69. Gideon Bohak, *Ancient Jewish Magic: A History* (Cambridge: Cambridge University Press, 2008), 117.

place upon which it was written was the golden plate (ציץ) on the high priest's forehead (Exod 28:36; 39:30; Lev 8:9).[70] Esther Eshel notes that "the oldest Jewish apotropaic prayer is the Priestly Blessing found in Numbers 6:24–26,"[71] which reads: "The Lord bless you and protect you! The Lord deal kindly and graciously with you! The Lord bestow His favor upon you and grant you peace!" (NJPS). This blessing, spoken by Aaron and his sons (6:23), appears on inscriptions and amulets dating as far back as the ninth century BCE.[72] It was found, for example, on an inscription from Kuntillet ʿAjrud as well as on a silver amulet from Ketef Hinnom in Jerusalem and in a number of scrolls found at Qumran.[73] Containing the name of YHWH, it provided powerful protection from evil spirits. This would assume that the Priestly Blessing, pronounced by the priests in a cultic setting, was also understood to restrain evil forces.

The importance of the Tetragrammaton or name and its ability to guard and protect also appears in the New Testament, where, for example, Jesus—in his so-called high priestly prayer in John 17—asks God to keep his disciples [safe] by God's name (τήρησον αὐτοὺς ἐν τῷ ὀνόματί σου) that he has given Jesus (17:11). Immediately after this Jesus indicates that he himself has guarded his disciples and kept them [safe] with the name that God had given him (ἐγὼ ἐτήρουν αὐτοὺς ἐν τῷ ὀνόματί σου ᾧ δέδωκάς μοι, καὶ ἐφύλαξα)—except for Judas, "the son of destruction [ὁ υἱὸς τῆς ἀπωλείας]" (17:12).[74]

These examples indicate that the cultic activity of the priesthood was frequently and significantly understood as warding off or preventing God's wrath, impending calamity, or evil of one sort or another. Martial terminology is a natural way to describe such oppositional rituals.

---

70. Ibid., 117–18.

71. Esther Eshel, "Apotropaic Prayers in the Second Temple Period," in *Liturgical Perspectives: Prayer and Poetry in Light of the Dead Sea Scrolls: Proceedings of the Fifth International Symposium of the Orion Center for the Study of the Dead Sea Scrolls and Associated Literature, 19–23 January, 2000,* ed. Esther G. Chazon, STDJ 48 (Leiden: Brill, 2003), 70.

72. Ibid.

73. Ibid.

74. Note that this same terminology (ὁ υἱὸς τῆς ἀπωλείας ["the son of destruction"]) occurs elsewhere in the New Testament only in 2 Thess 2:3.

The Thessalonian Restrainer Goes "Out of the Middle"

In 2 Thess 2 another difficult exegetical issue in relation to the restrainer has to do with the interpretation of the phrase ἐκ μέσου γένηται (2:7). Elsewhere the terminology occurs only in secular Greek, where it has the meaning of "be removed" or "disappear."[75] With such a meaning, it would essentially indicate that the restrainer would cease his restraining activity. With the restrainer in opposition to the man of lawlessness, this would make sense, since 2 Thessalonians would thus be indicating that the restrainer would stop restraining the mystery of lawlessness, thus making room for the appearance or revelation of the man of lawlessness at the right time (2:6–8). As Nicholl states, "the restrainer's present activity functions both to hold back the rebel's revelation until the appointed time and to prevent the premature unleashing of Satan's full power and full deception."[76]

But there is another attractive possibility for understanding the enigmatic ἐκ μέσου γένηται. According to Stephen G. Brown, the term "middle" (μέσος) contains mythic imagery, and he argues that it should be understood as "an archetypal symbol referring to a sacred center, a place where earth and heaven met originally."[77] Sigve K. Tonstad further notes that "this 'middle' is actually the 'garden of God' (Ezek 28:13) or even the 'mountain of God' (Ezek 28:14)."[78] He then notes that the same Greek terminology for "the middle" is used in Ezek 28:14, 16 LXX, describing where "the anointed cherub" walked before he was banished by God.[79] Assuming an Old Testament background for this allusion in 2 Thess 2 would also bring up possible references to the "middle" of the garden of Eden (Gen 3:3) or even Aaron standing "in the middle" (Num 17:13 LXX / 16:48 MT) of the living and the dead when he made atonement for the rebellious Israelites in the wilderness after the rebellion of Korah, Dathan, and Abiram.

---

75. E.g., Achilles Tatius, *Leuc. Clit.* 2.27.2; Plutarch, *Tim.* 5.3, *Comp. Nic. Crass.* 2.6.4, and *Quaest. conv.* 618 D1; Ps.-Aeschines, *Ep.* 12:6 (see Nicholl, *Hope to Despair*, 227 n. 8; BDAG, s.v. "γίνομαι" 6b).

76. Nicholl, *Hope to Despair*, 228.

77. Stephen G. Brown, "The Intertextuality of Isaiah 66.17 and 2 Thessalonians 2.7: A Solution for the 'Restrainer' Problem," in *Paul and the Scriptures of Israel*, ed. Craig A. Evans and James A. Sanders, JSNTSup 83 (Sheffield: JSOT Press, 1993), 264.

78. Tonstad, "Restrainer Removed," 146.

79. Ibid.

Since both architectural and literary descriptions of and references to the tabernacle and particularly the temple contained Edenic iconography and imagery,[80] the phrase could point to high priestly mediation in a sanctuary setting. If this were the case, it would indicate that the restrainer ceases high priestly mediation before the revelation of the man of lawlessness. This would make sense, though, since the text indicates that once the restrainer is "out of the middle," the revelation of the man of lawlessness happens immediately. Once cultic restraint ceases, evil is free to flourish.

Conclusion

I have attempted to sketch out the contours of the interpretation that the enigmatic reference to the restrainer in 2 Thess 2 obliquely alludes to Daniel's references to Michael in 10:13, 21, and especially 12:1. The dynamic description of Michael in the book of Daniel, along with the later understanding in various Jewish communities of Michael as a high priestly, intercessory figure, would make sense as the potential background for the restrainer in 2 Thess 2, particularly when one is cognizant of the various

---

80. Such descriptions include arboreal, cherubic, floral, fluvial, geographic, and lithic imagery. See the substantial discussions in, e.g., Margaret Barker, *The Gate of Heaven: The History and Symbolism of the Temple in Jerusalem* (London: SPCK, 1991; repr., Sheffield: Sheffield Phoenix, 2008), 57–103; G. K. Beale, *The Temple and the Church's Mission: A Biblical Theology of the Dwelling Place of God*, NSBT 17 (Leicester: Apollos, 2004), 66–80; Meredith G. Kline, *Images of the Spirit* (Grand Rapids: Baker, 1980; repr., Eugene, OR: Wipf & Stock, 1999), 35–42; L. Michael Morales, *Who Shall Ascend the Mountain of the Lord? A Biblical Theology of the Book of Leviticus*, NSBT 37 (Leicester: Apollos, 2015), 100–102; Terje Stordalen, *Echoes of Eden: Genesis 2–3 and Symbolism of the Eden Garden in Biblical Hebrew Literature*, CBET 25 (Leuven: Peeters, 2000), particularly 100–102; 355–56, 363–72, 376, and 409–31; Stordalen, "Heaven on Earth: Jerusalem, Temple, and the Cosmography of the Garden of Eden," *CBÅ* 13 (2009): 7–20; Stordalen, "Heaven on Earth—Or Not? Jerusalem as Eden in Biblical Literature," in *Beyond Eden: The Biblical Story of Paradise (Genesis 2–3) and Its Reception History*, ed. Konrad Schmid and Christoph Riedweg, FAT 2/34 (Tübingen: Mohr Siebeck, 2008), 28–53; J. T. A. G. M. van Ruiten, "Eden and the Temple: The Rewriting of Genesis 2:4—3:24 in The Book of Jubilees," in *Paradise Interpreted: Representations of Biblical Paradise in Judaism and Christianity*, ed. Gerard P. Luttikhuizen, TBN 2 (Leiden: Brill, 1999), 63–94; and Gordon J. Wenham, "Sanctuary Symbolism in the Garden of Eden Story," in *Proceedings of the World Congress of Jewish Studies, Jerusalem, August 4–12, 1985: Division A; The Period of the Bible* (Jerusalem: World Union of Jewish Studies, 1986), 19–25.

descriptions of priestly restraint against disaster and evil. The cessation of Michael's activity of restraint would thus refer to the cessation of his high priestly ministry of resistance to and restraint of evil. Daniel's "time of trouble" (12:1) would then ensue, mirroring the reference to the climactic rise and activity of the Thessalonian man of lawlessness. Consequently, it is possible to view the reference to the restrainer in 2 Thessalonians in the context of high priestly ministry of resistance and restraint—a cultic work that also had martial overtones.

Is resistance futile? In terms of the restrainer's resistance to the man of lawlessness in 2 Thess 2—no. But while it is not futile, neither is such resistance eternal.

Part 4
Temple and Priesthood: Rethinking Sacred Authority

Pillars, Foundations, and Stones: Individual Believers as Constituent Parts of the Early Christian Communal Temple

Timothy Wardle

Introduction

In *Against Apion*, Josephus famously remarks that Jerusalem is home to "the one temple for the one God" (2.193). This statement succinctly encapsulates the significance of the Jewish temple for late Second Temple Jews, as the Jerusalem temple, its priests, and its sacrifices stood at the center of first century Jewish religious life. In this one place God's presence was understood to dwell in a particular and immanent way, sins were forgiven, and restitution between the God of Israel and the people of Israel could take place. Even more, the temple embodied the unique relationship between the Jewish people and their God, and it stood as the symbol for Israel's election, the establishment of the covenant, and the locus of God's presence on earth. Due to the religious and symbolic importance of the temple in Jerusalem, two particular groups in the first centuries BCE and CE began to appropriate temple terminology and apply it to their respective communities. In so doing, the covenanters at Qumran and members of the early Christian movement made strong statements regarding their communal identity—God's presence now infused their respective communities, and purity and holiness were now expected. What had been true of the temple, they said, is now true of us. Their audacious claim is the focus of this paper. We will proceed in the following manner: after a brief review of the use of sacrificial and priestly language in the literature of both communities, we will turn our attention to the application of temple identity first to the Qumran community and then to the emerging community of Christians. Following this, we will more narrowly examine how and why early Christians appropriated particular structural elements of the temple and applied them to their community.

Cultic Metaphors in the Dead Sea Scrolls and Early Christian Literature

Before turning to the principal issues of the paper, we need to consider two related cultic matters: sacrifices and priests. Along with the appropriation of temple terminology, the Qumran sectarians and early Christians also repurposed the ideas of sacrifice and priest and used these concepts to strengthen their communal identities. We begin with the idea of sacrifice. Both the Qumran covenanters and many early Christians believed that the application of sacrificial terminology to their membership held rich theological promise, and they asserted that a life lived in devotion to the God of Israel, enacted through prayer, obedience, and the pursuit of holiness, could render atonement in ways equal to the sacrifices performed in the temple. At Qumran, this understanding is most clearly spelled out in the Rule of the Community, which states that a life of holiness, justice, and prayer may "atone for the guilt of iniquity and for the unfaithfulness of sin ... without the flesh of burnt offerings and without the fats of sacrifice" (1QS IX, 3–5).[1] Among early Christians, the apostle Paul is the earliest to use sacrificial metaphors to illustrate specific aspects of Christian life, as his description of the death of Jesus and the life that believers are now to live is, at times, cloaked in the language of sacrifice and atonement (e.g., Rom 3:25; 1 Cor 5:7; Rom 12:1).[2]

Priestly identity was also of elevated concern in both communities. As suggested by the hundreds of references to priests in the scrolls and the many explicit mentions of the Zadokites, priests with proper pedigrees held important positions at the Qumran site (e.g., 1QS I, 18–21; II, 1–11;

---

1. See, e.g., 1QS VIII, 3–10; 4Q174 frag. 1, I, 21, 6. Unless otherwise noted, all translations of the Qumran documents are from Florentino García Martínez and Eibert J. C. Tigchelaar, *The Dead Sea Scrolls Study Edition*, 2 vols. (Leiden: Brill, 1997–1998).

2. See also Acts 10:4; Rom 15:16; Phil 2:17; 4:18; 2 Tim 4:6; Heb 13:15–16; Rev 8:3–4. On the idea of sacrifice in early Christianity, see Michael Newton, *The Concept of Purity at Qumran and in the Letters of Paul*, SNTSMS 53 (Cambridge: Cambridge University Press, 1985), 52–116; John R. Lanci, *A New Temple for Corinth: Rhetorical and Archaeological Approaches to Pauline Imagery*, StBibLit 1 (New York: Lang, 1997), 7–19, 115–34; Stephen Finlan, *The Background and Content of Paul's Cultic Atonement Metaphors* (Atlanta: Society of Biblical Literature, 2004), 123–92.

V, 2-4; VI, 3-6; 1Q28a II, 19).[3] Moreover, priests played important roles in the eschatological outlook of the community, and the sectarians envisioned a prominent role for a priestly messiah (e.g., 1QpHab II, 7-8; 1Q19; 1QM II, 5-6; 11Q18 20; 1QS IX, 9-11; CD XII, 22-XIII, 1). Though the extent to which priestly figures were involved in the founding of the community remains disputed, it is clear that priestly identity played an important role in the maintenance of community ideology.[4]

Conversely, the early Christian community could claim very few of priestly descent among their numbers. Even if we take seriously Acts 6:7, which states that a great many of the priests became obedient to the faith, these priests appear to have held little significance in the overall mission of this small community. Rather, several early Christian texts begin to appropriate priestly language and apply it both to individual believers or the Christian community at large. In Rom 15:16, for example, Paul moves in this direction when speaking about his mission in sacerdotal terms. First Peter and Revelation go even further, with 1 Peter describing the recipients of this letter as a "holy" and "royal" priesthood (2:5, 9), and Revelation asserting that Jesus has made Christians "to be a kingdom, priests serving his God and Father" (1:6; cf. 5:10). These claims to priestly status in 1 Peter and Revelation are remarkable for many reasons, not least of which is that gentiles are now being granted the title of priests of God.[5]

More could be added to this very rudimentary discussion of the application of sacrificial terminology and priestly identity to the communities at Qumran and in early Christianity, but the above examples serve

---

3. Robert A. Kugler, "Priesthood at Qumran," in *The Dead Sea Scrolls after Fifty Years: A Comprehensive Assessment*, ed. Peter W. Flint and James C. VanderKam (Leiden: Brill, 1999), 93-103; Lawrence Schiffman, *Reclaiming the Dead Sea Scrolls: The History of Judaism, the Background of Christianity, the Lost Library of Qumran* (Philadelphia: Jewish Publication Society, 1994), 73-76.

4. Kugler, "Priesthood at Qumran," 93-116; John J. Collins, *Beyond the Qumran Community: The Sectarian Movement of the Dead Sea Scrolls* (Grand Rapids: Eerdmans, 2010), 122-56.

5. Martha Himmelfarb, *A Kingdom of Priests: Ancestry and Merit in Ancient Judaism*, JCC (Philadelphia: University of Pennsylvania Press, 2006), 139-42. Himmelfarb emphasizes the importance of this point when comparing the worldviews found in the New Testament and Dead Sea Scrolls. Whereas the Qumran sectarians may have begun moving down the path of stressing merit over ancestry in the Rule of the Community, the early Christians took the idea of merit over ancestry to its logical conclusion when including gentiles as priests of God.

to highlight the magnetic appeal of the temple for these two groups. For both communities the idea of the cult mattered, with particular aspects of the cult serving to reinforce each community's identity.

More germane to the focus of this paper, the Qumran and early Christian communities appropriated not only what happened at the temple (the sacrifices) and the identity of those who oversaw these sacrifices (the priests), but they also applied the very notion of the temple to their understandings of communal life as the people of God. In describing themselves as the temple, these two communities staked a claim to the idea that each now served as the distinct dwelling place of the God of Israel. This metaphor of the temple was most often applied broadly to the community; if the temple was where God's presence was most fully realized, then the application of this terminology to the community was another way of speaking of its sacredness. At other times, however, particular aspects of the temple were singled out and applied to individual members. This temple terminology could become quite specific, with the assignment of specific identities or roles to individual members, such as pillars, foundations, walls, stones, and the like. In what follows, we will (1) examine Qumran's application of the temple metaphor to the community; (2) investigate the parallel desire among early Christians to assign particular temple identities to believers within their community; and (3) explore the embedded christological implications in how this temple terminology connected individuals both to the figure of Jesus and to their fellow Christians.

Qumran

In the Dead Sea Scrolls, the temple was the primary metaphor by which the Qumran community constructed their sectarian identity and organized their communal life.[6] The weight the community placed on this metaphor is evident in the Rule of the Community, in which obedience to the community's rules results in the formation of a "house of holiness" in which God's presence is manifest.[7] First seen in column V with a mention of the

---

6. Cecilia Wassen, "Do You Have to Be Pure in a Metaphorical Temple?," in *Purity, Holiness, and Identity in Judaism and Christianity: Essays in Memory of Susan Haber*, ed. Carl S. Ehrlich, Anders Runesson, and Eileen Schuller, WUNT 305 (Tübingen: Mohr Siebeck, 2013), 56–57.

7. Among others, see Georg Klinzing, *Die Umdeutung des Kultus in der Qumrangemeinde und im Neuen Testament*, SUNT 7 (Göttingen: Vandenhoeck & Rupre-

"house of truth in Israel" (V, 5-6), this idea is expanded in column VIII where the community council is understood to be "founded on truth" and is described as "a holy house [בית קודש] for Israel" and "the foundation of the holy of holies [קודש קודשים] for Aaron" (1QS VIII, 5-6). Similarly, in column IX, the council of the community is presented as a "holy house for Aaron, in order to form a most holy community, and a house of the Community for Israel, those who walk in perfection" (1QS IX, 6; cf. XI, 6-9). In the Rule of the Community this temple identity does not come freely. Rather, the hard work of repentant and holy living actuates it and allows the community to embody their role as this "holy house." The Rule lists several preconditions for this temple identity, and here we once again use columns VIII-IX as examples. In column VIII, the community council was to implement truth and justice by preserving "faithfulness in the land" and "aton[ing] for sin by doing justice and undergoing trials" (1QS VIII, 3-4; also 1QS IX, 3-5). Column IX goes on to assert that this work of atoning "for the guilt of iniquity and for the unfaithfulness of sin" requires living according to the standards of the community, which would then produce "the spirit of holiness in truth eternal." Moreover, they must not intermingle with the men of deceit who do not walk in this perfection (1QS IX, 3-9). Through obedient and holy lives, striving for justice, and faithful adherence to the rules of the community, the Qumran sectarians would accomplish atonement for the sins of the community, thereby giving real force to the idea of a communal temple marked by purity and holiness.

The Florilegium (4Q174) also expresses this concept of the community as a temple. The opening of this midrash on 2 Sam 7 refers to an eternal, pure temple that God will build with his own hands. In ensuing lines, however, differing temples seem to be in mind, both a temple of Israel, which had been destroyed long ago due to Israel's sin, and an interim temple, a מקדש אדם.[8] Though the translation of the phrase מקדש אדם has been the subject of much debate, the most likely reading is that of a "temple of men" or "temple consisting of men."[9] Understood in this

---

cht, 1971), 50-74; Albert L. A. Hogeterp, *Paul and God's Temple: A Historical Interpretation of Cultic Imagery in the Corinthian Correspondence*, BTS 2 (Leuven: Peeters, 2006), 104-8.

8. There has been considerable discussion as to whether two or three temples are envisioned in 4Q174. For a review of the various possibilities, see Michael O. Wise, "4QFlorilegium and the Temple of Adam," *RevQ* 15 (1991): 103-32; esp. 107-10.

9. Bertil Gärtner, *The Temple and the Community in the Qumran Scrolls and the*

manner, the community at Qumran functioned as an interim temple, with the community's prayer and worship substituting for the sacrifices in the temple.[10] According to the sectarians at Qumran, this מקדש אדם, or interim temple consisting of members of the community, would, at the appropriate time, give way to the מקדש אדוני, or the temple which God himself would establish on earth without the aid of any human being.

In a few scrolls, the community is identified not only with the temple, but also with specific architectural features. In 1QS VIII, 4–10, the author moves from identifying the community as the temple to identifying the sectarian community with specific portions of the temple structure (1QS V, 5; 4Q511 XXXV, 3–5). Alongside descriptions of the community as a "house" and "dwelling," these texts depict the community in Isaianic language as "the tested wall," "precious cornerstone," and the "foundation of the holy of holies" (Isa 28:16). The use of these Isaianic architectural terms serves to reinforce the idea of the community as a temple and speaks to God's involvement with, and active presence in, the founding of the community.[11]

4Q164, a pesher on Isa 54:11–12, also identifies the community with specific building materials, that is, stones. In this case, however, the sectarians are identified not with the temple, but with the renewed city of Jerusalem. In this scroll, the glorious city will consist of various stones, and each stone has an equivalent in the Qumran community. The foundation of sapphires are the priests and those who laid the foundations of the community; the battlement of rubies are the twelve chief priests; and the gates

---

New Testament, SNTSMS 1 (Cambridge: Cambridge University Press, 1965), 16–46; George J. Brooke, *Exegesis at Qumran: 4QFlorilegium in its Jewish Context*, JSOTSup 29 (Sheffield: JSOT Press, 1985), 178–93; Michael A. Knibb, *The Qumran Community* (Cambridge: Cambridge University Press, 1987), 258–72; Jacob Milgrom, "Florilegium: A Midrash on 2 Samuel and Psalms 1–2," in *The Dead Sea Scrolls: Hebrew Aramaic, and Greek Texts with English Translations*, ed. James H. Charlesworth (Louisville: Westminster John Knox, 2002), 6B:248–63; esp. 248–51; Timothy Wardle, *The Jerusalem Temple and Early Christian Identity*, WUNT 2/291 (Tübingen: Mohr Siebeck, 2010), 155–60.

10. For a contrary view, see Daniel R. Schwartz, "Temple and Desert: On Religion and State in Second Temple Period Judaea," in *Studies in the Jewish Background of Christianity*, WUNT 60 (Tübingen: Mohr Siebeck, 1992), 29–43; esp. 38.

11. Wassen, "Metaphorical Temple," 60; Carol Newsom, *The Self as Symbolic Space: Constructing Identity and Community at Qumran*, STDJ 52 (Leiden: Brill, 2004), 156–57.

of glittering stones are understood to refer to the chiefs of the tribes of Israel. In both 1QS and 4Q164, then, the members of the community are identified with physical buildings or places, with the sectarians embodying specific architectural characteristics.[12]

From what has been seen above, the temple metaphor was a powerful one for the Qumran sectarians. At times, the community is identified with the temple, while at other times there are very specific connections made between the community and the architectural structures that made up the temple. But all of this temple imagery depends upon the obedience and faithfulness of the community members. In order to be a temple they had to live in purity, for only then would their community be a suitable place for God's presence to inhabit. Indeed, the Rule of the Community regarded this communal temple identity as something that could only come about through, and be maintained by, purity of life and separation from all that might pollute the holy character of the community. Any deviation from the rules of the community had implications not just for the individual but also for the holiness of the community and the very idea of the community as a temple.

Christian Transference of Temple Terminology to the Community

Early Christians also found the symbolism of the temple difficult to resist when contemplating the character of their own community. Paul is the first to make this theological move when he declares in 1 Cor 3:16–17: "Do you not know that you are God's temple and that God's Spirit dwells in you? If anyone destroys God's temple, God will destroy that person. For God's temple is holy, and you are that temple."[13] Similarly, in 2 Cor 6:16, Paul unabashedly states: "We are the temple of the living God." Following this, he asserts that God now lives in and among the community. As a result, the Corinthians need to separate from anything that would make them unclean, for associating themselves with anything or anyone that detracts from their individual and corporate holiness is at odds with their new identity as a temple. Paul is absolutely clear on this point—their new temple identity necessitates the purity and holiness of the community.

---

12. Revelation 21:14 moves in the same direction, as the names of the twelve apostles are inscribed on the twelve foundations of the new Jerusalem.

13. Unless otherwise noted, all biblical quotations are from the NRSV.

In concert with Paul's desire to see holiness as a marker of the Corinthian church, the temple metaphor likely had the dual purpose of promoting unity within the Christian community in Corinth.[14] They were having difficulty fully embracing their new reality as followers of Christ, with one consequence being the many divisions that threatened the community's very existence. Here the temple metaphor also mattered, for since there was "one" temple in Judaism, the temple functioned as a powerful unifying symbol for all involved in the worship of the God of Israel.[15] Holiness and unity were both essential, and the temple metaphor was elastic enough to include both. Since God's presence was now to be found in their community, the community must be both holy and unified.

Because of Paul's insistence that the *community* was now the temple of God, a third "temple" text in the Corinthian letters has prompted some discussion among commentators.[16] In 1 Cor 6, Paul raises the issue of sexual immorality (πορνεία) and urges the Corinthian believers to flee from all sexual immorality, which in this particular case, means not to be joined to a prostitute. Following this exhortation, Paul rhetorically asks: "Do you not know that your body is a temple of the Holy Spirit within you, which you have from God, and that you are not your own? For you were bought with a price; therefore glorify God in your body [τὸ σῶμα ὑμῶν]" (1 Cor 6:19–20). While the ethical norms that Paul here espouses are clear (glorify God in your body and do not engage in πορνεία), what is not as obvious is what "body" Paul here has in mind. Since Paul is talking about the "body" in the context of uniting it (or not) with a prostitute, it seems more appropriate to understand "your body" as referring to an individual and not to the community at large. But this individual reading is complicated by the puzzling grammatical combination of a singular

---

14. See Margaret M. Mitchell, *Paul and the Rhetoric of Reconciliation: An Exegetical Investigation of the Language and Composition of 1 Corinthians* (Louisville: Westminster John Knox, 1993), 99–105.

15. The Jerusalem temple was not, in point of fact, the only Jewish temple during the Second Temple period. The temple at Elephantine, the Samaritan temple on Mount Gerizim, and the Oniad temple at Leontopolis all attest to the existence of other Jewish temples contemporaneous with the temple in Jerusalem. None of these other temples, however, ever became serious rivals to the one in Jerusalem. For further details on these alternative Jewish temples, see Wardle, *Jerusalem Temple*, 98–139.

16. For a recent review of the discussion, see Nijay Gupta, "Which 'Body' Is a Temple (1 Corinthians 6:19)? Paul beyond the Individual/Communal Divide," *CBQ* 72 (2010): 518–36.

noun (τὸ σῶμα) and a plural genitive pronoun (ὑμῶν). Due to the singular noun and Paul's decided corporate emphasis throughout 1 and 2 Corinthians, many commentators prefer to read σῶμα as referring to the Corinthian community and thus in line with Paul's use of the temple metaphor in 1 Cor 3 and 2 Cor 6.[17] While this communal understanding of "body" in 1 Cor 6 does help align this passage with Paul's two references to the community as the temple (1 Cor 3:16–17 and 2 Cor 6:16), the emphasis of the argument in 1 Cor 6 seems clearly directed toward the necessity of individual Corinthian's behavior and holiness. My own sense is that the individual understanding of "body," and thus of "temple," is to be preferred here. Nonetheless, Paul's grammatical ambiguity has the effect of putting the emphasis on *both* the community and the individual, as Paul may well intend to draw attention to the importance of communal holiness while at the same time emphasizing the role that each individual has in maintaining this purity.[18] Since the community is made up of individuals, individual purity, or lack thereof, can either uphold or destroy the holiness of the community.

Paul suggests as much in his declaration of the community's temple identity in 1 Cor 6:19–20. As it is with the community at large (1 Cor 3:16–17; 2 Cor 6:16–17), so it is with each individual member of the church (1 Cor 6:19); they are to separate themselves from anything that would bring defilement. The indwelling Spirit of God within the Corinthian believers demands this holiness; each member of the Corinthian church must distinguish him- or herself from anything that would render the body impure.[19] Since each individual believer is a constitutive element of the whole temple-community, this focus on individual holiness has a decidedly corporate emphasis.[20]

---

17. See, for example, Paul Minear, *Images of the Church in the New Testament* (Philadelphia: Westminster, 1960), 180–82; Newton, *Purity*, 57–58; Kazimeirz Romaniuk, "Exégèse du Nouveau Testament et ponctuation," *NovT* 23 (1981): 199–205; see also Hogeterp, *Paul and God's Temple*, 338–41.

18. For a similar understanding, see Gupta, "Which 'Body,'" 522–23; Robert H. Gundry, *Sōma in Biblical Theology: With Emphasis on Pauline Anthropology*, SNTSMS 29 (Cambridge: Cambridge University Press, 1976), 220.

19. Gordon D. Fee, *The First Epistle to the Corinthians*, NICNT (Grand Rapids: Eerdmans, 1987), 263–65; Richard B. Hays, *First Corinthians*, IBC (Louisville, John Knox, 1997), 106.

20. Newton, *Purity,* 57–58; Hays, *First Corinthians,* 107.

The "templization" of the Christian community is not merely a Pauline idea. Among New Testament texts, Jesus's declaration that he would construct a temple "not made with hands" (Mark 14:58); James's directive in Acts 15:16 regarding the rebuilding of the ruins of the dwelling of David; Revelation's promise that the overcomers will become pillars in the temple of God (3:12); and 1 Peter's assertion that his addressees form a spiritual house (2:5); these may all be read as early references to the Christian community as an eschatological and metaphorical temple. Moreover, this appropriation of temple terminology continued unabated in the early second century. Ignatius refers to his readers as temples on four different occasions (*Eph.* 9:1; 15:3; *Magn.* 7:2; *Phld.* 7:2), and the Epistle of Barnabas explicitly equates his readers with the temple in his denigration of the Jerusalem temple (4:11; 6:15; 16:1–10). Though the temple metaphor for the community was only one among many metaphors for the early Christian community, and not the primary metaphor as it was at Qumran, the equation of community and temple became an increasingly important method of self-identification for the Christian community in the early centuries of the Common Era.[21]

Architectural Metaphors and Temple Identity

Both the sectarians at Qumran and the early Christians therefore found the idea of the temple deeply influential in formulating their respective communal identities. The early Christians, however, went beyond Qumran in assigning particular temple terminology to individuals.[22] This temple terminology proved to be quite nuanced from a very early period. Paul, in his letter to the Galatians, describes Peter, James, and John as pillars, an architectural designation usually understood as referring to their important role in the early Christian community and hence presupposing the idea of the community as a temple. Along with the idea of early Christians as pillars, other early Christians are named "foundations" and "stones" in this new temple. We now turn to these descriptions.

---

21. See William Horbury, "New Wine in Old Wineskins," *ExpTim* 86 (1974): 36–42.

22. 1QS VIII, 7–8 starts to move in this direction, but the extent to which this occurs is limited.

Pillars

In Gal 2 we encounter the earliest depiction of specific temple terminology being applied to individual believers. In the course of his adamant denial that he was dependent upon the Jerusalem apostles for his ministry, Paul states that these leaders in Jerusalem—James, Cephas, and John—were those "reputed to be pillars" (οἱ δοκοῦντες στῦλοι εἶναι). While some have argued that this pillar language refers to these apostle's standing in the community, the more likely referent is to pillars in the new, eschatological temple now comprised of early Christians.[23] Several lines of evidence point to this conclusion. First, as we have seen above, Qumran provides a subtle parallel to the *idea* of individuals as structural features in a new temple, as a few scrolls metaphorically describe members of the Qumran community as significant architectural components of both the temple and the new Jerusalem (i.e., as walls, cornerstones, foundations, and stones).[24] Second, Paul's discomfort with the term "pillars" (seen in his use of the term δοκοῦντες) being applied to the Jerusalem apostles suggests that this designation did not originate with him, and was instead a well-known and early title given to these three figures.[25] Indeed, Paul here seems stuck in the difficult position of trying to acknowledge the importance of these three leaders of the Jerusalem church while also asserting his own independence from them.[26] Third, the prevalence of communal temple imagery in portions of the New Testament outside of the Pauline epistles implies that this understanding of the Christian community as a temple gained traction in several branches of the early Christian movement and was not relegated to a single tradition. As a result, it seems likely that some of the foremost early Christian leaders—in this case James, Cephas, and John—held the

---

23. C. K. Barrett, "Paul and the 'Pillar' Apostles," in *Studia Paulina in honorem Johannis De Zwann Septuagenarii*, ed. J. N. Sevenster and W. C. van Unnik; Haarlem: Bohn, 1953), 10–19; Ulrich Wilckens, "στῦλος," *TDNT* 7:732–36, esp. 734–35; F. F. Bruce, *The Epistle to the Galatians: A Commentary on the Greek Text*, NIGTC (Grand Rapids: Eerdmans, 1982), 122–23; J. Louis Martyn, *Galatians: A New Translation with Introduction and Commentary*, AB 33A (New York: Doubleday, 1997), 205.

24. See especially 1QS VIII–IX and 4Q164; see also 1QS VII, 17; 1Q28a I, 12; 4Q171 III, 15–16.

25. It makes little difference here whether Paul is using δοκεῖν in an ironic or sarcastic fashion. What is important is that this term was so well-known that Paul could not deny it, even if he had wished to do so.

26. Barrett, "'Pillar' Apostles," 16–19.

title of "pillar" in deference to their work of supporting and sustaining this new temple community.

Further evidence that early Christian use of the term "pillar" referred specifically to pillars in the temple is found amidst the tapestry of temple images and motifs found in Revelation.[27] Among the letters to the various churches in Rev 2–3, the letter to the church in Philadelphia concludes with the following promise: "If you conquer, I will make you a pillar [στῦλον] in the temple [ναός] of my God, and you will never go out of it. I will write on you the name of my God, and the name of the city of my God, the new Jerusalem that comes down from my God out of heaven, and my own new name" (3:12). Though the source of this pillar imagery has been disputed,[28] the intention is more or less clear—steadfast faithfulness to the figure of Jesus results in great reward. In this case, the reward on offer is to be claimed by God through having God's name inscribed on that person, and for the faithful to be installed as pillars in the temple of God. As integral parts of God's temple, these faithful ones will never face the prospect of being away from the presence of God.[29] The language of Rev 3:12 delineates the Christian community as a new temple, with individual believers as permanent fixtures in it.[30]

This association of pillar language with prominent followers of Jesus also found its way into other early Christian literature. In referring to the many trials that Peter and Paul were forced to undergo, the author of

---

27. Robert A. Briggs, *Jewish Temple Imagery in the Book of Revelation*, StBibLit 10 (New York: Lang, 1999), 45–110; Gregory Stevenson, *Power and Place: Temple and Identity in the Book of Revelation*, BZNW 107 (Berlin: de Gruyter, 2001), 215–306; G. K. Beale, *The Temple and the Church's Mission: A Biblical Theology of the Dwelling Place of God*, NSBT 17 (Leicester: Apollos, 2004), 313–34.

28. For a review of the various theories and fuller discussion, see David E. Aune, *Revelation 1–5*, WBC 52a (Dallas: Word, 1997), 241–44; Briggs, *Jewish Temple Imagery*, 67–74; Stevenson, *Power and Place*, 244–51; Beale, *Temple*, 328–30.

29. This new and unmediated access to God is a thread running throughout the book, culminating in the mention of faithful ones who will worship God and will have God's name written on their foreheads in the new Jerusalem (Rev 22:3–4). This new city, now functioning as a temple due to the immanence of the presence of God and the Lamb, is the place in which the faithful ones will continually serve their God. See Jürgen Roloff, *Die Offenbarung des Johannes* (Zuürich: Theologischer Verlag, 1984), 61; Adela Yarbro Collins, *Crisis and Catharsis: The Power of the Apocalypse* (Philadelphia: Westminster, 1984), 86; Aune, *Revelation 1–5*, 242; Stevenson, *Power and Place*, 241–42, 50–51.

30. Klinzing, *Umdeutung des Kultus*, 201; Collins, *Crisis and Catharsis*, 67.

1 Clement states that the "greatest and most righteous pillars were persecuted and fought to the death" (5:2–4). Here we see pillar language applied to early Christian leaders, and in an ironic twist considering his equivocal use of the term in Gal 2, Paul himself has now become one of the early Christian pillars. The Shepherd of Hermas uses this pillar idea differently. In Vision 3, Hermas's guide singles out seven women and declares that, by the Lord's command, the tower/church is supported by, or sustained by, these seven women (Vis. 3.8 [16:2]). Though not explicitly called pillars, their role of sustaining and/or supporting the tower is an implied metaphor, for without their support the tower/church would fall into ruin.

Stones

Other early Christian texts describe individual members of the Christian community with a different architectural term: stones. First Peter 2:4 calls Jesus the living stone (λίθον ζῶντα), a description drawn from the ensuing citations of Isa 28:16 and Ps 118:22 in the following verses (1 Pet 2:6–8). Directly following this declaration about Jesus, his followers are also named as living stones (λίθοι ζῶντες, 2:5). These living stones, in turn, are described as being built up (οἰκοδομεῖσθε) into a "spiritual house" (οἶκος πνευματικός).

The meaning of this last phrase (οἶκος πνευματικός) has been the subject of some dispute, for much like the Hebrew בית, the term οἶκος can be variously understood as household, family/dynastic line, or physical building.³¹ John Elliott has argued that the structure of this passage and the communal emphasis in the book as a whole necessitates understanding the οἶκος πνευματικός of 1 Pet 2:5 as "household."³² In support of this idea, he notes that οἶκος does not refer to the temple in the New Testament outside of passages in which the temple is explicitly in view in the Hebrew Bible (e.g., quotations, allusions, or context) and that the early Christian term to describe the temple is always ναός, not οἶκος. Paul Achtemeier, however, argues that the term οἶκος πνευματικός clearly refers to a temple in 1 Pet 2:5.³³ As evidence, he notes that when the LXX uses the verb οἰκοδομέω

---

31. See BDAG, 698–99.
32. John H. Elliott, *1 Peter: A New Translation with Introduction and Commentary*, AB 37B (New York: Doubleday, 2000), 414–18.
33. Paul J. Achtemeier, *1 Peter: A Commentary on First Peter*, Hermeneia (Minneapolis: Fortress, 1996), 159. See also Gärtner, *Temple and Community*, 72–79; R. J.

to describe the building of the temple, the accompanying noun is usually οἶκος, that the Hebrew Bible and Dead Sea Scrolls often use בית to describe the Jerusalem temple, and that Jesus, in John 2:17, uses the term οἶκος when speaking of the temple.[34]

Alongside these arguments, Achtemeier asserts that the immediate context of 1 Pet 2:5 rules out any structures other than a temple, for the remainder of 1 Pet 2:4–5 locates this "spiritual house" as the place at which spiritual sacrifices would be offered to God by a holy priesthood.[35] As such, 1 Pet 2 is our earliest piece of evidence connecting individual believers with the stones of the temple. Collectively, these stones join together to form a "spiritual house," a temple in which spiritual sacrifices are offered up to God.

This identification of Christians as stones continues in ensuing decades. One example comes from the letters of Ignatius, as he describes his Ephesian readers as "stones of a temple, prepared beforehand for the building of God the Father" (*Eph.* 9:1). Similarly, the Shepherd of Hermas equates various groups of Christians with different types of stones in the building of the tower/church (Vis. 3.5 [13.1–3]). Stones that are square, white, and which fit smoothly into place are named as the apostles, bishops, teachers, and deacons of the church. Those stones brought from the deep places and that fit seamlessly are those who have suffered for the name of the Lord, and those who are culled from the dry land and placed into the building without need of a chisel are those who have followed the commandments and walked uprightly. Conversely, stones that are ill-shaped, cracked, or otherwise unfit for use in the construction of the tower are equated with the undisciplined, unfaithful, or double-minded (Vis. 3.6–7 [14.1–15.5]).

Foundations

A third way in which specific architectural features are applied to the Christian community is found in the Ephesian description of the foundations for

---

McKelvey, *The New Temple: The Church in the New Testament*, OTM (Oxford: Oxford University Press, 1969), 128.

34. Achtemeier, *1 Peter*, 156–59.

35. In agreement with Achtemeier, J. Ramsey Michaels, *1 Peter*, WBC 49 (Waco, TX: Word, 1988), 100, remarks: "it is difficult to imagine a house intended for priesthood as being anything other than a temple of some sort."

this holy temple.³⁶ Ephesians 2:19–22 relates that the Ephesians are "members of the household of God, built [ἐποικοδομηθέντες] upon the foundation [ἐπὶ τῷ θεμελίῳ] of the apostles and prophets, with Christ Jesus as the cornerstone." In him the whole structure is joined together and "grows [αὔξει] into a holy temple in the Lord; in whom you also are built together spiritually into a dwelling place for God." Here we have a specific description of the Ephesian believers as a temple coupled with the foundations of this temple being named as the apostles and prophets. In an interesting move, the construction of this temple is described in both past and present tenses. In Eph 2:20, the use of the aorist passive (ἐποικοδομηθέντες) indicates that the edifice has been built already and assumes God as the architect of this temple. The switch back to the present tense in 2:21 (αὔξει), however, implies that this sacred building is in a continual state of growth.³⁷ The Christian temple, therefore, is both an already established reality and an evolving structure.

On the strong and certain foundation, Ephesians implicitly describes others who believe in Jesus as constituting essential aspects of this temple. Whereas in 1 Peter the Christian believers are identified with stones, Ephesians provides no direct architectural terminology. Rather, the Ephesians are continually reminded that they are integral parts of this new temple: they are "built upon the foundation of the apostles and prophets," it is on Jesus as the cornerstone that the "whole structure is joined together and grows into a holy temple," and they are being "built together spiritually into a dwelling place for God." This entire temple structure is anchored by Jesus, who is described as its ἀκρογωνιαῖος (2:20). Though the exact meaning of this term is disputed (cornerstone or capstone),³⁸ it is clear

---

36. Andrew Lincoln, *Ephesians*, WBC 42 (Dallas: Word, 1990), 152–53. Following Lincoln, the genitive construction τῶν ἀποστόλων καὶ προφητῶν should be taken as appositional, i.e., that the apostles and prophets constitute a foundation, and not as a subjective genitive, i.e., that the apostles and prophets laid the foundation.

37. Ibid., 152; Ernest Best, *Ephesians*, ICC (Edinburgh: T&T Clark, 1998), 279–80. Cf. the personification of the temple in 4Q403 1 I, 41, where "all the fou[ndations of the hol]y of holies, the supporting columns of the most exalted dwelling, and all the corners of this building" are commanded to sing praises to the God of Israel.

38. For a discussion of the issue, see McKelvey, *New Temple*, 195–204; Markus Barth, *Ephesians 1–3: Introduction, Translation and Commentary on Chapters 1–3*, AB 34 (Garden City, NY: Doubleday, 1974), 317–19; Lincoln, *Ephesians*, 154–56; Best, *Ephesians*, 284–86; Joel Marcus, *Mark 8–16: Introduction, Translation and Commentary*, AB 27A (New Haven: Yale University Press, 2009), 808–9.

that ἀκρογωνιαῖος serves as the architectural element that ties together all other elements in this emerging temple. The point of this description of the community as a temple is explicitly laid out in 2:22; it is in this human temple that God now resides. Together, Christ as the cornerstone and the apostles and prophets as foundations provide strength and stability to this organically evolving temple.

Why These Particular Identifications?

We now turn to ask why these particular elements of the temple—pillars, stones, and foundations—were singled out and equated with individual believers. Several possibilities exist. One possibility is that the idea of equating architectural features with a community of people was "in the air," and that the early Christians simply found such metaphorical language satisfying. Above, we explored the community-as-temple idea at Qumran; and the Christian appropriation of specific temple architecture (foundations, stones, pillars) lines up reasonably well with the architectural elements (foundations, tested walls, cornerstones) applied metaphorically to the community in the Qumran scrolls. While it is unlikely that early Christians directly borrowed the temple-community idea from the sectarians at Qumran, it may well be that early Christians embraced ideas that also happened to have found their way into the ideological fabric of the community that lived along the shores of the Dead Sea.

Second, it seems more likely that christological reflection among early Christians paved the way for the identification of individual believers with architectural elements of the communal temple. Therefore, while the use of temple symbolism at Qumran and in early Christianity was carried out in similar ways, it was likely done for different reasons.[39] The temple identity at Qumran appears to have sprung from a desire to disassociate themselves from the physical temple and cult that they considered polluted, while still remaining true to the idea of the temple.[40] In so doing, the purity that befitted the temple was translated to the community itself, which is why one sees the heightened emphasis on purity in the Dead Sea Scrolls. This temple association, however, does not appear to have gone beyond the traditional Jewish ideas of covenant, election, purity, sacrifices

---

39. Gärtner, *Temple and Community*, 101.
40. Wardle, *Jerusalem Temple*, 150–62.

and the like. They stayed rooted in the traditions of Israel, even though they redefined what it meant to be the elect and, at least for an interim period, understood this idea as applying only to their community.

Christians, on the other hand, predicated their understanding of temple ideology on what they believed God had done in and through the figure of Jesus. The holiness that was urged on the community was a byproduct of this understanding of their community as a temple, for God's presence could not remain where holiness was not evident. Therefore, at the heart of the "templization" idea in early Christianity stands the figure of Jesus. This identification of believers with integral architectural features of this temple—foundations, stones, and pillars—relies upon a connection between Jesus and those who believed in him.

Christology and the Christian Community-Temple

In Eph 2:20, the apostles and prophets are described as the foundations of the communal temple. But this apostolic foundation for the temple does not stand alone. It is closely aligned with, and dependent on, the cornerstone of the entire building, which is Christ. On this cornerstone, the author of Ephesians states, "the whole structure is joined together and grows into a holy temple in the Lord, in whom you also are built together spiritually into a dwelling place for God." The apostles and prophets, while understood as foundational elements in the new Christian temple-community, are in turn reliant upon Jesus as the cornerstone that holds the entire building together.

More explicitly, in 1 Cor 3:11 Paul unequivocally states that Jesus is the foundation of the church, arguing that "no one can lay any foundation other than the one that has been laid, [and] that foundation is Jesus Christ." Paul then warns the Corinthians that they must exert extreme caution in how they build upon this foundation, for the day will disclose their work and the fire will test it. The Shepherd of Hermas conveys a similar understanding, asserting that the Son of God is the foundation upon which the entire framework of the temple/church is built (Sim. 9.14.9 [91.6]). In Ephesians, 1 Corinthians, and the Shepherd of Hermas, Christ is clearly the foundation of the temple structure. Individual members of the community function as foundations only insofar as they are, in a Pauline phrase, "in Christ."

In a similar manner, 1 Pet 2 establishes an intimate connection between the "living stone," Jesus, and the "living stones," members of the community who comprise integral parts of the spiritual building. This designation of individual believers as "living stones" links Christ and the early Christians, for they share both his identity (λίθος) and his life (ζάω).[41] On the one hand, this shared terminology—Jesus and individual Christians as stones—reveals no clear sense of differentiation or hierarchy. All are stones and each is a necessary component of this building. On the other hand, the readers of 1 Peter are encouraged toward faith in Jesus, and urged to "come to him, the living stone." Therefore, as the living stone, Jesus is the initial stone upon which all other stones are anchored. As we have seen above, this idea of Jesus as the chief stone, or the cornerstone, is also present in other early Christian literature. Just as all ancient buildings are dependent upon a cornerstone, so also individual believers are dependent upon Jesus for stability, life, and unity. Christ supports the church and is the preeminent stone in this temple building. All other stones derive their strength from him.

While close connections between Jesus and individual believers can be seen in the terminology of foundations and stones, a similarly close linguistic connection does not exist between Jesus as a pillar in the temple and the early Christian understanding of prominent members of the community as pillars in the communal temple. Jesus is nowhere described as a pillar. So whereas the application of stone and foundation terminology to individual believers is explicitly christological, the pillar language has no clear antecedent in Christ. On the one hand, this is to be expected. The conceptual identification of Jesus with the foundation, living stone, and cornerstone all convey the idea of support and stability. Each is a foundational element upon which the rest of the building, including the pillars, can be built. Therefore, if early Christian expectation of Christ's role was primarily to provide a strong and sturdy foundation, then we should not expect to find him described as a pillar. On the other hand, however, the idea of Jesus supporting the early Christian community is present in early Christian literature. Without pillars, the edifice would collapse, and it is in Jesus, Eph 2:21 says, that the "whole structure is joined together and grows into a holy temple." Similarly, Col 1:17 states: "in him all things hold together." In this sense, Jesus's work in supporting and joining together the temple sustains the coherence of the architecture of the building, and

---

41. Elliott, *1 Peter*, 413. A description of Christians as stones is also found in Ignatius, *Eph.* 9.1; Herm. Vis. 3.5–8; Herm. Sim. 9. Cf. McKelvey, *New Temple*, 181.

thereby maintains the unity of the temple-community. Just as Jesus is understood to join and hold together the Christian community, so also the "pillar" apostles in the early church were charged with supporting and maintaining the temple-community. Viewed in this light, the early Christian pillar terminology is inherently christological.

Implications and Conclusions

We are now in a position to assess the implications of the early Christian practice of applying architectural terminology to individual Christians.

First, the idea of the community as a temple necessitated living obedient, pure lives. Clear parallels exist with the Qumran community on this point: both Paul and the author of 1QS argue that temple identity demanded holiness. For both communities, this notion of the community as a temple likely functioned both descriptively and prescriptively, affirming both what was true of the community as well as serving as a continual reminder of the importance of maintaining communal purity.[42] But an implicit shift in emphasis may be seen in the early Christian decision to apply temple terminology to individuals within the community. By naming individuals as essential structural components, the emphasis on purity clearly and explicitly extends to each individual within the community. Holiness was demanded of each individual, for they comprised the very structure in which God's presence resided.

Second, the identity of those needing to be pure went way beyond what was seen at Qumran, for the early Christians democratized the idea of the temple by including faithful Jews *and gentiles*. This egalitarian understanding stood in sharp contrast to the exclusive nature of the Jerusalem temple, where gentiles were not allowed to participate in Jewish religious rituals. Now, however, gentiles were declared to be full members of the temple community, and faith instead of ethnicity became the instrumental means by which one could commune with the God of Israel in this temple community. One side effect of gentile inclusion is Paul's insistence on moral and not ritual purity.[43] Since gentiles were not subject to the ritual laws, these regulations were no longer appropriate for this new community.

---

42. Hogeterp, *Paul and God's Temple*, 384–85; Wassen, "Metaphorical Temple," 70.

43. Wassen, "Metaphorical Temple," 82; Jonathan Klawans, *Impurity and Sin in Ancient Judaism* (Oxford: Oxford University Press, 2000), 150–57.

Instead, Paul is specifically concerned with moral purity, and especially as this related to the avoidance of all sexual sin. As equal and essential components of the new temple-community, both Jews and gentiles were required to live lives of moral purity.

Third, in a manner similar to that found at Qumran, early Christians described their new temple identity in terms taken from the Jewish Scriptures. Passages such as Isa 28:16 provided fertile soil for both, as the Isaianic architectural terms of "foundations" and "cornerstones" readily found their way into the literature of each community. Yet early Christian reflection on texts such as Isa 28:16 differed in two important ways from that at Qumran. First, whereas the author of 1QS understood Isa 28:16 as relating to the community, the author of 1 Peter interpreted this same passage christologically. The focus was primarily on Christ, and only secondarily on the community. Second, alongside Isa 28:16, early Christians focused their attention on several "stone" passages linked together through the use of the term "stone" or "cornerstone." Psalm 118:22 and Isa 8:14–15, for example, speak of a rejected stone and one that would cause many to stumble. Of these two, Ps 118:22 played an especially formative role in early Christian proclamation of the identity of Jesus—its mention of "the stone that the builders rejected" becoming the "chief cornerstone" is found on the lips of Jesus (Mark 12:10 and parr.); in the mouths of Peter and John before the council (Acts 4:11); and in Eph 2:20 and 1 Pet 2:7, two texts discussed above that apply the idea of the temple to the community. The utility of these stone testimonia can be seen in 1 Peter's combination of Isa 8:14, 28:16, and Ps 118:22, in which the author distinguishes between those who do and do not belong to the new temple-community by way of observing who has rejected and stumbled over the chosen and precious cornerstone.[44] The broader context of 1 Peter reveals how easily Jesus's rejection could also be understood as applying to the community that bore his name (4:16), for the readers of 1 Peter were experiencing their own suffering and rejection. The language first applied to Jesus now also seemed to apply, to a certain extent, to those who were "in Christ," for their suffering and rejection was due to their identity as followers of Jesus.

---

44. See Elisabeth Schüssler Fiorenza, "Cultic Language in Qumran and in the New Testament," *CBQ* 38 (1976): 159–77; esp. 174; Joel Marcus, *The Way of the Lord: Christological Exegesis of the Old Testament in the Gospel of Mark* (Louisville, Westminster John Knox, 1992), 120.

Fourth, as noted earlier, there is a strong christological emphasis to the application of specific temple terminology to individual Christians. The description of individual Christians as stones, foundations, and pillars scattered throughout early Christian literature is emphatically tied to the understanding of Christ as the cornerstone and foundation of this communal temple; Christ is the one who provides stability and support to the whole structure. What is true of him becomes, to an extent, true of his followers. Stated differently, the very idea of believers as foundations, stones, and pillars and their functions in the Christian communal temple is clearly predicated upon the role already being played by Jesus. This differs from what we see at Qumran. While the community council and the Teacher of Righteousness both played important roles in the community, the ideology of the community as a temple is not predicated on, or dependent upon, the founder and leaders of the community. *In the early Christian conception it is.* Individual believers are explicitly connected to Jesus. Without him the temple idea is, quite literally, without foundation.

Finally, despite these christological connections, the communal temple idea found in the earliest Christian literature is never understood to be the temple of Christ. It is always the temple of God. As such, the presence of God, or the Spirit of God, inhabits this temple. So while the conception of the community as a temple connects individual believers to Jesus, the overarching image is emphatically theocentric in nature.[45] It seems likely, then, that one motivation for connecting individual believers to specific architectural features in this early Christian temple was to expand a clearly theocentric image into one that was also heavily christological in focus. Much as a plant is dependent upon its roots for life, so also the church was dependent upon Jesus for its nourishment and existence. Since Christ is the living stone and cornerstone, Christians are living stones. Since Christ is the foundation, the apostles and prophets are the foundation of the church. Since Christ supports and upholds the church, so also Christians, working together, are pillars in this temple-community. Individual believers are connected to Jesus in an intimate manner, and are thereby integral components of God's temple, in which the Spirit of God is at work. This is the power of the metaphor and why it left an indelible mark on early Christianity. The temple is God's, and Christ and Christians are constituent architectural items that support the entire sanctuary.

---

45. McKelvey, *New Temple*, 180–82.

"Not One Stone Will Be Left on Another": The Destruction of the Temple and the Crucifixion of Jesus in Mark's Gospel

Nicole Wilkinson Duran

Scholars attuned to themes of sacrifice in the Gospel according to Mark have tended to see Jesus as inherently opposed to the rituals and laws of the purity system, including temple sacrifice and indeed the temple itself. While a tension clearly exists between Jesus and what the gospel perceives as his ritual and religious environment, this essay will question whether Jesus in Mark expresses genuine opposition to the temple, to sacrifice, or to the purity system. I will argue that the gospel affirms the logic of sacrifice, in much the same way that Hebrew narrative did, and that the gospel does not see the temple's destruction as paving the way for Jesus's own brand of salvation, but grieves the event, as it grieves the crucifixion.[1]

One scholar of Mark sums up Jesus's relationship to the temple in this gospel thus:

> Whereas the temple was called by God to be the focal point of Israel's restoration and the ingathering of the nations, it has failed to fulfill this vocation and is declared by Jesus "a den of thieves," doomed for destruction. Through his passion narrative and especially his description of

---

1. Scholars who, in various ways, see the fall of the temple as a necessary step toward the kingdom of God that Jesus proclaims include Bruce Chilton (*The Temple of Jesus: His Sacrificial Program Within a Cultural History of Sacrifice* [University Park: Pennsylvania State University Press, 1992]; N. T. Wright (*Jesus and the Victory of God* [London: SPCK, 1996]); John Dominic Crossan (*The Historical Jesus: The Life of a Mediterranean Jewish Peasant* [San Francisco: HarperSanFrancisco, 1992]; and Marcus Borg (*Jesus in Contemporary Scholarship* [Valley Forge, PA: Trinity Press International, 1994]).

Jesus' death, Mark portrays Jesus as the cornerstone of a new temple that succeeds where its predecessor failed.[2]

In this reading and many others, Jesus's cursing of the fig tree, his protest in the temple, and his predictions of its demise together comprise evidence that Jesus is opposed to the temple and all that happens within it—legitimately or otherwise. Moreover, as in this citation, Jesus's opposition to the temple indicates its failure, the integral wrongness of it as a system and a symbol. In his person or in his community, according to this reading, Jesus intends to replace—indeed, to supersede—the temple. The temple that Jesus somehow becomes, generally in the institution of the Eucharist, gathers in the gentiles whom the temple at Jerusalem kept out.

The stakes of this interpretation rise particularly in connection with Mark's story of the temple action. Scholars with an interest in the historical events of Jesus's life generally maintain that the story of the temple cleansing reflects an event in the life of the historical Jesus.[3] The question then becomes not whether Mark believed that the temple was inherently wrong, but whether Jesus did—and for some influential historical scholars, the answer has been yes. Indeed, interpreters sometimes judge the historicity of Mark's account on the basis of whether or not it affirms Jesus's unmitigated hostility to the temple. Sanders doubts the historicity of the two scriptural allusions in Mark on this account. The idea that the "house of prayer for all nations" (Isa 56:7) has become "a cave of bandits" (Jer 7:11) is Mark's way of mitigating Jesus's action, Sanders argues.[4] The historical Jesus did not merely protest against the combination of trade and sacrifice present in the temple, as Mark implies, but against the very existence of the temple. Similarly, John Dominic Crossan considers Jesus's action in the temple not a cleansing, but a symbolic destruction: "It seems clear that Jesus, confronted, possibly for the first and only time, with the

---

2. Timothy C. Gray, "Jesus and the Temple: The Narrative Role of the Temple in the Gospel of Mark" (PhD. diss., Catholic University of America, 2006), 4.

3. E.g., Robert Funk, *The Acts of Jesus: The Search for the Authentic Deeds of Jesus* (Salem, OR: Polebridge Press, 1998), 122; Ben Witherington III, *The Gospel of Mark: A Socio-rhetorical Commentary* (Grand Rapids: Eerdmans, 2001), 314; E. P. Sanders, *Jesus and Judaism* (Philadelphia: Fortress, 1985), 66; Wright, *Jesus and the Victory of God*, 405; and Nicholas Perrin, *Jesus the Temple* (Grand Rapids: Baker Academic, 2010), who notes that the arguments against the historicity of the incident are few (82).

4. Sanders, *Jesus and Judaism*, 66. All translations of scripture are mine unless otherwise noted.

Temple's rich magnificence, symbolically destroyed its perfectly legitimate brokerage function in the name of the unbrokered Kingdom of God."[5]

There is much to unpack in this reading. The contrast in Crossan's phrasing between "the perfectly legitimate brokerage" of the temple and the "unbrokered" kingdom of God implies that the temple's actual destruction will be a positive, liberating development, ridding the faithful of the priestly middleman who heretofore brokered salvation. The understanding of Jesus's mission as breaking open (by tearing down) a metaphorically closed, and at times apparently fetid and airless temple ought to trouble us, from a history of religions perspective. The temple was the center of first century Judaism. Even the Qumran community, self-exiled to the desert and themselves claiming to be the true temple, dreamed not of the destruction of the temple, but of its renewal.[6] We ought then to be suspicious of a view that puts Jesus entirely in opposition to the religion he practiced. From various perspectives, criticism of sacrifice certainly arose in the ancient world. But, as post-Enlightenment intellectuals influenced by two Christian millennia, we ought to guard against the assumption that Jesus shared our lack of sympathy with temple sacrifice.

In Mark's Gospel, the disciples marvel at the temple, at the size of the stones with which is built. Their awe brings on Jesus's prediction of the destruction of the temple. But the disciples' awe requires consideration in itself, as an indicator of the significance of the temple for those living in or visiting Jerusalem. A building of its size and grandeur—even if it were not understood to be a holy place—demands emotional response.

In 1999, I witnessed the aftereffects of the earthquake that hit the region west of Istanbul, Turkey. Though I lost neither landmarks deeply meaningful to me nor loved ones, the destruction was shocking. No doubt like many others who saw those scenes, I was struck at some very basic level, at the sight of tall, impressive buildings smashed as under a gigantic foot, multi-story structures collapsed like a house of cards.

It may be that we all move through any city assuming that all the structures are permanent and secure, accepting them as part of the environment,

---

5. Crossan, *Historical Jesus*, xii.

6. Peter Schäfer, *The Origins of Jewish Mysticism* (Princeton: Princeton University Press, 2009), 115; Michael Newton, *The Concept of Purity at Qumran and in the Letters of Paul*, SNTSMS 53 (Cambridge: Cambridge University Press, 1985), 8; Bertil Gärtner, *The Temple and the Community in Qumran and in the New Testament*, SNTSMS 1 (Cambridge: Cambridge University Press, 1965), 122.

like mountains and weather. Americans continue to watch the 9/11 footage obsessively, in some kind of terrible awe—and, if we are honest, we do this not only because of the human death toll. The loss of the buildings themselves was a trauma. The massive tribute to human endeavor and our national identity that was the World Trade Center turns out to have been provisional, no more permanent after all than a tent. This realization—that what we thought was permanent was not—continues to resound in insecurity and grief.

When Ched Myers points out that "a temple was closely identified with a deity's existence," I am reminded of the sight of those collapsed buildings in Istanbul and of the footage of the twin towers falling straight down, each in its own cloud of smoke and dust.[7] Impressive, large, public buildings have power—that is why they are built. They speak to us of human power, implicitly ordained by the divine. This is why the powerful from ancient times through today invested and still invest so much money and time in building. The sheer size of our largest human constructions implies a potent mixture of human effort and divine presence or providence, an awesome confluence of divine and human power.

Thus, as Myers notes, the temple signified God's presence, God's existence in this place. At the same time, the temple must also have spoken of human significance, of the enduring quality of human civilization, at least as this one group of human beings defined it. The temple that Jesus knew was meant to speak of Herod the Great's power and ultimately, ironically, of the Roman support that had kept Herod in place. After Herod, the temple continued to speak of this kind of collaboration between Rome and the only Jewish hierarchy remaining in Judea, the high priests. In addition to its association with the divine, the temple spoke of past Jewish sovereignty, of the power of the priesthood, and of the Roman imperial limits on that sovereignty and that power.

Like the temple itself, the destruction of the temple is multivalent. Some first century Jews may have welcomed the symbolic hit to the legitimacy of the priests, even if that blow was dealt by Rome itself. Yet the temple in ruins would surely have been a profoundly disturbing image—raising the question to which Myers points, about the existence of this god,

---

7. Ched Myers, *Binding the Strong Man: A Political Reading of Mark's Story of Jesus* (Maryknoll, NY: Orbis Books, 1990), 304.

and the continuance of this people. For Myers, though, the question moves in a different direction. He goes on to say:

> One could not repudiate the temple without provoking the most fundamental crisis regarding Yahweh's presence in the world. Jesus directly challenges this identification, arguing that to abandon faith in the temple is *not* to abandon faith in God.[8]

But does Jesus himself abandon faith in the temple in this gospel? True, Jesus predicts its imminent destruction, and yet he continues to point to the power of God. But when Myers portrays Jesus as leaning away from faith in the temple, we are a step closer to the more troubling idea, expressed by N. T. Wright and others, that the historical Jesus sought to lessen people's hold on the physical temple, so as to replace it with a spiritual one.[9] Perhaps more troubling still, the place of the physical temple in this reading is also the place of the sacrificial system that it housed. Jesus's death in this reading becomes a sacrifice that replaces—or supersedes—temple sacrifice. As sacrifice, the temple authorities, and the temple edifice are elements of a complex religious system, so in biblical interpretation Jesus's attitude toward one of these elements is read as indicative of a complex rejection of all.

Thus Nicholas Perrin declares that in turning over tables in the temple, Jesus is "announcing the establishment of a new temple and himself as its messianic high priest."[10] Jesus in this reading appears in fact to be establishing Christianity. While Perrin here declares Jesus the "messianic high priest" of a new, spiritual temple, he argues throughout the book that Jesus is rather the new temple itself.[11] This Christology of Jesus as high priest is surely influenced by the epistle to the Hebrews, where Jesus is both high priest and unique sacrificial victim. In Hebrews, however, the heavenly temple is not Jesus but a platonic ideal, more real than the real temple, but existing on a heavenly plane. It requires Perrin to make Jesus all three—temple, priest, and, by implication, the unique sacrificial victim. He becomes the outward temple and all its inward moving parts—the entire temple-focused religion.

---

8. Ibid., 304–5.
9. Wright, *Jesus and the Victory of God*, 426.
10. Perrin, *Jesus the Temple*, 14.
11. Hence the title of Perrin's book, *Jesus the Temple*.

The idea that Jesus historically believed in a spiritual temple, or propounded a belief that he *was* a spiritual or heavenly temple, fits very ill with evidence in the earliest gospel. If anyone in the first century had what Myers calls "faith in the temple," then surely everyone had it. One does not have to ascribe to a particular practice or doctrine in order to believe in a large and grand edifice of stone. To abandon such faith would have been virtually impossible. To return to the example of my experience, I had no religious or even cultural investment in the taller apartment buildings of the Turkish skyline, but I did have faith in their endurance. I only realized I had this faith when I lost it—upon seeing the buildings in ruins. Even when it has no particular religious significance, the work of human hands, while it stands, elicits our faith and trust, regardless of our will. Not to believe in the temple, prior to its destruction, would have been like not believing in the mountain on which it stood. In Mark's Gospel, as we will see, there is no spiritual temple to take its place.

In John's Gospel, Jesus very early urges his enemies: "Destroy this temple and in three days I will raise it" (John 2:19). But in Mark, Jesus is *falsely* accused, before the Sanhedrin, of having said something similar. The narrator describes the accusations against Jesus as desperate attempts to incriminate him and tells us that: "some falsely testified, 'We heard him say, I will destroy this temple made with hands and in three days I will build another, not made with hands.' But not even so did their testimony agree" (Mark 14:58–59). The gospel's unambiguous denial that Jesus ever said such a thing is then complicated somewhat by a later taunt from those who pass by the cross. They quote the false testimony as though it were true: "Ha! The one who would destroy the temple and build it in three days, save yourself and come down from the cross!" (15:29).

Surely, neither the accusers at Jesus's interrogation nor those who mock him from the foot of the cross are reliable interpreters of his words. Perhaps precisely for that reason, the reader comes away with some uncertainty about what if anything Jesus actually said about his body and the temple, and what he meant by it. What we have learned is that, in the view of this gospel, if Jesus were to have made such a threat, evidence that he did so would be damning. But the reader has never heard Jesus make the threat.

In Mark, Jesus does not (as in Matthew) seem to establish the church, nor does he set himself up as an alternative to the temple. He does, however, predict its destruction, as indeed he predicts his own demise. Perhaps it is Mark's belief in Jesus's clairvoyance, his foreknowledge of the demise of the temple, that leads both his enemies in the gospel story and many readers of that story to conclude that Mark's Jesus desires its destruction. Jesus is, after all, angry in 11:15-17. He wreaks havoc in some kind of protest, turning over tables, making biblical accusations, and disturbing traffic patterns.

Within Mark's Gospel, the fact that the story of Jesus's action in the temple is an intercalation between parts one and two of the cursed fig tree story has been understood as supporting evidence that Jesus in this gospel welcomes the destruction of the temple: his disgust for the fig tree stands in for his disgust with the temple.[12] Neither the temple nor the tree has borne good fruit. Neither has nourished the people who come to them, and now neither ever will. In chapter 11, Jesus withers the fig tree with his angry words, and then seems to offer this destructive power to the disciples in a saying on prayer (Mark 11:22-15). He is, then, undeniably glad the fig tree is dead. Two chapters later, then, his prophecy about the demise of the temple seems to indicate that he exults similarly in the ultimate punishment of the temple. In this reading, Jesus's biblical citations as he turns over tables, that it has become "a den of thieves" or "a cave of bandits," are the reason that it must go, as the fig tree must. Jesus is glad to see it go; he would happily bring it down with his own bare hands.

But Jesus's reference to the cave of bandits—or "den of robbers" as the NRSV translates—mentioned in Jeremiah (Jer 7:11; Mark 11:17) deserves closer scrutiny. The temple is intended to draw attention to its worksmanship, as a testament to the labor of human hands as much as to divine power. Jesus cites Isaiah as he turns over tables, to the effect that the temple was to be called "a house of prayer for all peoples" (Isa 56:7)—that is, a building constructed for purposes of worship. But, he continues, switching to Jeremiah, it has been made into something like a cave of criminals—that is, a found refuge, a primitive shelter, used for illicit purposes. Unlike the usual implications of a future, spiritual temple "not made with hands," the cave Jesus sees in the temple is not loftier than the human-made one. It is rather *less* than human, uncivilized, outside of society, and thus the natural refuge of antisocial bandits. The image erases both the impressive human endeavor visible in the temple and the divine blessing on that endeavor. The temple is seen both as desecrated and reduced; the awe has been sucked out of it.

---

12. John P. Meier, *A Marginal Jew* (New York: Doubleday, 1994), 2:886-88.

Jesus thus uses the Jeremiah allusion to portray the temple as both abandoned by its rightful caretakers and used, exploited by others. Immediately before this verse in Jeremiah, God tells the people to stop repeating, like a mantra, "this is the temple of the Lord, the temple of the Lord, the temple of the Lord" (Jer 7:4). Yet God assures them that if they do justice to the alien, the orphan, and the widow, the presence of the Lord will indeed continue in the temple and with the people (Jer 7:5–7). Conversely, if they continue to transgress the commandments and worship other gods, they should not expect the temple to be a refuge. " 'Has this house, which is called by my name, become a den of robbers in your sight? You know, I too am watching,' says the Lord" (Jer 7:8–11). The prophet does not see temple worship in and of itself as inadequate or wrong-headed. Rather, the effectiveness of temple sacrifice and the divine presence there seem to be conditional upon the people's righteousness. Temple worship does not right all their wrongs, nor ought it to function as a place to hide oppression.

In Mark, Jesus's combination of prophetic citations leaves us with an invaded house, commandeered by bandits. The image calls to mind Jesus's somewhat mysterious saying in chapter 3, about entering a strong man's house, binding the owner and then looting his belongings (Mark 3:27). In both cases, the house is invaded and taken over, exploited and plundered. The immediate adversary in chapter 3 is "the scribes from Jerusalem." It seems unlikely, then, that in chapter 11 Jesus is criticizing or casting out the money-changers who happen to be present that day with this image of a house plundered and invaded by thieves: after Jesus's outburst in the temple, it is the scribes, along with the chief priests, who begin plotting to kill him (11:18). They seem to have understood themselves to be the invading thieves, illegitimate possessors and misusers of the house; undoubtedly, the reader is meant to make that connection as well.

If the house has been invaded and is being plundered, the first response is surely not to tear the house down. The plunder must be stopped, the bandits or thieves expelled, the house of prayer restored. Jesus in his actions and words in Mark 11 criticizes what has been done to the temple; he does not advocate its destruction nor offer himself as an alternative. What Jesus says in this gospel is that the temple should be one thing—a house of prayer—but that the ambiguous "you" have made it something else—a cave for bandits. Jesus seems then to be angry at "you" and what "you" have done to alter the very structure of the place. He does not seem angry at the temple itself, or at the sacrificial system that it makes possible. If the temple were being used for its intended purposes—implicitly including sacrifice—all would be well. Rather, the temple is, according to Mark's Jesus, being destroyed from within. Later he will prophesy about the future destruction of the temple from without; so there is betrayal from inside and there is persecution from outside. The same will soon be said in this gospel of Jesus himself. Indeed, the enemies of the temple, as Jesus defines them, are his own enemies, so its destruction becomes akin to his own. The connection between Jesus's body and the temple is not that Jesus will replace the temple, but that the two will suffer the same fate.

Interpreters often understand the story of Jesus's curse of the fig tree, which frames the temple incident, as an allegory, in which Jesus condemns the temple as represented in the fig tree.[13] Jesus comes off rather badly in this reading, if we are honest, petulant and unreasonable, expecting the tree to produce figs in the wrong season, and angry that it does not. The oddness of Jesus's anger at the tree is lost, though, because we are looking through the tree at the temple. In fact, there seems to be little investigation into the symbolism of the fig tree, or the story of its cursing, except as it points to the destruction of the temple. Perhaps embarrassed by an unreasonable Jesus, scholarship stops at the fig tree only long enough to speed their progress to the destruction of the temple.

But if we are trying to understand a kind of allegory involving a fig tree, we might pause and look for comparison to Judg 9, which features its own allegory involving a fig tree. In Judg 9:7–15, Jotham, the only surviving heir to the deceased King Jerubbaal, speaks out against Abimelech's usurpation of the throne, by way of a parable. In the parable, the trees go in search of a king to rule over them. The olive tree is first asked to rule and says no—because it is busy doing the more important job of producing olives and oil (9:8–9). The fig tree likewise says no; it must continue producing sweetness and figs (9:11). The grapevines also decline, since they are too busy producing wine (9:13). The brambles, however, since they produce nothing and so have nothing better to do, agree to be king (9:14–15). The message, in part at least, is that Abimelech has become king precisely because he was not occupied doing something worthwhile, because he is useless.

This parable could be relevant on several levels to the cursing of the fig tree and its context in Mark 11. First of all, Judg 9:7–15 is an allegory,

---

13. For a recent, example, see J. R. Daniel Kirk, "Time for Figs, Temple Destruction, and Prayer in Mark 11:12–25," *CBQ* 74 (2012): 509–27.

asking explicitly to be seen through. Although the story of Jesus cursing the fig tree is told as a narrative event, not as a parable, the history of interpretation would suggest that the placement and details of the story have invited readers to interpret it symbolically, if not allegorically. Like the incident in Mark, the Judges text is about trees that do, or do not, bear fruit. If the Judges text informs the Markan one, then it brings with it a concern for inappropriate rulers, rulers who only agree to rule, or who are only appointed to rule, because, like the bramble, they have no good to offer the world.

Suppose that Mark's storyteller has the Judg 9 story in mind as he relates the story of the fig tree's demise. A fig tree not bearing fruit, in Jesus's perspective somehow *purposely* not bearing fruit, would be making the wrong choice. It would be the Judges allegory gone wrong. Asked to neglect its fruit-bearing duties in order to wield power over others, the fig tree in Mark's Gospel has said yes. Unlike the bramble king Abimelech in Judg 9, the fig tree has other, more natural and productive, duties. If nothing else is clear from the story of Jesus's encounter with the tree, it is clear that the tree should by all rights be producing figs to feed the hungry, including and especially Jesus. If indeed the gospel has Judg 9 in mind, it would make sense of Jesus's anger at the tree's lack of figs. The tree has, in effect, refused to feed the hungry, opting to rule instead.

Surely this logic applies not to the temple, but to the group rising to the surface in this gospel as Jesus's opponents—again, the chief priests and scribes. Under Roman auspices, the chief priests and all those in power in Jerusalem have that power only to the extent and for the reason that they have chosen personal power over the interests of the people whom they serve. The power of the priests ought to nourish and feed, like the power of the fig tree. But these priests have been selected for and permitted power only to the extent that they do not have the people's deep interests at heart. They stand like a fruitless fruit tree, promising what they cannot deliver.

Under Roman occupation the high priests cannot bear real fruit; they cannot embody or empower the nation. No wonder it is not the season for figs, because it is the unnatural, world-upside-down time in which the fig tree has refused or been forbidden its natural role. In fact, depending on the placement of an accent, the Greek of 11:13 might be better translated, "it was not the time for fig *trees*." It was a time when fig trees were acting strangely, unlike what a fig tree must be, a time when they grew no figs.

Although the cursing of the fig tree remains an allegory about the temple in this reading, it becomes an allegory in which the fig tree does not represent the temple itself. Rather, it stands for a leader or group of leaders who have chosen to wield power over others, like a king, rather than to produce the good fruits that they were created to bear. The lesson of its cursing is not that the temple must fall, but that the leadership, since they have chosen to do no good, must fall.

Jesus is not punishing the temple in turning over tables there; he is in effect casting out demons from it, pushing out, however temporarily, those who have changed it from a house of prayer into a den of criminals. This seems to me very consistent with the overall message of Jesus in this gospel. It is a message supported, for example, both by the parable of the vineyard in Mark 12 and by the exorcism of the Gerasene demoniac in Mark 5.

Only a few verses away from Jesus's action in the temple is the parable of the vineyard. Like the cursing of the fig tree, this parable seems to contain an allusion to a story from biblical tradition. In this case, the Jesus of Mark's Gospel surely has Isaiah's parable of the vineyard in mind (Isa 5:1–6). As in Isaiah, we see the owner dig a pit for the winepress, and in both cases we see the owner set up a watchtower (Isa 5:2; Mark 12:1). Guarding one's vines against marauders or animals may have been common, but the detail of the watchtower is notable in both cases. The owner makes every attempt—building a fence as well, in Mark's Gospel—to protect the vineyard and guard its fruit. But in Isaiah, the vines seem to rebel; they bear the wrong grapes. We are told that the vineyard is the house of Israel and the people of Judah, and that God now intends to "remove its hedge" and "break down its wall, and it shall be trampled upon." Removing the protective boundaries, God will leave the people vulnerable to any and all destructive forces.

In Mark 12, the problem is not the vines themselves, nor is there anything wrong with the fruit. The problem is the tenants, appointed to care for the vineyard, who refuse to recognize the owner's sovereignty. If the owner in both passages is God, as seems to be the case, and the vineyard in both passages is the people of God, then the problem in the Mark passage is not with the people themselves, but with those individuals temporarily set over them, those acting as intermediaries between the people-as-vineyard and God-as-owner. Clearly, as in this entire section of the gospel in which the conflict with the chief priests rapidly escalates, it is the priests and not the people—not the temple or its divinely ordained practices—who will be replaced. Whereas in Isa 5 the vineyard will be opened up and trampled, in Mark 12 only the tenants suffer destruction; the vineyard—whole and still producing fruit—will be given to others.

When Jesus is done causing damage in the temple, and when the disciples realize that the fig tree he cursed on his way in is now dead, he concludes both episodes by telling them about the power of faith. "Have faith in God," he tells them. "Truly I say to you, if anyone says to this mountain, 'Be taken up and thrown into the sea,' and does not consider in his heart, but believes that what he says will become, it will be for him" (Mark 11:22–23). The relationship between the mountain's destruction, the death of the fig tree, and the protest in the temple has stumped many interpreters. In the traditional reading against which I argue here, the discussion of prayer pops up as a non sequitur.[14]

Indeed, it is striking that Jesus's example of the power of faith is a negative example—the power of faith to destroy something that is as accepted a part of the landscape as is "this mountain." By faith, the mountain will be taken up and thrown into the sea. The saying about faith here is usually understood apolitically. But if the fig tree represents the high priests, then the mountain, seemingly immobile, seemingly permanent, certainly powerful in its stability, yet undesirable for unexplained reasons, sounds like Rome itself. In the cursing of the fig tree and in the saying about the power of faith, then, the disciples are being told that their faith has power to change the very landscape, in a religious and political sense. They have the power to cut off useless leadership and to throw the weighty Roman powers into the sea.

To connect images once again in this gospel, the image of something thrown by spiritual, divinely given power into the sea recalls Mark's story of the Gerasene demoniac (Mark 5:1–20). There Jesus casts out a horde of unclean spirits who, when asked for a name, evoke the Roman occupying presence: "My name is Legion, for we are many" (Mark 5:9). At the demons' own request, Jesus casts them out and into the herd of swine and the swine in turn plunge headlong into the sea, and drown. Jesus thus cleanses the infested environment that is Gerasa in this gospel, ridding it of unclean animals and spirits at once. Articulating the eternal dream of the colonial subject, the nefarious and multi-pronged presence, analogous to the Romans themselves, has been driven into the sea.

In Mark's Gospel, Jesus has the ability, at least momentarily, to drive the Roman presence out. By protesting the temple leadership in Mark 11,

---

14. Ibid., 509; see also Christfried Böttrich, "Jesus und der Feigenbaum: Mk 11:12-14, 20-25 in der Diskussion," *NovT* 39 (1997): 328–59.

Jesus indirectly does exactly that. This would make better sense of the saying on prayer that follows both the temple action and the withered fig tree. When the disciples are amazed that Jesus's frustration with the leadership-as-fig tree has resulted in the withering of the tree, Jesus responds that faith is capable not only of withering the leadership, but of driving their Roman masters into the sea.

Jesus does, in this gospel, predict the destruction of the temple. Having made himself a roadblock in the temple, having killed a fig tree, and having returned to the temple for an extended period of teaching there (11:27; 12:35, 41), he comes out of the temple again and his disciples take a good hard look at the building. They are impressed by the sheer size of it and of the stones that were manipulated to build it (13:1). Jesus responds, "Not one stone will be left upon another stone. All will be thrown down" (13:2). Myers notes the parallelism between "Teacher, Look! What wonderful stones…" in 13:3, and "Rabbi, look! The fig tree that you cursed …" (11:21). Myers uses the parallel to read the fig tree as representing the temple.[15] Certainly, there is a parallel, but it is perhaps a more complicated parallel than Myers maintains. In 11:21, Peter points out Jesus's own destructive power: "Rabbi, look! The fig tree that you cursed has withered!" But in chapter 13 the disciples point out the sheer size of the temple, even of the stones that make up its walls; by implication, they are impressed with the power such size represents. The parallel would be neater if in chapter 11, Peter had been calling attention to the strength and size of the fig tree before it withered. In the case of the temple, the power the disciples note is, in a sense, the apparent power to resist destruction. This power, Jesus predicts, will disappear.

In Dereck Dachke's book on the destruction of the temple and Jewish apocalypse, the author quotes Sigmund Freud's essay, "On Transience." Remarking on the destruction left behind by the First World War, Freud notes:

> It shattered our pride in the achievements of our civilization…. It made our country small again and made the rest of the world far remote. It robbed us of very much that we had loved, and showed us how ephemeral were many things we had regarded as changeless.[16]

---

15. Myers, *Binding the Strong Man*, 304.

16. Quoted in Dereck Daschke, *City of Ruins: Mourning the Destruction of Jerusalem through Jewish Apocalypse*, BibInt 99 (Leiden: Brill, 2010), 5.

Bringing Freud's observation to Mark's Gospel, this is, it seems to me, what Jesus is saying in predicting the fall of the temple. There is no exultation here, but, in Mark's Gospel, an in-advance kind of trauma—what seems now changeless, to use Freud's words, is in fact terribly ephemeral. Not heavenly or eternal, just so fragile as to be blown away by the very next wind.

The disciples follow up Jesus's harsh predictions about the temple with the question, "When will this be?" Jesus explains the signs for which they should watch, the suffering that will be involved, throughout the rest of this apocalyptic chapter. The disciples understand that when Jesus predicts the unbuilding of the temple, he is predicting the upheaval of the world as it is. We need to understand, then, that when the prospect of the destruction of the temple appears in Mark, it is a terrible prospect, akin to the blotting out of the sun and moon (13:24). The temple is ground zero of the Markan apocalypse, which seems only to extend as far as Judea. Its destruction is survivable, but—like the blotting out of the sun and moon—it is only just survivable, and only by the merciful intervention of God, who has "cut short the days" (13:20). It is survivable only in the sense that in Mark the crucifixion is survivable: that which continues beyond the catastrophe cannot be seen or named, so that even the resurrection, even the surviving, leaves us frightened and speechless.[17]

The final moment of relationship between the temple and Jesus's body is, in fact, at the moment of his death: "Then Jesus gave out a loud cry and expired. And the curtain of the Temple was split into two, from above to below" (15:37–38). Christian readers never seem to tire of reading this moment as a triumph. Jesus has opened up the temple to gentiles; his death shreds the veil that kept people apart from God. But as I have argued elsewhere, the ripping of fabric is a ritual of grief, in this gospel and elsewhere in Jewish tradition.[18] We need only look to Jesus's trial before the Sanhedrin in the previous chapter to find an example of this symbolism. When Jesus makes his single claim to be, indeed, the messiah, the high priest tears his clothes in dismay or grief, perhaps to suggest that Jesus has thus extinguished his own existence as far as the high priest is concerned (14:63). The tearing of the temple curtain, like the ritual rending of

---

17. See Maia Kotrosits and Hal Taussig, *Re-reading the Gospel of Mark amidst Loss and Trauma* (New York: Palgrave Macmillan, 2013), 150–51.

18. Nicole Wilkinson Duran, *The Power of Disorder: Ritual Elements in Mark's Passion Narrative*, LNTS 378 (New York: T&T Clark, 2008), 105.

garments in grief, enacts and emphasizes the transgression of the body's boundaries in death. Jesus's death, the passing out of breath from his body, is simultaneous with the first breaching of the temple's own boundaries. In the tearing of the curtain, the temple grieves, or God does, or most likely of all, the gospel shows the depth of its grief to the reader. Like the darkness that falls over the earth in the three hours leading up to the death, the tearing of the curtain tells us the cosmic wrongness of the climactic moment of the gospel.

The message of the gospel overall is an apocalyptic one. The world is upside down and must be read as such.[19] What is good and holy will be destroyed because it is good and holy. Nevertheless, something survives. Evil is not the last word. Like Jesus, the temple is doomed—not because it is evil, but precisely because it is good. Because it is good, like Jesus it is betrayed from within and destroyed from without. What survives in this case is a torn curtain and the isolated stones, dispersed—unbuilt, unmade.

Yet we have already been told, at the close of the parable of the vineyard, that the stone that the builders rejected has become the cornerstone. We the readers are left to put these scattered textual blocks together, to put one upon the other. One was rejected, another thrown down. Yet there will be a building, one of these will be the cornerstone of something, but something much murkier than a spiritual replacement. The reader of the temple and its destruction in Mark's Gospel must remember that Jesus himself is not seen resurrected in this story. What we are left with in both cases is an emptiness where there should be a corpse. What will be built with the cornerstone that has escaped death is entirely unclear. The reader's best hope is not in a fully made spiritual temple, nor even in a visualized resurrected body, but in the unnerving claim that neither the destruction of the temple, nor Jesus's crucifixion are the end of the story.

---

19. Ibid., 121; see also Mary Ann Tolbert, *Sowing the Gospel: Mark's World in Literary-Historical Perspective* (Minneapolis: Fortress, 1996), 302.

"You Are What You Wear": The Dress and Identity of Jesus as High Priest in John's Apocalypse

Ross E. Winkle

Introduction

The Epistle to the Hebrews is the only New Testament document that explicitly calls Jesus Christ a high priest (ἀρχιερεύς), and it does so repeatedly in an attempt to explicate his priesthood and priestly ministry.[1] But Hebrews is not the only New Testament document that frequently uses terminology related to the tabernacle/temple cultus, of which the high priest was the chief figure and functionary. The book of Revelation also frequently uses such cultic terminology (e.g., tent/tabernacle, temple, lampstands, lamps, altar, censer, incense, ark of the covenant, etc.).[2]

---

1. Hebrews implies that Jesus is priest (ἱερεύς; 7:11, 15, 21; 8:4), quotes Ps 110:4 (109:4 LXX) to prove it (5:6; 7:17, 21), and describes Melchizedek with the same terminology as a type of Christ (7:1, 3). Notice the interplay in Heb 7 between "priest" (7:1, 3, 11, 14–15, 17, 20–21, and 23) and "high priest" (7:26–28), and see Paul Ellingworth, who concludes that Hebrews does not differentiate between ἱερεύς or ἀρχιερεύς in its discussion of Christ (*The Epistle to the Hebrews: A Commentary on the Greek Text*, NIGTC [Grand Rapids: Eerdmans, 1993], 183).

Hebrews uses the Greek term for high priest (ἀρχιερεύς) to describe Jesus's ministry (2:17; 3:1; 4:14, 15; 5:5, 10; 6:20; 7:26; 8:1; 9:11), just as it uses the same term to describe the earthly high priest (5:1; 7:27, 28; 8:3; 9:7, 25; 10:11 [variant]; 13:11). Hebrews 10:21 also calls Jesus the "great priest" (ἱερέα μέγαν), the only time this terminology is used in the New Testament, yet in line with its widespread usage in the LXX (Lev 21:10; Num 35:25, 28, 32; 2 Kgs 12:11; 22:4, 8; 23:4; 1 Chr 9:31; 2 Chr 24:11; 34:9; Neh 3:1, 20; 13:28; Hag 1:1, 12, 14; 2:2, 4; Zech 3:1, 8; 6:11; Jdt 4:6, 8, 14, 15:8; 1 Macc 12:20; 14:20; 15:2; 2 Macc 14:13; and Sir 50:1). The terminology of ἱερέα μέγαν is equivalent to the usage of ἀρχιερεύς; notice also ἀρχιερέα μέγαν ("great high priest") in 4:14 (see the discussion in Ellingworth, *Epistle*, 183).

2. Cf. the tent/tabernacle (13:6; 21:3), tent/tabernacle of witness (15:5), temple

Moreover, Revelation explicitly refers to its implied readers as priests not once but three times (1:6; 5:10; and 20:6). Consequently, one is not surprised to find that it utilizes high-priestly imagery, for example, in its visionary portrayal of the new Jerusalem in chapter 21.[3]

But it is high-priestly imagery in relation to Jesus Christ that remains contentious. After all, Revelation not once describes Jesus Christ explicitly as high priest, as the Epistle to the Hebrews frequently does. John W. Baigent utilized four evidentiary criteria to determine whether supposed New Testament evidence outside of Hebrews supported a possible high-priestly portrayal of Christ: (1) distinctive high-priestly functions; (2) place of such functions; (3) distinctive clothing; and/or (4) genealogical qualifications.[4] But Baigent saw nothing in Revelation that met his criteria,

---

(3:12; 7:15; 11:1, 2, 19; 14:15, 17; 15:5, 6, 8; 16:1, 17; 21:22), lampstands (1:12, 13, 20; 2:1, 5; 11:4), seven lamps (4:5), lamp (21:23; 22:5), altar (6:9; 8:3, 5; 9:13; 11:1; 14:18; 16:7), censer (8:3, 5), incense (5:8; 8:3, 4), ark of the covenant (11:19), etc. See Robert A. Briggs, *Jewish Temple Imagery in the Book of Revelation*, StBibLit 10 (New York: Lang, 1999), passim.

3. John's description of the city with its twelve foundation stones (21:19–20) apparently reflects the twelve stones that adorned the ephod of the high priest. Most scholars have acknowledged this relationship, e.g., David E. Aune, *Revelation 17–22*, WBC 52c (Nashville: Nelson, 1998), 1165; Richard Bauckham, *The Theology of the Book of Revelation*, NTT (Cambridge: Cambridge University Press, 1993), 134; G. K. Beale, *The Book of Revelation: A Commentary on the Greek Text*, NIGTC (Grand Rapids: Eerdmans, 1999), 1080–88; Joseph Comblin, "La liturgie de la Nouvelle Jérusalem (Apoc., XXI, I–XXII, 5)," *ETL* 29 (1953): 15; J. A. Draper, "The Twelve Apostles as Foundation Stones of the Heavenly Jerusalem and the Foundation of the Qumran Community," *Neot* 22 (1988): 41–63, esp. p. 43; Edmondo F. Lupieri, *A Commentary on the Apocalypse of John*, trans. Maria Poggi Johnson and Adam Kamesar, ITSRS (Grand Rapids: Eerdmans, 2006), 344; David Mathewson, *A New Heaven and a New Earth: The Meaning and Function of the Old Testament in Revelation 21.1–22.5*, JSNTSup 238 (Sheffield: Sheffield Academic, 2003), 130–49, 153–56; Robert H. Mounce, *The Book of Revelation*, rev. ed., NICNT (Grand Rapids: Eerdmans, 1998), 393; Grant R. Osborne, *Revelation*, BECNT (Grand Rapids: Baker, 2002), 755–58; Elisabeth Schüssler Fiorenza, *Revelation: Vision of a Just World*, PC (Minnneapolis: Fortress, 1991), 112; and Stephen S. Smalley, *The Revelation to John: A Commentary on the Greek Text of the Apocalypse* (Downers Grove, IL: InterVarsity Press, 2005), 554.

4. John W. Baigent, "Jesus as Priest: An Examination of the Claim That the Concept of Jesus as Priest May Be Found in the New Testament Outside the Epistle to the Hebrews," *VE* 12 (1981): 34.

and thus he ultimately declared that there is "no compelling reason" to view Christ as high priest there.⁵

Dietmar Neufeld, who has written the seminal studies on dress imagery in Revelation, underscored the significant role of dress in revealing identity when he noted the adage that "what you wear is what you are."⁶ In my discussion of Jesus's identity in Revelation, I will limit my remarks to just one of Baigent's four criteria: distinctive clothing or dress. I will focus particularly on Rev 1:13, the center of the debate over the question of the high-priestly identity of Jesus, and I will examine two dress items there in order to demonstrate that they do provide evidence of the role-related identity of Jesus as high priest in Revelation.⁷

---

5. Ibid., 37.

6. Dietmar Neufeld, "Under the Cover of Clothing: Scripted Clothing Performances in the Apocalypse of John," *BTB* 35 (2005): 67. See also Neufeld, "Sumptuous Clothing and Ornamentation in the Apocalypse," *HvTSt* 58 (2002): 664–89.

7. For a fuller treatment of this topic, see Ross E. Winkle, "'Clothes Make the (One like a Son of) Man': Dress Imagery in Revelation 1 as an Indicator of High Priestly Status" (PhD diss., Andrews University, 2012). The high priest's dress was a key indicator of his identity and status in Israelite society: Leviticus, for instance, describes the chief (or, high) priest as the one who has been consecrated to wear the garments (21:10), while Numbers provides the only biblical example of the transfer of power between one high priest and a new one by describing the apparent succession of the soon-to-be high priest putting on the high priest's garments (20:23–28). See the discussion in Deborah W. Rooke, "The Day of Atonement as a Ritual of Validation for the High Priest," in *Temple and Worship in Biblical Israel*, ed. John Day, LHBOTS 422 (London: T&T Clark, 2005), 348 n. 18, and 350. In later tradition, the high priest who wore the high-priestly garments was differentiated from the high priest who was anointed, since the anointing oil was believed to have been hidden during the time of King Josiah and no longer available (m. Hor. 3:4; b. Hor. 12a; b. Ker. 5b; see the discussion in Margaret Barker, *The Great High Priest: The Temple Roots of Christian Liturgy* [London: T&T Clark, 2003], 78). Analysis of high-priestly dress imagery thus presents itself as an important indicator not only of identity but also of the role and functions of the one thus identified, particularly when texts do not explicitly describe the one so identified as high priest (Neufeld, "Under the Cover," 70). Notice the comments of John R. Yeatts, who asserted with reference to Rev 1:13: "The symbolic significance of the Son of Man's attire aids our understanding of his role and identity" (*Revelation*, BCBC [Scottdale, PA: Herald, 2003], 41). Here Yeatts indicates that the dress of Jesus helps one understand not only his identity but also his role or work.

Dress and Identity in Contemporary Discussion

Social scientists and historians of dress have refined their understanding of the definition, nomenclature, and taxonomy of dress and related terms over the last forty years.[8] The work that has become foundational on this subject was written by Mary Ellen Roach-Higgins and Joanne B. Eicher in 1992.[9] They differentiated between appearance, clothing, dress, adornment or ornament, apparel, costume, and fashion, and they favored the

---

8. Differences of understanding still exist, however. See, e.g., Kim K. P. Johnson, Nancy A. Schofield, and Jennifer Yurchisin, "Appearance and Dress as a Source of Information: A Qualitative Approach to Data Collection," *CTRJ* 20 (2002): 125–37, esp. 125 n. 1. For a discussion of the difficulty in providing a "final or rigid definition" of these and related terms, see Malcolm Barnard, *Fashion as Communication*, 2nd ed. (London: Routledge, 2002), 10–11.

9. See Mary Ellen Roach-Higgins and Joanne B. Eicher, "Dress and Identity," in *Dress and Identity*, ed. Mary Ellen Roach-Higgins, Joanne B. Eicher, and Kim K. P. Johnson (New York: Fairchild, 1995), 7–18, particularly 7–10 on the taxonomy of dress. Many scholars have accepted this research as the standard in the field. See, e.g., Mary Lynn Damhorst, "In Search of a Common Thread: Classification of Information Communicated Through Dress," *CTRJ* 8.2 (1990): 1–12; Joanne B. Eicher and Sandra Lee Evenson, eds., *The Visible Self: Global Perspectives on Dress, Culture, and Society*, 4th ed. (New York: Fairchild, 2015), 5; Kim K. P. Johnson and Sharron J. Lennon, "Introduction: Appearance and Social Power," in *Appearance and Power*, ed. Kim K. P. Johnson and Sharron J. Lennon, Dress, Body, Culture (Oxford: Berg, 1999), 1–10; Nancy Lindisfarne-Tapper and Bruce Ingham, "Approaches to the Study of Dress in the Middle East," in *Languages of Dress in the Middle East*, ed. Nancy Lindisfarne-Tapper and Bruce Ingham (London: Curzon, 1997; repr., Oxford: Routledge, 2013), 1–39; Johnson, Schofield, and Yurchisin, "Appearance and Dress," 125 n. 1; and George B. Sproles and Leslie Davis Burns, *Changing Appearances: Understanding Dress in Contemporary Society* (New York: Fairchild, 1994), 7.

Their work, however, is not without criticism. Barnard critiques Roach-Higgins and Eicher's influential study because of its lack of any stand-alone definition, for their definitions must be distinguished from a host of other related words (*Fashion as Communication*, 11). He suggests that these terms may well be both resistant to singular definition and difficult to clearly separate from one another (ibid., 11–12).

For other definitions of clothing, dress, and related terms, see Barnard's brief summary (ibid.); Fred Davis, *Fashion, Culture, and Identity* (Chicago: University of Chicago Press, 1992), 25 n. 4; Robert Hillestad, "The Underlying Structure of Appearance," *Dress* 6 (1980): 117–25; Rebecca H. Holman, "Apparel as Communication," in *Symbolic Consumer Behavior: Proceedings of the Conference on Consumer Esthetics and Symbolic Consumption*, ed. Elizabeth C. Hirschman and Morris B. Holbrook (Ann Arbor, MI: Association for Consumer Research, 1980), 7–9; and Susan B. Kaiser, *The*

term "dress" over all other related terms because they believed that none of the other terms was as accurate or as comprehensive in nature.[10] Their resultant definition was simple yet broad in what it included: "an assemblage of modifications of the body and/or supplements to the body."[11] This definition consequently included not only garments, jewelry, and accessories, but also such body modifications as hair treatments, colored skin, body piercings, and fragrances and scents applied to the body.[12]

A few years before Roach-Higgins and Eicher set forth what came to be their foundational understanding of dress, Grace Q. Vicary wrote that

> the term "clothing" includes any artefactual addition to the body which changes its appearance. These additions can be *garments* (dress, costume, apparel, including headwear, footwear, underwear, designed for work, play, or formal occasions in a variety of environments); *ornaments* (beads, gems, chains, straps, buttons, metal bands, buckles, feathers, ribbons, laces, furs); *cosmetics* (dyes, paints, powders, oils, perfumes); *devices* (wigs, corsets, braces, padding, dentures, plastic fingernails); *treatments* (mutilations, massage, tattoos, hair dyeing, thinning, removing, straightening, curling); *equipment* (eyeglasses, watches, ice skates, pocketbooks, cameras, pipes, backpacks, masks, handkerchiefs, gloves, crutches); and *tools* (knives, combs, mirrors, scissors, pens, toothpicks, fans).[13]

Though there are differences in nomenclature and a different bias in foundational definitions, Roach-Higgins and Eicher remained generally in line

---

Social Psychology of Clothing: Symbolic Appearances in Context, 2nd ed. (New York: Fairchild, 1997), 3–11.

10. Roach-Higgins and Eicher, "Dress and Identity," 9. See their comparison and contrast of the term "dress" with "adornment" or "ornament," "apparel," "appearance," "clothing," "costume," and "fashion" in ibid., 9–10.

11. Ibid.

12. Ibid., 7. Hilda Kuper, in the introduction to her research article on Swazi dress in Swaziland, observes that clothing "can be described as part of the total structure of personal appearance which includes hairstyles, ornaments, masks, decorations and mutilations" ("Costume and Identity," *CSSH* 15 [1973]: 348). For a full discussion of Roach-Higgins and Eicher's categorization of dress, see Eicher and Evenson, *Visible Self*, 2–29.

13. Grace Q. Vicary, "The Signs of Clothing," in *Cross-Cultural Perspectives in Nonverbal Communication*, ed. Fernando Poyatos (Toronto: Hogrefe, 1988), 293–94 (emphasis original).

with Vicary's overall, expansive approach. What constitutes "dress" is thus much more comprehensive than the typical hat, dress, shirt, pair of pants, or pair of shoes that another is wearing.

Academicians of dress frequently stress that dress communicates.[14] First impressions of another that one comes into visual contact with typically include the "reading" of what her or his dress communicates. Vicary notes that "in random public encounters, clothing is usually perceived before voice can be heard or gestures and facial expressions seen. Thus clothing and adornment, as they modify appearance, become a universal, primary, nonverbal communication system."[15] The ability of humans to "read" another person via their clothing or dress prioritizes such communication over verbal communication.

The scope of what dress can communicate is simply astounding: "one's sex, age, group, nationality, religious affiliation, means of livelihood, social, economic, and marital status, political or military rank, personal achievements, loyalties, beliefs, and values, family connections, and trade."[16] Despite the vast amount of data dress can communicate, infor-

---

14. This assertion is virtually universal. See Linda Baumgarten, *What Clothes Reveal: The Language of Clothing in Colonial and Federal America; The Colonial Williamsburg Collection*, Williamsburg Decorative Arts Series (Williamsburg, VA: The Colonial Williamsburg Foundation, 2002), 54; Patrizia Calefato, *The Clothed Body*, trans. Lisa Adams, Dress, Body, Culture (Oxford: Berg, 2004), 5–13; Davis, *Fashion, Culture, and Identity*, 3–4, 191; Eicher and Evenson, *Visible Self*, 26; Johnson, Schofield, and Yurchisin, "Appearance and Dress," 125; John Norton, "Faith and Fashion in Turkey," in Lindisfarne-Tapper and Ingham, *Languages of Dress*, 149–77, esp. 149–51; Sproles and Burns, *Changing Appearances*, 5 and 218–24; and Penny Storm, *Functions of Dress: Tool of Culture and the Individual* (Englewood Cliffs, NJ: Prentice Hall, 1987), 102.

15. Vicary, "Signs of Clothing," 292. Vicary further notes that such communication is not typically ambiguous, since dress communication is "as complex, and precise, as most verbal language" (ibid., 293). Not all agree, however, that dress should be spoken of as a "language"; see, e.g., Kaiser, *Social Psychology of Clothing*, 239, and Grant McCracken, "Clothing as Language: An Object Lesson in the Study of the Expressive Properties of Material Culture," in *Material Anthropology: Contemporary Approaches to Material Culture*, ed. Barrie Reynolds and Margaret A. Stott (Lanham, MD: University Press of America, 1987), 103–28, particularly 113–14 and 117.

16. Neufeld, "Under the Cover," 68. See also Calefato, *Clothed Body*, 15–25; Davis, *Fashion, Culture, and Identity*, 191; Marilyn J. Horn and Lois M. Gurel, *The Second Skin: An Interdisciplinary Study of Clothing*, 3rd ed. (Boston: Houghton Mifflin, 1981), 30–34 and 186–204; Johnson and Lennon, "Introduction," 2; Kaiser, *Social Psychol-*

mation overload is not necessarily a danger to be concerned about, since humans are quite capable of decoding such data quickly.[17]

One of the pieces of information dress communicates is identity.[18] Diana Crane begins her work on fashion, for instance, by declaring that clothing "performs a major role in the social construction of identity."[19] Phyllis Culham, in her discussion of ancient dress, concluded: "There is surely no other item which identifies a person so immediately in so many ways as clothing."[20] *What* one wears can thus very well identify *who* one is. One can often identify, for instance, whether or not two people

---

ogy of Clothing, 272, 321; Roach-Higgins and Eicher, "Dress and Identity," 11; Jane Schneider and Annette B. Weiner, "Introduction," in *Cloth and Human Experience*, ed. Annette B. Weiner and Jane Schneider, SSEI (Washington, DC: Smithsonian Institution, 1989), 1–29; and Storm, *Functions of Dress*, 102–208.

17. Mary Lynn Damhorst, "Dress as Nonverbal Communication," in *The Meanings of Dress*, ed. Mary Lynn Damhorst, Kimberly A. Miller-Spillman, and Susan O. Michelman (New York: Fairchild, 2005), 67.

18. Cf. Barbara Burman and Carole Turbin, "Introduction: Material Strategies Engendered," *G&H* 14 (2002): 371–81; Davis, *Fashion, Culture, and Identity*, 25; Sandra Lee Evenson, "Dress and Identity," in *Berg Encyclopedia of World Dress and Fashion*, ed. Joanne B. Eicher and Phyllis B. Tortora (Oxford: Oxford University Press, 2010), 10:52, 54–55, 57; Bruce Ingham, "Men's Dress in the Arabian Peninsula: Historical and Present Perspectives," in Lindisfarne-Tapper and Ingham, *Languages of Dress*, 40–42; Kuper, "Costume and Identity," 365–66; Lindisfarne-Tapper and Ingham, "Study of Dress," 4–5; and Jane Schneider, "The Anthropology of Cloth," *ARA* 16 (1987): 412. For surveys of anthropological studies that include several underscoring the identifying powers of dress, see Joanne B. Eicher, "The Anthropology of Dress," *Dress* 27 (2000): 59–70; and Karen Tranberg Hansen, "The World in Dress: Anthropological Perspectives on Clothing, Fashion, and Culture," *ARA* 33 (2004): 369–92.

19. Diana Crane, *Fashion and Its Social Agendas: Class, Gender, and Identity in Clothing* (Chicago: University of Chicago Press, 2000), 1 (see also pp. 1–4). Notice also the relationship between clothing and identity in Stella Bruzzi, *Undressing Cinema: Clothing and Identity in the Movies* (London: Routledge, 1997), 14, 69–70, 102–3, 142–43, and 199.

20. Phyllis Culham, "Again, What Meaning Lies in Colour!," *ZPE* 64 (1986): 244. See also Rosemary Canavan, who also notes the immediacy of identity perception via clothing (*Clothing the Body of Christ at Colossae: A Visual Construction of Identity*, WUNT 2/334 [Tübingen: Mohr Siebeck, 2012], 41–42). Roach-Higgins and Eicher also note that dress has "a certain priority over discourse in the establishing of identity" because it can be seen before one says (or, writes) anything ("Dress and Identity," 12 [see also p. 13]). See also Gregory P. Stone, "Appearance and the Self," in *Human Behavior and Social Processes: An Interactionist Approach*, ed. Arnold M. Rose (Boston: Houghton Mifflin, 1962), 101.

are twins simply by the identical dress they wear.[21] Over forty years ago Gregory P. Stone mused about how the names of famous politicians had been established by—and consequently associated with—various articles of dress: Teddy Roosevelt and his pince-nez, Franklin Delano Roosevelt and his cigarette holder, and Thomas Dewey and his moustache.[22] Thus Hilda Kuper concludes that "it is no wonder that persons should view their clothing almost as an extension of themselves."[23] No wonder we are apt to say, as someone tries on an article of dress, "It's you!"[24]

One kind of identity that dress can communicate is occupational or role-related identity.[25] Upon initially glancing at a person wearing the dress of a police officer, for instance, it is improbable that one would doubt that the individual so dressed was a police officer.[26] As Richard Wentz observes, "The little boy is given toy soldiers and astronauts for his birthday. He knows those persons by their clothing. The professor wears a shapeless herringbone jacket with tan cotton twill pants, shoes with thick rubber soles—for comfort, he tells us. He *looks* like a professor."[27]

At times dress has become unusually successful at providing an indication of one's role-related identity. As a result, the name of a piece of dress has evolved into the name of a person's role or occupation. As such, the

---

21. As noted by Roach-Higgins and Eicher, "Dress and Identity," 13.
22. Stone, "Appearance and the Self," 95.
23. Kuper, "Costume and Identity," 366.
24. See Valentine Cunningham, "If the Cap Fits: Figuring the Space of the Human," in *The Anthropological Turn in Literary Studies*, ed. Jürgen Schlaeger, YREAL 12 (Tübingen: Narr, 1996), 51.
25. Role-related dress is similar to what others term "occupational dress": dress that communicates one's occupation or work responsibilities. I prefer to use the terminology of role-related dress. On this type of identity, see, e.g., Jennifer Craik, *Uniforms Exposed: From Conformity to Transgression*, Dress, Body, Culture (Oxford: Berg, 2005), 119–21 and 131–38; Holman, "Apparel as Communication," 8; Johnson, Schofield, and Yurchisin, "Appearance and Dress," 135; Kaiser, *Social Psychology of Clothing*, 240; Miller-Spillman, "Dress in the Workplace," in Damhorst, Miller-Spillman, and Michelman, *The Meanings of Dress*, 221; and Gregory P. Stone, "Clothing and Social Relations: A Study of Appearance in the Context of Community Life" (PhD diss., University of Chicago, 1959), 291–92, who recorded what a painter said during an interview: "I dress the same as anybody does in their profession. People see me, and they know I'm a painter" (292).
26. Cf. Richard Wentz, "Clothed in the Beauty of Possibility," *Parab* 19 (Fall 1994): 80.
27. Ibid., emphasis original.

particular feature of dress becomes a synecdoche, describing not just that particular article of dress but the whole person in order to convey identity: "bobby-soxer, zoot-suiter, redcoat, brown shirt, hard hat, blue-collar worker, blue stocking, man of the cloth, sans-culotte."[28]

In another vein, a particular sartorial element may stand for the entire set in the construction of one's role-related identity. For instance, a crown may symbolize the king and even the whole institution of the monarchy. This rhetorical use of metonymy consequently organizes the remaining elements of the sartorial set into foreground and background, "thereby obviating the need to examine every item of an individual's attire in minute detail to place him socially."[29] In the illustration just mentioned, the crown is usually enough to provide identification of the whole, while a scepter and other sartorial elements of royalty fade into the background. Here the crown as a "working symbol" in the foreground becomes what is known as a key or salient symbol.[30]

Dress and Identity in Revelation

One cannot underestimate the power and influence of dress in human history. Focusing on only a slice of that time, Alicia J. Batten, Carly Daniel-Hughes, and Kristi Upson-Saia write the following:

> Dress was a significant preoccupation for Judeans and Christians in antiquity. Dress, whether material or metaphoric, figured significantly in daily life, in texts, and in ritual practices. It functioned in a range of ways: as a way to construct and communicate identity, as a means to conform or distinguish, as a locus of dispute and resistance, or as a path to or expression of holiness.[31]

---

28. Calum M. Carmichael, "Forbidden Mixtures," *VT* 32 (1982): 406.

29. Nathan Joseph, *Uniforms and Nonuniforms: Communicating Through Clothing*, Contributions in Sociology 61 (New York: Greenwood, 1986), 20.

30. Ibid., 21. Other salient symbols include a police officer's badge, a military person's insignia, or a mace, staff, or wand carried by the faculty marshal at college and university graduation services.

31. Alicia J. Batten, Carly Daniel-Hughes, and Kristi Upson-Saia, "Introduction: 'What Shall We Wear?,'" in *Dressing Judeans and Christians in Antiquity*, ed. Kristi Upson-Saia, Carly Daniel-Hughes, and Alicia J. Batten (Farnham, UK: Ashgate, 2014), 1. For summary discussions on the significance of dress during both the Old Testament and New Testament periods, see, e.g., Edgar Haulotte, *Symbolique du vêtement*

Furthermore, in comparing the communicative role of dress in society in general with its communicative role in ancient Near East and Old Testament literary texts, for example, Jopie Siebert-Hommes suggests that "the impact of clothing objects and other insignia [in literary texts] *may be even more crucial* [than in society in general], because authors and writers often intentionally make use of special details about dress and garments to convey certain information about the main characters."[32] One needs only look at the repeated use of dress in the ancient literary texts about Joseph, Kings Saul and David, Queen Esther, the Maccabees, and Jesus to discover that dress communicated not only personal identity but role-related identity.[33] One did not function as high priest (or even priest) in ancient Israel, for example, without distinctive dress, as Heather A. McKay has astutely observed: "In the cult where divine power is channelled through cultic officials all the transactions are facilitated by special robes and insignia."[34]

Dress terminology and imagery are unusually pervasive throughout the book of Revelation. This includes not only their presence but also their absence. Nakedness has been commonly understood to be symbolic of the

---

selon la Bible, Théologie 65 (Paris: Aubier, 1966), 79–89; Jung Hoon Kim, *The Significance of Clothing Imagery in the Pauline Corpus*, JSNTSup 268 (London: T&T Clark, 2004), particularly 10–69 and 106–223; Harry O. Maier, "Kleidung II (Bedeutung)," *RAC* 21:22–40; and Christoph G. Müller, "Kleidung als Element der Charakterzeichnung im Neuen Testament und seiner Umwelt: Ein Streifzug durch das lukanische Erzählwerk," *SNTSU* 28 (2003): 187–214.

32. Jopie Siebert-Hommes, "'On the Third Day Esther Put on Her Queen's Robes' [Esther 5:1]: The Symbolic Function of Clothing in the Book of Esther," *LDiff* 3.1 (2002), par. 1 (emphasis added), http://tinyurl.com/SBL0393h.

33. For Joseph, see Gen 37:3, 31–33; 38:14, 18, 25; 39:11–20; 41:7–8, 14, 42; 43:31–32; and 45:3–4. For Saul and David, see 1 Sam 15:27; 24:1–10; and 28:8, 14. For Esther, see Esth 4:1; 5:1. For the Maccabees, see 1 Macc 1:9; 8:14; 10:20–21, 62, 64; 11:13; 14:41–47. As for Jesus, see, e.g., Luke 2:7; 8:26–39 and 43–48; 9:29; 23:11; and 24:12. Robert J. Karris has suggested that "in a sense Luke describes Jesus' life from beginning to end by means of the theme of clothing" (*Luke: Artist and Theologian: Luke's Passion Account as Literature*, Theological Inquiries [New York: Paulist, 1985], 86).

34. Heather A. McKay, "Gendering the Body: Clothes Maketh the (Wo)man," in *Theology and the Body: Gender, Text and Ideology*, ed. Robert Hannaford and J'annine Jobling, Canterbury Books (Leominster, UK: Gracewing, 1999), 99. See also McKay, "Gendering the Discourse of Display in the Hebrew Bible," in *On Reading Prophetic Texts: Gender-Specific and Related Studies in Memory of Fokkelien van Dijk-Hemmes*, ed. Bob Becking and Meindert Dijkstra, BibInt 18 (Leiden: Brill, 1996), 185–86, 189, 196–98.

loss of personal identity and thus shameful. In the ancient world, nakedness was considered a "costume," but as a costume, nakedness would not be a negative perspective of dress.³⁵ But four times in Revelation it is the *absence* of dress (3:17, 18; 16:15; 17:16) that constitutes the basis of either a condemnation or judgment (3:17; 17:16) or a warning (3:18; 16:15).³⁶ These explicit and repeated warnings against the *absence* of dress thus further underscore the significance of the *presence* of dress within Revelation's overall rhetoric.

With regard to the presence of dress references, Revelation describes the explicit or implied dress of a cast of generalized as well as specific characters in terms of cloth and clothing, crowns and victory wreaths, jewelry and precious stones, as well as in metaphorical dress, and it does so in at least twenty-four different texts.³⁷ Moreover, the frequency of seven verbs

---

35. For nakedness as a "costume" in the ancient world, see Larissa Bonfante, "Classical Nudity in Italy and Greece," in *Ancient Italy in Its Mediterranean Setting: Studies in Honour of Ellen Macnamara*, ed. David Ridgway et al., Accordia Specialist Studies on the Mediterranean 4 (London: Accordia Research Institute, University of London, 2000), 271–93, in particular, 271–72; and Bonfante, "Nudity as a Costume in Classical Art," *AJA* 93 (1989): 543–70, in particular, 544.

36. Notice also the use of the verb ποιέω in 17:16 to describe the stripping off of clothes. Neufeld notes that priests were singled out in the requirement to cover up one's nakedness ("Sumptuous Clothing," 675); this is intriguing within the light of Revelation's identification of God's people as priests (1:6; 5:10; 20:6).

37. See the following (twenty-four clusters of) texts: 1:13; 2:10; 3:4–5; 3:11; 3:18; 4:4, 10; 6:2, 11; 7:9, 13, 14; 9:7; 10:1; 11:3; 12:1, 3; 13:1; 14:14; 15:6; 16:15; 17:4; 18:12, 16; 19:8, 12, 13, 14, 16; 21:2, 11, 19; 22:14. Cf. Neufeld, who counted only sixteen ("Sumptuous Clothing," 677–78); it is likely that part of the reason for this discrepancy is because of the narrower dress definitions Neufeld utilizes.

The precious stone imagery (λίθος τίμιος) in 21:11 and 19 refers to the adornment and appearance of the new Jerusalem, but the language comes from that of dress. The same is true for the pearls in 21:21, which are part of the "necklace" of the bride, the new Jerusalem. See also 21:2, where the new Jerusalem is adorned (κεκοσμημένην) like a bride, while in 21:19 the foundations of the city are adorned (κεκοσμημένοι) with precious stones.

Metaphoric dress occurs when subjects are described as dressed in essentially nondress items or concepts (i.e., a god dressed in light or glory). See, e.g., H. A. Brongers, "Die metaphorische Verwendung von Termini für die Kleidung von Göttern und Menschen in der Bibel und im Alten Orient," in *Von Kanaan bis Kerala: Festschrift für Prof. Mag. Dr. Dr. J. P. M. van der Ploeg OP zur Vollendung des siebzigsten Lebensjahres am 4. Juli 1979: Überreicht von Kollegen, Freunden und Schülern*, ed. W. C. Delsman et al., AOAT 211 (Kevelaer: Butzon & Bercker; Neukirchen-Vluyn: Neukirchener Verlag,

of dress is not less than conspicuous, appearing twenty-three times.³⁸ The cumulative weight of these scattered, repeated, and sometimes striking references to dress in Revelation indicates that dress must be of critical significance within its overall rhetoric, underscoring Neufeld's observation that Revelation is "liberally strewn with clothes."³⁹ Neufeld also observes

---

1982), 61–74; Elena Cassin, *La splendeur divine: Introduction à l'étude de la mentalité mésopotamienne*, CeS 8 (Paris: Mouton, 1968), 118; A. Leo Oppenheim, "Akkadian *pul(u)ḫ(t)u* and *melammu*," *JAOS* 63 (1943): 31–34; Thomas Podella, *Das Lichtkleid JHWHs: Untersuchungen zur Gestalthaftigkeit Gottes im Alten Testament und seiner altorientalischen Umwelt*, FAT 15 (Tübingen: Mohr Siebeck, 1996), 4–9; and Nahum M. Waldman, "The Imagery of Clothing, Covering, and Overpowering," *JANESCU* 19 (1989): 161–70, particularly 162. In Rev 10:1 the mighty angel is "clothed with a cloud" (περιβεβλημένον νεφέλην), while in 12:1 the woman is "clothed with the sun" (περιβεβλημένη τὸν ἥλιον).

38. I.e., forms of ἐνδύω ("I put on, clothe": 1:13; 15:6; 19:14), κοσμέω ("I adorn": 21:2, 19), περιβάλλω ("I put around, clothe": 3:5, 18; 4:4; 7:9, 13; 10:1; 11:3; 12:1; 17:4; 18:16; 19:8, 13), περιζώννυμι ("I gird about, wrap around": 1:13; 15:6), and χρυσόω ("I gild, adorn with gold": 17:4; 18:16).

Two other verbs are not typically dress verbs, but in Revelation (as in other New Testament texts) they carry this meaning. The first one, ἔχω ("I have"), has a dress meaning in Rev 9:9 and 17. In those texts it respectively describes locusts and mounted troops wearing protective breastplates (cf. BDAG, s.v. "ἔχω," §4). Revelation also utilizes the verb to describe those who have hand-held items which could be classified as accessories or, according to Vicary's classification scheme ("Signs of Clothing," 293–94), dress treatments, equipment, or tools (e.g., 1:16 [metaphorical stars; but see 3:1], 18 [metaphorical keys; see 3:7 and 20:1], 5:8 [harps and bowls of incense], 6:2 [bow], 6:5 [scales], 8:2 [censer], 8:6 [trumpets; cf. 9:14], 10:2 [scroll], 13:17 [mark], 14:1 [name], 14:14 [crown and sickle], 14:17–18 [sickle], 15:1 [harps], 17:1 [vials/bowls], 17:4 [golden cup], 19:12 [name], 19:16 [name], 20:1 [key and chain], 21:9 [vial/bowl], and 21:15 [measuring rod]).

The second verb, λαμβάνω ("I take, receive"), is also not typically a dress verb, but in John 13:12 it has the meaning of "put on" with reference to Jesus putting on his garments after washing his disciples' feet. In several texts in Revelation λαμβάνω also works as a dress verb (14:9, 11; 19:20; 20:4). These texts refer to the reception of the mark of the beast, and in these cases the verb works as a periphrasis for the passive form "be marked" (BDAG, s.v. "λαμβάνω," §10, part C). Consequently, since the mark of the beast is similar to a brand or tattoo (see David E. Aune, *Revelation 6–16*, WBC 52B [Nashville: Nelson, 1998], 455 [on 7:3], 456–59, and 766–68 [on 13:16b]), this verbal usage would indicate verbal dress imagery.

39. Neufeld, "Sumptuous Clothing," 679. For further on the significance of dress in Revelation, see also James L. Resseguie, "Clothing: A Map of the Spiritual Life," in *Spiritual Landscape: Images of the Spiritual Life in the Gospel of Luke* (Peabody, MA:

with regard to Revelation that "clothes and jewelry are a part of each character's identity kit that aids in playing out assigned social roles,"[40] thus affirming the maxim that "you are what you wear."

Dress and the Identity of Jesus in Revelation

Whether or not the New Testament book of Revelation suggests high-priestly imagery for Jesus Christ has been a contentious exegetical battlefield. Revelation 1:13 has become the critical verse par excellence, typically springing from one's interpretation of the long, foot-length robe (ποδήρη) of the one "like a son of man" (ὅμοιον υἱὸν ἀνθρώπου)—not explicitly identified as Jesus Christ but certainly none other than him (see 1:18 and further confirmation in Rev 2–3). Numerous exegetes see priestly or high-priestly dress imagery here.[41] Nevertheless, opposition to such a

---

Hendrickson, 2004), 92, 93; and Resseguie, *Revelation Unsealed: A Narrative Critical Approach to John's Apocalypse*, BibInt 32 (Leiden: Brill, 1998), 41–42.

40. Neufeld, "Sumptuous Clothing," 679. See also ibid., 678, 686.

41. E.g., Brian K. Blount, *Revelation: A Commentary*, NTL (Louisville: Westminster John Knox, 2009), 44; L. A. Brighton, *Revelation*, ConcC (Saint Louis: Concordia, 1999), 49; G. B. Caird, *A Commentary on the Revelation of St. John the Divine*, HNTC (New York: Harper & Row, 1966), 25; Joseph Coppens, "Le messianisme sacerdotal dans les éscrits du Nouveau Testament," in *La venue du Messie: Messianisme et eschatologie*, ed. Édouard Massaux, RechBib 6 (Bruges: de Brouwer, 1962), 111; Gordon D. Fee, *Revelation: A New Covenant Commentary*, NCCS 18 (Eugene, OR: Cascade Books, 2011), 17; J. Massyngberde Ford, *Revelation: Introduction, Translation and Commentary*, AB 38 (Garden City, NY: Doubleday, 1975), 385; Robert H. Gundry, *Commentary on the New Testament: Verse-by-Verse Explanations with a Literal Translation* (Peabody, MA: Hendrickson, 2010), 99; James M. Hamilton Jr., *Revelation: The Spirit Speaks to the Churches*, Preaching the Word (Wheaton, IL: Crossway, 2012), 47; Alan David Hultberg, "Messianic Exegesis in the Apocalypse: The Significance of the Old Testament for the Christology of Revelation" (PhD diss., Trinity Evangelical Divinity School, 2001), 128–32; Craig S. Keener, *Revelation*, NIVAC (Grand Rapids: Zondervan, 2000), 94–95; Dan Lioy, *The Book of Revelation in Christological Focus*, StBibLit 58 (New York: Lang, 2003), 117; Ernst Lohmeyer, *Die Offenbarung des Johannes*, 3rd ed., HNT 16 (Tübingen: Mohr Siebeck, 1970), 15; Eduard Lohse, *Die Offenbarung des Johannes*, NTD 11 (Göttingen: Vandenhoeck & Ruprecht, 1971), 20; Mounce, *Book of Revelation*, 57–58; Neufeld, "Sumptuous Clothing," 677; Jon Paulien, "The Role of the Hebrew Cultus, Sanctuary, and Temple in the Plot and Structure of the Book of Revelation," *AUSS* 33 (1995), 249; William Riley, "Temple Imagery and the Book of Revelation: Ancient Near Eastern Temple Ideology and Cultic Resonances in the Apocalypse," *PIBA* 6 (1982): 91; Ugo Vanni, *L'Apocalisse: ermeneutica, esegesi, teo-*

sacral, cultic understanding has been persistent. When commenting on this verse in 1998, for example, Frederick J. Murphy firmly claimed that "Christ nowhere appears as high priest in Revelation."[42] In his magisterial commentary on Revelation, David Aune, in perhaps the most potent and substantial offense against the view that one can detect (high) priestly imagery for Jesus in Rev 1:13, recognized that the priestly interpretation was widespread. But in his detailed analysis he considered such an interpretation as without foundation and concluded that "there is therefore no clear intention on the part of the author to conceptualize the appearance of the exalted Christ in priestly terms."[43]

The evidence in John's inaugural vision in 1:12–20, however, does point toward high-priestly imagery. First, the locative context of John's first vision shows Jesus walking in the midst of seven golden lampstands (1:12–13). While this being explicitly explained to John that these lampstands represent the seven churches of Ephesus, Smyrna, Pergamum, Thyatira, Sardis, Philadelphia, and Laodicea (1:11, 20), they also resonate with temple imagery. Aune, for example, states that "this imagery suggests

---

logia, RivBibSup 17 (Bologna: Dehoniane, 1988), 126–28; and Ben Witherington III, *Revelation*, NCBC (Cambridge: Cambridge University Press, 2003), 81.

42. Frederick J. Murphy, *Babylon Is Fallen: The Revelation to John*, NTC (Harrisburg, PA: Trinity Press International, 1998), 90.

43. David E. Aune, *Revelation 1–5*, WBC 52A (Dallas: Word, 1997), 93, 94. For other opponents of such a (high) priestly view, see, e.g., G. R. Beasley-Murray, *The Book of Revelation*, NCB (London: Marshall, Morgan & Scott, 1978; repr., Grand Rapids: Eerdmans, 1981), 66–67; Peter R. Carrell, *Jesus and the Angels: Angelology and the Christology of the Apocalypse of John*, SNTSMS 95 (Cambridge: Cambridge University Press, 1997), 160 n. 38; R. H. Charles, *A Critical and Exegetical Commentary on the Revelation of St. John*, ICC (Edinburgh: T&T Clark, 1920), 1:27–28; Heinz Giesen, *Die Offenbarung des Johannes*, RNT (Regensburg: Pustet, 1997), 87–88; R. C. H. Lenski, *The Interpretation of St. John's Revelation* (Minneapolis: Augsburg, 1963), 65; Frederick David Mazzaferri, *The Genre of the Book of Revelation from a Source-Critical Perspective*, BZNW 54 (Berlin: de Gruyter, 1989), 303 n. 315, and 320; Leon Morris, *The Book of Revelation: An Introduction and Commentary*, rev. ed., TNTC (Leicester: Inter-Varsity, 1987), 54; Osborne, *Revelation*, 89; Pierre Prigent, *Commentary on the Apocalypse of St. John*, trans. Wendy Pradels (Tübingen: Mohr Siebeck, 2001), 136–37; Jürgen Roloff, *The Revelation of John: A Continental Commentary*, trans. John E. Alsup, CC (Minneapolis: Fortress, 1993), 36; Robert L. Thomas, *Revelation 1–7: An Exegetical Commentary* (Chicago: Moody, 1992), 98–100; and Albert Vanhoye, "L'Apocalisse e la lettera agli Ebrei," in *Apokalypsis: Percorsi nell'Apocalisse di Giovanni in onore di Ugo Vanni*, ed. Elena Bosetti and Angelo Colacrai, Commenti e studi biblici (Assisi, Italy: Cittadella, 2005), 262–64.

that a 'temple' is the ambiance for John's vision."[44] One would expect a priestly or high-priestly figure to be associated with the lampstand imagery in Rev 1, since they were the personnel historically associated with the lampstand(s) in the Israelite tabernacle and temple. While it is clear that the common priests were mentioned in association with rituals relating to the lampstand(s) in the holy place of Solomon's Temple (e.g., 2 Chr 13:10–11), it was not the common priests but instead the high priest who was specifically associated with the singular lampstand or menorah in the cultic legislation of the tabernacle traditions (Exod 27:20–21; 29:29–30; 30:8 Num 8:2–4; Lev 24:3–4).[45] The picture in Rev 1, with Jesus standing in the midst of the seven golden lampstands, appears more likely indicative of the high priest tending with care the golden lampstand(s) as he was delegated to do on a daily basis.[46] Thus, beyond the two cultic references in the introductory material, this locative contextual marker sets forth not only a sanctuary background but even a high-priestly one for the rest of John's inaugural vision.

Second, John describes Jesus dressed in a long, ankle-length robe (ἐνδεδυμένον ποδήρη) in Rev 1:13.[47] As for its usage in the New Testament, ποδήρης is a *hapax legomenon*, occurring only here. The LXX provides cru-

---

44. Aune, *Revelation 1–5*, 88. See also Gundry, *Commentary*, 99; Thomas B. Slater, *Christ and Community: A Socio-Historical Study of the Christology of Revelation*, JSNTSup 178 (Sheffield: Sheffield Academic, 1999), 96; and Iwan Whiteley, "A Search for Cohesion in the Book of Revelation with Specific Reference to Chapter One" (PhD diss., University of Wales [Lampeter], 2005), 159–60.

45. See, e.g., Rachel Hachlili, *The Menorah, the Ancient Seven-Armed Candelabrum: Origin, Form and Significance*, JSJSup 68 (Leiden: Brill, 2001); 176; Deborah W. Rooke, "Kingship as Priesthood: The Relationship between the High Priesthood and the Monarchy," in *King and Messiah in Israel and the Ancient Near East: Proceedings of the Oxford Old Testament Seminar*, ed. John Day, JSOTSup 270 (Sheffield: Sheffield Academic, 1998), 200; Rooke, "Day of Atonement," 350; and L. Yarden, *The Tree of Light: A Study of the Menorah: The Seven-Branched Lampstand* (Ithaca, NY: Cornell University Press, 1971), 14. Philo understood that the work of tending the lampstand was initially a high-priestly ministry, but it was delegated to subordinate priests as a result of indolence and negligence (*QE* 2.105).

46. The reference to the lampstand in Rev 1 would likely preclude a Yom Kippur or Day of Atonement meaning, since the lampstand was not integrally related to the rituals of that day any more so than any other day of the year.

47. The word ποδήρης is related to the word for foot (πούς [plural: πόδες]), and thus this term typically refers to or describes a robe that reaches down to the feet. See BDAG, s.v. "ποδήρης, ες."

cial information regarding ποδήρης, however, and this remains essential in determining the semantic range and contextual meaning of the word. There it occurs in twelve verses, eight[48] of which refer specifically and conclusively to an item of the high priest's dress. In three of the remaining four verses in the LXX, it describes the dress of the "man" in Ezek 9 who marks the foreheads of the inhabitants of Jerusalem.[49] The last LXX reference occurs in Sir 27:8, where it is part of a maxim that cannot be clearly associated with any particular occupation or role.[50]

The Greek term in the LXX translates two separate Hebrew terms (מעיל and מחלצות), and the majority of references in the LXX, its singular occurrence in the Letter of Aristeas, all of the seventeen references in Philo, and four out of the five references in Josephus indicate that a ποδήρης was typically considered part of the dress of the high priest.[51] It is probable that John derived the term, singular in the New Testament, from the LXX.[52] Although it may have had a wider meaning early on in its history, it appears that by the time of John it had apparently become a technical term, referring to the foot-long, hyacinth-colored garment of the high priest.[53]

---

48. With reference to the clothing of the high priest, it occurs in Exod 25:7; 28:4, 31 (adj.); 29:5 (adj.); 35:9; Zech 3:4; Sir 45:8; Wis 18:24.

49. Ezek 9:2, 3, 11. For arguments that it is understood as a high-priestly term in Ezekiel, see Winkle, "Clothes," 168–76.

50. See ibid., 180–81.

51. For a discussion of whether the Greek term translates two, three, four, or five Hebrew terms, see ibid., 161–98 and 286–88. The Greek term is also used in relation to the high priest's dress in the Letter of Aristeas 96; Philo, *Fug.* 185; *Her.* 176; *Leg.* 1.81; 2.56; *Mos.* 2.117, 118, 120, 121, 133, 143; *Mut.* 43; *Somn.* 1.214; and *Spec.* 1.85 (2x), 93, and 94; and Frag. 117 on Exod 28:27 LXX (text in *Philo*, LCL, 12:257); Josephus, *Ant.* 3.159; 8.93; 20.6; and *J.W.* 5.231. See also the T. Levi 8:2 and Barn. 7:9. For a discussion of the divided meaning of the term in Josephus, see Winkle, "Clothes," 190–93. While one might agree with Josephus in *Ant.* 3.153 (against Philo *Spec.* 1.83) that the tunics of the common priests reached to the feet, it is unlikely that in Rev 1:13 John would intend the same rare literary understanding of the term Josephus utilized there in view of the overwhelming use of the term in relation to the high priest found elsewhere.

52. Marko Jauhiainen, *The Use of Zechariah in Revelation*, WUNT 199 (Tübingen: Mohr Siebeck, 2005), 79.

53. As for the precise nature of this hyacinth color (Exod 28:31: תכלת MT / ὑακίνθινον LXX), E. P. Sanders asserts that "the precise description of colours is very difficult—in fact, impossible" (*Judaism: Practice and Belief: 63 BCE–66 CE* [London: SCM Press, 1992], 95). The colored yarns would be made out of wool, since linen is not

The Israelite high priest essentially wore two basic sets of ritual clothing: those worn during the normal course of the year (e.g., Exod 28:2–43), and special clothing for Yom Kippur (or, the Day of Atonement; see Lev 16:1–4). The ornate clothing for the former was studded with gems and precious stones, utilized gold in several places, and was multicolored. The simpler clothing for the latter lacked precious stones, gems, and gold and was not multicolored.[54] Since the foot-length garment of Jesus is hyacinth-colored, it cannot be referring to Yom Kippur or Day of Atonement imagery but rather imagery corresponding to the regalia worn by the high priest on every other day but that one.

Third, Rev 1:13 also states that Jesus is dressed around his chest at the location of his breasts (περιεζωσμένον πρὸς τοῖς μαστοῖς) with a golden belt or sash (ζώνην χρυσᾶν). The only two places in the LXX in which the ζώνη and the ποδήρης occur in relatively close proximity are Exod 28:4–29:9 and Ezek 9.[55] The dress of the high priest is clearly—though not exclusively—the focus of the former text. In the latter, the LXX counterpart to the "man in linen" in Ezek 9 (MT) is likely based on the high-priestly understanding of his ministry.[56] Consequently, since the only biblical contexts in which these two dress items occur in relative proximity explicitly or probably refer either to the high priest or to high-priestly imagery, one could infer that John's use of ζώνη in close proximity to ποδήρης in 1:13 was meant to underscore the high-priestly identity of Jesus.

John also describes the ζώνη as "golden." The priests of the sanctuary wore sashes, and they were made of fine linen and were multichromatic,

---

readily capable of being dyed (ibid., 95–96). Despite the assertion of Sanders, the hyacinthine color was likely a bluish-purple one. On this, see Manfried Dietrich, "Trumpet Snails and Purple Snails as an Indication of the Transfer of Religion and Technology in the Eastern-Mediterranean Region," in *Homeland and Exile: Biblical and Ancient Near Eastern Studies in Honour of Bustenay Oded*, ed. Gershon Galil, Mark Geller, and Alan Millard, VTSup 130 (Leiden: Brill, 2009), 51–54; I. Irving Ziderman, "Seashells and Ancient Purple Dyeing," *BA* 53 (June 1990): 98–101; and Ziderman, "Purple Dyeing in the Mediterranean World: Characterisation of Biblical *Tekhelet*," in *Colour in the Ancient Mediterranean World*, ed. Liza Cleland and Karen Stears with Glenys Davies, BARIS 1267 (Oxford: Hedges, 2004), 40–45.

54. For a detailed analysis of these garments, see Winkle, "Clothes," 130–255.

55. In the LXX see Exod 28:4 (ζώνη and ποδήρης); 28:31 (ποδήρης [adj.]); 28:39 (ζώνη); 29:5 (ποδήρης [adj.]); 29:9 (ζώνη); Ezek 9:2 (ζώνη and ποδήρης); 9:3 (ζώνη and ποδήρης); 9:11 (ζώνη and ποδήρης).

56. See Winkle, "Clothes," 168–78 and 311.

being embroidered with bluish-purple (hyacinth), reddish-purple (Tyrian purple), and scarlet needlework (Exod 39:29 MT; 36:36 LXX). The high priest's ζώνη in Exod 28:4–29:9 LXX was not golden at all. However, Josephus tells us that the high priest's sash in his day was different from that of the regular priests: while it was worn on the breast a little above the armpits like that of the other priests, it had a mixture of gold interwoven in it (Josephus, *Ant.* 3.159; see also 3.154). Apparently the interwoven gold was the element of the high priest's sash that distinguished his from that of the common priests. The golden sash situated at the breast of Jesus in Rev 1:13 would thus potentially allude to high-priestly dress imagery.[57]

With only two dress items discussed here, some might raise the concern that John cannot be referring to high-priestly dress in Rev 1 because too many characteristic dress elements of the high priest are missing from his sartorial portrayal. For instance, F. J. A. Hort argued more than a century ago that "even though the biblical associations of the word [ποδήρης] are chiefly connected with the high-priesthood," what "makes it somewhat doubtful whether that is distinctly meant here is the absence of any other clear sign of the high-priesthood."[58] Margaret Barker on her part argues that the ποδήρης cannot be the hyacinthine, foot-length robe of the high priest: "On balance, we should probably assume that the robe in Revelation 1.13 was the white linen worn by the high priest when he entered the holy of holies as no other vestments are mentioned. Had it been the long coloured robe worn elsewhere, he would have been wearing over it the embroidered tunic, the ephod, and the breastplate set with twelve gem stones. These are not mentioned."[59]

---

57. On the belt/sash, see Margaret Barker, *The Revelation of Jesus Christ: Which God Gave to Him to Show to His Servants What Must Soon Take Place (Revelation 1.1)* (Edinburgh: T&T Clark, 2000), 84–85, who cites this passage in Josephus as proof that only the high priest wore a sash interwoven with gold; see also Winkle, "Clothes," 306–25.

58. F. J. A. Hort, *The Apocalypse of St John: I–III: The Greek Text with Introduction, Commentary, and Additional Notes* (London: Macmillan, 1908), 16.

59. Barker, *Revelation*, 84–85. See also Aune, *Revelation 1–5*, 94; Heike Omerzu, "Women, Magic and Angels: On the Emancipation of Job's Daughters in the Apocryphal Testament of Job," in *Bodies in Question: Gender, Religion, Text*, ed. Darlene Bird and Yvonne Sherwood (Burlington, VT: Ashgate, 2005), 94; and Akira Satake, *Die Offenbarung des Johannes*, ed. Thomas Witulski, KEK 16 (Göttingen: Vandenhoeck & Ruprecht, 2008), 142.

Both of Hort's and Barker's objections assume that dress indicative of the high priest must include the whole dress ensemble—or at least several parts of it. But these contentions would be classic examples of incorrect expectations precipitating dress identity misperceptions. On the contrary, I would instead conclude that John's Jesus is wearing dress indicative of the high priest: over the hyacinthine ποδήρης he wears a golden ζώνη, equivalent to the high-priestly belt/sash which Josephus described as being intricately interwoven with gold.

Metonymical or synecdochical use of dress imagery in Rev 1 should not be ignored or discounted. John may well have used ζώνη metonymically or synecdochically to encompass the high-priestly ζώνη, ephod, and even breastplate, since they could be visually perceived to be attached to each other.[60] Such sartorial metonymy or synecdoche remains probable in several texts in the LXX and Philo.[61] The ποδήρης and the ζώνη would thus *not* have necessarily presented an incomplete and thus disconfirming depiction of Jesus as high priest.

Moreover, not all of Revelation's characters are, so to speak, "fully clothed." John portrays other characters in his work with what appears like an incomplete dress ensemble. For instance, John's sartorial description of the sixth plague's two hundred million horsemen includes only their breastplates colored in fire, hyacinth, and sulphur (9:16–17). Similarly, John describes the one "like a son of man" in 14:14 with only a golden crown or wreath on his head and a sharp sickle in his hand; certainly he

---

60. William H. C. Propp hypothesizes that the Old Testament "woven-band" may have been part of what constituted the ephod itself (i.e., "woven-band" + two shoulder-pieces); see his discussion in *Exodus 19–40: A New Translation with Introduction and Commentary*, AB 2A (New York: Doubleday, 2006), 436.

61. See LXX (Exod 25:7; 35:9) and Philo (*Her.* 176; *Leg.* 1.81; *Mut.* 43; *QE* 1.107–108; *Somn.* 1.216; see also *Mos.* 2.109–110) and the discussion in Winkle, "Clothes," 164–67 and 185–90. For another similar, apparently incomplete, priestly dress catalogue, see Ezek 44:17–19, where the only priestly garments mentioned are linen turbans and undergarments. Note also the incomplete references to high-priestly attire in 4Q405 23 II, 1–10, which list ephodim, the band of the ephod, and possibly the head ornament; see the discussion in Crispin H. T. Fletcher-Louis, *All the Glory of Adam: Liturgical Anthropology in the Dead Sea Scrolls*, STDJ 42 (Leiden: Brill, 2002), 356–73. See also Roy Gane and the literature he cites on the use of the *pars pro toto* principle (in which a part is taken for the whole) within the Israelite cult (*Cult and Character: Purification Offerings, Day of Atonement, and Theodicy* [Winona Lake, IN: Eisenbrauns, 2005], 190 n. 102).

would be wearing more than this, since the shame of nakedness is a concern elsewhere for John (3:18; 16:15). One must understand these clearly incomplete sartorial descriptions as purposely partial, and metonymical or synecdochical in nature. A similar understanding of the sartorial portrayal in Rev 1 would not only be prudent and reasonable but also useful in explaining the role-related identity of Jesus.

Conclusion

The Epistle to the Hebrews is the only New Testament document that explicitly states that Jesus has a role-related identity as high priest. But clothing and dress can implicitly communicate role-related identity as well. In the book of Revelation, a work that, like Hebrews, also utilizes cultic terminology and concepts, two dress elements in Rev 1:13 are indicative of a high-priestly, role-related identity for Jesus: the foot-length robe and the golden belt/sash.[62] Of these two, I would suggest that the foot-length robe strongly indicates high-priestly imagery, while at the same time not suggesting Yom Kippur or Day of Atonement concerns on account of its implied hyacinthine color. In fact, I believe it is the salient, foreground dress element indicating such an identity because of its textual prominence as the first dress element John sees in this vision. On the other hand, the golden belt/sash possibly indicates high-priestly identity, but more likely as a subsidiary or background dress indicator that supports the dress element of the foot-length robe.

Jesus as high priest in the book of Revelation? On the basis of the sartorial references in Rev 1:13, I would suggest an affirmative response. This particular dress imagery consequently provides arguable evidence that the cultic concerns regarding the high-priestly identity of Jesus in the Epistle to the Hebrews are not unique within the New Testament.

---

62. For a detailed discussion of another possible high-priestly dress image for Jesus in Rev 1:15 with reference to the enigmatic term χαλκολιβάνῳ ("bronze" NIV; "burnished bronze" ESV, NASB, NRSV), see Winkle, "Clothes," 325–56.

Bibliography

Achtemeier, Paul J. *1 Peter: A Commentary on First Peter*. Hermeneia. Minneapolis: Fortress, 1996.
Adler, Yonatan. "The Ritual Baths near the Temple Mount and Extra-Purification before Entering the Temple Courts: A Reply to Eyal Regev." *IEJ* 56 (2006): 209–15.
Allen, Leslie C. *The Books of Joel, Obadiah, Jonah, and Micah*. NICOT. Grand Rapids: Eerdmans, 1976.
Andersen, Francis I., and A. Dean Forbes. *Spelling in the Hebrew Bible*. BibOr41. Rome: Biblical Institute Press, 1986.
Andersen, Francis I., and David N. Freedman. *Amos: A New Translation with Notes and Commentary*. AB 24A. New York: Doubleday, 1989.
———. *Hosea: A New Translation with Introduction and Commentary*. AB 24. Garden City, NY: Doubleday, 1980.
———. *Micah: A New Translation with Introduction and Commentary*. AB 24E. New York: Doubleday, 2000.
Anderson, Lewis O. "The Michael Figure in the Book of Daniel." PhD diss., Andrews University, 1997.
Anderson, Megory, and Philip Culbertson, "The Inadequacy of the Christian Doctrine of Atonement in Light of Levitical Sin Offering." *AThR* 68 (1986): 303–28.
Aquinas, Thomas. *Summa Theologica*. Translated by Fathers of the English Dominican Province. 3 vols. New York: Benziger, 1947–1948. http://tinyurl.com/SBL0393a.
Armstrong, John. *The Idea of Holiness and the Humane Response: A Study of the Concept of Holiness and Its Social Consequences*. London: Allen & Unwin, 1981.
Astell, Ann W., and Sandor Goodhart, eds. *Sacrifice, Scripture, and Substitution: Readings in Ancient Judaism and Christianity*. CJA 18. Notre Dame: University of Notre Dame Press, 2011.

Auld, A. Graeme. *I and II Samuel: A Commentary*. OTL. Louisville: Westminster John Knox, 2011.
Aune, David E. *Revelation 1–5*. WBC 52A. Dallas: Word, 1997.
———. *Revelation 6–16*. WBC 52B. Nashville: Nelson, 1998.
———. *Revelation 17–22*. WBC 52C. Nashville: Nelson, 1998.
Bähr, Karl C. W. F. *Symbolik des Mosaischen Cultus*. 2 vols. Heidelberg: Mohr, 1837–1839.
Baigent, John W. "Jesus as Priest: An Examination of the Claim That the Concept of Jesus as Priest May Be Found in the New Testament Outside the Epistle to the Hebrews," *VE* 12 (1981): 34–44.
Bailey, Daniel P. "Jesus as the Mercy Seat: The Semantics and Theology of Paul's Use of Hilasterion in Romans 3:25." PhD diss., University of Cambridge, 1999.
Bandy, Alan S. *The Prophetic Lawsuit in the Book of Revelation*. NTM 29. Sheffield: Sheffield Phoenix, 2010.
Barker, Margaret. *The Gate of Heaven: The History and Symbolism of the Temple in Jerusalem*. London: SPCK, 1991. Repr., Sheffield: Sheffield Phoenix, 2008.
———. *The Great High Priest: The Temple Roots of Christian Liturgy*. London: T&T Clark, 2003.
———. *The Revelation of Jesus Christ: Which God Gave to Him to Show to His Servants What Must Soon Take Place (Revelation 1.1)*. Edinburgh: T&T Clark, 2000.
Barnard, Malcolm. *Fashion as Communication*. 2nd ed. London: Routledge, 2002.
Barr, James. *The Variable Spellings of the Hebrew Bible*. Schweich Lectures 1986. Oxford: Oxford University Press, 1989.
Barrett, C. K. "Paul and the 'Pillar' Apostles." Pages 1–19 in *Studia Paulina in honorem Johannis De Zwann Septuagenarii*. Edited by J. N. Sevenster and W. C. van Unnik. Haarlem: Bohn, 1953.
Barstad, Hans M. *The Myth of the Empty Land: A Study in the History and Archaeology of Judah during the "Exilic" Period*. Oslo: Scandinavian University Press, 1996.
———. *The Religious Polemics of Amos: Studies in the Preaching of Am 2, 7B-8; 4,1-13; 5,1-27; 6, 4-7; 8, 14*. VTSup 34. Leiden: Brill, 1984.
Barth, Gerhard. *Der Tod Jesu Christi im Verständnis des Neuen Testaments*. Neukirchen-Vluyn: Neukirchener Verlag, 1992.
Barth, Markus. *Ephesians 1–3: Introduction, Translation and Commentary on Chapters 1–3*. AB 34. Garden City, NY: Doubleday, 1974.

Barton, John. "The Prophets and the Cult." Pages 111–22 in *Temple and Worship in Biblical Israel*. Edited by John Day. LHBOTS 422. London: T&T Clark, 2005.

Basson, Alec. "'Friends Becoming Foes': A Case of Social Rejection in Psalm 31." *VEccl* 27 (2006): 398–415.

Batten, Alicia J., Carly Daniel-Hughes, and Kristi Upson-Saia. "Introduction: 'What Shall We Wear?'" Pages 1–18 in *Dressing Judeans and Christians in Antiquity*. Edited by Kristi Upson-Saia, Carly Daniel-Hughes, and Alicia J. Batten. Farnham, UK: Ashgate, 2014.

Bauckham, Richard. *The Theology of the Book of Revelation*. NTT. Cambridge: Cambridge University Press, 1993.

Bauer, W., F. W. Danker, W. F. Arndt, and F. W. Gingrich. *Greek-English Lexicon of the New Testament and Other Early Christian Literature*. 3rd ed. Chicago: University of Chicago Press, 2000.

Baumeister, Theofried. *Die Anfänge der Theologie des Martyriums*. MBT 45. Münster: Aschendorff, 1980.

Baumgarten, Albert I. "Setting the Outer Limits: Temple Policy in the Centuries Prior to Destruction." Pages 88–103 in *Redefining First-Century Jewish and Christian Identities: Essays in Honor of E. P. Sanders*. Edited by Fabian E. Udoh, Susannah Heschel, Mark A. Chancey, and Gregory Tatum. CJA 16. Notre Dame: University of Notre Dame Press, 2008.

Baumgarten, Joseph M. "The Law and Spirit of Purity at Qumran." Pages 93–105 in *The Dead Sea Scrolls and the Qumran Community*. Vol. 2 of *The Bible and the Dead Sea Scrolls: The Second Princeton Symposium on Judaism and Christian Origins*. Edited by James H. Charlesworth. Waco, TX: Baylor University Press, 2006.

———. "The Purification Liturgies." Pages 200–212 in vol. 2 of *The Dead Sea Scrolls after Fifty Years: A Comprehensive Assessment*. Edited by Peter W. Flint and James C. Vanderkam. Leiden: Brill, 1998.

———. "Some 'Qumranic' Observations on the Aramaic Levi Document." Pages 393–401 in *Sefer Moshe: The Moshe Weinfeld Jubilee Volume; Studies in the Bible and the Ancient Near East, Qumran, and Post-Biblical Judaism*. Edited by Chaim Cohen, Avi Hurvitz, and Shalom Paul. Winona Lake, IN: Eisenbrauns, 2004.

———. "Tohorot." Pages 83–92 in *Qumran Cave 4. XXV: Halakhic Texts*. Edited by Joseph M. Baumgarten et al. DJD 35. Oxford: Clarendon, 1999.

———. "Yom Kippur in the Qumran Scrolls and Second Temple Sources." *DSD* 6 (1999): 184–91.

Baumgarten, Linda. *What Clothes Reveal: The Language of Clothing in Colonial and Federal America; The Colonial Williamsburg Collection.* Williamsburg Decorative Arts Series. Williamsburg, VA: The Colonial Williamsburg Foundation, 2002.

Beale, G. K. *1–2 Thessalonians.* IVPNTC 13. Downers Grove, IL: InterVarsity Press, 2003.

———. *The Book of Revelation: A Commentary on the Greek Text.* NIGTC. Grand Rapids: Eerdmans, 1999.

———. *The Temple and the Church's Mission: A Biblical Theology of the Dwelling Place of God.* NSBT 17. Leicester: Apollos, 2004.

Beasley-Murray, G. R. *The Book of Revelation.* NCB. London: Marshall, Morgan & Scott, 1978. Repr., Grand Rapids: Eerdmans, 1981.

Bechtel, Lyn M. "Shame as a Sanction of Social Control in Biblical Israel: Judicial, Political, and Social Shaming." *JSOT* 16 (1991): 47–76.

Becking, Bob, and Meindert Dijkstra, eds. *On Reading Prophetic Texts: Gender-Specific and Related Studies in Memory of Fokkelien van Dijk-Hemmes.* BibInt 18. Leiden: Brill, 1996.

Beckwith, Roger T., and Martin J. Selman, eds. *Sacrifice in the Bible.* Carlisle: Paternoster, 1995.

Benjamin, Don C. "An Anthropology of Prophecy." *BTB* 21 (1991): 135–44.

Bergen, Wesley J. *Reading Ritual: Leviticus in Postmodern Culture.* JSOTSup 417. New York: T&T Clark, 2005.

Bergman, Jan, and Benjamin Kedar-Kopfstein. "דָּם." *TDOT* 3:234–50.

Best, Ernest. *Ephesians.* ICC. Edinburgh: T&T Clark, 1998.

Betz, Hans Dieter, ed. *Religion in Geschichte und Gegenwart.* 4th ed. Tübingen: Mohr Siebeck, 1998–2007.

Bibb, Bryan D. "The Prophetic Critique of Ritual in Old Testament Theology." Pages 31–43 in *The Priests in the Prophets: The Portrayal of Priests, Prophets and Other Religious Specialists in the Latter Prophets.* Edited by Lester L. Grabbe and Alice Ogden Bellis. JSOTSup 408. London: T&T Clark, 2004.

———. *Ritual Words and Narrative Worlds in Leviticus.* LHBOTS 480. New York: T&T Clark, 2009.

Blenkinsopp, Joseph. *Isaiah 1–39: A New Translation with Introduction and Commentary.* AB 19. New York: Doubleday, 2000.

———. *Isaiah 56–66: A New Translation with Introduction and Commentary.* AB 19B. New York: Doubleday, 2003.

———. *A History of Prophecy in Israel.* 2nd ed. Louisville: Westminster John Knox, 1996.

Blount, Brian K. *Revelation: A Commentary*. NTL. Louisville: Westminster John Knox, 2009.
Böcher, Otto. "Johannes der Täufer." *TRE* 17:172–181.
Böckler, Annette M. "Unser Vater." Pages 249–261 in *Metaphor in the Hebrew Bible*. Edited by Pierre Van Hecke. BETL 187. Leuven: Peeters, 2005.
Bohak, Gideon. *Ancient Jewish Magic: A History*. Cambridge: Cambridge University Press, 2008.
Bonfante, Larissa. "Classical Nudity in Italy and Greece." Pages 271–93 in *Ancient Italy in Its Mediterranean Setting: Studies in Honour of Ellen Macnamara*. Edited by David Ridgway, Francesca R. Serra Ridgway, Mark Pearce, Edward Herring, Ruth Whitehouse, and John Wilkins. Accordia Specialist Studies on the Mediterranean 4. London: Accordia Research Institute, University of London, 2000.
———. "Nudity as a Costume in Classical Art." *AJA* 93 (1989): 543–70.
Borg, Marcus. *Jesus in Contemporary Scholarship*. Valley Forge, PA: Trinity Press International, 1994.
Boring, M. Eugene. *An Introduction to the New Testament: History, Literature, Theology*. Louisville: Westminster John Knox, 2012.
Botha, P. J. "Honour and Shame as Keys to the Interpretation of Malachi." *OTE* 14 (2001): 392– 403.
Botterweck, G. Johannes, and Helmer Ringgren, eds. *Theological Dictionary of the Old Testament*. Trans. John T. Wills et al. 15 vols. Grand Rapids: Eerdmans, 1974–2006.
Böttrich, Christfried. "Jesus und der Feigenbaum: Mk 11:12–14, 20–25 in der Diskussion." *NovT* 39 (1997): 328–59.
Bourdillon, M. F. C., and Meyer Fortes, eds. *Sacrifice*. London: Academic Press, 1980.
Braun, Joachim. *Music in Ancient Israel/Palestine: Archaeological, Written, and Comparative Sources*. Grand Rapids: Eerdmans, 2002.
Brettler, Marc Zvi. *God Is King: Understanding an Israelite Metaphor*. JSOTSup 76. Sheffield: JSOT Press, 1989.
Breytenbach, Cilliers. "'Christus starb für uns': Zur Tradition und paulinischen Rezeption der sogenannten 'Sterbeformeln.'" *NTS* 49 (2003): 447–75.
———. "Gnädigstimmen und opferkultische Sühne im Urchristentum und seiner Umwelt." Pages 217–243 in *Opfer: Theologische und kulturelle Kontexte*. Edited by Bernd Janowski and Michael Welker. STW 1454. Frankfurt am Main: Suhrkamp, 2000.

———. "Versöhnung, Stellvertretung und Sühne: Semantische und traditionsgeschichtliche Bemerkungen am Beispiel der paulinischen Briefe." NTS 39 (1993): 59–79.

———. *Versöhnung: Eine Studie zur paulinischen Soteriologie*. WMANT 60. Neukirchen-Vluyn: Neukirchener Verlag, 1989.

Briggs, Robert A. *Jewish Temple Imagery in the Book of Revelation*. StBibLit 10. New York: Lang, 1999.

Bright, John. *Jeremiah: A New Translation with Introduction and Commentary*. AB 21. New York: Doubleday, 1965.

Brighton, L. A. *Revelation*. ConcC. Saint Louis: Concordia, 1999.

Brockelmann, Carl. *Hebräische Syntax*. Neukirchen-Vluyn: Neukirchener Verlag, 1956.

Brongers, H. A. "Die metaphorische Verwendung von Termini für die Kleidung von Göttern und Menschen in der Bibel und im Alten Orient." Pages 61–74 in *Von Kanaan bis Kerala: Festschrift für Prof. Mag. Dr. Dr. J. P. M. van der Ploeg OP zur Vollendung des siebzigsten Lebensjahres am 4. Juli 1979; Überreicht von Kollegen, Freunden und Schülern*. Edited by Edited by W. C. Delsman, J. T. Nelis, J. R. T. M. Peters, W. H. Ph. Römer, and A. S. van der Woude. AOAT 211. Kevelaer: Butzon & Bercker; Neukirchen-Vluyn: Neukirchener Verlag, 1982.

Brooke, George J. "Miqdash Adam, Eden and the Qumran Community." Pages 285–301 in *Gemeinde ohne Tempel: Zur Substituierung und Transformation des Jerusalemer Tempels und seines Kults im Alten Testament, antiken Judentum und frühen Christentum*. Edited by Beate Ego, Armin Lange, and Peter Pilhofer. WUNT 118. Tübingen: Mohr Siebeck, 1999.

———. *Exegesis at Qumran: 4QFlorilegium in Its Jewish Context*. JSOTSup 29. Sheffield: JSOT Press, 1985.

Brooks, Walter E. "The Perpetuity of Christ's Sacrifice in the Epistle to the Hebrews." *JBL* 89 (1970): 205–14.

Brown, Francis, Samuel R. Driver, and Charles A. Briggs. *A Hebrew and English Lexicon of the Old Testament*. Oxford: Clarendon, 1907.

Brown, Raymond. *An Introduction to the Gospel of John*. Edited by Francis J. Moloney. ABRL. New York: Doubleday, 2003.

Brown, Stephen G. "The Intertextuality of Isaiah 66.17 and 2 Thessalonians 2.7: A Solution for the 'Restrainer' Problem." Pages 254–77 in *Paul and the Scriptures of Israel*. Edited by Craig A. Evans and James A. Sanders. JSNTSup 83. Sheffield: JSOT Press, 1993.

Brown, William H. "From Holy War to Holy Martyrdom." Pages 281–92 in *The Quest for the Kingdom of God: Studies in Honor of George E. Mendenhall*. Edited by Herbert B. Huffmon, Frank A. Spina, and Alberto R. Green. Winona Lake, IN: Eisenbrauns, 1983.

Bruce, F. F. *The Epistle to the Galatians: A Commentary on the Greek Text*. NIGTC. Grand Rapids: Eerdmans, 1982.

Brueggemann, Walter. *Isaiah 1–39*. WesBibComp. Louisville: Westminster John Knox, 1998.

———. *To Pluck up, to Tear down: A Commentary on the Book of Jeremiah 1–25*. ITC. Grand Rapids: Eerdmans, 1988.

Brueggemann, Walter, Sharon D. Parks, and Thomas H. Groome. *To Act Justly, Love Tenderly, Walk Humbly: An Agenda for Ministers*. New York: Paulist, 1986.

Bruzzi, Stella. *Undressing Cinema: Clothing and Identity in the Movies*. London: Routledge, 1997.

Bultmann, Rudolf. *Neues Testament und Mythologie: Das Problem der Entmythologisierung der neutestamentlichen Verkündigung*. Edited by Eberhard Jüngel. BEvTh 96. Munich: Kaiser, 1988.

Burkert, Walter. *Kulte des Altertums: Biologische Grundlagen der Religion*. Munich: Beck, 1998.

———. *Homo Necans: The Anthropology of Ancient Greek Sacrificial Ritual and Myth*. Translated by Peter Bing. Berkeley: University of California Press, 1983.

———. *Homo Necans: Interpretationen altgriechischer Opferriten und Mythen*. RVV 32. Berlin: de Gruyter, 1972.

Burman, Barbara, and Carole Turbin. "Introduction: Material Strategies Engendered." *G&H* 14 (2002): 371–81.

Caird, G. B. *A Commentary on the Revelation of St. John the Divine*. HNTC. New York: Harper & Row, 1966.

Calabro, David. "Inalienable Possession in Early Egypto-Semitic Genitive Constructions." *QVO* 12 (2017): 91–106.

Calefato, Patrizia. *The Clothed Body*. Translated by Lisa Adams. Dress, Body, Culture. Oxford: Berg, 2004.

Calhoun, Robert Matthew. *Paul's Definitions of the Gospel in Romans 1*. WUNT 2/316. Tübingen: Mohr Siebeck, 2011.

Calvin, Jean. *Institution de la religion chrestienne: en laquelle est comprinse une somme de pieté, et quasi tout ce qui est necessaire a congnoistre en la doctrine de salut; Quatrième livre: L'existence de l'Église*. Geneva: Du Bois, 1541.

Campbell, Douglas A. *The Deliverance of God: An Apocalyptic Rereading of Justification in Paul*. Grand Rapids: Eerdmans, 2009.
Canavan, Rosemary. *Clothing the Body of Christ at Colossae: A Visual Construction of Identity*. WUNT 2/334. Tübingen: Mohr Siebeck, 2012.
Carey, Greg. Review of *Ritual and Metaphor: Sacrifice in the Bible*, Christian A. Eberhart, ed. *RBL* 7/2012. http://tinyurl.com/SBL0393b.
Carmichael, Calum M. "Forbidden Mixtures." *VT* 32 (1982): 394–415.
Carrell, Peter R. *Jesus and the Angels: Angelology and the Christology of the Apocalypse of John*. SNTSMS 95. Cambridge: Cambridge University Press, 1997.
Carroll, Robert P. "Halfway through a Dark Wood: Reflections on Jeremiah 25." Pages 73–86 in *Troubling Jeremiah*. Edited by A. R. P. Diamond, Kathleen M. O'Connor, and Louis Stulman. JSOTSup 260. Sheffield: Sheffield Academic, 1999.
———. *Jeremiah: A Commentary*. OTL. London: SCM, 1986.
Casas, Bartholomé de las. *In Defense of the Indians: The Defense of the Most Reverend Lord, Don Fray Bartolomé de las Casas, of the Order of Preachers, Late Bishop of Chiapa, against the Persecutors and Slanderers of the Peoples of the New World Discovered across the Seas*. Translated by Stafford Poole. DeKalb: Northern Illinois University Press, 1974.
Cassin, Elena. *La splendeur divine: Introduction à l'étude de la mentalité mésopotamienne*. CeS 8. Paris: Mouton, 1968.
Charles, R. H. *A Critical and Exegetical Commentary on the Revelation of St. John*. ICC 44. Edinburgh: T&T Clark, 1920.
Charlesworth, James H. "John the Baptizer and Qumran Barriers in Light of the Rule of the Community." Pages 353–78 in *The Provo International Conference on the Dead Sea Scrolls: Technological Innovations, New Texts, and Reformulated Issues*. Edited by Donald W. Parry and Eugene Ulrich. STDJ 30. Leiden: Brill, 1999.
Chester, A. N. "Hebrews: the Final Sacrifice." Pages 57–72 in *Sacrifice and Redemption: Durham Essays in Theology*. Edited by S. W. Sykes. Cambridge: Cambridge University Press, 1991.
Childs, Brevard S. *Isaiah*. OTL. Louisville: Westminster John Knox, 2001.
Chilton, Bruce. *The Temple of Jesus: His Sacrificial Program Within a Cultural History of Sacrifice*. University Park: Pennsylvania State University Press, 1992.
———. "Yohanan the Purifier and His Immersion." *TJT* 14.2 (1998): 197–212.

Clements, Ronald Ernest. *Isaiah 1–39*. NCBC. London: Marshall, Morgan & Scott, 1980.

Clines, David J. A., ed. *Dictionary of Classical Hebrew*. 9 vols. Sheffield: Sheffield Phoenix Press, 1993–2014.

Cohen, Shaye J. D. *From The Maccabees to the Mishnah*. 2nd ed. Louisville: Westminster John Knox, 2006.

Collins, Adela Yarbro. *Crisis and Catharsis: The Power of the Apocalypse*. Philadelphia: Westminster, 1984.

———. "The Son of Man Tradition and the Book of Revelation." Pages 536–568 in *The Messiah: Developments in Earliest Judaism and Christianity*. Edited by James H. Charlesworth. Minneapolis: Fortress, 1992.

Collins, John J. *Beyond the Qumran Community: The Sectarian Movement of the Dead Sea Scrolls*. Grand Rapids: Eerdmans, 2010.

———. *Daniel: A Commentary on the Book of Daniel*. Hermeneia. Minneapolis: Fortress, 1993.

———. "Prayer and the Meaning of Ritual." Pages 69–85 in *Prayer and Poetry in the Dead Sea Scrolls and Related Literature: Essays in Honor of Eileen Schuller on the Occasion of Her 65th Birthday*. Edited by Jeremy Penner, Ken M. Penner, and Cecilia Wassen. STDJ 98. Leiden: Brill, 2012.

Comblin, Joseph. "La liturgie de la Nouvelle Jérusalem (Apoc., XXI, 1–XXII, 5)." *ETL* 29 (1953): 5–40.

Considine, Patrick. "The Theme of Divine Wrath in Ancient East Mediterranean Literature." *SMEA* 8 (1969): 85–159.

Coppens, Joseph. "Le messianisme sacerdotal dans les écrits du Nouveau Testament." Pages 101–112 in *La venue du Messie: Messianisme et eschatologie*. Edited by Édouard Massaux. RechBib 6. Bruges: de Brouwer, 1962.

Coxon, Peter W. "Smith, William Robertson." *TRE* 31:407–9.

Craigie, Peter C., Page H. Kelley, and Joel F. Drinkard, Jr. *Jeremiah 1–25*. WBC 26. Waco, TX: Word, 1991.

Craik, Jennifer. *Uniforms Exposed: From Conformity to Transgression*. Dress, Body, Culture. Oxford: Berg, 2005.

Crane, Diana. *Fashion and Its Social Agendas: Class, Gender, and Identity in Clothing*. Chicago: University of Chicago Press, 2000.

Creason, Stuart. "*PQD* Revisited." Pages 27–42 in *Studies in Semitic and Afroasiatic Linguistics Presented to Gene B. Gragg*. Edited by Cynthia L. Miller. SAOC 60. Chicago: Oriental Institute of the University of Chicago, 2007.

Cross, Frank Moore. "Kinship and Covenant in Ancient Israel." Pages 3–21 in *From Epic to Canon: History and Literature in Ancient Israel*. Baltimore: Johns Hopkins University Press, 1998.

Crossan, John Dominic. *The Historical Jesus: The Life of a Mediterranean Jewish Peasant*. San Francisco: HarperSanFrancisco, 1992.

Culham, Phyllis. "Again, What Meaning Lies in Colour!" *ZPE* 64 (1986): 235–45.

Cummins, Stephen Anthony. *Paul and the Crucified Christ in Antioch: Maccabean Martyrdom and Galatians 1 and 2*. SNTSMS 114. Cambridge: Cambridge University Press, 2000.

Cunningham, Valentine. "If the Cap Fits: Figuring the Space of the Human." Pages 45–63 in *The Anthropological Turn in Literary Studies*. Edited by Jürgen Schlaeger. YREAL 12. Tübingen: Narr, 1996.

Damhorst, Mary Lynn. "Dress as Nonverbal Communication." Pages 67–80 in *The Meanings of Dress*. Edited by Mary Lynn Damhorst, Kimberly A. Miller-Spillman, and Susan O. Michelman. 2nd ed. New York: Fairchild, 2005.

———. "In Search of a Common Thread: Classification of Information Communicated Through Dress." *CTRJ* 8.2 (1990): 1–12.

Daniel, Suzanne. *Recherches sur le vocabulaire du culte dans la Septante*. EeC 61. Paris: Klincksieck, 1966.

Daschke, Dereck. *City of Ruins: Mourning the Destruction of Jerusalem through Jewish Apocalypse*. BibInt 99. Leiden; Boston: Brill, 2010.

Davila, James. "Heavenly Ascents in the Dead Sea Scrolls." Pages 461–85 in vol. 2 of *The Dead Sea Scrolls after Fifty Years: A Comprehensive Assessment*. Edited by Peter W. Flint and James C. Vanderkam. Leiden: Brill, 1999.

Davis, Fred. *Fashion, Culture, and Identity*. Chicago: University of Chicago Press, 1992.

Day, John. *God's Conflict with the Dragon and the Sea: Echoes of a Canaanite Myth in the Old Testament*. UCOP 35. Cambridge: Cambridge University Press, 1985.

De Troyer, Kristin. "Blood: A Threat to Holiness or towards (another) Holiness?" Pages 45–64 in *Wholly Woman, Holy Blood: A Feminist Critique of Purity and Impurity*. Edited by Kristin De Troyer, Judith A. Herbert, Judith Ann Johnson, and Anne-Narie Korte. SAC. Harrisburg, PA: Trinity Press International, 2003.

DesCamp, Mary Therese, and Eve E. Sweetser. "Metaphors for God: Why and How Do Our Choices Matter for Humans? The Application of

Contemporary Cognitive Linguistics Research to the Debate on God and Metaphor." *PastPsy* 53 (2005): 207–38.

DeSilva, David Arthur. *4 Maccabees: Introduction and Commentary on the Greek Text in Codex Sinaiticus*. BSCS. Leiden: Brill, 2006.

Detienne, Marcel. "Pratiques culinaires et esprit de sacrifice." Pages 7–35 in *La cuisine du sacrifice en pays grec*. Edited by Marcel Detienne and Jean-Pierre Vernant. Bibliothèque des histoires. Paris: Gallimard, 1979.

Dierichs, Angelika. *Von der Götter Geburt und der Frauen Niederkunft*. KAW 82. Mainz: von Zabern, 2002.

Dietrich, Manfried. "Trumpet Snails and Purple Snails as an Indication of the Transfer of Religion and Technology in the Eastern-Mediterranean Region." Pages 35–58 in *Homeland and Exile: Biblical and Ancient Near Eastern Studies in Honour of Bustenay Oded*. Edited by Gershon Galil, Mark Geller, and Alan Millard. VTSup 130. Leiden: Brill, 2009.

Dille, Sarah J. "Honor Restored: Honor, Shame and God as Redeeming Kinsman in Second Isaiah." Pages 232–50 in *Relating to the Text: Interdisciplinary and Form-Critical Insights on the Bible*. Edited by Timothy J. Sandoval and Carleen Mandolfo. JSOTSup 384. London: T&T Clark, 2003.

Dimant, Devorah. "4QFlorilegium and the Idea of the Community as Temple." Pages 165–89 in *Hellenica et Judaica: Hommage à Valentin Nikiprowetzky*. Edited by André Caquot, Mireille Hadas-Lebel, and J. Riaud. Leuven: Peeters, 1986.

Douglas, Mary. "The Go-Away Goat." Pages 121–41 in *The Book of Leviticus: Composition and Reception*. Edited by Robert A. Kugler and Rolf Rendtorff. VTSup 93. Leiden; Boston: Brill, 2003.

———. "Poetic Structure in Leviticus." Pages 239–56 in *Pomegranates and Golden Bells: Studies in Biblical, Jewish, and Near Eastern Ritual, Law, and Literature in Honor of Jacob Milgrom*. Edited by David P. Wright, David Noel Freedman, and Avi Hurvitz. Winona Lake, IN: Eisenbrauns, 1995.

Doukhan, Jacques. *Secrets of Daniel: Wisdom and Dreams of a Jewish Prince in Exile*. Hagerstown, MD: Review and Herald, 2000.

Downing, J. "Jesus and Martyrdom." *JTS* 14 (1963): 279–93.

Draper, J. A. "The Twelve Apostles as Foundation Stones of the Heavenly Jerusalem and the Foundation of the Qumran Community." *Neot* 22 (1988): 41–63.

Drexler, Joseph. *Die Illusion des Opfers: Ein wissenschaftlicher Überblick über die wichtigsten Opfertheorien ausgehend vom deleuzianischen Polyperspektivismusmodell*. Münchener Ethnologische Abhandlungen 12. Munich: Akademischer Verlag, 1993.

Dunn, James D. G. *Romans 1–8*. WBC 38A. Dallas: Word, 1988.

Dunnill, John. Review of *Ritual and Metaphor: Sacrifice in the Bible*, Christian A. Eberhart, ed. *RBL* 7/2012. http://tinyurl.com/SBL0393c.

Duran, Nicole Wilkinson. *The Power of Disorder: Ritual Elements in Mark's Passion Narrative*. LNTS 378. New York: T&T Clark, 2008.

Eberhart, Christian A. "Atonement: II. New Testament." *EBR* 3:32–42.

———. "Blood I. Ancient Near East and Hebrew Bible/Old Testament." *EBR* 4:201–12.

———. "Characteristics of Sacrificial Metaphors in Hebrews." Pages 37–64 in *Hebrews: Contemporary Methods, New Insights*. Edited by Gabriella Gelardini. BibInt 75. Leiden: Brill, 2005.

———. *Kultmetaphorik und Christologie: Opfer- und Sühneterminologie im Neuen Testament*. WUNT 306. Tübingen: Mohr Siebeck, 2013.

———. "A Neglected Feature of Sacrifice in the Hebrew Bible: Remarks on the Burning Rite on the Altar." *HTR* 97 (2004): 485–93.

———. "Qorban." *WiBiLex*. Stuttgart: Deutsche Bibelgesellschaft, 2010. http://tinyurl.com/SBL0393d.

———. "Sacrifice? Holy Smoke! Reflections on Cult Terminology for Understanding Sacrifice in the Hebrew Bible." Pages 17–32 in *Ritual and Metaphor: Sacrifice in the Bible*. Edited by Christian A. Eberhart. RBS 68. Atlanta: Society of Biblical Literature, 2011.

———. "Schlachtung/Schächtung." *WiBiLex*. Stuttgart: Deutsche Bibelgesellschaft, 2006. http://tinyurl.com/SBL0393e.

———. *Studien zur Bedeutung der Opfer im Alten Testament: Die Signifikanz von Blut- und Verbrennungsriten im kultischen Rahmen*. WMANT 94. Neukirchen-Vluyn: Neukirchener Verlag, 2002.

Ehrhardt, Arnold. "Jewish and Christian Ordination." *JEH* 5 (1954): 125–38.

Eicher, Joanne B. "The Anthropology of Dress." *Dress* 27 (2000): 59–70.

Eicher, Joanne B., and Sandra Lee Evenson, eds. *The Visible Self: Global Perspectives on Dress, Culture, and Society*. 4th ed. New York: Fairchild, 2015.

Eidevall, Göran. *Sacrificial Rhetoric in the Prophetic Literature in the Hebrew Bible*. Lewiston, NY: Mellen, 2012.

Eisenstadt, Samuel N., and Luis Roniger. *Patrons, Clients and Friends: Interpersonal Relations and the Structure of Trust in Society*. Themes in the Social Sciences. New York: Cambridge University Press, 1984.

Ellens, Deborah L. *Women in the Sex Texts of Leviticus and Deuteronomy: A Comparative Conceptual Analysis*. LHBOTS 458. New York: T&T Clark, 2008.

Ellingworth, Paul. *The Epistle to the Hebrews: A Commentary on the Greek Text*. NIGTC. Grand Rapids: Eerdmans, 1993.

Elliott, John H. *1 Peter: A New Translation with Introduction and Commentary*. AB 37B. New York: Doubleday, 2000.

Erbele-Küster, Dorothea. "Blutschuld." *WiBiLex*. Stuttgart: Deutsche Bibelgesellschaft, 2015. http://tinyurl.com/SBL0393f.

———. "Die Körperbestimmungen in Leviticus 11–15." Pages 209–23 in *Menschenbilder und Körperkonzepte im Alten Israel, Ägypten und im Alten Orient*. Edited by Angelika Berlejung, Jan Dietrich, and Joachim F. Quack. ORA 9. Tübingen: Mohr Siebeck, 2012.

———. "Gender and Cult: 'Pure' and 'Impure' as Gender-Relevant Categories." Pages 375–406 in *Torah*. Edited by Irmtraud Fischer and Mercedes Navarro Puerto. BW 1. Atlanta: Society of Biblical Literature, 2011.

———. *Körper und Geschlecht: Studien zur Anthropologie von Leviticus 12 und 15*. WMANT 121. Neukirchen-Vluyn: Neukirchener Verlag, 2008.

———. "Reading as an Act of Offering: Reconsidering the Genre of Leviticus 1." Pages 34–46 in *The Actuality of Sacrifice: Past and Present*. Edited by Alberdina Houtman, Marcel Poorthuis, Joshua Schwartz, and Joseph Aaron Turner. JCPS 28. Leiden: Brill, 2014.

Eshel, Esther. "Apotropaic Prayers in the Second Temple Period." Pages 69–88 in *Liturgical Perspectives: Prayer and Poetry in Light of the Dead Sea Scrolls: Proceedings of the Fifth International Symposium of the Orion Center for the Study of the Dead Sea Scrolls and Associated Literature, 19–23 January, 2000*. Edited by Esther G. Chazon. STDJ 48. Leiden: Brill, 2003.

Evans, Gillian R. "Anselm von Canterbury." *RGG4* 1:515–16.

Evenson, Sandra Lee. "Dress and Identity." Pages 10:52–58 of *Berg Encyclopedia of World Dress and Fashion*. Edited by Joanne B. Eicher and Phyllis B. Tortora. Oxford: Berg, 2010.

Falk, Daniel K. "Festivals and Holy Days." Pages 636–45 in *The Eerdmans*

Dictionary of Early Judaism. Edited by John J. Collins and Daniel C. Harlow. Grand Rapids: Eerdmans, 2010.

———. "Qumran Prayer Texts and the Temple." Pages 106–26 in *Sapiential, Liturgical and Poetical Texts from Qumran: Proceedings of the Third Meeting of the International Organization for Qumran Studies, Oslo 1998; Published in Memory of Maurice Baillet*. Edited by Daniel K. Falk, Florentino García Martínez, and Eileen M. Schuller. STDJ 35. Leiden: Brill, 2000.

Fauconnier, Gilles, and Mark Turner. "Conceptual Integration Networks." *CogSci* 22 (1998): 133–87.

Feder, Yitzhaq. *Blood Expiation in Hittite and Biblical Ritual: Origins, Context, and Meaning*. WAWsup 2. Atlanta: Society of Biblical Literature, 2011.

Fee, Gordon D. *The First Epistle to the Corinthians*. NICNT. Grand Rapids: Eerdmans, 1987.

———. *Revelation: A New Covenant Commentary*. NCCS 18. Eugene, OR: Cascade, 2011.

Feldman, Louis H., James L. Kugel, and Lawrence H. Schiffman, eds. *Outside the Bible: Ancient Jewish Writings Related to Scripture*. 3 vols. New York: Jewish Publication Society, 2013.

Ferngren, Gary B. *Medicine and Religion: A Historical Introduction*. Baltimore: Johns Hopkins University Press, 2014.

Finlan, Stephen. *The Background and Contents of Paul's Cultic Atonement Metaphors*. AcBib 19. Atlanta: Society of Bibilical Literature, 2004.

———. *Problems with Atonement: The Origins of, and Controversy about, the Atonement Doctrine*. Collegeville, MN: Liturgical Press, 2005.

———. "Spiritualization of Sacrifice in Paul and Hebrews." Pages 83–97 in *Ritual and Metaphor: Sacrifice in the Bible*. Edited by Christian A. Eberhart. RBS 68. Atlanta: Society of Biblical Literature, 2011.

Fischer, Georg. *Jeremia 1–25*. HThKAT. Freiburg im Breisgau: Herder, 2005.

Fletcher-Louis, Crispin H. T. *All the Glory of Adam: Liturgical Anthropology in the Dead Sea Scrolls*. STDJ 42. Leiden: Brill, 2002.

———. "The High Priest as Divine Mediator in the Hebrew Bible: Daniel 7:13 as a Test Case." Pages 161–193 in *Society of Biblical Literature 1997 Seminar Papers*. SBLSP 36. Atlanta: Scholars Press, 1998.

———. "Jewish Apocalyptic and Apocalypticism." Pages 1569–1607 in *The Study of Jesus*. Vol. 2 of *Handbook for the Study of the Historical Jesus*. Ed. Tom Holmén and Stanley E. Porter. Leiden: Brill, 2011.

———. "Jesus as the High Priestly Messiah: Part 1." *JSHJ* 4 (2006): 155–75.
———. "Jesus as the High Priestly Messiah: Part 2." *JSHJ* 5 (2007): 57–79.
———. "The Revelation of the Sacral Son of Man: The Genre, History of Religions Context and the Meaning of the Transfiguration." Pages 247–98 in *Auferstehung—Resurrection: The Fourth Durham-Tübingen Research Symposium: Resurrection, Transfiguration and Exaltation in Old Testament, Ancient Judaism and Early Christianity (Tübingen, September, 1999)*. Edited by Friedrich Avemarie and Hermann Lichtenberger. WUNT 135. Tübingen: Mohr Siebeck, 2001.
Ford, J. Massyngberde. *Revelation: Introduction, Translation and Commentary*. AB 38. Garden City, NY: Doubleday, 1975.
Frankfurter, David. "Ritual as Accusation and Atrocity: Satanic Ritual Abuse, Gnostic Libertinism, and Primal Murders." *HR* 40 (2001): 352–80.
Frazer, James G. *The Golden Bough: A Study in Magic and Religion*. 3rd ed. London: Macmillan, 1911–1915.
Freedman, David N., ed. *Anchor Bible Dictionary*. 6 vols. New York: Doubleday, 1992.
Fretheim, Terence E. *Jeremiah*. SHBC 15. Macon, GA: Smith & Helwys, 2002.
Frevel, Christian, and Christophe Nihan, eds. *Purity and the Forming of Religious Traditions in the Ancient Mediterranean World and Ancient Judaism*. DHR 5. Leiden: Brill, 2013.
Frey, Jörg. "Probleme der Deutung des Todes Jesu in der neutestamentlichen Wissenschaft: Streiflichter zur exegetischen Diskussion." Pages 3–50 in *Deutungen des Todes Jesu im Neuen Testament*. Edited by Jörg Frey and Jens Schröter. WUNT 181. Tübingen: Mohr Siebeck, 2005.
———. "Temple and Rival Temple—The Cases of Elephantine, Mt. Gerizim, and Leontopolis." Pages 171–203 in *Gemeinde ohne Tempel: Zur Substituierung und Transformation des Jerusalemer Tempels und seines Kults im Alten Testament, antiken Judentum und frühen Christentum*. Edited by Beate Ego, Armin Lange and Peter Pilhofer. WUNT 118. Tübingen: Mohr Siebeck, 1999.
Frey-Anthes, Henrike. "Sündenbock/Asasel." *WiBiLex*. Stuttgart: Deutsche Bibelgesellschaft, 2007. http://tinyurl.com/SBL0393g.
Frymer-Kensky, Tikva. "Pollution, Purification and Purgation in Biblical Israel." Pages 399–414 in *The Word of the Lord Shall Go Forth: Essays in Honor of David Noel Freeman in Celebration of His Sixtieth Birthday*.

Edited by Carol L. Meyers and Michael Patrick O'Connor. Winona Lake, IN: Eisenbrauns, 1983.

Funk, Robert. *The Acts of Jesus: The Search for the Authentic Deeds of Jesus.* Salem, OR: Polebridge Press, 1998.

Gane, Roy E. *Cult and Character: Purification Offerings, Day of Atonement, and Theodicy.* Winona Lake, IN: Eisenbrauns, 2005.

———. *Ritual Dynamic Structures.* GDR 2. Piscataway, NJ: Gorgias, 2004.

García Martínez, Florentino, and Eibert J. C. Tigchelaar, eds. *The Dead Sea Scrolls Study Edition.* 2 vols. Leiden: Brill, 1997–1998.

Gardiner, Alan Henderson. *Egyptian Grammar: Being an Introduction to the Study of Hieroglyphs.* 3rd ed. Oxford: Griffith Institute, 2005.

Gärtner, Bertil. *The Temple and the Community in the Qumran Scrolls and the New Testament.* SNTSMS 1. Cambridge: Cambridge University Press, 1965.

Gaventa, Beverly Roberts. *First and Second Thessalonians.* IBC. Louisville: John Knox, 1998.

Gelb, Norman. *Herod the Great: Statesman, Visionary, Tyrant.* Lanham, MD: Rowman & Littlefield, 2013.

Genest, Olivette. "L'interprétation de la mort de Jésus en situation discursive: Un cas-type; l'articulation des figures de cette mort en 1–2 Corinthiens." *NTS* 34 (1988): 506–35.

Gennep, Arnold van. *Les rites de passage.* Paris: Picard, 1909.

Gerstenberger, Erhard. *Leviticus: A Commentary.* OTL. Louisville: Westminster John Knox, 1996.

Gese, Hartmut. "Die Sühne." Pages 85–106 in *Zur biblischen Theologie: Alttestamentliche Vorträge.* 2nd ed. Tübingen: Mohr Siebeck, 1983.

Gesenius, Wilhelm. *Gesenius' Hebrew Grammar.* Edited by Emil Kautzsch. Translated by Arthur E. Cowley. 2nd ed. Oxford: Clarendon, 1910.

———. *Hebräische Grammatik, völlig umgearbeitet von Emil Kautzsch.* 28th ed. Leipzig: Vogel, 1909.

———. *Hebräisches und Aramäisches Wörterbuch zum Alten Testament: bearbeitet von F. Buhl.* 17th ed. Berlin: Springer, 1962.

Giesen, Heinz. *Die Offenbarung des Johannes.* RNT. Regensburg: Pustet, 1997.

Gilders, William K. *Blood Ritual in the Hebrew Bible: Meaning and Power.* Baltimore: Johns Hopkins University Press, 2004.

Girard, René. *Des choses cachées depuis la fondation du monde.* Paris: Grasset, 1979.

———. "Generative Scapegoating." Pages 73–105 in *Violent Origins: Walter Burkert, René Girard, and Jonathan Z. Smith on Ritual Killing and Cultural Formation*. Edited by Robert G. Hamerton-Kelly. Stanford, CA: Stanford University Press, 1987.
———. *La violence et le sacré*. Paris: Grasset, 1972.
———. *Violence and the Sacred*. Translated by Patrick Gregory. Baltimore: Johns Hopkins University Press, 1977.
Gnilka, Joachim. "Martyriumsparänese und Sühnetod in synoptischen und jüdischen Traditionen." Pages 223–46 in *Die Kirche des Anfangs: Festschrift für Heinz Schürmann*. Edited by Rudolf Schnackenburg. Leipzig: St. Benno, 1977.
Goldingay, John E. *Daniel*. WBC 30. Dallas: Word, 1988.
Goldman, Leon, Richard S. Moraites, and Karl W. Kitzmiller. "White Spots in Biblical Times." *Archives of Dermatology* 93 (1966): 744–53.
Goldstein, Jonathan. *2 Maccabees: A New Translation with Introduction and Commentary*. AB 41A. Garden City, NY: Doubleday, 1983.
Gorman, Frank H. "Sacrifices and Offerings." *NIDB* 5:20–32.
Gray, George Buchanan. *Sacrifice in the Old Testament: Its Theory and Practice*. New York: Ktav, 1971.
Gray, Timothy C. "Jesus and the Temple: The Narrative Role of the Temple in the Gospel of Mark." PhD diss., Catholic University of America, 2006.
Groß, Walter. *Zukunft für Israel: Alttestamentliche Bundeskonzepte und die aktuelle Debatte um den Neuen Bund*. SBS 176. Stuttgart: Katholisches Bibelwerk, 1998.
Grotius, Hugo. *Defensio fidei catholicae de satisfactione Christi adversus Faustum Socinum*. Salmurii: Pean, 1675.
Gruenwald, Ithamar. *Rituals and Ritual Theory in Ancient Israel*. BRLJ 10. Leiden: Brill, 2003.
Gundry, Robert H. *Commentary on the New Testament: Verse-by-Verse Explanations with a Literal Translation*. Peabody, MA: Hendrickson, 2010.
———. *Sōma in Biblical Theology: With Emphasis on Pauline Anthropology*. SNTSMS 29. Cambridge: Cambridge University Press, 1976.
Gupta, Nijay. "Which 'Body' is a Temple (1 Corinthians 6:19)? Paul beyond the Individual/Communal Divide." *CBQ* 72 (2010): 518–36.
Haber, Susan. "From Priestly Torah to Christ Cultus: The Re-Vision of Covenant and Cult in Hebrews." *JSNT* 28 (2005): 105–124.

Hachlili, Rachel. *The Menorah, the Ancient Seven-Armed Candelabrum: Origin, Form and Significance*. JSJSup 68. Leiden: Brill, 2001.

Hahn, Ferdinand. "Das Verständnis des Opfers im Neuen Testament." Pages 51–91 in *Das Opfer Jesu Christi und seine Gegenwart in der Kirche*. Edited by Karl Lehmann and Edmund Schlink. DiKi 3. Freiburg im Breisgau: Herder, 1983.

Hamilton, James M., Jr. *Revelation: The Spirit Speaks to the Churches*. Preaching the Word. Wheaton, IL: Crossway, 2012.

Hannah, Darrell D. "The Angelic Restrainer of 2 Thessalonians 2.6–7." Pages 28–45 in *Calling Time: Religion and Change at the Turn of the Millennium*. Edited by Martyn Percy. LSRS 2. Sheffield: Sheffield Academic, 2000.

———. *Michael and Christ: Michael Traditions and Angel Christology in Early Christianity*. WUNT 2/109. Tübingen: Mohr Siebeck, 1999.

Hansen, Karen Tranberg. "The World in Dress: Anthropological Perspectives on Clothing, Fashion, and Culture." *ARA* 33 (2004): 369–92.

Hanson, Ann Ellis. "The Medical Writer's Woman." Pages 309–38 in *Before Sexuality: the Construction of Erotic Experience in the Ancient Greek World*. Edited by David M. Halperin, John J. Winkler, and Froma I. Zeitlin. Princeton: Princeton University Press, 1990.

Hanson, K. C. "When the King Crosses the Line: Royal Deviance and Restitution in Levantine Ideologies." *BTB* 26 (1996): 11–25.

Harrington, Hannah K. "Examining Rabbinic Halakha through the Lens of Qumran." Pages 137–56 in *The Qumran Legal Texts between the Hebrew Bible and Its Interpretation*. Edited by Kristin De Troyer and Armin Lange. CBET 61. Leuven: Peeters, 2011.

———. *Holiness: Rabbinic Judaism and the Graeco-Roman World*. RFCC London: Routledge, 2001.

———. "Leniency in the Temple Scroll's Purity Law? Another Look." *Henoch* 36 (2014): 35–49.

———. "Purification in the Fourth Gospel in Light of Qumran." Pages 117–38 in *John, Qumran, and the Dead Sea Scrolls: Sixty Years of Discovery and Debate*. Edited by Tom Thatcher and Mary Coloe. EJL 32. Atlanta: Society of Biblical Literature, 2011.

———. *The Purity Texts*. CQS 5. London: T&T Clark, 2004.

Hartenstein, Friedhelm. "Zur symbolischen Bedeutung des Blutes im Alten Testament." Pages 119–37 in *Deutungen des Todes Jesu im Neuen Testament*. Edited by Jörg Frey and Jens Schröter. WUNT 181. Tübingen: Mohr Siebeck, 2005.

Hartley, John E. *Leviticus*. WBC 4. Dallas: Word, 1992.
Hasenkamp, Christoph Hermann. "Ueber die Opfer: Resultate einer biblisch-philosophischen Untersuchung." *Die Wahrheit der Gottseligkeit* 1/1 (1827): 7–33; 1/3 (1829): 245–349.
Haulotte, Edgar. *Symbolique du vêtement selon la Bible*. Théologie 65. Paris: Aubier, 1966.
Hays, Richard B. *First Corinthians*. IBC. Louisville, John Knox, 1997.
Heim, S. Mark. *Saved from Sacrifice: A Theology of the Cross*. Grand Rapids: Eerdmans, 2006.
Heger, Paul. *The Three Biblical Altar Laws: Developments in the Sacrificial Cult in Practice and Theology; Political and Economic Background*. BZAW 279. Berlin: de Gruyter, 1999.
———. *The Development of the Incense Cult in Israel*. BZAW 245. Berlin: de Gruyter, 1997.
Hendel, Ronald S. "Away from Ritual: The Prophetic Critique." Pages 59–80 in *Social Theory and the Study of Israelite Religion: Essays in Retrospect and Prospect*. Edited by Saul M. Olyan. RBS 71. Atlanta: Society of Biblical Literature, 2012.
———. "Prophets, Priests, and the Efficacy of Ritual." Pages 185–98 in *Pomegranates and Golden Bells: Studies in Biblical, Jewish, and Near Eastern Ritual, Law, and Literature in Honor of Jacob Milgrom*. Edited by David P. Wright, David Noel Freedman and Avi Hurvitz. Winona Lake, IN: Eisenbrauns, 1995.
Henten, Jan W. van. *The Maccabean Martyrs as Saviours of the Jewish People: A Study of 2 and 4 Maccabees*. JSJSup 57. Leiden: Brill, 1997.
———. "The Tradition-Historical Background of Romans 3:25: A Search for Pagan and Jewish Parallels." Pages 101–28 in *From Jesus to John: Essays on Jesus and New Testament Christology in Honour of Marinus de Jonge*. Edited by Martinus C. de Boer. JSNTSup 84. Sheffield: JSOT Press, 1993.
Henze, Matthias. "Additions to Daniel." Pages 122–139 in vol. 1 of *Outside the Bible: Ancient Jewish Writings Related to Scripture*. Edited by Louis H. Feldman, James L. Kugel, and Lawrence H. Schiffman. Philadelphia: Jewish Publication Society, 2013.
Herr, Moshe David. "Day of Atonement." *EncJud* 5:1376–84.
Hieke, Thomas. "Der Kult ist für den Menschen da: Auf Spurensuche in den Opfervorschriften von Levitikus 1–10." *BK* 64 (2009), 141–47.
———. *Levitikus: Erster Teilband: 1–15*. HThKAT. Freiburg im Breisgau: Herder, 2014.

———. *Levitikus: Zweiter Teilband: 16–27*. HThKAT. Freiburg im Breisgau: Herder, 2014.
Heike, Thomas, and Tobias Nicklas, eds. *The Day of Atonement: Its Interpretations in Early Jewish and Christian Traditions*. TBN 15. Leiden: Brill, 2011.
Hillers, Delbert R. "Therefore I Will Punish You." Pages 120–42 in *Covenant: The History of a Biblical Idea*. Seminars in the History of Ideas. Baltimore: Johns Hopkins University Press, 1969.
Hillestad, Robert. "The Underlying Structure of Appearance." *Dress* 6 (1980): 117–25.
Himmelfarb, Martha. *A Kingdom of Priests: Ancestry and Merit in Ancient Judaism*. JCC. Philadelphia: University of Pennsylvania Press, 2006.
Hobbs, T. R. "Reflections on Honor, Shame, and Covenant Relations." *JBL* 116 (1997): 501–3.
———. "Reflections on 'The Poor' and the Old Testament." *ExpTim* 100 (1989): 291–94.
Hodgson, Peter C. "Hegel, Georg Wilhelm Friedrich." *EBR* 11:705–8.
Hödl, Ludwig. "Anselm von Canterbury." *TRE* 2:759–78.
Hofius, Otfried. "Sühne IV: Neues Testament." *TRE* 32:342–47.
———. "Sühne und Versöhnung: Zum paulinischen Verständnis des Kreuzestodes Jesu." Pages 33–49 in *Paulusstudien*. WUNT 51. Tübingen: Mohr Siebeck, 1989.
Hogeterp, Albert L. A. *Paul and God's Temple: A Historical Interpretation of Cultic Imagery in the Corinthian Correspondence*. BTS 2. Leuven: Peeters, 2006.
Holladay, William. *Jeremiah. 1: A Commentary on the Book of the Prophet Jeremiah, Chapters 1–25*. Hermeneia. Philadelphia: Fortress, 1986.
———. *Jeremiah. 2: A Commentary on the Book of the Prophet Jeremiah, Chapters 26–52*. Hermeneia. Minneapolis: Fortress, 1989.
Holman, Rebecca H. "Apparel as Communication." Pages 7–15 in *Symbolic Consumer Behavior: Proceedings of the Conference on Consumer Esthetics and Symbolic Consumption*. Edited by Elizabeth C. Hirschman and Morris B. Holbrook. Ann Arbor, MI: Association for Consumer Research, 1980.
Horbury, William. "New Wine in Old Wineskins." *ExpTim* 86 (1974): 36–42.
Horn, Marilyn J., and Lois M. Gurel. *The Second Skin: An Interdisciplinary Study of Clothing*. 3rd ed. Boston: Houghton Mifflin, 1981.

Hort, F. J. A. *The Apocalypse of St John: I–III: The Greek Text with Introduction, Commentary, and Additional Notes*. London: Macmillan, 1908.
Howe, Bonnie. *Because You Bear This Name: Conceptual Metaphor and the Moral Meaning of 1 Peter*. BibInt 81. Leiden: Brill, 2006.
Hubert, Henri, and Marcel Mauss. "Essai sur la nature et la fonction du sacrifice." *Année Sociologique* 2 (1899): 29–138.
Huffmon, Herbert B. "The Treaty Background of Hebrew *Yāda'*." *BASOR* 181 (1966): 31–37.
Huffmon, Herbert B., and Simon B. Parker. "A Further Note on the Treaty Background of Hebrew *Yāda'*." *BASOR* 184 (1966): 36–38.
Hultberg, Alan David. "Messianic Exegesis in the Apocalypse: The Significance of the Old Testament for the Christology of Revelation." PhD diss., Trinity Evangelical Divinity School, 2001.
Hyatt, J. Philip. "The Translation and Meaning of Amos 5:23–24." *ZAW* 68 (1956): 17–24.
Ibita, Ma. Maricel S. "'O Israel, I Will Testify against You': Intensification and Narrativity in the Lament-Lawsuit of the 'Unsilent' God in Psalm 50." Pages 537–49 in *The Composition of the Book of Psalms*. Edited by Erich Zenger. BETL 238. Leuven: Peeters, 2010.
Ingham, Bruce. "Men's Dress in the Arabian Peninsula: Historical and Present Perspectives." Pages 40–54 in *Languages of Dress in the Middle East*. Edited by Nancy Lindisfarne-Tapper and Bruce Ingham. Richmond: Curzon, 1997. Repr., Oxford: Routledge, 2013.
Jacobsen, Thorkild. "Mesopotamia." Pages 123–219 in *The Intellectual Adventure of Ancient Man: An Essay on Speculative Thought in the Ancient Near East*. Edited by Henri Frankfort, H. A. Frankfort, John A. Wilson, Thorkild Jacobsen, and William A. Irwin. Chicago: University of Chicago Press, 1946.
Jaeschke, Walter. "Hegel, Georg Wilhelm Friedrich." *RGG4* 3:1504–8.
Janowski, Bernd. "Das Geschenk der Versöhnung: Leviticus 16 als Schlussstein der priesterlichen Kulttheologie." Pages 3–31 in *The Day of Atonement: Its Interpretations in Early Jewish and Christian Traditions*. Edited by Thomas Hieke and Tobias Nicklas. TBN 15. Leiden: Brill, 2012.
———. "Der Ort des Lebens: Zur Kultsymbolik des Jerusalemer Tempels." Pages 369–97 in *Temple Building and Temple Cult: Architecture and Cultic Paraphernalia of Temples in the Levant (2.–1. Mill. B.C.E.)*. Edited by Jens Kamlah with Henrike Michelau. ADPV 41. Wiesbaden: Harrassowitz, 2012.

———. *Sühne als Heilsgeschehen: Traditions- und religionsgeschichtliche Studien zur Sühnetheologie der Priesterschrift*. 2nd ed. WMANT 55. Neukirchen-Vluyn: Neukirchener Verlag, 2000.

Janowski, Bernd, and Gernot Wilhelm. "Der Bock, der die Sünden hinausträgt: Zur Religionsgeschichte des Azazel-Ritus Lev 16,10.21 f." Pages 109–69 in *Religionsgeschichtliche Beziehungen zwischen Kleinasien, Nordsyrien und dem Alten Testament: Internationales Symposion Hamburg 17. –21. März 1990*. Edited by Bernd Janowski, Klaus Koch, and Gernot Wilhelm. OBO 129. Friborg: Presses Universitaires; Göttingen: Vandenhoeck & Ruprecht, 1993.

Janowski, Bernd, and Michael Welker, eds. *Opfer: Theologische und kulturelle Kontexte*. STW 1454. Frankfurt am Main: Suhrkamp, 2000.

Janzen, David. *The Social Meanings of Sacrifice in the Hebrew Bible: A Study of Four Writings*. BZAW 344. Berlin: de Gruyter, 2004.

Jauhiainen, Marko. *The Use of Zechariah in Revelation*. WUNT 2/199. Tübingen: Mohr Siebeck, 2005.

Jenni, Ernst, and Claus Westermann, eds. *Theological Lexicon of the Old Testament*. Trans. Mark E. Biddle. 3 vols. Peabody, MA: Hendrickson, 1997.

Jenson, Philip Peter. *Graded Holiness: A Key to the Priestly Conception of the World*. JSOTSup 106. Sheffield: JSOT Press, 1992.

———. *Obadiah, Jonah, Micah: A Theological Commentary*. LHBOTS 496. New York: T&T Clark, 2008.

Jindo, Job Y. *Biblical Metaphor Reconsidered: A Cognitive Approach to Poetic Prophecy in Jeremiah 1–24*. HSM 64. Winona Lake, IN: Eisenbrauns, 2010.

Jobling, David. *1 Samuel*. Berit Olam. Collegeville, MN: Liturgical Press, 1998.

Johnson, Bo. "צָדַק." *TDOT* 12:239–65.

Johnson, Kim K. P., Nancy A. Schofield, and Jennifer Yurchisin. "Appearance and Dress as a Source of Information: A Qualitative Approach to Data Collection." *CTRJ* 20 (2002): 125–37.

Johnson, Kim K. P., and Sharron J. Lennon. "Introduction: Appearance and Social Power." Pages 1–10 in *Appearance and Power*. Edited by Kim K. P. Johnson and Sharron J. Lennon. Dress, Body, Culture. Oxford: Berg, 1999.

Johnson, Richard W. *Going outside the Camp: The Sociological Function of the Levitical Critique in the Epistle to the Hebrews*. JSNTSup 209. London: Sheffield Academic, 2001.

Jones, Larry Paul. *The Symbol of Water in the Gospel of John.* JSNTSup 145. Sheffield: Sheffield Academic, 1997.

Jonge, Marinus de. *Christology in Context: The Earliest Christian Response to Jesus.* Philadelphia: Westminster, 1988.

———. "Jesus' Death for Others and the Death of the Maccabean Martyrs." Pages 142–51 in *Text and Testimony: Essays on New Testament and Apocryphal Literature in Honour of A. F. J. Klijn.* Edited by Tjitze Baarda, A. Hilhorst, G. P. Luttikhuizen, and A. S. van der Woude. Kampen: Kok, 1988.

Joseph, Nathan. *Uniforms and Nonuniforms: Communicating Through Clothing.* Contributions in Sociology 61. New York: Greenwood, 1986.

Joüon, Paul, and Takamitsu Muraoka. *A Grammar of Biblical Hebrew.* SubBi 27. Rome: Biblical Intitute Press, 2006.

Kaiser, Susan B. *The Social Psychology of Clothing: Symbolic Appearances in Context.* 2nd ed. New York: Fairchild, 1997.

Karris, Robert J. *Luke: Artist and Theologian: Luke's Passion Account as Literature.* Theological Inquiries. New York: Paulist, 1985.

Kazen, Thomas. *Issues of Impurity in Early Judaism.* ConBNT 45. Winona Lake, IN: Eisenbrauns, 2010.

Keener, Craig S. *Revelation.* NIVAC. Grand Rapids: Zondervan, 2000.

Kellermann, Ulrich. *Auferstanden in den Himmel: 2 Makkabäer 7 und die Auferstehung der Märtyrer.* SBS 95. Stuttgart: Katholisches Bibelwerk, 1979.

———. "Zum traditionsgeschichtlichen Problem des stellvertretenden Sühnetodes in 2 Makk 7:37." *BN* 13 (1980): 63–83.

Kessler, Martin. "Editor's Introduction." Pages xi–xiv in *Reading the Book of Jeremiah: A Search for Coherence.* Edited by Martin Kessler. Winona Lake, IN: Eisenbrauns, 2004.

Kim, Jung Hoon. *The Significance of Clothing Imagery in the Pauline Corpus.* JSNTSup 268. London: T&T Clark, 2004.

Kirk, J. R. Daniel. "Time for Figs, Temple Destruction, and Houses of Prayer in Mark 11:12–25." *CBQ* 74 (2012): 509–27.

Kittel, Gerhard, and Gerhard Friedrich, eds. *Theological Dictionary of the New Testament.* Translated by Geoffrey W Bromiley. 10 vols. Grand Rapids: Eerdmans, 1964–1976.

Kiuchi, Nobuyoshi. *The Purification Offering in the Priestly Literature: Its Meaning and Function.* JSOTSup 56. Sheffield: Sheffield Academic, 1987.

Klauck, Hans Josef. *Unterweisung in lehrhafter Form: 4 Makkabäerbuch.* JSHRZ NS 3. Gütersloh: Mohn, 1989.

Klauck, Hans-Josef, et al., eds. *Encyclopedia of the Bible and Its Reception.* Berlin: de Gruyter, 2009–

Klauser, Theodor, et al., eds. *Reallexikon für Antike und Christentum.* Stuttgart: Hiersemann, 1950–

Klawans, Jonathan. *Impurity and Sin in Ancient Judaism.* Oxford: Oxford University Press, 2000.

———. *Purity, Sacrifice and the Temple: Symbolism and Supersessionism in the Study of Ancient Judaism.* Oxford: Oxford University Press, 2006.

Kline, Meredith G. *Images of the Spirit.* Grand Rapids: Baker, 1980. Repr., Eugene, OR: Wipf & Stock, 1999.

Klingbeil, Gerald A. *Bridging the Gap: Ritual and Ritual Texts in the Bible.* BBRSup 1. Winona Lake, IN: Eisenbrauns 2007.

Klinzing, Georg. *Die Umdeutung des Kultus in der Qumrangemeinde und im Neuen Testament.* SUNT 7. Göttingen: Vandenhoeck & Ruprecht, 1971.

Knibb, Michael. *The Qumran Community.* Cambridge: Cambridge University Press, 1987.

Knöppler, Thomas. *Sühne im Neuen Testament: Studien zum urchristlichen Verständnis der Heilsbedeutung des Todes Jesu.* WMANT 88. Neukirchen-Vluyn: Neukirchener Verlag, 2001.

Koch, Klaus. *Das Buch Daniel.* EdF 144. Darmstadt: Wissenschaftliche Buchgesellschaft, 1980.

———. "Sühne und Sündenvergebung um die Wende von der exilischen zur nach-exilischen Zeit." *EvT* 26 (1966): 217–39.

Koester, Helmut. "From Paul's Eschatology to the Apocalyptic Schemata of 2 Thessalonians." Pages 441–58 in *The Thessalonian Correspondence.* Edited by Raymond F. Collins. BETL 87. Leuven: Leuven University Press, 1990.

Koester, Craig R. "God's Purposes and Christ's Saving Work According to Hebrews." Pages 359–87 in *Salvation in the New Testament: Perspectives on Soteriology.* Edited by Jan G. van der Watt. NovTSup 121. Leiden; Boston: Brill, 2005.

Köhler, Ludwig. *Theologie des Alten Testaments.* 4th ed. NTG. Tübingen: Mohr Siebeck, 1966.

Koehler, Ludwig, Walter Baumgartner, and Johann Jakob Stamm, *The Hebrew and Aramaic Lexicon of the Old Testament.* Translated and edited under the supervision of M. E. J. Richardson. 4 vols. Leiden: Brill, 1994–1999.

Koltun-Fromm, Naomi. *Hermeneutics of Holiness: Ancient Jewish and Christian Notions of Sexuality and Religious Community*. Oxford: Oxford University Press, 2010.
Kotrosits, Maia, and Hal Taussig. *Re-reading the Gospel of Mark amidst Loss and Trauma*. New York: Palgrave Macmillan, 2013.
Kratz, Reinhard G. "Israel in the Book of Isaiah." *JSOT* 31 (2006): 103–28.
Kraus, Thomas J. "Angels in the Magical Papyri: The Classic Example of Michael, the Archangel." Pages 611–28 in *Angels: The Concept of Celestial Beings—Origins, Development and Reception*. Edited by Friedrich V. Reiterer, Tobias Nicklas, and Karin Schöpflin. DCLS Yearbook 2007. Berlin: de Gruyter, 2007.
Kraus, Wolfgang. "Der Erweis der Gerechtigkeit Gottes im Tode Jesu nach Röm 3,24–26." Pages 192–218 in *Judaistik und Neutestamentliche Wissenschaft: Standorte—Grenzen—Beziehungen*. Edited by Lutz Doering, Hans-Günther Waubke, and Florian Wilk. FRLANT 226. Göttingen: Vandenhoeck & Ruprecht, 2008.
———. *Der Tod Jesu als Heiligtumsweihe: Eine Untersuchung zum Umfeld der Sühnevorstellung im Römer 3,25–26a*. WMANT 66. Neukirchen-Vluyn: Neukirchener Verlag, 1991.
———. "Der Tod Jesu als Sühnetod bei Paulus: Überlegungen zur neueren Diskussion." *ZNT* 3 (1999): 20–30.
Kraus, G, and G. Müller, eds. *Theologische Realenzyklopädie*. Berlin: de Gruyter, 1977–2006.
Kreuzer, Siegfried. *The Bible in Greek: Translation, Transmission, and Theology of the Septuagint*. SCS 63. Atlanta: SBL Press, 2015.
Kugler, Robert A. "Priesthood at Qumran." Pages 2:93–116 in *The Dead Sea Scrolls after Fifty Years: A Comprehensive Assessment*. Edited by Peter W. Flint and James C. VanderKam. Leiden: Brill, 1999.
Kuper, Hilda. "Costume and Identity." *CSSH* 15 (1973): 348–67.
Kurtz, Johann H. *Das mosaische Opfer: Ein Beitrag zur Symbolik des mosaischen Cultus. Mit besonderer Berücksichtigung der neuesten Bearbeitung dieses Gegenstandes in der "Symbolik des mosaischen Cultus" von Dr. K. Chr. W. Fr. Bähr*. Mitau: Lucas, 1842.
Lacocque, André. *The Book of Daniel*. Translated by David Pellauer. Atlanta: John Knox, 1979.
Lakoff, George. "The Contemporary Theory of Metaphor." Pages 202–51 in *Metaphor and Thought*. Edited by Andrew Ortony. 2nd ed. New York: Cambridge University Press, 1993.

Lakoff, George, and Mark Johnson. *Metaphors We Live By.* Chicago: University of Chicago Press, 2003.

Lanci, John R. *A New Temple for Corinth: Rhetorical and Archaeological Approaches to Pauline Imagery.* StBibLit 1. New York: Lang, 1997.

Lange, Armin. "Gebotsobservanz statt Opferkult: Zur Kultpolemik in Jer 7,1–8,3." Pages 19–35 in *Gemeinde ohne Tempel: Zur Substituierung und Transformation des Jerusalemer Tempels und seines Kults im Alten Testament, antiken Judentum und frühen Christentum.* Edited by Beate Ego, Armin Lange, and Peter Pilhofer. WUNT 118. Tübingen: Mohr Siebeck, 1999.

Lasaulx, Ernst von. *Die Sühnopfer der Griechen und Römer und ihr Verhältnis zum Einen auf Golgatha: Ein Beitrag zur Religionsphilosophie.* Würzburg: Voigt & Mocker, 1841.

Lauterbach, Jacob Zallel. "A Significant Controversy between the Sadducees and the Pharisees." *HUCA* 4 (1927): 173–205.

Law, Timothy Michael. *When God Spoke Greek: The Septuagint and the Making of the Christian Bible.* Oxford: Oxford University Press, 2013.

Lawrence, Jonathan D. *Washing in Water: Trajectories of Ritual Bathing in the Hebrew Bible and Second Temple Literature.* AcBib 23. Atlanta: Society of Biblical Literature, 2006.

Lee, J. A. L. *A Lexical Study of the Septuagint Version of the Pentateuch.* SCS 14. Chico, CA: Scholars Press, 1983.

Lehmann, Karl, and Edmund Schlink, eds. *Das Opfer Jesu Christi und seine Gegenwart in der Kirche: Klärungen zum Opfercharakter des Herrenmahls.* DiKi 3. Freiburg im Breisgau: Herder; Göttingen: Vandenhoeck & Ruprecht, 1983.

Lemche, Niels Peter. "Kings and Clients : On Loyalty between the Ruler and the Ruled in Ancient 'Israel.'" *Semeia* 66 (1994): 119–32.

Lemos, T. M. "Shame and Mutilation of Enemies in the Hebrew Bible." *JBL* 125 (2006): 225–41.

Lenski, R. C. H. *The Interpretation of St. John's Revelation.* Minneapolis: Augsburg, 1963.

Lesses, Rebecca M. *Ritual Practices to Gain Power: Angels, Incantations, and Revelation in Early Jewish Mysticism.* HTS 44. Harrisburg, PA: Trinity Press International, 1998.

Leuchter, Mark. "The Fightin' Mushites." *VT* 62 (2012): 479–500.

Levine, Baruch. *In the Presence of the Lord: A Study of Cult and Some Cultic Terms in Ancient Israel.* SJLA 5. Leiden: Brill, 1974.

———. *Leviticus* ויקרא: *The Traditional Hebrew Text with the New JPS Translation*. JPS Torah Commentary. Philadelphia: Jewish Publication Society, 1989.

———. *Numbers 1–20: A New Translation with Introduction and Commentary*. AB 4A. New York: Doubleday, 1993.

Levison, John R. *Filled with the Spirit*. Grand Rapids: Eerdmans, 2009.

Levtow, Nathaniel B. *Images of Others: Iconic Politics in Ancient Israel*. BJSUCSD 11. Winona Lake, IN: Eisenbrauns, 2008.

Lichtenberger, Hermann. "The Dead Sea Scrolls and John the Baptist: Reflections on Josephus' Account of John the Baptist." Pages 340–46 in *The Dead Sea Scrolls: Forty Years of Research*. Edited by Devorah Dimant and Uriel Rappaport. STDJ 10. Leiden: Brill, 1992.

Lidell, Henry George, Robert Scott, Henry Stuart Jones. *A Greek-English Lexicon*. 9th ed. with revised supplements. Oxford: Clarendon, 1996.

Lincoln, Andrew. *Ephesians*. WBC 42. Dallas: Word, 1990.

Lindisfarne-Tapper, Nancy, and Bruce Ingham. "Approaches to the Study of Dress in the Middle East." Pages 1–39 in *Languages of Dress in the Middle East*. Edited by Nancy Lindisfarne-Tapper and Bruce Ingham. London: Curzon, 1997. Repr., Oxford: Routledge, 2013.

Link, Christoph. "Grotius, Hugo." *RGG4* 3:1303–4.

Lioy, Dan. *The Book of Revelation in Christological Focus*. StBibLit 58. New York: Lang, 2003.

Liss, Hanna. "Ritual Purity and the Construction of Identity." Pages 329–54 in *The Books of Leviticus and Numbers*. Edited by Thomas Römer. BETL 215. Leuven: Peeters, 2008.

Lohmeyer, Ernst. *Die Offenbarung des Johannes*. 3rd ed. HNT 16. Tübingen: Mohr Siebeck, 1970.

Lohse, Eduard. *Die Offenbarung des Johannes*. NTD 11. Göttingen: Vandenhoeck & Ruprecht, 1971.

———. *Märtyrer und Gottesknecht: Untersuchungen zur urchristlichen Verkündigung vom Sühntod Jesu Christi*. 2nd ed. FRLANT 46. Göttingen: Vandenhoeck & Ruprecht, 1963.

Lucas, Ernest C. "Sacrifice in the Prophets." Pages 59–74 in *Sacrifice in the Bible*. Edited by Roger T. Beckwith and Martin J. Selman. Grand Rapids: Baker, 1995.

Luciani, Didier. *Sainteté et pardon*. 2 vols. BETL 185. Leuven: Leuven University Press, 2005.

Lundbom, Jack R. *Jeremiah 1–20: A New Introduction with Translation and Commentary*. AB 21A. New York: Doubleday, 1999.

———. *Jeremiah 21–36: A New Translation with Introduction and Commentary.* AB 21B. New York: Doubleday, 2004.

———. *Jeremiah: A Study in Ancient Hebrew Rhetoric.* 2nd ed. Winona Lake, IN: Eisenbrauns, 1997.

Lupieri, Edmondo F. *A Commentary on the Apocalypse of John.* Translated by Maria Poggi Johnson and Adam Kamesar. ITSRS. Grand Rapids: Eerdmans, 2006.

Luther, Martin. "Vom Abendmahl Christi: Bekenntnis (1528)." Pages 261–509 in vol. 26 of *D. Martin Luthers Werke: Kritische Gesamtausgabe.* Weimar: Böhlau, 1909.

Maccoby, Hyam. *Ritual and Morality: The Ritual Purity System and its Place in Judaism.* Cambridge: Cambridge University, 1999.

Maier, Harry O. "Kleidung II (Bedeutung)." *RAC* 21:1–60.

Malina, Bruce J. "Authoritarianism." Pages 12–19 in *Handbook of Biblical Social Values.* Edited by John J. Pilch and Bruce J. Malina. Updated ed. Peabody, MA: Hendrickson, 2009.

———. "Mediterranean Sacrifice: Dimensions of Domestic and Political Religion." *BTB* 26 (1996): 26–44.

———. *The New Testament World: Insights from Cultural Anthropology.* 3rd ed., rev. and expanded. Louisville: Westminster John Knox, 2001.

———. "Patronage." Pages 151–55 in *Handbook of Biblical Social Values.* Edited by John J. Pilch and Bruce J. Malina. Updated ed. Peabody, MA: Hendrickson, 2009.

Marcus, Joel. *Mark 8–16: A New Translation with Introduction and Commentary.* AB 27A. New Haven: Yale University Press, 2009.

———. *The Way of the Lord: Christological Exegesis of the Old Testament in the Gospel of Mark.* Louisville, Westminster John Knox, 1992.

Martyn, J. Louis. *Galatians: A New Translation with Introduction and Commentary.* AB 33A. New York: Doubleday, 1997.

Marx, Alfred. "Familiarité et transcendance: La fonction du sacrifice d'après l'Ancien Testament." Pages 1–14 in *Studien zu Opfer und Kult im Alten Testament.* Edited by Adrian Schenker. FAT 3. Tübingen: Mohr Siebeck, 1992.

———. "Le sacrifice israélite de 1750 à nos jours: Histoire de la recherché." PhD diss., Université de Strasbourg, 1977.

———. *Les offrandes végétales dans l'Ancien Testament: Du tribut d'hommage au repas eschatologique.* VTSup 57. Leiden: Brill, 1994.

———. *Les systèmes sacrificiels de l'Ancien Testament: Formes et fonctions du culte sacrificiel à Yhwh.* VTSup 105. Leiden: Brill, 2005.

———. "Opferlogik im alten Israel." Pages 129–49 in *Opfer: Theologische und kulturelle Kontexte*. Edited by Bernd Janowski and Michael Welker. STW 1454. Frankfurt am Main: Suhrkamp, 2000.

———. "Sacrifice pour les péchés ou rite de passage? Quelques réflexions sur la fonction du *ḥaṭṭā't*." *RB* 96 (1989): 27–48.

———. "The Theology of the Sacrifice according to Leviticus 1–7." Pages 101–20 in: *The Book of Leviticus: Composition and Reception*. Edited by Rolf Rendtorff and Robert A. Kugler. VTSup 93. Leiden: Brill, 2003.

Massaux, Édouard, ed. *La venue du Messie: Messianisme et eschatologie*. RechBib 6. Bruges: Desclée de Brouwer, 1962.

Mathewson, David. *A New Heaven and a New Earth: The Meaning and Function of the Old Testament in Revelation 21.1–22.5*. JSNTSup 238. Sheffield: Sheffield Academic, 2003.

Mays, James L. *Hosea: A Commentary*. OTL. Philadelphia: Westminster, 1969.

Mazar, Benjamin. *The Mountain of the Lord*. Garden City, NY: Doubleday, 1975.

Mazzaferri, Frederick David. *The Genre of the Book of Revelation from a Source-Critical Perspective*. BZNW 54. Berlin: de Gruyter, 1989.

McCarter, P. Kyle, Jr. *I Samuel: A New Translation with Introduction, Notes and Commentary*. AB 8. Garden City, NY: Doubleday, 1980.

McClymond, Kathryn. *Beyond Sacred Violence: A Comparative Study of Sacrifice*. Baltimore: Johns Hopkins University Press, 2008.

McCracken, Grant. "Clothing as Language: An Object Lesson in the Study of the Expressive Properties of Material Culture." Pages 103–28 in *Material Anthropology: Contemporary Approaches to Material Culture*. Edited by Barrie Reynolds and Margaret A. Stott. Lanham, MD: University Press of America, 1987.

McKane, William. *A Critical and Exegetical Commentary on Jeremiah. Vol. 1: Introduction and Commentary on Jeremiah I–XXV*. ICC. Edinburgh: T&T Clark, 1986.

———. *A Critical and Exegetical Commentary on Jeremiah. Vol. 2: Jeremiah XXVI–LII*. ICC. Edinburgh: T&T Clark, 1996.

McKay, Heather A. "Gendering the Body: Clothes Maketh the (Wo)man." Pages 84–104 in *Theology and the Body: Gender, Text and Ideology*. Edited by Robert Hannaford and J'annine Jobling. Canterbury Books. Leominster, UK: Gracewing, 1999.

———. "Gendering the Discourse of Display in the Hebrew Bible." Pages 169–199 in *On Reading Prophetic Texts: Gender-Specific and Related*

Studies in Memory of Fokkelien van Dijk-Hemmes. Edited by Bob Becking and Meindert Dijkstra. BibInt 18. Leiden: Brill, 1996.

McKelvey, R. J. *The New Temple: The Church in the New Testament.* OTM. Oxford: Oxford University Press, 1969.

McLean, Bradley H. "The Absence of an Atoning Sacrifice in Paul's Soteriology." *NTS* 38 (1992): 531–53.

Medebielle, Alexis. *L'expiation dans l'Ancien et le Nouveau Testament.* Vol. 1. SPIB. Rome: Institut Biblique Pontifical, 1924.

Meier, John P. *A Marginal Jew.* 4 vols. New Haven: Yale University Press, 1991–2009.

Merklein, Helmut. "Der Sühnetod Jesu nach dem Zeugnis des Neuen Testaments." Pages 155–83 in *Versöhnung in der jüdischen und christlichen Liturgie.* Edited by David H. Ellenson, Klaus Kienzler, Hanspeter Heinz, and Jakob Josef Petuchowski. QD 124. Freiburg: Herder, 1990.

———. "Der Tod Jesu als stellvertretender Sühnetod: Entwicklung und Gehalt einer zentralen neutestamentlichen Aussage." Pages 181–91 in *Studien zu Jesus und Paulus.* Edited by Helmut Merklein. WUNT 43. Tübingen: Mohr Siebeck, 1987.

Meshel, Naphthali S. *The "Grammar" of Sacrifice: A Generativist Study of the Israelite Sacrificial System in the Priestly Writings with a "Grammar" of Σ.* Oxford: Oxford University Press, 2014.

Metzger, Paul. *Katechon: II Thess 2,1–12 im Horizont apokalyptischen Denkens.* BZNW 135. Berlin: de Gruyter, 2005.

Meuli, Karl. "Griechische Opferbräuche." Pages 185–288 in *Phylobolia: Festschrift für Peter von der Mühll zum 60. Geburtstag am 1. August 1945.* Edited by Olof Gigon and Karl Meuli. Basel: Schwabe, 1946.

Michaels, J. Ramsey. *1 Peter.* WBC 49. Waco, TX: Word, 1988.

Milgrom, Jacob. "Concerning Jeremiah's Repudiation of Sacrifice." *ZAW* 89 (1977): 273–75.

———. *Cult and Conscience: The Asham and the Priestly Doctrine of Repentance.* SJLA 18. Leiden: Brill, 1976.

———. "First Day Ablutions in Qumran." Pages 561–70 in vol. 2 of *The Madrid Qumran Congress: Proceedings of the International Congress on the Dead Sea Scrolls, Madrid 18–21 March, 1991.* Edited by Julio Trebolle Barrera and Luis V. Montaner. STDJ 11. Leiden: Brill, 1992.

———. "Florilegium: A Midrash on 2 Samuel and Psalms 1–2," Pages 248–63 in vol. 6B of *The Dead Sea Scrolls: Hebrew Aramaic, and Greek Texts with English Translations.* Edited by James H. Charlesworth. Louisville: Westminster John Knox, 2002.

———. *Leviticus 1–16: A New Translation with Introduction and Commentary*. AB 3. New York: Doubleday, 1991.

———. *Leviticus 17–22: A New Translation with Introduction and Commentary*. AB 3A. New York: Doubleday, 2000.

———. *Leviticus: A Book of Ritual and Ethics*. CC. Minneapolis: Fortress, 2004.

———. *Numbers* במדבר*: The Traditional Hebrew Text with the New JPS Translation*. The JPS Torah Commentary. Philadelphia: Jewish Publication Society, 1990.

———. "A Prolegomenon to Leviticus 17:11." *JBL* 90 (1971): 149–156.

———. "Sin-Offering or Purification-Offering?" *VT* 21 (1971): 237–39.

Miller, Patrick D. *They Cried to the Lord: The Form and Theology of Biblical Prayer*. Minneapolis: Fortress, 1994.

Miller, Robert D, II. *Covenant and Grace in the Old Testament: Assyrian Propaganda and Israelite Faith*. PHSC 16. Piscataway, NJ: Gorgias, 2012.

Miller-Spillman, Kimberly A. "Dress in the Workplace." Pages 217–24 in *The Meanings of Dress*. Edited by Mary Lynn Damhorst, Kimberly A. Miller-Spillman, and Susan O. Michelman. 2nd ed. New York: Fairchild, 2005.

Minear, Paul. *Images of the Church in the New Testament*. Philadelphia: Westminster, 1960.

Mitchell, Margaret M. *Paul and the Rhetoric of Reconciliation: An Exegetical Investigation of the Language and Composition of 1 Corinthians*. Louisville: Westminster John Knox, 1993.

Moore, Anne. *Moving beyond Symbol and Myth: Understanding the Kingship of God of the Hebrew Bible through Metaphor*. StBibLit 99. New York: Lang, 2009.

Moore, James. "Darwin, Charles: I. Darwin and the Bible." *EBR* 6:162–65.

Moraldi, Luigi. *Espiazione sacrificale e riti espiatori nell'ambiente biblico e nell'Antico Testamento*. AnBib 5. Rome: Pontifical Biblical Institute, 1956.

Morales, L. Michael. *Who Shall Ascend the Mountain of the Lord? A Biblical Theology of the Book of Leviticus*. NSBT 37. Leicester: Apollos, 2015.

Mørkholm, Otto. "Antiochus IV." Pages 278–91 in vol. 2 of *The Cambridge History of Judaism: The Hellenistic Age*. Edited by W. D. Davies and Louis Finkelstein. Cambridge: Cambridge University Press, 1989.

Morris, Leon. *The Book of Revelation: An Introduction and Commentary*. Rev. ed. TNTC 20. Leicester: Inter-Varsity Press, 1987.

Mounce, Robert H. *The Book of Revelation*. Rev. ed. NICNT. Grand Rapids: Eerdmans, 1998.

Moxnes, Halvor. "Honor and Shame." *BTB* 23 (1993): 167–76.

Müller, Christoph G. "Kleidung als Element der Charakterzeichnung im Neuen Testament und seiner Umwelt: Ein Streifzug durch das lukanische Erzählwerk." *SNTSU* 28 (2003): 187–214.

Müller, Friedrich Max. *Lectures on the Origin of Religion as Illustrated by the Religions of India: Delivered in the Chapter House, Westminster Abbey, in April, May, and June, 1878*. Hibbert Lectures. London: Longmans, Green & Co., 1878.

Murphy, Catherine. *John the Baptist: Prophet of Purity for a New Age*. Interfaces. Collegeville, MN: Liturgical Press, 2003.

Murphy, Frederick J. *Babylon Is Fallen: The Revelation to John*. NTC. Harrisburg, PA: Trinity Press International, 1998.

Myers, Ched. *Binding the Strong Man: A Political Reading of Mark's Story of Jesus*. Maryknoll, NY: Orbis Books, 1990.

Naiden, Fred S. "Rejected Sacrifice in Greek and Hebrew Religion." *JANER* 6 (2006): 189–223.

———. *Smoke Signals for the Gods: Ancient Greek Sacrifice from the Archaic through Roman Periods*. Oxford: Oxford University Press, 2013.

Neil, William. *The Epistles of Paul to the Thessalonians*. MNTC 12. London: Hodder & Stoughton, 1950.

Neufeld, Dietmar. "Sumptuous Clothing and Ornamentation in the Apocalypse." *HvTSt* 58 (2002): 664–89.

———. "Under the Cover of Clothing: Scripted Clothing Performances in the Apocalypse of John." *BTB* 35 (2005): 67–76.

Newsom, Carol. *The Self as Symbolic Space: Constructing Identity and Community at Qumran*. STDJ 52. Leiden: Brill, 2004.

Newton, Michael. *The Concept of Purity at Qumran and in the Letters of Paul*. SNTSMS 53. Cambridge: Cambridge University Press, 1985.

Neyrey, Jerome H. "Dyadism." Pages 53-56 in *Handbook of Biblical Social Values*. Edited by John J. Pilch and Bruce J. Malina. Peabody, MA: Hendrickson, 2009.

———. "Group Orientation." Pages 94-98 in *Handbook of Biblical Social Values*. Edited by John J. Pilch and Bruce J. Malina. Peabody, MA: Hendrickson, 2009.

———. "Limited Good." Pages 122-27 in *Handbook of Biblical Social Values*. Edited by John J. Pilch and Bruce J. Malina. Peabody, MA: Hendrickson, 2009.

Ng, Wai Yee. *Water Symbolism in John: An Eschatological Interpretation.* StBibLit 15. New York: Lang, 2001.
Nicholl, Colin R. *From Hope to Despair in Thessalonica: Situating 1 and 2 Thessalonians.* SNTSMS 126. Cambridge: Cambridge University Press, 2004.
———. "Michael, the Restrainer Removed (2 Thess.2:6–7)." *JTS* 51 (2000): 27–53.
Nielsen, Kirsten. *Yahweh as Prosecutor and Judge: An Investigation of the Prophetic Lawsuit (Rîb-Pattern).* JSOTSup 9. Sheffield: JSOT Press, 1978.
Nielsen, Kjeld. *Incense in Ancient Israel.* VTSup 38. Leiden: Brill, 1986.
Nihan, Christophe. "Forms and Function of Purity in Leviticus." Pages 311–67 in *Purity and the Forming of Religious Traditions in the Ancient Mediterranean World and Ancient Judaism.* Edited by Christian Frevel and Christophe Nihan. DHR 3. Leiden: Brill, 2013.
———. *From Priestly Torah to Pentateuch: A Study in the Composition of the Book of Leviticus.* FAT 2/25; Tübingen: Mohr Siebeck, 2007.
———. "The Templization of Israel in Leviticus: Some Remarks on Blood Disposal and *Kipper* in Leviticus 4." Pages 94–130 in *Text, Time, and Temple: Literary, Historical and Ritual Studies in Leviticus.* Edited by Francis Landy, Leigh M. Trevaskis, and Bryan D. Bibb. HBM 64. Sheffield: Sheffield Phoenix, 2015.
Nitzsch, Friedrich. *Die Idee und die Stufen des Opferkultus.* Kiel: Universitäts-Buchhandlung, 1889.
Noam, Vered. "Stringency in Qumran: A Reassessment." *JSJ* 40 (2009): 342–55.
Norton, John. "Faith and Fashion in Turkey." Pages 149–77 in *Languages of Dress in the Middle East.* Edited by Nancy Lindisfarne-Tapper and Bruce Ingham. London: Curzon, 1997. Repr., Oxford: Routledge, 2013.
O'Hagan, A. "The Martyr in the Fourth Book of the Maccabees." *SBFLA* 24 (1974): 94–120.
Olmo Lete, Gregorio del, and Joaquín Sanmartín. *Dictionary of the Ugaritic Language in the Alphabetic Tradition.* HdO 67. 2 vols. 3rd ed. Leiden: Brill, 2015.
Olyan, Saul M. *Rites and Rank: Hierarchy in Biblical Representations of Cult.* Princeton: Princeton University Press, 2000.
———. "Honor, Shame, and Covenant Relations in Ancient Israel and Its Environment." *JBL* 115 (1996): 201–18.

Omerzu, Heike. "Women, Magic and Angels: On the Emancipation of Job's Daughters in the Apocryphal Testament of Job." Pages 85–103 in *Bodies in Question: Gender, Religion, Text*. Edited by Darlene Bird and Yvonne Sherwood. Burlington, VT: Ashgate, 2005.

Oppenheim, A. Leo. "Akkadian *pul(u)ḫ(t)u* and *melammu*." *JAOS* 63 (1943): 31–34.

Oppenheimer, Aharon. *The ʿAm ha-ʾAretz: A Study in the Social History of the Jewish People in the Hellenistic-Roman Period*. Translated by I. H. Levine. ALGHJ 8. Leiden: Brill, 1977.

Osborne, Grant R. *Revelation*. BECNT. Grand Rapids: Baker Academic, 2002.

Oswalt, John N. *The Book of Isaiah: Chapters 1–39*. NICOT. Grand Rapids: Eerdmans, 1986.

Otzen, Benedikt. "Michael and Gabriel: Angelological Problems in the Book of Daniel." Pages 114–24 in *The Scriptures and the Scrolls: Studies in Honour of A. S. van der Woude on the Occasion of His 65th Birthday*. Edited by Florentino García Martínez, A. Hilhorst, and C. J. Labuschagne. VTSup 49. Leiden: Brill, 1992.

Pagolu, Augustine. *The Religion of the Patriarchs*. JSOTSup 277. Sheffield: Sheffield Academic, 1998.

Pape, Wilhelm. *Griechisch-Deutsches Handwörterbuch*. 3rd ed. Braunschweig: Vieweg, 1880.

Patai, Raphael. *The Arab Mind*. New York: Scribner, 1973.

Paulien, Jon. "The Role of the Hebrew Cultus, Sanctuary, and Temple in the Plot and Structure of the Book of Revelation." *AUSS* 33 (1995): 245–64.

Perrin, Nicholas. *Jesus the Temple*. Grand Rapids: Baker Academic, 2010.

Péter, René. "L'imposition des mains dans l'ancien testament." *VT* 27 (1977): 48–55.

Peterson, David. *Engaging with God: A Biblical Theology of Worship*. Downers Grove, IL: IVP Academic, 1992.

Petropoulou, Maria-Zoe. *Animal Sacrifice in Ancient Greek Religion, Judaism, and Christianity, 100 BC–AD 200*. OCM. Oxford: Oxford University Press, 2008.

Philo. Translated by F. H. Colson et al. 12 vols. LCL. Cambridge: Harvard University Press, 1929–1962.

Pilch, John J. "'Beat His Ribs While He Is Young' (Sir 30:12): A Window on the Mediterranean World." *BTB* 23 (1993): 101–13.

———. "Forgiveness." Pages 59–64 in *The Cultural Dictionary of the Bible*. Collegeville, MN: Liturgical Press, 1999.

———. *Introducing the Cultural Context of the Old Testament*. Hear the Word! 1. Eugene, OR: Wipf & Stock, 2007.

———. "Parenting." Pages 145–48 in *Handbook of Biblical Social Values*. Edited by John J. Pilch and Bruce J. Malina. Peabody, MA: Hendrickson, 2009.

Piller, Michael. "The Best of Both Worlds, Part 1." DVD, Episode 26 of Season 3 of *Star Trek: The Next Generation*. Directed by Clif Bole. Hollywood, CA: Paramount Pictures, 2013.

Plevnik, Joseph. "Honor/Shame." Pages 106–14 in *Handbook of Biblical Social Values*. Edited by John J. Pilch and Bruce J. Malina. Peabody, MA: Hendrickson, 2009.

Podella, Thomas. *Das Lichtkleid JHWHs: Untersuchungen zur Gestalthaftigkeit Gottes im Alten Testament und seiner altorientalischen Umwelt*. FAT 15. Tübingen: Mohr Siebeck, 1996.

Porter, Stanley E. καταλλασσω *in Ancient Greek Literature, with Reference to the Pauline Writings*. EFN 5. Cordoba: Ediciones El Almendro, 1994.

Prigent, Pierre. *Commentary on the Apocalypse of St. John*. Translated by Wendy Pradels. Tübingen: Mohr Siebeck, 2001.

Pröbstle, Martin. "Truth and Terror: A Text-Oriented Analysis of Daniel 8:9–14." PhD diss., Andrews University, 2006.

Propp, William H. C. *Exodus 19–40: A New Translation with Introduction and Commentary*. AB 2A. New York: Doubleday, 2006.

Rajak, Tessa. *The Jewish Dialogue with Greece and Rome*. AGJU 48. Leiden: Brill, 2001.

Rapp, Ursula. "The Heritage of Old Testament Impurity Laws: Gender as a Question of how to Focus on Women." Pages 29–40 in *Gender and Religion: European Studies*. Edited by Kari E. Børresen, Sara Cabibbo, and Edith Specht. Quaderni 2. Rome: Catocci, 2001.

Regev, Eyal. "The Ritual Baths Near the Temple Mount and Extra-Purification before Entering the Temple Courts." *IEJ* 55 (2005): 194–204.

———. *Sectarianism in Qumran: A Cross-Cultural Perspective*. RelSoc 45. Berlin: de Gruyter, 2007.

Reich, Ronny. "*Miqwa'ot* (Jewish ritual immersion baths) in Eretz-Israel in the Second Temple and the Mishna and Talmud Periods." (Hebrew). PhD diss., Hebrew University of Jerusalem, 1990.

———. "Two Possible *Miqwāʾōt* on the Temple Mount." *IEJ* 39 (1989): 63–65.

Rendtorff, Rolf. *The Covenant Formula: An Exegetical and Theological Investigation*. Translated by Margaret Kohl. OTS. Edinburgh: T&T Clark, 1998.

———. *Die Gesetze in der Priesterschrift: Eine gattungsgeschichtliche Untersuchung*. FRLANT 62. Göttingen: Vandenhoeck & Ruprecht, 1954.

———. *Leviticus 1,1–10,20*. BKAT 3/1. Neukirchen-Vluyn: Neukirchener, 2004.

———. *Studien zur Geschichte des Opfers im Alten Israel*. WMANT 24. Neukirchen-Vluyn: Neukirchener Verlag, 1967.

Resseguie, James L. "Clothing: A Map of the Spiritual Life." Pages 89–100 in *Spiritual Landscape: Images of the Spiritual Life in the Gospel of Luke*. Peabody, MA: Hendrickson, 2004.

———. *Revelation Unsealed: A Narrative Critical Approach to John's Apocalypse*. BibInt 32. Leiden: Brill, 1998.

Riley, William. "Temple Imagery and the Book of Revelation: Ancient Near Eastern Temple Ideology and Cultic Resonances in the Apocalypse." *PIBA* 6 (1982): 81–102.

Ringgren, Helmer. "עָמַד." *TDOT* 11:178–87.

Rissi, Mathias. *Die Theologie des Hebräerbriefs: Ihre Verankerung in der Situation des Verfassers und seiner Leser*. WUNT 41. Tübingen: Mohr Siebeck, 1987.

Roach-Higgins, Mary Ellen, and Joanne B. Eicher. "Dress and Identity." Pages 7–18 in *Dress and Identity*. Edited by Mary Ellen Roach-Higgins, Joanne B. Eicher, and Kim K. P. Johnson. New York: Fairchild, 1995.

Robertson Smith, W. *Lectures on the Religion of the Semites*. Burnett Lectures 1888–1889. London: Black, 1894.

Robinson, Clayton David. "The Laying On of Hands, with Special Reference to the Reception of the Holy Spirit in the New Testament." PhD diss., Fuller Theological Seminary, 2008.

Robinson, John A. T. "The Baptism of John and the Qumran Community: Testing a Hypothesis." Pages 11–27 in *Twelve New Testament Studies*. SBT 34. London: SCM, 1962.

Röcker, Fritz W. *Belial und Katechon: Eine Untersuchung zu 2 Thess 2,1–12 und 1 Thess 4,13–5,11*. WUNT 262. Tübingen: Mohr Siebeck, 2009.

Röhser, Günter. *Stellvertretung im Neuen Testament*. SBS 195. Stuttgart: Katholisches Bibelwerk, 2002.

———. "Sühne II: Biblisch 2. Neues Testament." *RGG4* 7:1844 –45.
Roloff, Jürgen. *Die Offenbarung des Johannes*. ZBK NT 18. Zurich: Theologischer Verlag, 1984.
———. *The Revelation of John: A Continental Commentary*. Translated by John E. Alsup. CC. Minneapolis: Fortress, 1993.
Romaniuk, Kazimeirz. "Exégèse du Nouveau Testament et ponctuation." *NovT* 23 (1981): 195–209.
Römer, Thomas. "The Formation of the Book of Jeremiah as a Supplement to the So-called Deuteronomistic History." Pages 168–83 in *The Production of Prophecy: Constructing Prophecy and Prophets in Yehud*. Edited by Diana Edelman and Ehud Ben Zvi. Bible World. London: Equinox, 2009.
Romney Wegner, Judith. "'Coming before the Lord': The Exclusion of Women from the Public Domain of the Israelite Priestly Cult." Pages 451–65 in *The Book of Leviticus: Composition and Reception*. Edited by Rolf Rendtorff and Robert A. Kugler. VTSup 93. Leiden: Brill, 2003.
Rooke, Deborah W. "The Day of Atonement as a Ritual of Validation for the High Priest." Pages 342–364 in *Temple and Worship in Biblical Israel*. Edited by John Day. LHBOTS 422. London: T&T Clark, 2005.
———. "Kingship as Priesthood: The Relationship between the High Priesthood and the Monarchy." Pages 187–208 in *King and Messiah in Israel and the Ancient Near East: Proceedings of the Oxford Old Testament Seminar*. Edited by John Day. JSOTSup 270. Sheffield: Sheffield Academic, 1998.
Ruane, Nicole J. *Sacrifice and Gender in Biblical Law*. Cambridge: Cambridge University Press 2013.
Ruiten, J. T. A. G. M. van. "Eden and the Temple: The Rewriting of Genesis 2:4–3:24 in The Book of Jubilees." Pages 63–94 in *Paradise Interpreted: Representations of Biblical Paradise in Judaism and Christianity*. Edited by Gerard P. Luttikhuizen. TBN 2. Leiden: Brill, 1999.
Sabourin, Leopold. *Rédemption sacrificielle: Une enquête exégétique*. Studia 11. Brussels: de Brouwer, 1961.
Sakenfield, Katherine Doob, ed. *New Interpreter's Dictionary of the Bible*. 5 vols. Nashville: Abingdon, 2006–2009.
Sanders, E. P. *Jesus and Judaism*. Philadelphia: Fortress, 1985.
———. *Judaism, Practice and Belief: 63 BCE–66 CE*. London: SCM Press, 1992.
Satake, Akira. *Die Offenbarung des Johannes*. Edited by Thomas Witulski. KEK 16. Göttingen: Vandenhoeck & Ruprecht, 2008.

Schäfer, Peter. *The Origins of Jewish Mysticism.* Princeton: Princeton University Press, 2009.
Schellenberg, Annette. "More than Spirit: On the Physical Dimension in the Priestly Understanding of Holiness." *ZAW* 126 (2014): 163–79.
Schenker, Adrian. "Das Zeichen des Blutes und die Gewißheit der Vergebung im Alten Testament: Die sühnende Funktion des Blutes auf dem Altar nach Lev 17.10–12." *MThZ* 43 (1983): 195–213.
———. "Einführung." Pages v–viii in *Studien zu Opfer und Kult im Alten Testament.* Edited by Adrian Schenker. FAT 3. Tübingen: Mohr Siebeck, 1992.
———. "Interprétations récentes et dimensions spécifiques du sacrifice ḥaṭṭāt." *Bib* 75 (1994): 59–70.
———. *Versöhnung und Sühne: Wege gewaltfreier Konfliktlösung im Alten Testament; mit einem Ausblick auf das Neue Testament.* BiBe 15. Fribourg: Schweizerisches Katholisches Bibelwerk, 1981.
Schiffman, Lawrence H. "Purity and Perfection: Exclusion from the Council of the Community in the *Serekh ha-'Edah*." Pages 373–89 in *Biblical Archaeology Today.* Edited by J. Amitai. Jerusalem: Israel Exploration Society, 1985.
———. *Reclaiming the Dead Sea Scrolls: The History of Judaism, the Background of Christianity, the Lost Library of Qumran.* Philadelphia: Jewish Publication Society, 1994.
———. *Sectarian Law in the Dead Sea Scrolls: Courts, Testimony and the Penal Code.* BJS 33. Chico, CA: Scholars Press, 1983.
———. *Texts and Traditions: A Source Reader for the Study of Second Temple and Rabbinic Judaism.* Hoboken, NJ: Ktav, 1998.
Schmidt, F. *La pensée du temple, de Jérusalem à Qoumrân: Identité et lien social dans le judaïsme ancien.* Paris: Édition du Seuil, 1994.
Schmidt, Nathaniel. "The Son of Man in the Book of Daniel." *JBL* 19 (1900): 22–28.
Schmidt, Werner H. *Das Buch Jeremia: Kapitel 1–20.* ATD 20. Göttingen: Vandenhoeck & Ruprecht, 2008.
Schneider, Jane. "The Anthropology of Cloth." *ARA* 16 (1987): 409–48.
Schneider, Jane, and Annette B. Weiner, "Introduction." Pages 1–29 in *Cloth and Human Experience.* Edited by Annette B. Weiner and Jane Schneider. SSEI. Washington, DC: Smithsonian Institution, 1989.
Schröter, Jens. "Sühne, Stellvertretung und Opfer: Zur Verwendung analytischer Kategorien zur Deutung des Todes Jesu." Pages 51–71 in *Deu-*

tungen des Todes Jesu im Neuen Testament. Edited by Jörg Frey and Jens Schröter. WUNT 181. Tübingen: Mohr Siebeck, 2005.

Schüngel-Straumann, Helen. *Gottesbild und Kultkritik vorexilischer Propheten*. SBS 60. Stuttgart: Katholisches Bibelwerk, 1972.

Schüssler Fiorenza, Elisabeth. "Cultic Language in Qumran and in the New Testament." *CBQ* 38 (1976): 159–177.

———. *Revelation: Vision of a Just World*. PC. Minnneapolis: Fortress, 1991.

Schwager, Raymond. "Christ's Death and the Prophetic Critique of Sacrifice." *Semeia* 33 (1985): 109–23.

Schwartz, Baruch J. "The Bearing of Sin in the Priestly Literature." Pages 3–21 in *Pomegranates and Golden Bells: Studies in Biblical, Jewish, and Near Eastern Ritual, Law, and Literature in Honor of Jacob Milgrom*. Edited by David P. Wright, David Noel Freedman, and Avi Hurvitz. Winona Lake, IN: Eisenbrauns, 1995.

Schwartz, Daniel R. *2 Maccabees*. CEJL. Berlin: de Gruyter, 2008.

———. "Temple and Desert: On Religion and State in Second Temple Period Judaea." Pages 29–43 in *Studies in the Jewish Background of Christianity*. WUNT 60. Tübingen: Mohr Siebeck, 1992.

———. "Two Pauline Allusions to the Redemptive Mechanism of the Crucifixion," *JBL* 102 (1983): 259–68.

Scurlock, JoAnn. "The Techniques of the Sacrifice of Animals in Ancient Israel and Ancient Mesopotamia: New Insights through Comparison, Part 1." *AUSS* 44 (2006): 13–49.

Seeley, David. *The Noble Death: Graeco-Roman Martyrology and Paul's Concept of Salvation*. JSOTSup 28. Sheffield: JSOT Press, 1990.

Seow, Choon-Leong. "Ark of the Covenant." *ABD* 1:386–93.

Shea, William H. *Daniel: A Reader's Guide*. Nampa, ID: Pacific Press, 2005.

Shogren, Gary S. *1 & 2 Thessalonians*. ZECNT. Grand Rapids: Zondervan, 2012.

Siebert-Hommes, Jopie. "'On the Third Day Esther Put on Her Queen's Robes' [Esther 5:1]: The Symbolic Function of Clothing in the Book of Esther." *LDiff* 3.1 (2002). http://tinyurl.com/SBL0393h.

Simkins, Ronald. *Creator and Creation: Nature in the Worldview of Ancient Israel*. Peabody, MA: Hendrickson, 1994.

Sklar, Jay. *Sin, Impurity, Sacrifice, Atonement: The Priestly Conceptions*. HBM 2. Sheffield: Sheffield Phoenix, 2005.

Slater, Thomas B. *Christ and Community: A Socio-historical Study of the*

Christology of Revelation. JSNTSup 178. Sheffield: Sheffield Academic, 1999.

Smalley, Stephen S. *The Revelation to John: A Commentary on the Greek Text of the Apocalypse.* Downers Grove, IL: InterVarsity Press, 2005.

Smith, Henry Preserved. "The Laying-On of Hands." *AmJT* 17 (1913): 47–62.

Soranus Ephesius. *Soranus' Gynecology.* Translated from the Greek with an introduction by Owsei Temkin. Baltimore: Johns Hopkins Press, 1991.

Sproles, George B., and Leslie Davis Burns. *Changing Appearances: Understanding Dress in Contemporary Society.* New York: Fairchild, 1994.

Stanley, Christopher D. *Paul and the Language of Scripture: Citation Technique in the Pauline Epistles and Contemporary Literature.* SNTSMS 74. Cambridge: Cambridge University Press, 1992.

Stansell, Gary. *Micah and Isaiah: A Form and Tradition Historical Comparison.* SBLDS 85. Atlanta: Scholars Press, 1988.

Staubli, Thomas. *Die Bücher Levitikus, Numeri.* NSKAT 3. Stuttgart: Katholisches Bibelwerk, 1996.

Stefanovic, Zdravko. *Daniel: Wisdom to the Wise: Commentary on the Book of Daniel.* Nampa, ID: Pacific Press, 2007.

Stegemann, Hartmut. "The Qumran Essenes—Local Members of the Main Jewish Union in Late Second Temple Times." Pages 83–166 in vol. 1 of *The Madrid Qumran Congress: Proceedings of the International Congress on the Dead Sea Scrolls, Madrid, 18–21 March, 1991.* Edited by Julio C. Trebolle-Barrera and Luis V. Montaner. STDJ 11. Leiden: Brill, 1992.

Stemberger, Günter. "Yom Kippur in Mishnah Yoma." Pages 121–37 in *The Day of Atonement: Its Interpretations in Early Jewish and Christian Traditions.* Edited by Thomas Hieke and Tobias Nicklas. TBN 15. Leiden: Brill, 2012.

Stevenson, Gregory. *Power and Place: Temple and Identity in the Book of Revelation.* BZNW 107. Berlin: de Gruyter, 2001.

Stiebert, Johanna. *The Construction of Shame in the Hebrew Bible.* JSOTSup 346. New York: Sheffield Academic, 2002.

Stöckl, Albert. *Das Opfer nach seinem Wesen und seiner Geschichte.* Mainz: Kirchheim, 1861.

Stökl Ben Ezra, Daniel. "Fasting with Jews, Thinking with Scapegoats: Some Remarks on Yom Kippur in Early Judaism and Christianity, in Particular 4Q541, *Barnabas* 7, Matthew 27 and Acts 27." Pages 163–87 in *The Day of Atonement: Its Interpretations in Early Jewish and Chris-*

tian Traditions. Edited by Thomas Hieke and Tobias Nicklas. TBN 15. Leiden: Brill, 2012.

———. *The Impact of Yom Kippur on Early Christianity: The Day of Atonement from Second Temple Judaism to the Fifth Century*. WUNT 163. Tübingen: Mohr Siebeck, 2003.

Stone, Gregory P. "Appearance and the Self." Pages 19–39 in *Human Behavior and Social Processes: An Interactionist Approach*. Edited by Arnold M. Rose. Boston: Houghton Mifflin, 1962.

———. "Clothing and Social Relations: A Study of Appearance in the Context of Community Life." PhD diss., University of Chicago, 1959.

Stordalen, Terje. *Echoes of Eden: Genesis 2–3 and Symbolism of the Eden Garden in Biblical Hebrew Literature*. CBET 25. Leuven: Peeters, 2000.

———. "Heaven on Earth—Or Not? Jerusalem as Eden in Biblical Literature." Pages 28–57 in *Beyond Eden: The Biblical Story of Paradise (Genesis 2–3) and Its Reception History*. Edited by Konrad Schmid and Christoph Riedweg. FAT 2/34. Tübingen: Mohr Siebeck, 2008.

———. "Heaven on Earth: Jerusalem, Temple, and the Cosmography of the Garden of Eden." *CBÅ* 13 (2009): 7–20.

Storm, Penny. *Functions of Dress: Tool of Culture and the Individual*. Englewood Cliffs, NJ: Prentice Hall, 1987.

Stott, Wilfrid. "The Conception of 'Offering' in the Epistle to the Hebrews." *NTS* 9 (1962): 62–67.

Strong, John T. "Egypt's Shameful Death and the House of Israel's Exodus from Sheol (Ezekiel 32.17–32 and 37.1–14)." *JSOT* 34 (2010): 475–504.

Stulman, Louis. *Jeremiah*. AOTC. Nashville: Abingdon, 2005.

Surkau, H. W. *Martyrien in jüdischer und frühchristlicher Zeit*. FRLANT 36. Göttingen: Vandenhoeck & Ruprecht, 1938.

Sweeney, Marvin A. "The End of Eschatology in Daniel? Theological and Socio-Political Ramifications of the Changing Contexts of Interpretation." Pages 248–61 in *Form and Intertextuality in Prophetic and Apocalyptic Literature*. FAT 45. Tübingen: Mohr Siebeck, 2005.

Sykes, Stephen W., ed. *Sacrifice and Redemption: Durham Essays in Theology*. Cambridge: Cambridge University Press, 1991.

Talmon, Shemaryahu. "Yom Hakkippurim in the Habakkuk Scroll." *Bib* 32 (1951): 549–63.

Taylor, Joan. *The Immerser: John the Baptist within Second Temple Judaism*. SHJ. Grand Rapids: Eerdmans, 1997.

Taylor, Vincent. *Jesus and His Sacrifice: A Study of the Passion-Sayings in the Gospels*. London: Macmillan, 1948.

Thiel, Winfried. *Die deuteronomistische Redaktion von Jeremia 1–25.* WMANT 41. Neukirchen-Vluyn: Neukirchener Verlag, 1973.
Thomas, Robert L. *Revelation 1–7: An Exegetical Commentary.* Chicago: Moody, 1992.
Tiemeyer, Lena-Sofia. "The Priests and the Temple Cult in the Book of Jeremiah." Pages 233–64 in *Prophecy in the Book of Jeremiah.* Edited by Hans M. Barstad and Reinhard G. Kratz. BZAW 388. Berlin: de Gruyter, 2009.
Tiwald, Markus. "Christ as Hilasterion (Rom 3:25): Pauline Theology on the Day of Atonement in the Mirror of Early Jewish Thought." Pages 189–209 in *The Day of Atonement: Its Interpretation in Early Jewish and Christian Traditions.* Edited by Thomas Hieke and Tobias Nicklas. TBN 15. Leiden: Brill, 2012.
Tolbert, Mary Ann. *Sowing the Gospel: Mark's World in Literary-Historical Perspective.* Minneapolis: Fortress, 1996.
Tonstad, Sigve K. "The Restrainer Removed: A Truly Alarming Thought (2 Thess 2:1–12)." *HBT* 29 (2007): 133–51.
Trawick, Paul, and Alf Hornborg. "Revisiting the Image of Limited Good: On Sustainability, Thermodynamics, and the Illusion of Creating Wealth." *CA* 56 (2015): 1–27.
Troxel, Ronald. *The Prophetic Literature: From Oracles to Books.* Malden, MA: Wiley-Blackwell, 2012.
Tucker, Gene M. "Prophetic Speech." *Int* 32 (1978): 31–45.
Tylor, Edward B. *Primitive Culture.* London: Murray, 1920.
Ullucci, Daniel. *The Christian Rejection of Animal Sacrifice.* Oxford: Oxford University Press, 2012.
———. "Contesting the Meaning of Animal Sacrifice." Pages 55–74 in *Ancient Mediterranean Sacrifice.* Edited by Jennifer W. Kunst and Zsuzsanna Várhelyi. Oxford: Oxford University Press, 2011.
Ungerer, Friedrich, and Hans-Jörg Schmid. *An Introduction to Cognitive Linguistics.* 2nd ed. Learning about Language. Harlow: Longman, 2006.
Vahrenhorst, Martin. "Levitikon/Leviticus/Das dritte Buch Mose." Pages 325–430 in vol. 1 of *Septuaginta Deutsch: Erklärungen und Kommentare zum griechischen Alten Testament.* Edited by Martin Karrer and Wolfgang Kraus. Stuttgart: Deutsche Bibelgesellschaft, 2011.
Vanhoye, Albert. "L'Apocalisse e la lettera agli Ebrei." Pages 257–75 in *Apokalypsis: Percorsi nell'Apocalisse in onore di Ugo Vanni.* Edited by Elena Bosetti and Angelo Colacrai. Commenti e studi biblica. Assisi, Italy: Cittadella, 2005.

Vanni, Ugo. *L'Apocalisse: ermeneutica, esegesi, teologia.* RivBibSup 17. Bologna: Dehoniane, 1988.

Vaux, Roland de. *Studies in Old Testament Sacrifice.* Cardiff: University of Wales Press, 1964.

Vawter, Bruce. *Amos, Hosea, Micah with an Introduction to Classical Prophecy.* OTMes 7. Wilmington, DE: Glazier, 1981.

Vernant, Jean-Pierre. "Théorie générale du sacrifice et mise à mort dans la θυσία grecque." Pages 1–39 in *Le sacrifice dans l'Antiquité: Huit exposés suivis de discussions; Vandœuvres-Genève, 25-30 août 1980.* Edited by J. Rudhardt and O. Reverdin. EAC 27. Geneva: Fondation Hardt, 1981.

Versnel, H. S. "Making Sense of Jesus' Death: The Pagan Contribution." Pages 215–94 in *Deutungen des Todes Jesu im Neuen Testament.* Edited by Jörg Frey and Jens Schröter. WUNT 181. Tübingen: Mohr Siebeck, 2005.

Vicary, Grace Q. "The Signs of Clothing." Pages 291–314 in *Cross-Cultural Perspectives in Nonverbal Communication.* Edited by Fernando Poyatos. Toronto: Hogrefe, 1988.

Vis, Joshua M. "The Purification Offering of Leviticus and the Sacrificial Offering of Jesus." PhD diss., Duke University, 2012.

Vogel, Winfried. *The Cultic Motif in the Book of Daniel.* New York: Lang, 2010.

Volz, Paul. "Die Handauflegung beim Opfer." *ZAW* 21 (1901): 93–100.

Vorwahl, Heinrich. *Die Gebärdensprache im Alten Testament.* Berlin: Ebering, 1932.

Wagner, J. Ross. "Isaiah in Romans and Galatians." Pages 117–132 in *Isaiah in the New Testament.* Edited by Steve Moyise and Maarten J. J. Menken. NTSI. London: T&T Clark, 2005.

Waldman, Nahum M. "The Imagery of Clothing, Covering, and Overpowering." *JANESCU* 19 (1989): 161–70.

Waltke, Bruce K. *A Commentary on Micah.* Grand Rapids: Eerdmans, 2007.

Waltke, Bruce K., and Michael Patrick O'Connor. *Introduction to Biblical Hebrew Syntax.* Winona Lake, IN: Eisenbrauns, 1990.

Wangemann, Hermann Th. *Das Opfer nach Lehre der heiligen Schrift Alten und Neuen Testaments: Eine apologetische Darstellung des biblisch-kirchlichen Opferbegriffs.* Berlin: Schultze, 1866.

Wardle, Timothy. *The Jerusalem Temple and Early Christian Identity.* WUNT 2/291. Tübingen: Mohr Siebeck, 2010.

Waschke, E.-J. "רָמַס." *TDOT* 13:509–11.

Wassen, Cecilia. "Do You Have to Be Pure in a Metaphorical Temple?" Pages 55–86 in *Purity, Holiness, and Identity in Judaism and Christianity: Essays in Memory of Susan Haber*. Edited by Carl S. Ehrlich, Anders Runesson, and Eileen Schuller. WUNT 305. Tübingen: Mohr Siebeck, 2013.

Watts, James W. *Leviticus 1–10*. HCOT. Leuven: Peeters, 2013.

———. *Ritual and Rhetoric in Leviticus: From Sacrifice to Scripture*. Cambridge: Cambridge University Press, 2007.

Watts, John D. W. *Isaiah 1–33*. WBC 24. Waco, TX: Word, 1985.

Webb, Robert. "John the Baptist and His Relationship to Jesus." Pages 179–229 in *Studying the Historical Jesus: Evaluations of the State of Current Research*. Edited by Bruce Chilton and Craig A. Evans. NTTS 19. Leiden: Brill, 1998.

Weima, Jeffrey A. D. *1–2 Thessalonians*. BECNT. Grand Rapids: Baker Academic, 2014.

Weinfeld, Moshe. "Jeremiah and the Spiritual Metamorphosis of Israel." *ZAW* 88 (1976): 17–56.

Wellhausen, Julius. *Israelitische und jüdische Geschichte*. 9th ed. Berlin: de Gruyter 1958.

Wenham, Gordon J. "Sanctuary Symbolism in the Garden of Eden Story." Pages 19–25 in *Proceedings of the World Congress of Jewish Studies, Jerusalem, August 4-12, 1985: Division A; the Period of the Bible*. Jerusalem: World Union of Jewish Studies, 1986.

———. "The Theology of Old Testament Sacrifice." Pages 75–87 in *Sacrifice in the Bible*. Edited by Roger T. Beckwith and Martin J. Selman. Grand Rapids: Baker, 1995.

Wentz, Richard. "Clothed in the Beauty of Possibility." *Parab* 19 (Fall 1994): 80–81.

Werman, Cana. "The Concept of Holiness and the Requirements of Purity in Second Temple and Tannaitic Literature." Pages 163–79 in *Purity and Holiness: The Heritage of Leviticus*. Edited by Marcel J. H. M. Poorthuis and Joshua Schwartz. JCPS 2. Leiden: Brill, 2000.

Werrett, Jan C. *Ritual Purity and the Dead Sea Scrolls*. STDJ 72. Leiden: Brill, 2007.

Westbrook, Raymond. "Social Justice in the Near East." Pages 143–60 in *The Shared Traditions*. Vol. 1 of *Law from Tigris to the Tiber: The Writings of Raymond Westbrook*. Edited by Bruce Wells and F. Rachel Magdalene. Winona Lake, IN: Eisenbrauns, 2009.

Wevers, John William. *Notes on the Greek Text of Leviticus*. SCS 44. Atlanta: Scholars Press, 1997.
Whiteley, Iwan. "A Search for Cohesion in the Book of Revelation with Specific Reference to Chapter One." PhD diss., University of Wales (Lampeter), 2005.
Wilckens, Ulrich. *Der Brief an die Römer: Röm 1–5*. EKK 6/1. Neukirchen-Vluyn: Neukirchener Verlag, 1978.
Willi-Plein, Ina. *Opfer und Kult im alttestamentlichen Israel: Textbefragungen und Zwischenergebnisse*. SBS 153. Stuttgart: Katholisches Bibelwerk, 1993.
Williams, James G. "Kings and Prophets: Sacred Lot and Divine Calling." Pages 129–62 in *The Bible, Violence, and the Sacred: Liberation from the Myth of Sanctioned Violence*. Valley Forge, PA: Trinity Press International, 1995.
Williams, Jarvis J. *Christ Died For Our Sins: Representation and Substitution in Romans and Their Jewish Martyrological Background*. Eugene, OR: Pickwick, 2015.
———. *Maccabean Martyr Traditions in Paul's Theology of Atonement: Did Martyr Theology Shape Paul's Conception of Jesus's Death*. Eugene, OR: Wipf & Stock, 2010.
———. "Martyr Theology in Hellenistic Judaism." Pages 493–521 in *Christian Origins and Hellenistic Judaism: Social and Literary Contexts for the New Testament—Early Christianity in Its Hellenistic Context*. Edited by Stanley E. Porter and Andrew W. Pitts. ECHC 2. Leiden: Brill, 2012.
Williams, Sam K., *Jesus' Death as Saving Event: The Background and Origin of a Concept*. HDR 2. Missoula, MT: Scholars Press, 1975.
Wink, Walter. *John the Baptist in the Gospel Tradition*. SNTSMS 7. Cambridge: Cambridge University Press, 1968.
Winkle, Ross E. "'Clothes Make the (One Like a Son of) Man': Dress Imagery in Revelation 1 as an Indicator of High Priestly Status." PhD diss., Andrews University, 2012.
Wise, Michael O. "4QFlorilegium and the Temple of Adam." *RevQ* 15 (1991): 103–32.
Wißmann, Hans. "Frazer, James George." *EBR* 9:632–34.
Witherington, Ben, III. *1 and 2 Thessalonians: A Socio-rhetorical Commentary*. Grand Rapids: Eerdmans, 2006.
———. *Revelation*. NCBC. Cambridge: Cambridge University Press, 2003.
———. *The Gospel of Mark: A Socio-rhetorical Commentary*. Grand Rapids: Eerdmans, 2001.

Wolff, Hans W. *Joel and Amos: A Commentary on the Books of the Prophets Joel and Amos*. Translated by W. Janzen, S. D. McBride Jr., and C. A. Muenchow. Hermeneia. Philadelphia: Fortress, 1977.

Wright, Christopher J. H. "Atonement in the Old Testament." Pages 69–82 in *The Atonement Debate: Papers from the London Symposium on the Theology of Atonement*. Edited by Derek Tidball, David Hilborn, and Justin Thacker. Grand Rapids: Zondervan, 2008.

Wright, David P. *The Disposal of Impurity: Elimination Rites in the Bible and in Hittite and Mesopotamian Literature*. SBLDS 101. Atlanta: Scholars Press, 1987.

———. "The Gesture of Hand Placement in the Hebrew Bible and in Hittite Literature." *JAOS* 106 (1986): 433–46.

———. "Hands, Laying On of: Old Testament." *ABD* 3:47–48.

———. "Unclean and Clean (OT)." *ABD* 6:729–41.

Wright, N. T. *Jesus and the Victory of God*. London: SPCK, 1996.

Yadin, Yigael. *The Temple Scroll*. 3 vols. Jerusalem: Israel Exploration Society, 1977–1983.

Yarden, L. *The Tree of Light: A Study of the Menorah: The Seven-Branched Lampstand*. Ithaca, NY: Cornell University Press, 1971.

Yeatts, John R. *Revelation*. BCBC. Scottdale, PA: Herald Press, 2003.

Yerkes, Royden K. *Sacrifice in Greek and Roman Religions and Early Judaism*. Hale Lectures. New York: Scribner, 1952.

Zenger, Erich. "Das Buch Levitikus als Teiltext der Tora/des Pentateuch: Eine synchrone Lektüre mit diachroner Perspektive." Pages 47–83 in *Levitikus als Buch*. Edited by Hans-Josef Fabry and Hans-Winfried Jüngling. BBB 119. Berlin: Philo, 1999.

Ziderman, I. Irving. "Purple Dyeing in the Mediterranean World: Characterisation of Biblical *Tekhelet*." Pages 40–45 in *Colour in the Ancient Mediterranean World*. Edited by Liza Cleland and Karen Stears with Glenys Davies. BARIS 1267. Oxford: Hedges, 2004.

———. "Seashells and Ancient Purple Dyeing." *BA* 53 (June 1990): 98–101.

Zimmermann, Ruben. "'Deuten' heißt erzählen und übertragen: Narrativität und Metaphorik als zentrale Sprachformen historischer Sinnbildung zum Tod Jesu." Pages 315–73 in *Deutungen des Todes Jesu im Neuen Testament*. Edited by Jörg Frey and Jens Schröter. WUNT 181. Tübingen: Mohr Siebeck, 2005.

Contributors

David Calabro (dcalabro22@gmail.com) is Lead Cataloger of Eastern Christian and Islamic Manuscripts at the Hill Museum and Manuscript Library at St. John's University (Collegeville, Minnesota, USA). He holds a PhD in Near Eastern Languages and Civilizations from the University of Chicago. His book on ritual hand gestures in the Northwest Semitic world is under contract with Eisenbrauns. Calabro has published several articles and book chapters on aspects of Near Eastern culture and language, including "Egyptianizing Features in Phoenician and Punic Inscriptions from Egypt," in *Studies in Semitic Language Contact*, ed. Aaron Michael Butts (Leiden: Brill, 2015), 97–113. His research encompasses the cultural history of the Near East from the Bronze Age to modern times, dwelling particularly on ritual practice, body language, historical linguistics, and the intertextuality of religious narratives.

Nicole Wilkinson Duran (nhawduran@gmail.com) has published various articles on Hebrew Bible and New Testament topics and served on the editorial board of the Global Bible Commentary. She is the author of two books: *Having Men for Dinner: Deadly Banquets and Biblical Women* (Cleveland: Pilgrim Press, 2006) and *The Power of Disorder: Ritual Themes in Mark's Passion Narrative* (London: T&T Clark, 2009). She has been editor and coeditor of a number of other collections of essays. She received her PhD in Religion from Vanderbilt University in 1997 and has taught in a variety of contexts, from South Africa to South Carolina. She is ordained in the Presbyterian Church, USA, and currently serving as a chaplain in the Presbytery of Philadelphia.

Christian A. Eberhart (ceberhart@uh.edu) is Professor of Religious Studies at the University of Houston, Texas (USA). He is also Director of the Religious Studies Program and Chair of the Department of Comparative Cultural Studies at this university. He is the founder and former chair of the Sacrifice, Cult, and Atonement section of the Society of Biblical Literature Annual Meeting and the founder and convener of the international Hebrews research group for the Society of New Testament Studies. He has published many essays and articles on the Hebrew Bible, the Septuagint, and early Christian literature. His books include *The Sacrifice of Jesus: Understanding Atonement Biblically* (Minneapolis: Fortress Press, 2011), *Kultmetaphorik und Christologie: Opfer- und Sühneterminologie im Neuen Testament* (Tübingen: Mohr Siebeck, 2013), and *What a Difference a Meal Makes: The Last Supper in the Bible and in the Christian Church* (Houston: Lucid Books, 2016). He also edited the volume *Ritual and Metaphor: Sacrifice in the Bible* (Atlanta: Society of Biblical Literature, 2011). Christian is originally from Hannover in Germany.

Göran Eidevall (goran.eidevall@teol.uu.se) is Professor in Biblical Studies, especially the Hebrew Bible, at Uppsala University (Sweden). His main area of research is the prophetic literature. Eidevall has studied the use of metaphors and the construction of enemy images in various biblical texts. In a recent project he has analyzed attitudes toward the sacrificial cult in the entire corpus of prophetic literature. Eidevall is the author of *Grapes in the Desert: Metaphors, Models, and Themes in Hosea 4–14* (Stockholm: Almqvist & Wiksell International, 1996), *Prophecy and Propaganda: Images of Enemies in the Book of Isaiah* (Winona Lake, IN: Eisenbrauns, 2009), *Sacrificial Rhetoric in the Prophetic Literature of the Hebrew Bible* (Lewiston, NY: Edwin Mellen, 2012), and a forthcoming commentary on the book of Amos for the Anchor Yale Bible series (New Haven: Yale University Press, 2017).

Dorothea Erbele-Küster (erbelek@uni-mainz.de) is currently fulltime Visiting Professor of Old Testament Studies at the Ruprecht-Karls-University in Heidelberg, Germany. She has been Professor of Old Testament at the Protestant Theological Faculty in Brussels, Belgium, and lecturer of Biblical Studies at the Protestant Theological University in Kampen, Netherlands, and at the Johannes Gutenberg University of Mainz, Germany. She has published broadly on ritual questions and hermeneutics. The revised version of her monograph *Körper und Geschlecht: Studien zu Leviticus 12 and 15* from 2001 is forthcoming in English as *Body, Gender and Purity* (London: T&T Clark, 2017). Besides the above-mentioned topics, her current research focuses on ethics in the Hebrew Bible.

CONTRIBUTORS

Aaron Glaim (glaim@ohio.edu) is a Visiting Assistant Professor in the Department of Classics and World Religions at Ohio University in Athens, Ohio (USA). His research examines sacrificial terminology in biblical and extracanonical literature of the First and Second Temple and Roman periods. He is presently completing a book manuscript, forthcoming with Oxford University Press, that argues for consistency in the reciprocal logic undergirding the performance and understanding of this practice in the majority of Israelite and later Judean religion. Beyond these materials, his work on sacrifice has been enriched by ethnographic observation of contemporary animal-sacrificing temples or rites in India, Nepal, and Indonesia.

Hannah K. Harrington (hharrington@patten.edu) is Professor of Old Testament at Patten University, Oakland, CA (USA). Harrington began her extensive work with the Dead Sea Scrolls at the University of California Berkeley, where she studied under the Biblical scholar Jacob Milgrom and earned both the MA (1985) and PhD (1992) in Near Eastern Studies. She has written over sixty publications (books, articles and reviews) on the Dead Sea Scrolls and other topics relating to holiness and ritual purity in Second Temple Judaism. Notable examples include: *"Leviticus"* in the *Women's Bible Commentary* (Louisville: Westminster John Knox, 2012); *Purity Texts* (Sheffield: Sheffield Academic, 2004); *Holiness: Rabbinic Judaism and the Graeco-Roman World* (London: Routledge, 2001) and, currently in progress, *Ezra and Nehemiah* (Grand Rapids: Eerdmans) and *Purity and Sanctuary of the Body in Second Temple Judaism* (Göttingen: Vandenhoeck & Ruprecht). Harrington has received four National Endowment for the Humanities Grants. She and her husband, Dr. Bill Harrington, organize study tours to Israel.

Ma. Maricel S. Ibita (maricel.ibita@gmail.com) is Assistant Professor at the Department of Theology of the Ateneo de Manila University, Quezon City, Philippines. She is also a guest lecturer at the St. Vincent School of Theology–Adamson University. She finished her dissertation, "Micah 6:1–8: Rereading the Metaphors for YHWH, Israel and Non-human Creation," from the Faculty of Theology and Religious Studies of the Katholieke Universiteit Leuven in Belgium in 2015 and was granted both civil and ecclesiastical degrees. Her publications and research interests concern narrative, poetry and metaphor studies in the Bible; the use of the Old Testament in the New Testament; women in the Bible; migration and the

Bible; liberation, social science, postcolonial, and ecological hermeneutics; and the interdependence between Jewish and Christian sources for biblical interpretation, among others.

Joshua M. Vis (jvis@rca.org) holds a PhD from Duke University; he is the Church Engagement Facilitator for Israel/Palestine for the Reformed Church in America (RCA). In this role, Vis leads study trips to Israel/Palestine with the aim of teaching participants about the biblical stories, the history of the land, the archaeology, the geography, and the complexities of the contemporary conflict. He enjoys studying and teaching on the sacrificial system of Israel, the Synoptic Gospels, the historical Jesus, Herod and his building projects, the politics of Israel/Palestine and the United States, and much more. This spring Vis will begin to discern how the RCA can further educate its members on the Israeli/Palestinian conflict and give them opportunities to be advocates for peace and reconciliation in this region.

Timothy Wardle (tim.wardle@furman.edu) is assistant professor of New Testament and Christian Origins at Furman University in Greenville, South Carolina (USA). His current teaching and research interests include the early histories of Judaism and Christianity, the gospels, and the city of Jerusalem. He is the author of *The Jerusalem Temple and Early Christian Identity* (Tübingen: Mohr Siebeck, 2010), along with several articles and book chapters.

Henrietta L. Wiley (hwiley@ndm.edu) is Associate Professor of Sacred Scripture at Notre Dame of Maryland University (USA). Previous appointments include Denison University and Mount Agnes Theological Center for Women. She received her PhD from Harvard University in Hebrew Bible. Among her research interests are gender dynamics in the ancestral narratives, representations of slavery and servitude throughout the Hebrew Bible, and ancient Israelite religion in its ancient Near Eastern and Eastern Mediterranean context. She was formerly cocoordinator of the Sacrifice, Cult, and Atonement section of the Society of Biblical Literature. She is also an ordained priest in the Episcopal Church and has held office, including that of president, for many years on the board of the Anglican Association of Biblical Scholars.

Jarvis J. Williams (jwilliams@sbts.edu) is Associate Professor of New Testament Interpretation at The Southern Baptist Theological Seminary in Louisville, Kentucky (USA). He is the author of *Maccabean Martyr Traditions in Paul's Theology of Atonement: Did Martyr Theology Shape Paul's Conception of Jesus's Death?* (Eugene, OR: Wipf & Stock, 2010); *For Whom Did Christ Die? The Extent of the Atonement in Paul's Theology* (Milton Keynes, UK: Paternoster, 2012); "Martyr Theology in Hellenistic Judaism and Paul's Conception of Jesus's Death in Romans 3:21–26," in *Christian Origins and Hellenistic Judaism: Social and Literary Contexts for the New Testament—Early Christianity in Its Hellenistic Context*, edited by Stanley E. Porter and Andrew W. Pitts, vol. 2 (Leiden: Brill, 2012); *Christ Died For Our Sins: Representation and Substitution in Romans and Their Jewish Martyrological Background* (Eugene, OR: Pickwick, 2015); *A Commentary on Galatians* (Eugene, OR: Wipf & Stock, forthcoming); and *Christ Redeemed "Us" from the Curse of the Law...: A Jewish Martyrological Reading of Galatians 3:13* (New York: T&T Clark, forthcoming 2018). He is also the author of articles on the function of Jesus's death in Paul's soteriology in Romans and in the Letter of Ephesians.

Ross E. Winkle (rwinkle@puc.edu) is Professor of New Testament at Pacific Union College in Angwin, California (USA). His teaching areas include New Testament Greek, Jesus and the gospels, parables of Jesus, the book of Revelation, and biblical eschatology. He has a longstanding interest in the theological meaning of the architecture, rituals, and cultic clothing associated with the Israelite tabernacle and later temples. He is currently cowriting a commentary on 1 Peter while continuing research on metaphorical pneumatology.

Ancient Sources Index

Hebrew Bible

Genesis
Reference	Page
1:2	86
3:3	284
4	152
4:3–5	129, 130
6:7	134
6–8	134
8:20–21	16, 135
8:21	136
9:6	205
9:12–13	217
12:3	181
15	217
18:16–19:29	181
18:22–33	181
27	133
27:41	133
29:35	272
30:9	272
32:12	133
32:14	133
32:20 ET	216
32:21	216
32:7–8	133
32–33	133
33:10–11	133
33:8	133
34:1–27	279
35:1–3	82
37:3	336
37:31–33	336
38:14	336
38:18	336
38:25	336
39:11–20	336
41:7–8	336
41:14	336
41:42	336
43:31–32	336
45:3–4	336
48	124
48:14	99, 124
48:17	99, 124
48:18	99, 124

Exodus
Reference	Page
	15, 119
7:2–11:10	181
12	207, 242
12:1–28	215
12:25–26 LXX	242
12:29–32	181
13:5 LXX	242
15:11	73
19:14	83
19:14–15	90
19:14–16	78
21:20 LXX	255
23:14–17	218
24	138
24:1–11	217
24:3–8	207
25–40	230
25:7	342
25:7 LXX	345
25:17–20	260
25:17–22	228
25:18–22	260
25:30	278
26:4	271
26:24	271

Exodus (cont.)

27:20	278
27:20–21	341
28:2–43	343
28:4	342
28:4 LXX	343
28:4–29:9	343
28:4–29:9 LXX	344
28:17	271
28:27 LXX	342
28:29	278
28:30	278
28:31	342
28:31 LXX	343
28:33–35	282
28:36	283
28:38	278
28:39 LXX	343
29	112, 118
29:5	342
29:5 LXX	343
29:9 LXX	343
29:9–10	115
29:10	99, 100, 101, 105, 107, 211
29:12	212
29:13	212
29:15	100, 101, 105, 107
29:19	100, 101, 105, 107
29:20	114, 203
29:21	203
29:29–30	341
29:33	226
29:36	36, 37, 51, 226, 257
29:36–37	36, 38, 41
29:37	37, 41, 51, 226
29:38–42	278
29:44	203
30:8	278, 341
30:10	34, 35, 51, 220, 226, 243, 257
30:10 LXX	261
30:15	66, 226
30:16	66
30:19	114
30:20	78
30:21	114
31:7	260
32:1–9	181
32:9–14	181
32:12	256
32:14 LXX	260, 261
32:26–29	279
32:30–34	181
32:33	256
33:12–34:9	259
33:20	73
34:23	218
35:9	342
35:9 LXX	345
35:12	260
36:11	271
36:29	271
36:36 LXX	344
37:6–8	260
37:6–9	228
39:10	271
39:29 MT	344
39:30	283
40:31	114

Leviticus	15, 28, 47, 56, 65, 66, 70, 72, 74, 82, 119, 198, 201, 213, 215, 219, 221, 233, 249, 260, 329
1	65, 112, 116, 199, 213
1–6	237, 243
1–7	28, 64, 66, 199, 200, 213–15, 217
1–16	33, 37
1:1–7:6	263
1:1–16:28	42
1:2	63, 215
1:2–4	121
1:3	65, 156, 215
1:3–4	214
1:4	66, 100, 101, 107, 112, 137, 187, 214, 215, 261
1:4 LXX	105
1:5	200
1:9	199, 214
1:9 LXX	237
1:10	107, 215
1:10 LXX	100, 105

ANCIENT SOURCES INDEX 401

Reference	Pages
1:13	199, 214
1:13 LXX	237
1:17	199, 214
1:17 LXX	237
2	200, 213, 214
2:1	215
2:1–2 LXX	237
2:2	214, 215
2:4	215
2:5–7 LXX	237
2:9	214
2:11 LXX	237
2:15 LXX	237
3	108, 109, 112, 116, 118, 213
3:1	215
3:1 LXX	237
3:2	100, 101, 105, 107, 112
3:5	214
3:8	100, 102, 105, 107, 112
3:11	214
3:13	102, 105, 107, 112
4	35, 63, 112, 116, 206, 207
4–5	16, 66, 133
4:1–5:13	25, 26, 33, 39, 41, 46, 47–50, 54–57, 200, 207, 213
4:4	100, 102, 105, 107, 112, 187, 200, 211
4:5–7	200, 212
4:6	201
4:7	200
4:8–10	214
4:10	212
4:15	100, 102, 105, 107, 112, 187, 211
4:16–18	200, 212
4:17	201
4:19	212
4:19–20	214
4:20	46, 49, 51, 54, 66, 200, 214, 217, 261
4:21	199
4:23	215
4:24	100, 102, 105, 107, 112, 187, 211
4:25	201, 212
4:26	46, 49, 50, 51, 54, 56, 66, 200, 212, 214, 215, 217, 261
4:28	215
4:29	100, 102, 105, 107, 112, 211
4:30	201, 212
4:31	46, 49, 51, 54, 66, 200, 212, 214, 215, 217, 261
4:32	215
4:33	100, 102, 105, 107, 112, 211
4:34	201, 212
4:35	46, 49, 51, 54–56, 66, 200, 212, 214, 215, 217, 218, 261
4:46	66
5	64
5:3	85
5:5–7	64
5:6	46, 49, 50, 51, 54, 56, 66, 261
5:9	212
5:10	46, 49, 50, 51, 54, 56, 66, 261
5:11	215
5:11–13	65, 214
5:12	217
5:13	46, 49, 51, 54–56, 66, 214, 215, 261
5:13 LXX	237
5:14–6:7 ET	213
5:16	66, 215, 261
5:18	64, 66, 215, 261
5:25	64
5:26	66, 261
5:30	64
5:34	64
6:2 LXX	237, 238
6:7–16	214
6:13	278
6:14–18 ET	214
6:16 LXX	237
6:23	34, 51, 261
7:1–7	213
7:7	51, 261
7:18	137
7:21	85
7:38	215
8	77, 112, 118
8:6	77
8:9	283
8:11	38

Leviticus (cont.)

8:14	100, 103, 105, 107, 112, 211
8:15	37, 51, 64, 212, 220
8:16	212
8:18	100, 103, 105, 107, 112
8:18–21	263
8:21	214
8:22	100, 103, 105, 107
8:24	114
8:34	66
9:1–10:2	252
9:1–16:30	263
9:1–16:34	257
9:7	34, 35, 39, 40, 51, 214, 215
9:22	111, 116
10:6	115
10:7	66
10:17	51
11–15	59, 71, 74, 84, 93, 94
11:1–47	237
11:15	84
11:45	74
12	26, 59–61, 64–70
12:1	61
12:2	61, 69
12:4	59, 60, 61, 62, 67, 69, 208
12:4–6	44
12:5	59, 60, 61, 67, 69, 208
12:6	61, 62, 63, 69
12:6–7	206
12:6–8	218
12:7	43–45, 50, 51, 54–56, 61, 65, 66, 67, 68, 207–9
12:8	52, 55, 61, 63, 65, 66, 68
12:26	64
12:31	64
12:35	64
13–14	61
13:6	37
13:7	70
13:13	37
13:17	37
13:23	37
13:28	37
13:34	37
13:37	37
13:58	37
14	223, 224, 230
14:1–32	223
14:2	70
14:7	37, 224
14:9	45
14:14	209
14:18–21	66
14:19	43, 44, 50, 52, 55
14:19–20	84
14:20	44, 215
14:23	70
14:29	66
14:31	52, 55, 66
14:32	257
14:48	37
14:49	37
14:51	223
14:52	37, 224
15	61
15:13	70, 257
15:14	63
15:15	50, 52, 55, 56
15:16	78
15:19–26	61
15:25	66
15:30	50, 52, 55, 56, 66
15:31	38
16	25, 28, 34, 38–43, 46–49, 56, 57, 79, 198, 199, 202, 204, 206, 220, 222–25, 231, 237, 243, 246, 250, 257–59
16–17	258, 259, 262
16:1–4	343
16:1–28	25, 33–36, 38, 42, 45, 46, 48, 56
16:1–30	263
16:2	42, 260
16:2–28	42
16:2–34 LXX	243
16:3	42, 199, 254
16:3–24	263
16:3–28	243
16:3–34	244

16:5	199, 254	16:33	34, 39, 42, 45, 49, 53, 55, 66, 202, 225
16:5–20	258		
16:5–34	258	16:34	33, 34, 42, 43, 45–50, 53, 55, 56, 66, 225, 254
16:6	16:6 33–35, 39, 40, 52, 225, 226, 254		
		17	41
16:7–8	220	17:11	15, 17, 21, 47, 48, 66, 204
16:8 LXX	223	17:11 LXX	258
16:9	254	17:12	258
16:10	34, 35, 52, 198, 215, 220, 224–26	17:15	42
		18–19	74
16:11	33–35, 39, 40, 52, 217, 225	18:5	237
16:13	281	18:26	42
16:13 LXX	237	18:28–29	74
16:13–15	260	19:1–4	74
16:14	35	19:2	74
16:14–15	201, 212, 260	19:2–20:26	77
16:15	42, 202, 217	19:5	214
16:15–16	201, 217	19:5–7	137
16:16	33–36, 38, 39, 41–43, 47, 49, 50, 52, 55, 56, 226, 252, 257, 263	19:7	214
		19:22	66
16:16–18	225	19:34	42
16:17	33, 34, 35, 39, 40, 42, 52	20:2–8	74
16:18	33, 34, 35, 36, 37, 38, 43, 49, 52, 55, 220	20:3	73
		20:8	72
16:18–19	37, 38, 202, 212, 217	21:10	329
16:19	36, 37	21:10 LXX	327
16:20	33, 34, 35, 36, 38, 39, 42, 45, 49, 52, 55, 202, 222	22:19	214
		22:19–21	156
16:20–22	20, 198, 215, 220, 221, 230	22:19–23	137
16:21	47, 100, 103, 105, 108, 111, 112, 116, 122, 187, 222, 254	22:20	130, 214
		22:23	130
16:23	42	22:32	73
16:24	34, 39, 40, 42, 199, 212, 214, 215, 217, 225	23:26–32	42, 197
		23:27–32	243
16:25	212, 217, 254	23:28	53, 66
16:27	42, 52	23:32	42
16:29	42, 48, 197, 241, 261	23:42	42
16:29–30	244	24:2–4	278
16:29–31	42	24:3–4	341
16:29–32 LXX	262	24:8	278
16:29–34	36, 41, 42, 45, 47	24:14	100, 103, 105, 108
16:30	33, 34, 42, 43, 45–50, 52, 54–56, 66, 252, 254, 257, 263	24:16	42
		25:9–10	243
16:31	42	26:14–39	74
16:32	53, 226	26:25	255

Leviticus (cont.)		18:5	280
26:37 LXX	281	19	71, 74
27:18	100	20:23–28	329
27:23	100	25:1–13	279
		25:13	66
Numbers	119	27:16	122
1:1	271	27:18	104, 105, 108, 111, 116
1:50	122	27:18–20	122
1:53	280	27:23	104, 105, 108, 111
3:10	122	28:3	278
4:7	278	28:6	278
4:16	278	28:10	278
4:20	73	28:15	278
5:8	66, 261	28:22	53, 66, 261
6	64	28:23	278
6:11	53, 66, 261	28:24	278
6:23	283	28:30	53, 66, 261
6:24–26	283	28:31	278
7:89	260	29:5	53, 66, 261
8:2–4	341	29:7–11	198, 243
8:6–7	77	29:11	261
8:10	100, 103, 105, 108, 122	31:50	66, 261
8:12	34, 53, 66, 100, 103, 105, 107, 113, 261	35:25 LXX	327
		35:28 LXX	327
8:19	66, 261	35:32 LXX	327
8:21	34, 45, 53, 66, 77, 261	35:33	39, 205
10:9–10	137		
11:18	84	Deuteronomy	
14	256	3:18	280
14:18	257	4:25–28	237
15:22–29	133	5:32–33	237
15:25	53, 66, 261	7:1–6	73
15:28	53, 66, 261	7:13 LXX	281
16	152, 281	7:24 LXX	281
16:46	280	8:1	237
16:46–47	282	9:2 LXX	281
16:46–47 ET	215	11:8–9	237
16:47	280	11:18–25	237
16:48	280	11:25 LXX	281
16:48 MT	284	11:28	237
17:11	66, 261	12	163
17:11–12	215	16:16	218
17:12	66, 261	21:1–8	256
17:13 LXX	284	21:6	114
18:3	73	21:8	226

23:9 LXX	281	1 Samuel	
23:9–14	84	1	144
25:18 LXX	281	2:2	73
27–28	249	3:14	215
28:1–14	237, 249	3:15	216
28:1–68	249	4	279
28:7 LXX	281	6:20	73
28:15–68	237, 249	7:8–10	143
30:15–16	237	9:27	272
30:17–20	237	15	152, 211
32	247, 249	15:1–3	181
32:4	171	15:8–9	181
32:6	171	15:22–23	140, 176
34:9	100, 104, 105, 108, 111, 122	15:23	152
32:36	248	15:27	336
32:36 LXX	248	17:1–58	210
32:41	255	17:7	281
32:43	255	17:10	211
		17:20	280
Joshua		17:36	211
1:5 LXX	281	17:41–51	181
2:19	122	17:45–47	211
3:2	78	24:1–10	336
3:5	84	25:39	122
6	211	26:19	135, 136
6:2–20	279	28:8	336
7:13–14	84	28:14	336
10:13	272	29:13–14	176
22:27 LXX	242		
		2 Samuel	
Judges		2:28	272
2:14 LXX	281	7	293
6:21–23	134	8:9	280
6:24	134	11:2	84
9	320, 321	11:4	84
9:7–15	320	12:20	216
9:11	320	17:9	271
9:13	320	18:28	113
9:14–15	320	21:3–4	133
9:57	122		
13	133, 134	1 Kings	
13:16	134	3:14	261
13:19–23	134	8:10–11	216
13:22	73	10:17	281
13:23	134	14:26–27	281

1 Kings (*cont.*)		1:10–20	180, 192, 193
15:20	280	1:11–12	193
19:13	73	1:11–14	184
		1:11–15	182, 183, 186, 187
2 Kings		1:12	188
2:13	261	1:13	182
4:6	272	1:13–16	180
5:14	82	1:14–15	189
10:2	281	1:15	184, 188, 192
10:7	115	1:15–16	182, 187, 188
12:11 LXX	327	1:16	179, 181, 189, 190
13:18	272	1:16–17	184, 187, 188, 192
17:20	126	1:16–18	182
17:22–23	237	1:16–20	174
19:20–28	181	1:17	181, 191
21:3	260	1:18	191, 194
22:4 LXX	327	1:18–19	188
22:8 LXX	327	1:18–20	182, 192
23:4 LXX	327	1:19–20	182, 192
23:26–25:11	237	1:20	142, 181, 182, 184, 192
		2:6–3:26	180
Isaiah	131, 188, 193	5	322
1	176	5:1–6	322
1–39	144	6:3	73
1:1–20	27, 169, 176, 177, 181, 187	8:14–15	308
1:2	142, 178, 184, 185, 193	19:19–20	131
1:2–3	178	19:19–21	144
1:2–4	174, 180, 192, 193	22:12–13	190
1:2–8	178, 181, 182, 187, 194	27:8–9	144
1:2–10	180, 193, 194	27:13	131, 144
1:2–20	172, 174, 179, 182, 192	28:16	294, 301, 308
1:3	142, 178, 185, 193	43:23–24	132
1:3–4	180, 185	49:15	171
1:4	142, 178, 185, 186, 190, 192	53	247, 251
1:5–6	142, 181	53 LXX	247
1:5–8	182	53:11 LXX	247
1:5–20	174	53:4–6 LXX	247
1:6	190	53:8 LXX	247
1:7	142	53:10–12 LXX	247
1:7–9	192	54:11–12	294
1:8	142	56:6	132
1:9	142	56:6–7	131
1:9–10	186	56:7	132, 312, 317
1:10	178, 182, 187, 188	60:7	131, 132
1:10–17	135, 141–143, 176, 244	60:10	132

66:21	132	16:9	165
		17:19–27	164
Jeremiah	131	17:22–23	164
1:9–10	123	17:24–26	131, 148
3:16	201	17:26	151, 153, 161, 164, 166
5:1	256	18:4	256
5:7	256	18:23	41, 226
6:6	146	23:14	186
6:11	146	25:10	165
6:15	146	26:9	281
6:16–17	145	27:20	256
6:16–19	156	31:2–14	148
6:16–21	145, 176	33:1–13	165
6:19	146, 156, 157	33:10	165
6:19–20	148, 158	33:10–11	151, 161, 165
6:20	135, 145, 146, 148, 149, 151, 153, 156, 157, 166	33:11	165, 166
		33:14–26	166
6:21	145, 156, 157	33:17–18	131, 148
7:1–15	159, 160	33:18	151, 161, 166
7:4	318	38:34	256
7:5–7	318	41:5	163
7:8–11	318	43:3	256
7:8–15	160	46:9	282
7:11	312, 317		
7:16	147, 159	Ezekiel	
7:16–20	159	1:22	115
7:16–24	147	7:18	115
7:18	147	9	343
7:21	135, 146, 149, 151, 159–62, 166	9 LXX	342
7:21–23	137, 148, 163, 244	9:2	342, 343
7:21–26	148, 176	9:3	342, 343
7:21–28	159, 161	9:11	342, 343
7:22	161, 162	10:14	271
7:22–23	161–63, 167	16:46–49	186
7:22–28	159, 161, 163, 164	20:1–38	181
7:23	162	20:40	131
7:24	147	20:40–44	131
7:34	165	20:41	132
11:1–17	181	20:43	131
11:14	159	20:44	131
11:15	148	24:23	115
14:10	158	27:30	115
14:11	159	28:13	284
14:11–12	147, 158, 166	28:14	284
14:12	149, 158	28:14 LXX	284

Ezekiel (cont.)		Amos	
28:16 LXX	284	1:2	139
32:27	115	2:4–5	131
34:18–19	188	2:6	136
36:25	86	2:8	128
43:14–20	260	3:2	185
43:20	37, 261	3:14	139
43:22	37, 261	4:4	139
43:25–26	41	4:11	186
43:26	37	5:5	139
43:27	131	5:9–12	136
44:17–19	345	5:16–20	136
44:20	115	5:21–22	244
45:15	66, 215	5:21–24	131, 176
45:17	261	5:21–27	135, 136, 138, 139
45:18	37	5:22	130
45:22	34	5:24	137
		5:25	137
Hosea		5:26	138
3:4–5	131, 141	7:2	256
4:15	141	7:10–17	131
6:4–7	135, 139	9:11–15	139
6:6	140, 176, 244		
6:9	140	Jonah	
6:10	140	1:15	272
7:1–3	140	3:5–10	181
7:4	140		
7:12–13	140	Micah	188, 193
8:4–5	141	1:2–16	181
8:13	135, 141, 146	1:8	182
9:4	156	3:12	190
10:5	141	4:1–13	131
10:14–15	141	6	176
11:8	186	6:1–2	182
11:9	73	6:1–3	145
12:11	141	6:1–5	181
12:14 ET	205	6:1–8	27, 169, 172, 173, 176, 177, 179, 181, 182, 187, 192–194
12:15	205		
13:2	141	6:3	178, 182, 185, 192, 194
13:8	171	6:3–5	180, 186
		6:4	145
Joel		6:4–5	173, 184, 186, 193
2:12–27	181	6:5	180, 185, 187, 188, 192, 193, 194
		6:6	144, 186, 190
		6:6–7	173, 178, 182, 184, 186

6:6–8	135, 144, 176, 183, 188, 244	Psalms	
6:7	144, 187	5:1	171
6:7–8	192	5:13	281
6:8	144, 173, 180, 182, 184, 186, 188, 189, 191, 192, 193	10:5	186
		24:4	77
6:9–12	192	24:5	185
6:9–16	182	32	181
6:12–13	145	33:10	181
6:13	180	40:6	176
6:13–16	182, 192	50	176, 181
6:14–16	181	50:1–5	181
6:16	145, 192	50:21	188
7:9	185, 255	51	181, 244
		51:2	190
Nahum		65:4	226
2:9 MT	272	68:32	256
3:3	281	78:38	226
		79:9	41, 226
Habbakuk		80:15–16 MT	122
3:11	272, 281	80:18 MT	122
		84	216
Haggai		90:4	281
1:1	271	96:9	73
1:1 LXX	327	105:30	260, 261
1:12 LXX	327	109:4 LXX	327
1:14 LXX	327	110:4	327
2:2 LXX	327	111:9	73
2:4 LXX	327	118:22	301, 308
		120–134	218
Zechariah		140:2 LXX	282
3:1 LXX	327	141:2	282
3:4	342	146:9	181
3:8 LXX	327		
6:11 LXX	327	Job	
7:2	260	1:6	82
8:22	260	2:12	115
12:10	86	5:12	181
13:1	86		
		Proverbs	
Malachi		16:14	261
1	127		
1:7–8	127	Lamentations	
1:13	127	3	171
3:4	132, 156		

Esther		3:38 LXX	237
4:1	336	3:38–40 LXX	237, 256
4:16	78	3:38–40 LXX Th.	238
5:1	336	3:39 LXX	238
9:2 LXX	281	3:40 LXX Th.	238
		4:2	256
Daniel		7	275, 276
1–6 MT	234	7:1	271
1:1	271	7:10	276
1:1–2:49 LXX	236	7:13 LXX	275
1:2	271	7:22	276
1:3	271	7:26	276
1:4	272	8	278, 279
1:4 LXX	236	8:3	272
1:5	272	8:4	272
1:6	271	8:6	272
1:8–9 LXX	236	8:7	272
1:8–19 LXX	236	8:9	271
1:12–19 LXX	236	8:10	278
1:19	272	8:11	276, 277, 278
1:21	271	8:13	270
1:21 LXX Th.	271	8:15	272
2:2	272	8:17	272
3 MT	234	8:18	272
3 LXX	234, 236	8:22	272
3 LXX Th.	238	8:23	272
3:23 LXX	234	8:25	272, 276, 277
3:24–25 LXX	235	9:1	271
3:24–40 LXX	234	9:2	271
3:24–90 LXX	233, 245	9:2 LXX Th.	271
3:24–97 LXX	234	9:7	271
3:27 LXX	235	9:11	271
3:27–28 LXX	236	9:20	271
3:28 LXX	235, 236, 238	9:27	270
3:28–29 LXX	246	10	271, 277
3:28–37 LXX	235	10–12	265, 266, 270, 273, 274, 277, 279
3:28–90 LXX	242		
3:29 LXX	235	10:1	277
3:30–31 LXX	235	10:4	271
3:32 LXX	235, 236	10:5–6	276, 278
3:33–36 LXX	236	10:10–12:4	270
3:34–35 LXX	236	10:11	272
3:36 LXX	236	10:12	271
3:36–37 LXX	236	10:13, 21	28, 270, 271, 272, 274, 276, 278, 285
3:37 LXX	236, 246		

10:13 LXX	277	3:37	226
10:16	272	4:5 ET	226
10:17	272	4:11	281
10:20 LXX	277	7:1	122
10:21	28, 270, 271, 274, 276, 278, 285	10:34	66
11	270, 277	13:28 LXX	327
11:1	271		
11:1–4	272	1 Chronicles	
11:2	272	5:18	280
11:3	272	6:34	66, 260, 261
11:4	272	9:31 LXX	327
11:6–8	272	15:5–10	278
11:11	272	16:40	278
11:13–17	272	23:28	257
11:15–16 LXX	281	24:5	278
11:16	271	26:7	280
11:20	272	27:22	278
11:21	272	28:1	278
11:25	272	28:13 LXX	242
11:31	270, 272	29:6	278
11:36–37	270		
11:41	271	2 Chronicles	
12	28	2:4	278
12:1	28, 270–274, 276, 285, 286	5:12	137
12:1 LXX	272	6:25–27	256
12:10	270	6:39	256
12:11	270	7:14	256
		8:13	218
Ezra		13:10–11	341
3:6	271	20:6 LXX	281
5:13	271	20:12 LXX	281
6:3	271	21:3	281
7:9	271	23:9–10	281
8:21	271	24:11 LXX	327
8:24	278	24:18	216
8:29	278	26:17	280
8:32–33	78	28:6	280
10:16	271	29:23	100, 104, 105, 107
10:17	271	29:24	66, 260, 261
10:18–19	113	30:18	261
		32:5	281
Nehemiah		34:9 LXX	327
2:11–12	78	36:14	278
3:1 LXX	327	36:19–20	237
3:1 LXX	327		

Deuterocanonical Literature

Tobit
- 1:4 — 245
- 4:10–11 — 246
- 8:3 — 274
- 12:9 — 246

Judith
- 2:25 — 281
- 4:6 — 327
- 4:8 — 327
- 4:14 — 327
- 6:4 — 281
- 6:12 — 281
- 9:1 — 282
- 11:18 — 281
- 14:11 — 281
- 15:8 — 327

Wisdom of Solomon
- 1:8 — 255
- 11:3 — 281
- 14:31 — 255
- 18:11 — 255
- 18:21 — 281
- 18:21–25 — 281
- 18:22 — 281
- 18:23 — 282
- 18:24 — 282, 342
- 18:25 — 282

Sirach
- 3:3 — 261
- 3:30 — 261
- 5:6 — 261
- 14:18 — 205
- 17:31 — 205
- 20:28 — 261
- 27:8 — 342
- 28:5 — 261
- 34:18 — 237
- 34:19 — 261
- 35:5 — 237
- 45:8 — 342
- 46:6 — 281
- 45:16 — 261
- 45:23 — 261
- 46:16 — 237
- 50:1 — 327
- 50:13 — 237
- 50:14–21 — 243
- 50:17–19 — 244

Susanna
- 1:34 — 100, 105, 108

1 Maccabees — 238, 244, 245
- 1 — 239, 247, 249
- 1–2 — 241, 247
- 1:1–63 — 240
- 1:1–64 — 255, 263
- 1:9 — 336
- 1:10–64 — 241
- 1:11 — 239
- 1:11–15 — 237, 239, 248
- 1:16–19 — 239
- 1:20–24 — 239
- 1:25–28 — 240
- 1:29–32 — 240
- 1:29–50 — 239
- 1:33–50 — 240
- 1:35 — 281
- 1:36–2:13 — 240
- 1:41 — 239
- 1:41–42 — 239
- 1:41–45 — 237
- 1:41–59 — 245, 263
- 1:41–64 — 240, 257
- 1:43 — 242
- 1:44 — 239
- 1:45–47 — 239
- 1:48–49 — 239
- 1:50 — 240
- 1:52 — 240
- 1:54–61 — 240
- 1:62–2:28 — 240
- 1:64 — 252
- 2:20–22 — 241
- 3:58–59 — 237

4:36–58	243, 245	5:11–16	240
4:36–59	245	5:15–16	249
4:41–59	243	5:15–20	237
4:54–60	237	5:17	246
5:32	255	5:17–18	252, 257
5:43	281	5:18	247
6:2	281	5:20	252, 253
6:4	281	5:20–7:32	248
6:60	256	5:20–7:38	259
8:11	281	5:20–8:5	254
8:14	336	5:21–6:11	252
10:20–21	336	5:27–6:6	249
10:62	336	5:35	240, 257
10:64	336	6	246, 248
11:13	336	6:1–5	240
11:38	281	6:4–6	243, 245
12:20	327	6:6	240
14:20	327	6:12–16	247, 253
14:41–47	336	6:12–17	248, 252, 255
15:2	327	6:12–7:38	263
		6:13–16	253
2 Maccabees	234, 238, 244–46,	6:15	257
	248, 249, 251, 254, 257, 263	6:18	254, 255, 257
1:5	240, 246, 248, 251–53, 257	6:18–7:42	252, 253
1:7–8	251	6:18–8:2	252, 253
1:10–2:18	245	6:18–8:5	253
1:18	257	7	247, 248
1:26	255	7:1	246
2:16	257	7:2–41	246
2:17–18	251	7:6	248
2:18	252, 253	7:16	248
2:19	242, 257	7:18	246, 247, 263
2:19–22	252	7:28–29	246
2:19–15:37	251	7:30–32	248
2:22	242	7:31	248
2:23	252	7:32	246–50, 254, 255, 257
3:32	255	7:32–38	248, 249, 253, 254, 257, 263
4:1–6:31	255	7:33	243, 246–48, 250, 253, 263
4:16–17	255	7:37	253, 254
4:40	282	7:37–38	246, 250
5:1–11	252	7:38	248, 250, 254
5:1–7:38	249	8	253
5:1–8:5	247, 249, 251–254	8:1–4	253
5:4	240, 257	8:1–5	251
5:11–14	252	8:4	253

2 Maccabees (cont.)		7:8	259, 263
8:5	252, 263	7:11	282
8:5–7	253	8:14	256
8:11	256	8:22	256
8:13	256	9:9	256
8:29	246, 248	9:15	256
10:4	247	9:24	256
10:5	257	9:32	256
12:39–42	263	11:3	256
12:42	257	11:22	282
14:13	327	12:4–16	256
15:11	282	12:12	256
15:32–37	252	12:17	256
15:37	252, 253	13:16	282
		17:10	259
3 Maccabees		17:19–20	260
5:38	282	17:20	262
		17:20–21	257
2 Esdras		17:21	257–59
20:34	261	17:21–22	254, 255, 257–59, 261–63
		17:22	256, 259–62
4 Maccabees	234, 238, 245, 246, 248,	18:4	259
	254, 257, 263	18:22	256
1:11	240, 256		
3:12	282	Pseudepigrapha	
4:10	282		
4:13	256	Assumption of Moses	
4:19–20	255	9:6–7	259
4:20	240	10:2–10	259
4:21	255, 256, 263		
4:23	240, 255	3 Baruch	
5:1–6:30	240	14:2	279
5:4–6:40	255	11:4–9	279
5:4	254, 257		
5:6	255	1 Enoch	
5:19	257	10:4	274
5:35	254, 257	10:11–12	274
6	247, 249, 254	20:1–7	274
6:1–8	255	40:9	274
6:6	255		
6:28	250, 255, 256	Jubilees	
6:28–29	256–59, 262, 263	5:6	274
6:29	255–58	5:17–18	243
7:4	282	10:7–13	274
7:6	257	22:16–18	237, 263

22:16–22	243	VIII, 3–10	290
25	124	VIII, 4–10	294
25:14	100, 124	VIII, 5–6	293
34:18–19	244	VIII, 7–8	298
48:15–19	274	VIII–IX	293, 299
		IX, 2	78
Letter of Aristeas		IX, 3–5	290, 293
96	342	IX, 3–9	293
139, 142	243	IX, 4–5	82
152–153	237, 263	IX, 6	293
		IX, 9–11	291
Liber antiquitatum biblicarum		XI, 6–9	293
13:6	243		
		1QS^a	
Psalms of Solomon		I, 12	299
2:2	237, 263		
3:8	243	1Q19	291
Qumran		1Q28a	
		II, 2–4	85
CD		II, 19	291
VI, 18–19	198		
X, 2	81	1Q34	
XII, 22–XIII,1	291	2 + 1 6–7	244
XV, 15	75		
		1QapGen^{ar}	20, 124
1QpHab		20:21–22, 28–29	124
II,7–8	291		
		1QH	
1QS	295, 307, 308	XIX, 10–13	85
I, 18–21	290		
II, 1–11	290	1QH^a	
III, 4	244	IV, 27–30, 35	80
III, 4–12	89	V, 20–22	80
III, 6–8	81	VIII, 18–21	80
III, 10–13	81		
V, 2–4	291	1QM	
V, 5	294	II 1–3	280
V, 5–6	293	II, 5–6	291
V, 14–20	81	VII, 3–6	85
V, 20	78	XV 4–7	280
VI, 3–6	291	XVI 13–14	280
VI, 16–22	75	XVII, 7	275
VII, 17	299		
VIII, 3–4	293		

4Q23	108	4Q512	81, 86
		42–44 II	81
4Q164	294, 295, 299		
		4QMMT	
4Q171		B 55–58	74
III, 15–16	299	B 71–72	84
4Q174		11Q5	
1–2,21 1.1–10	78	XXVII, 2–11	243
frag. 1, I, 21, 6	290	XIX, 13–14	80
4Q213a	83	11Q18	
1 I 6–10	83	20	291
4Q255		11Q19	
II, 1–4	81	L, 12–16	84
		XLV, 11–18	78
4Q265		XLV, 7–12	78
1 II, 3–9	75		
		11QT	
4Q266		25:12–31:10	242
9 ii 1–4	84		

Ancient Jewish Writers

4Q274–279	81		
		Josephus, *Against Apion*	
4Q284a		2.193	289
1.4	74	2.24, 193	242, 245
4Q403		Josephus, *Jewish Antiquities*	
1.1.41	303	3.153	342
		3.154	344
4Q405		3.159	342, 344
23 II, 1–10	345	3.230–232	204
		8.93	342
4Q414		12.316–326	245
10 VII	86	14.102	269
2 II, 5–6	81	14.357	269
		15.417	237
4Q504		19.116–119	89
1–2 V, 15	86	20.6	342
4Q511		Josephus, *Jewish War*	
35.3–5	294	1.662	269
		2.11	269
		2.40	269

2.139	75	2.203	244
2.150	76	7.431	244
2.159	83		
2.213	269	Philo, *De vita Mosis*	
2.214	269	2.23–24	243
2.267	269	2.24	244, 254
3.127	269	2.109–110	345
5.219	201	2.117	342
5.231	342	2.118	342
5.454	269	2.120	342
6.260	269	2.121	342
6.345	269	2.133	342
7.48	269	2.143	342

Josephus, *Life*

1.43, 60	269	Philo, *Legum allegoriae*	
		1.81	342, 345
		2.56	342
Philo, *De decalogo*		3.11	218
11	84		

Philo, *De fuga et inventione*

		Philo, *Legatio ad Gaium*	
		306	243, 245
185	342	308	245

Philo, *De mutatione nominum*

		Philo, *Questiones et solutiones in Exodum*	
43	342, 345	1.107–108	345
		2.105	341

Philo, *De somniis*

1.214	342	Philo, *Quis rerum divinarum here sit*	
1.216	345	176	342, 345
1.216–17	245		

New Testament

Philo, *De specialibus legibus*

1.11.67–69	241, 242	Matthew	316
1.68–70	218	3:16	90
1.83	342	3:16–17	88
1.85	342	4:3	275
1.93	342	14:15	272
1.94	342	16:17	205
1.186	244	24:34	272
1.193–203	243	26:28	228, 229
1.198–204	109, 110	27:15–23	231
2.11.67–69	245	27:17	231
2.193–94	241	27:28	231
2.196	244		
2.196–199	244		

Mark	29, 311–313, 316, 318, 321, 325, 326		2:22	257
1:4		89	3:3	89
1:44		257	3:4–9	91
2:23–28		230	3:7	91
3:1–6		230	3:7–14	89
3:27		318	3:12	91
5		322	3:17	91
5:1–20		323	3:21–22	90
5:9		323	4:42	267
5:27–30		230	5:14	257
11	318, 320, 323, 324		8:15	268
11:13		321	8:26–39	336
11:15–17		317	8:43–48	336
11:15–19		230	9:29	336
11:17		317	11:21	282
11:18		318	14:9	268
11:21		324	18:13	228
11:22–15		317	22:20	230
11:22–23		323	23:11	336
11:27		324	24:12	336
12		322		
12:1		322	John	
12:10		308	1	90
12:35		324	1:19–28	91
12:41		324	1:26	92
13		324	1:29	90
13:1–2		230	1:31	89, 90, 92
13:2		324	1:33	90, 92
13:3		324	1:41	92
13:20		325	2:6	257
13:24		325	2:17	302
13:31		272	2:19	316
14:24		229	3:5	88
14:58		298	3:25	257
14:58–59		316	7:37–39	88, 92
14:63		325	13:1–17	88
15:17		230	13:12	338
15:26		229	17	283
15:29		316	17:11	283
15:37–38		325	17:12	283
			18:3	281
			19:19	229
Luke				
1:8–11		341	Acts	
2:7		336	4:11	308

6:7	291	6:16	295, 297
10:4	290	6:16–17	297
15:16	298	10:4	281
21:24–26	94		
21:27	237, 243, 263	Galatians	
21:27–30	245	1:4	255
27:9	272	2	299, 301
27:40	268	2:20–21	255
		3:13	230, 255
Romans		4:4	230
1:18	267		
3:25	21, 228, 229, 260–262, 290	Ephesians	
5:6–11	255	2:13	21
5:9	21	2:19–22	303
7:6	268	2:20	303, 305, 308
8:32	255	2:21	303, 306
12:1	290	2:22	304
13:12	281		
15:16	290	Philippians	
		2:17	290
1 Corinthians	305	4:18	290
1:13	255		
3	297	Colossians	
3:11	305	1:17	306
3:16–17	295, 297	1:20	21
5:7	290		
6	296, 297	1 Thessalonians	266
6:19–20	296, 297	2:18	275
10:1–3	90	3:5	275
10:16	21	4:16	274
11:2	268	5:10	255
11:24	255	5:21	268
11:25	21, 229		
11:27	21, 229	2 Thessalonians	28, 267, 268, 270, 273, 274
15:2	268		
15:3	255	2	28, 265, 266, 270, 273, 274, 284–86
15:50	205	2:1–2	266
		2:1–12	265–67, 274
2 Corinthians		2:3	268, 283
5:14–15	255	2:3–4	266
5:17	272	2:4	270, 277
5:21	255	2:6	266, 268
6	297	2:6–8	284
6:7	281	2:7	266, 284
6:10	268	2:7–8	268

2 Thessalonians (cont.)		9:20	229
2:8	268	9:21–22	229
2:8–11	266	9:25	327
2:9	275	10:11	327
3:3	275	10:19	21
		10:21	327
2 Timothy		10:23	268
4:6	290	10:29	21
		13:11	327
Philemon		13:15–16	290
13	267		
		1 Peter	291, 303, 306, 308
Hebrews	327, 346	1:6	291
2:17	228, 327	1:19	21
3:1	327	2	302, 305
3:6	268	2:4	301
3:14	268	2:4–5	302
4:14	327	2:5	291, 298, 301, 302
4:15	327	2:6–8	301
5:1	327	2:7	308
5:5	327	2:9	291
5:6	327	4:3	272
5:10	327	4:16	308
6:20	327	5:10	291
7	327		
7:1	327	2 Peter	
7:3	327	1:9	257
7:11	327		
7:15	327	1 John	
7:17	327	1:7	228
7:21	327	2:2	227
7:26	327	4:10	227
7:26–28	327		
7:27	327	Revelation	291, 300, 327–38, 346
7:28	327	1	341, 344, 346
8:1	327	1:6	328
8:3	327	1:9	340
8:4	327	1:12	328
9:1–5	229	1:12–13	340
9:5	227	1:12–20	340
9:6–7	229	1:13	29, 328, 329, 337–43, 346
9:7	327	1:15	346
9:11	327	1:16	338
9:12	21	1:18	338, 339
9:14	21	1:20	328, 340

2–3	300, 339	11:2	328
2:1	328	11:3	337, 338
2:5	328	11:4	328
2:10	337	11:19	328
3:1	338	12:1	337, 338
3:4–5	337	12:3	337
3:5	338	13:1	337
3:7	338	13:6	327
3:11	337	13:16	338
3:12	298, 300, 328	13:17	338
3:17	337	14:1	338
3:18	337, 338, 346	14:9	338
4:4	337, 338	14:11	338
4:5	328	14:14	337, 345
4:10	337	14:15	328
5:8	282, 328, 338	14:17	328
5:10	328	14:17–18	338
6:2	337, 338	14:18	328
6:5	338	15:1	338
6:9	328	15:5	327, 328
6:11	337	15:6	328, 337, 338
7:1	21	15:8	328
7:1–3	274	16:1	328
7:3	338	16:7	328
7:9	337, 338	16:15	337, 346
7:13	337, 338	16:17	328
7:14	337	17:1	338
7:15	328	17:4	337, 338
8:2	338	17:16	337
8:3	328	18:12	337
8:3–4	290	18:16	337, 338
8:3–5	282	19:8	337, 338
8:4	328	19:12	337, 338
8:5	328	19:13	337, 338
8:6	338	19:14	337, 338
9:7	337	19:16	337, 338
9:9	338	19:20	338
9:13	328	20:1	338
9:13–15	274	20:1–3	274
9:14	338	20:4	338
9:16–17	345	20:6	328
9:17	338	21	328
10:1	337, 338	21:2	337, 338
10:2	338	21:3	327
11:1	328	22:3–4	300

Revelation (cont.)	
22:5	328
21:11	337
21:14	295
21:15	338
21:19	337, 338
21:19–20	328
21:21	337
21:22	328
21:23	328
22:14	337

Early Christian Writings

Barnabas	
4:11	298
6:15	298
7	230
7:9	342
7:10	231
16:1–10	298

1 Clement	301
5:2–4	301

Gospel of Peter	
11	230

Ignatius, *To the Ephesians*	
9.1	298, 302, 306
15.3	298

Ignatius, *To the Magnesians*	
7.2	298

Ignatius, *To the Philadelphians*	
7.2	298

Shepherd of Hermas, Similitudes	
9	306

Shepherd of Hermas, Visions	
3.5	302
3.5–8	306
3.6–7	302
3.8	301
13.1–3	302
14.1–15.5	302
16:2	301

Rabbinic Works

m. Hagigah	
2:5	72, 76
2:6	76, 93
3:1	93
3:1–2	72

m. Horayot	
3:4	329

m. Menahot	
9:8	110

m. Middot	
1:6	93

m. Sheqalim	
8:4	93

m. Sotah	
9:15	86

m. Tevul Yom	
2:2–3	84

m. Yadayim	
2:20	88

m. Yoma	
3:2–6	93
3:3	79
4:2	222, 230
5:2	201
6:2	222
7:3–4	93

b. Horayot	
12a	329

b. Kerithot		Greco-Roman Literature	
5b	329		
9a	84	Homer, *Iliad*	
b. Menahot		18.409, 412	281
93b	112	Homer, *Odyssey*	
110a	279	14.346	281
		2.430	281
b. Shabbat		21.390	281
87a, 88b	84		
		Plutarch, *Comparatio Niciae et Crassi*	
b. Yevamot		2.6.4	284
46a	84		
		Plutarch, *Quaestionum convivialum libri IX*	
b. Yoma		618 D1	284
5a	198		
19b	276	Plutarch, *Timoleon*	
30a–b	79	5.3	284
31a	79		
36a	110		
53a	276		
b. Zebahim			
6a	198		
62a	279		

Midrash and Related Literature

Abot Rabbi Nathan
   2   84

Mekilta de Rabbi Shimon
   96–97   84

Mekilta Yitro   84

Midrash Psalms
   Ps 134, sect. 1   279

Pesiqta Rabbati
   Piska 44, sec. 10   279

Subject Index

Aaron 17, 26, 33–37, 42, 45, 47, 53, 77, 101–3, 105, 111, 114, 122, 125, 201–3, 215, 220–22, 225, 243, 244, 279–84, 293
Abednego 234
Abel 129, 130, 152
Abimelech 319, 320
ablution 25, 71, 72, 75–84, 86-92, 94
acceptance 26, 35, 80, 81, 100, 126–28, 130–34, 136, 137, 141, 144, 146, 147, 149, 152, 153, 156, 158, 189, 191, 199, 215, 216, 249, 251, 256, 260, 269
adytum 34, 35, 47, 49
Akkadian 39, 101, 113, 185, 226, 338
altar 3, 14, 19, 35, 36, 37, 38, 41, 44, 45, 46, 47, 63, 64, 66, 70, 82, 101, 102, 109, 127, 128, 131, 132, 134, 135, 139, 160, 189, 200, 204, 207, 209, 215, 216, 217, 220, 221, 226, 239, 245, 278, 327, 328
altar base 200
altar horns 35, 36
altar of burnt offering 189, 212, 214, 278
Amarna 185
Ananias 234
ancient Near East 1, 2, 24, 175, 205
animal slaughter 10, 14, 16, 205, 214
Antiochus (VI Epiphanes) 238–41, 243, 245–49, 251–53, 255–57, 263
Aquila 273
Aquinas 3, 4
Aramaic 79, 80, 82, 83, 88, 113, 115, 215, 227, 271, 280, 294
archangel 270, 274, 275
Aristotle 3
ark of the covenant 260, 279, 327
army 142, 211, 252, 253

Assyrian 126, 139, 141–44, 192, 217
atonement 1, 2, 12–24, 26, 27, 29, 66, 68, 75, 77, 80, 82, 83, 86, 87, 89, 91, 92, 95, 101, 103, 121, 122, 124, 198–200, 202–5, 207, 209, 210, 212–22, 224, 226, 227–30, 232, 233, 237, 240, 243–46, 250, 255, 258–62, 280, 281, 284, 290, 293
Augustine 3, 12, 184
authorities 1, 12, 17, 26, 149, 229, 233, 234, 241, 315
authority 28, 81, 106, 116, 119, 124, 172–75, 177, 187, 190–93
Azarias 234
Azazel 45, 47, 198, 220, 223, 225
Babylon, Babylonian 126, 234, 340
Beersheba 139
belt 28, 343–46
Bethel 127, 138–41
blend 170, 171
blended space 171
blending theory 26, 169, 171, 193
blessing 74, 81, 82, 86, 92, 95, 99, 111, 118, 124, 133, 244, 252, 254, 283, 317
blood 3, 8, 14–18, 20, 22–25, 27, 36–39, 43, 44, 47, 59–62, 64, 65, 67–70, 101, 102, 109, 110, 114, 122, 142, 143, 180, 183, 184, 198–210, 212–14, 217, 219, 220, 222–24, 226–29, 244, 253, 256, 257–60, 262, 263, 279
blood application rite 23, 27, 199, 201, 204, 205, 208–10, 213, 214, 217, 219, 220, 222, 224, 226, 229
blood flow 25, 60, 70, 208
blood of purification 25, 59–62, 67, 69, 70

-425-

blood of the covenant 230
blood rite 8, 14, 15, 198, 199, 203, 205, 206, 207, 210
blood, impure 25, 43, 60, 67, 68, 208
bloodguilt 205
bloodshed 3
bread 3, 4, 17, 278
breastplate 338, 344, 345
brother 133, 134, 241, 246–48, 250, 252–54, 265, 279
bull 36, 37, 101–3, 113, 202
burning rite 8, 27, 199, 212, 214, 215, 217–19, 221
burnt offering 8, 16, 19, 39, 63, 101–3, 153, 156, 158, 160, 161, 164, 199, 206, 207, 212–14, 217, 218, 226, 278
Cain 129, 130, 152
Calvin, Jean 4, 5
censer 215, 280, 282, 327, 328, 338
cereal offering 19, 200, 213–15
chariot 148
childbirth 60, 205, 209, 218
Chislev 241
Christian 3, 24, 28, 226, 229, 257, 289, 290–92, 295, 298, 299, 302, 304–9, 335
christological 16, 17, 21, 23, 28, 200, 229, 309
Christology 23, 249, 250, 275, 305, 339–41
client 178, 179, 182, 185, 194
clothes 77, 325, 338, 339
commemoration 4
communal identity 28, 289
communion offering 213, 215
community 8, 10, 27, 28, 42, 45, 64, 65, 69, 72, 74–76, 78, 81, 87, 99, 118, 122, 155, 163, 164, 167, 177–79, 182–84, 186–88, 190, 192, 197, 200, 203, 209, 219, 228, 233, 237, 238, 247–50, 252, 285, 289–309, 312, 313
consecration 8, 36–38, 41, 53, 88–90, 105, 116, 118, 119, 188, 203, 208, 210, 219, 238, 260, 262, 279, 329
contagion 71, 79
cornerstone 294, 303–6, 308–9, 312, 326
covenant 128, 135, 139, 140, 148, 169, 176, 180–85, 188, 192–94, 207, 217, 229, 230, 236–38, 241, 248, 249, 252, 260, 279, 289, 304, 327, 328
cross 4, 9, 21, 229, 316
crucifixion 21, 28, 230, 311, 325, 326
cult-critical 125, 234. *See also* prophetic cult-criticism
cult-disabled 61, 67
curse 118, 135, 230, 320
Daniel 234–38, 246, 270, 271, 276, 278, 285
daughter 69, 180, 207
Day of Atonement 3, 12, 19, 24, 27, 40, 55, 56, 70, 73, 79, 99, 105, 197–201, 204, 206, 212, 217, 218, 220, 221, 224, 226, 227, 229–32, 241, 244, 276, 281, 329, 341, 343, 345, 346. *See also* Yom Kippur
death 4, 9, 10, 12, 13, 15, 19–21, 24, 73, 74, 148, 172–74, 184, 192, 205, 229, 230, 233, 234, 238, 240, 241, 246–48, 250, 252–60, 262, 282, 290, 301, 312, 314, 315, 323, 325, 326
Decalogue 162, 180
deification 18
desecration 139, 188, 240–43, 245, 263, 270, 317
destruction 2, 8, 13, 28, 29, 112, 125, 132, 135, 138, 140, 157, 160, 175, 176, 200, 217, 228, 245, 253, 283, 311–18, 320, 322–26
diaspora 155, 163, 164, 167, 234
disease 71, 72, 203
dishonor 80, 181, 182
dove 63
dress 28, 282, 329–39, 342–346
Eleazar 122, 246, 248, 250, 252–58
Elephantine 215, 228, 296
elimination ritual 215, 223, 231
Esau 133, 134, 216
Essene 75, 83, 87
Eucharist 2, 3, 4, 17, 228, 229, 312
expiation 8, 14–16, 18–21, 27, 44, 82, 133, 187, 220, 233, 259

SUBJECT INDEX

family 35, 69, 133, 177–80, 218, 242, 245, 254, 260, 301, 332
father 5, 17, 26, 133, 169–72, 175, 176–79, 182, 184, 185, 187, 190–94, 244, 291, 302
feast 3, 8, 136, 142, 148, 165, 242, 245, 259
female 59, 61, 69
festival 27, 87, 129, 136–39, 143, 148, 197, 198, 229, 240, 241, 243, 245
flesh 81, 141, 160, 204, 205, 255, 290
forgiveness 16, 27, 46, 50, 54, 64, 66, 87, 89, 133, 182, 185, 188, 200, 214, 216, 217, 228, 233, 238, 244, 249, 257, 258, 263
foundation(s) 7, 28, 29, 145, 292–95, 298, 299, 302–6, 308, 309, 328, 337, 340
frame 175, 252
garments 82, 128, 326, 329, 331, 336, 338, 343, 345
generic space 171
Gerizim 228, 296
gesture 3, 4, 12, 15, 16, 19, 25, 99–101, 104–9, 111, 112, 116, 117, 120–24, 130, 134, 222, 224, 240, 332
Gibeonites 133
gift 6, 16, 22, 69, 110, 125, 126, 128, 130, 133, 134, 137, 140, 141, 146, 147, 152, 153, 157, 180, 215, 228
Gilgal 139, 141
Goliath 210, 211
grain offering 153, 158, 164, 213, 215
Greco-Roman 1, 3, 73
Greek 3, 8–11, 13, 21, 25, 60, 67–69, 101, 104, 109, 129, 152, 201, 202, 206, 212, 213, 220, 223, 226, 230, 234, 235, 238, 239, 247–49, 251, 255, 267, 269, 271–73, 277, 278, 281, 284, 294, 299, 321, 327, 328, 342, 344
guilt offering 8, 15, 16, 203, 209, 213, 215
hand placement, hand-leaning 15, 16, 19, 25, 77, 99–101, 104–6, 108, 110–12, 115–17, 120–24, 211, 222

Herodian temple 79
high priest, high priestly 17, 27, 28, 40, 41, 79, 204, 249, 255, 260, 263, 265, 266, 271, 275, 276, 278–83, 285, 286, 315, 325, 327–29, 336, 339–46
holiness 25, 28, 38, 71–80, 83, 84, 86–88, 90, 92, 94, 187, 189, 191, 289, 290, 292, 293, 295–97, 305, 307, 335
Holiness Code 34, 41, 42, 73
holy of holies 202, 226, 245
holy spirit 80, 81, 86, 90
honor 3, 24, 177–82, 185, 186, 191, 192, 194, 279
horse 148
household 82, 133, 175, 301, 303
husband 176
Ibn Ezra 112, 116
idolatry 82, 128, 135, 140, 147, 261
immersion 72, 76, 77–80, 83–87, 92–94
impurity 38, 40, 41, 44, 53, 59, 60, 61, 62, 65–82, 84–88, 90, 93, 94, 118, 203, 204, 207, 208, 210, 216, 217, 245
incarnation 13, 18, 229
incense 3, 132, 142, 145, 146, 148, 153, 164, 201, 215, 237, 278, 280–82, 327, 328, 338
injustice 80, 110, 169
inner sanctum 64, 201, 202, 220
innocence 9, 110, 136, 192, 205, 228, 247, 253
input space 170, 171
intercessor 27, 147, 175, 275, 279, 285
Israel 7, 8, 11, 12, 19, 22, 26, 27, 29, 35, 38, 42, 47, 59, 63, 71, 72, 74, 77, 78, 81, 83, 85, 86, 90, 93, 100, 103, 104, 126–28, 131, 132, 135–37, 139–49, 152, 156, 159, 162, 169, 171, 175–94, 202, 204, 206, 208, 210, 211, 215–23, 226, 233, 235, 237, 238, 240, 242, 244–58, 260–63, 265, 266, 271, 275, 276, 278–82, 284, 289, 290, 292, 293, 295, 296, 303, 305, 307, 311, 322, 329, 336, 341
Israelite(s) 14, 19, 25, 26, 33, 34, 37, 40–48, 56, 63, 77, 99, 105, 106, 121,

Israelite(s) (cont.)
  124–29, 131, 132, 135–39, 141–45, 149, 152, 172, 189, 197, 207, 217, 228, 279, 280, 284, 329, 341, 343, 345
Jerusalem   1, 26, 78, 85, 93, 94, 127, 131, 132, 139, 141–44, 146–49, 153, 154, 160, 163–65, 197, 198, 200, 201, 218, 228, 240, 249, 252, 283, 285, 289, 294–96, 298–300, 302, 304, 307, 312, 313, 318, 321, 324, 328, 337, 342
Jerusalem temple   1, 132, 294, 296, 304
jewelry   331, 337, 339
Judaism   1, 2, 9, 12, 14, 21, 24, 27, 29, 59, 70, 71, 73, 74, 80, 81, 84, 86, 87, 90, 92, 126, 162, 197, 198, 201, 213, 221, 228, 229, 231, 233, 238, 239, 241–45, 255, 274, 276, 278, 279, 285, 291, 292, 296, 307, 312, 313, 342
Judas Maccabaeus   245, 253
justice   13, 128, 136–38, 143, 144, 156, 182, 183, 186, 191, 194, 290, 293, 318
killing   9, 10, 186, 205, 215, 222, 223, 246, 279
king   78, 104, 136, 141, 145, 152, 169, 170–172, 175, 176, 181, 182, 184, 185, 187, 190, 191, 193, 194, 216, 235, 236, 237, 241, 242, 252, 277, 320–22, 335
kinship   178, 180, 185, 193
lawsuit   26, 169, 175, 176, 192, 193
leper   203, 209
loyalty   139, 140, 144, 180, 183, 191
Luther, Martin   4
Maimonides   79
male   59, 61, 63, 105
Manoah   134
Mari   185
martyr   27, 233, 234, 246–55, 257–63, 282
martyrology   27, 233, 234
meal   3, 5–8, 10–12, 123, 160, 207, 230
meal offering   8
meal rites   12, 207
Melanchthon, Philip   4
Melchizedek   327
menstruation   61, 67, 68, 93, 205

mercy seat   201, 202, 229, 260, 261, 281
Meshach   234
messenger   134, 138, 240
metaphor, metaphorical   26, 113, 142, 169–72, 175, 177, 193, 194, 228, 290, 292, 295–98, 301, 304, 309, 337, 338
Michael   27, 265, 266, 269–77, 279, 285, 286
ministry   27, 88, 91, 92, 231, 279, 280, 281, 286, 299, 327, 341, 343
Misael   234
mother   43, 69, 80, 205, 246, 248, 252, 253
Naaman   82
Nebuchadnezzar   234
Noah   16, 135
obedience   12, 17, 72, 128, 138, 140, 143, 146, 163, 183–85, 192, 237, 290, 292, 295
object marker   33–35, 37
observance   8, 27, 162, 164, 165, 197, 233, 237, 240, 242, 243, 245–47, 255, 260
offerer   14, 20, 22, 25, 39, 40, 44–50, 53–57, 64, 65, 70, 104, 106, 109, 118, 119, 122, 133, 212, 218, 219
offering   3, 5, 8, 17, 19, 23, 24, 34, 35, 39–41, 44, 46, 48–50, 54, 57, 63, 64, 65, 70, 77, 79, 82, 101–3, 106, 109, 110, 116, 118, 121–23, 127, 128, 132, 134, 135, 137, 141, 143, 144, 148, 149, 153, 160, 162, 164, 165, 166, 199, 200, 202, 207, 212, 213, 215, 217–19, 231, 237, 238, 239, 244, 245, 263, 278
pagan   3, 7, 10, 13, 159, 234, 240, 262
parturient   44, 60, 63, 208, 209. *See also* postpartum woman
Passover   94, 207, 215, 218, 230, 242
patron, patronage   177–79, 181, 182, 184, 185, 191, 194
peace offering   213
pigeon   207
pillars   28, 292, 298–301, 304–6, 309
plagues   181, 281
pleasing odor   214–219

postpartum woman 59, 61. *See also* parturient
power 6, 71–74, 76, 80, 84, 87, 118, 122, 152, 172–74, 177, 179, 181, 191, 193, 204–5, 211, 229, 256, 268–69, 272, 284, 309, 314–15, 317, 321–24, 329, 335–36
prayer 82, 83, 87, 88, 132, 143, 147, 158, 181, 182, 184, 229, 234–38, 243, 244, 248, 250, 251, 253–56, 258, 281–83, 290, 294, 312, 317, 318, 322–24
priest 3, 12, 14, 17, 25, 28, 35, 40, 43, 44, 46, 48–50, 54, 61, 63–68, 70, 73, 77–79, 91, 93, 99, 101, 106, 109, 114, 122, 127–29, 131, 132, 140, 148, 149, 151, 155, 156, 166, 189, 197, 201, 203, 207, 217, 223, 226, 227, 239, 242, 243, 245, 260, 275, 276, 278–81, 283, 289–92, 294, 314, 315, 318, 321–23, 325, 327–29, 336, 337, 341–45
Priestly source 33, 200
prophet 7, 83, 86, 125, 127–31, 138–40, 143, 149, 158, 160, 161, 169, 180, 182, 190, 193, 201, 303–5, 309, 318
prophetic cult-criticism 26, 135, 151, 156, 176, 194
propitiation 6, 27, 233, 241
purgation 25, 33–50, 53–57, 68, 80, 81, 204, 207, 209, 226
purification 19, 37, 38, 42–45, 55, 63, 66–70, 79–86, 88–90, 93, 94, 203, 207–9, 243–45, 250, 251, 257–60
purification offering 22, 38, 39, 44, 55, 56, 63–65, 69, 213
purification ritual 1, 19, 25, 60, 61, 64, 65, 68–70, 87, 91, 203, 223
purity 25, 28, 46, 50, 59–62, 65, 68–72, 74–77, 81, 82, 84, 86, 87, 91–93, 208, 244, 245, 289, 293, 295, 297, 304, 307, 308, 311
Qumran 28, 72, 74, 75, 77, 78, 80–83, 85–90, 92, 197, 280, 283, 289–95, 298, 299, 304, 307–9, 313, 328
ram 37, 101, 103, 203
recipient 25, 104, 106, 121, 123, 124, 130

reciprocity 128, 130, 146, 152
reconciliation 6, 22, 27, 133, 144, 148, 182, 184, 216, 233, 247, 248, 250–54
rejection 4, 5, 13, 125, 126, 127, 128, 130, 131, 136–39, 141, 143–46, 151–53, 156–58, 160, 163, 166, 182, 187, 191, 308, 315, 326
relationship (primarily YHWH–Israel/believers) 125, 129, 132, 137, 138, 140, 143, 144, 149, 157, 165, 188, 216, 217, 220, 226, 229, 276, 289, 328, 333
relationship, broken 192
relationship, mutual asymmetric 172–74, 177, 179, 185
relationship, reciprocal 125, 130–32, 139, 152, 153, 157, 180
relationship, triangular 70
relationship, vertical 218
reparation offering 213
repentance 81, 82, 89, 229, 244
restrainer 27, 266–68, 284
righteousness 136, 137, 138, 159, 185, 191, 231, 318
ritual purification 71, 77, 80, 82, 83, 85, 86, 90, 91, 94, 190
ritual washing 75, 81, 82, 83, 92
robe, foot-length 28, 339, 344, 346
Roman 3, 4, 13, 16, 21, 73, 74, 94, 201, 213, 229, 230, 233, 269, 270, 291, 314, 321, 323, 324
Roman Catholic 3, 4, 16
sacrament 3, 4
sacredness 1, 8, 10, 27, 72, 74, 79, 84, 86, 93–95, 205, 224, 226, 284, 292, 303
sacrifice 1–19, 21–26, 28, 29, 35, 40, 41, 44, 47, 49, 64, 70, 72, 79, 82, 89, 106, 108, 112, 118, 119, 121, 125–41, 143–53, 155–67, 169, 176, 180–88, 190, 192–94, 198–203, 206, 209, 212–18, 221–24, 229, 230, 237–46, 257–61, 263, 278, 289, 290, 292, 294, 302, 304, 311–13, 315, 318, 320
meaning of 214
types of 15, 19, 163, 213–15, 217, 219

sacrifice of communion   156, 161, 213
sacrificial animal   14, 16, 19, 20, 109, 110, 112, 116, 120, 123, 190, 202, 211, 212
sacrificial blood   14, 22, 200, 202, 203, 205–9
sacrificial cult   7, 8, 14–17, 25, 26, 105, 108, 111, 124, 127, 131, 151–53, 155, 156, 158, 161, 163–67, 215, 217
sacrificial material   214
sacrificial offering   64, 214
sacrificial ritual   2, 3, 7, 9, 12, 19, 23, 27, 199, 200, 208, 212–14, 218, 220, 222, 223, 227
Samaria   127, 141
Samaritan   228, 296
Samson   134
sanctification   70, 74, 77, 81, 83, 84, 86, 87, 189, 203, 227, 245, 246
sash   28, 343–46
scapegoat   19, 27, 105, 112, 118, 119, 122, 123, 199, 215, 220–24, 226, 230–32, 250
Second Temple   2, 24–27, 29, 71, 72, 74, 86, 87, 89, 90, 92–95, 155, 159, 166, 167, 197, 201, 221, 227, 228, 233, 234, 238, 239, 241–45, 274, 279, 283, 289, 294, 296, 341
sectarian   28, 75–77, 80–82, 85, 87–89, 92, 290–95, 298, 304
servant   80, 133, 184, 189, 222, 246–48, 250, 253, 281
Shadrach   234
shame   80, 146, 177, 179–82, 192, 194, 238, 346
sin offering   8, 15, 16, 19, 22, 24, 25, 37, 63, 102, 103, 104, 199–202, 206, 207, 209, 211–15, 217, 220, 222, 225, 230
sinner   12, 14–16, 46, 81, 234, 246, 247, 260
sister   279
slaughter   8–10, 16, 23, 65, 101, 102, 109, 191, 202, 221
social values   26, 176, 177, 193, 194
Solomon's temple   26, 167
Son of God   90, 305
sons   82, 101–3, 114, 115, 122, 145, 178, 186, 193, 203, 241, 246, 248, 249, 252, 253, 256, 271, 277–80, 283
soteriology   12, 16, 17, 21–23, 228, 234, 246, 247, 260
sprinkle   37, 86, 101, 102, 110, 201, 202, 223
substitute   184, 215, 255–57
suzerain   26, 169, 176, 179–82, 185, 186, 188, 189, 191
Symmachus   273
temple   1, 24–29, 72, 78–80, 82, 83, 86, 87, 92–94, 109–13, 124, 125, 127, 131, 138, 141, 146, 149, 153, 154, 157, 159–61, 163–66, 189, 200, 201, 215, 216, 218, 219, 226–28, 231, 237–49, 251–55, 257, 259, 263, 266, 270, 277, 280, 285, 289, 290, 292–309, 311–18, 319–25, 340, 341
tent of meeting   63, 101, 102, 207, 221, 225
Theodotion   105, 271, 272, 277
theology, theological   3, 12, 14, 16, 17, 19, 20, 24, 26, 42, 56, 125, 151–53, 155, 158, 161, 163, 166, 203, 210–12, 219, 225, 227, 229, 290, 295
theosis   18
Tishri   197, 241
tribute   130, 132–37, 142–44, 147, 148, 216, 314
turtledove   63, 207
Ugaritic   113, 185
uncleanness   33, 37, 47, 189, 192
veneration   12
victim   5, 8, 9, 16, 64, 106, 109, 127, 315
warfare   27, 281
wife   84, 134, 176
wine   3, 4, 17, 128, 229, 236, 237, 320
woman   25, 43, 59–63, 65, 67–70, 110, 134, 147, 171, 206–9, 279, 301, 338
worship   24, 26, 29, 126, 127, 138, 146, 148, 151, 153, 161, 163, 176, 188–91, 194, 229, 230, 234, 240–45, 251, 263, 277, 294, 296, 300, 317, 318

Yom Kippur 27, 33, 34, 40, 42, 45–48, 197, 201, 204, 222, 229, 233, 237, 238, 240–46, 250, 254, 256–60, 262, 263, 276, 281, 341, 343, 346

Select Greek and Hebrew Terms

ἀφίημι 200, 214
δῶρον 109, 212, 215
ἐξιλάσκομαι 200, 203, 214, 226
ἐπιτίθημι 201
θυσία 200, 213, 278
θυσία σωτηρίου 213
ἱλάσκομαι 21, 22, 200, 226, 227
ἱλαστήριον 202, 227, 228
ὁλοκάρπωμα 212
ὁλοκαύτωμα 206, 213
ὀσμὴ εὐωδίας 214, 215
περὶ τῆς ἁμαρτίας 202, 213
περὶ τῆς πλημμελείας 203, 213
ῥαίνω 201

אהל מועד 53, 101, 102
אשם 203, 213
זבח 110, 136, 137, 141, 144, 156, 160, 161, 164, 166, 213
זבח שלמים 213
חטא + את 37
חטא + על 37
חטאת 33–36, 40, 41, 44, 46, 48–50, 54, 56, 57, 63, 64, 65, 102, 103, 187, 199, 202, 213
טהר 37, 44–46, 54–56, 62, 68, 81, 85, 203
טהרה 43, 51, 52, 59, 61, 62, 70, 206, 208
כפר 12, 15, 24, 25, 33–51, 54, 56–58, 65, 66, 101, 103, 121, 122, 133, 197, 200–204, 206, 209, 214–16, 220, 222, 225–27, 280
כפר + את 24, 34, 36, 38–41, 43, 45, 46, 49, 50, 56, 57
כפר + בעד 33–35, 39–42, 47–49, 66
כפר על 33–39, 41, 43, 45, 46, 48–50, 56, 57
כפרת 34, 35, 201

מזבח 35–38, 52, 215
מנחה 130, 133, 135, 137, 142, 148, 158, 164, 166, 200, 213, 214, 216
משפט 136, 137
סלח 46, 200, 214
סמך 25, 99, 101–4, 107, 122, 124, 220
עלה 63–65, 101–103, 156, 158, 160, 161, 188, 199, 206, 212, 213, 217
פשע 41, 47, 52, 103, 187, 222
צדקה 136, 137, 185, 194
קדש 35, 38, 42, 201, 202, 225, 278, 293, 294
קרבן 63, 212, 214–16, 218
ריב 145, 169, 176, 182, 188, 193, 194
ריח ניחוח 134, 214, 215, 218

www.ingramcontent.com/pod-product-compliance
Lightning Source LLC
Chambersburg PA
CBHW032136010526
44111CB00035B/590